Lee Kuan Yew
The Critical Years
(1971–1978)

Lee Kuan Yew
The Critical Years
(1971–1978)

(Facsimile Edition)

Alex Josey

Marshall Cavendish
Editions

© 1980 Alex Josey
Cased edition first published in 1980 by Times Books International

This paperback edition published in 2013 by
Marshall Cavendish Editions
An imprint of Marshall Cavendish International
1 New Industrial Road, Singapore 536196

Reprinted 2013

Other Marshall Cavendish Offices
Marshall Cavendish Corporation. 99 White Plains Road, Tarrytown NY 10591-
9001, USA • Marshall Cavendish International (Thailand) Co Ltd. 253 Asoke,
12th Flr, Sukhumvit 21 Road, Klongtoey Nua, Wattana, Bangkok 10110, Thailand
• Marshall Cavendish (Malaysia) Sdn Bhd, Times Subang, Lot 46, Subang Hi-Tech
Industrial Park, Batu Tiga, 40000 Shah Alam, Selangor Darul Ehsan, Malaysia

Marshall Cavendish is a trademark of Times Publishing Limited

National Library Board, Singapore Cataloguing-in-Publication Data
Josey, Alex.
Lee Kuan Yew : the critical years : (1971-1978) / Alex Josey. – Facsimile ed. –
Singapore : Marshall Cavendish, 2013, c1980.
p. cm.
ISBN : 978-981-4408-31-8 (pbk.)

1. Prime ministers – Singapore – Biography. 2. Singapore – Politics and
government – 1945-1963 I. Title.

DS610.73.L45
959.5705092 – dc23   OCN823774795

Printed in Singapore by Markono Print Media Pte Ltd

For Mum in her 99th year,

still reading books and enjoying her crossword puzzles

CONTENTS

Note on hanyu pinyin

Names of Chinese personalities and places have been spelt in accordance with Chinese phonetics (hanyu pinyin) wherever they appear except in quotations.

INTRODUCTION

Volume Two of *Lee Kuan Yew*, like Volume One, is intended to be a source book, a convenient reference to which historians and others can turn in their moment of need to find out what Lee actually said, or did, or what posture he took, at a certain time, on a certain issue. Here, in Volume Two, is the continuing story of Singapore's remarkable development from the beginning of 1971 to the end of 1978, as told by Lee himself, in his own words, more than 275,000 of them.

Here are Lee's fears, his hopes, his triumphs and his failures, his analytical judgements, his looks into the future, his valuations, his beliefs, his unswerving faith in the ability of the average Singaporean to understand what his Prime Minister is talking about; his supreme confidence that Singapore will survive as an independent, if inter-dependent, sovereign State, and be successful.

Early in 1979, seven by-elections were held to fill parliamentary vacancies caused by six resignations (some enforced by the PAP Central Committee), and a death. Under Lee's leadership, the Peoples Action Party won them all easily with a reduced "protest" vote. In effect, the results provided clear evidence that Lee's status continues to expand, not diminish, with the passing years. We are thus left with the tantalizing thought that more volumes of *Lee Kuan Yew* have yet to be written before Lee completes his contribution to the creation of modern Singapore.

August, 1979

Alex Josey

THE YEAR 1971

I

ON January 2, 1971, Dr. Benjamin Henry Sheares, a gynaecologist and obstetrician of international repute, was sworn in as the new President of the Republic. He had been unanimously elected by Parliament on December 30, 1970, following the death the previous month of President Yusof bin Ishak, Singapore's first President.

The Prime Minister, in moving Dr. Sheares' election, revealed to Parliament that he had explained to Dr. Sheares that within a fortnight he would have to receive the Heads of various Commonwealth delegations arriving for the Commonwealth Conference. Lee said that although Dr. Sheares was without experience in the political or diplomatic fields, his readiness to bring a disciplined intellect to bear on a new field augured well for Singapore. Dr. Sheares was sixty-three when he took office.

In his New Year Message, the Prime Minister said that workers, union leaders and grass-root leaders in the constituencies had to be told the facts of life: it would be foolish and dangerous to take for granted Singapore's stability, progress and prosperity. He warned: "We face multiple problems which, if most were to happen at the same time, will knock the bottom out of Singapore's development. The economic crunch will come in October this year, 1971. By then nearly all British service families would have left. By January 1972, there will only be 2,200 British servicemen, as against the 30,000 now. Added to this are serious anti-pollution problems, air, and especially water. We must develop our water resources to

1

the full. We should be able to collect and use between 25 — 35 per cent of the daily average of 700 million gallons of rainfall (95 inches per year) by 1975-80. This requires stiff anti-pollution measures to reduce mineral particles and acid fumes in the air, and extensive sewerage works. All sullage water from toilets, kitchens and bathrooms must go into the sewers. Then the run-off rain water can be pumped into reservoirs. Sewerage works, reservoirs, and filtration works all cost a lot of money and use up limited and valuable land.''

The government and the statutory boards must improve their organisational efficiency. Officers must make a habit of being polite and courteous. The quality of recruits into the public service must be improved: ways must be found of retaining the best amongst the younger generation in the face of competition from the private sector offering richer rewards. "We are within reach of solid, substantial progress in industry, on to middle technology."

The Prime Minister knew there were some hardships caused to individuals by resettlement required for development, resiting of hawkers, anti-pollution measures, and the re-vamping of bus and taxi services. However, the pace of these changes could not be slowed down. Lee said he understood the concern of the Malay community. They saw their progress as small compared to that made by the Chinese, Indians and Eurasians. But they had made some progress since 1959. And more progress could be made as the younger ones acquired more technical skills for the better jobs. Singapore had done well for 1970. But if Singapore was to get beyond simple manufacture and assembling in low value-added industries, "if we are to move up to more sophisticated industries with more value added, because of higher technology", then wages would have to remain competitive. American and West European investors, looking for bases for offshore manufacturing, constantly compared the benefits of cheaper and often harder-working labour in South Korea and Taiwan. True, Singapore had certain advantages. A strategic location. A better educated people more easily trained. There were more engineers, technicians and people with management expertise. Moreover, Western industrialists were happier when they could communicate with their workers, with administrators in the government, in the Public Utilities Board, and other semi-government authorities. The English language made this possible. "We offer long-term political stability, and high social standards of public health and social amenities. The point is, all these must not be jeopardised. We intend Singapore to be successful. We also intend that she be strong. Let us together resolve to demonstrate in 1971 that these are not empty slogans."

Commonwealth history was made when, from January 14-22, the Commonwealth Heads of Government met in Singapore for the first time in general conference away from London. With Tonga, Western Samoa and Fiji attending for the first time, more members were represented than ever before. From small informal gatherings of five Prime Ministers, the conference had become a meeting of thirty-one Presidents, Prime Ministers and senior Ministers. Nevertheless, said Lee in his address of welcome, though there had been a change of style and pattern, he hoped everyone would speak frankly and freely. A wide spectrum of political views reflected the different economic, social and cultural characteristics of thirty-one nation states. All sought a better future for their people. But, given the different circumstances of natural and human resources, agricultural or industrial backgrounds, and industrial and technological competence, different courses towards that goal had to be charted.

On some political issues, Lee said, strong views were held. "My work as chairman will be made easier if we do each other the courtesy of being frank and trenchant, and polite, if only coldly so." He referred to the months of controversy over the sale of British arms to South Africa, and the opposing views about the use of force in Rhodesia. His first duty as chairman was to enable all issues to be thoroughly discussed. But no issue should exclude adequate consideration of other equally important issues concerning all the six continents represented at the conference. Lee felt that if the conference could not contain current differences over the proposed arms sales, then it was unlikely that the Commonwealth, "as at present constituted", could long endure. Graver differences on vital world issues had to be faced.

Most associations of nation states were held together by a formal framework of rules which promoted some common national interests. In the United Nations, the Communists and the anti-Communists, the Arabs and the Israelis, all had found it necessary to sit in the same Assembly, however bitter their conflicts, because they all were in search of peace. They were also in search of solutions to common problems, one of which was the ever-widening rift between the rich and the poor nations, between the more and the less developed. Other associations like the European Economic Community had tight rules. These rules bound them closer together with the passage of time. Over the 1960s, these rules had brought them into a common economic mould. Further agreements among them in the 1970s might make the EEC countries have a greater say in the joint defence of Western Europe. Eventually some European union might emerge to help them chart a common destiny. The Commonwealth had no such rules. "We are unlike the French community. France and the French-speaking nations overseas, linked through past association in empire, are linked in present association through French membership of the EEC, and the former French dependencies being associated states. We were unfortunate that Britain was not a signatory of the Treaty of Rome on 25th March, 1957. Had she been, many of us might have been able to enjoy the benefits of a wider market for our produce and simple manufactures. Indeed, some African countries in the Commonwealth have sought and obtained some advantages of association with the EEC. On the other hand, the trading benefits in Commonwealth preferences have been slowly eroded. They will disappear when Britain joins the EEC.''

Successive Kennedy rounds had sought to lower tariff barriers to liberalise trade. But there was now a grave danger that the United States Congress might go through with legislation to slap quotas upon any import which was more than 15 per cent of her consumption of any product produced domestically. If this trigger-mechanism of the Mills Bill was re-introduced and passed in the 1971 Congress, it might lead to tariff wars between economic blocs. In this event, the concessions agreed to in principle at the UNCTAD meeting in Geneva in October 1970 would become derisory. If the total volume of world trade shrank, tariff concessions by developed countries to the less developed, without giving them also to the developed, as required by GATT (General Agreement on Tariffs and Trade), would not be much of a boost to the industries of the less developed countries. Declared Lee: "We should not leave the impression that thirty-one Commonwealth Heads of Government failed to take this opportunity to underline this threat to all our economies. If world trade shrinks as a result of protectionist tendencies in the United States or the EEC, we all stand to lose. Our interest are best served by getting more liberal trade policies pursued by the United States and the EEC. This will become more important when the EEC enlarges its membership from six to ten.''

Both the developed and the less developed countries had forged new links in regional and international groupings. Singapore was trying to find a wider base in regional development in ASEAN with Malaysia, Indonesia, Thailand and the Philippines. At the same time, Singapore continued defence arrangements in a Commonwealth Five — Malaysia, Australia, New Zealand and Britain. Australia and New Zealand had been associated with Singapore's defence in the Second World War. They had helped in the development of Singapore's defence capabilities since then. Singapore students were in Australian, Canadian and New Zealand universities, as in Britain. Nearly a third of Singapore's university graduates were from Commonwealth universities. "But we would be naive if we did not expect Australia and New Zealand, good friends though they are, from time to time to re-assess how best their resources can be re-deployed. It is in their interests, and ours too, that their nearer neighbour, Indonesia, is helped to greater stability and economic progress. For Indonesia can then become a stable and rich area for raw materials and, eventually, good markets for Australian and New Zealand exports.''

Lee believed the developed nations might be prepared, for the

4

present, to spread some of their external aid on Commonwealth countries for reasons of sentiment. Whether they continued to do so in the future would depend on whether such aid was likely to advance the economic, security, and other interests of the donor country. It was useful to have shared a common experience. But it was the future that concerned them more. Seven Presidents, a Vice-President, seventeen Prime Ministers and five senior Ministers in government leading their delegations, had not travelled thousands of miles to meet in Singapore if they did not believe in the Commonwealth. "However, we must build up multiple mechanisms to increase our mutual interests in joint endeavour."

There were over two hundred and fifty different Commonwealth associations, from the professions to youth groups, from Commonwealth press associations to Commonwealth educationists. All these were of value. But how were these organisations financed and kept alive and abreast of developments? Were these get-togethers of professional, educational and scientific elites sufficient? The Commonwealth partnership must give mutual advantage if it was to receive financial support from all partners, and be further developed to meet new situations.

If Britain joined the EEC, which was unlikely in the next few years, painful adjustments would have to be made by those who exported produce to Britain. Whether it was butter from New Zealand, grain from Canada and Australia, or sugar from the Caribbeans and Mauritius, all would be affected. In any case, regardless of British membership of the EEC, textiles from India, Pakistan, Singapore, and even Hong Kong, would lose their UK quotas by January 1972.

"How do we give a new content to this Commonwealth partnership in these circumstances?" There were probably answers but they would not be found if delegates became so preoccupied with immediate issues that the broader picture was distorted or blurred. "We shall then be the poorer for it. But if we can see the vistas on the horizon, further develop the many intangible ties born out of a common experience, and build on their foundations, we can all derive satisfaction and advantage from it."

Those, Lee said, were the realities of the present world, and of the probable future, seen from Singapore. He looked forward to hearing colleagues from East Africa. They could tell how they viewed the world, the difference between East African states which had, and those which did not have, common boundaries with white-dominated southern Africa. He thought the West African view of the world might be somewhat different from that of the Caribbean.

Canada and Australia, both on the rim of the Pacific basin, saw America and Japan in different perspectives. One had the United States as an immediate neighbour. Whilst in no danger from external aggression, there was the perpetual possibility of a nuclear exchange taking place over Canada's clear, unpolluted skies. Australia did not have the advantage of distance of the wide Pacific separating her from the problems of Asia. Even New Zealanders did not quite see the world exactly as the

5

Australians. They, the most "British" of all Commonwealth countries, might be hurt most when Britain joined the EEC. "We all have different problems, not excluding Britain. But we live in one small world. If we can give the Commonwealth a new relevance, a fresh validity, it will be a more agreeable place for all of us." Deliberations at the Conference should strive to give the Commonwealth a framework for future development. "If we evolve new patterns of economic and technological co-operation, making for more joint effort and mutual benefit, the Commonwealth could mean more to all of us."

The Conference discussed the international situation in general, economic problems affecting developing countries and the consequence of Britain entering the Common Market. But of major and historic importance was the agreement on the first Commonwealth Declaration, based largely on a draft prepared by President Kaunda of Zambia. It defined the Commonwealth as a "voluntary association of independent sovereign states, each responsible for its own policies, consulting and co-operating in international understanding and world peace." Within its diversity of culture, traditions and constitutions, the central principles they held in common were spelt out. They opposed racialism, colonialism and the existing wide disparities of wealth. The most controversial issue of racialism which focused on relations with South Africa, reached final resolution in the statement that: "We recognise racial prejudice as a dangerous sickness threatening the health development of the human race, and racial discrimination as an unmitigated evil of society. Each of us will vigorously combat this evil within our own nation. No country will afford to regimes which practise racial discrimination, assistance which, in its own judgement, contributed to the pursuit or consolidation of this evil policy." In pursuing their principles, they believed that they could "provide a constructive example of the multi-national approach which is vital to peace and progress in the modern world".

Lee was in philosophical mood when he spoke at the close of the meeting. Briefly, he restated Singapore's position on the question of the transformation of Africa. "We stand with our African colleagues in the Commonwealth in combating this evil of racism. We stand committed to the principle of human equality and dignity in the struggle against racism, and towards this end we are prepared to help by way of education and finance." But white racist-supremist theories could only be demolished by clearly demonstrating that the whites were not superior. It was not from weakness that one commanded respect. However desirable it might be to persuade white South Africans through contact and not isolationism to think and behave differently, Lee feared history would prove that it could only be done otherwise, more by force than reason.

The Prime Minister continued: "We cannot despair either for the white, black, brown, or the yellow man. There are in every ethnic group the outstanding intellect, that percentage of high-flyers. Ralph Bunche or Arthur Lewis, in diplomacy or scholarship, or James Baldwin and

Richard Wright in literature, many blacks have made outstanding contributions in open competition with a mainly white population. But the problem the less developed countries face is not that we do not have the individuals with exceptional qualities. The problem is that we are judged by our performance as a group, not as individuals. And for group performance, more than a few men of outstanding qualities are required. The cultural ballast, the value patterns, the social discipline, the organisational framework of effective government within which individual endeavour is made rewarding, and collective performance becomes a source of national pride — these are crucial ingredients. Then we will command equality, both as individuals, and as ethnic and social groups.

"History, deciphered from stone relics and parchments, has many instances of the rise and fall of many empires. Great civilisations have flourished and perished. Who would have believed when the Romans conquered Britain in the early years of the Christian era, that the barbarians they found there would, by the end of the nineteenth century, become the supreme naval and industrial power of the world? Who could have foreseen that this people, in the process of three hundred years of naval supremacy, seeded colonies in the New World, which have overtaken them, both in technological supremacy and material wealth? But who can say what will happen to America if she does not solve her own problems of over-abundance, the listlessness which leads to drugs, permissiveness, the near breakdown of civilised living in the urban ghettos as violence and organised disorder become a way of life? Some twenty-five million American negroes are not going to disappear from the face of North America by the year 2000. Their problems of large families, poor education, poverty and deprivation of human dignity must be solved. But how? Unless the family unit is recreated after being destroyed in slavery, and family care and pride keep the numbers of children down to a few who can be nurtured and nourished, all the money spent on the Vietnam war diverted to black housing, education and job opportunities, cannot solve them.

"The world has become too small for us all. It will become even smaller with the jumbos, the supersonics, the hydrofoils, and the hovercraft. It is becoming ever more economically inter-dependent. But we shall be disappointed if we believe that this dissolving of primeval prejudices will happen overnight. Behind the intellect is the primordial nervous system, reacting involuntarily with fear and prejudice to the strange and the unaccustomed. Worse, this is reinforced in so many ways by the portraying of inferiority of certain ethnic groups in literature, on television, and even in dolls. In a multitude of ways, this Conference has mirrored in miniature some of the the irreconciliables the world community faces. They must be made less irreconciliable. It will become too costly and painful for mankind if these conflicts are not tempered by the spirit of common brotherhood."

As Lee bid the delegates a safe journey home, he asked them to remember that Singaporeans did not pretend to be virtuous. Hypocrisy was not a feature of Singapore's leadership. Each different racial, cultural and linguistic group had its strength and weaknesses. But by education, by economic and social policy, Singapore hoped to lessen these weaknesses. Those entrusted with authority for the time being, from his colleagues and he in the Cabinet, to the teacher in school, to the foreman, all made a conscious effort towards a more equal and a more just society. "I hope if you re-visit us in the 1980s, you can find that we have moved along with the rest of the world, into a more easy and equable relationship between different racial, religious and linguistic groups."

III

A couple of weeks after the Commonwealth Conference, the Prime Minister, in a press interview, was asked about the naval dockyard which the Singapore Government was about to take over from the British. In peace time, in normal circumstances would he have any objections to "people like the Russians, say" making use of the dockyards for their naval vessels?

Replied the Prime Minister: "We would have no objections. However, I know that the British, Australians and New Zealanders would be happier not to share facilities in Singapore with the Russians. We understand this."

Lee was also asked if he thought there was a possibility of Malaysia and Singapore getting together again 'in the very long term' in a federation. Lee replied: "There is no advantage in talking about re-federation. It is not a possibility. The realities of the situation at the moment, both in Malaysia, make any talk about it counter-productive. The less we talk about re-federating, the more co-operation we shall develop on many matters, which over the eighties and nineties can lead to closer collaboration in foreign affairs and defence."

Questioned about investment in Singapore, the Prime Minister said that his government was flexible about local equity participation. When it was thought that a venture was going to be successful, Singapore might bargain for a share. "For instance, Rollei cameras. They wanted to give us 25 per cent equity. The Development Bank of Singapore wanted 30 per cent equity. In high technology, very capital-intensive, automated and cybernated, like oil refineries, Shell, Esso, Mobil, British Petroleum and Caltex are wholly-owned subsidiaries. But we are ourselves setting up our own refinery, with American participation, in free competition with the others. It's a profitable industry and we are conveniently situated."

In conclusion, the reporters asked about communal problems. Lee said that human beings liked to be able to recognize their offspring. "We are all egotistical. However, quite a number of Singaporeans do not look like each other. We do not have to force them to become like each other. A certain amount of crossing of ethnic lines voluntarily takes place. Some people marry others of a different ethnic stock, often to the unhappiness of their parents, who like to see their grandchildren in their own likenesses. But this crossing of ethnic lines is very marginal, too slow for us to be an assimilated society by the year 2000. The only alternative is to take each other for what we are, to be more tolerant to each other, and to lessen irrational prejudices."

IV

Singapore knew that during 1971, the Republic would have to take over from Britain full responsibility for Singapore's defence, and establish its own pattern of defensive alliance with Malaysia, Australia, New Zealand and Britain. The Singapore Armed Forces were rapidly expanded. Officers had to serve an extra year of service, and at a commissioning ceremony on 31 January, the Prime Minister referred to the failure, in one company, of fifteen men of more than average education and enough leadership qualities. Lee suspected that the extra year of service may have caused them not to try hard enough. He announced that in future all HSC (Higher School Certificate) and university graduates would go on to the Section Leaders' Courses after their basic training. Even if they failed as officer cadets they would still have to do two and a half years' national service, as corporals instead of officers. He congratulated the first eight pilots trained in Singapore's own SAF Flying School, who that day received their wings, and the six helicopter pilots sent to America for training. All six passed.

In a Chinese New Year speech on 11 February, the Prime Minister noted that 1971's celebrations marked a change in Singapore's style. The firing of Chinese crackers was prohibited. In 1970, firecrackers had caused six deaths, sixty-eight injuries and $361,200 damage to property. There were no deaths or damage in 1971, though Lee remarked that some people missed the noise and spectacle. He warned that in future the law against the firing of crackers would be enforced more strictly. Times had changed.

Three days later, in another speech at Sims Avenue Community Centre, the Prime Minister spoke about the need to nurture a polite, well-mannered and gracious society. "We have to be a rugged society to survive. But we should also have the social graces of a cultivated people. In an old established society, whether China, or Japan or India, or Britain or the European countries, good manners lubricated social life. They made life less brusque, less rough. But in migrant societies most people inherited the rough time pioneers had in making a living. Such people, whether in the wild west of America, or in Singapore, found little time for the civilities and courtesies of life. It was time to smooth out the rough and sometimes uncouth behaviour of children. Schools would have to begin to teach

9

the young to be polite and well-mannered. From the schools good manners would get into the homes. The Prime Minister also stressed the importance of children learning a second language as early as possible. In due course children would be admitted to primary schools at the age of five instead of six.

At a People's Action Party meeting on 7 March, Lee Kuan Yew spoke of the great changes that had taken place in Singapore in the sixteen and a half years since the PAP was formed. "From an inchoate, disorganised, disparate group of diverse racial, clanish, sub-clanish, linguistic and dialect groups, further fragmented by different cultural and religious differences, we have become a more tightly-knit society." There was now a consciousness that personal interests rested on national interest. "From a riotous, volatile, unstable, unpredictable society we have become stable and predictable, politically and economically."

Economic growth was no longer the result of random activity, without co-ordination or planning. Economic strategy had been carefully thought out, various alternatives weighed before decisions were made. Institutions had been created to accelerate the achievement of these economic goals. From the Economic Development Board, the Development Bank of Singapore, to the Monetary Authority, there was growing comprehensiveness in planning the future. There was a definite shift from schools geared to producing clerks, lawyers and doctors to ones also training technicians, engineers, architects, managers, and economists. Boys had to be healthy and vigorous to do their national service.

All this had been brought about because there was a hard core of people who, for a number of reasons, put cause before self. They were prepared to lose, in monetary and social rewards. "In 1954 if you joined the PAP, you were joining a group whose future was unpredictable and believed by intelligent people to be pessimistic. Now if you want to make more than an average contribution to Singapore's well-being and progress, one way is to join the PAP, and argue for your policies to be adopted by the PAP."

Lee said that to join the PAP one must prove sincerity and demonstrate convictions. "Then you can be a cadre member. As a cadre member you influence party and so government policies. If you are able and energetic, you can become an MP. Then you have direct access to the Ministers who formulate and implement government policies. And in the not-too-distant future, within the next five to ten years, you may begin yourself to decide on and implement policies. These decisions can make Singapore a better place to live in, make Singaporeans a better educated, a more healthy, and a more cultivated people. If you leave it to others less honest or able or sincere you will get frustrated watching them make a mess of Singapore and your future."

The party was extremely selective in taking in active members, and who were nurtured as cadre members. Today there was little risk of social stigma or economic sacrifice by joining the PAP. There was not the automatic eliminator of the early years, or even of the years when Singapore was in Malaysia, with the power of the police and armed forces in the hands of the Central Government. To join the PAP then, needed courage and convictions. Many did join. Because of them, Singapore today was in a happier position. But all this progress and development could so easily disintegrate, if the hard core or men monitoring performance, modulating policies and reconciling conflicting interests, were to fade away without equally hard digits to replace them. Nobody owed Singapore a living. But the Singapore Government owed Singaporeans the duty of giving everybody equal opportunities for schooling, working, a decent home, medical treatment, adequate recreational activities and a secure future. The standards of all these depended on first, the quality of a people, and next, the verve of their leadership. Businessmen expanded their enterprises, foreign companies invested to manufacture electronic goods, consumer durables, cameras and so forth, not for sentimental reasons. "We provide them with the stability for long-term planning. We provide them with one of the best-educated groups of workers in South and Southeast Asia — a people willing to work hard, quick to learn, and with the stamina for intense and sustained effort."

But all those assets to be put to advantage needed an inner core of modulators and monitors. Hence, the importance of recruiting new talent to ensure continuity. Active honest Party members, cadres with political convictions, helped the selection and election of good Members of Parliament. From these Members of Parliament, good ministers could be made. Then Singapore would thrive in the seventies and eighties and beyond. Self-renewal required a younger generation sensitive and with a deep commitment to their fellow Singaporeans to create a more just and equal society. The young must be given the opportunities to gain experience and confidence. The PAP's problem was not winning elections. The crucial problem was to provide for the continuity of effective leadership, with the conviction born out of a social conscience for the well-being of fellow citizens. Young men and women willing to work together to build a more just Singapore, could join the PAP. "From each his best, to each at least a fair share for his contribution, that will make for a stronger and better Singapore."

V

On 19 March, the Prime Minister gave an interview to a news agency. He was asked about the possibility of an American military base in Singapore. He replied: "We do not want a US base in Singapore. I have just got through all problems of unemployment and dislocation of employment as a result of the British forces being drastically run down. Being the bartender, the dry-cleaner, the grocer and so on, is not my idea of economic advance. What we want is to learn how to repair, maintain and make

11

components of sophisticated machines like aircraft. Ships we already do. That is fairly simple." In reply to another question, Lee said he did not want either an American base or a Russian base. He was quite happy with the modest force of British, Australians and New Zealanders, stationed in Singapore.

At the Pek Kio Community Centre, towards the end of March, Lee recalled August, 1965, when Singapore left Malaysia. "If we had not stood firm on our rights, imagine our position today. We would have been brow-beaten, and the economy in shambles. We would have had a lot to complain about, but we would not be in a position to complain publicly." Lee reminded his listeners that by 1971, instead of massive unemployment, there was now a shortage of workers. In this speech, Lee said that the NTUC could help organize big co-operative supermarkets which could keep down prices of consumer goods.

Lee sent a message to the International Planned Parenthood Federation (Southeast Asia and Oceania region) meeting in conference in the Philippines. Tradition, social values and taboos, he wrote, preserved a society from harm that came with unnecessary experimentation. They stood in the way of rapid change. Unfortunately, rapid change in social habits, in the begetting of large families, was urgently required. Otherwise a country never got out of being under-developed. In Singapore, nation-wide family planning programme helped to raise living standards, and to cultivate the more gracious side of life. "But we had to overcome, and indeed still meet, biases and antipathies more relevant to an age where infant mortality was high, and plagues and pestilence periodically kept the population within bounds." Lee sent his best wishes to the association in their necessary work to save man from the misery of his old habits of prolific procreation.

At the end of April, the Prime Minister took part in a youth seminar. He said that new countries like Singapore faced many problems: a lack of instruments for effective government, not enough trained administrators, engineers, technicians, not enough capital, and scarce technological expertise. Further, poor organisation of whatever meagre manpower there was, made the problem worse. But, given tough-minded and honest political leadership, these problems could be slowly overcome. "We have to live with what has happened. Events which took place before you were born, in 1945, and again in 1948, when the Malayan Communist Party staged its revolt in an armed bid for power, shaped our destiny. You have inherited the past, including the mistakes and the successes of those before you."

Lee said that there was as yet no large core of people in Singapore to provide the reflexes for national, as against individual survival. Singaporeans must become conscious that their very existence as a distinct people, in a poor and troubled Asia, depended upon their ability to react quickly and in unity to defend their interests. Many were too young to know how bad things were. They took for granted Singapore's orderly progress and continuing prosperity as the natural order of things. Those who did remember, knew that the present stability and prosperity had been built upon the cohesion, the determination and the planning of a small band of men. Singapore had a good chance of continuing to be a successful nation if the next generation understood the ingredients of success. They were first, a stable political situation, second, a well-educated and trained population ready to work and pay for what it gets. Third, the ability to attract higher-level technology industries. Fourth, better standards of life in a cleaner, greener and more gracious Singapore. Fifth, the competence of the defence forces to ensure that no one believed they could just walk in and take over what had been created and built.

The main burden of current planning and implementation rested on the shoulders of some three hundred key persons. They included key men in the **PAP, MPs** and cadres who mobilised mass support and explained the need for policies even when they were temporarily inconvenient or against sectional interests. Outstanding men in civil service, the police, the armed forces , chairmen of statutory boards and their top administrators — they had worked the details of policies set by the government and seen to its implementation. These people came from poor and middle-class homes. They came from different language schools. Singapore was a meritocracy. And these men had risen to the top by their own merit, hard work and high performance. Together they were a closely-knit and co-ordinated hard core. "If all the three hundred were to crash in one jumbo jet, then Singapore will disintegrate. That shows how small the base is for our leadership in politics, economics and security. We have to, and we will, enlarge this base, enlarging the number of key digits." It was strange, but true, that the fate of millions often turned around the quality, strength and foresight of the key digits in a country. They decided whether a country would gain cohesion and strength in orderly progress, or disintegrate into chaos.

Lee explained what he called "one special feature" about Singapore. The population was mixed. Even the majority community, 76 per cent Chinese, was composed of different groups: the older generations were dialect-speaking. Then there were the Chinese-educated and the English-educated. Next, Malays, Indians, Ceylonese and Eurasians. They had different languages, religions and cultures. It was not easy to get these various groups to see politics alike. But the government had to reconcile different views and get people to support policies to further the interests of all.

There could be few places in the world where it was necessary for senior Cabinet Ministers to read three sets of newspapers every morning, one in Malay, two in Chinese and three in English. In the past few months, a Malay newspaper had been talking of nothing but Malay problems, and advocating "bumiputra" policies. One Chinese newspaper, on the other hand, had been playing up pro-Chinese communist news, and working up Chinese language issues. It was worth noting that this newspaper did not

13

do this in its Malaysian edition. But the line taken by this paper had forced the other major Chinese paper to compete in drumming up chauvinistic and xenophobic sentiments. The English press, particularly one English language newspaper, financed by capital from obscure sources nominally from Hong Kong, had been playing up permissiveness in sex, drugs and dress-style. On national service, whilst giving lip-service support, this newspaper worked up a campaign to fault it on every count. These three newspapers set off three different pulls in three contrary directions. Unless checked, they would tear Singapore society asunder. Any government of Singapore that did not keep these divisive and disruptive activities in check, was guilty of dereliction of duty. "We must get the next generation on to more common ground to build their future upon. We must give our children roots in their own language and culture, and also the widest common ground through a second language, on which all can compete equally."

Lee promised that these problems would be overcome. Policies for effective bilingualism would be implemented. Then there would be less problems in reconciling different values and attitudes. "Then we shall become more cohesive a people, all rooted in their traditional values, culture and languages, but effective in English, a key to the advanced technology of the West, from where nearly all our new and more advanced industries come. These new factories making cameras, electrical and electronic products, chemicals and pharmaceuticals are providing the better paid jobs to technicians, engineers and executives. Japan learned and borrowed her technology from the West. Even China, today, had to buy her aeroplanes and sophisticated heavy machines from Russia or the West."

If the political situation remained stable, "if we do not allow communists or opportunists to upset the prevailing confidence in the future of Singapore", then there would be rapid economic progress. Western industrialists would invest in Singapore, exporting to Singapore not goods, but factories, and with the factories, the technological knowledge and skills to make sophisticated products. This was the way to better jobs, better homes, better schools, hospitals, dental clinics, parks and recreation centres. "Then we can afford to pay for security, through well-trained national servicemen under high calibre, professional combat and staff officers using highly sophisticated and expensive weapons." All this required leadership, a well-educated, well-trained and disciplined population. Sound politics led to good economic development, which in turn resulted in healthy social conditions and the wherewithal to ensure our security and your future."

VI

In his May Day Message, the Prime Minister thought that by May Day 1972, they should know whether the economy was going to slow down as a result of a massive and rapid withdrawal of British troops taking place in 1971, or whether it was going to press ahead to higher levels. There were abundant signs of prosperity and wealth. A large portion of it was from foreign investments, in other words, the confidence foreign industrialists and bankers had in Singapore's development. Singapore citizens and the government were also investing for the future. Hence the widespread building activity, office blocks, hotels, roads, flyovers, Housing Board flats, new schools, polytechnic and university and, most important of all, factories. Jobs were easy to come by. Anybody who was skilled or not choosy could get a job at adequate wages. Unemployment was at an all-time low.

But many economists believed that the expected American economy recovery would not be as rapid as planned. Worse, economic expansion showed a slowing down in Western Europe. This could lead to slower growth in world trade and affect investments in off-shore manufacturing bases like Singapore. These factors together could give Singapore a chill.

Lee said it was "terribly important" that several new middle-technology industries which were investing in Singapore were successful. They decided to site them in Singapore because of the climate of confidence, and the discipline, skills and industriousness of Singapore's workers. Big companies, like Plessey, Beechams, Rollei, General Electric, Timex, and several others were calculating on a long-term basis. They came with an already built-up export market for their telecommunications equipment, industrial machinery and tools, cameras, optical lenses, flashes and so on. They were from countries that had full employment and high wages. These countries did not want to import more foreign workers, preferring to export their factories. These new factories had expensive sophisticated machines. They required intelligent, well-educated and easily trained workers. To be profitable, workers and unions must work hard to learn new skills quickly and increase productivity rapidly. Then workers could be paid higher wages, and because wages form a comparatively small percentage of the unit cost of each product they could be paid more than the older low-capital high-labour industries.

VII

In July, 1970, foreign interests had established in Singapore a new English-language newspaper, the *Singapore Herald*. On 8 May, 1971 the Prime Minister publicly referred to the general Press situation in Singapore. (The previous week the editor-in-chief of the *Nanyang Siang*

Pau had been arrested, together with other officials of the newspaper for indulging in Chinese chauvinism and "glamourising the communist way of life"). Lee said he wanted to talk about "black operations" (meaning international conspiracies). He said Singapore occupied a very important geographical position, right at the southernmost tip of Asia. To the west were the Straits of Malacca, leading into the Indian Ocean. There was a contest going on for naval supremacy. The South China Sea and the Pacific were to the east. Several major countries had a deep interest in trying to get things in Singapore go the way they wanted them to go.

"First, I will tell you what Dr. Subandrio once told me before Confrontation. He passed through Singapore, before Malaysia, in the middle of 1963. Confrontation was just beginning. We met. He tried to persuade me not to go on with Malaysia. In the course of the conversation, he tapped me on the knee and said, 'What is Malaysia? What is the Tunku and what are the British? I have more agents in Singapore and Malaya than the British and the Tunku can handle.' I knew he had agents. The former Indonesian Consulate officials were very busy — giving *satay* parties, *kenduris* — collecting supporters, fixing their 'Kakis'. When we joined Malaysia, when Confrontation was full on, some of his agents caused trouble. But the police had been following the activities of the Consulate, and were able to negate them before they could create big trouble. There was a White Paper, published by the Central Government in Kuala Lumpur, exposing all this."

Lee returned to "black operations". He said that not so long ago, he had received information that Chinese Communist agents in Hong Kong had given a certain Singapore newspaper proprietor nearly HK$8 million — an equivalent of $4 million Singapore. The Singapore Government had checked and obtained corroboration of this. Curiously, the newspaper (later revealed as the *Eastern Sun*) took an anti-communist line. The communists allowed it to continue that policy. "They are very patient people. They were not in a hurry. They were planning, not for tomorrow, but for next year, for ten years' time." They were watching what was happening in Singapore's schools. They knew that more and more students, both in English schools and in Chinese schools, read English language newspapers. So they wanted a foothold. They had other plans in addition to this. "We have not moved in, so far. The paper has not become effective yet. But we are keeping a close watch, before we act."

Lee went on to speak about *The Singapore Herald*. It had been taking on the government since its publication in July, 1970. The registered largest share of this newspaper belonged to a firm called Heeda & Co. in Hong Kong. It was not a limited company, but a registered partnership, with two names, dummy names. Foreign capital coming to Singapore to start a newspaper did not take on the government, if it wanted to make money. It was only prepared to take on the government if it was after something other than money, and was prepared to lose money. "We stopped government advertisements. We stopped press facilities. The

16

newspaper carried on. Finally, realising its position would become too exposed and untenable, the editor, who was instrumental in organising the newspaper, stepped down, and went back to Kuala Lumpur.''

Now, new investors were said to be putting in money. One of them was supposed to be Miss Aw Sian who owned a Hong Kong newspaper. She was said to have pledged 1.5 million Singapore dollars. She was a' hard-headed business woman. Lee said he had a chat with the new editor, Mr. Ambrose Khaw, and asked him who put up the money, the first lot, from Heeda & Co., Hong Kong. He said he thought Lee knew, that it was Donald Stephens. "I then asked whether he really believed that Donald Stephens — sorry, his name is now Fuad Stephens — would take 1½ million dollars of his own money, to lose it in a Singapore newspaper which took on the Singapore Government. He agreed that this was difficult to believe.'' Lee then asked whether Khaw really believed Miss Aw Sian, a hard-headed business woman, would put her own money in a sinking newspaper. He said no. But he said the newspaper was only losing $60,000 per month, and with more advertisements, could break-even. Lee asked, "Whose money is it?" Khaw said he didn't know. Lee finally told him to let him know if he ever found out.

Referring to the *Nanyang Siang Pau* arrests, Lee said it was a very strange case. The General Manager, Lee Mau Seng, did not read or write Chinese; he came down from Kuala Lumpur after the riots in 1969. Then a Chinese Muslim, called Shamsudin Tung, came from Kuala Lumpur in 1970 and joined the paper. Immediately, crime in Singapore was played up, government news played down, whilst on the other hand, in their Malaysian edition, government and political news in Malaysia were played up and crime played down. They also tried to bring in a known MCA activist from Kuala Lumpur to be the editor of the Singapore newspage. Later, they worked up more and more Communist news, slanted and played up. And this was long before the ping-pong business. It started in the latter half of 1970. "There was something fishy. We kept the matter under surveillance. By February 1971, this paper was getting bold, as nothing had happened. Unlike the other newspaper I told you about which was financed 7 to 8 million Hong Kong dollars, from Hong Kong, this newspaper was in too great a hurry. It got hold of a well-known opportunist and a Chinese chauvinist, called Ly Singko. He had repeatedly been warned when he was writing editorials in *Sin Chew Jit Poh*. *Nanyang* paid him more money to come over to work up, to stoke up heat over Chinese language, education and culture. This campaign was beginning to generate some heat among the Chinese educated. We had to move in to check this 'black operation'. The case is by no means closed.''

Why should all these things happen? Because, explained Lee, Singapore appeared to be doing too well. Some people wanted to sour up the ground. Also, Singapore was an important centre. So the capacity to generate emotions could have an unsettling effect, could be used to push the government one way or the other. This could be useful to whoever wanted to influence the government. "We would be foolish if we are not alert to all these furtive activities. Perhaps, later, I may disclose more. But we do not take action for nothing. Finally, I give this piece of advice to all those who are either willing or unwitting pawns: sooner or later the game will be up, and they will be the sorrier for it."

At a party gathering on 13 May, the Prime Minister reminded Singaporeans that Singapore was one of the few countries in the world where the colonial power had withdrawn and a people had taken charge of their own destiny, raised the standard of social organisation and administration, and were visibly making progress. "You make faster progress when you have less internal dissensions. Do not stoke up heat over languages, cultures and religions. Live and let live. Let us all find common ground." He urged his listeners to learn the lessons of other countries like Ceylon, East and West Pakistan. In Ceylon, the Tamils and the Sinhalese quarrelled over language and religion. The whole economy declined. The Punjabis in West Pakistan and Bengalis in East Pakistan quarrelled and finally clashed in bitter conflict. Now the country was on the verge of collapse and bankruptcy.

As Singapore progressed, some people compared themselves to the European countries in the world and believed that Singapore's welfare standards were too low. But that was what Singapore could afford. "We should compare ourselves to the Japanese. Even they have lower social welfare standards compared to the West." If Singapore wanted to be like the Japanese in their progress and economic achievements, it would take at least another fifteen years of hard work. "My advice is not to get soft by talking as if we had arrived as an affluent society."

Two days later, at an NTUC Courtesy Campaign dinner, Lee said that manners reflected a history of a people. "Our effort to be courteous is not solely meant to boost the tourist trade. We want people to be polite because that makes life more agreeable for everyone, a courteous, tolerant, forbearing and agreeable society, not a hard, unfeeling, selfish, brutish society."

On 19 May, the Prime Minister, at a press conference, announced that Mr. Kwant of the Chase Manhattan Bank had decided to recommend to his head office to foreclose on *The Singapore Herald*. Briefly the facts were as follows: The *Herald* had exhausted some $3.2 million working capital before the end of 1970 and by November they sought an overdraft from Mr. Robert Quek, the Credit-Marketing Officer of the Chase Manhattan Bank, because Letters of Credit for paper and other things were falling due. Mr. Quek recommended the overdraft. By the end of 1970 they had overdrawn $180,000, making a total indebtedness to the bank of $830,000.

Acording to Mr. Jimmy Hahn, the General Manager of the *Herald*, he was introduced to Miss Aw Sian of Hong Kong by Mr. Adrian Zecha in January, 1971. She said she believed she could make a go of the *Herald*, and she parted with $500,000. She had now decided, after meeting the

18

Prime Minister, that she would not put any more of her own money in. The $500,000 had been spent. Miss Aw had no document to show on what terms she entered into this investment and how she was going to gain control of the newspaper. Mr. Hahn said that the *Herald* needed between $120,000 and $200,000 a month to keep going. It had a circulation of about 13,500.

A newspaper reporter asked the Prime Minister if the government had any inherent objection to foreign investment in Singapore newspapers. The Prime Minister said the government had a "very keen interest" to know what foreign capital came in, for what purpose, and, if it goes into newspapers, was "very anxious" to know whether it was coming in to make money, sell news, sell advertisements, or for what other purposes. Another questioner asked if the Prime Minister was satisfied that *The Singapore Herald* had nothing to do with any black operation. Lee said promptly that he was very far from satisfied.

"Suppose the *Herald* had Singapore finance, would the government's attitude be different?" asked another reporter. Lee replied: "I think, if it was genuine, local finance, with people here in Singapore, I think the attitude would be different, because not only would they have the right to make money, they would have a right to make politics. And I think I would acknowledge that right." He closed the conference by saying that the government had no intention of allowing people to come into Singapore, prepared to lose money, in order to create a climate which was hostile for Singapore's continued survival. The Prime Minister tabled two documents: one signed by Miss Aw which stated her investment in the *Herald* was limited to $500,000, and that she had no intention of putting any more of her own money in it. The other document signed by J.J. Hahn, read as follows: "To the best of my knowledge the money from Heeda Limited, a private limited company incorporated in Hong Kong, came from Tan Sri Donald Stephens and Mr. Lim Hong Ghee, Managing Director of Nabahu Co., Sdn. Bhd., of Kota Kinabalu. I appealed to Tan Sri Stephens to help the *Herald* financially after the major backers of Francis Wong pulled out following the racial riots in Malaysia in May 1969. The funds from Heeda Limited was remitted to me mainly through the Hong Kong Shanghai Bank by instalments starting from about December, 1969. Francis told me that he had cleared Heeda's participation with Mr. Rajaratnam and Dr. Goh Keng Swee on the undertaking that Heeda would have no editorial control. Heeda accepted this condition. I appealed to Miss Aw Sian to participate in the Herald financially on a purely business basis. Late in December 1970 Miss Aw Sian met Mr. Wee Cho Yaw in Hong Kong and they both agreed to invest in the *Herald*. Later Mr. Wee changed his mind and Miss Aw Sian said she would be responsible for arranging the necessary equity. Miss Aw told me that she would ask a few of her publisher friends to invest small amounts in the *Herald*.

"Our bankers are the Chase Manhattan and we owe them approximately $700,000 to date. Mr. Robert Quek of Chase approached my Chief Accountant before we commenced publication in July 1970 to urge us to bank with Chase. The other official I have had talks with in Chase is Mr. Anthony Lord. Mr. Adrian Zecha was instrumental in introducing me to Miss Aw Sian whom I had known for some time. Adrian also introduced me to Mr. Chin-ho, the Hawaiian property millionaire, and Mr. Michael German, the Managing Director of the *Bangkok Post*, a Thomson-owned newspaper. I resigned from *Reuters* because I was unhappy working under the then Editor-in-Chief, Mr. Brian Horton. Francis Wong approached me about April/May 1969 and offered me the position of General Manager of the *Herald* under quite favourable terms. In addition to a salary of $3,500 a month, 180,000 option shares and 2 per cent of the potential profit before tax. Mr. Sim Kee Boon of Intraco knows the background of Francis Wong's efforts to raise local capital.

"Miss Aw Sian has remitted to *The Singapore Herald* via FNCB the sum of S$500,000 in three instalments. Of this sum, $300,000 covered an applicaton for 300,000 shares of the *Herald* at $1 each fully paid. The balance of $200,000 was described as a loan. Miss Aw Sian has only received receipts for her funds — no share certificates. If Miss Aw Sian does not support the *Herald* financially, then I will have no alternative but to recommend to the Board of Directors the closure of the newspaper."

Later in the month, after efforts to find Singapore financial sponsors for the *Herald* had failed, the government revoked the *Herald's* printing licence. About the same time the *Eastern Sun* voluntarily ceased publication.

On 28 May, the Prime Minister's office issued the following statement: "On 24 May, at about 3.00 p.m., the Prime Minister received a long distance call from Brussels from Mr. David Rockefeller. Mr. Rockefeller explained that it was most unfortunate there was this misunderstanding, about the Chase Manhattan Bank's unsecured overdraft to the *Herald*. He told Mr. Lee that it was a standing rule of the Chase Manhattan Bank not to lend any money to newspapers for the very reason that newspapers got involved in politics. Unfortunately, Mr. Rockefeller said, Mr. Hendrik Kwant, Manager in Singapore, did not know of this ruling. Hence the overdraft was given. However, he was sending out Mr. Stankard, Vice-President, Zone Executive, Far East and Oceania Zone, to make an on-the-spot assessment.

"Mr. Lee suggested that he should get Mr. Stankard to clarify the Bank's position, that it was a standing rule not to lend to newspapers and in fact there was no secret guarantor or security for the overdraft. Mr. Rockefeller agreed to speak to Mr. Stankard. On 25 May, at 12 noon, Mr. Stankard, Mr. Kwant and Mr. Bish met Mr. Lee and the Minister for Foreign Affairs, Mr. Rajaratnam. Mr. Stankard said he had taken note of the situation. He admitted that the assets of the *Herald* were going to waste, and that there was going to be a loss to the Bank for what was due from the *Herald*. He acknowledged that the ball was in his court and said

20

that the ball game would begin. Mr. Lee said he would judge the Bank from their actions whether they were acting as prudent bankers would in the circumstances, or whether they had other considerations. Mr. Stankard said he had phoned Mr. Rockefeller. Mr. Rockefeller confirmed the statement he had made to Mr. Lee about the Bank having a standing rule not to lend to newspapers. However, Mr. Stankard stated that he did not believe it was universally promulgated throughout the Bank and he had tried to tell Mr. D. Rockefeller this, but the telephone connection was bad."

Shortly after this, the Prime Minister explained at a celebration at the Kampong Sungei Tengah community centre, why it had been necessary to deal with *Nanyang Siang Pau*. First he reminded his listeners that things were getting better all the time: in the next five years, he was confident, short of a major disaster beyond Singapore's control, the Republic could achieve almost as much as what had already been achieved in the past ten years. But, he warned, "we must be constantly aware of the special conditions in Singapore. Singapore has not got a homogeneous people".

Lee said that "our Malay brethren, their religion and problems required quiet sympathy and encouragement", though when necessary the government had to be firm. Lee recalled two big riots, one in 1950 over the Maria Hertogh trial, the second in 1964 at the Prophet Mohammed's birthday procession. On both occasions religion was involved. The first was caused, almost absent-mindedly, by a British judge sending a Eurasian convert to a convent. The second was caused by political exploitation of religion, using race riots for political intimidation. So religious communal issues had to be handled sensitively.

As for the Chinese-educated, they were very sensitive over their language and culture. "If you make the Chinese feel that the Chinese language and culture will disappear, or worse, that the government is supressing it, there will be an explosion." No Singapore government could want to destroy the Chinese language, education or culture. In fact it was the driving force of the economy, the drive and industry of workers. Anybody who tried to work up communal feelings, on spurious and specious grounds, over fictitious dangers to Chinese language and culture would be firmly dealt with. Hence, the action against the four *Nanyang Siang Pau* executives and editors. "We have allowed the paper to go on. They are still protesting about the detention of their editors and executives. But they have stopped filling the paper with Communist news, and there is no more inflammatory stuff on Chinese language, education, and culture. I think they know that if they re-prime the line they were taking, the government must act again."

Lee said that when Ly Singko was in *Sin Chew Jit Poh* he did not write as virulent editorials and articles as he did when he was transferred to *Nanyang Siang Pau* from February, 1971. Why? Aw Kow had received about $4 million communist money. Yet he, as managing-director of *Sin Chew,* kept Ly Singko under restraint. But when Ly was transferred to

21

Nanyang, he went all out to stoke up feelings. Why did the *Nanyang* owners let him do that? They claimed open trial. But they knew, and so did the government, that bringing them to trial at the moment meant that all this communal arsenic would be regurgitated in the press, putting further poison into the society.

The English-educated were a different category. Those not rooted in their own cultural traditions tended to unthinkingly imitate the West, whether relevant or irrelevant. Some got caught up with airy-fairy abstractions, like academic freedom — whatever they believed it meant. Some were naive enough to believe that freedom of the press was sacrosanct and unlimited. They did not, or perhaps could not, understand that freedom of the press really meant the freedom of the owner, the man who owned the newspaper, who hired and fired the journalists. But the English-educated as a whole did not riot as a rule. So, even though a little froth was being generated about the freedom of the press, in the *Herald* case, no harm would be done to Singapore's social and political stability.

The Indians, by and large, were English-educated. The parents of those sent to Tamil schools usually went back to India. So the Indians in Singapore were not riotous or violent in their mass behaviour.

It was in those circumstances that a government of Singapore had to govern in the interests of all or, when that was not possible, in the interests of the majority. "We cannot allow anyone to stir up things and upset our political stability." Trouble and instability would upset progress and economic growth. Then there would be no more new factories, no jobs waiting for the National Servicemen going out into the reserves, and none for the school leavers. Then social unrest and more riots would be the result. The latest example of this vicious cycle was Ceylon.

If anyone wanted to destroy Singapore, he would work on the different weaknesses of those three different language groups. Often they pulled in contrary directions. "Accentuate these contradictory pulls and you cause chaos." Lee gave a recent example. The Malay Teachers' Union had recommended a national-type school, using English as the medium of instruction, Malay as the National Language which is compulsory, and Chinese or Tamil as a what they call "second language", but in fact a third language. In effect, it meant closing down the Chinese schools and teaching Chinese as a third language, next to first English, and second Malay. "If any government is mad enough to accept this proposal it can only provoke the Chinese-educated to hostility. Perhaps most Chinese-educated know that the present Singapore government will never agree to this. That is why there has been no violent outcry from them."

Meanwhile on the opposite side, *Nanyang Siang Pau* had been demanding that the government should publish the *Government Gazette* in Chinese, since it was the language of the majority. They even complained that car-park attendants spoke English. The logical demand they were working up towards, was that Chinese should be **the** official language, and used as the language of administration and the courts. The result of such a

22

move would be bloody, literally bloody riots, as the non-Chinese, Malays, Indians, Eurasians, some 25 per cent of the population were squeezed out. They could never hope to learn Chinese and compete for places and jobs with the Chinese, if Chinese was **the** language.

That was what happened in Ceylon. There, Sinhalese and Tamils used to meet on common ground, in English. Then 20 per cent Tamils were squeezed out as the 80 per cent Sinhalese became the official language, and Buddhism the official religion. Ceylon was then in shambles. This was the sort of trouble-making the Singapore Government would not allow. It was the responsibility of the government to ensure that there was stability, that there was economic growth, a decent life for everyone. "For your children, there should be better education and higher skills, better social and medical facilities. We must move towards a more just and equal society, where everyone gets a share, fair compared to what he has put into society."

A bout of flu on 4 June prevented the Prime Minister from speaking personally to a gathering to form a Nantah academic staff association and his speech was read for him. He said he wanted to raise two matters on the future of Nanyang University and her graduates. The first was the need to produce bilingual graduates. Whenever practical, Chinese and English should both be used for instruction.

The second point was the academic standard required for admissions. Nantah's cut-off point based on Pre-U II results was in accordance not with what was the minimum academically desirable, but varied with supply and demand, supply of places in different departments and demands for admission to these different departments. This practice must be changed or it would lower the reputation of all the Nanyang degrees, and create problems for the graduates by unfairly lowering the prestige of Nantah's good degrees in Mathematics, Science, Accountancy, Business Administration and Management.

"You have now the support for the policy of effective bilingualism from the government, the Nanyang University Council and the Guild of Graduates. Nanyang student graduates who have a sound grounding in English in addition to their Chinese, will be in great demand. For they will be valuable to the new industries, particularly as personnel managers, because they can discuss matters with directors without interpreters, and with Mandarin and one, two or three dialects can create rapport with the many Chinese-speaking skilled and semi-skilled workers. This is something not many University of Singapore graduates can do."

The Prime Minister came back to the *Herald* affair when he spoke on "The Mass Media and New Countries" at the general assembly of the International Press Institute in Helsinki on 9 June. The obvious reference to the paper, though not named, did not come until the end of the speech. Lee began by reviewing the effect of the printed word on people, the effect of the mass media in general. He thought it not improbable that the sustained plugging of a line could mould public opinion on political issues and policies. In practice, new countries, particularly the smaller ones, could not altogether insulate themselves from outside views and news. In just about all new countries, radio and television were controlled by the State. When power was handed over from a colonial government to the first elected government, they remained in state control, with varying degrees of latitude for dissenting views. But the problem, despite ownership and control of television and radio stations, was that the economics of operation made it necessary to buy foreign programmes. At best, these programmes entertained without offending good taste. At worst, they could undo all that was being inculcated in the schools and universities. This was particularly so in the new countries where the English language was widely used.

Their newspapers, even if nationalised, carried reports from the well-organised world-wide news agencies of the West. There was also a whole range of American and British language magazines and journals to cater for all tastes. At a time when new nations required their peoples to work hard and be disciplined to make progress, their peoples were confused by the watching and reading of the happenings in the West. They read in newspapers and saw on television violent demonstrations in support of peace, urban guerillas, drugs, free love and "hippieism". Many people were uncritically imitative. A report of the hijacking of an airplane led to a rash of hijackings in other unexpected places. A report of a foreign diplomat being kidnapped for ransom by dissident groups was quickly followed by similar kidnappings in other countries. Some monks burned themselves to death in South Vietnam in acts of gruesome protest. Others in Ceylon and elsewhere followed suit.

Was it not possible to take in only the best of the West? Why did television in new countries not cut out the sensational and the crude, and screen only the educational, the aesthetic, the scientific and technological triumphs of the West? This had been tried in Singapore. However, as the costs of acquiring good programmes became higher, the less popular they were with other potential buyers in the region. Thus Singapore was caught in the lowest common denominator of viewers in the region.

As for the newspapers. the vernacular press, before independence, had usually joined in the anti-colonial crusade. After independence, they often sought an uncritical reversion to a mythical, romantic past. In the second phase, the more intelligent of these papers tried to find some balance in retaining the best of the old, whilst absorbing the best of the new in the West. But in any case, foreign news and features were still extensively translated and published. The English-language press in new countries, however, were by and large, unenthusiastic about independence in colonial times. They were often owned by Western investors. Most changed ownership after the colonial governments relinquished power. In countries like India and Ceylon, there had been a plethora of anti-establishment newspapers. How much of the confusion and dissensions in these new countries were compounded by the daily outpourings of hundreds of anti-establishment newspapers, no one would know.

What role would men and governments in new countries like the mass media to play? "I can answer only for Singapore. The mass media can help to present Singapore's problems simply and clearly and then explain how if they support certain programmes and policies these problems can be solved. More important, we want the mass media to reinforce, not to undermine, the cultural values and social attitudes being inculcated in our schools and universities. The mass media can create a mood in which people become keen to acquire the knowledge, skills and disciplines of advanced countries. Without these, we can never hope to raise the standards of living of our people."

If they were to develop, people in new countries could not afford to imitate the fads and fetishes of the contemporary West. The strange behaviour of demonstration and violence-prone young men and women in wealthy America, seen on television and the newspapers, was not relevant to the social and economic circumstances of new under-developed countries. The importance of education, the need for stability and work discipline, the acquisition of skills and expertise, sufficient men trained in the sciences and technology, and their ability to adapt this knowledge and techniques to fit the conditions of their country, these were vital factors for progress. But when the puritan ethics of hard work, thrift and discipline were at a discount in America, and generally in the West, the mass media reflecting this malaise could, and did, confuse the young in new countries. "We have this problem in a particularly acute form in Singapore. We are an international junction for ships, aircraft and telecomunications by cable and satellite. People from the richer countries of the West, their magazines, newspapers, television and cinemá films, all come in. We are very exposed. It is impossible to insulate Singaporeans from the outside world. One consoling thought is Arnold Toynbee's thesis that crossroads benefit from the stimulation of ideas and inventions from abroad. To take in Western science, technology and industry, we find that we cannot completely exclude the undesirable ethos of the contemporary West. This ethos flakes off on Singaporeans. So we must educate Singaporeans not to imitate the more erratic behaviour of the West." Lee said he realised that whatever the side-effects of importing Western science and technology, not to do so would be worse. To compound Singapore's problems, the population was not homogeneous. There were several racial, linguistic, cultural and religious groups. But with nearly all sectors of the population, the deleterious influence from the mass media of the West was an increasing problem. "Fortunately, we have not gotten to the stage of mod styles, communal living, drugs and escapism."

An interesting question was whether the mass media could affect a people to an extent where over a sustained period they not only determined social behaviour but also sparked off political action. Lee believed every now and again they did. People were affected by the suggestion of the printed word, or the voice on radio, particularly if reinforced by the television picture. He used to believe that when Singaporeans became more sophisticated with higher standards of educaton, these problems would diminish. But watching Belfast, Brussels and Montreal rioting over religion and language, he wondered whether such phenomena could ever disappear.

"Finally, making for more pressures in the interest in Singapore of our smaller neighbours and that of several great powers. The smaller countries do not have the resources or the stamina to be a threat. But in the growing contest for maritime supremacy of the Indian Ocean and the South China Sea, the great powers are prepared to spend time and their money to influence Singaporeans towards policies more to their advantage. They play it long and cool. Radio reception on handy transistors gives Singaporeans a whole variety of programmes, from the Voice of America to Radio Peking, and also the Voice of the Malayan National Liberation League clandestine radio station. The Malayan Communist Party wants to liberate not only West Malaysia, but also Singapore. On top of this, foreign agencies from time to time use local proxies to set up or buy into newspapers, not to make money but to make political gains by shaping opinions and attitudes. My colleagues and I have the responsibility to neutralise their intentions. In such a situation, freedom of the press, freedom of the news media, must be subordinated to the overriding needs of the integrity of Singapore, and to the primacy of purpose of an elected government. The government has taken, and will from time to time have to take, firm measures to ensure that, despite divisive forces of different cultural values and life-styles, there is enough unity of purpose to carry the people of Singapore forward to higher standards of life, without which the mass media cannot thrive."

VIII

Back in Singapore, the Prime Minister continued his visits to PAP branches. At Toa Payoh, on 19 June, he spoke of the government's plans to create satellite towns with small and large flats, more space reserved for playing fields, gardens, swimming pools, a stadium, schools and clinics. It would take time. The line between the better-off and the poorer-off must never be pronounced. Mobility from the lower to the middle income group must be possible for those who tried. Ability and effort, the contributions a man made to the society, could get him up the economic and social ladder.

One of the government's plans was to make it possible for almost every family to own their own home. This was possible only if families were planned. People with large families would find owning their own homes very difficult. No government, however efficient, could provide adequate housing, education, health and social services, if people continued to have six to twelve children in a family. "We can reach a point when Singapore becomes so crowded that life is unpleasant and unbearable. Slums in America, the richest country in the world, are warning examples. The poor, mostly blacks, are packed together in rotting tenements." The ideal family was that with two children. "If you must, then three. Only in this way can we make Singapore a clean, green and gracious place to live in, a garden city in which we can nourish and nurture our young for a better future. Then our economy will blossom for all to enjoy, as we mechanise more and more jobs, increase productivity, and raise wages."

Singapore was booming. There was a shortage of skilled workers. Unemployment was around 21,000. There were people who did not want to do hard, manual work. Over 53,000 work permits had been issued, mostly to West Malaysians. They were for skilled, semi-skilled and heavy, manual jobs. But there were thousands of others without work permits on construction sites. Without work permits, contractors avoided paying CPF contributions. There was an acute shortage of construction workers. "But we must get contractors to register these workers for work permits, to legalise and regularise the position."

This economic bustle was because Singapore did not shirk unpleasant and unpopular measures. Firm, fair and consistent policies brought about this climate of confidence. Hence rapid investment by foreign industrialists, accelerating economic growth — the new factories, new hotels, new shopping complexes, new homes and schools. This growing prosperity would eventually spread to all. The immediate aim of the government was to consolidate these economic gains. "We will not let down those who have shown confidence in us and who have invested in Singapore. And for you — shopkeepers, clerks, workers and hawkers, the increased revenue from this economic growth will improve standards of life. In co-operation, workers, management and government, we will achieve this."

Finally, it was worth remembering that the business of a government was to govern. "Our stability and progress were made possible because of fair and firm government, supported by an honest and effective administration. Without these basic factors, Singapore would have gone down the drain."

"The jumbo jet age has come to Singapore. With our rapid progress towards middle-technology industries, Singapore is becoming the industrial and technological centre in Southeast Asia," the Prime Minister told over six hundred Ho Clansmen at Duxton Road on 5 July. Lee advised them that young men and women must make the effort to be trained for industrial jobs. Children must be better educated, especially in technical education, in order to have a good future in the Singapore of the 1980s. "To continue as hawkers and unskilled labourers," he said, "is to be frustrated and deprived." After his address the Prime Minister talked with his constituents. He held his first election rally there sixteen years earlier, and on the platform was a young Ho who remembered the meeting, when he was only eight years old. He reminded Lee of this.

IX

President Sheares opened the Second Session of Parliament on 21 July. Reading the speech prepared for him by the Prime Minister, the President said that after six years of separate independence, Singapore was seen to be viable and less dependent on the entrépot trade. The Republic was developing into a centre for manufacturing, servicing, transportation and communications. When the British Government announced in January 1968 that they were going to pull out their forces by the end of 1971, there was widespread fear of unemployment. Unions, management and the government worked hard to create the conditions for rapid and massive investment. "We succeeded. At present, there is a temporary shortage of workers. Work permits are freely issued to skilled and semi-skilled workers, and to unskilled workers for heavy manual jobs. Block permits are given to building contractors so that work is not slowed down all over Singapore, from urban renewal, to new satellite towns, factories, roads, flyovers, canals and reservoirs."

The President said it was important that the industrialisation programme should not stall for lack of skilled, or if unskilled, the educated, industrious and easily trainable, workers. The policy of free work permits would continue until the re-cycling of national service recruits had evened out. In about three years, the national service intake would not exceed the numbers going into the reserves. Then conditions of full employment would have been reached. Meanwhile, the government had plans to systematically mechanise laborious and repetitive work. The private sector would be encouraged to do the same. "There is a limit to the inflow of unskilled non-citizen workers we can absorb if the fabric of our society is not to be strained. We want economic growth to raise the standards of living of our people."

Singapore must become viable in defence. Through the Commonwealth Five-Power defence arrangements, stability and security were assured for several years ahead. But use must be made of this time to consolidate Singapore's own defence capability. The Ministry of Defence had to overcome many problems. They were the result of very rapid expansion in the past few years. In the next few years, the heavy expenditure for the purchase of arms and equipment for defence would level off. Then a greater share of revenue could go into education, health and social services. Meanwhile, the rapid pace of development was making land more scarce, and resettlement more difficult, especially for farmers. As the economic position was now stronger, the government had decided to give higher rates of compensation to tenants and *ex gratia* payments to squatters for resettlement. Shops and industries in government-owned or acquired premises would now get resettlement *ex gratia* payments. Genuine farmers would be given more generous terms of resettlement.

"If we want to continue our rapid growth, we have to import part of the capital, and most of the technology, the management and marketing expertise. A considerable part of the wealth, increasingly evident since the past two years, in expensive shopping complexes, hotels, office blocks and factories, represents imported capital. It will take time and experience to build up our own corps of managers, engineers and marketing experts. With time, our people will increase their participation in the owning and the running of the new enterprise." But, for the present it was foolish not to admit that however shrewd and wealthy Singapore merchants were, many had not yet learned how to run a modern corporation, where ownership was separate from management. Investors and entrepreneurs had to develop new attitudes necessary for the management of industries and other enterprises. "Recently, a British group of stock market operators quietly bought the majority stocks of a Singapore company, then sold the company's holdings in a bank and in newspapers, for considerable profits, all at no risk, in little time, and without much effort. It is a sad and painful example of how poorly we run some of our limited companies listed on the stock exchange. We have to acquire sophistication and expertise to run large corporate holding companies and their subsidiaries. We must not allow anyone to take such easy pickings. We believe our young executives and accountants have the ability to acquire their expertise quickly in the next five to ten years. We shall the more rapidly develop this expertise if we increase the number of our own professionals by attracting highly qualified and able professionals, who will come not just to work, but also to settle permanently in Singapore."

The way forward was clear. Through land reclamation, effective anti-pollution measures, good zoning and planning, a gracious environment could be developed. Through family planning and a combination of incentives for small families and disincentives on having more than three children, the population growth could be kept in check. This was the only way for the quality of life to go up. Food alone was not enough to bring up a good citizen. Every child needed care and years of education and training. In many new countries, the population explosion had brought life down to the dirty ditches of the countryside or the filth and squalor of the pavements in the cities. It was fortunate that most Singaporeans had accepted the realities of life in present-day Singapore. Their approach to problems was generally practical and tolerant. "If we are to remain a cohesive people, we must concentrate on the factors which bind us together, and not which will divide us. We cannot allow anyone to work up heat on the gut issues over language, culture and religion, grating the raw nerves of our people. No one, and especially any one working in the mass media has the right to play with the emotional reflexes of our different communities. Partly as the result of recent politicking in the press over language and culture, now even designs of commemorative stamps, which were intended to be light-hearted and quite innocent, have been convoluted and inflated into a serious issue about culture and religion. Provided we keep these sensitive issues of language, culture and religion muted, we

29

have the capacity to transform our once disparate peoples into a modern industrialised island-nation. We must not be deflected from our course towards this goal."

X

National Day, 9 August, was celebrated with the usual enthusiasm. Lee, in his National Day broadcast, said that immediate prospects were good. Many new factories, shopping complexes and hotels were being planned and built. Many prospering enterprises were expanding production. All those willing could get a decent living. The background for Singapore's continuing progress was stability, both political and geo-political. Great changes were in the offing. The American government had set out to thaw their relations with China. They were also committed to wind up their military involvement in Vietnam and as soon as possible. For a new geo-political equilibrium to be established, there might have to be trade-off's across the board. New demarcations of spheres of influence might become part of the Asian political landscape. Some countries might be allowed to go neutral. Some might become pro-communists. "For you and me in Singapore, the well-being of our immediate neighbours affects our future. We shall play our part in regional economic co-operation. The better off they are, the better it is for us. We will participate in all joint projects for mutual benefits. Provided there is no sudden deterioration in the stability of the area, the future augurs well for us all."

Lee was much more relaxed and informal during an off-the-cuff speech in the National Theatre on 15 August. It went out live over television. He said he was not there to preach blood, sweat and tears or talk about the apocalypse. His message was that Singapore had done well — six superb years, a magnificent performance against all odds. "We made it so"; it did not just happen. But the hard work must be sustained. He referred to the "new generation leadership". Successors could not be nominated. All that could be done was to provide a group of able, honest and, he hoped, dedicated men. Out of them somebody would emerge as the captain of a new team. Men like Ong Pang Boon (seven years younger than the Prime Minister) would bridge the gap. Lee added that the present team would be here "for this decade".

In Jurong, a fortnight later, Lee, in a speech, referred to the mental outlook, the work and social disciplines of the new Singaporean. Without the necessary changes in attitudes and social behaviour, it would not have been possible to convert Jurong, a fishing village only ten years ago, into an industrial estate. A gratifying instance of this new self-discipline was the response of the people to the call to cut down water consumption.

By mid-April, it was known that a dangerous problem was ahead, as a result of one of the driest four months in many years. Two choices were open. One was to start rationing water supply by May. The other was to appeal to the people to cut down the use of water, first to keep it below 100 million gallons per day, then try to cut down further, to 90 million gallons per day if the drought continued. "We decided to make the appeal to reason and social responsibility. The first alternative of immediate rationing would cause hardship, particularly to people like hawkers. They would probably have to go out of business because, without water for cooking and cleaning, there would be outbreaks of infectious diseases like cholera, dysentry. This would deprive thousands of hawkers of income for weeks, and months, while rationing was on. To achieve a reduction of 20 per cent in water consumption by appealing to reason was considered doubtful. But we succeeded. There was a splendid group response, a demonstration of social discipline. We can take pride in this. We have got it in us as a people, to make the grade. It was not done in a few months. The reorientation of our people's outlook was done over the past decade."

There were still problems and the Prime Minister mentioned some of them in a long speech ten days later. Singaporeans, he said, were getting a little on the soft side. Young men after a few years in school refused to do heavy manual work: they did not like sweating and getting dirty. That would have to be changed.

Lee also spoke about the second generation leadership. A team of younger men, able, emotionally stable, sincere in their political beliefs, men who would not melt under heat and pressure, were being gathered together. Lee admitted that the final test of whether "we in the PAP" had succeeded or failed was whether "after us" the continuity of leadership had been provided for. "The dearest prize my senior colleagues in the Cabinet and I would treasure is that three years after we have ceased to hold office, we can attend a gathering like the one tonight, and see that life for Singaporeans has got better, and the environment greener and cleaner. Then we will know that we have done all that is required of us."

XI

When he addressed a large gathering of graduates on 11 September, Lee reminded them that one reliable yardstick of development and the wealth a society could generate, was the percentage of the population that had more than twelve years of education. In the USA, the figure was 30 per cent. In Nigeria, the largest African state, the figure was 0.01 per cent. In Singapore, the percentage was just above 1.3 per cent. The Prime Minister said that the nub of his message was that there were crucial non-economic factors that made for growth. These factors, unless monitored and prevented from getting out of control, would undermine social stability which in turn would cause a loss in confidence, leading to a drop in investments, setting a chain-reaction in motion. He referred to the social tensions which arose as a result of unequal earnings. "Singapore has been built on free enterprise, with high skills and disciplined brain power rewarded accordingly. Since 1819 our tradition has been competition. We thrive on the ability to flourish freely." Lee argued that this should continue. Well-qualified Malaysians should never be kept out of Singapore. If Singapore's doors were closed to them they would go further away, perhaps never to return. This would constitute a loss for Singapore and for Asia.

Lee warned against swank living. The less well-trained and well-off found it very hard to accept, especially when they saw Singaporeans spending in one night what they earned in a month. These social tensions must not become uncontrollable. The better-off should do something to identify with the well-being of the majority. They should make a contribution to the hopes and aspirations of the workers who made privileged situations possible, by helping in charitable work, or in other ways doing something for the less fortunate.

Speaking to the Employers Federation a week later, Lee came out in favour of the bonus system. He said it was a form of enforced annual saving. It was one of the contributing factors in the Japanese economic miracle, lower wage rates supplemented by bonuses twice annually, leading to higher savings and re-investments.

The Prime Minister also spoke of the need for Singapore not to import completely unnecessary social divisions and antagonisms. "In Singapore a person is judged by what he is, by what he can do, and not what accent or social mannerisms he has. He can be a coolie, when he started life. He can, and many do, end up as respected tycoons and head of their clan associations." It was imperative that Singapore continued with easy social relations, great social and economic mobility. They contributed towards relaxed industrial relations. Lee gave two instances of how not to improve management-labour relations. One concerned a British foreman hitherto working in Nigeria. He treated Singapore workers like uneducated Africans. The workers looked upon him as a barbarian. Result was strikes and go-slows. The shoe factory collapsed. The second instance was a crude Australian supervisor in a motor assembling plant. There was a strike because of his vulgar and obscene language. The management had to get rid of him to restore good management-labour relations and work discipline. Fortunately, very few Europeans behaved like those two. Moreover, the non-British Europeans, like the Germans, were anxious to establish good working relationships, even before production began. They set up works councils. They set out to give their workers a sense of belonging, a sense of participation.

Coming back to the problem of wages, the Prime Minister said that not all the strength of a determined government could have held wage increases to a moderate level, but for the understanding of union leaders, and their members, that it was in the national interest to press on the economic accelerator. Work permits were issued to sixty thousand non-citizens. Another fifteen thousand were on block permits for construction work, making a total of seventy-five thousand. There were many illegal

32

no-work-permit non-citizens. These would have to be stopped, but the policy would be to continue allowing non-citizen workers into Singapore until the annual intake into National Service equalled the numbers recycled into the reserves, and into productive jobs, by 1973-75. "We know what we are doing. We also know the price we have to pay. Employers ought to know that there are ways which can keep the relaxed situation on the industrial front as it is."

Singapore's young women workers were under-utilised. After child-birth, they often stopped working because wage rates for women workers were not enough to make it worth their while to leave their children to be cared for by someone they must pay to do this. Lee said the government would consider sharing dollar for dollar the capital cost of creches and full day kindergartens near or in factories. Employers would have to bear the cost of running them, treating it as part of wage costs. "Then we can have full use of an untapped work force between the ages of eighteen and thirty-eight, of over two hundred thousand, over a quarter of our present work force."

The Prime Minister pointed out that this would mean doubling the income of the skilled, semi-skilled and unskilled families. "It will lessen tensions. It will also help keep family size down. So my successor in office will have an easier situation to tackle in the 1980s."

XII

Opening an extension to Mount Alvernia Hospital on 21 September, the Prime Minister remarked that dedication was a commodity in scarce supply. But in the little that there had been in Singapore, both in education and the running of hospitals, the Catholic Church had made a significant contribution to raising standards. In the course of the next five to seven years, Singapore would become an important medical centre for the region. "We can provide specialist medical treatment over a wide spectrum of specialities for anyone who seeks them." Private practitioners and specialists could use specialist equipment in government hospitals, with all trained ancillary support, in return for undertaking to teach post-graduate students. Then excellent post-operation care, in hospitals like Mount Alvernia, could provide a valuable recuperative centre. Singapore offered opportunities to those who sought education, dental or medical treatment. "As we progress, so we offer some benefits in education and health to those of our neighbours who wish to take advantage of them."

On 1 October, the Prime Minister opened a "Keep Singapore Pollution Free" Campaign. He observed that some things in life could only be enjoyed by a whole society. No amount of private wealth could ensure clean and healthy, green and gracious surroundings. The absence of mosquitoes, flies and other noxious insects, and noise nuisance could only be ensured for, and enjoyed by, a whole society. Everyone must share the responsibility to keep up such an environment. Otherwise life became unpleasant and even unbearable for all. The government's responsibility was to see that the administrative machinery for these amenities was efficient. It was up to the people to mantain high standards of conduct. "We can educate, persuade and bring social pressure to bear on the wayward. Finally for a miscreant minority which refuses to conform, they must be punished when they violate the laws."

Lee promised, and it was a promise he kept, that in the next few years, in several planned phases, Singapore's rivers, streams and canals would be pollution-free. In the long run, keeping homes, roads and parks clean must be a matter of personal habit. The higher the density of population, the more difficult it was to achieve this. "In the main city area, we are living at around thirty thousand per square mile. And with bigger and higher satellite towns, these densities will increase. So it is all the more necessary the better to organise our lives. We must enable people to get from their homes to their offices or factories with a minimum of traffic jams. We must keep down traffic noise, cutting down noisy exhausts. We must lower the volume of all loudspeakers."

All non-citizens working in Singapore on work permits must be inducted into this way of life in orientation courses. Anti-social habits were not acceptable in Singapore. The punishment for repeated violation of the keep-the-city-clean laws must lead to the withdrawal of work permits and expulsion. The volume of radios and television sets must be kept down and not intrude on neighbours' privacy. "We must restore some of the tranquility and serenity of life in our city. We must bring back that appreciation of nature and beauty, of trees and birds, flowers and fountains. These are the hallmarks of a cultivated society."

XIII

On 16 October, the Prime Minister gave a farewell dinner to the British Commander-in-Chief at the Istana. The President attended. In his speech, Lee said that since January 1968, he had, from time to time, speculated on the circumstances in which he would bid farewell to the last four-star British Commander-in-Chief, Far East. One circumstance was a continued British presence on a smaller scale. "So, as Far East Command winds up, and we bid Sir Brian and Lady Burnett farewell, we welcome the ANZUK Commanders, British, Australians and New Zealanders. This makes the break with the past less momentous and the transition into a new era easier."

It was difficult to estimate the contribution the British forces had made to the stability and security of the Malaysia-Singapore area. But for the forces of Far East Command during the years of "Confrontation", it would have been a different Southeast Asia, with a very different successor to the late Dr. Sukarno. For had Dr. Sukarno's techniques of political pressure and military harassment worked, then instead of construction and progress, chaos and confusion would have been the lot of Southeast Asia. The Secretary of State for Defence in the past British Government said that they did not expect gratitude when the Government undertook these obligations. "Nevertheless, we would like to record our recognition of what the British, Australians and New Zealanders did. The continued existence, progress and prosperity of Singapore would never have been, but for them."

In comparison with Far East Command, ANZUK was a modest task force, with a two-star Commander to mark its different size and role. But it was still a significant naval and air presence, its credibility underlined by the presence of an ANZUK brigade. It was unlikely that British forces would ever be engaged on the same scale, as in the years of "Confrontation" or in the years of the "Emergency". Hence the urgency with which the Malaysians and Singapore had pursued the expansion of their own forces. "We hope to be able more adequately to look after our own internal security and, together, we should be able to ward off common threats." Every year made a great difference. When told in January 1968 of the plans for complete rundown by 1971, it was shock treatment. "It either galvanised us to more intense action, or it could have knocked us out. It was a close thing. But we have not keeled over." Singapore looked forward to regular visits from British Commanders. Lee hoped that the two-star command in ANZUK would be a certain stepping-stone to the highest command positions in Britain, Australia and New Zealand, as Commander-in-Chief, Far East Command, had been for British officers for so many years. Lee presented Sir Brian and Lady Burnett with a salver to remind them of their brief, but he hoped, happy stay in Singapore, as the last Commander-in-Chief, Far East Command.

XIV

Before the end of October Lee went to Europe. In Zurich, he spoke at a reception given by the Union Bank of Switzerland, about the scope for economic collaboration between Switzerland and Singapore. Singapore already ranked as the third most important Asian market for the Swiss watch industry, next to Hong Kong and Japan. The Swiss had chosen Singapore as their first site in Asia for a watch accessories factory. It was already in operation. The Swiss watch industry had also established a technical and service centre in Singapore for Southeast Asia.

Meanwhile, especially in the past six years, Singapore's traditional role as a collection centre for regional raw materials, and a distribution centre for Western and Japanese manufactured products, had changed in emphasis. "We are becoming more a centre for assembly and manufacturing." Improving and more developed banking, insurance, shipping, airlines, and telecommunications services supported this new role. "We have also deliberately encouraged the development of Singapore as a financial centre. We have provided the home for the Asian dollar market. We also have an active gold market." Singapore had set out to be to Southeast Asia, what Switzerland was to Europe, a money and gold market. "We are a small country with a population of 2.1 million. We have little in natural resources. We have no choice but to organise ourselves in an orderly way, and work hard to make a living in the highly competitive international market. Our people have learnt the importance of maintaining political stability and a climate of confidence. They know that their standard of living depends on their educational standards and their productivity. They know that any upset in international trade through the unsettled currency parities and the 10 per cent American import surcharge will affect them, since about 31 per cent of Singapore's GNP is generated through external trade."

Singapore was surrounded by the sea, situated in the centre of the archipelago in Southeast Asia, linking east and west. Singapore, in terms of ships using it, was the fourth busiest port in the world. It was the largest petroleum-refining, shipbuilding and repairing centre, between Europe and Japan. Hence Singapore provided the supporting services for oil exploration and production in the region. Singapore was linked with continental Asia via a causeway. More workers could be made available by drawing upon a pool of keen and easily trainable young workers from surrounding countries, where wages were lower and unemployment high. These workers were not foreigners. Many of them had relatives in Singapore. "The workers we take in on work permits are those who are hardy and readily assimilable, because they are of the same stock."

Perhaps Singapore's most important asset was the confidence of management and workers in each other's reasonableness. The government enjoyed general electoral support, having been in office for twelve and a half years. And there was close identification of views between the government and the unions. In the past five years, Singapore's GNP increased at an annual average rate of 13 per cent at constant prices. At the same time, the cost of living of the workers had been kept down to a 1.2 per cent inflation rate per year for the past decade. This was partly because of the reduction in prices of rice and other necessities, and the constant cost of rents for public housing.

Then there was the growing market in Southeast Asia itself, with a population of over two hundred and fifty million. Companies operating in Singapore looked forward to exporting to Japan, as the Japanese liberalised their trade, especially with Southeast Asian countries. However, the China market can only be in sophisticated factory equipment, and not consumer durables. Swiss manufacturers of machinery, precision and optical instruments, fine chemicals and pharmaceuticals could find Singapore a stable off-shore base for their manufacture. Rather than import foreign workers, the Swiss might consider exporting their factories to places like Singapore, where political conditions were stable, workers disciplined and hardworking, and the economic infrastructure more than adequate. "We are also changing the emphasis from physical services to brain services. There is a growing demand for engineering design, fabrication, installation and other technical services."

From Switzerland, the Prime Minister flew to London where at the Albert Hall on 2 November he addressed the Institute of Directors. He said it was fortunate for Singapore that all the super and major powers had an interest in keeping the sea-lanes, from East to West through the Straits of Malacca, and from North to South from Japan to Australia, open for the free passage of their ships. Singapore was as much a cross-roads of the twentieth century as it was in the nineteenth when Raffles founded it. And living on a cross-roads one developed a keen sensitivity to regional and international events. The two most fateful events for Asia in 1971 were not the Che Guevarist insurgency in Ceylon, not the horrendous tragedy in East Pakistan. They were the two sudden changes in policy by President Nixon which startled Asia and the world. First the announcement in mid-July of his visit to Beijing before May 1972. And as if that was not sufficient a shock to the inscrutable Japanese, the second followed in mid-August, a 10 per cent import surchage, and non-convertibility of the American dollar. A new series in the world ball game had begun. Nixon had put paid to all the rumpus over the Pentagon papers and the Laotian debacle.

Lee thought that the Japanese would probably continue their high growth rates at 8 per cent to 10 per cent, whatever the higher parity of the yen to the dollar, and however they liberalised foreign imports and investments into Japan. It was because they would remain "Japan Inc.", Japanese workers and managers would continue to be loyal to their companies. And workers, managers and company directors would be loyal, first and last, to the Emperor. But the Japanese might continue to be unliked in nearly all of Asia. About the only place where they were not disliked was Singapore. Perhaps it was because Singaporeans were also a hard driving people. Singapore's growth rates over the past three years had been 14.6 per cent per annum at constant prices. Immediate neighbours, Malaysia, made 7.8 per cent, and Indonesia, 6.6 per cent. Singaporeans might become less loved. Singapore's per capita GNP for 1970 was £396, over two and a half times that of Malaysia, and twelve times that of Indonesia. So Singapore was encouraging investments, in both Indonesia and Malaysia, by exempting from taxation, specified investments in those countries. Singapore investment was the sixth highest foreign investment in Indonesia, with America and Japan as leaders. The British were ninth. Meanwhile, British exports in Southeast Asia were systematically being overtaken by Japanese exports, of cars, radios, television sets, casette recorders, refrigerators and, now, giant tankers and power stations. This was happening in many other traditional markets of Britain. It took a long time to set a trend. It took an even longer time to reverse it.

Lee predicted that in the years after Mao, China was likely to go more expert than Red. Then they would make rapid progress. Once they gave up working things out from first principles, guided by the Thoughts of

Chairman Mao, and instead imported technology under licence, they would accelerate their growth rates. They would cut out the heavy costs of research and development and the lead time lost in R. and D. Unlike Japan, they would not be so dependent on external sources for raw materials, and external markets for exports. They would want to buy, not consumer durables, but capital equipment and industrial know-how, not just civil aircraft, but the know-how and capital equipment to build the aircraft. "Before the late eighties, China will have enough economic weight to make herself felt by the smaller countries bordering her, from North Korea down to Vietnam, Laos, Cambodia, Thailand, Burma, and the Himalayan States. She will increasingly play the role of Japan in the years before the war, in providing cheap exports in low and middle technology products, price-cutting to establish markets for her goods."

Lee thought it might take many years to refurbish and modernise the economic infrastructure of Indonesia. The absence of proper teaching and training in the twenty-five profligate years of the Sukarno era had left them little by way of professional and management competence, or industrial skills. Every service had to be bought from consultants at the best prices. Even in Singapore, where most international tenderers had set up their branch regional headquarters, technological expertise, industrial know-how, professional and management competence were in great demand.

Fortunately, money could be easily mobilised in Singapore. The Asian dollar market based in Singapore was now handling around US$900 million. At its past rate of growth, it would reach US$1,300 million by 1975, even if the US balanced their payments. Entrepreneurs who could identify feasible projects in Singapore and the surrounding areas should have no difficulty in raising capital in Singapore. The Americans were pouring into the area, withdrawal from Vietnam notwithstanding. The West Europeans had also re-entered the region.

There was a challenging role for Britain in Europe and for the nations of Western Europe, in the third world. It was as yet a poor third. But there were select areas where, because enterprise and high performance were highly rewarded, and because the people's threshold for pain was higher, growth rates had been high, and held out promise of getting even better. In Asia, the areas were South Korea, Taiwan (though the future was less certain now), Hong Kong, Malaysia and Singapore. Now Indonesia looked like joining the growers. On every continent, the super powers and the major powers would contend for trade, for economic and political influence. Britain and the other West Europeans could be valuable countervailing economic and political forces in an increasingly tripolar world of the 1980s as China developed the economic strength to make her influence felt around the rest of Asia.

Japanese economic and political influence would increase as the Americans decreased theirs. Russia and China would not be left out. The West Europeans jointly could be a benign and stabilising influence in

A relaxed Lee at the
Conference

The British Prime Minister,
Edward Heath, arriving at
the Conference

The Queen and Mrs Lee Kuan Yew chatting at the Istana while Lee looks on

Queen Elizabeth and the Prime Minister
at dinner in Singapore in 1972

Tun Abdul Razak, Prime Minister
of Malaysia, paid a friendly visit to
Singapore in 1973.

The round table at the Commonwealth Conference held in Singapore in 1971 (above)

Lee greeting President Julius Nyerere of Tanzania at the 1971 Commonwealth Conference

widening the areas of peace and progress. "For the British, French and Dutch, through long centuries of association in empire, knew, and still know, the Asian peoples and their cultures better than the Americans or Japanese, the Chinese or Russians. Separately, neither the British, nor French, nor Dutch, can match the economic punch of the Americans, Russians or Japanese. But multi-national European corporations can be a match. In the new dispositions of power and influence in Asia, the West Europeans should be represented. West Europeans should revive their interests and renew their participation in the economic affairs of Asia, and of the world beyond Europe, or both Asia and Europe, and the world, will be the poorer for it."

XV

In a BBC forum the following evening, Lee was questioned about ANZUK. He said that the psychological impact of the five-power agreement was more important than the realities of the agreement. The psychological impact of a small ANZUK presence would deter any adventurism. The real danger was the gradual build-up of guerilla insurgency which was a technique pursued in South Vietnam, Laos, Cambodia, and Thailand. "And if they go under, then it will go south into Peninsular Malaya. In that situation, troops won't make much of a difference. But it's going to take a long time for them to come down, even if they do. But, in the meanwhile, acts of piracy, acts of adventurism, are less likely to happen."

Lee said he was as satisfied with the force as constituted. He thought a lot of people in Southeast Asia, outside Singapore and Malaysia, were secretly and privately relieved that there was a residual force. "It's going to take some time for the Japanese to build up their navy which I am sure they will. And I don't think the People's Republic of China will just stop with missiles and ICBMs and the infantrymen. I think they will also develop their navy. The Russians are going there in increasing numbers and the Americans use this phrase called — it is a contradiction in terms — 'peaceful harassment'. And the more ships you have to put throught the Straits because you need oil from the Gulf and sending your manufactures to Western Europe and carrying things from Western Europe back — the more you can be politically harassed if you have not got somebody there who would see that the rules of peaceful passage of the high seas are observed."

Lee added: "I don't believe for one moment that the British, the Australians and the New Zealanders can match the Russians, ship for ship. It is just not possible. I mean it's a question of priorities, of what British consumer wants and what the Russian consumer wants but doesn't get. He gets more ships. But the very fact that there is a base in Singapore means that instead of one mothership having to cater for three or four ships, you can have one base catering for a whole fleet, if and when the time arises."

Asked again about China, Lee thought that for some while, the Chinese would be pre-occupied with their long 4,000 to 6,000-mile border — "6,000 if you include Outer Mongolia with the Soviet Union, the Ussuri and the Amur Rivers and large vast tracks of territory which, up till 1860 and 1870, were all part of Imperial China". The other pre-occupation was that nobody should step into the shoes of the Americans in supplying the people in Taiwan with modern equipment and hence make the re-absorption of Taiwan too prohibitive for the People's Republic of China. "I don't anticipate seeing Chinese armies over-running the rest of Southeast Asia. But I do see 'make-it-yourself' revolutions with Chinese equipment — as in South Vietnam and North Vietnam and Laos. I do see 'advisers' on the use and maintenance of this equipment which will be supplied on either free or very 'soft' terms. And I think this is the kind of problems which we will have to live with, for a very long time. The Chinese believe, I think quite wisely, in low-cost, low-risk, maximum damage to all the imperialist powers of the world."

On the future of Japan, Lee said he would first make the distinction between being a nuclear power and a non-nuclear power. "I think the first step the Japanese would take would be a very powerful non-nuclear potential. For them to go nuclear is a very traumatic step forward, because they suffered the two big bombs. And they are so small and compact in Honshu — the middle island — that ten bombs could knock them out. And so, if they are going to go nuclear, they have to go underwater. In other words, for a second strike or an assured destruction capability. That takes about five to seven years a time jump — a quantum jump as the Americans call it. And I would not rule that out altogether, because the way they have been treated by the Americans, first in July on China, Nixon's visit to China; secondly, this 10 per cent surcharge — I think there must be a large number of young Japanese in their early thirties and forties, with no sense of guilt or any memory of the last war, who would question the validity of the assumption that the American umbrella is there."

Asked about the American presence in the region, Lee pointed out that the Americans were spending some money developing Diego Garcia and he did not think that could be just an absent-minded vote being lost down in the Indian Ocean. He thought the very fact that the Americans had depended on the British and Britain's allies to look after the Gulf and the Indian Ocean and the Straits, must mean now that the transition between this small ANZUK presence and some future arrangement would depend largely upon whether the Americans regained their self-confidence and took an interest in the outer world beyond the immediate waters washing her shores. "If the Americans do not regain this poise and this composure and this interest in the outside world, then I think we are in for very, very serious trouble. And I doubt whether ANZUK will be such a powerful cornerstone of Australia, New Zealand and American security arrangements unless the Americans recover this poise."

XVI

Lee went up to Liverpool to accept from the University an honorary degree of Doctor of Laws. He discussed student unrest. In America, he said, he had met the president of an ivy league American university. He had just relinquished office. Lee asked him for an explanation for the restless, demonstration-inclined, militantly anti-Establishment students then in American universities. Why was it that hippism, psychedelic music, drugs and free sex had begun to infect even the ivy league universities where student populations were small, and student-teacher ratios were low? Why was it that the wealthiest society man had ever created was at odds with itself? Was it, as de Gaulle had suggested in May 1968, after the student and worker uprisings in Paris, because of the impersonalised and dehumanising nature of the age of automation? Were students and workers cogs in a complex machine, unable to get fulfilment either from their work or their leisure, living in large urban sprawls? Lee said he had inquired because he had a deep and vested interest in the causes of the social problems in the West. The Singapore Government had actively encouraged the introduction of Western industry and know-how into Singapore. With Western industries had come Western technologists and executives, their wives and children, and their life-styles. Some of them gave visible demonstration of the new hedonist cult. By their personal example, they added to the insidious daily erosion of conventional Eastern morality by so many Western television features, the cinema, magazines and newspapers. The continuous appeal to the baser instincts was found in too many Western-made or Western-style television advertisements, whether selling soft drinks or soap. American weeklies carried discussion of drugs, promiscuity and perversion, often without a word of disapprobation. "Already we have the beginnings of drug taking among some students in Singapore together with the pop songs and psychedelic music. And the strange dress-styles and imitative behaviour of some of our Western educated youth are causing concern to parents and the government." Lee's American friend gave him a perceptive analysis of the problems of the young in the contemporary West. The new mood in America, he said, had evolved gradually over the decades. The pace of change has been speeded up in the years since the end of the last world war, especially since the war in Vietnam. With each major scientific advance and mastery of the universe, young people had moved away from their Christian belief in God. Man was not only unravelling the secrets of his physical universe, he was also able to intervene in the biological processes. Pills could prevent conception. Pills could give euphoria and pleasure. Pills brought sleep, rest for a troubled mind. With disbelief in God and religion, fear of punishment for evil done had gone. Expectations of reward for good deeds had vanished. There was only this world, to make the most of.

Young people had never really known depression and mass unemployment. To aggravate this, affluence had been taken for granted in America. The younger generation now believed that the advances in industry and technology, and in methods of government, had made it possible for everyone to enjoy the good life. Immediate and instant pleasure was available for all. If they did not get their share of it, then it had to be due to the waywardness of the legislators, or the iniquity of the executive, or the villainies of the industrial-military complex. And welfare programmes had helped to make the Protestant work-ethic irrelevant. Why work hard and save for the rainy day, when the state could provide for lay-abouts, better than if they did not lay about?

Lee said his reaction was that if these were the basic causes of the so-called counter cultures of the West, then the introduction of Western industries and technology to Asia should not necessarily bring in its train this reckless tendency to experiment with one's body and psyche, ending up with drug addiction. If the breakdown of the work-ethic was the result of material abundance and over-ample welfare cushions for unemployment, then underdeveloped countries, like Singapore, were not in grave danger of contagion or sickness or other misfortunes.

Moreover, the East Asians, Chinese, Japanese, Koreans and the Vietnamese were pragmatic in their approach to life. As Confucianists and Buddhists, they believed that the hereafter was not much different from the present. To have a decent life in the next world, one's progeny must ensure that there was enough for one's needs in the next world. Any son who buried his parents without providing for their needs in the next world must be an ingrate. He must symbolically place food and wine on the alter (where the ancestral tablet is placed), and also burn miniature paper houses, carriages and money, so that they could reach his departed ancestor. This was repeated every year on the oriental All Souls' Day (*Cheng Meng*). The *raison d'etre* for Buddhist ancestor worship, with its forms and rituals, was that a man should look after his departed ancestors so that they would look after his welfare in this world, and so that the man's children will do likewise for him.

Eastern societies were patriarchal as yet unassailed by women's liberation movement, which might not come even after legal and economic equality of women was accepted as a country industrialised. The family unit was still tightly-knit, making up for any deficiency in state welfare. This way of life, living in accordance with strict codes of conduct, could continue well after the metaphysical basis may no longer be believed in. This was especially so when welfare benefits were meagre compared to British standards, and could not adequately buffer people from unemployment, sickness or old age. Hence Japanese workers had so far not shown the malaise of their American and Western counterparts, even though they had become production digits, in an increasingly automated, computerised world, and despite the monotony of assembly-line production. James Reston, an American commentator who had recently visited China, and had his appendix removed in Beijing, discovered that Chinese

42

workers in iron and steel mills were not only hardworking, but enthusiastically so, trying to raise production norms. Lee believed, however, that the solving of physical and biological conundrums had, nevertheless, created problems, requiring adjustments in social behaviour, not only in the West but also in the East. For example, new discoveries in medicine had reduced infant mortality and deaths due to infectious diseases. Modern medicine in new countries in Asia had resulted in population explosions in so many of them. Family planning had become a necessity for economic progress. But it was hard to change the public esteem for a father with many sons and daughters, which in the old days meant more workers for his rice-fields. It was only after Singapore girls had all become educated, held their own jobs after marriage and moved to better housing, that family planning was able to bring population growth rates down from nearly 4 per cent in 1960 to 1.7 per cent in 1970.

Big continents like China could insulate their people from the West and control contact with them. Foreign diplomats in Beijing lived in a diplomatic capsule, unable to make free contact with ordinary people. But a world made ever smaller by the inventiveness of Western man in communications and transportation left small underdeveloped countries with Hobson's choice. For Singapore not to bring in new industries and technology from the West would mean cutting themselves off from the mainstream of material progress. "By importing Western technology, we have achieved economic growth rates of over 13 per cent per annum, at constant prices, for the past five years, more than doubling the GNP in five years, and more than trebling it in the last decade. But the price for this material progress is the risk of eroding traditional value and culture patterns, and upsetting decorous social behaviour." This problem was made more acute because Singapore was an international junction for ships, aircraft and telecommunications by cable and satellite. It was not possible to insulate Singapore from the world, though it was possible to inoculate and immunise the people, through their cultural and social values, from the contemporary maladies of the West.

"We have been more successful in doing this with those parts of the population where their primary education has been in their mother tongues, reinforcing the influence of their homes and emphasising the attitudes which uphold the family unit as sacrosanct. And because no one believes that abundance and generous welfare are the natural order of things, society is not indulgent to those who opt out and expect their needs to be met out of public expenditure." Perhaps Singapore's best safeguard against the decline of the work-ethic in the West was that hard work was rewarding. So long as higher performance brought rewards, most people would do their best. Another fact was that undeveloped countries could not afford to feather-bed those who did not strive to make their contribution to the success of the society. Countries which wanted to develop quickly could be a little soft-hearted, but they could not afford to be soft-headed.

But then, what happened when Singapore had developed, when there was enough prosperity to spread around? With rapid modernisation came urbanisation and new styles of life. There would be the tendency for the society to become less patriarchal, as women, with equal education, get equal pay. Then the relevance of traditional social mores might be challenged. Before then, Lee hoped the West, which invented the pill, would also have established a new social equilibrium, absorbing the impact of all these discoveries on social behaviour. New discoveries, particularly the pill, might have made the old constraints appear out-of-date. But he doubted if constraints were irrelevant to social stability and collective endeavour in any society, East or West. The fabric of civilised living might be torn asunder if new norms for public manners and public morality were not established. For, whatever the differences in social systems and behaviour norms between the East and the West, these problems of the West could still spill over to those parts of the East which were on the jet routes linking the West and the East, unless these problems were resolved in the West itself.

At the University of Sheffield, Lee was given an honorary LL.D. In his address, Lee predicted that, by the 1980s, it would be at least a tripolar world, with China's re-emergence into the international community as a potential super-power. A combined Western Europe and Japan would be able, if they so decided, to throw their respective weights on the side of freer trade and economic co-operation. This would make for a safer world, one less introvert, trading and co-operating within and beyond economic blocs. A world where movement of goods, experts and expertise were free and easy; these were the conditions in which British talent found fulfilment during three hundred years of empire. The British, compared to other nations, had always had more than their average share of discoverers and inventors, in science and engineering. When these conditions of freer movement of goods, experts and expertise were re-established in a new framework in an outward-looking Europe, with a minimum of tariff barriers between economic blocs, British talent would again find fulfilment. These were the conditions which would also bring the most benefits to all countries, the developed and the less developed. But forecasting was a hazardous business. Futurology was still not a recognised discipline in British universities, as it was in American think-tank institutions. "And since I was tutored in a British university, I think it is unwise to sketch anything beyond the clearly discernible trends. For anything more would be in realms of speculation."

From Sheffield, Lee travelled to Cambridge where he gave the commemorative lecture at Fitzwilliam College, his old college. He recalled that Kipling in 1889, in "The Ballad of East and West", had predicted that "East is East and West is West, and never the twain shall meet". Recent history had provided an ironic rebuttal in over half a million Asians, mostly Indians and Pakistanis, now permanently settled in Britain. East had met West. Together with over fifty million Britons, half a million

Indians and Pakistanis would have a second generation soon born and bred in Britain, knowing nothing of India or Pakistan. Cheap, convenient, safe and rapid mass transportation had resulted in considerable immigration of peoples. From their former dependencies, people from Asia, Africa and the Caribbean had moved into the high leisure-seeking societies of Britain, France and Western Europe. They took up jobs, mostly in the lower social and income brackets. East and West had met, albeit unequally, in one society, in the West.

When the West first sailed out to the East, they met on unequal terms. Large areas of Asia were colonised by the superior naval and industrial strength of the West. The only country to avert Western domination was Japan. Even China had to grant extra-territorial concessions in her main ports. Twenty-three years after independence for India and Pakistan, in 1971, East met West, still on unequal terms. The exception was Japan. China would dispute this. They probably considered themselves more than equal to the West. Certainly, they believed theirs to be a superior society, cleansed of selfishness and the profit motive, freed from the clutches of greedy capitalists. But Japan and China were East Asia. For South and Southeast Asia, whether it was the Westerner who visited the East, or the Easterner who visited the West, both were conscious of the inequality of their respective positions. As individuals, there were many East and South Asians, whose ability and competence in their professional fields, were equal to the best of the Europeans and Americans. But why, in group performance as nation states, except for East Asia, had they not been able to equal the West? Why could they not organise themselves, maintain effective administrations, ensure political stability and provide proper sanitation, clean potable water, reliable electric supply? Why had they not controlled population growth? Why had they not widened the base and raised the levels of education of their people, and trained them in industrial techniques and technology? Why had they not made better use of machinery and equipment they bought, on soft loans, from the West, and made the economic and social progress which would have made them equal to the West?

The great Hindu and Sinic civilisations, going back well beyond 2,000 and 3,000 years respectively, could only have been created by peoples of considerable talent. They must have had the capacity for organisation and administration to sustain cultivated living over long periods of time. They must have maintained a surplus in agricultural and pastoral production, to enable a significant portion of their people to cultivate the arts. For music, literature, painting, sculpture and architecture flourished. The genius expressed in solid granite, chiselled and carved into the Ellora Caves near Aurangabad in Maharashtra, in the sixth to seventh centuries, the temples of Mahabalipuram near Madras in the seventh and eighth centuries, more recently, in the seventh century under the Mogul emperor, Shah Jehan, the Taj Mahal, these monuments of South Asian civilisations surpass any architecture of the same period in the West. In modern times, the poetry of

Tagore bears witness to Bengali artistry in both the English and Bengali languages, whilst India was still under the British Raj. What is it that has made Japan such an outstanding exception to the long catalogue of other not so successful attempts at modernisation and industrialisation in the East?

Just over a century after the Meiji Restoration, in 1868, Japan had the second highest GNP in the non-Communist world, although in per capita income, she ranked below West Germany. In 1969, Japan had surpassed Italy. Now, China appeared as though by another thirty years, she will have most of the intermediate technology implements between the shovel and the satellite, between the bicycle and the ICBM. In order to learn the technology of the West, the Japanese sent scholars abroad. They learnt the languages of the advanced nations. In a thoroughly eclectic manner, they chose from each his best: from the Prussians, their military system and strategic doctrines, from the British, their shipbuilding. The French also made a contribution to Japan's transformation. "But, unfortunately, to this day, the grapes grown in Japan will not make wines like French wines." And this was not for want of trying.

By the beginning of this century, the Japanese had defeated the Russian fleet. They grew in strength and confidence. They systematically learnt from countries more advanced than themselves. They bought the sophisticated products of the West, took them apart, studied the components, then reproduced almost identical products, albeit of unequal quality. However, a generation was now growing up, where the label "Made in Japan" denoted high quality at medium prices.

In their attempts to identify the factors that made the West superior in the sciences and technology, the Japanese even copied the dress-styles of the West. The black hat and grey gloves, striped trousers and black tails, became part of Japanese protocol. But now they tailored all these out of their own felt, textile and leather. At the same time, they had preserved as much as they could of their traditional forms of dress, styles of architecture and way of life. After their defeat in World War II, and during the years of American occupation, they decided that perhaps their diet was deficient. This might have been a factor accounting for the better performance of the Americans. So, with characteristic thoroughness and zeal, Japanese leaders set out to get their people to consume more animal protein and wheat, in addition to their traditional diet of fish, pickled vegetables and rice. It was not by accident that one of the cheapest drinks available in Japan today was pasteurised milk, subsidised by a government determined to ensure that their next generation would grow up taller, stronger and brighter. In fact, they had produced a taller generation. Some doctors said that the extra inches were due as much to animal protein as to a change in habits, sitting at tables, instead of on the floor, thus improving blood circulation in the legs.

What could South and Southeast Asian nations, some with ancient and glorious civilisations, learn from the experience of Japan? Could they industrialise and modernise the faster, with Japan having shown the way? Could they avoid the fanatic excesses of the Chinese communists? What were the mistakes they should avoid repeating, like the despoliation of Japan's once beautiful and gracious environment, the pollution of her air, rivers and beaches? Could they do it without the monotonous communist exhortation to hard work and self-sacrifice? Could it be done without the zealous regimentation of the Chinese communists, or the intense patriotism of the Japanese?

China and India had set out to catch up in science and technology by two different political systems. The Chinese had been successful in detonating hydrogen bombs and sending a satellite into space whistling "the East is Red". But this was in spite, not because, of the isolationism they imposed upon themselves. The men who made possible their technological advance were Chinese scientists, who had worked long years in American research establishments on nuclear and astro-physics, and aerospace sciences. Also, from 1949 to the time of their conflict with the Russians in the early sixties, they received Russian machinery and know-how. Until the split became open, Russian was the first foreign language taught in schools and universities in China. Now English had again become the first foreign language. In theory, it should now be easier for the less developed to develop. There was the recent UNCTAD agreements in-principle at Geneva, in October 1970. The developed countries could now reduce tariffs on the manufactured products of the less developed, without having to give the same concessions to all, including the developed, as required by GATT (General Agreement on Tariffs and Trade). New countries should be able to sell more of their simple manufactures for foreign exchange, buy more capital machinery and industrialise further. World Bank soft loans, United Nations agencies, bilateral and multi-lateral aid programmes, all were designed to ease the painful and difficult process of industrialisation, to make it less strenuous and exacting an effort. In theory, these concessions should shorten the time taken for industrial transformation.

But there were some harsh realities which had to be recognised, and several contradictions to overcome, by new countries before they could advance. Only then could they the better refurbish their societies, and have their old civilisations made more relevant to the mass-production, high consumption age. High consumption and high leisure came only after sustained endeavour. Looking at the great relics of past Hindu and Buddhist civilisations in South and Southeast Asia, Mahabalipuram, the Ellora and Ajanta Caves in India, Borobudur in Java, Angkor Wat in Cambodia, what was forgotten was that there were long periods of order and discipline, provided by a firm framework of administrative efficiency and discipline. Whenever incentives failed to work, coercion or compulsion was applied. Otherwise, their architects and engineers could not have created, in granite, sandstone, or marble, the ideas and the imagination of their artists. For some of these monuments took several centuries, and five times as many generations, to complete.

The first contradiction South and Southeast Asian societies faced was how to revamp their value systems and culture patterns, to meet the needs of an industrial society. It was not possible to move from the agricultural economies of Asia, equivalent to those of fifteenth and sixteenth century Western Europe, into the "technetronic" era the Americans had created and named, without jettisoning parts of the value systems and culture patterns of the past. Some of them inhibited, instead of encouraging, punctuality, work discipline, the desire to increase production norms, the acquisition of scientific knowledge and engineering techniques. Industrial status could be achieved only if new value systems and behaviour patterns were grafted on the old. It was in part the difference between the more intense and exacting Sinic cultures of East Asia and the less intense and less demanding values of Hindu culture of South and Southeast Asia, that accounted for the difference in industrial progress between Eastern and Southern Asia. The softer and more benign Hindu civilisation spread through Burma, Thailand, Laos and Cambodia, meeting the Sinic civilisation on the borders of Vietnam, hence the name, the Indo-China Peninsula.

It required bold and determined leadership to eradicate those values which hampered the advance of a people into the higher sciences. It required a strong will to force the adoption of values and attitudes which could quicken the pace of change. Rapid acquisition of knowledge in the sciences, industrial know-how, management expertise, marketing techniques and higher manipulative skills were only possible if the people were intense in the pursuit of these goals. They did not go with a relaxed culture, in which fatalism was a tranquiliser for anxiety over failure. Further, it required a practical turn of mind to modify these new disciplines and techniques, so as to fit them into the different social and cultural moulds, which their different histories had imprinted on South and Southeast Asian peoples.

Gunnar Myrdal, in his "Asian Drama" voluminously set out the reasons for lower achievements among these peoples. He termed them "soft societies". Their expectations and desire for achievement were lower. Had he studied the Sinic civilisations of East Asia — Korea, Japan, China and Vietnam — he would have come to the opposite conclusion that these were hard societies. Of course, there was a price to be paid for it. A recent survey by Americans doctors of the anxiety ratings of different ethnic nation groups, placed the Japanese at the top. They were the most anxiety-ridden of all peoples. The doctors were unable to evaluate the Chinese. The Germans were high up. The Americans were well down the neurosis ladder. The British even lower. But this happy state of serenity could only be afforded by those who had already arrived, like the British.

To compound the problem for the less developed, the Protestant work ethics of the West which made virtues of diligence, thrift and enterprise, were at present being discounted in the West. The youth of the West was seen to be rejecting these virtues. The abundance of Western post-industrial societies had been accompanied by an ostentatious flouting, by students and unionised workers, of those conventional values, without which the wealth and leisure could not have come about in the first instance. This confused students and workers of the less developed countries. It was more comfortable to believe that with the latest industrial innovations, hard work, thrift and industry were no longer necessary to lift their agricultural and pastoral economies on to the higher income levels of the industrial economy. It was more congenial, if the application of science and technology to industry could do the trick, without sweat and toil, which made for a strenuous life. For the less developed in South and Southeast Asia to achieve standards of life comparable to those of the post-industrial West, two or more generations might have to toil away. The result was that many professionally competent, but impatient, young men in the less developed parts of Asia chose the easier way out. By migrating, they could, and did, immediately enjoy standards of life of developed societies. And many did so. Because most of them were English-speaking, they had gone to the English-speaking countries of the West — Britain, Canada and America. American officials went out of their way to facilitate this brain drain. For example, they held examinations for doctors trained under the British system in India, Pakistan, Ceylon, Malaysia and Singapore, to enable them, ostensibly, to pursue research in America. The Indian and Pakistani governments had prohibited the holding of these examinations. So did Singapore. But the Malaysians still allowed the Americans to hold such examinations. The result was that hundreds of Indian and Pakistani doctors found the means to fly to Kuala Lumpur in West Malaysia to take these annual examinations. Too few took the patriotic road, because it meant a long period of self-denial, and hard work, for which the only reward was the satisfaction of helping to raise the quality of life for one's own people.

The second major contradiction to be resolved was that of language. Pride in one's past was necessary for self-confidence and morale, essential ingredients of success. With independence came a revivalist, romanticist streak. The indigenous language, modes of dress, even manners and mannerisms, were resurrected and given pre-eminence. Often they were the external manifestations of a supposedly glorious past. It was a phenomenon to be found not only in older civilisations. The pre-occupation of the American Negroes with Afro-American studies, new hair and dress-styles, were assertions of their right to a dignified and not inferior past. And it was worth noting that the Japanese had preserved as much of themselves, as was compatible with the industrial society. To get access to new knowledge, the best course would be to continue using the language of the former metropolitan power, particularly where this happened to be English. The contradiction between pride of one's own language, and the mastery of a foreign language, could be reconciled. The developed foreign

49

language was a useful legacy of empire. It should continue to be taught and used, whilst the indigenous language, over the decades, could be modernised and enriched by extensively borrowing ideas and words from the languages of the developed. Eventually, it could develop its own modern literature. In this way, scholars could go abroad. More important, the textbooks, journals and publications of the developed countries could be imported, enabling more students to acquire the knowledge and disciplines for industrial advance. Professors and experts from advanced countries could visit the universities of the less developed, and instruct much larger numbers of students than could be sent abroad.

This was what the Japanese did. They had some of their best students learn the languages of the advanced countries of the West, and sent them abroad to learn what the West had, which Japan did not. After several decades, the Japanese built up their own technical institutes and universities, using Japanese language textbooks for even technical and scientific subjects. But even today, they had scholars studying English, French and German going abroad, and keeping abreast of the latest developments in the higher sciences. They also imported foreign publications and kept in touch with contemporary work in all important fields. The assiduous learning of the language of an advanced country, and the fostering of one's own, were complementary, not inconsistent, policies.

But, so many new countries deliberately stifled the foreign language they had inherited and which could give them access to superior technology. Sometimes, this was done, not so much to elevate the status of the indigenous language, as to take away an advantage a minority ethnic group had by having greater competence in the former colonial language. This had been damaging. It blindfolded the next generation to the knowledge of the advanced countries. Worse, it led to an exodus of the professionally trained. They could emigrate to the advanced countries, and did, because they did not intend to allow their children to be crippled by language blinkers. No matter how good the translation from the English, Russian, French or German text, it often took two to three editions to have it translated and sent to the printer. Another two or three editions would have passed before the publication of the translated texts were available. Further, the range of books or journals which could be translated was narrow and limited. Translations could never equal access to direct sources, nor could they enable direct communication with specialists in the advanced countries.

Western science and technology had created one ever smaller world. It had led to mutual exposure of peoples of the West and less developed East. It was difficult to ward off external influences. To close a society, rigid controls had to be constantly maintained. Even the Russians found this unprofitable. Their "Intourist" now encouraged more travellers from the wealthy countries of the West, both to see their achievements, and to get more convertible currency. Their ballet and cultural troupes performed abroad. Their scientists and scholars attended congresses in the West, despite occasional defections. This trend was unlikely to be reversed. For the meeting of minds trained in similar, but somewhat different, disciplines could lead to a creative stimulus, when ideas were exchanged and disciplines cross-fertilized.

The question leaders of less developed South and Southeast Asia had to answer was not whether or not to modernise. Affluent tourists and the mass media had already aroused the appetites of their peoples for the sophisticated products, particularly consumer durables, of the advanced countries. The question to which they must find an answer was how rapidly to modernise and, equally important, how much of their traditional past could they retain, so that they were not just poor imitations of the West, with all the fads and fetishes, the follies and foibles of the contemporary West. One world need not mean a dull, grey or uniform one. The science, the technology, the computers, the automation, and the cybernetics for the mass-production of high-consumption economies had to be the same, based as they were on the physical sciences. But the architecture, social mores, styles of life, modes of dress, they need not be the same. The intake of calories, proteins, minerals and vitamins might have to approximate certain optimum levels. But the culinary arts need not be the same.

"Each leadership must decide what to keep and what to jettison of the old, to make progress and yet to keep enough to remain one's own distinctive self. Cultural continuity is compatible with the absorption of new technology. It will also lessen the problems of disorientation consequent on rapid changes in ways of working and modes of life."

Another major problem for many of the less developed countries was that they had to raise not only levels of knowledge and skills, but levels of intelligence, ability and dexterity. The controversy over whether ethnic differences correlated with low or high IQ would never be resolved so long as political and emotional considerations prevented dispassionate academic research and discussion. Whether it was nature or nurture, one problem especially acute in the societies of South and Southeast Asia was that the abler and more educated segments of their population tended to have much smaller families than the less educated. Even if genetics had no bearing on ability, and it were the environment, opportunities, diet, care and education which determined performance, very large families amongst the poor was still a grave problem. But if it turned out that nature as much as nurture decided the level of achievements, then some system of incentives and disincentives must be found to make sure that, with each succeeding generation, standards of education and skill, levels of performance and achievement, would rise both as a result of nature and of nurture. Whether it was genes, or the environment, or both, to catch up with the technology and match the capital accumulation of the developed, the problem of population control must be squarely faced. The solutions once decided upon must be vigorously implemented. Then standards of life would rise as levels of education and performance rose. Over the next few decades, there would be more in the East who could meet the West on equal terms. By the end of this century, there could be over a thousand millon people in East Asia who would equal the West in the sciences, technology, and in the arts. But most of South or Southeast Asia would probably be still unequal. It was more than a coincidence that those Asian countries which were able the better to resist Western domination were the ones that had emerged or were emerging into strong industrial nations. Japan and China, Korea and Vietnam (if they could be re-united), were meeting the West, especially the Canadians and Americans across the Pacific, and were dealing more on equal terms. China was anxious not to have to develop all her middle and higher technology industries from first principles, the way she developed her hydrogen bomb, her satellite and missile systems. China wanted to widen her field of potential collaborators in science-based industries in the West. Suspicious that the Americans would be the hardest to get industrial know-how from, China was cultivating the West Europeans and the Canadians.

But it was only the East Asians who were self-confident when dealing with the West. Both had put satellites into orbit, which only America, Russia and France had done. Pride in their long and glorious past was reinforced in the case of China, of having nuclear bombs and rockets, and in the case of Japan, of knowing that they make them. They were both confident that it was only a matter of decades before they were equal to most of the West. Meanwhile, in the less developed countries of South and Southeast Asia, disillusionment and near despair had set in because of their failure to make the grade. The despondency was all the greater because of earlier beliefs that growth was the natural and effortless result of the transference of capital equipment and work techniques from the developed to the less developed. This had not happened because there never was this easy ride towards the industrial society. The absurdities of the Che Guevarist insurgency in Ceylon, the terrifying tragedy of Bangladesh, and India's difficulties in dealing with over eight million refugees in West Bengal, underscored the present sorry state of affairs. The willingness of the developed West, and of the developed East in the case of Japan, and later China, to pass on the technology, capital equipment and skills on terms which were not too onerous, might regenerate optimism, and on a more realistic basis. An appreciation of each other's cultural differences which made for a higher or lower speed in developing the human and natural resources of each country would also help relations across ethnic and national boundaries.

When the South and Southeast Asians understood that the developed could, and were willing to help them, but that the decisive factor was the quality of their own leadership and the intensity of their own efforts, then East-West relationships would improve. "If South and Southeast Asians can re-establish the firm framework of administration which is competent and not corrupt, if social and work discipline can be re-imposed, then self-confidence will be restored. Then mutual respect will be established between most of the East and all of the West."

Lee passed through India on his way home to Singapore. At a banquet in his honour on 22 November, the Prime Minister of India, Mrs Indira Gandhi, referred to him as "a dynamic young leader of a dynamic young nation which has made tremendous progress". Lee, in his speech, reflected that: "Those of us who have been in political life know now that there are strange things happening in a world which is growing into monolothic economic blocs — the American economy forcing its problems on to the West Europeans, the Japanese, the Australians, to all others in the non-communist world; Western Europe trying to get together. Perhaps, we may never learn this lesson in Asia: that however much we disagree with each other, it is best if we do not settle disagreements by force. Europe went through two horrendous World Wars to discover that many of her problems could not be resolved by force of arms". So whilst the achievements of the advanced countries were admired, perhaps there were orthodox conventional oriental values which might provide the framework on which to rebuild a modern industrial society, keeping identities and not just becoming poor imitations of the West. Lee had no doubt that the Indian people had the capacity to do this.

Back in Singapore, the Prime Minister addressed a party meeting on 4 December. He said that every time he returned from a journey abroad, he was reinforced in his view that, in ten to twenty years, Singapore could reach the present standards of the advanced countries of the West. "We have the ability and dexterity, energy, enterprise and willingness to learn. As a people, we have settled for orderly progress." But Singaporeans had to learn quickly about corporate companies, their organization and the efficiency of management and labour. Singaporeans must also become more knowledgeable about share market operations. The Singapore Transport Company failure was because of both bad management and bad work discipline. It was a long story. Nearly twenty years earlier, corruption started to become rife, with conductors pocketing fares. They did not issue tickets for the full fares, or gave used tickets. Inspectors and drivers joined in the thieving. Corruption spread. Gangsters got involved in protecting this racket. The trade union could not enforce honesty and discipline. To protect the company's interest, the STC had to hire special European supervisors to check on the inspectors and conductors. Eventually, the management became top-heavy, costly and inefficient. Corruption sporadically continued. The STC slowly went down.

By 1964, the major British shareholders knew that there was no future in the STC. They sold out to local investors. And from 1964 to 1971, with the exception of 1970, no dividends were declared. Year by year, the losses accumulated. Finally, there was nothing left, except the buses, two pieces of land, office equipment and furniture and a $3.5 million overdraft. In

March 1971, when the government reorganised the bus network system, and gave equal treatment to all the bus companies, the authorities knew that the STC had either to reorganise, to become more efficient, and the workers had to stop corruption and be better disciplined, or to collapse. Nine months later, even before the year was out, it had collapsed. The story was not over. The drivers and conductors were being taken into the three Chinese bus companies. But if these workers carried on as they did in the STC, the Chinese bus companies would also go down. So the three Chinese bus companies had made it quite clear that the workers were on probation. They must work like the Chinese bus companies' workers: no corruption, harder work with slightly longer hours, little fringe benefits and higher pay. If they could not change and rid themselves of their bad habits, they must be out, or the Chinese bus companies would go bankrupt.

There was another lesson to be learnt from the STC story. Before 16 November, the STC shares in the stock market were below 60 cents. In Lee's view, these shares were already overvalued at that price. Then the shares suddenly went up. A firm of stockbrokers circulated a report that they estimated the land owned by the STC in McKenzie Road and Upper Aljunied Road were 5 acres and 20 acres respectively, when in fact, they were only 3½ acres and 5 acres respectively. Speculation on STC shares began. From 56½ cents, the shares went up to 83 cents in a matter of days. Share market manipulation could not be ruled out. In the course of three weeks, from 16 November until 3 December, $9½ million worth of shares changed hands. About $5½ million of these were paper transactions, delayed one-month turnovers. Those who gambled on the basis that the STC owned a lot of valuable property, and were going to be taken over by another bus company, got their fingers burnt. "It is unwise to speculate on the stock market unless you are a professional gambler. And it is not safe to rely on reports of stockbrokers. The newspapers are not well-informed. Often, they print incorrect information. Ordinary people who knew little about the real financial position of the STC have been the victims."

Singaporeans must learn not to be credulous. Never believe a story, just because it was printed whether in a newspaper or a magazine. Never act on speculative reports without investigation and checking. Singaporeans had a great deal to learn about corporate companies and shares. Earlier, in June, Haw Par had been taken over by Slater Walker. They made millions just creaming off Haw Par shares, which were undervalued. Corporate companies must be run by competent managers, not relatives. Labour must be disciplined, and good management-labour relations maintained. "All these we must learn quickly, or there will be more pain and suffering."

At another party meeting the following week, Lee said that few countries had the promise of rapid advancement which Singapore had. Similarly, few countries had the problems Singapore faced as the island was in one of the most troubled regions of the world. There were three troubled areas at the moment — the Middle East, Vietnam, and now, the Indian-Pakistani sub-continent. Two of these three areas were not very far from Singapore. This presented Singapore with a challenge that generated an alert and activist approach to life. Nobody could afford to sit under a coconut tree in Singapore, waiting for coconuts to ripen and fall. The maximum use of every opportunity must be made. But rapid progress had its dangers. It generated problems within the society. There were those who were unable to keep up with the pace of change. It also generated unhappiness amongst those who were less successful in making the grade.

Lee said that when he travelled abroad he often heard people attribute Singapore's progress to its 80 per cent Chinese population. They said the Chinese were hardworking and shrewd. Therefore, Singapore had made progress. It was a shallow analysis. Taiwan was 100 per cent Chinese. Yet it made less progress than Singapore. There were other factors which had made Singapore different. Unlike China or Taiwan, Singapore could not take the future for granted. People in Taiwan knew that in the long run they were part of China, and the whole of China knew that they were a potential super-power. They accepted the hard work and sweat as part of life. Their rewards: enough food to eat, adequate clothes to wear, and little else except high thinking. They sacrificed the present for the future. The position of Singapore was quite different. Living standards were high by comparison. Yet the future was troublesome because the whole region was not stable. The biggest challenge to be faced was how to transform Singapore from a trading outpost of empire, into a modern manufacturing, banking and financial centre for the region, helping its economic growth and generating stability. "To do this, we need to attract industrial know-how, banking and financial expertise. They will be attracted only if we offer them the certainty of good returns through an industrious, disciplined and skilled work force, an efficient and effective administration and a healthy and stimulating environment. Then we shall go forward and upwards with benefits accruing to all, each in accordance with his contribution to the economy."

XVII

At the opening of the Singapore International School on 15 December, the Prime Minister said he had last visited this school three years previously when he knew that the school, then the St. John's School, would be handed over to the Singapore Government at the end of 1971. He and his colleagues had decided that its best use would be as a private school for British and other students. "We knew many parents in Southeast Asia

55

would want their children to have a good education, in Singapore, where they would be nearer to their parents than if they were sent to schools in Britain or elsewhere." So the British community in Singapore, through the International Chamber of Commerce, was invited to undertake the task of setting up the school. Lee said he was confident that it would meet a real need. The problem was to gather a nucleus of good senior teachers and a headmaster to start the school, around which the staff should be built. Successfully launched and developed over the years, the Singapore International School could be a valuable asset to Singapore. Amongst other things, it could be a source of new ideas, of new teaching and learning methods. Innovations tested and proved sound and practical could be adapted and adopted. Anything which could add to the teacher-pupil relationship, crucial to learning, would be of value to Singapore, particularly because the student-teacher ratio in Singapore schools was high. He hoped all, headmaster, teachers and students, would find their stay in Singapore socially agreeable, professionally satisfying, and educationally rewarding. However, he added a caution. There were certain areas of social conduct "where we are not interested in experimentation, either in or outside this or any other school in Singapore. These taboos are well-known to your Board of Governors. But it should not cramp your style. Indeed, your parents and your headmaster may not disapprove of our aversion to drug taking and other pernicious maladies of the contemporary world. By all means high thinking, without low living. What is forbidden is living it high".

Lee was present at the closing ceremony of the Southeast Asia Pugilistic championship on 18 December. He said that the growing numbers of young men and women joining the various pugilistic associations in Singapore, and the larger numbers who watched this Championship, was a healthy sign. Drugs, permissiveness, hippism and psychedelic music had hypnotised so many young people in the developed countries, and also in the less developed countries which were exposed to these influences from the West. It was, therefore, gratifying to see evidence that this was not so in Singapore. Escapism in drugs, psychedelic music and promiscuity did not go with the rigorous training demanded of strong and healthy constitutions which the pugilistic arts demand. And in many community centres and other social and sporting organisations in Singapore, young men and women were practising judo, karate, fencing, basket-ball, and other sports. Lee also congratulated the various schools of Chinese martial arts in overcoming their old rivalries and sectionalism, and getting together in the Singapore National Pugilistic Federation.

As Secretary-General of the People's Action Party, Lee spoke at the party congress on 19 December. He said that from time to time, a political party must make a review of its position and then decide on what had to be done in the next phase of its life. The PAP had never been so sturdy and strong as at the end of 1971. "We have more widespread and more constant support. We have better leadership material, in intellect, energy and

56

education, than before. We are attracting people of ability and integrity to active participation in the party. The ground organisations to mobilise support for the party and for the government, both at national and at constituency levels, embrace every street, high-rise Housing and Development Board flat, and kampong." Party history explained the present strength. Even before formal inauguration as a party on 24 November, 1954, a group had already spent nearly ten years preparing for the launching of the political movement. "We had worked amongst intellectuals in the universities here and in Britain. We had organised and mobilised support in the trade unions, first in the public sector, then in the private sector. Then through joining forces with a pro-communist group in a united front, we enlarged our base to include the Chinese-educated workers and intellectuals."

During the united front period, party strength built up rapidly. By June 1959, office was assumed after winning a decisive election. "We survived all the shocks and upheavals of 1961 and 1962 when the united front broke up." In the end, contrary to many pessimistic forecasts, the non-communist, democratic socialists remained in control of the party and the government. Rebuilding rapidly the party machinery, the party won the general elections again in September 1963. "We had brought Singapore by consent into the Federation of Malaysia. In the Federation, we stood our ground in the years of great crises, 1964 and 1965 when communalism replaced communism as the primary threat to the integrity and survival of our people. Suddenly we were unceremoniously asked to leave the Federation in August 1965. As a party and a government, we pulled Singaporeans together despite the shock of separation. Another shock came in January 1968 when the British Government announced its decision to withdraw all their forces by the end of 1971." A plan was worked out to generate enough expansion and momentum in the economy to absorb the loss of 20 per cent of the GNP, in just over three years. "We won the 1968 elections, unopposed in fifty-one seats, and winning the other seven contested seats. And we have not let the people down. Today, Singapore is stronger economically. Singaporeans are more cohesive and united. Singaporeans have a greater capacity to ensure Singapore's own security."

Meanwhile, systematically, new blood had been infused into the party. The party had been restyled to be more relevant and sensitive to the problems of the 1970s. A younger generation has grown up not knowing the old problems of colonialism, poverty and illiteracy. Today, they took independence and successful development for granted. They did not know of the struggle, the fears of total collapse in failure, the planning and effort that had created the jobs for anyone willing to work. There were decent homes at low rents, with water, electricity and modern sanitation for every citizen within a matter of months of registering. Education was heavily subsidised, and with a wide variety of training to suit individual ability and aptitude, from university, polytechnic, to technical and

57

vocational institutes. Good medical services at normal charges, and a wide spread of social amenities were part of the ordinary social landscape. "The trials of twelve and a half years in office have given us considerable experience in anticipating and dealing with all manner of awkward problems. We shall transmit to a younger generation within the party this accumulated knowledge, and the expertise on how to mobilise people in Singapore, and for what purposes. Many of us here today paid an enormous price, and some nearly lost their lives, to learn all these. We must ensure that the next generation is worthy of the task they will inherit and able to preserve and improve upon it. Our past is an indicator of our future performance."

XVIII

In his message for the New Year, put out on 31 December, Lee judged 1971 to have been a successful year. It could have been a disaster. 17,000 civilian employees working with the British forces were retrenched, and 15,000 British troops left with their families. Yet the registered unemployed, 35,953, was lower than New Year's day the previous year, 43,655. "We have also made economic progress, though not as high as the 15 per cent growth for 1970." Preliminary figures showed that external trade went up by 14.5 per cent; manufacturing establishments increased output by 24.1 per cent; census value added up by 30.4 per cent; direct exports by manufacturers up by 24 per cent; and payroll tax, an indicator of employment and wages, up by 23 per cent, from $16.5 million in 1970, to $20.3 million in 1971, with 510,000 workers contributing over $220 million to the Central Provident Fund, as against 449, 813 workers contributing $156,355,094 in 1970. The Housing and Development Board built 16,147 units. This year we plan to build more than 17,500 units. 37,000 people are now owner-occupiers of HDB flats. By the end of this year, an additional 7,000 citizens can expect to be owner-occupiers.

"So long as we keep up that spirit of endeavour, and maintain that work discipline necessary for success, we shall grow stronger. It is the willingness to work, to put in an honest day's work for an honest day's wage, that is essential for success. We have entered a new era. All the worries of massive unemployment and the dislocation of our economy caused by the rapid withdrawal of British forces, are behind us. Before us is the prospect of an expanding economy which can pay for our enhanced security."

THE YEAR 1972

I

General elections (which the ruling PAP won), a visit in February by the Queen of England, (accompanied by the Duke of Edinburgh and Princess Anne), as Head of the Commonwealth, and journeys later in the year by the Prime Minister to Kuala Lumpur and Europe, marked another eventful year. The Prime Minister of Australia, Mr. William McMahon, was a welcomed guest of the Singapore Government in June.

Lee's first speech of the year was to the students of the Singapore Polytechnic. He spoke about education and economic development. He said the lesson for Singapore had been learned dramatically over the past few years. Over thirty thousand redundancies in the British bases, and those who found jobs were people who were skilled technicians or otherwise useful production digits. Those who did not get jobs were the clerks, the storekeepers and the unskilled. He did not want to leave the impression that development meant everybody must become a skilled technician or an industrial worker. It depended upon each country's level of development and the planning and programme which a government, given that kind of society, could take its people forward to the next phase. What he thought was universally true of most new countries was that they inherited a system of education, which very often was carried on unthinkingly by indigenous independent governments for five, ten years with very serious repercussions, for their own development, and resulting in unemployment.

Countries like Ghana, for instance, which is in West Africa had been exposed to contacts with the West for several centuries. Before the British, there were the Danes and the early slave traders. The Ghanians were people who had acquired quite a degree of sophistication, the ones on the coast as distinct from the ones in the hinterland. The British had produced amongst them Greek scholars, Latin scholars: the Vice-Chancellor of the University of Ghana was a Greek and Latin scholar. But the British did not produce engineers and technicians who could have run the Volta High Dam for them. Or perhaps more relevant, they did not produce good scientists in agriculture, in fertilisers, in how to make their economy move from a relatively simple, agricultural, pastoral base into something more productive. At the other end of the scale was India and Pakistan — highly developed sectors, universities well-endowed and prepared. They got into a position where they were producing unemployed engineers because the economic development did not keep pace with the engineers they were producing. The net result was that their doctors migrated. As British doctors migrated to America for better jobs, Indians and Pakistanis filled British hospitals. The lesson was that everybody had got to take a hard-headed look at his own position, decide in the context of his own base, the potential that it had, what was the next step forward.

"And for us the most important single thing is, of course, the development of our human resources, exploiting our strategic location which makes possible certain industries." Lee dealt with the question of what sort of industries Singapore should concentrate on. Broadly all those items of manufacture which contained a very high added skill value which, for instance, would be the case in a small country like Switzerland.

How many engineers did you produce for a certain number of skilled workers and technicians? Well, for the time being, the government had decided that probably it would be more sensible for Singapore to produce more technicians than engineers. This policy would have to be reviewed from time to time. The guiding factors would be what was the best possible way, given Singapore's peculiar, almost unique, circumstances, to mobilise manpower and train them. At the end of it all, the question must be asked: What was the optimum economic growth as against the social cost of economic growth? "In other words, do you want to keep on expanding until finally the main island and all the outer islands are crowded up with people and factories or do you come to a cut-off point and you say: right, this is the optimum kind of population, this is the optimum size of industries and types of clean industries, leaving the population with the maximum of social, aesthetic amenities. So beaches are unpolluted, people have reasonably comfortable homes, green spaces and so on." Lee thought it was possible to make only part of those momentous decisions immediately. Perhaps by 1980, a younger generation with more data would decide what was in the best interest of the population, of the people, of the country, of the society, whether by then they had reached cut-off point.

Meanwhile, there were certain things which they did not want to do. "You know that the great thing now is pollution or what they call in Japan 'public nuisance'. So there are countries which would like to export all their industries which cause 'public nuisance'. And if you want iron and steel mills or petro-chemicals or better still, wood and paper products which will pollute up the whole of your coastlines, stink us out, well they are too ready to come." Singapore would have to decide in about five, maybe at the latest, ten years, just where the cut-off point was: how many square miles for industries, how many for recreation, how many for education and residents. What kind of industries? The answer was quite simple. In broad yardsticks — clean, very little pollution, very little noise, high added skills to high wages, and world-wide markets, so as to avoid becoming pawn to any single regional market. The Prime Minister thought some of these problems would be very difficult to resolve. There was the temptation, the thrill, the enthusiasm generated within a machine — whether it was the Economic Development Board and its promotion officers, whether it was the Finance Ministry saying: "Well, why shouldn't we have a real big iron and steel mill with five million tons capacity? Never mind the pollution. Site it at the eastern end of the island where the prevailing winds will blow it away and miss us. Or put it in Pulau Tekong. Why shouldn't we have an aluminium smelting industry? It will pollute, but it will just miss us."

Lee thought that as a people, sometime about the second half of the seventies "we will have to make up our minds on this. Do we say no. You keep that, just like the Swiss? They do not make aluminium, they do not make steel. They buy all the steel and non-ferrous metals that they require from the Rhur, elsewhere. And Switzerland is relatively clean except for chemicals and pharmaceuticals which go into their lakes. These decisions decide what kind of training to give to the Poly student, what kind of training to give to the vocational institute student. And because for the time being we like to leave these options open, therefore the importance of a broad basic grounding to enable our students maximum versatility, in case our decisions and the operational open market forces make us go into lines which as of now we are unable to see."

II

On 10th February, the Prime Minister entertained a group of senior military and police officers to dinner at the Istana. In colonial times, he said, Singapore had no armed forces of its own. As for the Police Force, the upper ranks were reserved for Europeans. The net result was a set of values built into the population, which was not relevant to the post-colonial phase. Every high-flyer wanted to be a professional: an engineer, a computer programmer, quantity surveyor, architect, accountant or

61

medical specialist. It was only in recent years that people had come to recognise the importance of the Police and the Armed Forces as a career.

Times had changed. Thirty years ago, those who joined the Police Force had no expectations of rising to command positions. It was not so now. But it took some time to get the older Police Force officers to accept a component of good University graduates into their officer cadre. Some graduates left the Police Force, partly because they did not have the strength of character to withstand the earlier ganging up against them. But quite a number survived the trials and had got themselves accepted in their own right, on the strength of their character and ability. In the end, it was strength of character and performance that counted. The Commissioner of Police was commissioner not because he was a non-graduate or a graduate, but because he was the best man for the job. So it would be in the SAF.

"We must match the two, our experienced reliable officers and our bright ones, that cluster of trained intellects which will generate ideas, and stimulate new ways of solving old problems. Some of them may combine ability with a practical touch. These are the people who will reach the top. Unless we recruit men of quality to help make the maximum use of the considerable resources we are putting into defence, it will all be a fearful waste." But however spectacular the new induction into the officer cadre, Singapore must depend on that framework of reliable and steady officers, men whose judgement, commonsense, and experience could be relied upon to keep up the continuity of the force. As in the Police Force, so the new graduate officers would fit into the fabric of the command structure of the SAF.

III

"This Chinese New Year heralds in a new era. We are heading for full employment," declared Lee in his Chinese New Year Message. But he warned that full employment must not be allowed to blunt that keenness to strive and to achieve, so essential for further success. "We must consolidate our economic and social gains. As labour becomes more skilled and productive, in a steady and gradual way wages will go up. The signs are this will be a prosperous year. May I wish you a happy one."

IV

At a private dinner given by the Prime Minister in honour of the Queen and the Duke of Edinburgh and Princess Anne, at Penthouse Negara, on 19 February, Lee said there were many things he could tell her Majesty about Singapore and the British. But it could not be done in a few minutes.

Instead, he narrated a conversation he had several years ago with a minister of one of the EEC countries. He had just been to Southeast Asia. He said his countrymen used to believe that if they had good comfortable homes and well-paid jobs, they would be a happy people. They had lost their empire and this seemed a reasonable enough ambition. Now, said he, his people had comfortable homes and good wages to pay for all the things that make life agreeable. But they were not a happy people. It was not simply boredom. It was the absence of adventure. They, a maritime nation, had always found adventure in travel and enterprise overseas. So he had come back to Southeast Asia to re-forge these links, for economic, and perhaps more important, for psychological considerations. He remarked, in passing, that he feared his British friends might be making the same mistake. The British, he said, were also coming to believe that a comfortable future was in a cosy Europe. The Minister was a good raconteur, added the Prime Minister. Lee said it was impossible for him to recapture the Minister's gestures, his facial expression, the quizzical look in his eyes. They all vividly conveyed the disappointment the Minister feared might be in store for those who believed in a purely European formula.

"My generation is that of Prince Philip and of your Majesty. After the Second World War, I knew there were going to be vast changes in the direction and thrust of world power and politics. Looking back, it is easy to see how inevitable some of the trends were, that America would lose her overwhelming economic and military predominance, even though she remained the strongest single power in the world; that the countries of Western Europe would recover their economic strength and acquire renewed purpose in an economically integrated Europe; that Britain had to join Europe a little later and pay a higher price as a consequence of missing the opportunity of being a founder member; that Russia and China would inevitably be at odds over their vast border regions; that the patriotic and intense Japanese would turn Japan into the busiest workshop of Asia. However, looking forward is difficult. It is impossible to chart the twists and turns of super-power politics. Much is uncertain. I must hope that a stronger Europe, with Britain a member, will play a more active role in widening the areas of economic interests of Europe to Asia. Finally, may I say how happy I am to have Your Majesty and Your Royal Highnesses visit Singapore. Some twenty-five years ago, as a carefree undergraduate, I joined my fellow students at Cambridge in taking the morning off lectures to celebrate the marriage of the heir to the British throne to the Duke of Edinburgh. It was an auspicious day and good reason for festivity, thought somewhat early in the day for 'Audit Ale'. I did not know that I was to have the great pleasure to ask you, ladies and gentlemen, tonight, in Singapore, to join me in drinking to the good health of Her Majesty, Prince Philip and Princess Anne."

In response, the Queen thanked the Prime Minister (who is an honorary British Knight and a Companion of Honour). "We have had two very full and thoroughly interesting days here and all three of us have been deeply impressed by everything we have seen. To be a modern, thriving and humane community demands a great variety of talents and effort. We have seen something of the care for the life of the people in the housing estate at Toa Payoh. We have visited schools and universities without which no community can hope to prosper and develop. We have seen the remarkable industrial development at Jurong. At the Armed Forces Training Establishment we have seen the expression of that essential factor in every successful community, the will to defend itself. It is impossible to miss the signs of commercial and industrial activity which alone can generate the prosperity necessary to sustain the struggle towards a better life. We have also been delighted to see that this better life is interpreted in its widest sense and to include the control of pollution, the conservation of nature, and the opportunity to express all that is best in man through every kind of cultural and artistic activity.''

All these things were only the outward display of the administrative, commercial and humanitarian energies and the competence of the people of Singapore. "These are the people, Mr. Prime Minister, whom you have led and inspired through the last decade of dramatic development. Singapore today would do credit to the most advanced and homogenous community anywhere in the world. That this has been achieved in a multi-racial and multi-religious community speaks volumes for the good sense, tolerance and patriotism of all the communities and their leaders in the island. It has been a privilege and a pleasure to witness these things. Singapore is a story of success and you have done more than anyone to write it.''

The Queen told the Prime Minister she was most grateful for the smooth efficiency of the complicated arrangements made for her visit, "and finally I would like you all to know how deeply touched I have been by the warm and generous welcome given to me by so many people. And now, before you take us on your personally conducted tour of Singapore at night, I raise my glass to the President, and to you, our host this evening, and to your family, and wish you all health, happiness and success''.

A few days later, the Prime Minister addressed trade unionists at the NTUC annual delegates conference at the Conference Hall. He said that the end of 1971 had marked the close of an era in the nation's economic history. "From chronic high unemployment, we have entered a period of full employment.'' Today, Singapore's position was analogous to that of Germany or Holland in the early 1960s. Then their economy was booming, and they began to increase the number of "guest-workers'' from other countries. "We have the choice of controlled and steady wage increases and real growth, or of taking quick gains in artificially high and sudden increases in wage rates and bonuses, but thereby jeopardising future growth. Old habits of thinking and working, relevant in the past two decades of chronic unemployment, must be discarded, or they will hinder us from attaining our new goals." Now the opportunity had come to raise the level of skills of workers and degree of sophistication of industries. Then better wages to workers would be possible. Unions, management and government together would have to re-think their respective positions and roles, to reframe policies for very different social and employment conditions. If management, unions and the government were realistic in their approach to questions of wages and rewards in the context of full employment, and with an economy likely to grow at about 10 per cent plus per annum for the next five years, Singapore should be able to achieve solid gains in this decade, better wages and good returns on capital. There were many projects already in the pipeline. For the time being, industrialists would be allowed to recruit as many skilled and semi-skilled workers as they would wish to train, on work permits. "But, in five years, by 1976, we will have to decide just how much industrial growth we want, so that we can have a balanced allocation of our limited land resources. We want industries, but we must have enough reserved for housing, schools, hospitals, leisure and recreation."

Meanwhile, the government would be mechanising as much and as quickly as possible. Private employers would be wise to plan likewise. As wages went up steadily, in an orderly way, it would become uneconomical not to equip the worker with mechanical aids. One danger to be faced with full employment was growing complacency, leading to lower productivity. The Japanese were able to avoid this malaise. The Dutch and the Germans suffered from this disease only marginally, and that only very recently. The British had been suffering from it for many years and now it had become chronic. And the malady persisted in spite of high unemployment. "What happens to us will depend, first, on the cultural and work habits of our people; second, the soundness of the social and economic policies we are pursuing; and third, the manner in which management and unions co-operate in a sensible and realistic way in sharing an ever bigger cake."

The Prime Minister told the residents of Windsor Park a few days later that "whether it is in Housing Board high-rise flats or privately developed housing estates, like Windsor Park, a new community requires several years to take root. It is when people feel they are a unit, with common interests, that they have become a community. To quicken the pace, some people have to make the effort to get them together, get common user facilities attended to, whether drains be properly graded or streets lit up, some nuisance quashed or recreational facilities established or improved. Slowly, the new inhabitants develop a sense of belonging to a group, and to identify their common interests". The Prime Minister said it is most important to get people to live at ease with each other, especially when they were in geographical proximity.

In a message on the second anniversary of the Singapore Industrial Labour Organisation (SILO), Lee said that the keenness and diligence of the workers had been an important factor of Singapore's economic progress. This was especially so in new industries. The industrial and

65

manufacturing sector registered a 30 per cent growth rate in 1971. Without good labour-management relations, Singapore could not have survived the shock of separation in 1965 and the rundown of the British bases since 1968. He congratulated the Singapore Industrial Labour Organisation for representing more than 15,000 industrial workers. SILO had an important role to play in the nation's economic and social development. SILO could make workers place national interests before their own trade union 'sectarian' interests. It was the unwillingness to do this, that did so much harm to the British economy. Conversely, it was the placing of country before company or union, that has made Japan an outstanding success.

V

From 22 to 24 March, the Prime Minister and his wife paid an official visit to Malaysia at the invitation of the Prime Minister of Malaysia, Tun Abdul Razak. Lee was accompanied by the Minister for Finance, Mr. Hon Sui Sen, and senior government officials. The Prime Minister and Mrs. Lee had an audience with Seri Paduka Baginda Yang di-Pertuan Agong and Raja Permaisuri Agong. Lee met Tun Razak and the Deputy Prime Minister, Tun Dr. Ismail, and other Cabinet Ministers, discussed matters of mutual interest and exchanged views on the current world political situation. In view of the close relations between the two neighbouring countries, both governments agreed, on a reciprocal basis, to keep to a minimum the protocol formalities required in such visits.

At a dinner given by Tun Razak, the Prime Minister said: "We are not strangers. We have known each other well, as students from way back in 1940, and we have had a lot to do with each other in the early 1960s. In more recent years, because of the different circumstances we were placed in, our policies, on which our expectations rest, have developed differently. The different experiences we have gone through have left their different imprints on us and our peoples. So much, also, has altered in the surrounding circumstances. The background of world power and politics has altered. Many old familiar landmarks, we used to take for granted, have disappeared. But some things have not changed — the geography and the close ties of families on both sides of the Causeway. There is a continuing inter-dependence on security and stability, which is unlikely to change."

Lee said it would be too good to be true to suppose that there had not been differences of interests, or misunderstandings between the two governments. These differences however had been kept within their proper proportions. "Both of us have overriding interests in stability and confidence, so essential for development and progress. Much of our economic and social plans for our peoples depends upon our ability to see these difficulties and differences in the perspective of the greater issues at stake. We shall have to live with an ever more complex and complicated interplay of forces of the super and major powers. We owe it to ourselves and to our peoples not to be taken unawares. What we seek is peace and stability, in order that development and progress can bring about the better life for our peoples." So it was valuable to meet from time to time to exchange views on matters of common interest and concern. Their own minds had not remained static. Imperceptibly, like signatures, attitudes and thoughts had changed with the years. There was a need to review and revise assessments and expectations, plans and policies. Even though it was just over a year ago since they'd last met, several of the unspoken premises on which they had based their projections had been overtaken by events.

Tun Razak extended the Prime Minister a cordial welcome to Malaysia. It was, he remarked, Lee's first official visit to Kuala Lumpur since the separation. Razak reminded the Prime Minister that once he (Razak) had said that Singapore and Malaysia were like Siamese twins which had been separated by careful and intricate surgery but which still retained close ties of history, geography and common interest. It was true that for several years after Separation, both faced difficulties of adjustment to the new situation. But he felt that so long as both realised that Singapore and Malaysia were two independent sovereign States which must carry out their dealings with one another on this basis, "and so long as we both are genuinely desirous of working together for our common interest and mutual benefit", whatever difficulties or differences there were could be resolved. By being close neighbours, with dealings in many matters, they were faced with difficulties and irritations from time to time. With a genuine spirit of goodwill and friendship, Razak was confident all these problems could be resolved.

"Today, as a result of your visit here we have resolved one important matter which has been outstanding for so long, that is, the distribution of residual assets and profits of the Currency Board. I am very grateful to Mr. Lee for his understanding on this matter. I have no doubt that the two countries will work together in future. I am sure, Mr. Prime Minister, you will agree with me that this co-operation and friendship must continuously be sustained and refreshed by frankness and sincerity in all our dealings. I hope that your short visit here will mark a new period of sincere co-operation between our two countries. I wish to say here that we would like you to come again to Kuala Lumpur or anywhere in Malaysia either privately or officially and that you are always welcome."

VI

National health has always been a matter of considerable importance to Lee. Addressing a meeting of general practitioners on 25 March, Lee recalled that in 1966, there was one doctor to every 1,968 Singaporeans. Five years later, in 1971, the figures were one to 1,404. But this was still about twice the ratio for Australia and Japan. The drop had been 564 in 5 years, or approximately less than 6 per cent per annum. On a linear projection, it would take Singapore over ten years to reach the Japanese-Australian ratio. But no such linear projection was reliable. In a society where doctors were free to migrate in or out, the number of doctors would depend not so much upon the number of graduates trained but upon what kind of life a doctor could have, and, more important, what kind of future there was for his family.

According to income tax returns in 1969, amongst the professionals, architects and engineers had the second best average earnings of $40,000 per annum. Doctors had an average of $27,000 per annum. "But these figures were from income tax returns. In the course of time, as book-keeping and accounting improve, and as more doctors are engaged in company practice, I am sure doctors will move up the tax ladder to the level of engineers and architects."

At the end of 1971, there were 1,517 doctors registered in Singapore. 1,189 were with first degrees, 450 in government or University, and 739 in private practice. 328 had higher or specialist degrees, 162 in government or University, 166 in private practice. One of the immediate aims was to raise the quality of the health services generally, and also to become a centre of excellence for specialist medical services in Southeast Asia. "We have to improve health services without massive annually escalating costs, as with the British Health Service. It became so prohibitive that even a British Labour Government had, in 1968, to check the over-use of these services by the re-imposition of prescription and other charges. But even more deleterious has been its effect on industrial production. On 1 September 1971, the Office of the Health Economics, an independent fact-finding body set up by the British drug industry, reported that the cost of working time lost through minor ailments in Britain for 1970 was £800 million a year. Time-off for all kinds of illness worked out at an average of fifteen days a year for every worker in Britain. They said: This is reflected in the increase in absence for relatively minor causes of sickness, such as nervousness, headaches, sprains and strains ... Minor ill health is now no longer ignored or tolerated. On the other hand, Singapore must avoid the crippling cost of medical services in America, where, without heavy insurance cover paid either by the employer or employee himself, any serious illness was an economic calamity for the family.

At this stage of Singapore's development, the government could not provide for more than the essential medical services. The loss of a medical officer in the government service to private practice did not mean a loss to the health services available to the community. So long as the government medical services could expand at a rate commensurate with economic development, Singapore was doing well. "And we must allow free economic forces to settle the kind of medical services available in private practice." The question was how to make fuller and better use of outstanding specialists in private practice. Considerable investments were being made in medical specialities at great cost in buildings and equipment, and in the training of supporting staff. A start had been made in neuro-surgery, cardio-thoracic surgery, plastic and re-constructive surgery, paediatric surgery and nephrology. The expansion would eventually range over every speciality where the advances were not merely experimental. The University had been able to reconcile the competing interests of government medical officers and University teachers. A number of government doctors had been made Clinical Professors, Associate Professors and Clinical Teachers. They, and some private practitioners, helped in the training of undergraduate and post-graduate students.

Lee thought it should be possible for a body of eminent specialists from the government service, the University and some in private practice, to agree on a list of outstanding specialists who were known not to be self-seekers and who deserved honorary teaching or consultancy status for the contribution they could make in treating poorer patients and in teaching students. When their fields included the use of specialist medical equipment, they would be allowed use of these facilities. The best use must be made of manpower resources. Selfishness in not wishing to impart the knowledge and experience, clinical skills and surgical expertise, could only stultify the capacity to pass on these skills to the next generation. In every branch, most postgraduate training had to be done abroad, most of them on scholarships. And there had been tiresome instances where specialists had to be smacked for trying to dissuade Royal Colleges in Britain from recognising work done in Singapore hospitals as exempting them from a similar period to work in a British hospital.

Singapore now was able to, and would, invest extensively in medical specialisation. Over $100 million would be spent either to rebuild and refurbish the General Hospital in Outram Road, or to build a new teaching hospital at Kent Ridge. "With the right formulae to balance the competing interests of public and private sector general practitioners and specialists, we can raise standards of medical training, treatment and specialisation, to the advantage of all who live or seek treatment in Singapore."

VII

Singapore's industrialization programme took another historical step forward on 29 March when the Prime Minister opened Jurong Shipbuilders (Pte) Ltd. This company was incorporated in December 1968 as a joint venture between IHI (Ishikawajima-Harima Heavy Industries Co. Ltd.), Jurong Shipyard Limited and the Singapore government. Lee declared it officially open on the day the first vessel built by JSBL in

Singapore — a 14,000 ton Freedom type vessel — was being launched. This was a modest beginning, and there was considerable room for expansion and diversification. "We have always been a ship-repairing centre. We have also been a shipbuilding centre. But the shipbuilding was confined to small boats, craft, tugs and coastal vessels. This is the first ocean-going vessel built in Singapore." Shipbuilding was a much tougher business than ship-repairing. To the builders of ocean-going vessels, Singapore had to be internationally competitive. The future of ship-building in Singapore depended on several factors, some outside, and others within, Singapore's control. The demand for 14,000 ton general cargo vessels to take the place of the ageing Liberty ships would depend on the rate of increase of world trade, how much of it would be carried by containers, and how much by general cargo vessels.

If world trade expanded in this decade, as it did in the last, at 8.6 per cent per annum, and if wages in both Western and Eastern Europe and Japan went up as they did in the past, "then if our wages go steadily up but still less than half that of the Japanese, JSBL will be kept busy. But Singapore workers must be as efficient and productive as the workers of the IHI Shipyards in Japan". Then it would soon be worthwhile to instal automatic machines in the shipyard to increase the speed of production. Shipbuilding was high on labour content. In some advanced countries, wages were going up faster than automation could cut down on total wage costs. In America, where wage rates were very high, ships could not be built without substantial subsidies from their Government. In Germany, they had stopped building general-purpose cargo vessels. Shipbuilders concentrated on specialised vessels like containers, where the design or innovative content was so high that they could carry the higher wage costs.

Lee predicted that in the course of the next two decades, Japan's economic growth would carry the wages of her shipbuilders up. Japan might find herself in the position the Germans were in, concentrating on specialised vessels where the brain contribution was especially high. In standardised vessels, automation, computerisation and cybernation would be used to cut down the need for labour. But there was a limit to what automation, computerisation and cybernation could do. So the building of standard vessels would move to those countries, like South Korea, Taiwan and Singapore, where wages were lower than those of the industrialised countries and where the workers were diligent and could be trained to high skills. The national shipping line, the Neptune Orient Line, could give this shipyard a start. But JSBL's future depended on good management and technology, skills and productivity of the workers, and the reputation it must build for itself as a dependable shipyard which met its contracts on time and up to specifications.

Lee's sympathetic awareness of the difficulty of the Malays to adjust to rapid industrialisation was evident in the message he sent to the Singapore Malay Teachers' Union on their 25th anniversary. From 1965, when Singapore became independent, policies had constantly to be reviewed. The fundamental issue was how to make a living as a nation on its own. One answer was rapid industrialisation, encouraging industrialists of the advanced countries to export not manufactured goods to Singapore for re-export, but their factories, technological management expertise and marketing know-how. This fundamental change in policy, of industrialisation geared to a world export market, and not to a protected Malaysian market, had many consequences. One of them was its impact on education. It meant first that the emphasis would be on vocational and technical training, engineering and management. It also meant more widespread use of English, for this was the language of the investing industrialists, whether Americans, Japanese, Germans, Swiss, French or British.

This posed a problem for the Malay, Chinese and Tamil language streams. More and more parents had registered their children for the English stream schools. This led to sporadic and spasmodic reactions from the Chinese and Malay language newspapers, unions of school teachers, and literary and cultural groups. But, despite successive campaigns, parents continued to place the future careers of their children first, before any cultural or linguistic patriotism. This was mainly because they knew that in an English school, their children would learn their mother tongue as a compulsory second language. As a result of this, not enough student teachers were being recruited into TTC from the English stream. Malay and Chinese stream student teachers, were, however being recruited because the intention was to strengthen the teaching of the second language in the English schools. It would be a tragedy if the teaching of the second language and an appreciation of their history and culture in the English schools was not successfully done. "For then we may produce a population completely deculturised, cut off from its origins, with problems of disorientation because a whole generation will be unable to see themselves in historic perspective."

The Singapore Malay Teachers' Union had to overcome these problems of consequential adjustment. Malay children must be trained, so that they could find a satisfying and rewarding career for themselves in an industrialised Singapore of the 1980s. Boys and girls must understand how to work the machines in the factory, how to receive and give instructions. But there would still be need for gifted, literary people, to continue the Malay tradition in language and culture. There would be the need for Malay language teachers to teach Malay students, and others who choose to study Malay, the literature, history and culture of the Malay people, and how in Singapore they came to be part of the multi-racial society. "If the Singapore Malay Teachers' Union looks ahead to meet these problems, I feel confident that the adjustments will be made, and the Union will help our Malays to keep their balance in a period of rapid change."

71

VIII

Lee dipped again into contemporary history when he opened new union premises on 2 April. He recalled that it was over twenty years since Mr. K.M. Byrne, Dr. Goh Keng Swee and he started organising the government unions. "We rallied the ground for two purposes. First, to improve their economic and social lot. Second, to mobilise political pressure for independence. Vast changes have taken place since then. These changes have affected the government service." Twenty years ago, the government service set the pace for wages and conditions of service in Singapore. Then the government was the largest single employer. The public sector employees, including the services employees, comprised one-third of the working population. Today, the government was no longer employing such a major and decisive portion of workers. It only employed one-fifth of the working population. It was the private sector that had been expanding and would continue to expand. It was the private sector which had been thriving because of government's plans to stimulate and increase economic activity to make up for the rundown of the British bases.

These plans had produced results. As the economy improved, so would living standards. But some would go up faster than others, especially skilled workers, technicians and top-quality administrators and professionals. This was already manifest in the private sector. It was the rate for the job. The public sector would also have to observe the rate for the job if it was not to lose good and important digits. There was one special obligation in the public service which entitled government servants to a pension. It was that extra integrity demanded of them. The public servant exercised more power over the lives of Singaporeans than an employee of the most important private enterprise in Singapore. A government servant's decisions must be based on public interest. Singapore was a new country where the government and administration did not tolerate corruption, nepotism or favouritism. This had been a most important asset in national development and progress.

The public service also demanded efficiency and courtesy. In the private sector, rude or ill-tempered behaviour hurt the employer immediately. The employee responsible was immediately removed, or business would be lost to competitors. By the nature of government, there were no competitors. "Hence we must be constantly on the alert against waywardness. In private business, extra diligence, efficiency and courtesy bring extra rewards. They must be also rewarded in government service, especially through promotions." Lee hoped that high considerations of service, which had been the hallmark of the administration, would remain the distinguishing feature that marked out government servants from other workers.

"The tribute I paid to this Mission Hospital and to the Anglican Church 8¼ years ago was well-deserved," the Prime Minister told the Rt.

Reverand Chiu Ban It, the doctors, the nurses, the staff and guests, on 4 April when he officially opened the Outpatient Department and the Specialist Clinics of the St. Andrew's Mission Hospital for Children. He said that when he ran through the distinguished list of specialist consultants to the Hospital printed on their letter to him, he found the name of one of Singapore's ambassadors who had been abroad for more than five years. So he asked another on the list how much work he did at the Hospital. He admitted that he had not been very active. But he "had given all his subordinates the opportunity to exercise their talent and skills, doing service for free to treat the poor, and also keeping up their competence and expertise".

The Prime Minister went on to say that dedication was a rare commodity. "When conduct akin to dedication has been successfully induced by helping to further the skill and establish the reputation of the specialist, then those who manage this Hospital have done well. They have combined their desire to serve the community with the realities of life making people give of their time for the benefit of the sick."

"Of our post-secondary educational institutions, the Polytechnic has been a most worthwhile investment," the Prime Minister told the Singapore Polytechnic Guild of Graduates on 8 April. From 1960 to 1971, it produced a total of 3,729 graduates: 246 were degree graduates in Accountancy and Engineering. The Polytechnic had helped start these two faculties which were transferred to the campus of the University of Singapore in 1969: 591 were professional diploma graduates in Accountancy, Architecture, Building, Quantity Surveying, Valuation, Civil Engineering, Electrical Engineering and Mechanical Engineering: 520 were craft graduates. 2,372 were technician graduates, 2,169 diplomas and 203 certificates. Within six years, by the end of the academic year 1976 – 77, the number of technician graduates from the School of Industrial Technology was expected to rise from 2,372 to 9,783.

When the present government took charge in June 1959, the Polytechnic was not geared to turn out the professional and technician skills in the numbers required for rapid industrialisation. That it had been able to adapt, expand and progress, spoke well of the Board of Governors, of the Principal, Mr. Edis, and of the senior staff who supported him. Students of the Polytechnic, because of the tone set by the Principal and the teaching staff, and because of the nature of their training and disciplines, had had little time or inclination to tilt at windmills. In the 1960s, it was the university student activists from the Humanities who frittered their time away in mock heroic gestures on behalf of university autonomy and academic freedom. They echoed the irrelevant slogans of their teachers, people recruited from a different generation, who were out of touch with the main stream of thought and action, post-independence. Had it not been for Singapore's success in industrialising, there would have been real issues to agitate about, as unemployment steamed up unrest and frustration. As it was, these student activists had to thank the graduates of the

Polytechnic for helping to make a success of industrialisation, thereby creating the spin-off in jobs for graduates in the Humanities, in an expanding economy.

The cost of training students in the vocational stream was more than twice that of students in academic streams: academic stream $380 per student per annum, vocational stream $960 per student per annum. The average cost of a Polytechnic student per annum was $2,300. These were investments which had to be if the population was to be brought up to higher levels of skills, to improve total performance. Graduates of the Polytechnic had had no difficulty in getting jobs suitable to their training and skills. Among the committee members of the Guild were architects, quantity surveyors, planners, engineers and technical assistants. They reflected the important roles played by Polytechnic graduates in the economy. Lee was sure the expansion of the Polytechnic would be more than justified. "Your Guild of Graduates should have an ever growing membership, as over 1,300 graduates per year with diplomas and certificates join your ranks between now and 1977."

IX

Lee reviewed ASEAN's progress at the Fifth ASEAN Ministerial Meeting on 13 April. The ASEAN Declaration was signed in Bangkok in August 1967. The Declaration's two major objectives were to accelerate economic growth, and to promote regional peace and stability. ASEAN had developed cohesion in the past five years. It was becoming an institution which had been able to ride several upheavals that had shaken Southeast Asia in the five years since it was founded. Five years was not time long enough to measure progress in regional co-operation. Nevertheless, there had been progress. In the implementation of recommendations made by ASEAN committees, there had been steady advance. In the first year, August 1967 to August 1968, there were 102 recommendations. None were implemented. In the second year, August 1968 to December 1969, of 161 recommendations, 10 were implemented, 6.2 per cent. In the third year, December 1969 to March 1971, of 207 recommendations, 22 were implemented — 10.6 per cent. In the fourth year, March 1971 to April 1972, of 215 recommendations, 48 were implemented — 22.3 per cent. "I mention these figures not to denigrate what has been achieved, but rather to remind us of what more needs to be done. However, headway has been made in the fields of tourism, mass media, ASEAN Pavilion, co-ordination of civil aviation operation facilities, training courses, seminars and workshops, and exchange of information." But in trade and industry, progress had been slower. Intra-ASEAN trade, or trade between ASEAN partners, increased by US$380 million from US$1,712 in 1966 to US$2,092 million in 1970, or 5.2 per cent per annum. Total ASEAN trade with the world grew at 9.1 per cent. However, world trade went up at a higher rate by 11.4 per cent per annum for those five years. And as a percentage, trade within ASEAN to total ASEAN trade with the world dropped from 18.3 per cent in 1966 to 15.7 per cent in 1970. In other words, ASEAN partners decreased their trade amongst themselves and increased their trade with the rest of the world, from 81.7 per cent to 84.3 per cent. With Japan and the United States, ASEAN trade went up from 37. 6 per cent (US$3,510 million) to 44.6 per cent (US$5,924 million), and with Western Europe, from 8.5 per cent (US$798 million) to 12.9 per cent (US$1,709 million). "We must remember, however, that the exports of ASEAN countries are of a similar nature, mainly agricultural products, minerals, timber and oil. Consumers for them are to be found in the industrial countries. ASEAN imports are mainly of machinery and manufactured products from the industrial countries."

ASEAN had not yet attempted to create a common market, nor a free trade area. But an ASEAN advisory committee had been working with a UN Study Team investigating the possibilities of co-operation in trade and industry, monetary and financial matters, forestry and forest industries, and agriculture and shipping. Lee understood that a number of reports relating to these studies had been produced, and that the final report would be presented soon.

From the records of ASEAN proceedings, he gained the impression that in recommending projects, ASEAN committees had generally made a distinction between what was desirable and what was possible, and concentrated on the possible. For the present, ASEAN did not aim at integrating a regional economy. ASEAN's main aim was to strengthen and consolidate domestic economies. It would, therefore, be unrealistic for ASEAN to propose programmes or projects which did not fit into and assist in the consolidation of the respective economic development plans of the five countries. Perhaps the most valuable achievement of the four Ministerial Meetings, which were followed by meetings of ASEAN secretariats, had been the greater understanding of each other's problems. An atmosphere of goodwill had been generated following meetings and working groups of the senior officials of ASEAN members. This understanding and goodwill had helped to lubricate relationships which could otherwise have generated friction. Members had learned of the similarities of their economic and social problems and had been educating each other on the reasons why different methods were adopted to solve them. He felt sure member governments would want ASEAN to consolidate itself. ASEAN must achieve institutional strength to survive and endure the changes which the future had in store for everyone.

X

In a message to the Public Utilities Board Staff Union in its Fourth Anniversary souvenir programme, Lee said that the next few years would see a rapid expansion PUB services to meet increasing power, water and gas demands. New power stations at Senoko in Sembawang and the Kranji-Pandan reservoir schemes were some of these projects PUB workers had a special responsibility in the industrialisation programme. Without constant and steady power supply, reliable clean potable water, and increasing quantities of industrial water at especially low rates, production was bound to be affected. Then new investors would be wary of investing in Singapore. PUB workers must see that the reliability of supplies and the speed of repair and maintenance servicing were never in doubt.

"A whole generation has grown up, graduated from schools, some in universities, in jobs, or in National Service since 1954, when the PAP first organised activities in Tanjong Pagar," the Prime Minister told about 2,000 members of the PAP Tanjong Pagar Branch gathered to celebrate its 18th anniversary on 15 April. "Since 1959 when the PAP took office," Lee said, "our livelihood has improved, the kind of homes in which we live, the factories, offices, and wharves where we work in. Three factors made this possible. First, this is a striving people, willing to work, always doing something, trying to forge ahead. We do not sit idly under the coconut tree, waiting for the coconuts to fall onto our laps. Second, as the party in government, we have given the people leadership. Policies which were temporarily unpopular were implemented if they were necessary for progress. We have placed national interests over and above party interests."

Mr. Lee added, "Some political parties have won elections and got into governments in Asia on promises of giving things away for free. These promises could not be carried out because there was no money or foreign exchange to pay for promises of free rice, for example. The result has been economic collapse and revolution, roads unrepaired, no new houses, no new factories or investments, only more babies, more unemployment, more revolution." In a way, such people brought the troubles upon themselves because they were foolish to believe that the politicians could give them things for free, without plans to work the resources, to generate the revenue, to pay for the things to be given away for free. "The third factor is because we are well-organised. It is not just the government or the PAP. It is the whole society. It is capable of organising itself to get things done. Fortunately, Singaporeans are prepared to work and pay for the better life we all want. And we have been calculating in terms of the next ten, the next twenty years, the next generations. We have never sought a soft way out of our difficulties."

Earlier, Lee pointed out that all inner-city constituencies were becoming depleted of the bright and successful younger men and women. They married and moved out to the new satellite towns or suburbs. This left the older city areas with only the older people and the very young. But the alternative to this would be hurried and poorly planned urban renewal projects. It was better to put up with this decanting for several more years "as we plan to have the city rebuilt in such a way that none of it will be used only during office hours as in the City Hall, Empress Place, Raffles Place and Shenton Way areas. There facilities were under-utilised, roads, car parks, restaurants. Our planners were trying to weave into the city areas blocks for domestic residence, so that there could be a resident population to use these facilities throughout the day and night." This must be achieved even if it meant government intervention in planning and reduced development charges, and if this was not enough, then direct building.

XI

Lee's May Day Message was optimistic. "May 1972 will always be a proud milestone in the history of modern Singapore. Instead of massive unemployment, economic hardship and gloom, we have full employment, economic buoyancy and the prospect of rapid industrial expansion for the next five years. Now we must watch out for the different problems of full employment. We must guard against becoming slack and easy-going. As wages go up gradually and steadily, more jobs will be mechanised. A worker with the help of machines will be able to do more work. This will justify better pay. We cannot afford the mistakes of workers in advanced countries. For instance, as the British worker's life became better, he became snobbish. He refused to do work which he considered 'infra-dig' or socially inferior. So Indians, Pakistanis and West Indians were taken to do these so-called 'dirty' or 'heavy' jobs. This resulted in social and communal tensions. It simply will not do for Singapore."

It took a long time to get an economy on the move. Now that Singapore's was, the momentum had to be kept up. If they kept up the effort, workers would deserve the rewards that came with each successful year. If union leaders and workers had not realised how grave the situation was in 1965, at separation, and again in 1968, when the British bases began their rundown, Singapore would have gotten into a real mess. "Our concern now is no longer how to create more jobs. It is how to upgrade the skills of our workers, to increase productivity, to generate more revenue, to pay for better homes, schools, clinics and hospitals, sports and recreational facilities — to create a gracious Singapore worthy of a people who have striven hard, and are still hard at it, and deserve to go up the ladder of success."

77

XII

Lee never stopped looking ahead. He told the Singapore Chinese Middle School Teachers' Union: "In the next ten years, we shall raise the quality of our education. We shall improve facilities in schools, provide more and better trained teachers, and reduce the numbers of students per class. With widespread family planning and lower birth rates, we should be able to achieve all these objectives. The new junior colleges and secondary schools, when built, will mean that more secondary schools will be single-session schools."

The more important objective in education was to have students effectively articulate and literate in two languages — their mother tongue and English. Hence, unless parents chose otherwise for their children, the emphasis, starting from Primary I, would be on the command of these two languages. Learning depended on language. If understanding in a language was poor, then learning of any subject through that language must be poor. The number of Chinese teachers in English schools would be increased so that there would be smaller classes and more personal attention to students. The immediate target was three teachers for two classes. When the shortages of English teachers was overcome, the same would be done in Chinese schools — more English teachers to teach smaller classes.

Oral tests in the second language had formed part of the Primary School Leaving Examinations since 1969. Similar oral tests would be introduced in the Secondary IV Examinations in 1973, in addition to written papers. Grades would be awarded accordingly. For a language was first heard and spoken, before it was written and read. The Chinese Middle School Teachers' Union naturally looked after the interests of school teachers. But if they wished to win the respect and support of parents and the government, they must put the interests of the pupils placed under the care of teachers first and foremost.

XIII

On 28 May, the Prime Minister addressed a conference of the Asia-Pacific Socialist Bureau of the Socialist International. This conference of the Asia-Pacific Socialist Bureau of the Socialist International marked, he said, the second time socialist parties in Asia had gathered together for co-operation and co-ordination in an organised way. The first effort was at the Asian Socialist Conference in Rangoon in 1953. That was a different era. Then socialism seemed so obviously the way towards a better and more just society for the newly independent countries of Asia, in search of progress and equality. But after another meeting held in Bombay in 1956, the effort lapsed. "If we are to make the Asia-Pacific Socialist Bureau a more enduring organisation, giving impetus to democratic socialist move-

78

ments in the region, we must be realistic and practical. Only in this way can this Bureau become an organisation in which our different experiences can be shared, and our struggles for more just societies derive encouragement and strength.''

The fraternal parties represented in the Bureau could be divided broadly into three categories. First, the Australian Labour Party and the New Zealand Labour Party. They were well-established parties in wealthy and developed countries. These parties had held office for long periods on many occasions in the past. Their systems of government were stable and well-established, modelled after the British parliamentary tradition. Second, the Socialist Party of Japan and the Japan Democratic Socialist Party. Like Australia and New Zealand, Japan was a wealthy country. Japan had a longer history than either Australia or New Zealand. But, unlike Australia and New Zealand, the present Japanese parliamentary system was new, set up after the Second World War. The parliamentary tradition of two or more main contending political parties taking and relinquishing office in turn, as a result of the vote of the electorate in general elections, might become established in Japan. But the Liberal Democratic Party had ruled almost continuously for over twenty years. There were two shortlived coalitions of the Socialist Party and Democratic Party — from May 1947 to March 1948; and March to October 1948. But no Japanese socialist party had ever been in office alone, or as the senior partner. In the third category were the Democratic Action Party of Malaysia, the Socialist Party of India, the United Socialist Party of Korea and the People's Action Party of Singapore. These parties were from new countries, less developed, with comparatively low GNP and per capita income. Except for the PAP in Singapore, none of the parties had ever assumed office. "I must not, of course, forget the Israel Labour Party. They are a class by themselves — *sui generis*. Their country, though new, is well-developed. The Israel Labour Party has been in office as a major partner in successive governments for many years since 1948.''

After the Second World War, communism and socialism seemed the wave of the future. Many believed, then, that state central planning for the communist countries would bring about a golden age. For Western Europe, democratic parties, operating in mixed economies, as in Britain, France and Scandinavia, sought economic advancement and social progress through nationalisation of basic industries, coal, electricity, transportation, iron and steel, but leaving consumer products primarily to private enterprise. It was the more humane way towards a more equal and just society. Today, nearly three decades later, the golden age had yet to come, for both the communist and non-communist systems. The communist countries had made material progress. Their advances in the pure sciences and military technology were at least equal to those of the West. What had eluded them so far had been the application of science and technology to industry, for mass production of high quality consumer goods, to match the high-consumption societies of the free enterprise West.

Moreover, people now knew that the communist system did not necessarily transform agricultural societies of the less developed world into industrial technological giants, especially where technological and economic aid had not been forthcoming from the more advanced communist or non-communist countries. So whether it was Cuba, North Korea, China, or North Vietnam, the post-industrial society of abundance was still a long way off.

However, the lustre of the social democracies of Western Europe had somewhat diminished, in spite of prosperous societies. Idealism and revolutionary fervour did not burn as fiercely in the new permissive generation born to the warriors of the Second World War. Democratic socialism in West European countries had set out to achieve full employment as a basic target. In nearly all instances, these efforts were accompanied by higher inflation rates and higher personal taxes for more social benefits and welfare schemes. Sometimes, they had led to lower economic growth rates. With affluence, and without the fear of hunger or deprivation through poverty and unemployment, young people seemed more devoted to pleasure and leisure than to increasing the well-being of their community, let alone to help put right the many wrong things in the world around them, except to demonstrate violently about Americans in Vietnam. Their concern was more about the relatively few Americans being killed than about the appalling devastation wrought on the Vietnamese. A poverty of motivation to work and to achieve appeared a widespread problem. And when right-inclined governments had taken over from socialist governments in Western Europe, they had not been able to discontinue the welfare programmes, probably because it had become too difficult electorally to do so. At most, they had trimmed some of the welfare benefits and made their availability more selective.

In newly independent countries, the story of the past twenty-five years had been very different. "Socialism" had been an elastic word. Nearly every political party, in or out of power, claimed to be socialist. Even military councils, which had displaced inept civilian regimes, declared that they had socialistic objectives. But almost everywhere, the pervading poverty contrasted sharply against the obscene wealth of the corrupt or fortunate few. Economic development had been painfully slow, with high unemployment, and precious little wealth generated. Whatever the ideology of the political leadership of a new country, to modernise and develop, the leadership must resolve the non-economic hindrance to growth. Nearly all new countries inherited a plurality of cultures, languages, ethnic and religious groups. Heterogeneous societies were what the colonial powers brought together into one administrative boundary and what new countries had to live with. These non-economic factors could negate development programmes unless these inter-ethnic, inter-linguistic, inter-cultural and inter-religious rivalries were defused in a sympathetic and intelligent manner and potential conflicts muted.

The first problem of a less developed country was how to develop.

Only then could people think or talk of more social services and welfare programmes. "Some of us have learned through painful years of experience that adopting the outward trappings and norms of developed Western social democracies can only compound our problems. The five-day week, of forty or less hours, fully paid holidays of a month a year, free medical services, heavily subsidised housing, and high personal income tax, are worse than irrelevant. They will cripple our economy." Under-developed countries, whatever the system of government or ideology of the party in office, had to find the capital needed to import capital equipment, technological know-how and management expertise. Some did not have sufficiently educated workers to be trained for skilled jobs. The same was true of even the less developed countries of Eastern Europe. Of these countries, in 1945, Bulgaria had been most backward. She had been stultified by over five hundred years of Ottoman rule. Today, Bulgaria was registering more economic growth and technological advance than most other East European countries. The considerable input of capital equipment and the considerable transmission of know-how and skills from Russia had made possible this rapid transformation.

"What modest advances we have made in Singapore have been due to our willingness, over the past thirteen years, to face up to unpleasant realities. We needed, and did import, machinery, technological know-how, management expertise and even some technical skills. We accepted the reality that unless we could prevent emigration of trained talent, there were limits to narrowing the differentials in rewards between the high performers and the average performers, between managers and technocrats and clerical workers, or between technicians and skilled workers and unskilled manual workers. Had we attempted to go beyond these limits, diminishing rewards for those with the ability and the drive, would have led to a brains drain."

Assuming Singaporeans had it in them, with intensive education and training, and learning on the job, citizens could, over the years, take over nearly all the middle, and a part of the higher management and engineering positions. Only then could Singapore claim to be a country that had passed out from the ranks of the "developing countries". The quantitative test of at least US$1,000 per capita GNP was misleading in qualitative terms. "We may have broken through this arbitrary ceiling. But we are nowhere near 'developed' status, just as the oil states of the Gulf are 'developed' only in their consumer tastes, which oil royalties, dependent on Western technology and Western technocrats, have allowed them to cultivate. We inherited a colonial economy, geared to an imperial system — little industry, some banking and commerce. There was excessive dependence on the entrepot trade, exporting the region's primary products to Britain, Europe and America, and importing their manufactured products for distribution around the region. But we were fortunate in inheriting good transportation, roads, harbours and airports. We also inherited an honest and effective administration. Most important of

81

all, we were fortunate in having a hardworking and intelligent people. Through universal education, we have been able to increase performance of both brain and manual workers. So we have been reasonably successful in promoting the growth of middle-level technology."

With the increased resources as a result of economic growth, Singapore had been able to provide better academic and technical education, better medical services at nominal fees, improved public housing and more social amenities. Perhaps their most socialistic achievement had been the equality of opportunities, especially in education. Regardless of wealth or status, everyone had an equal opportunity to make the best of his potential and get a job in accordance with his training, ability and skill. "We have mitigated the exploitation of man by his fellow men through the possession of wealth. We have not tried to prevent a man doing better than his fellow men through his own ability, training and hard work. Compassion for the less fortunate moves our policies. But we are conscious that people can improve their lives only if these policies can get them to try for themselves. We can be soft-hearted. But we cannot afford to be soft-headed."

Lee concluded his speech expressing the hope that in the course of the meetings and work of the Asia-Pacific Socialist Bureau, "we can compare and contrast our experiences in tackling sometimes similar, but often different, situations. I am sure we in the PAP can learn from the experiences of our fellow socialist parties elsewhere".

Alas! Very little was heard of the Asia-Pacific Socialist Bureau of the Socialist International after this conference.

XIV

Lee took the opportunity at a dinner in honour of the visiting Australian Prime Minister, Mr. William McMahon, on 9 June, to review briefly world events. He said that in the past eighteen months, there had been momentous political changes in the world. President Nixon's visits to Beijing in February, and to Moscow in May, made most countries re-examine their positions and to assess what changes the future had in store for them. The easy assumptions of cold war politics were no longer valid. But it did not necessarily follow that there would be any immediate or precipitated change in the political and security climate which had so far kept Southeast Asia, outside of Indo-China, an area of relative tranquility. "Change there must be. For my own part, I would prefer the dust stirred up by all these dramatic events to settle, before coming to firm conclusions on which to base any changes in policies. Certainly it is not necessary to start changing our friends, though nothing is lost by making new friends of old adversaries of cold war days." The recent series of accords between America and Russia reinforced the trend towards the acceptance by the super powers of their desire and now their declared policy to avoid confrontation against each other. They had accepted the division in Europe, since the Second World War, as a fact of life for the foreseeable future. By the recent series of agreements between the West Germans and the Russians, West Germans and the Poles, the agreements in Moscow and the Berlin Four Power agreement, the Europeans had substantially cut down the dangers of conflict in Europe itself. Unfortunately, there had been no such accords over Asia. One probable result of President Nixon's earlier discussions in Beijing was to lessen the likelihood of a collision between America and China. There were other major powers with long-term interests in Asia and in the Indian and Pacific Oceans. They were not present at the Beijing discussions. Further, they had not yet reconciled their different view of the shape of things to come. America, China, Japan and Russia might take some time to agree what the limits of their respective capacities to influence events in the different countries of Asia were. Nor was it clear how much naval power could add to their economic and political influence on the littoral states of Asia adjoining the Indian and Pacific Oceans, and on the island nations lying off the Asian Continent.

"Meanwhile, the war in Indo-China grinds on. We must hope there can be a negotiated settlement that will enable American forces to withdraw, and not in disgrace, that the South Vietnam these forces leave behind can be allowed to sort their future out by themselves without external interference by force. If this could happen, then a confident Thailand will act as a buffer for Malaysia and Singapore. Then we can have more time to adjust ourselves to the changing forces acting on Asia, the Pacific and Indian Oceans." Lee said the Australian Prime Minister's visit came at a time when the whole region was preparing to adjust to the altered situations consequent upon the dramatic changes in policy of the great powers. It was still not altogether certain what these changes would be. There was nothing alarming about uncertainty, provided the future was not placed in jeopardy by hasty reaction. "Amidst all these uncertainties, it was a source of satisfaction that we were able to maintain steady co-operation between Australia and Singapore." They contributed to the climate of confidence which helped Singapore ride through some difficult times in the past few years. Such progress as was made, despite the adverse turn of events in 1965 and 1968, was due, in part, to the quiet understanding and support of friends, of which Australia was one. And the defence arrangements of the Commonwealth Five had provided continuing stability to an area important to Singapore, the people who live in it, and perhaps to Australasia. There ·vas no reason why "we should not make further progress in regional co-ope. ·on, to consolidate the present stability of the region. With a little luck, Southeast Asia should be able to withstand drastic changes in the Indo-Chinese situation. In these matters, we have common interests."

XV

"Like the rest of Singapore, Tanjong Pagar will see a transformation in the next decade," the Prime Minister told a gathering of over 900 Ho Clansmen at Duxton Road on 23 June. He pointed out that "as long as we maintain our spirit to work and to achieve we shall make rapid growth. There will be all-round improvement. But the large numbers of children I see around here tonight appall me. We must make greater efforts to practise family planning. Even China, with its huge land-mass and resources, has a vigorous policy of birth control. China has to do this to forge ahead as a great power. China places her national interests above individual or sectional interests. In implementing this policy, China has no place for sentimental considerations. When our trade delegation visited China last year, and a group of our doctors earlier this year, they were treated with utmost courtesy, but as guests. All of them were treated as Singaporeans, and not as overseas Chinese. It is in the interest of China to do this. Her national interest dictates that she makes friends with other peoples of different ethnic origins in this part of the world. The present decade — the 1970s — is ushering in a new era. It is a period of great flux and change, as the super-powers change the framework within which they compete for influence and power."

Lee again spoke about family size on 25 June. He said: "We cannot afford to have eight, ten, twelve children per family, if we want better schools, smaller classes per teacher, better training in technical education. No government, no parent can provide for eight, ten, twelve children, particularly if the parents are only earning $200 to $300 per month. We must taper off the population growth. Then we can spend more per individual child — feed him or her, nurture and train him or her, so that his or her performance will be higher. To have a better quality of life, we must invest more in each child. This we can do only if we have three, or better still, only two children per family. We just cannot multiply infinitely. It is just not possible to keep on reclaiming the sea, reclaiming marsh land like reclaiming Kallang Basin, building more factories, building more high-rise flats. We want not any factory, but those factories with higher skills, more for sophisticated manufacture; for such factories can pay workers more. Then our workers can live in better homes, rear better children, and have a better environment. In the next decade, we must set out to achieve in qualitative terms what we have already achieved in quantitative terms in the past decade."

The future continued to dominate Lee's thinking: "It is time we ask ourselves: What kind of Singapore do we want to live in? Just more and more factories, with more and more homes, all crowded together? Or can we not make our lives more agreeable, in a more gracious Singapore, with less overcrowding." "We have," he told a party gathering on 30 June, "to import all the rice and wheat we eat, since land is too precious for agri-

84

culture. We have to concentrate development on quality, not on quantity. We must become a highly trained, skilled and organised society, even higher up the technological ladder. To do this, we must raise the quality of our people. We must, therefore, invest more in each child — good pre-natal care, earlier training from kindergartens to primary and secondary schools, to Polytechnics and universities. But this cannot be done if there are more than three children per family."

At present, Singapore had 500,000 schoolchildren between the ages of six and eighteen. School doctors reported that 10 per cent of them were undernourished, not eating enough meat, or drinking enough milk. They were weak and feeble. They came from poor homes with large families. If parents earning under $300 a month had three or more children, then none of them would be properly nourished. None would grow up healthy and active. Doctors knew that a protein deficiency in mother and baby could lead to the baby's brain being permanently impaired. More parents must know these simple facts. By the time the child goes to school at the age of six, supplementary feeding of milk, or of reinforced soy bean paste, is too late to reverse the brain impairment. But, nevertheless, this supplementary feeding could improve their physical health.

"As a small country in a strategic position, we must have a highly educated, highly trained population, capable of generating the means for a good life, always able to surmount new problems and unexpected awkward situations. By ability, training and organisation, we must be able to react rapidly to any fresh situation."

Meanwhile, advances already made must be consolidated to create a firmer foundation for the next generation to build upon and to reach out for higher goals. "We must further improve the level of our physical and brain services." Singapore was becoming a centre for aeroplane repairing, ship-repairing and shipbuilding, as well as a financial centre for Asia. Singapore's currency must continue to be one of the most stable in this part of the world, to enable the Republic to be the home of the Asian Dollar.

The Singapore Armed Forces must now grow in sophistication to safeguard security. Without security, nobody would bring in capital or expertise to build sophisticated industries in Singapore. "Never expect something for nothing. Nothing is ever for free. Whenever a people get into the habit of wanting more and more for less and less work, then however advanced they are, they run into grave economic and social problems. As a country, as yet not even adequately developed, we will perish if we seek this easy way of life. We need the social discipline, the determination to be self-reliant, the will to subordinate sectional interests to the national interests. Only then shall we continue to go forward and upwards."

"There is an air of well-being in Blair Plain (a dock-workers' area) tonight. The conditions are much improved compared to what they were a few years ago in 1965. But I understand that you are worried about your housing, and that you also want a revision in wages — something I would like too," the Prime Minister told a big gathering of people when he declared open the Blair Plain Residents' Association on 2 July. He gave the workers "an undertaking that no government, no Port of Singapore Authority can ask workers to move out of their quarters until there is alternative HDB accommodation to which they can move". At the moment there was a building boom. The Housing and Development Board had to compete with the private developers of shopping complexes, and high-rise office blocks along Shenton Way, Collyer Quay and elsewhere for building workers and materials. But given a little time, this problem would be solved and the rate of building by the HDB would be increased.

Between the years 1961 and 1971, the tonnage of ships using Singapore had more than doubled, from 23,079 ships totalling 76 million net registered tons to 39,426 ships totalling 155.9 million net registered tons. The general mineral-oil and bulk cargo handled had almost trebled from 18.3 million tons to 48.1 million tons. Today, the PSA had over 10,000 workers, of whom nearly half were housed by the PSA itself.

The Prime Minister also pointed out that "the Port will have to expand, and in the not too distant future, Blair Plain, or a part of it, will have to be developed as part of the Port complex. We have to keep ahead in the facilities we have, and the efficiency of our operations. Above all, be competitive in costs." Turning to the question of an upward revision in wages, the Prime Minister said that "the thirteenth month payment is not just for this year: it will be paid every year". He also said a committee, under the chairmanship of Mr. S.R. Nathan, had investigated the scales of wages for the daily-rated workers in the government service and made certain recommendations. These recommendations, with amendments, would be implemented shortly.

The Prime Minister assured PSA workers that although the terms and conditions of service for daily-rated workers in the government and those in the PSA had not been exactly the same, the considerations which prompted the appointment of the Nathan committee to look into the government workers' scales would, in fairness, also apply to workers in the PSA. So a committee would be appointed to correlate the categories and grades of workers in the government service to categories and grades in the PSA service and then the new wage structures could be adopted by the PSA wherever they were appropriate. He told the workers that the more hardworking the gangs are, the more bonus rates go up. As mechanisation increases, productivity goes up. The prosperity of Singapore is to a considerable extent tied up with the efficiency with which the PSA operates.

"We do not manufacture just for Singapore or for the regional market. We manufacture and export to the world market. In the next ten to fifty years, there will be changes in modes of transportation. But it is unlikely that sea transportation can be beaten for its low cost. And good, efficient, sea transportation, with a fast turn-around of ships in our harbour, has helped our rapid industrialisation. All the countries in this region want to develop their own harbours to handle their imports and exports. It is only natural that they should want to do so. So this is a challenge to the PSA, your efficiency, our ability to plan ahead, and your disciplined and efficient operations. It is because you work hard, and have good supervisors, it is because the PSA has a hardworking staff under a hard-driving chairman, that our harbour will continue to be the most efficient and competitive in the whole of South and Southeast Asia between Japan and Europe. Together, we must make sure that it continues to stay on top. That is the way to ensure your children a healthy and promising future.''

Lee spoke to bank workers later in the week. Banks were now amongst the top employers in Singapore. This was because the economy was on top, and because Singapore had set out to become one of the financial centres of the world. ''The fact that you are in an industry on the up means that you have a responsibility serving an industry which will affect the rest of Singapore. You must justify the higher salaries and the generous thirteenth month annual payment by providing efficient and courteous service, which all customers expect of their banks. The trend in banks the world over, including Singapore, is the greater use of labour-saving machines, like computers, But I do not think in the next few years you need have any anxiety.''

Lee said that the government was allowing more international banks to establish themselves in Singapore. They would help the expansion of the Asian Dollar market and improve the services available. Hence, staff in banks would expand. But this was a highly competitive world. It was no longer just local banks competing against one another and against established British banks. Big international combines — American-Japanese, Singapore-Japanese, European-American — were establishing offices in Singapore. This meant keener competition in increasing the efficiency of their services.

Lee reminded the bank workers that they were doing well because the banks were doing well. Banks in Singapore were doing well because Singapore was doing well. Why was Singapore doing well? Because four-and-a-half years ago, when confronted with a grave crisis, ''we had the guts and gumption to take unpleasant decisions to help overcome these problems. One of the decisions was a permanent change in workers' attitudes, embodied in the Employment Act. The result is today's relative prosperity. If you want to do well, the first thing is to keep Singapore doing well. Then the banks will do well. My advice is: Do not rock the boat. Do not do anything that may shake confidence in the keenness to work of Singapore workers. Then you will share in Singapore's prosperity.''

XVI

China sent a ping-pong team to Australia and New Zealand and on the way called in on Singapore. At a party gathering on 14 July, Lee said this had been an interesting and important experience for Singapore. "The question is: Has the majority of our people learnt that, although nearly 80 per cent of them are ethnic Chinese, they are Singaporeans? Or are they bemused enough to think that, being ethnic Chinese, they can identify themselves as members of a potential super-power? It is tempting to indulge in a sensation of greatness, without having to undergo the hardships and sacrifices of the people of China and, at the same time, as Singaporeans, enjoy the freer and better life here. When I watched the ping-pong on television the first night, I was slightly bewildered and angered. Instead of giving support and encouragement to our players, who were up against world-class opponents, a part of the crowd booed whenever our players played badly. I was also told that about forty persons shouted slogans, wishing Chairman Mao long life. But there was no response to this from the bulk of the audience. However, from the second night on, there was no more booing. Instead, there were cheers whenever the visitors or our players acquitted themselves well in any rally."

The Prime Minister said that no one could ask of Singapore Chinese not to be ethnic Chinese. "And it would be unnatural not to feel pleasantly reassured that, as Chinese, we are not unequal to other major ethnic and cultural groups in the world; that the Chinese, either because of ethnic or cultural attributes or both, are not inadequate and can make the grade, whatever the political system. But there are many people who are interested to know whether this ethnic, cultural and linguistic affinity will make us susceptible to manipulation through tugging at the heartstrings of our people and making them more Chinese orientated and less Singaporean."

After the past week, Lee's assessment was that a portion could still be manipulated. But, unlike ten years ago, the majority were now Singaporean. The situation should get better with each passing year. The orientation in schools, and the experience of the past twenty years, had brought about this change. "I believe a definite majority in Singapore are aware that our future, our destiny, depend on our ability to discern our collective interests, and to protect these interests. For neither China, nor any other country or government, will protect us or our interests, just because we happen to be ethnic Chinese."

There would be more contacts over the years — basketball, netball, other sports, exchanges of cultural troupes, missions of merchants, doctors or acupuncturists. At the end of each meeting, visitors from China would go back to China. And when Singapore's ping-pong team went to Beijing, they would come back. And they would learn how valuable and important it was to have a Singapore to return to.

The visiting players were very considerate, wiping the ping-pong table, not only on their side, but also the Singapore players' side. When two Singapore players won their matches, they were congratulated and, with elaborate courtesy, offered drinks. These exemplary acts of courtesy and humility were the result of training and social discipline in a political system where every aspect of life was well-organised. They inculcated different standards, values and had methods to induce the social conduct they considered desirable. "I do not know what the team from China thought of Singapore, our social habits and political system. But we have a reasonable standard of life and a different style of living with considerable room for individual choice, in work and recreation. All this will continue but only if we never forget to protect our collective interests."

XVII

"Your personal duty to defend Singapore does not end with your Run out Date (ROD)," warned Lee at a commissioning ceremony for infantry officers at the Padang on 15 July. "Under the Enlistment Act, you have another ten years of yearly reservist training to keep you in trim. In the event of mobilisation of the reserves, other ranks can be called up till the age of forty. As officers, you can be called up till the age of fifty." As Singapore developed and became more prosperous, people's attitudes to discipline and work could develop in two possible ways. "We could follow the course some West Europeans and Americans have taken. In these countries, affluence has blunted the keenness of young people to strive and achieve. They want to be excused from the physical and emotional discipline in military service. So national service is considered a chore which competing political parties promise to abolish. And where, as in Britain, they have abolished national service, the young have tended to be more pleasure-seeking and less eager to strive and to achieve. The whole moral tone of the new generation in the West has altered as they go for the soft life. If we follow this trend, then Singapore will go down the drain. We have no NATO alliances which guarantee super-power support if we are attacked. So the more prosperous Singapore is, the more likely that she will be gobbled up if she were weak."

The other course was the one the Swiss had taken. They kept up their economic development, with higher rewards for higher performance, but with a keen awareness that their defences must be always kept up. The Swiss knew and accepted compulsory military service as part of their way of life. So it must be for every Singaporean. "We have a lot to protect, and everything to lose, if we are unable to defend ourselves. The only way we can defend ourselves with a small population, of just over two million people, is the way other small countries, like Switzerland, Finland and Israel, have done: by compulsory military service, and building up through the reserves of an armed force of considerable numbers if the

89

reserves are mobilised. For such a force to be credible, an elaborate programme of reservist training is essential. For ten years after your ROD, you will be kept on your mettle.''

Nearly 20,000 were already in the reserves. Each year, 12,000 national servicemen would go into the reserves, Infantry, Combat Engineers, Specialist Engineers, Artillery, Armour, Field Logistics, and so on. The annual build-up of reservists would grow from 12,000 to 16,000 in the next few years. No matter how relaxed and pleasure-loving the wealthy industrial societies of the West could afford to be, Singapore would be finished if Singaporeans became a hedonist society. Economic advance had been won the hard way. It could be sustained if the verve and vitality were kept up, if the society remained well-organised with a well-trained defence force. An attitude to life must be cultivated where nothing was taken for granted. Alertness, cohesiveness and the determination to stand up for their rights would decide whether in fact Singaporeans had to fight and die for them. ''The strange thing is that the more people know you are prepared to fight, and can fight well, the less likely is it necessary to do so.''

XVIII

When Lee spoke at the dinner of the Singapore Air Transport Workers' Union the next day, he told them that the newly formed Singapore Airlines would inherit twenty-five years of experience. Malayan Airways had started off in Singapore twenty-five years ago with three ''Air Speed Consul'' aircraft. There was little to choose between aircraft. All major airlines now used standard proven aircraft. Between established major airlines, there was also little difference in standards of maintenance, or the professionalism of engineers and technicians or pilots. The differences there were lie in the efficiency of the organisation and management, which took years to build up, and labour and wage costs.

The major airlines of the industrialised countries had established reputations for getting people, more or less, punctually to their destinations. But there was scepticism whether airlines run by countries not yet industrialised could provide such services. ''Fortunately, we are establishing ourselves as one of the few countries which, though still in the process of being industrialised, has already developed the habit for tip-top maintenance and a zeal for efficiency. It is reflected in a people's philosophy of life — either easy-going and tolerant of sub-standard work, or active and insistent on nothing less than the best achieveable.''

Lee confessed he knew little of the mysteries of advertising and of the soft sell. But he believed no magic set of initials, no logo could sell to more than the first few something which was not good. By skilful publicity, the P R man could attract attention and get across an idea. But if the idea got across did not tally with the reality, the value of the advertisement, however attractive, was soon dissipated. "Our best asset is in the reputation of Singapore itself. To most people abroad — in governments, in finance, in business, and to many ordinary newspaper readers in the main cities of the world — 'Singapore' means a hardworking and hard-headed people, a thrusting new nation rapidly climbing up the technological ladder. This is a reputation forged out of our struggle for survival. A reputation earned this hard way is a durable one, and very different from the 'image' created by skilful image-makers. The future of Singapore Airlines depends more on the reality SIA leaves behind on their passengers than any advertisement. To improve efficiency of organisation, promptness and friendliness of service, these must be our constant aims." Reputations were continually made and lost. Within a matter of months, Singapore could either enhance the reputation inherited from MSA, or fritter it away. What passengers actually experienced and passed on to their friends was far more effective than any glossy advertisement, however useful in selling an airline.

Singapore ran an airline not for reasons of prestige, but for plain economic benefit. "We are a centre of the main North-South and Northwest-Southwest jet routes. Other countries will give us landing rights, because they want to land in Singapore. But if we cannot make profitable use of any of these landing rights, we should have no compunction in closing a service down. This is our approach to life. We are not flying in a restricted and protected home market. We are flying the international jet routes in competition with major world airlines. Our standards must always go up, never slide down. We have to go into new aircraft as soon as they are proven after profitable operations by major airlines. You must match our faith in you, but never letting Singapore be apologetic for your slovenly or slack work."

One great advantage Singapore had over the major airlines of the wealthy world was service. As Americans and Europeans became more and more affluent, their people were less eager to please customers whether in shops or in aircraft. But the never tiring courtesy and efficiency of Singapore's cabin crew had won recognition from all seasoned travellers, who had sampled all the major airlines. This would help make Singapore's airline.

Government emphasis continued to be placed on community centres. On 18 July, Lee officiated at the opening of the Eunos Community Centre. He said that this new community centre was an example of how a community could help itself. A group of people voluntarily contributed funds to build their own community centre. The more fortunate helped to provide amenities and recreation for everybody else. Such activities generated a sense of cohesion and developed community pride. Five years ago conditions were very different. There was increasing unemployment and in Kampong Kembangan too. As a result of the Employment Act, the willingness of people to face realities and their determination to overcome

91

problems, the political and industrial climate of Singapore underwent a great change. Investments flowed in from abroad. There was now a shortage of certain types of skilled and semi-skilled workers and, in the building industries, even of unskilled workers. Women workers were in demand in the transistor and garment factories. More married women were wanted to join the work force. Creches and kindergartens would be built to enable more married women to work.

Meanwhile, with nearly full employment more people wanted new homes. This spurt in demand put great pressure on the HDB. They could not built enough at present because of a shortage of building construction workers. But the Board and the government were working out plans to increase the rate of building. One way was to mechanise more. Another was to slow down the building in the private sector, by postponing certain urban renewal projects. As for plans to develop Kampong Eunos and Kampong Kembangan, they were geared for completion in six to eight years' time though work would start earlier. The reason was the need for special planning required in this area. Because it was near the airport, low level buildings had to be planned for the whole area for both industrial and domestic use. High-rise factories or flats could not be built. Flats, factories and godowns could not go higher than five storeys. This made it even more difficult to plan adequate space for parks and playgrounds.

But in six years, great changes would take place throughout Singapore and in Kampong Eunos. More wives would be working, doubling the family income. This new generation of working husbands with working wives was already finding the supermarkets more convenient than the small sundry shops. Small shopkeepers had to combine together to streamline their business to meet changing conditions. He spoke on family planning too: "A better life for yourself and your children is only possible if you have a family of less than three children. Every child must be well-fed, cared for and trained. A family with two children is ideal if you want to give them the maximum benefits in health, education and training for a better job. Then, your children will have a better life". Those who had large families of six or more were just bringing up children to be poorly fed and trained, and whose future would be so much poorer than the children of the small families.

XIX

Newsweek of 24 July carried an interview with the Prime Minister. He was asked if the Vietnam War had really bought time for Singapore and other countries in Southeast Asia. Lee answered: "Definitely it has bought some time. What use has been made of the time? Well, it varies from country to country; but I hope I have made some use of that time, but then what is the point of that, if in the end the Thais come under pressure from a communized Indochina and yield, and then the West Malaysians come under pressure and then us?''

Asked if he still thought that was possible, Lee replied: "Oh! I would think it very much on the cards."

Newsweek: You've just restated the domino theory.

Lee: No, I'm not interested in playing dominoes. I am interested in seeing where my troubles can come from and how they can be avoided. I don't believe there is one monolithic communist movement, which is the basis of the so-called domino theory. As the Viet Cong and North Vietnamese have shown, there is a momentum in a liberation movement on its own. As the Chinese and Russians have discovered recently, in the last resort it is the leaders in North Vietnam who decide what game to play.

The Prime Minister was asked what the aims of the Soviet Union in Southeast Asia were. He replied: "It is definitely not one of their crucial areas like Western Europe or their frontier with China or their missile balance with America. These are matters of life and death for them. But assuming that these areas do not flare up, we will see more peaceful Russian competition for economic and political influence out there. Also, it is fair to assume that their navy is going to play an increasing role in extending this trading and political influence, particularly in the Indian Ocean and around the Straits of Malacca."

Newsweek asked Lee if he expected the Japanese to play a stronger political and perhaps military role in Asia in the next few years. Lee replied: "No. The Japanese will do what they consider to be in their long-term interests and I don't believe they will see it in their long-term interests to get involved militarily in Southeast Asia. When the U S has found it so unprofitable, why should they find it profitable? They may want to ensure the safety of their lines of communication to sources of oil and raw materials, but beyond that I would be surprised if they engaged in any military activity or commitments. I also believe they will continue to extend their trade ties in this area."

Newsweek: You don't seem as worried about Japanese economic penetration of Asia as the Thais and Indonesians appear to be.

Lee: It is a psychological problem. We in Singapore know economic cooperation with Japan is not an equal matter. We make their ships in our shipyards with our cheaper labour. Nonetheless, we pay them a royalty for their design and the more advanced parts of the ships are manufactured in Japan and carried here in Japanese bottoms. So obviously they have got more out of every ship we build than we do. But we accept that. What's the choice?

Newsweek: You don't believe this hinders your political manoeuverability as a nation?

Lee: Not unless the Japanese are overwhelmingly the dominant economic partner. If we were in the position of South Korea where Japanese investments and interests outweigh those of the Americans and all others, then we would be a little concerned because then the Japanese can lean on you. But not here where the Japanese are only one of many foreign investors.

XX

On the eve of National Day, Lee appeared on television to give his message. He said that 1972 marked the successful conclusion of a period of great trials and tribulations — first merger with Malaysia, then "confrontation", 1964 communal riots, 1965 separation, and finally the British military rundown. "Since the early 1950s, we have had chronic unemployment. By the first half of this year, we have overcome the redundancy problems. Today, there is only frictional umemployment — workers on the move in search of better jobs. Now we have to take some fundamental decisions on what kind of society we want to be. I say let us raise our sights, let us aim at quality and not quantity, From now on, we will choose industries which are more skill-intensive, more sophisticated in production, and can therefore pay higher wages. With a lower birth rate, we can reach out for higher goals. We can achieve a better standard of living and a higher quality of life. With smaller families, we can invest more in each child, better health, education and training, and higher performance."

Some people wondered whether Singaporeans would not become easy-going as they got less lean and less hungry. He did not think that would happen. Like the Swiss or the Japanese, Singaporeans simply had to maintain keenness. The Swiss and the Japanese were more prosperous than Singaporeans, but had not lost their drive. Because they had no abundance of natural resources, they knew they could not afford the soft life. So it was for Singaporeans.

The past few years of wage restraint had contributed to Singapore's rapid industrial expansion. Now that problems of redundancies were over, the National Wages Council had recommended an 8 per cent increase for 1972. If there were no economic upsets, wages should go up annually, in a steady and orderly way. "I believe we can achieve an annual 10 per cent plus growth rate for several years. If that is achieved, we can afford a 5 per cent plus wage increase annually. We have kept the cost of food, rent and other essentials stable for the past decade. The cost of living has risen in the past few years because of the rise in costs of imports from Europe and America, and, after the revaluation of the yen, even from Japan. This has affected many people, because standards of living have gone up. Many people now consider scooters, small cars, TV and refrigerators necessities, not luxuries."

There were over 60,000 families waiting for new homes. Because of the enormous expansion in private building of office blocks, hotels and shopping complexes, the government had not been able to build enough

HDB flats to meet the great demands resulting from higher incomes and rising standards of living. "This year, we are building 20,000 flats, twice the rate four years ago. We shall build more every year. All those on the waiting list will get them, some sooner than others, but on a fair basis."

The servicing and manufacturing sectors would continue to expand. A home for the "Asian Dollar" would be provided, developing banking and financial expertise. This could help the financing of development in the region. And the more the region developed, the more likely there would be peace and tranquility. Meanwhile, Singapore's overseas assets backing the currency had grown stronger each year. They were $336.2 million in 1959 when the PAP government took office. They had multiplied thirteen times in thirteen years to $4,230 million in June 1972. The Singapore Dollar had to be strong for Singapore to be the home of the "Asian Dollar".

"Without a hinterland to support us, many people, only seven years ago when we separated from Malaysia, thought we could not survive. But we have. Indeed, each year, we have added to our capital assets. And we are rebuilding the old city and also building several new towns. For more than thirteen years, we were beset by so many daunting problems. A faint-hearted people would have given up long ago. We never gave in, never mind giving up. For that alone, we deserve to succeed. If we press on, in twenty years we shall build a great metropolis, worthy of a hardy, resilient and stout-hearted people."

Lee went into greater deal in a rousing speech at the National Day rally in the National Theatre. He described 1972 as a very special year for Singapore. It marked a significant turning-point in history. It was never intended that Singapore should be an independent country, let alone one that had every promise of thriving and prospering. "Seven years ago, many wrung their hands in despair — how were we to solve all the enormous problems which even with British tutelage and more or less an integrated or a linked economy with Peninsular Malaya or the Federation of Malaya could not solve our unemployment problems then. How were we after we were out of Malaysia, to solve it? And when in 1968, just four and a half years ago, we were told that 20 per cent of our GNP was to be knocked off, people just gave us up for lost."

He thought they had cause that evening for rejoicing. Only a tough-minded people united in their resolve to make the grade could have done it. And it was so easily done, once everybody looked back on the seven years and the past four years. They said, "But of course, workers had the Employment Act to guide them, make them work; then investments flowed in." But it worked because workers, employers and government pulled in the same direction; all knew what was at stake and the price that would have to be paid for failure. "And we were determined not to fail."

Lee thought it useful to take stock of the position. In thirteen years — since taking office, thirteen and a quarter to be accurate — overseas assets had grown from $320 million — thirteen times — to $4,200

95

million. That was just the overseas assets. But Singapore's own development — the increase in wealth, the infrastructure, the generating stations, the wharves, container terminals, reclaimed land — on paper, another $4,000 million had been added. In round figures, external and internal assets had increased in wealth to $10,000 million, which meant about $5,000 per person — men, women and children.

Like a family or a limited company, a nation's output depends on the capital assets it has. This increase in the social, economic infrastructure meant that incomes trebled in the past decade. In 1971 it was over $3,000 per person.

Perhaps one of the important reasons why Singapore became different from the other countries was that Singapore never believed anything was for free, not even the water that they drank or the cool air that they breathed. Fans meant oil which meant royalties to the OPEC countries. And hence it was important that nobody in Singapore should ever drift into a position where they believed that things were for free.

Lee chided the thousands of gamblers who had put money in chit funds. He confessed there were many things that went on in Singapore without his knowledge, without the knowledge of colleagues. "We did not know that there were such things as chit funds that go every day. Well, those who gambled, they deserve it. But there were housewives, teachers, pensioners, who believed that this was an attractive way of increasing their savings with interests ranging from 20 per cent to 40 per cent, sometimes even 50 per cent. It was strange that there were no news or rumours of any default or malpractice at any time, although Gemini started business from as early as 1964 and Stallion started from 1970. When MAS — Singapore Monetary Authority — accountants discovered the astonishing facts, the government acted at once to minimise losses. Maximum restitution is our aim. All assets must be frozen and all property ferreted out and recovered. All subscriptions from those who have bid must be collected as and when they are due — whether daily, weekly or monthly. Maximum recoveries of all monies, properties and assets that can be got at is the primary objective. And when all these monies have been collected the Official Receiver will distribute them — pro rata to all 'live' subscribers, which means those who have contributed but have not yet drawn on the chit funds. Needless to say, I believe the Attorney-General knows that his duty will be to see that justice is fully and publicly done in our courts."

Lee thought it would be wrong to prejudge whether these monies were lost through ill-advised investments or for other reasons. But he thought Singaporeans must become more sophisticated. He warned them against the people with get-rich-quick schemes. They came from all the wealthy countries — Americans, Europeans, Australians.

"We just cannot go on being silly. The world's fastest, growing country, Japan, has been growing at a rate of 15 per cent per annum, which means that some of their best companies may make 25 per cent. So, if you lend or you invest in something which promises you 50 per cent, 60 per cent, I suggest you better see a good friend who knows what this is all about, because it just isn't true. Never believe just what you see, better delve deeper into it."

Sophistication is an essential factor in growing up. All want to make money. All want to increase savings. Lee advised that the safest way to save was in the Post Office. He reckoned that perhaps $70 million had been lost. Some very poor people were involved. That was why every single cent must be recovered.

Lee turned to the international situation. This was changing rapidly. There was an American election coming up. Maybe, there would not be spectacular changes. There was an Australian election coming up. Singapore acknowledged the right of any Australian Government to act in accordance with what they considered to be their national interest. If the Australian Labour Party became the Australian Government and said they wished to withdraw their troops and their Mirages, well, it was within their sovereign right, indeed all they needed to do under the ANZUK arrangement in any case was to hold consultations.

It was against this backdrop that Singapore planned for the future. As one set of problems was solved, new and bigger problems emerged. "We have got through the shock of communist riots, arson, assassinations. We went through the shock of communal riots, first time in our history in 1964. We got suddenly separated from Malaysia. The British pound suddenly devalued in November, 1967 and now it is floating and we have got, I think, more than 36 per cent of our assets in pound sterling. But all these problems we have overcome." The lesson was that in the last analysis, Singapore had only themselves to depend on. "If we lack the guts and gumption to stand up for ourselves, then I say write it off, forget it. All this that we have built, just give it away. I say it is through a series of crises, if you like, stresses and strains that forges a nation out of a group of loosely-linked people. Our forefathers came here because they were looking for the pot of gold at the end of the rainbow. Some found that pot of gold, many didn't. They sweated their guts out and built this city out of mudflats. We've inherited it, we have added to it. And I say it is worth defending it."

And so the defence capability which had been built up over the years. "Mind you, if the Russians or the Americans decide they want to capture Singapore, well, that is a different proposition altogether. It is like the Japanese Imperial Guards marching down the Peninsular Malaya right into Singapore and 90,000 British, Indian and Australian troops were captured. But I saw them fight. I saw the British blow their bagpipes across the Causeway. I saw them marched to captivity. And I say they were brave men. And that is what we have got to be. We have to be brave. And we need not necessarily fight the Japanese Imperial Guards. All we need do is to have the capacity to ward off any sneak attack for a week to a fortnight and the UN Security Council can intervene. But, of course, if you can't, and you are captured within twenty-four hours, then the whole thing is over. It is a *fait accompli*. And if we have this defence capability, then it is a defence capability which is not insignificant. And we are prepared to co-operate with all our neighbours to ensure the peace, stability and well-being of Southeast Asia, so that all of us can concentrate our energies and resources to the building up of better-fed, better-clothed, better-educated, more productive and more satisfying societies."

Finally, Lee said how proud he was that 1972 saw Singapore not in the depths of despair which many a wiseacre predicted in 1968, but comfortably resilient, buoyant ..... "We don't want to be booming too much. It is no good. It is just a mild boom, keep it up. Last year it was 14 per cent. I say, let us be on the conservative side. So 10 per cent plus which means every year 5 per cent plus. And all those who want to save — and we make sure that some save in the CPF (Central Provident Fund) — please choose wisely, and nothing better than putting your money in constructive purposes in Singapore."

XXI

In accordance with Article 49(3) of the Constitution, the Prime Minister advised the President to dissolve Parliament as from the 16th August. The President accordingly issued Writs of Elections naming Wednesday, 23 August, as Nomination Day. In a statement, the government said that the principal mandate on which the PAP had been elected to office on 13 April, 1968, was to see Singapore through the problems brought about as a result of the rundown of the British military bases. This task had been successfully completed.

The present government had therefore decided to seek a new mandate. For the next five years, the government's main aim was to raise standards of skills and technical competence, and to improve professional, management and technological expertise. Only higher standards could help Singapore achieve more sophistication in her industrial, commercial and servicing sectors, and enlarge her role as an international banking and financial centre, providing a home for the Asian Dollar. These new objectives required a change in policy emphasis, with the accent on quality.

Immediately after nominations on 23 August, Lee told a press conference that this was the fourteenth year of PAP government. "We have a team with a wide spread of trained abilities in planning and administration, and considerable experience. The record of successive PAP Cabinets from 1959 to 1972 is one of honest government, practical policies and efficient implementation. Our primary aim now is that every citizen should be educated to his fullest potential, to hold a job equal to his training and ability, and as his performance and output increase, so will his pay increase. In 1959, Singapore was a riotous place heading for destruction. Today, it is an orderly and constructive society. All of us have a stake in keeping it stable, hardworking and productive. We sweated the last seven years to get a stagnating economy, with chronic unemployment, moving forward and upwards, now with considerable buoyancy. To allow anyone to disrupt this trend towards a better society would be dereliction of our duty.''

Lee recalled that every time elections were about to be held, the same old political gamblers, and a few new punters, formed political parties to try their luck, many with other people's money. They believed they could win a lottery by promising to give the voters everything cheaper, or for free. To them, an election was an auction, a bidding contest to give away free houses, free medical services, more licence to the voter to do whatever he wanted. None of them could tell the voter how Singapore, an island of 2.1 million, at 10,000 per square mile, could create and increase total wealth before anything could be given away. "We never promise what cannot be done, and we make a practice of doing what we have promised. Given imaginative leadership, we in the PAP believe Singapore can make more out of our now increased economic infrastructure, and put the professional, industrial and commercial ability of our people to more rewarding pursuits in a fast-changing part of the world. It is only natural that our neighbours want to do their own exports of rubber, pepper and other produce. We must move to new fields, in brain servicing, banking and finance, ship repairing and shipbuilding, and be a base for middle technology manufacture by multi-national corporations with a world-wide market. Our second most important duty is to provide Singapore with a next generation leadership, with experience in government. The most crucial experience is how to mobilise our people in support of national policies to give Singaporeans an ever better future, with stability and security enhanced by a stronger economic and social base.''

The election campaign lasted no more than a few days, but Lee played an active part. Nomination Day was 23 August and the people voted on 2 September. Lee in his main rally speech on 29 August told a lunch-time crowd that it was a pity that not all the sixty-five seats were being contested, because he wanted those financing quite a number of "this bunch of seventy-five opposition candidates", to know where the people of Singapore stood. A majority of the seventy-five were political riff-raff, ragamuffins who would do anything to try their luck, for money was what they needed. One had even been charged and convicted for Criminal Breach of Trust.

It was nine years since there was a full contest for the hearts and minds of Singaporeans. Was there such a thing as a Singaporean? "Or are we just Chinese — English-educated Chinese, Chinese-educated Chinese — Malays, Indians, Ceylonese, Eurasians and others?''

Why were "the people" financing some of these candidates? Well, they could buy electoral registers easily, and particularly with computers, it was possible to break down the constituencies into racial, religious and almost linguistic components. Several governments, some friendly and some not so friendly, would also be interested to know. "We also want to know on the morning of 3 September, how many people are against the government in each constituency, and for what reasons, ethnic, religious, economic or personal grievances." A lot of people were interested to see whether the Malays would vote for Malays, how the Indians would go. How the Chinese voted — the difference between the English-educated and Chinese-educated, and so on. From the results, they would know, first, whether, if some people wanted to make use of some citizens, they could succeed. Second, the big powers, the super powers — Americans, Russians and Chinese — would be interested to see whether in the long run, Singapore was going to be a nation of Singaporeans, whether Singaporeans would be just Chinese, Indians, Malays and others. Lee said he got a lot of advice from diplomats and Western experts. Sometimes, he picked up valuable points. A lot of what they recommended was just irrelevant, and might be harmful.

In new countries, elections often became a farce, in which promises which could not be fulfilled, were made. Ministers became corrupt because they were not sure whether they could win the next elections. It was not possible to be corrupt without somebody knowing. Another person was involved. That other person would probably be getting the money from some other source. So it would go down the line from Ministers to secretaries to clerks to messengers. It had happened in many countries. Once a country had gone down that slippery slope, it ended at the bottom as a broken-back state. Recovery would be difficult. "If you have Mr. Vetrivelu, Mr. Jeyaretnam and Mr. Murugason in charge, we will be a broken-back state in no time. We are not a broken-back state. I know a lot of foolish candidates going around saying that the government is corrupt. I do not bother to issue summonses during the elections. But they are fools. We are not. If you can believe what they say, I am happy and prepared to step down."

Politics in new countries was literally a matter of life and death. Especially was this so in Singapore. Singapore had no natural wealth. All Singapore had was many intelligent people with skilful fingers. It was a hardworking population well-organised at ten thousand per square mile. Packed so closely, people could get very irritable, but there was no mugging in Singapore as there was, for example, in New York.

Lee referred to the "utter, lunatic things" the opposition candidates said. "If ever these people came into power, even God cannot help you from disaster. They are going to give you flats for free, medicine for free, everything you can ask or think of. The British tried that and they went near bankrupt. Now they charge about $5 for one visit to a doctor. And the British pay their National Insurance weekly for all their social benefits and pensions. But our opposition will give all of this for free. There is no need to pay. In fact, there is no need to work. We can all go home and sit under the banana tree."

100

In Ceylon, there was a left-wing coalition government of Sri Lanka Freedom, Trotskyites, the Communist Party of Ceylon and one or two left-wing groups. Ceylon could not go further left than that. Sri Lanka was great friends with China. What Mr. Zhou En-lai told Mrs. Bandaranaike made Lee feel deeply for her troubles. The Sri Lanka Government had promised to double the rice ration. There was no foreign money in the Treasury. They had to pay for the rice. So (to the question), "Please can you give me some rice?" Zhou said, "Nothing is for free. There is a limit to our help." Lee said he had never gone anywhere in his travels asking for anything for free. It was shameful. "I told Mr. Harold Wilson this in 1968. He said, 'Never mind, we will give you some aid.' I said, 'Harold, you are under no obligation to do so. If you want to give, I shall be happy to accept. But if I lead my people to believe that their survival depends on aid, they will die.' So, he gave us £50 million, one-quarter outright grant and three-quarters loan with interest. The loan to be repaid. We thanked them. But our present strength did not depend on that 50 million pounds."

Singapore's GDP since 1968 had more than doubled. It went up at an average of 15 per cent a year, "by your work and our planning. In the seven years of separate independence, we have found a new way to make a living".

Lee spoke about the armed forces. Why should Dr. Goh spend money buying expensive military hardware, training soldiers, sailors and airmen, when he was a thrifty soul? He was Defence Minister in 1965 – 67 and again from 1970. He was a tough-minded, resolute and able administrator. He built up a defence force from almost nothing. At that time, half of the two Singapore Infantry Regiment battalions were Malaysians. Most of the officers were Malaysians. Defence costs millions. Defence expenditure in 1966 was about 2 per cent of GDP; in 1972 about 10 per cent. No country disclosed its detailed defence expenditure. Men were trained with live bullets and mortar shells. Every year, some 16,000 to 20,000 went into the army. "At the end of 1980, if it became necessary at the press of a button, we will have 250,000 in the Armed Forces. To attack one battalion in a prepared defence position, three battalions are usually needed. Even then, you cannot be sure of capturing it. When we have got 250,000, whoever wants to take us over must have 750,000. That is quite a big-sized army. We can afford this only because of a national service army. What it is that your opposition tell you? Abolish it. Can Singapore maintain a 100,000 standing army? We would go bankrupt. This is an investment, not one that produces direct money interest, but one that produces an indirect interest in your security, and by giving confidence, not only to overseas investors, but also to our people with money."

This election was a test for Singapore's future. Foreign governments were interested. Americans, Russians, the Chinese were interested to know what Singapore was becoming. Naturally, the Malaysians and Indonesians, being close neighbours, would like to know what the breakdown was between loyal Singaporeans and those who were not. This was a real test for citizens as much as for the Singapore Government, a test in which the governments in the region and the super-powers had a long-term interest, because Singapore happened to be in a strategic position.

"If you are easily taken in, then all any goverment need do is to pump in US$100 million or more over ten years and they can take over. This time they were foolish. The *Herald* was openly anti-Singapore, anti-national service, long hair, drugs and everything with-itism. Next time, more mature operators would not have to buy *The Straits Times*. Just buy a few people, starting off with a convivial dinner, with wines and good cuisine."

Lee urged his listeners to vote in a way that all the super-powers might know that "whether you are Chinese-educated, English-educated, or bilingual, whether Indians, Eurasians, or Malays, you are voting as Singaporeans. We allow a certain latitude. We do not want to repress people. But let nobody be in any doubt what the game is all about. Vote in such a way that nobody believes that money can buy out Singapore. Once they can get a few mercenaries in, then proxies, and one day, they may get a majority, and in three readings in Parliament in one day of an emergency sitting, all that we have built up is gone. Then our commander-in-chief will have to salute whoever is sent down to take over because that is the present constitutional rule of the game. We will work out a constitution that will prevent any change constitutionally in three readings."

In an eve-of-poll broadcast, Lee urged that a decisive vote for the PAP would be good for the people and for Singapore. First, it would demoralise and discourage those who wanted to see Singapore go down. It would prove that all their money and plotting, working through proxies in Singapore, would not work. They would have to accept Singapore for what it was, and deal fairly and openly with them. Next, it would give a great impetus to investments, giving good jobs. It would also generate revenue which could pay for more social amenities. Western industrialists were now facing labour shortages, or difficult trade union problems. "Your massive support for the PAP will convince them that Singapore is the place to site their enterprises. It is crucial such people should know that our workers and trade unions are wholeheartedly in support of our policy to attract manufacturing and banking capital, management know-how and marketing enterprise."

None of the opposition parties had the remotest intention of developing into a loyal opposition: that is, an opposition which supported the nation's fundamental interests, "first, like how we are to defend ourselves; second, how to maintain harmony in a multi-racial society". Instead, the opposition, although not reported in the more responsible press, were exploiting issues over race, language and religion, willing to risk conflict and race riots, just for a few votes. Make no mistake, warned the Prime Minister, the opposition parties were not for Singapore, either in their thinking or speeches. They were a motley crew. Their only common factor was crude denunciation of the government and their attack of all policies, "the very policies which have brought you, and

Queen Elizabeth II of England visited Singapore in 1972 with Prince Philip, Duke of Edinburgh, and their daughter, Princess Anne. They are pictured here with President and Mrs Sheares, and Mrs Lee Kuan Yew

The Prime Minister presenting the sword of honour to a newly commissioned officer during a parade at the Padang (1973)

General Ne Win of Burma with Lee at the Istana

Governor Ronald Reagan and Mrs Reagan of the United States visited Singapore in 1973.

Lee paid his first official visit to the Soviet Union in 1970. Here a smiling Lee watches as the Soviet Prime Minister, Alexi Kosygin greets the Foreign Minister, S. Rajaratnam

Pre-Watergate. Lee with Richard Nixon, US President, in the grounds of the White House

them, a better life. Their formula for winning an election is to give things away for free, and to abolish laws, like the Employment Act, which have ensured work discipline and productivity. They have no plans for your security, economic advancement, or social development. To tell you the truth, they have no idea how the present sound state of affairs came about. So how can they improve upon it?"

The PAP had seen the people through two major crises in seven years — separation in 1965, accelerated British withdrawal in 1968. "Hard work and realistic policies brought us through. Now we are on top of our problems. The prospects look good for the immediate future. We are building 20,000 HDB flats a year. We will be increasing the rate to 30,000 a year. If you remain keen to learn and to work, you will get better jobs, with higher productivity by using more machines, and be better paid. We can make Singapore a metropolis pleasant to live and work in, with green parks, clean beaches, recreational areas, a civilised city with a gracious environment for everyone."

Politics in newly independent countries depended on two fundamental factors; first, the nature of a people, their innate character and cultural attributes, second, the quality of their leadership. To make the grade, people in new countries must work hard towards common goals. They could not afford to fritter away their energies on issues which divided and confused them. Instead, they must pour their efforts into constructive projects and pursuits. To get a people as a whole to do this, they needed leadership which is honest and effective, resolute but flexible. They must be prepared to do what was necessary for the good of all, even when policies were temporarily unpopular. "We are fielding sixty-five men, honest, hardworking, and willing to slog for you, and march with you towards a better future. We in the present leadership have not let you down. We fought the British for independence, we fought the communists for merger and Malaysia, we fought the racialists for equality in Malaysia."

Now major changes had taken place in the relationships of the superpowers. They affected the whole world. The future would be very different. "However, you know from your past experience and watching our performance over thirteen and a quarter years that whatever the threats, together, you and the government, we will respond swiftly to meet any crisis, any challenge in this fast-changing world. Do not put your future at risk. Vote solidly for the PAP. We have never let you down."

As generally expected, the PAP won all sixty-five parliamentary seats. At a Press Conference held at two o'clock in the morning of 3 September, Lee was asked how he felt about the 30 per cent of the vote which was recorded against the PAP. Lee said he was concerned, but pointed out that people voted against the PAP for a variety of reasons. In that respect it was not a solid anti-PAP protest vote.

Lee said he thought the problem of getting an intelligent constructive opposition had to be solved; Singapore just hadn't got the kind of people

103

coming into politics who were likely ever to develop into a coherent, constructive, loyal opposition. "So we are toying at twenty minutes past two in the morning, with the idea of getting some university seats — Nanyang and Singapore University graduates voting for one candidate and TTC plus (the Teachers' Training College plus), the Polytechnic and the Ngee Ann College voting for another two or three, so that they don't have to belong to the PAP, they don't have to be obliged to us. They can take us on — they are intelligent enough, I hope, to point out where we are wrong. I mean, we are not infallible." Nothing ever came of this early morning thought.

In a statement on 3 September, Lee stated: "The people have given us their decisive support. Votes cast in favour of PAP candidates were positive votes, 522,000 or 69.1 per cent. Votes against were 224,500 or 30.9 per cent. They went to a variety of opposition parties, and an even greater variety of candidates. They were votes more against the PAP than for the opposition. We have no illusions over this. Every political party and every candidate have had their full say of what they thought of the PAP government and our policies. Some candidates went well beyond the ambit of the law of libel and sedition. Politicking started from early 1971, over eighteen months ago, not just in these few weeks. As the government, we have bent backwards to let the opposition have their say, as long as they do not use violence, or incite people to violence. Now it is our duty to continue to govern fairly, and sometimes firmly, for you, the majority of the people of Singapore. Our object is the mostest good for the mostest people. We shall be analysing the reasons for the 30.9 per cent protest votes. Some are for personal disappointments, permits or licences refused. More are for dislocation of their way of life and their livelihood, as a result of rapid industrialisation and urbanisation, and urban renewal. And, let us face it, in at least two constituencies, simple ethnic, linguistic and religious issues were exploited to the fullest by the opposition. Where people have grievances which are even partially well-founded, it is our duty to do our best to put them right. But where people are against the government because they want to have special treatment for themselves over and above other citizens, this just cannot be done. Popular government does not mean the government must be popular all the time, with all the people. Democratic representative government, one man one vote, means that the governing party must have the support of the majority of the people, for the main aims and policies of the government, for most of the time, especially election time, every four to five years, when the mandate should have been fulfilled."

The Prime Minister called on the President later in the day and asked that the current Cabinet continue in office until the following week. Lee wanted time for discussions with several of his Cabinet colleagues before settling the new Cabinet. The new Cabinet, with Lee as Prime Minister, was sworn in on 16 September.

XXII

The importance of the English language was underlined by Lee in an address at the official opening of the Regional English Language Centre Building on 18 September. He said Singapore was privileged to be the host to this Regional Centre to train teachers of English as a second language. In an ever smaller world, with mass rapid transportation, people from all parts of the world travelled and met. For the time being, more people from the wealthy, developed West travelled to see the East, than the other way around. Whether Americans, Japanese or West Europeans, most of them spoke English.

At the height of the Roman empire, from about 250 B.C. to 50 A.D., Latin was the speech of a large part of Europe, North Africa and Asia Minor. After the Roman Empire disintegrated, Latin still continued to be spoken, with varying degrees of corruption with local dialects. Latin was the language for the educated which, of course, included the clergy. In the Middle Ages, Latin was the international medium of communication between persons of culture. From the Renaissance, up to the second half of the 19th century, Latin was dominant in the curriculum of all continental schools, and also of the grammar and public schools of Britain. It was a discipline to sharpen the mind. It also helped them understand their own languages better for so many of the words of their own languages were derived from Latin. Latin also gave them a sense of continuity of western civilisation. Right up till 1687, when Isaac Newton published his *Principia,* he wrote it in Latin, for Latin was the language considered appropriate for learning philosophy, theology and science.

In East Asia, for many centuries, the Chinese written script was the language of the literati, of diplomats and government officers. The Chinese ideograph was adopted by the Japanese, Koreans and the Annamese between the 3rd and 10th centuries. This borrowing had had a profound influence on the vocabulary, phraseology and even the mono-syllabic pronouncement of words in these different languages. Scholars and diplomats in the whole of East Asia could understand each other in written classical Chinese, *wen yen*. The Japanese had evolved their own phonetic alphabets in Katakana and Hiragana. They had even Romanised their script. But they had not been able to drop Kanji without loss in the richness of the language. After the Second World War, nationalistic sentiments became dominant. The Koreans and the Vietnamese had gone completely phonetic in their scripts. But their own names, whether it was Park Chung Hee, or Kim Il-Sung, Nguyen Van Thieu, or Le Duc Tho, were three Chinese characters, written and understood by the educated throughout East Asia.

French was the premier language of international diplomacy in the three centuries right up till the Second World War. But it was the British colonies that thrived and took over the French colonies in North America.

So a huge nation with a powerful economy grew in size and churned out books, magazines, films, TV features and comic strips, all in the English language. In 1946, at Lake Success, at the first session of the United Nations General Assembly, English and French were the working languages. There were other official languages, like Chinese, Russian and Spanish. But the business of translating documents and making sure that the world's leaders were talking about the same things, reduced the working languages to these two. When the Russians and East Europeans were asked what language they wanted their documents in, they chose English. By this decision, they hastened a process that had already begun, when the English-speaking colonies dominated and Americanised the whole of North America, except Quebec. But even Quebec understood American English.

When ASEAN leaders met all understood each other perfectly. "We do not speak perfect English as the English or the Americans do. But then what is perfect English?" Before the War, it was that of the English ruling classes, from the famous public schools and Oxbridge, or of the eastern seaboard of America, schools like Groton, universities like Harvard, Yale, Princeton, and a few select others of the Ivy league. But the Australians spoke perfect Australian English. And they were understood, albeit with a little effort, by those who heard them for the first time.

"So long as people learn the basic norms in basic English, they can speak to, and be understood by, Americans, British, West Indians, Africans, Indians, Pakistanis, Burmese, Ceylonese, Malaysians and Singaporeans. And, with a little effort, they should be able to understand all the mutations in pronunciation, diction and idiom, as the English language is taken over and freely developed by these peoples of non-British stock. A great service would be done to this smaller world by increasing understanding and rapport when people meet without the need for interpreters. For, if they understand and can speak directly and privately to each other, perhaps there will be a more peaceful world."

XXIII

President Sheares addressed the newly elected Third Parliament on 12 October, after Professor Yeoh Ghim Seng had been re-elected Speaker. Of the sixty-five PAP Members of Parliament, eleven took their seats for the first time. The President said that Parliament met in circumstances vastly different from those prevailing when the previous Parliament was opened on 6 May, 1968. Then the prospects were grim. "We faced the stark question of survival, how to hold up the economy, to generate jobs of any kind, to prop up massive unemployment." The will to succeed was decisive. Sheer determination, hard work and realistic planning enabled Singapore to make the grade. The current continuing and controlled boom was giving Singapore that glow of success. There was a boom which would spread from the city to the new towns and through to the villages and kampongs in the rural areas. Now the challenge was to maintain and continue this rapid pace of growth. "We can become a centre for excellence in all fields important to our economies and cultural life."

On constitution and security matters the President said the past few years had shown that some safeguards were necessary. Constitutional amendments would be made early in the current session of Parliament, so that no surrender of Singapore sovereignty, or any part thereof, by way of incorporation into, or federation with, any other country was possible unless two-thirds of the total electorate voted positively for it in a referendum. It was, President Sheares added, criminal negligence to allow foreign interests with large financial resources to manipulate Singapore's internal politics, professional, academic and other groups, to try to beguile domestic opinion, especially if their efforts were insidiously multiplied by purveying them through mass media set up and supplied generously with funds for that purpose. No foreign interests could be allowed to take over Singapore though financing and manipulating political parties through their naive or vain, self-proclaimed leaders. Whether fools or knaves they must be saved from their own follies or villainies when powerful groups set out to use them.

XXIV

Whenever he had time, Lee was ever willing to take part in academic discussions. He spoke at the 5th Asian-Pacific Congress of Cardiology held in Singapore on 13 October. He said he was overawed to find himself in the presence of so many eminent heart specialists. "It's a daunting prospect to have to talk to some 500 people who, even as I speak, will run their professional eye up and down me, checking my age against my weight, height, the amount of alcohol I may be showing, either on my countenance or the lack of crispness in my speech. The reason I am here, of course, is that your Chairman gives me an annual check-up to see whether the old ticker is degenerating faster than it should. Every year, we go through the routine: ECG lying down, ECG sitting up, ECG — after going up and down steps at a certain speed for several minutes, ECG to discover how quickly the pattern returns to normal after this exercise. Each time I leave a little encouraged. He knows I am suspicious. So he never tells me that all is well. His is the subtle approach — a quiet nod, and a hum of satisfaction as he runs through the stream of paper graphing my heart-beat, and the very audible asides to my general physician about an athlete's heart. It gladdens mine. He knows that I read up all the medical articles in magazines ostensibly meant for more than just the average layman. He knows I cut out saturated fat — lean meat, preferably beef, only selected parts of mutton and pork, and that only occasionally. Even in vegetable oils some are to be avoided, like coconut, which is saturated."

107

Yet despite all this hotch-potch collection of dos and don'ts from articles, and tips from friends like Professor Monteiro, he had all this while laboured under a grave misconception — that the heart should never be strained, that as one got older one should be careful not to push the ticker too hard. So violent exercises like badminton and squash were to be eschewed. More leisurely ones, unlikely to induce cardiac failure, like golf or swimming, were for him. Then one day, Lee said, he was playing golf with a surgeon friend. He had read up the latest on aerobics. He said the heart should be pushed to its uttermost limits to dilate all the arteries throughout the body and in the heart itself, and to increase the pulse rate to its maximum, for as long as possible. It would improve heart muscle tone, and after a few weeks the lethargic feeling would go. Lee asked him if he had tried it out himself. Well, he said, running on the spot for him, bringing his knees as high up to his chest as possible, was difficult because he was well in his fifties. So he walked on the spot. But he assured Lee that he had got quite a few friends who had complained of feeling lethargic, and slothful — to run on the spot, more and more minutes each day, and now they were almost bursting in song with a spring in their steps. None had dropped down dead. Lee asked him whether they were his friends or his guinea-pigs. He countered that it was the results of experiments by a Canadian heart specialist. He recounted a case of a Canadian pilot invalidated because of heart problems. After one year of aerobics, he had his pilot's licence and status restored.

This sounded convincing. So Lee tried it, but cautiously. He walked on the spot. Nothing happened. So he began to run, but gently, on the spot. Still no ill-effects. So he increased it day by day. Then one day after a round of golf, he ran for five minutes. He got his surgeon to take his pulse rate. So he said it was normal, 70 plus. After five minutes, "Marvellous, 140". After four minutes, back to 70 plus. Marvellous! Young man's heart was his verdict. "If only I had known earlier," said Lee, "I would have been younger at heart all these past years!" His belief was that life was better short, healthy and full than long, unhealthy and dismal. "We all have to die. I hope mine will be painless. As de Gaulle said, 'Never fear, even de Gaulle must die' and he did. And how lucky — heart-failure during sleep." Of course, it was preferable to die at home in one's bed. "Tonight, I have a unique occasion of some 500 heart specialists as a captive audience. Can I say that the kindest thing you can do for me — if ever I have a partial cardiac failure or a stroke, is to let me die as painlessly as possible. Nothing is more pitiful than to have stroke after stroke after stroke. With each one both physical movement and intellectual capacity are reduced until one becomes a vegetable."

XXV

Progress and comparative affluence brought their own problems. Lee spoke about some of them at a constituency function the following evening. The social and economic problems Singapore would meet in the years ahead he predicted would be very different from those of the past. The roads around Tiong Bahru and in many other areas, were lined with parked cars, packed like sardines. Housing Board estates, theoretically low-cost housing, had now to provide car parks. It was a sign of growing wealth spreading more widely. But it presented the government with grave decisions which had to be taken. "Are we to keep on multiplying people, flats, cars, roads, flyovers until the whole of Singapore is nothing but Housing Board flats, office blocks, hotels, shopping complexes, car parks, flyovers? Or do we reserve sufficient areas of green places for lung space, leisure, quiet, peace and recreation?"

The first thing to slow down multiplying was people. Stop large families — have only two per family, then automatically each in Singapore could have more per person. "Then we can have space for factories, offices, and homes, hospitals, parks, beaches and all the other things that make for a high standard of living with quality in our environment." The crying need for vacant space has led the new MP for Henderson to complain that no land was available for his constituency to build a Community Centre, a basketball court and a playground for children. His complaint was valid. A Community Centre would be built in Henderson. The open space required for the people of this new constituency must be found. People living in twelve-storied flats needed open space where they could go out to look at the sky.

"There were times when he had to build under pressure. When we built Bukit Ho Swee after the big fire in 1962, we had to build many one-room flats, block after block. It met an urgent need. But now very few trees and no grass grow there. There are just too many childrens' feet trampling the grass dead, and knocking the saplings down. Now we have to knock down the walls, reconstruct, and redesign one-room into two-room flats. We have been learning from experience. We did better in Queenstown than in Bukit Ho Swee, and better in Toa Payoh than in Queenstown." In Toa Payoh sites had been reserved for schools, parks, playgrounds. Primary schools should be so sited that no child below twelve need go more than two miles. Lee was astonished when he met a school-boy in Toa Payoh a few days earlier and learned that he had to travel one hour each way to school in Siglap. His parents had moved from Siglap. There was, at the moment, not enough schools in Toa Payoh. Fortunately, the land for schools had been set aside.

But the problem of road congestion needed a more fundamental solution. Singapore had over 170,000 private cars. Every month over 1,000 new cars were registered, an 8 to 10 per cent per annum increase.

"We cannot build 8 – 10 per cent more roads (80 miles), more bridges (8), per year, especially in the city centre. And there is a limit to road widening and one-way streets. So we have traffic jams. They will become worse each year unless we reverse the trend. It may become easier to walk half a mile than to take a car or a taxi." Part of the solution was to discourage people using big cars, and one family owning two or three cars. Increases would continue in registration fees, in annual road tax, and in parking fees. More and more people would find it worthwhile to use buses and taxis, and to use smaller cars when going to the city centre. Of course, public transport must be improved. Buses must be cleaner and their schedules more regular. "By the 1980s we must have settled and built our MRT (mass rapid transport), either above ground or underground or partly above and partly underground."

All wanted a more gracious environment. There were many things in life which could be enjoyed privately, but not clean air and water. Either all of Singapore would have dirty air and dirty water, or all of Singapore must have cleaner air, and cleaner water. A new Ministry had been created to look after this. "Let us rethink and replan our future to make life more agreeable for everyone. Let us have more factories. They should be good factories, clean, making quality products requiring high skills, and so paying higher wages. High skills mean longer training in vocational schools, the polytechnic, the universities. It means more money to be spent on each student, as more students go up the education pyramid. But we can only do this if we have two children per family. If we start now, shifting from quantity to quality, in ten years' time we will have a cleaner, quieter and more gracious Singapore, and a healthier people better trained and educated, with more aesthetic and cultivated appreciation for music, art and literature."

XXVI

Interviewed by United Press International on 28 October, the Prime Minister said he believed the Nixon administration would back Thailand as the buffer against communist expansion southward into Malaysia and Singapore after a ceasefire and US military withdrawal from South Vietnam. If Indo-China were to go communist, there was no question that Asian communism would expand if it could — and in the direction of this economically booming island state. But Lee said he believed there was also no question that the Nixon government would seek to halt such a trend. "Mr. Nixon has affirmed that it is peace with honour. How can you have honour unless you do not abandon those whom you have persuaded to go into battle with you?" Lee said. He said he was convinced that Nixon, assuming he was re-elected on November 7, would not abandon all his Asian allies, in this particular case Thailand. He must provide the Thais with the psychological and material equipment to fight the threat of communist insurgency and infiltration, if it came.

What made Thailand the most likely buffer between communist and non-communist countries in Southeast Asia, said Lee, were the uncertainties of a non-communist government's ability to survive in South Vietnam, and the doubtfulness of Cambodia and Laos assuming a buffer role. The communists in Vietnam were unified in what they wanted to achieve. But, the question was could the other two sides in this three-cornered coalition stick together, the non-communist (or neutralists) and the anti-communists. Were they able to unite around a common cause?

A close and skilled observer of all of post-World War II Asia, Lee said unity of national purpose in warding off a communist imposition had eluded the non-communists and anti-communists in Vietnam before, and might again. There was every likelihood that the communists would 'fragment' their opposition through guile, playing on personal vanities, animosities and ambitions, and probably take over. If South Vietnam went neutralist, and then pro-communist, then communist, he did not see Laos and Cambodia surviving as non-communist states either, "in which case we fall back on Thailand". Without Thailand as a buffer region, Lee said, the spread of indigenous communism, supported by fraternal parties in neighbouring countries, was almost a foregone conclusion. He said: "Communist expansion has always been through accretion from contiguous areas. They've always had sanctuaries from which they expanded. They island-hopped or leapfrogged in Cuba and Chile ... but the real communist heartland, until China and Russia fell apart, was created by expansion from the heartland of Eurasia. Before they can get a communist Malay Peninsula, Thailand must either be communist, or willing to go along with it."

Despite China's softening of hostility towards non-communist states, Lee said, a communist liberation movement in this part of Southeast Asia would receive Beijing's, at least, moral support, and Hanoi's more than moral support. In North Vietnam, China showed how far the Chinese were prepared to go in support of her contiguous neighbour. Thus, said Lee, now more than ever, Thailand should be psychologically reassured they are not being abandoned. "I think the Thais also know, like the rest of Southeast Asia, that Americans are not going to fight any more ground battles in Asia, particularly against irregular guerilla forces. But if there were an American presence in Thailand, the Thais would be assured that the Nixon doctrine of supplying arms and economic aid would apply to them. That's crucial to give them confidence, whether they will have the will to resist, or whether they go along with the other side, because they believe it's the winning side." Lee suggested, along with material aid, the United States might station a small military force in Thailand as well — "not to do the fighting, but as 'earnest' in American lives of the Nixon doctrine to help the Thais to help themselves."

Lee said "if Nixon wins the election on November 7, I believe he will leave a token force there as a symbol that his Guam doctrine is in operation." History proved that Lee misplaced his hopes on the occasion.

XXVII

Wishing all Hindus in Singapore a happy and felicitous "Festival of Lights", the Prime Minister in his Deepavali Message said that the festival originated in a cultural tradition which placed a great emphasis on tolerance and forbearance. Multi-racial and multi-religious Singapore needed such values in abundance. Like Chinese New Year, Christmas and Hari Raya, Deepavali had become a common Singapore festival, in which Singaporeans of all races partook. Deepavali symbolised the victory of the Power of Light over the forces of darkness and obscurity.

Thirty years ago, the Prime Minister told the Singapore Teachers' Union on 5 November, there was not in Singapore the same equality of opportunities which they had now. As a result, men with considerable ability and dedication to their society went into the teaching service. In the years prior to independence, they played a significant role in the fight for self-determination. Many today were social and political leaders. Now with universal education, free primary schools, nominal fees for secondary schools, and ample number of scholarships and bursaries, the sieving process had become more thorough. It was much more difficult to get some of the best into the teaching service.

Lee said he would like to pose to them not the role which as unionists alone they should concern themselves, but their role as teachers. The English stream had now nearly 9,700 teachers; the Chinese stream about 6,000. Unless this trend was reversed, the ratio would widen in favour of the English stream which they represented. This fact conferred on them greater responsibilities, especially when confusion of values and selfishness of purpose were now perversely affecting men in many developed English-speaking countries. "We now read of teachers and doctors of developed countries on strike — a sign of a disordered society. We have not come to such a sad situation. I hope we never will."

As a union, their function was to see that teachers acquired their fair share of material rewards. But in the context of the Singapore of the 1970s, Lee believed it was more important that their status in society was enhanced. No amount of monetary rewards could match what an enterprising man could get in the private sector. It was status in society, the respect which fellow citizens held them in, which was crucial in attracting to, and retaining within, the teaching service, a hard core of men and women in the schools who could maintain the high standards.

The accent in the next five years was on quality. How was this to be achieved in the schools? The professionals in the Education Ministry say they had done marvellously. In 1971, 53 per cent (47,000) passed their Primary School Leaving Examination. In 1972, nearly 62 per cent (53,000) or 6,000 more pupils passed Primary 6, and were entitled to enter Secondary I. Did this reflect an increase in teaching quality? Or was it the dropping of history-geography as an examination subject, and the testing of basic intelligence and learning capacity in the first and second languages, mathematics and science to go on to Secondary I?

In the English stream, nearly 63 per cent passed. In the second language, 62 per cent passed in Chinese; 82 per cent passed in Malay; 62 per cent in Tamil. "We are now suddenly faced with 6,000 more students for Secondary I next year, a shortage of classrooms, a shortage of teachers. We have to improvise — gymnasiums, extra classrooms and other facilities. Schools which have single sessions will be used by other schools for Secondary I classes. All this we can do and more, provided we keep the birth-rate down."

The other simple alternative was to do what the Finance Ministry said ought to be done — decide on a "cut-off" point. Last year, 47,000 went to Secondary I. So 47,000 ought to be the "cut-off" point. Lee said he believed this would be wrong. "We have to respond to the consequences of adjustments we have made, more Primary 6 passes partly because of the better teaching in English schools where most of the pupils are, and partly because of the adjustment in the examination syllabi." The first basic target was to lower the birth rate.

The second was to get well-balanced and well-trained teachers to discharge their duties to the children. Then there would be a society with much more ballast. How to teach enough to a child so that he or she wanted to go on reading and learning after the years in school are over? With one language, and the mother tongue, in a British, a French, or German society, it was difficult enough. In Singapore's society it was doubly difficult. The average Chinese boy who went to an English school was really learning two non-mother languages. He learnt English, which was not his mother tongue. He learnt Mandarin as a second language. It was also not his mother tongue because often the dialect was the language of the home. This presented a very grave challenge.

It was possible of solution, provided it was understood that all those who passed — the 62 per cent — could not be expected to be simultaneous translators. A language was first heard and spoken before it was read and written. Children should be taught enough for them to understand and to speak freely in two languages. But let them choose which one to use as the master language in which to articulate their thoughts effectively. It was important that this be done very early in schools. It was easier for a European to command two languages, perhaps English and French, or English and German. They were cognate languages. But English and Chinese were completely different, one Greco-Roman and Anglo-Saxon in its base, the other not spelt or pronounceable from the idiographic script, monosyllabic and tonal. To be able to speak both fluently required a great deal of effort. "I am convinced that this effort has to be made, if we are to survive as a distinctive society, worth the preserving. Or we will become completely deculturalised and lost. If we become like some societies speaking pidgin English, mindlessly aping the Americans or British with no basic values or culture of their own then, frankly, I do not believe this is a society or nation worth the building, let alone defending."

The minimum that must be achieved was to teach enough, in the mother tongue, of the basic values and culture. Even if the boy or the girl was unable to recite a Confucian classical passage or a pantum or whatever its equivalent in Tamil poetry, he had imbibed enough to know, when he looked at the cinema or the television screen, "or more and more the young people who come through on charter flights from Australia, New Zealand, Britain, America and Europe, that they are they, and we are ourselves." This was absolutely crucial.

Americans rioted in their universities, in their capital, because their soldiers were being killed in Vietnam. They could not lick the Vietcong and the North Vietnamese as easily as their think-tanks had prophesied they could. Canadians and Britishers unconnected with this problem imitated and joined in demonstrations. Australians who had a vital interest in a favourable outcome of the war in Vietnam also demonstrated and rioted. The nexus of the common language and a not very dissimilar culture gave them a common net. Or, if you like, the lowest common denominator pulled them down, as sometimes it raised them up in nuclear and astrophysics.

If Singapore failed to resolve effectively their problem of languages, and to preserve what was best in their respective cultural values, "we could become an even more unfeebled version of the deculturalised Caribbean calypso-type society. They were brought over as slaves and have lost any trace of the African in them. The few Indians and the Chinese amongst them have also been deculturalised: the island-in-the-sun, steel-drum-beating and rum-brewing-and-drinking, happy-go-lucky life."

Lee did not believe people could survive in Singapore with that way of life. "Eventually we may evolve a common culture for Singapore. Meanwhile, it is the hard framework of basic cultural values and the tightly-knit Asian family system that have enabled us to achieve what we have. The achievement was not that of economic planners alone. Every time you pass a construction site, cast your eye and see who is the brick-layer, plumber, electrician. Who is the man who gives the finish to your woodwork and tiles? They have that urge to work, to save, and to achieve."

Two military officers were sent from Singapore to sit in two courts martial in Trinidad nearly two years earlier. A mutiny had taken place. They had only one battalion. Yet they mutinied. Lee read the reports of the two officers with great interest. They had never been to that part of the world, nor had they been to Britain where one could meet people from the Caribbean. These two officers came back and recited their experience, not only of the courts martial, but of a way of life. A court martial that could have taken two weeks, dragged on for more than three months. Every now and again they had a fiesta. Everybody enjoyed himself for weeks on end. A holiday was not just for one day. A holiday ran for whole weeks. So the court martial was suspended and everybody had a jolly good time. "Well, if we were in the Caribbean maybe we could survive doing our own thing. You have a wealthy and benign American civilisation that likes to seek holidays in the sun. So you build hotels by the beaches, and large parts of your population consists of nothing but servers and hangers-on. That was one of the reasons for the mutiny. It is Black Power in an island where blacks are in political control. But the blacks found themselves in an unsatisfying position as servers to whites, who have the cash.''

Lee asked the teachers to note that when he spoke of bilingualism, he did not mean just the facility of speaking two languages. It was more basic that, "first, we understand ourselves: what we are, where we came from, what life is or should be about, and what we want to do. Then the facility of the English language gives us access to the science and technology of the West. It also provides a convenient common ground on which the Chinese, Indians, Ceylonese, Malays, Eurasians, everybody competes in a neutral medium.''

He said the government was determined to succeed with bilingualism. He knew it could be done and it must be done early in life. "I paid for it bitterly because I was foolish enough, when I was young, not to listen to my grandmother who sent me to Chinese school to learn Chinese, because the method of teaching was wrong. I spent only two years in a Chinese school. They made me recite passages parrot-fashion, I scrubbed it out of my mind when I went to English school. And I have had to study Chinese since the 1950s and I am still doing so. And it is not just learning the language. With the language goes the fables and proverbs. It is the learning of a whole value system, a whole philosophy of life, that can maintain the fabric of our society intact, in spite of exposure to all the current madnesses around the world. My wife and I took the decision to send our three children to Chinese school and also get them educated in English. I know it can succeed. I will not accept anything less from our teachers.''

Lee said it was the union's responsibility as a union of teachers not only to find adequate material rewards and status for their members. This was necessary if people were to be attracted, recruited and retained who could educate the young in a balanced and rounded way, and also instil into them that desire to work and to achieve. Unless that was done Singapore would slide downhill. Life in Singapore was not just more hotels and more dinners, bigger and bigger banqueting halls, more motor-cars, more flyovers, more one-way streets, more pay, more thirteenth-month payments, though all these were necessary. But all would lead to futility if in the process "we lose our way, if we are unable to identify ourselves, and confuse ourselves with that which we are not''.

Lee, in his Hari Raya Puasa Message wished all Muslims in Singapore Selamat Hari Raya Puasa. He said the fast during Ramadhan required spiritual strength and faith. "In multi-religious Singapore, our peoples have always enjoyed each other's religious holidays. There is a place for all religions in Singapore. With further industrialisation and urbanisation, all of us, Muslims, Buddhists, Hindus, Christians, and followers of other faiths, must accommodate and adjust ourselves to changing social and economic circumstances, for example the need to be punctual for work schedules on an assembly line." Lee was sure all Muslim citizens could and would adapt to changing circumstances, and "be equal to the challenges we have ahead of us".

XXVIII

The power of the mass media was a factor of present-day life. It started off with the printing press and the billboards. Then came the radio and the cinema. Now it had found its most comprehensive and powerful weapon in television, and via satellite. The efficacy of the mass media in shaping attitudes and influencing behaviour, the Prime Minister said in a lengthy speech to the Press Club on 15 November, was beyond doubt. Over a sustained period, it could influence people's attitudes towards ideas and beliefs, policies and programmes. What amazed him was that this powerful instrument did not require of its practitioners special professional training nor codes of conduct to govern them. "You can be a journalist without understanding the impact on the minds of millions when you write smut and circulate it through millions of copies to literate and semi-literate people. You can be a powerful influence for good or for bad by just having a good television personality. But special qualifications and acceptance of a code of ethics are not demanded. To be a doctor, a surgeon, a lawyer, an engineer, you have to pass stringent professional examinations. The governing body of experienced practitioners decides whether or not you are qualified to join their ranks. If they pass you, you have to abide by certain rules of conduct, which experience over the decades has made necessary. Those who breach these rules are punished by disciplinary committees for improper conduct. Hence doctors abusing their position of trust can be struck off the register. Perhaps the mass media, especially TV, is a relatively recent innovation. Perhaps governing bodies and rules will grow out of the problems TV is creating."

In this respect, the communist countries were thoroughly consistent. They had decided that the mass media was a very powerful instrument. They did not let anyone use it, other than those who would advance the cause of the communist state and to advance its current policies. The Russians even objected to anybody beaming any television programme on them without their consent. This was in anticipation of the next stage through satellite dissemination, when simple television sets could receive programmes via satellite.

For developing countries the mass media, developed in the West, presented a specially sensitive problem. Its impact was bad enough in devel-

116

oped countries. Most western democracies had problems in getting majority governments. Most governments were returned on a minority vote, whether it was in Canada or Britain. If there was *laissez-faire* in dissemination of views, regardless of whether they were truthful, sound or relevant, but because they sounded smart or witty, the end result tended to be very erratic. However, when it came to garnering votes, "provided you are allowed to get your point of view across, however hostile the press or the TV commentators", a determined and effective political leadership could beat them. This was because the more hostile the media, the more people made a mental discount of criticism and attacks. Those who lived through the Japanese occupation of Singapore knew how the newspapers and the news broadcasts were interpreted. "When the Japanese said they had a famous victory in the Coral Sea, we looked for the small print to see how many ships they claimed to have sunk. Then we waited a few weeks to see how many hospital ships came back to harbour." But the mass media, particularly the TV, had an insidious and dangerous way of influencing values and changing behaviour patterns.

Television time had to be filled. Stations were opened at 5.30 p.m. It had to be kept going till midnight and on two channels. It cost thousands of dollars, creative minds and good supporting technicians, to make a good feature. So it was easier to fill up by buying programmes, usually American or British. "I have seen Perry Mason in Cairo, speaking Arabic. I watched in astonishment. Here was a country absolutely against the American system and establishment. But they faced the problem of filling time. There are many such popular series. But these programmes convey the whole ethos of the producer society." Similarly with newspapers. They had to fill the pages. What was easier than to buy features? Some features were good. "I enjoy reading James Reston, even though from time to time I disagree with his views." But many features were of indifferent quality, and some were positively bad.

The most dangerous part of the mass media was its power of suggestion. People were imitative. If nobody reported hijacking, or how easy and successful hijacking could be, there would not have been so many hijackings. Lee believed the Pilots' Association was right when they suggested all the hijacking failures should be reported but all hijacking successes, blocked out particularly details of how they were successfully executed. The craze spread by imitation, until the impossible happened — a Soviet aircraft was hijacked. That took some doing. Obviously, despite the Iron Curtain, ideas leaked through.

"This brings me to Singapore. I read a recent series in the *New Nation*. It was imitating what the Western journalists are doing. It was ostensibly respectable. First, a serious study of homosexuality. Then a protracted series on lesbianism. Then unwanted babies. The Lord Chief Justice of Britain said in a recent case of pornography, that if anybody showed the muck in a case before him to his daughters, he would take the man and wring his neck with his own hands. How did it come to such a

117

pass? By a gradual, insidious process of suggesting that this is all right, that there is nothing wrong with it. It has led to 'anything and everything goes'."

Fortunately for Singapore, the *New Nation, The Straits Times*, or for that matter the *Herald*, and the *Eastern Sun*, did not, and does not, have the same impact on the population. The Chinese or the Malay press and, in a more limited way, the Indian Press, in the mother language, made much more emotive and powerful appeals. They pulled at the heart-strings. That was why in the case of *Nanyang*, "though I did not twist their necks, we took firm measures". And the business was not over yet. "Twisting the necks of language and culture chauvinists would not have best served our purposes. They deserve special treatment."

Although the *Straits Times* prided itself on a very large circulation, of 120,000 on week-days and 150,000 on Sundays, the total Chinese press circulation, *Nanyang, Sin Chew, Shin Min, Min Pao*, was double that. Every copy of a Chinese newspaper had at least two and a half to three times the readers of an English newspaper. Not only were the families who bought them larger, Chinese papers were found in all coffee shops, clan associations, clubs, eating places. The Bertha Hertog riots took place not because of *The Straits Times*, but because of *Utusan Melayu*, though both printed pictures of the Dutch Eurasian Muslim convert in a convent. The Malay paper tugged at Muslim emotions in a way the English paper could not.

"We are a very exposed society. We cannot adopt either the Russian or Chinese method. We cannot shut off the outside world, jamming broadcasts and banning imports of publications. Even jamming is a difficult and expensive game. Whether it is on permissiveness or pornography, or on any subject, your duty, as indeed it is that of RTS, is to inform, educate and entertain. Inform people of what is happening in Singapore, and in all parts of the world, of events relevant to us. Educate them, not just in the three Rs, but continue the process which we are doing in the schools, inculcate values which will make Singapore a more cohesive society, and viable nation. Entertain to sell your papers, but this can be done without unnecessary salacious or blue jokes. Even in business, news must be factual and correct. Let me read you the chairman's statement of a British investment company called Hume's Holdings Ltd., from their 46th annual report, September 1972. A sound, balanced chairman of an investment trust said this of his financial press. 'Whoever is responsible for our business pages should take this to heart. Take-overs. A major factor affecting activity in the stock and share markets during the past year was the continuing and growing turnover in the 'take-over' market. Genuine mergers arising from quiet and objective negotiations between company boards with a view to commercial and industrial efficiency seem to be out-dated. The spotlight of publicity given to the emotive and sometimes intemperate arguments employed by offeror companies with a view to promoting vast industrial conglomerates, followed by greater commercial and industrial power in fewer hands, seems to be a fashion which some people may regard as being extremely inimical to the public interest'."

Lee said that the important part was: The investor and the consumer, under these conditions, (meaning emotive reporting) must find it increasingly difficult to judge the efficiency of and the fair price for the component parts of the various industrial and commercial processes which produce the end-product or service. Whether in the background of the special interest of those concerned in negotiating and promoting these mergers, the public is presented with an entirely objective view of these matters by spokesmen in the city and by the financial press, must be open to question. He did not want to invite a libel suit, hence his phrase an open question. Lee advised the Press Club not to be overawed just by the technical competence of the production. Because people in advanced countries wrote well in polished rounded phrases, it did not mean the content was right. "We should not follow them, imitating them stupidly and mindlessly. We should exercise our own moral judgment on whether that is good or bad for us."

Singapore had many cultural, many linguistic groups. One of the dangers of bilingualism was that one day, sooner or later, large numbers of the population would be exposed to communist Chinese publications. Lee believed the risk was a calculated one, and minimal. Provided a person was also educated in the English language, he had a window open to another world. Then, he could read communist literature and propaganda with some detachment, and exercise his own critical judgment. But when communist literature was banned, the Western press applauded. Nobody questioned the rightness of that policy. These were dual standards imposed by the West. If freedom of the press was not affected by banning most communist Chinese publications, then why not ban Western publications? But imagine the howl of protest every time *Time* or *Newsweek* was banned in Saigon or Thailand. The Western press had praised Manila as one of the great centres for freedom of expression, for giving liberty to the human soul and spirit. Lee said he was amused to read that the gentleman who came to see him in 1971 on behalf of the Press Foundation of Asia, Mr. Roces, had recently been arrested and detained. Now he was under house arrest.

"Every morning, my task begins with reading five, four now, newspapers. It can be tiresome. I note the scurrilous, the scandalous. I can live with that. But when any newspaper pours a daily dose of language, cultural or religious poison, I put my knuckle dusters on. Do not believe you can beat the state. Mr. Nixon, with Mr. Agnew's help, demonstrated that. I watched a programme one night four years ago, when Mr. Nixon introduced his Cabinet, after he had just won the elections. Mr. Agnew quite rightly said he, at least, had been voted for by the people and spoke for the majority. But these wiseacres, the skilful commentators, who can convey so much just by the right twinkle of an eye as they read the news — who voted for them? What right have they to pass hasty value judgements and tear down a President's policies the instant they were announced?".

As Mr. Nixon presented his first Cabinet, CBS had a panel of very quick, agile and nimble minds ready to go. The moment Nixon was over, this panel of demolishers came on. They included John Kenneth Galbraith of the "Affluent Society". He had a very felicitous turn of phrase which could be quite waspish. He and most of the others began to shoot down every one of Nixon's team. "It made quite an impact on me. The Governor of Massachusetts, a Mr. Volpe, was appointed Secretary for Transport. The Governor had been voted for, and had won his election. Most probably he would have beaten Galbraith if ever Galbraith stood for election against him. Galbraith said: As for Governor Volpe, Massachusetts can well do better without him when he goes to Washington. I am paraphrasing him. I cannot convey the derisive nuances." This panel did not know who would be in Mr. Nixon's team, or what job each member would be doing until it was announced that night. The panel had no time for considered judgements. The attitude was one of showbiz: Right, let's have some fun. They shot the Nixon team down like clay pigeons — or so they thought. But in the end Mr. Nixon won in spite of a hostile press and TV. Lee said he was interested to see how *Time Magazine* quickly switched over support from McGovern and hailed the victor.

Now, if in a developed society, they could have such disorders aggravated, if not partly caused, by the mass media, commentators and journalists in developing countries should not unthinkingly toss poison and pollution into the pool. "I know even RTS trips up. I watched a programme one night at 11.30 p.m. There was one feature of a series. It must have cost very little to produce. All it had was a girl in a night dress, a married man putting his clothes on and a telephone through which she was talking to all her other lovers. I wondered: Is it Channel 5 or Channel 3? I pressed again. It was Channel 5. First thing next morning, I shot off a note. RTS said it had been vetted. They put up a plausible explanation. A young university lady graduate thought the feature was good since it debunked the permissive society. This married man had got the seven-year itch. He needed to reassure himself of his virility. Telecasting it would show up the hollowness of the permissive society. When the middle-aged married man discovered that he was one amongst seven lovers one for every day of the week he collapsed, discomfitted and demoralised. In the conversations over the phone, it turned out that none of the other six minded his having his one day a week!" Filling time on television by buying feature serials allowed this pervasive mood of promiscuity from the West to float in. It had to be fought.

Twenty years ago, Singapore boys and girls would not have been seen walking about arms around each other's waists. British boys and girls did that. Singaporeans did not. Their parents would have frowned upon it. Their friends would not admire them for having a boy friend fondling them round the waist and parading them round the streets. But, gradually, through the daily exposure, they had come to accept this as normal decent behaviour. But there were certain norms of public conduct which, unless maintained, must affect the whole texture of that society. It was not possible to sustain the moral fibre of society if everything goes. Everything did not go in Singapore. There were incentives and disincentives which would be applied. Some had a special responsibility — people in the news media, the PR man who drew posters, the producers of snippets for television or cinema advertisement.

Only one society was more exposed than Singapore, Hong Kong. "There, everything goes. But nobody cares. Nobody is trying to build a nation in Hong Kong. If they try, Peking will come down on them. Nor does Hong Kong have one man one vote every five years. So everything goes, from the US 7th Fleet, to agents from Taiwan, to communist officials working in the Bank of China on top of which is the neon slogan Long Live Chairman Mao!" The few Britishers in charge read the *South China Morning Post* and the *Hong Kong Standard*. The English press influenced about 5 per cent of the population. Lee said that when he was in Hong Kong, he made a point of reading the Chinese press. If they tried representative government, one man one vote, Hong Kong would be ruined.

"We can control the input of the pernicious and the vicious and prevent our people from over-exposure to what is bad. I believe the safest way is cultural inoculation. Steeped early in our own traditional values, we can watch the temporary aberrations of the West, without harm to ourselves. Americans can afford to lose five to six years in riotous, drug-induced madness. They can continue to grow and not collapse, because 208 million people have that momentum to carry them through these lost years. Nevertheless, I was astounded to learn how this madness had penetrated even their institutions of excellence. When I saw the decorations outside, I thought it was a bit early for Christmas. Then they told me it was for Thanksgiving! My mind went back to one Thanksgiving at Harvard not long ago. The whole college was closed for Thanksgiving. There was nothing to eat. So the Master of the College invited me to his home. And he had also invited several of his brightest students. The discussion turned to drugs. The brightest of them all said he had tried LSD. This discussion was absolutely deadpan. There was no disapproval, no approbrium, expressed by anyone. The Master expressed surprise. He inquired what it was like. The student said, that is exactly the point. Lots of people like to know about it. I think I might write about it in the next issue of the college magazine!" In 1968, Lee was told that 40 per cent smoked marijuana at weekends. In 1970, 60 per cent smoked marijuana regularly. They claimed it did no harm at all.

One night, in October 1970, somebody pressed the fire alarm at 12.30 a.m. Dogs, cats, boys, girls, who should not have been there, all tumbled down into the quadrangle. But the young in America had reached a stage where "if you were a girl, and you had no boy to go to for the weekend, you feel there must be something wrong with you". Maybe a new society would evolve in which roles were switched. All a male had to do would be to spawn away. The female would look after herself and the children. Women were qualified to work. They could, if necessary, nurture any accidental or intended children. It did not matter whose child it was. Maybe such children would grow up less inhibited and more creative. The idea of knowing one's father and mother might become old-fashioned.

But, Lee said, he would like to see this brave new world tried out elsewhere than Singapore for at least one generation. He was not in favour of experimentation until it had been proven. Until it was demonstrated that the change was for a better, stronger society, this experimentation was not for Singapore. Many a once scandalous conduct had become acceptable. Traditional values were being gradually eroded. There was a reason for taboos in society. For instance, in the old days, a divorcee was not invited to Buckingham Palace. The reason was to discourage divorces and remarriages. Not that adultery did not take place. But then Cabinet Ministers divorced their wives and remarried. Things became complicated. Eventually, their wives had to be accepted at the Palace. Because ministers had set an example, others followed. A principle once breached was easily demolished.

Singapore must inoculate herself from this epidemic. When children were young, they should be made to understand that there were basic traditional values to which they should hold fast. What was good, what was bad, what was to be admired, what was to be despised, who was a hero, who a villain. "This is what we are trying to do in the schools through bilingualism. Do not shoot this down. If you do, you have got to fight me. I feel strongly about certain things, and this is one of them."

Bilingualism must be thorough, the values inculcated when young and impressionable, for the inoculation to be successful. The unsuccessful bilingualist, the monolinguist, in Singapore's situation, was a dangerous person. A completely monolingual Chinese-educated person who read only the Chinese script was as dangerous as a completely monolingual Malay-educated person who read the Jawi script. Remember what happened? Communist-led riots, and Muslim religious riots. The innocent were casually murdered. "We must hold on to the quintessence of 4,000 years of civilised living, although it was punctuated by intermittent periods of disorder, chaos, famine, pestilence. But continuous civilisation was maintained and made possible only by certain precepts. They existed 4,000 years before Mao. I have a feeling they will survive 4,000 years after Mao. And I do not know what the equivalent is in Tamil. But I am sure the Tamil language and culture which lasted 3,000 years must have been sustained by certain fundamental precepts. One of the fundamentals is the sanctity of the family unit. Of course, man is adulterous. So is woman. And there is considerable hypocrisy about. But hypocrisy helps to maintain public decorum. Only when certain norms of public conduct obtain, is orderly, cultivated living possible."

As might have been expected, Lee's speech about the Press in Singapore and his critical references to Hong Kong aroused criticism in the British colony. The Hong Kong Government spokesman said that Lee's statements were "absurdly wide off the mark". He added that the fact that in Hong Kong there was a tremendous amount of press freedom obviously irked Lee. One prominent Chinese in Hong Kong said that the Prime Minister's remarks were "tantamount to interfering in Hong Kong's internal affairs".

XXIX

On 24 November Lee left for Europe. He did not return to Singapore until 28 December. He visited Cairo on his way back. He had meetings with leaders in Britain, France, Belgium, Italy and Holland. Lee's main interest was the question of Singapore's trade with the enlarged European Economic Community. In London he met Mr. Heath, the Prime Minister, had lunch with Harold Wilson, leader of the Opposition; dined with the Queen; met Service chiefs. He addressed the Royal Institute of International Affairs, and spent three days on a private visit to his old college in Cambridge. In Brussels he addressed the conference of the Atlantic Institute. At length and in some detail he reviewed Europe's past trade links with Asia. They went back some 500 years. He also dealt with the present and allowed himself the luxury of speculating on the future.

His first assumption was that there was no nuclear conflict between the super powers, no pre-emption by Russia on China. Then nuclear rationality would prevail in China, as it had done in America and Russia. Any other supposition led to such pessimistic conclusions that it was not worth speculation. Then, it was in the interests of all the five economic power-groups to maintain peace, order and stability in the world. If there were no major wars between the major powers, then, was self-sufficiency in economic "blocs" the most fruitful system for all?

Was it in the interests of the non-communist world that it should be compartmentalised in self-sufficient economic blocs? Could Europe of the Nine afford to have close links only with the rest of Western Europe, with the Mediterranean Basin and Africa in a special relationship: wealthy, self-sufficient and self-satisfied? What about Japan? Was it possible for Japan to achieve self-sufficiency without changing her boundaries — a proposition dangerous for the peace of the world? Even an attempt at a Japanese economic bloc could turn Southeast Asia into a dangerous area of conflict. Could Japan survive as a powerful economic super-state without an American nuclear umbrella? Or, if this nuclear umbrella was not credible, would not Japan go for a second strike capability and make this a more dangerous world? And, could Europe survive as a powerful economic and political bloc if there was no NATO with a credible American commitment?

So one must hope that though the present economic blocs would remain, enlightened national and bloc interests would lead to ever freer trade, by lowering of tariffs, and removal of non-tariff barriers, and not only between America and Western Europe. The Japanese were learning that they had to exercise their ingenuity in ways other than making it impossible for Europeans and Americans to sell to, or invest in Japan. Their new Prime Minister, Mr. Tanaka, had publicly displayed realisation of this, that trade and investments must be reciprocal. With the Japanese, however, old habits died hard, and from Prime Ministerial recognition to bureaucratic change in policy, there might be quite an interval. Even so, the era was over, when trade for Japan meant the export of finished products, the result from the imports of technology from the developed West, and raw materials from the under-developed South and Southeast Asia.

If transportation costs had not inhibited Japanese exports to Europe, neither should they inhibit European exports to Southeast Asia, Japan and China. For specific middle-technology products, with high labour and skill content, Europeans could fight back by judicious selection of sites in East and Southeast Asia for offshore manufacture. For there were several urban centres where there was political stability and good industrial climate, with labour skills as high as, and costs lower than, those in Japan. And when Suez was re-opened one day, it would stimulate trade between Europe and Asia as its first opening did in 1869. The high growth rates in developed countries in the 1950s and 1960s, reflected also in their external trade, were partly due to the rehabilitation of Western Europe and Japan. Fundamental technological innovations, like the jet engine, nuclear power, petrochemicals and electronics, were in large measure the spin-off from military research and development during and after the last war. They stimulated consumer demand and increased trade.

It had been suggested that one of the reasons for the slow-down in economic growth and in world trade, was that most of these new industries had reached maturity. As more countries produced goods which had been the preserves of one or two, exports were becoming a "zero sum" game. Instead of more exports stimulating more imports and expanding trade, an increase of the share of total exports by any major country diminished the share of the rest. Hence the tendency to protectionism. Research on rocket and space programmes had not led to a spin-off in civilian user, except for communications, earth and weather satellites, and the miniaturisation of certain components. These innovations and inventions had not yet given a boost to world trade.

But, for the next two decades, a potential powerful stimulus to world trade could come from the opening of China to the world. China could become a vast new frontier for existing middle and higher technology, machinery and know-how. This would generate growth both in the developed countries and in China itself, with spin-off benefits for Third World countries in aid and trade. With a population estimated at over 750 million, in nearly 10 million sq. kilometres, China had an effective administration, and an adequate infrastructure of power, water, transportation, basic education and skills. Unlike most of the new countries, China had the capacity to absorb, and effectively use, inputs of technology, both machinery and knowhow. But China had not got enough foreign exchange to pay for such massive purchases unless extensive credits were made available.

There were signs that China wanted closer economic ties with the developed West. First, cultivation of West European governments by China even before President Nixon's visit to Beijing. Next, China's symbolic purchase of three Concordes. China had publicly supported the expansion of the E.E.C. Now Japan had severed diplomatic relations with Taiwan, and was to have direct diplomatic and trade relations with China. Some Japanese believe America would have established close diplomatic and direct trade relations with China soon enough to enable China's leaders to be present in Washington to join in celebrations in the spirit of 1976. China would want to import technology on the most competitive terms, and on the best credits offered, from Europe, Japan and America.

For most of the Third World, development would be uneven and patchy. Trade concessions and UNCTAD resolutions were important in easing the painful and slow process of educating and disciplining agricultural communities and transforming them into industrial-urban societies. But the decisive factors were a people's ethnic and cultural characteristics, the cohesiveness of their social organisation, their administrative competence, plus their leadership to provide the will to a whole people to make strenuous and sustained efforts. But the flame of hope, however small and flickering, must be kept alive.

It was not a coincidence that those countries which the West found most difficult to subjugate, like Vietnam, or to extract Treaty Ports and extra-territorial concessions from, like China, were also the ones which had demonstrated their capacity for effective administration and for economic progress, with the promise of high growth rates if capital, machinery and knowhow were made available. East Asians shared a common intense culture. Their main characteristics were a high threshold for pain, a capacity for concentrated work over long periods, a willingness to postpone present consumption for greater capital formation. They were quick learners. Hence, they had been more successful in industrialisation, and they had the fastest growth rates — South Korea, Japan, Taiwan, and, but for the war, Vietnam.

Lee said his second assumption for these projections was that the Americans would regain their self-confidence and poise and maintain their interests abroad in NATO, the Middle East, East and Southeast Asia. Only then was Mr. Nixon's generations of peace and prosperity without war, likely. Japan and Europe could help to repair the terrible devastation in Indo-China and add to Mr. Nixon's US$7 billion rehabilitation programme. And if the Russians and the Chinese also pitched in, if only to help the communist side, then, for once, all major power groups were on the same side doing the right thing for mankind. But if, on the other hand, the Americans became self-centred, filled with self-pity, resentful that their generosity in restoring Europe and Japan to prosperity had gone unrequited, their efforts to keep out communism and uphold the right of self-determination for South Vietnamese unappreciated, they might become interested only in themselves. This would make for a dangerous world.

Four years of a US Presidency was a relatively short time in the history of nations. Perhaps, it was because the Americans were such a young nation that they were impatiently waiting to celebrate their 200th anniversary. They were generous and idealistic. But the onerous and tedious burdens of a super-power also demand patience, stamina and endurance. And it had taken the European in Kissinger to get America to play a long game.

"If we are to move towards a more peaceful and stable world, the major countries must move now towards a more multilateral sharing of world responsibilities in trade and finance. The Atlantic Institute has already got Japanese corporations as active and contributing members, although it is the Pacific, not the Atlantic, that washes Japanese shores. If Europeans take an interest beyond just the Mediterranean Basin and Africa, they will help make this a more prosperous and stable world. After all, it was the Europeans who opened up East and Southeast Asia long before the Americans or Russians." And it was significant that when Indonesia was sorely in need of rehabilitation after twenty prodigal years of Dr. Sukarno, the Americans insisted on the IGGI (Inter-Governmental Group for Indonesia) formula: one-third USA, one-third Japan, one-third Western Europe. For Southeast Asians, European multilateral sharing of responsibilities could be critical. 350 years of the Dutch in Indonesia, 150 years of the British in Malaysia and Singapore, and about 100 years of the French in Indo-China, had left a profound imprint on their lives. Ties of language, culture and sentiment were not easily cut and forgotten. In part, it was nostalgia in the face of the more demanding super-powers. The donor-donee relationship with a super-power was not always an agreeable one.

Many in Southeast Asia had found the Russians willing to give aid, but people who could be rough when baulked. The Americans could be generous. But they twisted arms readily and brutally to get their way. And the Japanese brought up memories of the Second World War to the conscious surface every time a hard-headed and hard-hearted Japanese team negotiated a deal to extract timber, minerals or oil. The Southeast Asians had re-discovered that the Europeans, especially their former imperial power, were perhaps amongst the more cultured of the developed peoples. Of course, Europeans put their national or company interests first, like all others. But they maintained the civilities and courtesies that made arm-twisting less of a painful business.

It was more than symbolic that the first European country Indonesia's

126

President Suharto visited was Holland. And he sent a special message to the European Heads of Government when they met in October. He followed this with a visit to Paris and Brussels. It might not be possible immediately for the EEC to let in agricultural products from Southeast Asia on the terms granted to the African states of the Yaounde Convention, or even the East African states of the Arusha Agreement. But Southeast Asia was watching what twenty Caribbean and other sugar-producing countries might be getting. Some concessions to Southeast Asia, for psychological, as much as for economic reasons, were in everyone's interests.

However, concluded Lee, Southeast Asians were more likely to benefit from exports to the EEC of the Nine of manufactured middle technology products — not textiles or transistors, over which there were many vexing problems for Europe as there were for America. If the Nine allowed an annual increase of at least 15 per cent of the GSP (Generalised System of Preferences) quota, accompanied by liberalisation in the rules of origin of raw materials, Europe could contribute substantially towards a more stable, peaceful and prosperous world, where a freer exchange of goods and services diminished reasons for conflicts.

In Brussels, the Prime Minister met the Belgian Prime Minister and senior Ministers, and paid a call on the King and Queen. He also met the Chairman and Commissioners of the EEC. Then he went to Paris to meet President Pompidou, the French Prime Minister, and other Ministers. In Rome, he met the Italian Prime Minister and the Pope. He visited Cairo before returning to Singapore.

In an official statement put out in Cairo after meeting the Egyptian Prime Minister, Dr. Aziz Sidky, Lee said that Dr. Sidky had explained the Middle East situation with lucidity and realism. "We also discussed the problems for medium and small countries in a changing situation where the super-powers may reach understanding among themselves, which will affect the disposition of smaller countries. Medium and small countries must be on the alert to this new development. They must be careful that their interests are not sacrificed as the super-powers seek a new accommodation of their interests. Southeast Asia, the war in Indo-China, and a satisfactory solution to the tragic conflict was considered in this context. Singapore's friendship with the Egyptian and Arab peoples and my personal relations with Egyptian leaders are good. We want to develop them further from the sound base on which it was established with the late President Nasser."

THE YEAR 1973

I

In his New Year Message, the Prime Minister optimistically predicted five more years of success. "We enter 1973," he said, "with the satisfaction of having accomplished five continuous and successful years in re-orienting our economy." Singapore had shaken off dependence on British military expenditure, developed a significant industrial sector, built up the Republic as a banking and financial centre, increased sophistication as a serving centre, both physical and brain services. "In the next five years we can achieve as much as in the past five years. But the emphasis will be on quality, not quantity." Lee was confident that barring accidents, Singapore could maintain high growth rates in the next five years, provided workers, employers and the government continued to work together towards agreed goals.

Alas, the Prime Minister was not to know then that 1973 was to be a year of economic turbulence, arising from the disarray of the international monetary exchange rates and global inflation. The price of crude oil was quadrupled, a matter of crucial importance to Singapore as the world's third largest centre for oil-refining.

Lee thought that the dangers might come in eight to ten years, when the State had reached what he called the "comfort line". He feared that once Singapore achieved comfortable standards, the Republic might go the way of several Western countries, like Britain. "We may lose our keenness to work, to strive and to achieve. We could so easily loosen social

128

and work discipline. We can become a people who only want to enjoy life.'' This was a curious phenomenon in several developed Western countries. The result of growing abundance and affluence had been a loss of verve and the setting in of an ennui. Traditional virtues of hard work for higher rewards, thrift, economic and social advancement were lost. There was a reluctance to perform personal services. The only developed industrial country which had, so far, avoided such erratic behaviour was Japan. Lee believed it had a lot to do with the culture of a people, their basic values, their attitudes to life, to work, to personal and national discipline. Cultural values determined what a people considered to be desirable goals for the individual and the nation. If a people believed that happiness was obtained by enjoyment, by consuming more of the good things they saw advertised, they would fall prey to the hedonist cult. The consumer society tended to make pleasure the main purpose of life. The stimulation of the physical senses, whether by food, alcohol, tobacco, drugs, sex, was regarded as the chief good and an end in itself.

Even Asian civilisations, like China and India, had from time to time gone into periods of decadence. Officials became corrupt and pleasure-loving, as emperors and their retinue became more and more debauched. They oppressed the peasantry to pay for their pleasures. Then the whole society broke up.

"Therefore, even as we make economic and material progress never forget that it is only a means to other ends. We must consciously imbue our younger generation with the values which will prevent them from becoming soft, leisure-seeking and pleasure-loving. Work and social disciplines are absolutely necessary for achieving higher material goals. More, they are intrinsically good in themselves for the individual and the nation. The greatest satisfaction in life comes from achievement. To achieve is to be happy. Singaporeans must be imbued with this spirit. We must never get into the vicious cycle of expecting more and more for less and less. Sensual pleasure is ephemeral. Solid satisfaction comes out of achievement, the overcoming of obstacles which lie in the path of an individual or a nation seeking success. It generates inner or spiritual strength, a strength which grows out of an inner discipline. As we approach this comfort line in eight to ten years, personal and group behaviour can become undisciplined, or even anarchic. Let us inculcate in our children the tried and tested values of our traditional cultures. Man does not live by bread alone. 1973 will be another good year, as we keep in trim, eager to learn, to strive, and to achieve.''

Lee's optimism proved, in the end, to have been justified: Singapore made adjustments to external and internal policy which not only kept the economy operating but expanding, though at a reduced rate.

II

On 8 January, the Prime Minister went to Thailand on an official visit lasting a week. It was the first time a Singapore Prime Minister had officially visited Thailand. At a banquet speech, Field Marshal Thanom Kittikachorn, Thailand's Prime Minister, said that Singapore's economic achievement served to demonstrate what a small developing country could accomplish through dedication and diligence of the people, coupled with inspired leadership and management.

Lee, in his speech, said the Kingdom of Thailand was unique. It was the only country in Southeast Asia which had not been turned into a colony by the West. This suggested that the Thai leadership had always had political perception and diplomatic skills of a very high order. Lee jocularly hoped that Field Marshal Thanom would share with him the not too closely guarded secrets of Thailand's politics of survival. In a more serious vein, Lee said that in "the next few years", survival under ever-changing economic, political and security conditions would be one of the major features of the region. The disengagement of American forces from Indo-China ended one phase in the history of the region. The phase that followed might not necessarily be characterised by peace and stability, "though this is what we hope it will be". For American military disengagement did not alter several basic forces which might make for the continuation of some of the problems that had troubled the region.

Nor would the new phase mean that the super and major powers would not continue to exert their influence on events within the region. There had always been external pressures working on, and within, the region. "We cannot wish nor will these external pressures away." But external influences need not necessarily be disastrous, or even malevolent, especially if the countries in the region were able to develop the capacity to meet the challenges inherent in the new situation. And it was conceivable that co-ordination and co-operation within the region could even turn these external influences to advantage. "But first a realistic assessment of our respective separate capabilities and a formulation of rational policies are necessary." The Kingdom of Thailand had always demonstrated this capacity for realism and rationality, or Thailand would not have successfully avoided destruction of its integrity as a sovereign state.

Lee hoped Singapore would be able to develop a similar capacity for objective, realistic assessments of new trends and developments, and, like Thailand, "ride the changes that lie before us". The countries of Southeast Asia today were less insulated from what happened to each other than ever in the recent past. The survival and political integrity of each country would affect the security, and perhaps even the survival, of the others. This one fact had become increasingly apparent in recent years. "If we all take this fact into account, particularly those of us in ASEAN, then prospect for peace and prosperity, for each of us, is enhanced." For all in

ASEAN, this was a period of intermission, waiting for the end of one phase of history and the start of another more promising era.

In a joint communique at the end of the visit, both countries pledged "increased co-operation and consultation in economic, political, technical and strategic matters within the pattern of closer Southeast Asian relations". It continued: "After fruitful and friendly exchange of views covering matters of common interest and concern, the two Prime Ministers acknowledged there was need for the two countries, together with other like-minded nations in the region, to co-operate and co-ordinate their views, with a view to contributing to the strengthening of the fabric of peace and stability in Southeast Asia."

III

Back in Singapore, a few weeks later, Lee, in his Chinese New Year Message, expressed the hope that the "Year of the Ox" would bring opportunities to enlarge Singapore's horizons in politics and economics. With the end of the American military involvement in Vietnam, the countries of Southeast Asia must, he said, reach out for a new equilibrium. If there was orderly adjustment, then economic and social progress could bring a better life to the peoples of Southeast Asia. In 1972, drought in many countries had caused grave shortages in rice, wheat and other grains. Millions were still suffering from privation. World prices of rice, wheat, sugar and essential foodstuff had gone up. This would have affected Singapore much more, but for prudent stockpiling of rice. Economic growth had enabled Singapore to meet these increased costs of imports of foodstuff. No working family went underfed. "Let us hope that the harvest for 1973 will be bountiful and that food prices will return to normal. Meanwhile, we must work with unremitting vigour. This will ensure that we enjoy a happy and prosperous new year."

In a speech on 17 February to representatives of the Citizens Consultative Committees and Management Committees of the community centres, Lee elaborated this theme. He said it might be useful to recall the hard facts of life. The current heady boom in the stock market did not reflect the true economic position of the companies, either the value of their assets, their earning potentials, or likelihood of future growth. The bubbly market had been caused by considerable speculation. The Hong Kong stock exchanges had worked themselves into a tizzy. Singapore had been infected by this. There was a crazy streak that one could get something for nothing, of buying in the morning and selling in the afternoon at a profit. Meanwhile, the corporate raider who used paper with a highly inflated value to acquire property and assets was doing this at very little cost to himself, but at the expense of the investing public which ultimately had to foot the bill. The big time operators, with inside know-

131

ledge, would know when to get out. It would be the small time amateurs, hoping to make a bit on the side, who would be landed with the bulk of the share scrips when the price was knocked down from the unreal levels.

Singapore could not build a sound economic base on the basis of gambling. The transformation of the economy was a painful one. "One adversity was hardly overcome before another befell us. It was sheer determination, good planning and the hard work of our people, that saw us through these difficulties." The present climate of confidence was the result of a combination of social and work discipline, plus honest and efficient administration. "We have the basis for steady growth for the next five years, especially in the manufacturing and servicing sectors." If there were no setbacks in international trade, Singapore should make over 10 per cent in annual growth. "And it is our intention to see that the workers get the benefits of their hard work. The average worker must find it worthwhile to be thrifty, to save part of his increased earnings. For those who want to gamble, there is little that any government can do to save them from their own greed and folly. Many have lost money on chit funds, chasing impossibly high interest rates. Those who speculate on the stock exchange do so at their own peril, particularly when they have little knowledge of stock companies or the international money market and the problems of currency parities and short-term speculative inflows of money. When the economy is developing at about 10 per cent per annum, it is not possible to make 10 per cent per week. The bubble must burst."

Lee reminded them that Singapore had grown stable as a result of hard work. To get rich quickly without hard work was a pipe dream. That was why the Turf Club never lost. "If you can afford a flutter, go ahead. But remember it is a flutter."

IV

Speaking at the NTUC COMFORT anniversary dinner on 11 March, Lee reminded trade unionists that three years earlier, pirate taxis were rampant, bus companies were going bankrupt, and traffic conditions were deplorable. "We then decided that before the roads became chaotic and public transport broke down completely, to clean up the pirate taxis, improve the bus and taxi services." As an act of faith in the ability of the NTUC and workers to co-operate in a transport co-operative, COMFORT was launched to give the taxi drivers — many of whom were formerly running pirate taxis and others were being exploited by taxi owners — a chance to own taxis and the mini buses. This act of faith had proved not misplaced. But there were a lot of headaches and heartaches, and sometimes plain nastiness when the old system of lawless road behaviour stopped and discipline enforced where indiscipline had been a way of life. To get taxi drivers to co-operate needed organisation, patience, good human relationship, and, above all, firmness of purpose. The NTUC and workers had acquitted themselves well. Those qualities were not lacking. The plan was to give every taxi driver a chance to own his taxi, and after paying off the instalments, to start saving to buy a new taxi whilst, at the same time, saving to buy his Housing Board flat.

All this needed planning, careful calculations and a capacity on the part of the organisers to understand the motivations of the people they were dealing with. Only then could they get the members of the co-op to work the system being established, giving them adequate rewards and including others also to conform. COMFORT now ran 1122 taxis, more than one-fourth of all taxis, and 265 mini-buses. "I hope the energy, enthusiasm and organisation that launched COMFORT will carry it forward to further success, and the day will come when COMFORT will help most taxi drivers to have a chance to own their taxis."

V

Welcoming Mr. Dzemal Bijedic, President of the Federal Executive Council, Socialist Federal Republic of Yugoslavia, on 17 March, the Prime Minister said that Mr. Bijedic's visit to Southeast Asia could not have come at a more opportune moment. The end of the war in Vietnam marked a new phase in the politics of this region and, indeed, of the world. The peace treaty over Vietnam was a consequence of the new direct relations the great powers were establishing between themselves, over the heads of small nations. The outlines of this new pattern of great power politics were already clear.

"After a quarter of a century of bi-polar politics, the great powers have abandoned the former system of getting the smaller nations to be in alliance with them, or sympathise with their cause on the bi-polar issues. Over the past decade, they believe that competing for support of the smaller nations had hampered, rather than assisted, in the settlement of momentous issues of peace and war. So two recent major issues — the question of the People's Republic of China and the Vietnam war — were resolved not in co-operation or consultation with some 130 nations in the UN, but through secret negotiations between Washington and Peking, and Washington, Moscow and Peking."

This new phase had come about because of the changes in the respective strength of America, the Soviet Union, Western Europe, Japan, and the emergence of China as a great power with a growing nuclear capacity. So, from the bi-polar alignments of the Cold War, the great powers were moving towards a more flexible position of balanced co-existence. But most significant for small nations was that the great powers were no longer moved by ideological considerations. They were no longer as fervent as they were a decade ago that they had a mission to make the world safe for capitalism, socialism or communism. Their primary concern was the safeguarding and maximising of their national interests. This fundamental change from the old Cold War position required a rethinking and reformulation of the content of the concepts of non-alignment. For small countries, the question now was not how to avoid being sucked into the warring camps of the two great powers, but how to have their interests taken into consideration when the great powers reached their compromises. "I hope the energies in co-ordinating the views of the middle and smaller countries, which Your Excellency has set out to do, will help the small nations to maintain their independence and integrity during this new period of greater uncertainties, but, perhaps also greater opportunities."

In his reply, Mr. Bijedic remembered Lee's visit to Yugoslavia in late 1971. Then, in a friendly and cordial atmosphere, "we conducted a comprehensive exchange of views on the international problems of that period and on ways of promoting bilateral co-operation." It gave him, he said, satisfaction to note that thanks to identical or similar views, Singapore and Yugoslavia had been able to co-operate very closely and usefully in the United Nations, during UNCTAD sessions, at non-aligned gathering, and at various international meetings convened with the objective of safeguarding peace, solving the economic problems of developing countries and promoting international co-operation in general.

VI

In Parliament, three days later, the Prime Minister announced changes in Cabinet salaries. He pointed out that it was eighteen years ago when the salary for the post of Chief Minister, and subsequently Prime Minister, was fixed at $3,500. The position for Ministers became intolerable by 1970, when an adjustment had to be made. It was time to do a more complete revision of these salaries. Lee said he had discussed this matter with colleagues in Cabinet and decided as follow:- (1) All Cabinet Ministers would be paid the salary of $7,000, $500 more than Superscale Grade 'A' ($6,500) (2) Dr. Goh Keng Swee, "who acts for me from time to time", would fill the post of Deputy Prime Minister. It would carry a salary of $8,000. (3) Dr. Toh Chin Chye would have a charge allowance of $7,000 for discharging the duties of Vice-Chancellor of the University of Singapore, as well as being Minister for Science and Technology. (4) Senior Minister of State would be equivalent to Superscale Grade 'C' ($4,500), Minister of State equivalent to Superscale Grade 'D' ($3,500), Senior Parliamentary Secretary equivalent to Superscale Grade 'F' ($2,750), Parliamentary Secretary equivalent to Superscale Grade 'G' ($2,500), and Political Secretary, $1,750. (5) The Prime Minister's salary would be $9,500. (6) The President's emoluments would be raised from $4,000, which was tax-free, to $12,000, with $4,000 tax-free. However, the President had requested him to inform the House that he did not wish to make use of this increase in his salary. As in the case of civil servants, these salaries would be effective from 1 March 1973, and they would be revised and consolidated every four to five years.

Lee said that in making these adjustments in salaries, two considerations had been uppermost in their minds. Firstly, the need for some rough correlation with the Civil Service pay scales. Secondly, they should be sufficiently realistic, so that in the years ahead, it would be not so much of a sacrifice to give up a job in the private sector in order to take on the responsibilities of public office. It was seldom possible to pay a man in his Ministerial position as much as what he would get, either in running a business or practising his own profession. Some sacrifice was inevitable. But too great a disparity between Ministerial rewards and what Ministers, with business experience and professional qualification, could earn outside would make it increasingly difficult to assemble a successor government.

But no salary, however generous, could ensure the complete honesty and integrity with which Ministers must discharge their duties. Honest mistakes, or errors of judgment, by Ministers, however costly, were not as damaging to a country as the suspicion of bias because of corruption. Once a government was tainted with this, the contamination spread throughout the administration. "Then we shall go down the slippery slope, at the bottom of which are carcasses of so many corrupt governments whose peoples have had to suffer for the dishonesty and greed of those of authority."

The Prime Minister thought it might not be possible to gather another team as the one thrown up by the challenge of tumultuous events and cataclysmic changes, from Japanese occupation to guerilla insurgency to self-government to merger to separate independence. But it was possible to set standards of integrity and competence and to establish them as minimum norms for persons holding public office.

VII

On 24 March, the Prime Minister left for America to participate in seminars and to give some lectures before going to Washington, to meet President Nixon, Dr. Henry Kissinger, and US industrialists. He returned to Singapore in mid-April.

At Le High University, Pennsylvania, Lee gave three "Jacob Blaustein" lectures. The first was "Southeast Asian View of the New World Power Balance in the Making". "We live in stirring times," Lee began. "Not for some time has the world witnessed such dramatic changes in the relationship of the great powers as in the past two years. We are witnessing the shifts in the balance of power as the weighting has changed. And the great powers are learning to live peacefully with each other, despite the urge in each to be more influential than the others. At this juncture in post-War II history, I venture this Southeast Asian view of the new power balance in the making, and their implications for the smaller countries of Asia."

1972 – 73 saw some remarkable turns in the kaleidoscope of international relations. Mr. Nixon's discussions in Beijing and in Moscow changed the scenario for Hanoi. Hanoi knew their position was weakened. Hence in October, it was Hanoi that announced a 9-point agreement which had been agreed in-principle with Dr. Kissinger. Peace was around the corner. But it was not to be signed until after Mr. Nixon's re-election, and after another period of massive bombing of North Vietnam, from December 18 till they were suspended before the New Year. Talks were resumed. The agreement was finally signed on January 27.

After all this pulverising of North Vietnam, the North Vietnamese Prime Minister, Mr. Pham Van Dong, cordially received Dr. Kissinger in Hanoi on 11 February. The old, fixed divisions of the Cold War appeared fluid and nebulous. Washington had moved from confrontation to negotiations with both Beijing and Moscow. For whatever their different reasons, both communist powers wanted the war in Vietnam scaled down and America allowed to withdraw honourably. So President Thieu was still President and in control, when North Vietnamese and Vietcong officers arrived in Saigon for the setting up of the Joint Military Commission. And Madam Binh, the Foreign Minister of the PRG (Provisional Revolutionary Government), attended a reception in Paris given by the South Vietnamese Foreign Minister, Mr. Tran Van Lam, to shake his hand. Foes had seemingly become friends. America was more friendly to China, a Leninist-Maoist state, than to India, a democratic state, with a free representative system of government. China, for her part, showed greater cordiality towards capitalist America and Japan than towards communist Russia. Paradoxically also, India had become closer to Russia. Ideological divisions appeared to be less relevant. For the time being, national interests seemed the most reliable guide for the actions and policies of governments.

A staunch, anti-communist ally of America, Japan, was now cause of considerable irritation in America. Japan was under pressure to change her trade and monetary policies which had caused an American balance of payments deficit of $4.5 billion for 1972. Further, America's relations with her allies in Western Europe were not all that free from friction. America saw the EEC, whose formation she had urged and encouraged, as over-protectionist, and not only in the EEC's common agricultural policy. There was growing annoyance at reverse preferences for the EEC from states associated with it. Even NATO solidarity, for many years unquestioned, needed to be re-stressed. There were many spiky problems over the talks on Mutual and Balanced Force Reductions, defence burden sharing, and the lowering of force levels of some European countries of the NATO alliance even without MBFR (Mutual and Balanced Force Reductions) agreement.

Naturally, there was much confusion in Southeast Asia over all these developments. It was the speed and suddenness of these shifts in policy that caught many an Asian government off balance. The plain black and white contrasts of the Truman and Eisenhower Administrations were too simplistic for the realities of the 1970s. Nothing more vividly spelt out the change in moods and policies than American Presidential addresses. In 1949, President Truman warned against the "false philosophy" of communism and stated that "the US and other like-minded nations find themselves directly opposed by a regime with contrary aims and a totally different concept of life". In 1961, President Kennedy's words rang out in clear and crisp terms: "Let every nation know, whether it wishes us well or ill, that we shall pay any price, bear any burden, meet any hardship, support any friend, oppose any foe, in order to assure the survival and success of liberty." But whether it was in defence of liberty or in opposition to communist dictatorship, the US found herself helping to defend governments in Asia not particularly reputed for democratic practices, nor enthusiastic supporters of the liberty of the individual. Perhaps, said Lee, these countries could not afford democratic liberties when they were open to exploitation by communist subversion and insurgency. However, by January 1973, President Nixon, in his inauguration, said: "The time has passed when America will make every nation's conflict our own, or make every nation's future our responsibility or presume to tell the people of other nations how to manage their own affairs."

In place of direct military intervention on behalf of governments, without much to show by way of popular support, the Nixon doctrine, announced at Guam in 1969, was that America would help those who wanted to, and presumably could, defend their freedom with economic and military aid. It assumed that the American President and Congress believed that such aid was in America's interests. These changes had been a long time in gestation. From 1946–71, America had spent $74.7 billion on economic aid and $35.3 billion on military aid to all under-developed countries. The results had been less than satisfactory, whether in economic development or military stability, internally or externally. And on Vietnam, American military expenditure was $108 billion, and economic expenditure $8.5 billion. But the most grievous cost of Vietnam was in domestic strife and dissension.

Meanwhile, Russia had grown into an equal nuclear power. Together with Eastern Europe, Russia had more in conventional arms in Central Europe than the West. But she had become increasingly worried over China and her growing nuclear capacity. China had become alarmed at Russia's intentions and subordinated everything to the threat from Russia of a pre-emptive nuclear strike. On the other hand, although the American economy was the world's most dominant, its pre-eminence was no longer so assured, compared with the combined GNP of the West Europeans of $609 billion for 251 million people, or to Japan's $243 billion for 105 million people.

Now, it was generally accepted that China's intervention in the Korean War in 1950 was defensive and precipitated by the closeness of General MacArthur's advance to the Yalu River, China's frontier with North Korea. "Since China's aggressive attitude in Southeast Asia, and Vietnam in particular, is now regarded as an American misreading of the situation, is it not best for America to reassess the whole security situation in Southeast Asia?"

Lee said that whatever the rights or wrongs of the intervention in Vietnam, one beneficial result of the conflict, and the way it had ended, was that it had broken the spell on other Southeast Asians, that the wave of history was on the side of the communists. Their victory was shown not to be inevitable. The fact that there were viable non-communist countries in Southeast Asia today, whatever their varying claims to democratic government, was because that streak of communist wins in China and North Vietnam was checked. Otherwise, people in the rest of Southeast Asia might have been stampeded into the communist millenium.

By 1959, the monolithic communist movement had begun to crack between Moscow and Beijing. By 1963, the schism had become vociferously public. And, after all the acrimony and genuine Chinese fears of a pre-emptive strike, this schism might never be healed, however much the successors of the present leaderships in Russia and China tried to reestablish the unity of the communist movement. But, in any event, China had, for the time being, abandoned the rhetoric of the countryside surrounding and conquering the cities, one of Lin Piao's less famous last dogmas. It could well be that after the Indo-Chinese experience, however much dogma will continue to be chanted, in the next decade, particularly with a new generation in charge, China's support for guerilla insurgency might become more moral than material. And, like the Russian leadership, they might learn that it was easier to deal with governments in established authority than guerilla revolutionary groups. But, on the other hand the present trends towards rational and friendly government-to-government relations might well change with a new generation in leadership in Beijing.

For the present, America was making carefully parallel progress in her negotiations with both Russia and China towards an easing of relations. Any détente must appear to be *pari passu*, and must not give an impression of exploitation of Russo-Chinese differences. It was only to be expected that the middle and small nations, whose interests might be affected, were concerned with the dangers of direct super-power diplomacy, that super-power differences being settled over their heads might well be at their expense.

With growing rapport between China and America, the Japanese, fearful of a march being stolen on them, moved with alacrity in October. They dropped Taiwan and established diplomatic relations with China at ambassadorial level. The Japanese did not fear communist subversion and had more to gain than lose in establishing closer relations. So too, the

138

Australians and New Zealanders, after their elections in December 1972. But the smaller countries nearer China and Indo-China had been more cautious. South Korea made tentative approaches for a dialogue and regular meetings with North Korea. However, the South Korean President thought it necessary to strengthen his grip on events by enlarging his constitutional powers. Thailand, nearest to Indo-China, and with only fifty miles of Laos between her and China at their nearest boundaries, wanted more time to see how events would develop before making any changes in policy. Malaysia, on the other hand, with Thailand between her and China and Indo-China, could believe that diplomatic exchange with China would show her own ethnic Chinese guerilla movement how hollow their struggle had become, as Beijing's representative presented himself at the court of the Malaysian King, and observed the rules of non-interference in Malaysian internal affairs.

But Indonesia, with memories of recent interference with her internal communist problems, was less convinced of correct behaviour. She was not enamoured of an early re-establishment of relations with China. Hence, when the Australian Prime Minister in February suggested that some new grouping for regional co-operation in security and economic matters could include China and Japan, the Indonesians let it be known that it was not feasible for the time being, though the proposal had merit in the long term. Singapore, with three quarters of her 2.1 million population of Chinese ethnic descent, was happy to continue trade and economic relations through existing non-diplomatic channels and let her neighbours take the initiative of opening official and diplomatic relations with China. The Philippines, more engrossed in domestic constitutional changes, had alleged Maoist support for guerilla groups, before and after exploration was made in Beijing by representatives of President Marcos.

By and large, the greater the correlations between domestic problems of subversion and the closer the nexus between their own guerilla insurgents and Beijing, the less the enthusiasm for any speedy change in policy and establishing of diplomatic representation. In the end, how these matters sorted themselves out would depend in part on the developments in Indo-China, and on how America, Russia and China were seen to get the North Vietnamese, Vietcong and South Vietnamese, to honour the terms of the Paris agreement.

"These are anxious and uncertain times for the smaller countries of East and Southeast Asia," continued Lee. Peace and prosperity without war for the great powers must mean a change in posture, strategy and tactics from the years of bipolar division, between the communists and the Free World. The meaning and consequences of the new triangular politics between America, Russia and China had been poignantly demonstrated to Hanoi in the past eighteen months. And, what about the interests of America's powerful allies, Western Europe and Japan? Even for them, it must mean critical re-appraisals of the new power balance and their place in it. For, in the negotiations for a new balance of power, their interests might not always coincide with those of America. An economic heavy-weight like Japan had had to respond quickly to the implications of these changes. Japan could not do without the US security umbrella for quite some time, especially to protect her from nuclear blackmail. Moreover, Japan's trade with America was almost one-third of her total external trade. Geographically, Japan was next door to both China and Russia, each of whom could do with her technological and economic co-opera-tion. But, both Russia and China could become more of a problem for Japan after she had extended such technological and economic co-operation.

In the case of China, even if Japan did not take the initiative, it was likely that the West Europeans, with excess industrial capacity, would find it difficult to resist extending credits to China for heavy plants and know-how. Indeed, the West Europeans had a long-term interest in keeping Russia more occupied in the East than in the West. An industrialised and stronger China in no way ran counter to Western European security or economic interests. America must also recognise that, with or without trade and transfer of technology, China would make the grade. It was only a question of time. China would take many more years to do it the hard way, like the Japanese did before the war, by imitation, industrial espionage and experimentation on her own. But if China had to do it all on her own, it would probably lead to quite unnecessary and more implacable hostility for many years ahead. This was what happened to Japan before World War II. The obstacles placed in the path of Japan's industrial-isation compounded her animosities towards the white peoples. To major power rivalries was added racial antagonism.

On the other hand, the generosity of America in rehabilitating Western Europe, including defeated Germany, under the Marshall Plan 1947 – 49, at $13 billion in three years or 2 per cent of her then GNP for three successive years, was as much to stop the advances of communism, as the result of lessons learned from World War I, of an embittered and revanchist Germany. So, also, American help in rehabilitating Japan with some $4.3 billion aid from 1946 – 71. It was as much to check what was then monolithic communist expansion as to give Japan a reasonable place in the world, repaired from the ravages of war.

If peace and prosperity without war was to be achieved, it must mean nuclear co-existence. But, in economics and politics, there would be both competition and co-operation, across ideological, racial, continental and regional barriers. In the current phase during which America was trying to find a world power balance between America, Russia and China, with Western Europe and Japan on America's side of the security balance, fundamental differences, whether in ideology or in political and economic systems, between the free enterprise and communist systems, must be muted. But these differences continued to exist. It was extremely doubtful if any amount of collaboration and co-operation would make the communist system open up their basically closed economies to the free enterprise of the West.

Russia intervened in Czechoslovakia in 1968 to prevent any gradual opening up and liberalisation of the political and economic system in Czechoslovakia, because the Soviet Union considered it a threat to the security of Russia, through setting an attractive and, for Russia, a dangerous example for her other East European buffer states. Ordinary national competition for power and influence over third countries was part of the game of peaceful co-existence, but not where such competition intruded upon the security of Russia and the communist bloc. Hence, whatever the contemporary differences, over defence burden-sharing, balance of payment deficits, currency parities, tariff and non-tariff barriers to trade between America and Western Europe and America and Japan, the three together comprised an open non-communist world system, distinct from the closed economic systems of the communist powers of Comecon and China.

Any significant part of the Third World over which a communist government was established meant that the free world system was that much diminished. Professor Thomas Schelling said in 1966 before a Sub-Committee on the Far East and Pacific Affairs, "Hearings on United States Policy Towards Asia": "The great danger, if all Asia goes communist, is really exclusion of the United States and what we call Western civilisation from a larger part of the world that is poor and coloured and potentially hostile. The worst aspects of that exclusion are not military, but are social, political, spiritual, philosophical ... "

This was only one result. The greater loss in the long run was the shrinking and weakening of the economic base of the non-communist world, and a corresponding expansion and increase in the base of the communist world, divided though it might be between Russia and China. For, however much confrontation between the communist and non-communist powers was reduced by negotiations to co-existence, it still meant only co-existence, the abjuring of the use of force in any conflict which might directly involve the super and major powers directly. This era of negotiations had led to co-operation in space. But, on earth, including the oceans, it meant continuing competition for influence. For with a new country joining one or the other of the competing sides, there was a gain to that side in the access to resources of more population and territory, whilst denying the same to the other competing sides.

In this kind of peaceful co-existence, with more or less peaceful competition for influence, America offered a formidable challenge to the other great powers, given her enormous industrial capacity, technological superiority and her multi-national corporations. The alternative was for America to opt out of South and Southeast Asia. Then she was out of the Indian Ocean, and, eventually, out of Asia, and her global influence must shrink as that of Russia expanded.

Lee added: "The dramatic advances in communication and transportation technology in the past three decades were made primarily by

141

America. American jumbo jets, and instant communications through American satellites placed in stationary orbit, have made for a smaller and more inter-dependent world. It would be an irony of history if America were to give up areas where her influence has been considerable, and has not met with antagonism. Peace and prosperity are more likely to be preserved if the burdens of stability, and opportunities of trade and investments, are shared between the super and major powers, and no small country is forced to join one or other of the contending political and economic systems, because of the predominant presence of one and the absence of the other. This is the best, for the time being, Southeast Asia can hope for in this search for stability and progress."

In the second lecture, "Decolonisation and the Non-economic Factors of Developments in New Countries in Southeast Asia", Lee said that when Roosevelt and Churchill promulgated the Atlantic Charter in 1941, they gave a psychological impetus to the right of self-determination. It was to lead to the irreversible dissolution of the European Empires. It unscrambled a European balance of power in Asia, which first started in 1486, when Diaz went round the Cape of Good Hope. At the outbreak of World War I, there were only four sovereign states in Asia — Afghanistan, China, Japan and Thailand. Only Japan was effectively sovereign. India and Pakistan became independent in 1947, Burma and Ceylon in 1948.

China became communist in 1949, in a revolution based on a dispossessed peasantry, not an industrial proletariat. Meanwhile, the Cold War had already set in on Europe. Decolonisation widened the area of contest to these new under-developed countries. Each side wanted to collect more followers and territory to its system of governing and ordering society. Technical assistance, economic aid and supply of arms were part of the techniques to win new followers. When the Cold War started, America was the anchorman on the Allied side. Britain was exhausted and divested of the largest of her overseas possessions, and France had yet to recover from German occupation. Hence, America mounted the Marshall Plan and founded NATO to stop Europe from being eroded. For the Middle East, there was CENTO, and for Southeast Asia, SEATO.

In Vietnam, the Americans switched their policies from support for freedom movements to support of the French in resisting Ho Chi Minh and the Viet Minh. The object of all this was some restoration of the balance of power and the containment of communist power — Russia, and China, then believed to be the ideological ally of Russia. There was a string of military bases all the way from South Korea, through Japan, Taiwan, the Philippines, Thailand, to Turkey, to contain the monolithic communist land mass of Russia and China. Broadly speaking, America succeeded in preventing the expansion of the communist bloc.

But the Americans found themselves more and more alone in carrying the main burden of global balance of power. It led to the present period of negotiations. With Russia, America reached agreement on SALT (Strategic Arms Limitation Talks), and now talks were being held on MBFR (Mutual and Balanced Force Reductions) for a new balance in Europe with fewer, and less costly, American ground forces in Europe. With China, America had opened up a friendly dialogue. With Taiwan becoming a non-issue, there could be a gradual movement towards a new quadrilateral balance among China, Japan, Russia and America in East Asia and the Western Pacific generally. But what of Southeast Asia? The Japanese were psychologically unable for the time being, to expand their self-defence forces for sharing the burden of maintaining security and stability outside of Japan's own immediate surroundings. A sizeable Japanese naval task force on its own, and not part of a United States-Japan security arrangement, might at present be received with reservation in some countries in Southeast Asia.

Meanwhile, as far back as 1955 – 6, Russia had seen the opportunities of encouraging anti-imperialism to further weaken Western strength in South and Southeast Asia. In 1955 – 6, Khrushchev and Bulganin visited India, Burma and Indonesia. So, non-aligned India and Indonesia and, to a lesser extent, Burma, drew aid from both sides, the West and Russia. In the case of Indonesia, the Russians saw an opportunity to exploit the situation against the West. They armed Sukarno's Indonesia for the liberation of West New Guinea. They gave $378 million worth of economic aid for prestige projects, like steel mills, and another $630 million worth of military aid, to make up a billion dollars up till 1966.

In those heady days of the Bandung era, it was believed that large land masses, with huge populations had only to gain independence, and stop being exporters of raw materials to the metropolitan powers of Europe, in order to grow rich. They would become processors and manufacturers in their own right. But they learned that modernisation and industrialisation were not so simple. So Indonesia's Sukarno turned to external adventure to divert attention from internal misery. His first target for rhetoric and diversion was West New Guinea, the remnant of Dutch colonialism in Southeast Asia. His alibi for non-development, and indeed economic decline, was that the Indonesian people had to sacrifice to finish the struggle against colonialism. When the Americans got the Dutch to promise to give up West New Guinea in 1962, after a UN team survey, and handed it over to Indonesia in 1963, Sukarno had to find a new diversion. He found it in the Federation of Malaysia, established in September 1963. He alleged that it was a neo-colonialist plot. Against it, he mounted "confrontation". But the bubble burst in September 1965, when, in a coup and counter-coup, hundreds of thousands of communists and their followers were killed, and a billion dollars worth of Russian aid went down the drain. Indeed, so did aid from China for prestige projects like the stadium for "GANEFO" (Games for the Newly Emerging Forces). Loans from the West, including $408 million from America, up till 1967, had also to be re-scheduled.

143

"It is now generally understood that without security and stability, economic development is difficult to achieve. People in Asia have seen the path to recovery and development of Japan and South Korea. They have seen the less spectacular, but still substantial, results of progress made by Thailand, Malaysia and Singapore. With this perception of what needs to be done, a different mood now prevailed in South and Southeast Asia. On the Indian sub-continent, after fratricidal tension and strife for over twenty-four years since partition in August 1947, India was the dominant power in the sub-continent." It might take some time for the dust to settle, and for Pakistan to adjust to the changed circumstances. Now, perhaps all these countries of South Asia, India, Pakistan and Bangladesh, could and would concentrate their energies and resources on constructive development.

It was true that Russia's standing in India and Bangladesh had never been higher. But it did not follow that, because the Russians had given considerable economic and military aid to India, therefore India would necessarily be in bond. Notwithstanding her defence industries, India needed a constant flow of essential spares for the more sophisticated military hardware already supplied. But, as in the case of Indonesia, it was possible, at great cost, to change suppliers.

For America in South Asia, it meant the slow and tedious process of repairing relations with India. If nothing else, this would enable India to exercise a greater freedom of choice in economic and political policies. American disappointment over economic and military aid to India and other developing countries should not cloud the view of the future. The poor results of economic aid to new countries were not foreseen, mainly because economic planners in the West did not take sufficient account of the non-economic factors that determine development. Inputs of capital and know-how alone did not produce greater wealth. Ethnic, cultural, religious characteristics, social values, the existence or absence of an effective leadership, able to establish and run an honest and efficient administration, and the drive in a people — these were critical factors. And cultural, religious and social values, if not orientated to endeavour and achievement, took a long time to change, if changeable at all. And if they were to change, it must be because both leaders and people wanted a change.

In the 50s and early 60s, many in the West, and in the less developed world, believed it was essential that the performance of democratic India should not be seen to compare unfavourably with the performance of a totalitarian system in China, and that help must be given to ensure that this did not happen. US aid alone to India, from 1946 — 67, both economic and military, amounted to $7.14 billion. India also received aid from Britain, West Germany and Russia. But her performance, as reflected in her GNP of $79 per capita and a growth rate of 3.4 per cent for 1960 – 71, was short of the Chinese performance of $150 per capita for 1971, at a 4 per cent annual growth rate.

What were the reasons? Was the aid to India inadequate? But China had no aid to speak of, after her break with Russia in 1959. It was difficult to generalise and lay down broad principles. But at the risk of reducing complex truth into over-simple generalisations, Lee ventured the following explanations. It was a fallacy to compare the two countries. They had more dissimilarities than similarities. The respective performances were not simply the result of different ideological, political and economic systems. There were other more important factors which exerted immeasurable influence on the results. "We are comparing two fundamentally different nations, with different histories, different culture and value systems, and attitudes to modernisation and progress. The two peoples and their cultures had been tempered and shaped over the centuries by the different climates of these two sub-continents. The results were two very different civilisations."

Historically, India was never united to the same degree of stability and duration as China had been since the 3rd century B.C. As Ghandi once said, India was united by the English language and the railway system the British built. At independence, she suffered grievously as a result of the massacres that followed partition into three components, East and West Pakistan and India. But even this smaller India had undergone further divisions into smaller linguistic states, until there were now twenty-two states, and eight Union Territories. The Hindu peoples of the Indian sub-continent absorbed successive waves of invasion by a technique peculiar to themselves. By the Hindu system of caste, they could serve their new rulers, whether Moghul emperors, or the British Raj, in a secular capacity even though they could not eat off the same table, nor inter-marry without losing caste and becoming outcasts. And so, Indian society preserved clearly defined and different ethnic and linguistic groups despite centuries of Moghul and British rule. This made for a more disparate India.

Chinese history and civilisations, on the other hand, proceeded differently. Successive conquerors from the North and Northwest, both before and after the Great Wall was built about 200 B.C., were always absorbed into Chinese culture and ethnically assimilated as Chinese. Sinic culture was like a minting machine, relentlessly setting out to a stamp all who came under its influence into exactly the same mould. Successive invaders were absorbed and assimilated by the Chinese. So, ethnically, the Chinese were more homogeneous than the Indians. Linguistically, all Chinese used the same script, however different the dialect pronounciation of the Chinese ideograph might be in different parts of China. This cultural unity the Chinese communists inherited and used to considerable advantage. China's authoritarian communist system made it easier to implement the tough policies necessary to bring a backward, agricultural people into the industrial society. India, with one man one vote, and the need to govern by consent of the majority expressed in periodic elections at not more than five-yearly intervals, had to make repeated concessions to vociferous dissenting minorities of linguistic or racial sub-groups. "From my observation of the Asian scene, I am prompted to the belief that East Asians — Koreans, Japanese, Chinese and Vietnamese — are intense peoples. The South and Southeast Asians are, by and large, of less intense cultures." Two broad conclusions could be drawn from this. "First, that when it comes to modernisation and industrialisation, the more intense peoples tend to make more rapid progress, whether they work the free enterprise system like Japan and South Korea, or the communist systems like China, North Korea and, before the massive bombings, North Vietnam. Second, that the disgruntled intense East Asian was more likely to take to communism than the dissatisfied but culturally less intense South and Southeast Asian. The less intense South and Southeast did not see the point of sustained and prolonged hating and plotting to kill the class enemy."

It was Russia's lack of intimate knowledge of the histories and cultures of the peoples of Southeast Asia that led the Soviet Union to invest in the Indonesian Communist Party via Sukarno. What other communist party but one of a less intense culture would be so exposed and above ground that they and their supporters could be rounded up and eliminated by hundreds of thousands?

Equally, it was lack of understanding of the intense East Asian communists in Vietnam that got America embroiled in Vietnam. In the Vietnamese communists, Americans got locked in combat with an intense adversary who would not give up despite all the punishment of the sophisticated firepower of the world's mightiest industrial nation.

But whatever the reasons, China achieved recognition as a great power which must be a part of any arrangement for peace and stability in Asia. China's bellicose statements in support of revolution and guerilla insurgency in the past, however, had left the smaller countries of Asia with doubts as to the sincerity of China's peaceful attitude of correct non-interference in the national affairs of other countries. In this period of transition into a new era, an American presence was re-assuring for most small countries even as they came to terms with this new China, and learnt to live with her, as they all must. "It will take some time before the picture is clearer, what kind of quadrilateral equation comprising America, Japan, Russia and China can ensure peaceful co-existence in East and Southeast Asia, whilst they compete for economic and political influence in third countries."

In the final lecture, "Security and Stability Essential for Development of New Countries in Southeast Asia", Lee argued that Japan and China, as integral parts of Asia, would in the long run, willy-nilly, exercise their influence on East and Southeast Asia. Russia was completely open in pursuit of influence as a global power. The West Europeans had chosen, for the immediate future, to concentrate their energies and interests on the Mediterranean Basin and Africa in pursuance of EEC policies. It was, therefore, important for Southeast Asia that America's global outlook should not be distorted by unhappy experiences in Vietnam. What the smaller countries of Asia wanted was non-interference with their independence and integrity. Since it was not very likely that all the great powers would, in the forseeable future, guarantee non-interference and neutrality, it was the balance between the great powers which would promote stability and enable the smaller countries to choose their partners for progress from amongst the most advanced countries.

In the economic field, there could be more multilateral sharing of responsibilities for trade, aid and development among America, Japan and Western Europe. A good example of this was the Inter-Governmental Group for Indonesia formula for aid to Indonesia — one-third America, one-third Japan, and one-third Western Europe. But the security and stability of the region, without which development could not take place, could, for the time being, be provided only by an American presence. Russia's naval presence could not, and would not, be excluded from the region. If it was the only presence, then a single superpower hegemony would be established, changing the whole geo-political picture.

The countries in Southeast Asia, watching the mood in America and reading Senator McGovern's policy to quit Southeast Asia immediately, started re-examining their security positions. At a meeting in December 1971, the Foreign Ministers of the Association of Southeast Asian Nations (ASEAN) — Indonesia, Malaysia, Philippines, Singapore and Thailand — discussed the possibilities of a neutral zone for the area, its neutrality guaranteed by America, Russia and China. They realised it was not easy to get the three great powers to agree to this. But it was set down as a long-term objective, which might or might not be achieved. Meanwhile, American forces were stationed in Thailand and the Philippines, and British, Australian and New Zealand forces were stationed in Singapore, with an Australian air force contingent in West Malaysia. No great power had campaigned for these forces to be withdrawn. The presence of these forces did not conflict with the declared long-term ideal of neutralisation. As a new balance was reached between America, Russia, China and Japan, it was not unlikely that most of these bases would be dismantled.

This meeting of ASEAN Foreign Ministers was an exercise to discover a way to check the spread of insecurity and instability, if Senator McGovern's policy to quit Southeast Asia immediately had carried the day. As it turned out, there would be another four years of President Nixon. But four years was not a long time in the history of peoples. So the doubts on long-term instability remained. A bi-partisan foreign policy for a U.S. naval task force to stay indefinitely in the area, always there to balance Russia's growing naval presence, would increase the stability of the region.

There were two crucial areas of the world over which the West European powers used to exercise a stabilising influence: the first was the Middle East, the oil countries of North Africa, Arabia and the Gulf. The second was South and Southeast Asia. Perhaps, many of the problems of instability that had arisen in the Middle East might have been avoided, if the Arabs had been given more of a choice in their economic and political policies through the US providing alternatives. Instead, after the refusal of Foster Dulles to finance the Aswan Dam, he left the Egyptians to go all the way with Russia. This led to a situation where Western oil supplies had become precariously dependent on the continuance of friendly rulers in Saudi Arabia and the Sheikh Emirates of the Gulf. So the world energy crisis had taken an awkward dimension as a result of unforeseen consequences of the spurning of Egypt's desire to build the Aswan Dam, opening the door to Russia's influence.

This experience should perhaps underline the importance of not creating a power vacuum in Southeast Asia. Southeast Asia straddles the sea passages between the Indian and Pacific Oceans. A vacuum was most likely to lead to conflict. Russia could fill this vacuum rapidly. China could not. But China would not want to be outflanked in this way. Nor would Japan be happy to see the Russian navy astride a critical route to the Gulf, from which nearly 90 per cent of Japan's oil came. Other smaller countries too, might not be unhappy to see a Russian presence balanced by an American one.

Lee said: "You may well ask: What is there in Southeast Asia for America, apart from its geo-political importance?" Lee turned to the past for an answer. In December 1941, when President Roosevelt placed an embargo on oil, rubber, tin and other essential supplies to Japan, until the Japanese agreed to quit China, Japan chose war. Japan grabbed Southeast Asia for its oil, rubber, tin and other raw materials. But Southeast Asia today supplied only 9.2 per cent of Japanese imports, mostly raw materials, and absorbed 11.7 per cent of Japanese exports, mainly manufactures. The region had a population of about 293 million people, almost three times that of Japan, but with a total GNP a little more than one-sixth that of Japan's. The region's development, which varied from country to country, was not as spectacular as the East Asian countries. But it was certainly higher than South Asia. From 1965 – 71, real GNP growth rates of Southeast Asia ranged from 1.7 per cent for South Vietnam, to over 12 per cent for Singapore. Five countries of Southeast Asia enjoyed growth rates in excess of 6 per cent.

The explored and known reserves of oil amounted to some 2 per cent of total world reserves. Indonesia, Brunei and Malaysia produced about 1 million barrels per day in 1971. In 1970, based on the UN Geological Survey, the Chase Manhattan Bank forecast that some $36 billion would be spent on oil exploration up to 1980. So far, although there had been strikes of oil, these strikes had been of relatively small pockets, not the huge fields comparable to those of the Gulf States or in Saudi Arabia. But such strikes might still be possible.

In any case, with the increasing price of crude oil, as a result of stronger bargaining power of the OPEC countries, natural rubber went up in price, with the slowing down in expansion of synthetic production. Southeast Asia produced 85 per cent of the world's natural supply, 69 per cent of world copra, and 39 per cent of world palm oil supply. The region had 6.9 per cent of wild forest reserves, soft woods and hard woods. It also produced 64 per cent of the world's tin supply.

Given the choice, apart from the three communist countries of China, North Korea and North Vietnam, there was little doubt in the minds of Asians that their chances of modernisation and development were much better if they could gear into the economy of the West. The way in which trade had diversified in Southeast Asia since decolonisation bore this out. During the period of colonial rule, all these countries had their economies vertically integrated with that of the metropolitan power in Europe. Since independence, trade with, and investments by, the West Europeans had continued, but they had been completely outpaced by the Americans and Japanese.

Trade with Russia had always been more a question of politics. Trade between India and Russia had more than doubled between 1958 and 1970, from $181 million to $420 million, or 2.1 per cent to 5.9 per cent of Russia's external trade. On the other hand, Russia's trade with Southeast Asia, following the collapse of the Indonesian Communist Party in 1965, declined from 1.9 per cent in 1965 to 1.2 per cent in 1969.

Chinese trade with Southeast Asia was negligible. Chinese total external trade for 1970 was estimated at $4.2 billion as compared to Hong Kong's $5.4 billion for a population of just 4 million as against China's 773 million. China's trade with all Southeast Asian countries amounted to only $245 million, or 1.6 per cent of total Southeast Asian trade.

If China was able to get sizeable credits for industrialisation, it was likely that trade with Southeast Asia would grow rapidly. For, through trade via Hong Kong and countries in Southeast Asia, China could obtain hard currencies, which would help meet instalments due on those credits.

On the whole, the future for Southeast Asia, outside the countries of Indo-China, was a shade more optimistic now in 1973 than it was in 1964, when the war escalated in Vietnam. The most dramatic change had taken place in Indonesia. Today, Indonesia's economy is in much better shape; currency was stable, and investments were increasing. The Indonesian government of President Suharto had set its mind on economic progress and development. The same concern for economic development was evident in Thailand, Malaysia and Singapore. Only in the Philippines, where martial law had been invoked to deal with domestic problems, was there doubt whether economic progress matched the expectations of the people.

"As for Indo-China itself, there are three scenarios I can envisage. First, where despite low level violence and small violations of the Paris agreement, the peace provisions are in the main honoured by the South Vietnamese, North Vietnamese and the Vietcong. In this case, the contest will be primarily political. The outcome will depend on the economic and social performance of the South Vietnamese government to hold on to its political ground. In such a situation, the ceasefire in Laos will continue, and the fighting in Cambodia will peter out with a possibility of some political settlement. The second scenario is an all-out offensive by both the North Vietnamese and the Vietcong as soon as they believe they can overwhelm the armed forces of the South Vietnamese government. However, the North Vietnamese will always have to consider the possibility of an American reaction to a flagrant breach of the Paris agreement where North Vietnamese forces are openly involved. The third scenario is where the North Vietnamese, to avoid unnecessary risks, ostensibly honour all that is required of them under the Paris agreement. They leave it to the Vietcong in South Vietnam, with North Vietnamese infiltrators to add to their strength, to make a bid for power, at first, perhaps, by political means, and then by a graduated escalation of violence and insurgency to prevent any economic and political consolidation by the South Vietnamese government."

There were other permutations and combinations of these scenarios. The course of events was not easily predictable, because the situation in Laos and Cambodia was nebulous and was not covered by specific provisions in the Paris agreement for a ceasefire and a political settlement. Three-fourths of Laos was under de facto control of the Pathet Lao, a situation which they achieved primarily with the help of the North Vietnamese. Two-thirds of Cambodia was in the hands of the various Cambodian insurgent groups, again only because they were backed by Vietcong and North Vietnamese forces. The Laotians and Cambodians were people of less intense cultures. They needed the intense North Vietnamese and the Vietcong to give them that stiffening which helped them against their own non-communist Laotians and Cambodians.

But if the Vietcong did eventually establish its control over South Vietnam, and the South was slowly re-united with the North, it did not necessarily mean the rest of Southeast Asia would go communist. The Thais were more prepared psychologically to face up to such a situation. Now, the possibility of even more neutralist, (or even pro-communist) governments in Laos and Cambodia was a contingency the Thais have taken into their calculations. The crucial factor, however, was whether they felt they could depend on American military and economic aid, as spelt out under the Nixon doctrine. If they could, then they could be confident. With the spread of the benefits of economic developments that Thailand had enjoyed in the past twenty years, it was unlikely that any indigenous Thai guerilla insurgency could overthrow the established government. For the Thai communists were culturally less intense Southeast Asians, not intense East Asians like the North Vietnamese or Vietcong. It was true that there was one means of exporting more experienced insurgents via the Pathet Lao. There were four million Laotians in Northeast Thailand, compared to 2 million in the whole of Laos itself — the result of an expedition in the early nineteenth century, when the Thai Kingdom pushed its boundaries northwestwards, and absorbed these people into Thailand. But the Pathet Lao were gentler

Hindu-influenced types, who did not go in for self-immolation like the intense East Asian Buddhist monks of South Vietnam.

For the rest of Southeast Asia, excluding Indo-China, cautious optimism might well be justified. The danger of external communist aggression was remote. It was not part of communist revolutionary doctrine. Perhaps, amongst other reasons, it carried a high risk of painful retaliation. If ordinary people could see a serious attack on poverty and feel improvement in standards of life, then communist guerilla insurgency would find it very difficult to get going. This was especially so because the peoples of Southeast Asia were culturally less intense than the East Asians of Vietnam, and less prone to guerilla insurgency. It was in Indo-China itself, where the issue was left open by the nature of the Paris agreement. The final outcome could go either way. It must be so, or there would have been no agreement.

Whilst no valid comparison could be drawn from the performance of India and China to determine what influence, ideology, or political and economic systems had on economic performance, a comparison of North and South Korea could give some insights. North and South Koreans were basically the same people, with the same ethnic, cultural and social values, but run under different economic and political systems. North Korea was the part which was more industrialised by the Japanese. The South was richer in agriculture. Both sides received aid from their allies. From 1960 – 71, the free enterprise system in South Korea had registered growth rates of 9.3 per cent per annum. The latest available data showed the South having a GNP of $8.3 billion or $259 per capita (population: 31.9 million). North Korea's GNP was $3.8 billion or $280 per capita (population: 14.3 million).

Whether development along similar lines could take place in South Vietnam depended, first, on whether the South Vietnamese government was able to hold its ground and maintain security to enable economic development to proceed. Second, it depended on mobilising capital and enterprise to convert a war economy to a peace-time economy. Some of the vast military complexes could be put to civilian user. New industries must be established. Enough of the refugee population in the towns must be given adequate security and induced to return to the countryside to get agricultural production going again. The lack of revolutionary zeal in the leadership, and in the people at large, could be made up through substantial inflows of capital and know-how, put to work efficiently by private enterprise. If security and stability were established, massive injections of aid and the operations of efficient multi-national corporations could bring about rapid economic growth. Once rapid growth had started, the chances of guerilla insurgency succeeding were correspondingly reduced. But the Vietcong knew this, and could be expected not to acquiesce in this process.

America helped rehabilitate a devastated Western Europe, including a ruined West Germany. America also helped rebuild Japan. South Korea today was growing prosperous and viable because of American investments. The offer to rehabilitate Indo-China, if conditions allowed this aid to be used constructively, might help to heal part of the devastation the war had wrought on the peoples of that unhappy peninsula of Asia. Perhaps it would also give the people of South Vietnam a better chance to determine their own future.

On 10 April, President Nixon entertained Lee Kuan Yew to dinner at the White House. The President said: "We honour tonight, and we welcome here, a world statesman of the first rank, who has contributed with his intelligence, with his understanding, in helping us develop the kinds of policies that will maintain a world in which freedom can survive for larger countries like the United States, and for smaller countries like Singapore. There is no more articulate and intelligent spokesman for what I would call free society in the world than the Prime Minister of Singapore, Mr. Lee Kuan Yew .. "

In his response, Lee congratulated the President on his negotiations with Beijing and Moscow, and on disengaging America from Vietnam with honour. Peace and prosperity without war was not just an American dream but a world vision of the future, reassuring for all mankind who had to live in an ever smaller, more interrelated and more interdependent world. "May I express this hope," concluded Lee, "that in your second term you will be able to complete the new chapter which you have started in your first term through the policies which you initiated with such great promise." Fate determined otherwise. Soon came the Watergate Scandal, and the resignation of President Nixon from high office.

Interviewed over NBC's "Meet the Press" television feature on 11 April, the Prime Minister answered a series of topical questions. Included among them was whether he thought America achieved peace with honour in Vietnam. Lee replied: "You disengaged from Vietnam in an honourable way. Whether there is peace in Vietnam is another matter."

At New York airport before flying back to Singapore, Lee told the media that he had come to learn the mood in America after the disengagement from Vietnam. And from the Administration he got to know of their policies for this new phase — post-Vietnam.

VIII

Less than a fortnight later, Lee addressed an important conference of the National Trades Union Congress. He told the delegates: "We have perhaps a decade in which to ensure continuity in the close relationship between the government and the labour movement. This present relationship will continue perhaps for another decade. To understand this relationship, you have to dig up the past, and educate your younger members on what went before. Then they can pick out what is relevant for the future. The fundamental position of strength which Singapore enjoys is the relationship of trust and confidence between workers and the political leadership. Nobody doubts that policies are framed, and decisions are made, in the interests of the majority of the people. How did this come about?"

Lee thought it would be useful if a group of people were commissioned to objectively describe this historical development, in the labour and the political movements. Some time in 1923, the communists became the first organised political force. In the 1930s and 40s, the communists built up the first organised trade unions, mainly underground. They reached the peak of their strength, in open organisations, in 1963. "We became part of that political-cum-labour movement in the 1950s and 60s. Having assumed power in 1959, the line got drawn between the communists and the non-communist factions of the political and labour leaderships. It should analyse how it was that, after 1963, communist stocks went steadily down. And, gradually, painfully, picking up the bits and pieces, today we have the NTUC working in a framework of a relatively sound security with stable employment and industrial expansion."

Knowledge of this past was necessary in understanding why the present was what it was, and why those conditions could be expected to continue for a decade. But what would follow? A people did not live just for a decade. Therefore, it was necessary not only to discuss the technological changes which were coming, and with it the consequential forms and styles in which the trade union movement would operate. More important was the question of how this intimate partnership between the political and the union leaderships was to be maintained. "We have inducted into the political leadership some of the younger, more promising trade union leaders, those with the potential to mature and develop a broader and wider perspective. We hope that they will provide that continuity. They will be entrusted, or have thrust upon them, the responsibility, not simply easy matters, like asking for more wages and better benefits, but also to weigh and carry the burden of the consequences of affording these increased wages and benefits on the economy as a whole. For they must take into account the economic base on which our well-being, indeed our survival, depends."

The Prime Minister went on to refer to the "special and unique economic and political base within which we operate in Singapore". Perhaps the older union leaders had it inbuilt as part of their psyche so that they did not need to discuss these problems. "We were the heart of an empire. In 1945, we were truncated from the rest of the British Empire in Southeast Asia. We had been the administrative and entrepot centre, the trading, processing, collecting and distributing point for Southeast Asia. We faced a changed situation. First, we tried to reform a broader economic base through merger, in Malaysia, in 1963. But we had to completely change our strategy, in 1965, when we were out of Malaysia. We moved on to a new role, one which we can continue to play only if we have that added edge in better organisation and higher efficiency, so that we keep moving from traditional entrepot to manufacturing and servicing — and from physical services to brain services, including international banking and finance.''

If this basic point was overlooked, all these papers on technological progress would end in the wastepaper basket. To survive, to thrive, Singapore had to get better all the time. Services had to be provided which nobody else could do at that speed, quality or price. "And because we provide security and stability, investors can amortise their capital outlays over periods of ten, fifteen and more years, not one to three. Unless you get your younger union leaders to understand and to remember, at all times, the framework within which we have built this relative prosperity, then all may go down the drain one day. I say relative prosperity, because compared to the Japanese, our wages, skill for skill, are about one-third that of the Japanese. But for engineers, managers and professionals, we are about four-fifths that of the Japanese. This is another reality which union leaders and members have to recognise. Those in the upper brackets, the professionally trained, can sell their services across national boundaries by migrating. When we held wages down from '68 to '72, five years of restraint, we lost quite a number of high-calibre men. They moved out to the private sector, and got paid the rate for the job. Otherwise they would have moved out of Singapore altogether."

A first-class engineer, whether in electronics, chemical or civil engineering, or computers could cross national boundaries. He could sell his services in Western Europe, North America or Australasia. The skilled worker, even the technician, could not. Hence, considerable adjustments had to be made in the public sector this March 1973, to match rewards in the private sector for the top administrators and professionals. These were fundamental data, without which younger unionists would never be able to understand their limits for manoeuvre. These were realities which the government accepted in 1965. Lee reminded the unionists that he posed them to the delegates in that hall in 1965 and the solutions required for survival were discussed. "You accepted the challenge. Together we faced up to these realities. So today we are not dead, nor crawling on all fours, as many thought we would. But do not forget that the basic facets of our economic position have not altered. Gloss over them, take liberties with ourselves, only if we are prepared to unscramble all that has been built. Change is of the essence of life, whether in the individual or in a people, or in the world. But for us, our basic position means that we cannot afford to be a soft or easy-going society. I hope nobody will ever write about Singapore, that after enjoying remarkable growth for some two decades, the next generation leaders forgot the basis on which that growth and development were possible, and allowed the firm framework of good government to go slack, and work and social discipline went down, and prosperity soon evaporated."

There were two basic factors for strength. First, rapport between the political and union leaderships. This enabled entrepreneurs to confidently predict their returns from their investments for ten, fifteen or more years.

154

Second, whether or not there would gradually be more economic regional co-operation, like a free trade area, or a common market for specific combined projects. "We make our plans on the basis of the least favourable of economic and political circumstances. Therefore, we cannot allow any loss of verve, or blunting of our keenness. Loss of that cutting edge in our competitiveness means a lowering of our standards of life."

Lee believe that if these realities were kept in mind, and discussions were held against that backdrop, "we should be able, in this decade, to groom a generation of union leaders who have got their heads screwed on properly and their feet firmly planted on hard realities".

In his May Day Message, Lee hoped that normal harvests for rice, wheat, sugar and the other basic commodities would during the year bring the cost of living down. Then the increase in wages granted in 1972, and again in 1973, by the National Wages Council, would be enjoyed in fuller measure by all. For despite all the calculating and planning, the worldwide poor harvests could not be anticipated. Nature had always been unpredictable. But, however capricious nature was, life would have been a great deal harsher if work and social discipline had not enabled Singapore to make economic progress. It was this economic progress that made increased wages possible, and so warded off hunger and privation, despite crop failures in grain-producing countries.

IX

A week later, the Prime Minister left for Japan for talks with Japanese leaders. During his stay in Tokyo, the Prime Minister met the Japanese Prime Minister, Mr. K. Tanaka, the Foreign Minister, Mr. M. Ohira, and other senior Government leaders for an exchange of views on the current world situation. In addition, the Prime Minister also met Mr. K. Uemura, the Chairman of the Japan Federation of Economic Organisations, and other important Japanese industrialists, to discuss matters of mutual interest. The Prime Minister was accompanied by Mrs. Lee, who launched a ship in Nagasaki named Neptune-World built by the Mitsubishi Heavy Industries for the World Neptune Shipping Investment Inc. This was the first vessel launched for the company which is a subsidiary of Singapore Neptune Orient Line.

At a press conference in Toyko, Lee was asked what influence Beijing had over the Chinese in Singapore. Lee replied that the state of relations between Beijing and Singapore was cordial and correct. "We have always maintained close economic relationships without diplomatic exchange of representatives, mainly because the British recognised the People's Republic of China in 1949 and they inherited all these state-owned banks of Nationalist China — the Bank of China, the Kwangtung Bank — and

155

several insurance companies, and so trade has gone on without the necessity to have embassies in Peking and Singapore. That there will be embassies between Peking and Singapore is absolutely inevitable because it is a matter of time before our neighbours, Singapore's neighbours, also wish to deal direct with Peking for both economic and political reasons. So in the same way as you feel suspicious that because Singapore is more than 75 per cent Chinese and the ambassador from Peking need not need an interpreter to speak to me or my colleagues, therefore, people feel that something is being said which they don't know about. Therefore suspicion is aroused. And therefore, I would like to give my neighbours the honour of being first in establishing relations.

"As for the influence that they can bring to bear on the Chinese in Singapore, I would categorise them in different layers. There is the older generation born in China, who have been in Singapore thirty, forty, fifty years. They have memories of their villages or their towns and a great deal of sentiment. They are the older generation and growing smaller in the percentage of voters in Singapore and of influence. The growing bulk of the population are born in Singapore, brought up in Singapore's schools, bilingual, learning both Chinese and English, and their interest is one which they will calculate and can calculate for themselves, namely that they are better off in Singapore with all the consumer products of the whole world at their disposal and within their purchasing power, so long as Japanese and West Europeans and Americans keep on helping us in our painful climb up the technological ladder than if they were given blue denim to make into rather sombre and hardwearing clothes. And in the long run, I have not the slightest doubts that they will calculate for themselves and reach decisions which are in their own interests, just as you would not expect the 'Neisay' or the 'Sunsay' in Brazil to be voting for Japanese interests. If they were only educated in Chinese and they have only access to Chinese literature from the People's Republic of China, then, of course, the influence would be considerable. But they are also educated, all of them, in English, and this gives them binocular vision, 3-D in colour, stereophonic sounds, and they can therefore see in depth. And if it were not so, I would not have been elected for four successive elections."

X

To strengthen mutual understanding and friendly relations between Indonesia and Singapore, the Prime Minister led a strong delegation to Jakarta on 25 May. The visit also provided the opportunity for talks between President Suharto and Lee Kuan Yew, and also for the signing of a border agreement between the two countries by the two Foreign Ministers.

At a State banquet, President Suharto welcomed the Prime Minister and spoke at length about the importance of ASEAN, of which both

Indonesia and Singapore were members. He said the friendship and co-operation of the two countries had been further emphasized that afternoon by the signing by the Foreign Ministers of the Border Agreement on Territorial Waters. Lee thanked the President for his warm welcome. He said he had expected to see a Djakarta vastly different from the one he last saw over a decade ago. Although he was psychologically prepared to see a modern metropolis taking shape, he was nevertheless impressed by the physical transformation. However, he was even more impressed by the transformation in the outlook and policies of the government of Indonesia under Suharto's leadership. "The emphasis you, Mr. President, have publicly placed on economic and social development has enhanced peace and stability for the whole region. You have courageously set out to accomplish these goals, knowing that they cannot be easily or quickly accomplished."

In retrospect, perhaps it had been as well that they had a few years to carefully and quietly reach the perception they had of each other. Lee said he and his colleagues knew how difficult it must have been "to have so firmly set your face against any easy way out of the economic and social problems which you inherited. Your different style we easily recognised. But it took us some time to realise how determined you were to mobilise the energies of over 120 million Indonesians and concentrate them into tapping the vast resources of over 3,000 major islands. Perhaps it was because of your quiet style, that we took some time to recognise that you and your government were establishing a rational and pragmatic series of policies to repair the ravages of the last war, and neglect of the economy for some twenty years after the war. But after the systematic dampening of politicking and the refusal to be deflected from your constructive line of action, we realised that a profound and fundamental change in direction had taken place. It was a turning-point in the long history of Indonesia, a turning towards construction and development, towards a better tomorrow for Indonesia."

On the other hand, Lee said he hoped that the past seven years might have enabled Suharto and his government to have a better understanding of Singapore; that the making of a fast buck, the absence of scruples in the pursuit of wealth, associated with merchant adventurers, is a caricature which bore no resemblance to the establishment in Singapore, "nor to the kind of society we have set out to build".

Further, he ventured to suggest that if Singapore were not Southeast Asian in orientation and instinctive reflexes, "we would not have found such an identity of approach to many of the major issues we discussed this afternoon. The swift and sudden changes in the international scene, following detente between America and China, and America and the Soviet Union, may well have left us at variance on how to meet and to adjust to these shifts in the international scene. I believe that our discussions this afternoon have brought us closer and enabled us to have a better understanding of our respective thinkings on the common problems that face us in Southeast Asia."

Lee recalled that since they had met in Lusaka nearly three years ago, quiet co-operation and co-ordination had been increasing between the two governments. It freed the discussions of unexpected difficulties or fundamental differences of opinion. He hoped those contacts would continue and broaden at all levels. It was in the interests of all to have the economies of ASEAN countries grow and prosper, adding to each other's economic and social well-being. Lee said he was confident that under Suharto's leadership, the Indonesian government and the Indonesian people would continue to make ever increasing progress. "Indeed, the peace and stability which you so painstakingly restored in Indonesia restored international confidence in the future of the region and generated greater economic activity for us all."

The joint communique said that the Heads of Government "noted with satisfaction, the increasing cordiality in the relations between the two countries" and "agreed to strengthen the trade and economic relations between them." The communique continued: "The President of the Republic of Indonesia explained to the Prime Minister of Singapore the Indonesian efforts to develop its own as well as regional resilience. In this context, the President of the Republic of Indonesia emphasised the significance of the archipelago principles to the concept of national resilience, particularly in order to maintain national unity and cohesion, political stability, economic progress and national security. The Prime Minister of Singapore was sympathetic to, and expressed his support for, the Indonesian efforts to strengthen its own national resilience as well as regional cohesiveness. He also appreciated the importance of the archipelago principles to Indonesia. The Prime Minister of Singapore explained the effort of nation building currently being pursued in Singapore in order to create a Singaporean national identity, and assured the President of the Republic of Indonesia that such an effort would contribute to stability and harmony in Southeast Asia. The President of the Republic of Indonesia expressed his appreciation for the effort of nation-building in Singapore and expressed his conviction that the Singapore nation will find its rightful place within the Southeast Asian context."

XI

On 21 July, the Prime Minister formally opened the National Stadium. "Let me say what we hope to achieve. We have invested nearly $30 million for the building, and over $20 million for the land, car parks and ancillary facilities. This $50 million will not produce any profits. In fact, we shall be lucky to get enough receipts to pay for the annual administrative and maintenance costs. In other words, we are putatively losing over $5 million a year, a 10 per cent return on $50 million per annum, and several millions more for annual depreciation. However, as a social investment, fully and

158

properly used, it can be made a great asset." People would be encouraged to watch, and then to personally take part in sporting activities. Healthy, wholesome exercise and recreation could make up for the passive entertainment which filled the lives of many people, the TV, cinemas, floor-shows and exhibitions. With a population of just over two million, "let us not waste time going especially out of our way to produce gold medallists, whether for Olympic, Asian or SEAP games. There are no national benefits from gold medallists for smaller countries. For the super powers, with large populations, superiority in sports is national propaganda to persuade other people of the superiority of their competing political systems. But it is foolish and wasteful for the smaller countries to do this."

From time to time, Singapore would throw up a few natural record-breakers. But, warned Lee, any Olympic sports council member, or an affiliate club, which sets out to persuade above-average sportsmen or sportswomen to devote the best years of their lives merely to training and becoming gold medallists, would find their zeal misplaced, and funds cut off. For they could do an injustice to these persons. First, they were unlikely to achieve world class. Second, what happened to record-breaking aspirants when their prime years were over? "We live an artificial city life. Too many people take the lift, briefly amble to a bus stop, and take another lift to work. Many do not make daily exercise a habit. Sports can help. This stadium should be used to encourage not just watching games, but, after watching, to engage in sports and athletics. Inter-school and inter-university semi-finals and finals for students can be held here. So also inter-constituency sports amongst the younger adults. And we should also encourage inter-constituency veterans' sports. Keeping fit is a lifelong exercise. Perhaps watching people keep fit may encourage others to do so."

From time to time, there would be spectacular, world-class, star-studded teams, clashing in this arena. They could show what some human beings could do, if they were born with the physical attributes — co-ordination of the eye and muscle — plus intense and professional training. "But let us not deceive ourselves that there are any credits for us in our trying to do this. Our best return is to generate healthy, vigorous exercise for the whole population, young and old, enhancing the valuable qualities we have — a keen, bright, educated people who will lead better and more satisfying lives if they are fit and healthy."

XII

The following day, the Prime Minister spoke at the opening of the Consumer Co-operative (WELCOME) in Toa Payoh. He said there had been several consumer co-operatives after the war in the late 1940s and early '50s. They all failed. Firstly, they did not have professional and efficient management. Secondly, wholesalers were not keen to break their own network of retailers. So they kept fashionable goods in great demand only for their retailers, withholding these goods from the co-ops. Thirdly, the co-op shop did not have enough support from the people. They then lacked the spirit of community effort to protect community interests. Lee said the WELCOME co-op supermarket must be different. Firstly, it was going to be efficiently managed just like any commercial supermarket — competitive prices, good display of items housewives want, strict control on shoplifting, and proper accounting to show a clear profit. This would attract more customers and many would join as co-op shareholders. Secondly, any wholesaler who withheld popular or fashionable goods in great demand from this co-op supermarket, to give it to his pet retail network, would be bucking not only the labour movement but also the government. Any goods found in any other supermarket could and would be found in this supermarket, if buyers wanted them. Thirdly, more people had taken to the co-op idea. In the next two to three years, given hard-headed management, buyers from this supermarket would get back 5 – 10 per cent of what they had spent in purchases.

For the government, there was one compelling reason why this supermarket must be a success. People always grumbled that between wholesalers, middlemen, and retailers, profiteering was going on. "We import rice, all staple foods, and almost all other foodstuffs. We have to pay the world market prices of these commodities. At present, wholesale prices have shot up, because there is a world-wide food shortage. Worse, there is a loss of confidence in paper money. Big companies in America, Western Europe and Japan are hedging against inflation by converting paper money into commodities, including perishable foodstuffs, pushing prices up further. Even pigs, chickens and eggs, which we produce, have gone slightly up. This is because their feedstuff comes from ricebran, maize, soybean cake and other animal feeds. Their prices have gone up with the world increase in food prices. If this supermarket is well-supported, and well-managed, we shall know what the wholesale price is, and what the retail price, with profit, can be. Then we shall have a yardstick to measure by how much other retailers are putting up prices. We shall know definitely whether they are profiteering, or whether they cannot get the goods at normal wholesale prices at which the supermarket buys, because of market manipulation, by wholesalers or other middlemen."

There were, however, some difficulties which this co-op supermarket must overcome. First, it could not give credit. The provision shopkeeper could, because he knew which of his customers were credit-worthy, and would pay their debts. Second, some small shopkeepers short-weighted their sales and made prices look cheaper. Third, shoplifting would eat into the profits of this co-op. NTUC's WELCOME must make sure that shoplifting be kept to a minimum by close surveillance, both through plain-clothes detectives, and closed circuit television. But these problems could be overcome. The small shopkeepers would find it increasingly difficult to compete against the supermarkets, because overhead costs were lower for the supermarkets. "So I advise these shopkeepers to get together and form their own supermarkets, or they will lose out. We have chosen Toa Payoh because the least number of small shopkeepers are affected. You will get more value for your money buying here. Further, you should also get a return of 5 – 10 per cent back every year on your purchases. And the more shares you buy into the Co-op the more you will get back."

XIII

At the opening of the new Raffles Institution on 28 July, Lee Kuan Yew said that nearly seven years earlier, he and his colleagues in the Cabinet had to decide whether to renovate Raffles Institution, reinforcing and rebuilding the inside but keeping the external structures of the buildings, or demolish these buildings and rebuild Raffles Institution on the same site, or build a new R.I. on a new site. Had they been stone buildings, architecturally unique and artistic, they might have been justified in refurbishing them at great cost. But they were not. The continual repair and maintenance would become increasingly uneconomic. There were too many old timber struts.

Rebuilding on the same site was uneconomic. The area had become part of the business centre, with heavy traffic. "Many of my colleagues in the Cabinet and I had been educated at the old Raffles Institution. It was a difficult, but, I believe, the right decision to move it to this site in Grange Road. It is a handsome site to resite a famous old school. It was in the suburbs. We thought traffic would be easier, though the traffic problem has increased even in Grange Road. In my days as a student, one advantage R.I. had over all other schools in Singapore was that it drew the best students from all the government primary schools throughout Singapore. A student got in on the basis of merit, not his father's status or wealth. It was student meritocracy. It brought together the best students from all segments of our society. I did not know then that I was to be in politics. But being in R.I. turned out to be an advantage. I got to know and to get along with boys, rich and poor, of various races and cultures, and not only from Singapore, but other parts of Southeast Asia. This quality R.I. must maintain."

Another feature of R.I. was its pride in consistently high performance. This was the result of bright pupils stimulating good teachers to give of their best effort. It was an educational institution of excellence. R.I.'s objective was to nurture the well-rounded individual — a scholar, a sportsman, an organiser — so that he could meet the problems and the challenges of his time. No education in any school, however good, in another part of the world, could teach a Singaporean to meet the problems of life in Singapore. Unfortunately, some wealthy parents, partly for reasons of social snobbery, believed they could buy their children a better future, by sending them to expensive private schools in Britain, America,

Australia, or elsewhere. But, in fact, they were doing their children great harm. If they wanted their children to emigrate to that country, that was another matter. But to be trained in one's teens, at a most impressionable age, in British schools geared to British society, or Australian schools designed for meeting Australia's evolving society, and then to come back to Singapore, was to be gravely handicapped. "We are forging a nation. It can only be done in Singapore, by Singaporeans, in the home, in our schools and in the armed forces. We are inculcating common values necessary for national survival. We are acquiring the will and the wherewithal, to advance, and to protect our national interests. A new generation is growing up, sharing a common experience, having more of a common perception of a common future, prepare to act jointly to protect its collective security and well-being. The most important years for the development of these attitudes are those in school and the armed forces." R.I. could, and would, make a valuable contribution to this end. The principal and teachers would inculcate values and disciplines that could make old Rafflesians proud of those who came after them, better prepared for their roles in a vastly different Singapore. The presence of so many distinguished old Rafflesians symbolised this continuity between the old and new R.I. R.I. must compete with other schools in training students not simply how to get on as individuals, but most important how to get on as a distinct people, able to care and fend for themselves.

XIV

At the Commonwealth Conference in Ottawa in August, the Prime Minister made two speeches and gave several television interviews and press conferences. In a long speech which covered many subjects, including the worth of the Commonwealth, Lee on 3 August, started off with a reference to a speech by the Prime Minister of Fiji. Lee said the Prime Minister of Fiji was searching for Shangri-la. "So are we. Fiji has a better chance of achieving it for its wonderful land. It is in the South Pacific. There may be some nuclear fallout, but there is no great contest for influence between the super and major powers in the vast expanse of the South Pacific. I am not so fortunately placed. Singapore is at the southern tip of Asia, the crossroads between the Pacific and Indian Oceans, the half-way point between Northern Asia and Southern Australasia, and a key communications centre. It is not due to any special virtue or attractiveness of my people that we receive considerable attention from the Americans, the Soviet Union, the Chinese and the Europeans, who were first there. I hope they will continue to be interested and may add to a more stable balance of influence. I have to face reality, otherwise I must perish. I too like to have Singapore turned into a Shangri-la with a tranquil Indian Ocean and a Pacific Ocean, pacific in the literal sense of the word."

Détente between America and China, America and the Soviets, had reduced the dangers of nuclear and even conventional war between America and the Soviet Union, and America and China. The Chinese were not yet convinced that the changed situation had lessened the danger of a pre-emptive nuclear strike on them by the Soviets. However, the contest for influence and supremacy still continued in Southeast Asia, especially between the Soviet Union and China. The Soviet Union had a growing fleet of modern naval vessels. "Nothing we can say or do here in Ottawa can or will exclude the Soviet navy from the Indian Ocean, the Straits of the Archipelago, including the Straits of Malacca, and the South China Sea. Nor can the Japanese prevent them from sailing through the Inland Sea of Japan up to Vladivostok. These are the facts of life. And lest we forgot, the nuclear-powered aircraft carrier, the *USS Enterprise*, sailed through the Straits of Malacca into the Bay of Bengal at the time when Pakistani troops were retreating from the Indian Armed Forces."

When the Prime Minister of Australia said that because Singapore had a large ethnic Chinese population, the Soviet ships could not come to Singapore, the Soviet Union immediately diverted four Soviet tenders, feeder ships, to Singapore for repairs, to see whether Singaporeans were Chinese or Singaporeans. "We repaired them. I would ask him not to provoke the Soviets, for the next time they will send, not a feeder ship, but a missile destroyer or even a nuclear vessel. The fact is, as the President of Tanzania has said, when elephants fight, the grass suffers. The thought occurred to me that when elephants flirt, the grass also suffers. And when they make love, it is disastrous."

In mid-1971, after Mr. Nixon's dramatic broadcast that he was to visit China, he announced a visit to the Soviet Union and he bombed Hanoi and mined Haiphong when the North Vietnamese launched their attack in the spring of 1972. Nevertheless, he received the full red carpet treatment in Moscow. This had become, what the Americans would call, a different ball game. "It has repercussions for all of us here. It has been suggested that the Americans allowed the Soviets to catch up and reach nuclear parity in order that there could be a successful SALT Agreement. Perhaps, one day, both the Americans and the Soviet Union will be wise enough to allow China to reach parity. Then, and only then, will China be a party of any SALT Agreement."

Indo-China, next to the Middle East, was the most troubled part of the world, with all the potentials for conflict. The Soviet Union, for its own reasons, had decided to mute the dangers of violence in the Middle East, so that at least it would not be drawn into collision with America. The Soviet Union wanted American technology, American wheat, the good things in life. How long that phase would stay, no one knew. China, for its own reasons, also wanted détente with America. Then it would have only one front. China also wanted friends all over the world to outdo and isolate the Soviet Union. China openly exhorted the EEC to succeed. Then the Soviet Union would be kept busy in the West and have two fronts to keep it busy.

Lee said: "This big power game is acute in Southeast Asia. We are trapped in the schemes of the great powers. There are two alternatives for us. One, to create a Shangri-la in our minds. The ASEAN countries, Indonesia, Malaysia, the Philippines, Singapore and Thailand, have asked, 'Please, can we have neutralisation? Can we have a zone of neutrality, guaranteed by the big powers?' " The only major power that responded was China, but China was not yet in a position to guarantee it. The other two which could guarantee it, the Soviet Union and America, had not responded. "So we are whistling in the dark, through the cemetery of Indo-China. We have to guess what China's willingness to guarantee neutrality will be when it has a blue water fleet that can police the Straits of Southeast Asia, the South China Sea and the Indian Ocean."

Lee warned that collapse in Indo-China would bring advanced threat of guerilla insurgency to Singapore's doorsteps by way of Thailand and West Malaysia. He did not ask his colleagues from Australia, or Britain, or New Zealand to defend Singapore from this. They could not. This had been painfully demonstrated in Vietnam. "This problem we will face ourselves."

Lee said he disagreed with the Chairman's proposition that because the major and superpowers had eased their relations with each other, therefore, the world was safer and, by implication, Singapore was safer. "On the contrary, I am in a more uncomfortable position. I believe even the middle powers of Western Europe are concerned, though they do not show it. The Europeans had to take a public position in matters such as MBFR (Mutually Balanced Force Reductions). Soviet forces go back five hundred miles. They could be back in a matter of hours. American forces go back 4,000 miles, three thousand five hundred of it, the waters of the Atlantic. This could mean the gradual Finlandisation of Europe." There were ABMs around Moscow and around Washington, as a result of the SALT Agreement. Estimates were that America and the Soviet Union had over 2,500 nuclear warheads. Britain say, had fifty. When it really came to the crunch, eye-ball to eye-ball, one had over 2,500 and the other, fifty missiles. Could they really use it against Soviet cities without ABMs? This was the problem for the West European powers.

"But what of us? We all want to live in peace. Let us all destroy offensive weapons and only have defensive weapons for internal security. But where is the dividing line between offensive hardware and defensive hardware? Australia has given a squadron of Sabres to our friends, the Malaysians, and another squadron of Sabres to our friends, the Indonesians. I believe they are defensive. But I am forced to buy from Britain two defensive squadrons of Hunters. But they are old, second generation, refurbished aircraft. They will augment our joint defensive capability. But what good are these aircraft against the most likely threat of guerilla insurgency. They are in the jungles with M-16s, hand-launched rockets and mortars. The Vietcong, at the height of the war, bogged down

164

560,000 American troops, one brigade of Australians, one company of New Zealanders, 50,000 Koreans, Thais and Filipinos. So Shangri-la is not for Southeast Asia, unless one seeks the poppy variety."

Lee thought that the longer-term threat to the peace and security was the widening disparity between the wealthy and the poor. The whites were the wealthy, and the non-whites were the poor. The only exceptions were the Japanese and the oil-rich states. This was going to be so for a long time. "Whether we meet at UNCTAD, GATT, the UN or Commonwealth meetings, the barely concealed feeling is the unfairness of it all. With every passing year, short of a fundamental change in human nature, this disparity will widen. Many countries may never take off at all. When you compound race with poverty, then I believe, we have got the makings of complicated problems."

Southern Africa had become the best arena for conflict. For the moment the South African Whites had become more wealthy and more powerful. "But the day the Soviet Union and China decide that it is time to cut down the West, this is the safest and cheapest way." All they needed to do was to supply more and more weapons. And the Africans would learn to use more and more sophisticated ones. Many Africans would die. But die they must if they wanted to have justice in Rhodesia, South Africa and the Portuguese colonies. The price was terrible. And it would not be Soviets or Chinese who would die. "We all want peaceful solutions. But there are situations where peaceful solutions are pipe dreams."

Developing nations needed all their trained talent and skills to jack up their societies. The Australians now said they would let in Asians. But it was professionally trained Asians they wanted, professional expertise. "I think it is rather unkind. Unless we can have a clear understanding of our respective positions, however good Australian Universities may be, we cannot send our students there. We cannot afford to lose them. We have to pull ourselves up by our bootstraps. We live in the same part of the world as Australia. That Australia is wealthy, I know only too well. We are much poorer but we want to be less poor. Is it not possible to help us, not just by token words but by sincere and hard projects like an integrated iron and steel complex which can benefit the whole region. Why not send Australian iron ore and coke to Indonesia to be smelted? Why not bring Japanese expertise, better and cheaper than most in the developed world? The under-developed countries of Southeast Asia can make the other products, steel plate, jigs, tools and dies and so on. One integrated regional project like that will make the Australian slogan 'We are part of Asia' more than a slogan."

At the end of the conference, the BBC interviewed, separately, both Mr. Gough Whitlam, the Australian Prime Minister, and Lee about the comment each had made about the other in the conference. Whitlam said that Lee and Heath, the British Prime Minister, were the last two Conservative leaders left. Whitlam also wondered why the Singapore Prime Minister had not sent troops to Vietnam if he was so concerned about security in Southeast Asia. Further, if Singapore was so keen to get its nationals back from Australia for military service, why not ask for them to be extradited?

Lee told the BBC that he was amused to find himself in the same class as Ted Heath. As for sending troops to Vietnam why should he, he asked. "I thought the intervention in Vietnam by Foster Dulles was a mistake. But the mistake having been committed, it affected the whole of Southeast Asia, and not to go through with it, having dug their toes in, in Vietnam, to scuttle out meant to jeopardise the rest of us in Southeast Asia."

As for Whitlam's suggestion that he should extradite Singapore students, Lee said he was quite happy to do that, but the Australian Immigration Minister would not permit him to do so. Lee explained that trained manpower was Singapore's only precious natural resource — the good marketing man, the manager, the engineer — those were the types the Australian Prime Minister wanted. "If he wants the chaps on the factory floor we can send him thousands of them." Lee agreed with the BBC interviewer that he preferred to have these face-to-face confrontations in a Commonwealth Conference than in the mass media.

Before the conference ended, Lee made a contribution to the discussion on Intra-Commonwealth Relations. He said that if the British had not been so immersed and imbued with their sense of destiny as an overseas nation, a people who found adventure and greatness overseas, founded civilisations in North America, perhaps none of the Prime Ministers would that day be gathered in Ottawa. "We are here, in a way, to decide whether such further meetings are to have such relevance. It is useful having Heads of Government meet. But it could become as disadvantageous as holding Olympic Games. People used to make bids for Olympic games, but they discovered it was not worth it. That is the crux of what intra-commonwealth relations is about. Is it worth it?" Lee thought there were the following advantages: there were no other forums, whether the UN, OAU, ASEAN, the Caribbean Grouping, OAS, ASPAC (for East Asia, now in cold storage), where diverse peoples from al the continents of the world could be brought together. There had been changes. "Instead of our lines all going to London we are having lines with our immediate neighbours. And most important, lines to Washington, Moscow, Brussels, Peking, Tokyo, for these are the centres where the big decisions made are going to affect us all, whether we like it or not."

Commonwealth countries shared several qualities which none of the other organisations had. "When we meet at other conferences we have got to put earphones on. In the EEC, they used to speak French as their working language. Now with the British, Danes and the Irish in as members, more members speak English than French. But the key people make it a point of speaking French, just as they do in Quebec, even though they speak perfect English. However, we do not pretend that we do not speak English. We all do. The direct exchanges have helped in this last week of discussions. We got to know each other better since we last met.

We felt the mood of this conference. If we go on in this constructive vein, some governments will find it politically worthwhile to have another meeting in two years' time. I hope this time, it will be at a climatically more congenial time of year. We were not in favour of August. Neither were my friends from Jamaica and Britain. But we came, nevertheless. Because we hoped it would be useful, that perhaps this conference may not be the last. If it has to be, let us give it a decent burial. But I think that would be a pity. It is because there are all these new regional groupings which will pull us away from each other (when we meet in stylish settings like the non-aligned summits in Belgrade, Lusaka, now in Algiers, and in September, the UN), that we should keep on this regular informal meeting of minds of Heads of Government. At other forums, we tend to make set speeches, designed to impress, designed to gather votes. They are not really conducive to understanding the other persons's point of view. This is one forum where we can speak frankly and generate least rancour. We can keep this up. We have got a group, not so intimate as it used to be when it was a white five. Or even after it became sixteen or seventeen. The next time we meet, we shall have two more, to make thirty-four Heads of Government. Nevertheless, we have the same backgrounds, use the same terms of reference. We inherited basic institutions and concepts of government and society. We understand each other better than any other group do. We use the same diction and concepts. It does not mean that we all stay put. We are all evolving and discovering our own personalities. Just following the forms and institutions of the British, or the Canadians, or the Australians or New Zealanders, or God forbid, of South Africa, is not what will bring about cohesive societies and effective government to raise our people's standards of life. For this generation, we have all been brought up in similar institutions, with ideas and ideals which make it possible for us to speak with an informality and intimacy which is not possible elsewhere. Whether our successors can keep this up is another matter. But if we are going to use this as a forum to harangue and harass each other, then what is the purpose of another meeting?''

Lee thought that they would all be going to be more and more preoccupied with regional groupings. There was a grave danger in this for all small and middle countries. The big economic blocs of the non-communist world, wealthy and powerful — America, the EEC, Japan — were going to come to terms with each other. They had to. They had preserved peace, stability, and prosperity for themselves. The British felt the pinch of Japanese ball bearings and TV sets. And on shipping, the whole of Europe was being pushed against the wall by Japan. The Europeans just could not compete against the efficiency of the Japanese shipbuilding industry except in specialised vessels with a higher innovative content. But if they and the Americans shut off Japan, there would be big trouble. Japan's trade with Southeast Asia was very small — only 12 per cent of her total exports, and imports only 8 per cent of total imports. Japan's productive capacity was for the whole world. If Japan was cut off she would have to make up her mind, either to go with the Soviet Union or China. And if it was going to be along race lines, then this might become far from a peaceful world.

Lee said he made no apologies for being in Singapore. "My great grandfather went there as a coolie, seeking the jackpot at the end of the rainbow. He found a small one. He went back. But his wife and children did not. So I am in Singapore. But we helped build a city out of a mud flat. We did not kill any Red Indians. We did not kill any Aborigines. We want to be friends with all, those who were there and those who migrated there in the British period. We want to help development, and not only in our immediate region. It is this dialogue which may make the Commonwealth a worthwhile association after empire. Marlborough House was bequeathed by the British, in the expectation that the Commonwealth would amplify Britain's voice in world affairs. It is a very experienced voice as those of us who have had dealings with her know so well. Unfortunately, she has no longer got the economic strength to use effectively the accumulation of wisdom over three and a half centuries of empire. The Commonwealth has not got the cohesiveness of the French community because the French hand out aid and subvention. It is not the associate status of the associated states that keeps them in the EEC. It is because France makes it worth their while to vote for France in world forums, like the UN. The ironic tragedy for Britain was that she left us with effective institutions that have enabled many of us to become viable and we have voted in accordance with our wishes against Britain on crucial issues. Compare this to the French community. When there is a revolt in Chad, the French foreign legion helped to keep the revolt down. So they know who their friend is. I think I know who my friends here are. I can speak frankly and forcefully, only because I know Ted Heath, Gough Whitlam, Norman Kirk, Pierre Trudeau and other leaders well. And in this forum the others understand what we are talking about. Perhaps we shall go back feeling only subjectively not only better. But we shall also mull over what has been said. If we make the Commonwealth valuable for this kind of interchange, it is something one day which even the British will find it to their interests to help sustain. I was asked yesterday whether Britain had not deliberately downgraded the Commonwealth. I said benign neglect was appropriate. For in Britain, there is still considerable sentiment for the Commonwealth, this aftermath of empire. We are peoples whom they had used for their interests. Two million Indians fought and thousands died in the last war. There are monuments in Ottawa, Canberra, Wellington, and Singapore for people who died in two wars which did not directly concern them. The British have no legal obligations. They have been scrubbed off with independence. But we are all human beings at the end of the day and that is why we are here. And because we are human beings temporarily endowed with powers which affect the lives of many other human beings, perhaps if we understand each other's problems and difficulties, we may help each other and make for a slightly better world. That, I hope, will be the result of this conference."

XV

Lee was away from Singapore on National Day, but he spoke at a National Day rally at the National Theatre on 26 August. He said that since the beginning of 1973, large parts of the world had been beset by shortages of grain and other foodstuffs, leading to very high food prices. Inflation and monetary problems in America and several countries of Western Europe had made for uncertainties, leading to wildly fluctuating parities of major currencies. This had been primarily caused by inflation and loss of confidence in the American dollar. The problem was compounded by the Watergate crisis. It did not help the American Administration in taking effective action to stabilise the American economy and strengthen the dollar. Because of uncertainties over the value of floating currencies, industrialists, financiers and traders in the developed countries hedged against all paper currencies by buying into commodities. This led to a steep rise in the prices of commodities, both agricultural products and minerals. For a long time, the commodity producers of the Third World suffered. As the industrial goods they imported cost more and more, the raw materials they produced and exported were sold for less and less. It was ironic that only when financiers and industrialists were caught in their own inflation and temporarily lost confidence in their own paper money, that prices of commodities went up. Manufacturers and speculators had been buying forward in commodities, i.e. buying commodities even before they were needed or ready to be handed over.

This mood, for the first time in several decades, reversed the unfavourable position of commodity-producing countries. Of course when the international currency crises were sorted out, hedging in commodities would stop. Then commodity prices would go down again. But some experts believed that in several items, prices might not go down to such low levels as in the past. Meanwhile, cocoa has gone up three times, helping countries like Ghana. Copper had doubled in price in the past year. Rubber nearly doubled in price this year, and palm oil up two and a half times. All countries had been very hard-hit by the sharp increase in the prices of food. No one, at the end of last year, foresaw the disastrous crop failures, especially in rice. This had made the world market price go up between two to two and a half times. As Singapore had no significant agricultural sector in grains, the Republic was affected by the world prices of grains, mutton and beef and other imported foods.

"It was unfortunate that just at the time we were about to enjoy the increased benefits of several years of hard work, such a large part of our wage increases have had to go in higher food prices. And, with the big floods now in Pakistan and India, the rice situation may not go back to normal before the 1974 harvests. But, perhaps, it is worth reminding ourselves how fortunate we have been that, because of industrialisation and the development of physical and brain services in Singapore, we have had the foreign exchange to pay for our needs. No one has suffered starvation or mulnutrition. But it underlines the importance of our staying keen and efficient. We cannot afford to slacken and become easy-going. For once we are soft or disorganised, we will never be able to survive world crises of the kind the world is presently facing — food shortages, currency uncertainties, and, if the crisis in America is prolonged, a danger of a possible down-turn in international trade. Such a recession will affect the whole world."

On the other hand, if the situation improved and monetary and trade problems were resolved, Singapore would stand very much to benefit. For when confidence in paper currencies was restored as new currency exchange rate regulations were settled, commodity prices would come down, whilst industrial and servicing sectors would surge forward. "We must stay well-organised, keen and hardworking, to be able to take advantage of an upturn in international trade, especially in manufactured products, when the present troubled political and financial situation is settled. By then, prices of basic foods like rice should go down dramatically with normal harvests. In this way, we can ride over the presently rough economic conditions and, gradually, but steadily, raise our real living standards."

XVI

On 16 September, the fifteenth group of officer cadets passed out at SAFTI, the Singapore Armed Forces Training Institute. Lee spoke at the commissioning parade. He observed that some who started the course including university graduates, had not passed, although others with Higher School Certificates and School Certificates had. Academic grading did not coincide with the attributes required of an officer — leadership, initiative, responsibility and character, calm and collected in an unexpected situation. It could be that the tests were not perfect. It could also be that standards were set on the high side. It was necessary from time to time that the methods of instruction, examination and grading be reviewed. Subjective personal biases must be reduced to a minimum. For instance, those with problems over language of commands must be given extra tuition and time to adjust and pick up the confidence to articulate their thoughts. Those who had the qualifications, but did not make the grade as officers, were put at a disadvantage. They had to overcome the natural resistance of employers, who would want to know why they did not become officers. It was not an insurmountable obstacle, but an unnecessary one, particularly if they could have made it either by trying harder, or by more effective instruction. However, if SAFTI instructors and assessors were right, and qualities of leadership were lacking, they would never be more than functionaries anyway.

"For those of you who have made it, and are passing out today, you will now have to practise the art of leadership. Many of you will now be sent to take charge of raw recruits, to train them, as you yourselves were once trained. You will discover that the first problem is effective communication. You must be simple, clear, to be easily understood. You have to win the confidence of the men in your charge. You must exercise authority without being authoritarian. And if you also convince them that you have their welfare and progress at heart, then you stand a good chance of becoming a good leader. No test, examination, observation or trial can be the same as the actual task of having to take charge of men, instilling confidence, in your subordinates, for your leadership, and in your superiors for your judgement. I wish you well for the future."

XVII

That day, 16 September, Lee celebrated his fiftieth birthday. He had been continuously in office, as Prime Minister, since 1959. In his honour, the National Trades Union Congress (NTUC) produced a book *Towards Tomorrow*, dedicated to him. It was presented to him at a dinner at the Mandarin Hotel. The President was among the guests.

Accepting the book, Lee admitted that he usually found personal occasions in his honour somewhat embarrassing. He always felt the compliments should be for someone else present and subconsciously he looked around the table. On this occasion he could not avoid the spotlight. He was moved by the sincerity of the felicitations from friends and colleagues who, at the instigation of Devan Nair, had contributed to the book. He thanked them all, those who had organised, and those who graced the occasion by their presence. He was grateful that the evening's proceedings had not become an exercise in mutual back-slapping. It would not have been in keeping with their forms and styles. The worth of a man's contribution to society could be objectively judged only after his life-time. Hence, the wise British convention of putting up statues of their national heroes only after they had departed from the scene. Even then, they made mistakes. "But I promise Devan Nair that I shall try my best not to give him reasons to regret the compliments he has paid me. He and I, and the group of men now in their late forties and fifties, comprised the original band who prepared the ideological and the mass foundations of the PAP, before its inauguration in 1954. We were as much the product of our times, as of our visceral and cerebral compulsions. We had lived through a momentous period of human history, when we were young enough not to be emotionally and psychologically incapacitated by the shock of the war, and the collapse of then conventional values and wisdom. We saw the old colonial society crumble under the attack of the then much under-rated Japanese. We survived the ordeal of occupation. But we had sufficient resilience to rise to the challenge after the war, to want to assume leader-

171

ship at a time when it seemed so obviously foolhardy to do so. The strains and stresses before and after we took office in June 1959 could so easily have ripped us apart, and torn our determination and cohesion to pieces. We held, and stayed as a team because we had convictions. We believed we had a cause worth fighting and dying for.''

And because together they went through some fearful crises, and skirted near disasters, they had forged bonds of trust and camaraderie. Successive crises also demonstrated that both the leaders and the people were undaunted by the prospect of disaster. Indeed, they had drawn on their reserves of courage and strength when confronted with crises, and put in that extra effort to overcome it. This trust and confidence between the leadership and the people, grown out of common travail, was one of their most precious assets. "We must nurture it and pass as much of it on as is possible to our successors.''

With every passing year, a generation was growing up that took for granted what were only dreams two decades ago. However, all the wonders and marvels of modern technology notwithstanding, he doubted if full employment, rising real wages and higher consumption, in a better environment, could be sustained without real effort and social discipline. They were not the natural course of things, and certainly could not be achieved, unless population growth was rapidly choked down. There were times when, Lee said, he got glimpses of the challenges facing the next generation. "I believe they will be even greater than those we have faced. In one finite world, where national ambitions can often be achieved only at the expense of the national interests of others, it requires great qualities of leadership, indeed of statesmanship, magnanimity and breadth of vision to see ourselves and our neighbours in one whole human society. More and more, the next generation will have to seek goals which are not only satisfying for themselves, but which will also leave open similar goals to be achieved by their neighbours.'' With the passing of time, people must slowly recognise that the traditional national hero was inadequate. Whether it was the centurion of the Roman legions, or the fighter pilot of World War I, or national leaders like Churchill, Roosevelt, de Gaulle, Lenin, Stalin or Mao, it was no longer enough to be cast in the mould of national heroes. If the world was to survive, there must be world heroes, people who had greater vision and feeling for mankind, and not just their own national segment of it.

It was not enough that the leaders of the great powers should lessen the dangers of nuclear conflict between themselves, whilst they competed for power, wealth and influence over other countries of the world, and sometimes at other people's expense. In a world shrunken by scientific and technological advances, made inter-dependent by trade and travel, the export of ideas and ideologies, and also machinery for production and destruction, rivalries based on national-ethnic-cultural-religious chauvinisms could be as destructive and futile as conflicts of differing ideological-economic-political systems. Every region of the world, to thrive and to prosper, must throw up leaders able to see beyond contemporary and conventional horizons. However, the immediate task was to widen the basis upon which rested the security and economic well-being of Singapore and Singaporeans. "We must do this without hampering similar efforts by our neighbours. Indeed, where co-operation is possible, we should help advance their interests as we advance our own."

The past was not pre-ordained. Nor was the future. There were as many unexpected problems ahead, as there were in the past. Those who were prepared to face their problems, those who educated and trained their people to meet unexpected hardships with quiet courage and resolution, were the people who deserved to thrive and to prosper. "In responding to the toast, may I express my hope that the people of Singapore will deserve a place for themselves."

XVIII

On 4 October, the Prime Minister took part in a conference organised by *The Financial Times* on "Business Opportunities In The Pacific Basin". He said it was with some reservations that he proffered his thoughts. First, it was a vast area, the eastern rim of which was not well-represented at the Conference. There were no Canadians, or Latin Americans. Second, for the countries on the western rim, they had heard speakers, better qualified than he was, on business opportunities, ranging from Japan, Taiwan, Hong Kong, Thailand, Malaysia, Indonesia, the Philippines and Australia. They were people whose work and experience had given them a keen sense to pick up opportunities for profitable commerical or industrial enterprise. A large number of participants were from Europe. Lee hoped that as a result of the conference, their interest in this part of the world was rekindled. "You must have discovered that Southeast Asia would welcome greater economic and commercial collaboration with the EEC to balance the growing trade with, and investments from, the US and Japan."

Lee produced tables showing how EEC and Japanese trade with Southeast Asia was expanding. The graph illustrating Southeast Asia's trade with the EEC was like a DC-3 taking off, that with America, like a second-generation jet, and that with Japan, almost like a STOL. So it was with new investments, post-independence. The Americans were leading, followed by the Japanese. He expected the Japanese to overtake the Americans. Both in trade and in new investments, the EEC of the Six and now of the Nine were lagging behind the Americans and the Japanese. Perhaps it took some time to recover from the aftermath of empire. First, there was the preoccupation with Europe and with each other in the EEC. Second, and more pertinent, the Europeans had not trained a post-World War II generation who could seize the opportunities of the Pacific Basin, especially in East and Southeast Asia. Individually, the countries of

173

Western Europe had no longer the economic weight to compete against the US or Japan in Southeast Asia. But together, the EEC could match either of them — provided the EEC had the desire to widen her horizons beyond the Mediterranean and Africa. Besides the GSP concessions to developing countries, there could be agreements for commercial and economic co-operation to help the flow of investments, machinery and know-how from Europe to Southeast Asia, and of raw materials and simpler manufacture from Southeast Asia to Europe.

It was accepted that the Pacific Ocean was an integrator, now that ocean transport had become cheaper with bigger and bigger ships requiring smaller and smaller crews. It was already cheaper to ship cars from Tokyo to San Francisco than to send them from Detroit to San Francisco. In cost terms, transportation across the Pacific was not much greater than the transportation costs across the Atlantic. Telephone communications had become cheaper with the satellite. Indeed, it was as cheap to make a call from Bogota to Tokyo, as it was from Singapore to Tokyo. And if supersonic aircraft overcame its population and range problems, it would be another great integrator for the Pacific Basin countries, more so than for countries washed by the Atlantic.

The industrial dynamo of the Western Pacific was Japan. But the country with the greatest potential for growth was the People's Republic of China. "I also have a table which shows how ridiculously small China's external trade was in 1970. With a population of 760 million, an area of over nine and a half million sq. km., a GNP of nearly US$100 billion, China had in 1970 an external trade of US$4.2 million, compared with Hong Kong's US$5.4 billion for the same year, with a population of 4 million in 1,000 sq. km. and with a GNP of US$2.5 billion." China appeared to be seeking her technology from the widest spread of competitors, between Japan, America and Western Europe. In the higher technologies, Western Europe might be a more willing supplier of capital equipment and know-how than either her nearer neighbour, Japan, or the United States.

If transportation costs had not inhibited Japanese exports to Europe, neither should they hinder European exports to Japan, China and Southeast Asia, through which the ships must pass, in any case. It was the search for this trade with fabulous Cathay that made the British come to Southeast Asia and establish forward bases in Penang, Singapore and Hong Kong. Earlier, the Portuguese had established themselves in Formosa and Macao. And when the Suez Canal was re-opened, as eventually it must be, this trade would receive a greater boost than when the Canal was opened in 1869. Nearer to Singapore were the ASEAN countries and Indo-China. The growth rates of ASEAN countries were much higher than those for the Indian sub-continent, or for most of the countries of Africa other than the oil producers. The annual average per capita rate of growth ranged from 7 per cent for 1965 – 70 for Indonesia (at constant prices) to 7.8 per cent for the Philippines, 3.9 per cent for Malaysia (before the sharp rise in commodity prices for 1973), 6.8 per cent for Thailand, and 11.4 per cent for Singapore. The per capita GNP for ASEAN countries was more than twice that for African countries. Some sample figures from the latest World Bank report for 1973, released in Nairobi, were:

Mali	..	US$70
Tanzania	..	US$110
Nigeria	..	US$140
Kenya	..	US$160
Senegal	..	US$240
Indonesia	..	US$80
Thailand	..	$210
Philippines	..	US$240
Malaysia	..	US$400

The biggest plus in favour of rapid development in Southeast Asia was the political climate. Southeast Asia had learnt the terrible lessons of conflict. The ruin and devastation that overwhelmed both North and South Vietnam, Laos and Cambodia, were in striking contrast to the steady and rapid progress of Thailand, Malaysia and Singapore. This was very much in the consciousness of the leaders and of the peoples of the countries in Southeast Asia. Then there was the experience of the Indonesian people. After nearly twenty profligate years under the late Dr. Sukarno, Indonesia, after painful beginnings, had now set course for economic development, seeking investments and rapid growth.

It was conceivable that in some thirty years, Southeast Asians might have become relatively so prosperous that they might have afforded themselves the luxury of narrow nationalism, and turned against the multinationals which had brought with them higher technology and made for better standards of life. But for the next thirty years, it might well serve Southeast Asia's interest to have those that had made the grade, berate and even ill-treat the multinationals. This might make them turn to Southeast Asia. Bad news for the multinationals in Australia, as their shares, both on the Australian and British stock markets, went down, might be good for the countries in Southeast Asia. And it might also help Latin America, despite their proneness to coups and military juntas. For the Japanese would prudently seek alternative sources for raw materials, particularly minerals. "And, in a different context, every time I read of American or European workers wanting more pay for less hours in a four-day week, in order to have a longer weekend to enjoy their higher pay, I am cheered. For this is better than aid. It means that the European entrepreneurs will have to seek out stable areas of the world where workers are keen and industrious, to expand their production, at lower wage costs. Only the Japanese have not as yet got into this more-pay-less-work-more-leisure syndrome. But one must not rule out this possibility, however remote it may seem for the time being."

175

To sum up, the prospect for stability and rapid growth was more than fair on the western rim of the Pacific Basin. For Southeast Asia in particular, inputs of capital and technology from Japan, America, and Western Europe would increase this rate of growth. There were only two riders which clouded the horizon. The first was population growth. It was still too high. Most countries in Southeast Asia had population growth rates of between 2½ per cent to 3½ per cent. This did not bode well for long-term economic progress and political stability. However, the trend might change as education became more widespread and the benefits of economic growth flowed from the towns into the rural areas. The second was the problem of guerilla insurgency. It was difficult to predict the future. However, even if Cambodia did grow neutralist or pro-communist, South Vietnam might still be standing. And if the Thais were given time, on Mr. Nixon's Guam Doctrine of economic and military aid for countries to defend themselves, Thailand should uphold her independence without compromise. "A Chinese proverb says: *Sai wung shih ma, yen chih huo fu*. Literally, it means: old man of frontier lost horse, who knows, misfortune or good fortune? He lost his horse, a misfortune. But then his horse came back, accompanied by another horse, good fortune. His son mounted the new horse, fell and broke his thigh, another misfortune. Because of this injury, he missed a battle in which his friends were slain. Of course, this is a most non-Marxist, pro-Maoist proverb. But that does not invalidate its philosophical basis. If I could elaborate on the proverb, the son, from this experience, learnt prudence, without losing his nerve. For those of you who have, like the son of the old man of the frontier, learnt from past experience, and acquired perception, prudence and judgement without losing the gumption to take calculated risks, there are opportunities to be seized, for fortune awaits the enterprising in this part of the Pacific Basin."

XIX

At a variety show presented by an athletic association on 19 October, the Prime Minister took the opportunity to warn parents against demanding too much of their children. The young had to be nurtured, encouraged, restrained and taught, to prepare them to meet the future. But parents were prone to two mistakes. First, because of the highly competitive society and the intense nature of most of the people, some parents pushed their children too hard to achieve success. Such parents believed success in examinations could be achieved by their children through maximum effort, regardless of what their children could accomplish. Thus considerable numbers of young boys and girls had been forced beyond the limits of their ability and endurance. Students and young people had even committed suicide, some on the eve of examinations, others after the results were out. And for every suicide, there were many others who had their personalities cracked under excessive pressure to score well.

Each child had his or her own gifts. These gifts might not be in academic matters. Parents must carefully judge what their children's limits were. Their teachers could usually help them decide this. Where a child was able but lazy, then he needed to, and should, be pushed. But never push a hard worker to go beyond his limits. At the other extreme were parents who had a difficult time in their youth, but had succeeded in life. They wanted to give their children all the things they themselves had missed when young — expensive toys, watches, clothes, too much pocket money, outings at expensive restaurants, expensive holidays abroad before they were old enough to appreciate what they saw on their travels. They ended up with spoilt children.

Life in any society, especially in a highly urbanised, industrial and commercial setting like Singapore, demanded constraints, resolve and a philosophical approach to one's share of success and failure. The young had to be encouraged to do their best. They had to be taught self-discipline and self-restraint, and to eschew self-indulgence. Every boy or girl had his or her own special combination of attributes and capacities. Parents must ensure that the child was encouraged to develop to the best of his or her ability. But no one could do more than his best. Whatever might be the best that a child was capable of, that was what he or she had got to learn to do with in life. Most important of all, parents should have small families. Two was enough. In fact, many families could barely afford to adequately feed and bring up two children. Each child needed a balanced diet, proper care and adequate educational toys and facilities before kindergarten and school to develop and become well-trained and educated. "Then we will have a better equipped generation capable of taking Singapore to a higher level of economic, intellectual and cultural achievement."

XX

"Deepavali and the other religious festivals in Singapore remind us of the need to be a tolerant society," said Lee on 24 October. "From different cultural and ethnic origins, more common values will emerge over the years as a younger generation share a common experience. I wish all a Happy Deepavali."

Hari Raya Puasa followed shortly after. Said Lee: "Muslims, like Buddhists, Christians and others, in response to changing environmental conditions, are learning how to carry on the essence of their traditions, whilst adjusting the outward forms. As we rebuild Singapore, people move from villages and kampongs to high-rise new towns. Now Malays are asking for earlier resettlement. Our Malay Muslims have successfully adapted to new styles of living, including the way they celebrate their festivals. A tolerant and equable approach to changing living conditions has helped. I wish all Muslims in Singapore Selamat Hari Raya Aidilfitri."

XXI

On 30 October, the Prime Minister opened the 7th World Congress of the International Federation of Petroleum and Chemical Workers. Lee said that when he agreed to attend the opening, little did he know how grave the world energy problem would become. Before the latest war between the Arabs and Israelis, the outlook had been grim enough. With consumption rising much faster than new discoveries of oilfields, if consumption patterns went unchanged, known deposits of fossil oils would be exhausted by the first half of the next century. Price increases were inevitable. But no one could have forseen the pace at which they had taken place, in spasmodic fits of conferencing between the oil-producing countries and the oil companies, all of which were reconciled to regular revisions of agreements. And with each revision, the oil companies were left with a smaller share of the equity. Eventually, they would become just management and marketing consultants for the oil-producing countries. The last price increases to oil companies had already led to increases of over 30 per cent to consumers like Japan.

As if to underline the need for economy, apart from an increase in price, Arab oil countries had banned exports to the United States and Holland. And after cutting down immediately by about 10 per cent they had undertaken to cut down future production by at least 5 per cent per month, until a just and satisfactory solution to the troubles of the Middle East was found. All that had been achieved up to date was an in-place ceasefire, with United Nations peace-keeping forces being deployed to demarcate where those forces were. It looked as if the world, both the developed and developing parts of it, would be in for a period of increasing shortage of oil. A just and durable peace would require months of difficult and tortuous negotiations on how to implement UN Security Council Resolution 242 of 1967. For six years, from 1967 to 1973, no progress was made to define what constituted "secure and recognised boundaries" for Israel, in order to facilitate withdrawal from occupied Arab lands. When this problem was resolved, there was the more delicate task of reconciling the right of all countries in the area, including Israel, to peace "within secure and recognised boundaries", with that part of Resolution 242 which required a "just settlement of the refugee problem".

There was no shortage of ingenious minds which could work out a series of compromises which could be seen to implement Resolution 242 in all its parts, as called for by the American-Soviet sponsored resolution. The difficulty would be in finding the trust or faith required of the parties to the conflict to leave the past behind them, and move forward towards a constructive and peaceful future. For this was what the Israelis and the Arab peoples, including the Palestinians, must have in some measure, to make work any set of proposals to implement Resolution 242. Lee thought it might take many months, if not years, to reach the minimum levels of

178

trust, or faith, without which there could be little hope of a just and durable peace for Israel or the Arabs. Meanwhile, what were the consequences of the increasing scarcity and higher prices for oil on the economies of the industrialised and industrialising parts of the world? Increased costs of production or even diminished production? Was it possible for the non-industrial world to avoid being affected, by such increased costs and possibly diminished production of goods they imported from the industrialised countries? "I am sure many economists and other experts of governments are feeding varying sets of data into computerised mathematical models to find how their economies will be altered as a result of smaller oil supplies at higher prices. But I have not been able to read any reputable journal with any forecast of the repercussions of these developments. Perhaps no expert is willing to risk his reputation, or, if there is any such forecast, no journal is prepared to print it and risk its own standing."

Perhaps, out of "this imminent oil crisis that is coming upon us", a tremendous spurt would be given to research to bring other sources of energy into practical operation sooner than would have happened. And patterns of consumption of fossil-oil energy would also have to change permanently. Meanwhile, the great oil game for control of, or access to, oil in North Africa and the Middle East went on between the super-powers. The Soviet Union was independent of oil imports. The United States could, for the time being, get on without the import of Arab oil, which comprised some 8 per cent of her total consumption. Otherwise there would have been no ceasefire and continuing US-Soviet détente. But both super-powers were playing for longer-term stakes, which included Middle East oil, the Suez Canal and other areas of strategic importance. Even after the Arab-Israeli problems had been resolved, the problems of diminishing oil resources remained with all its implications in economics and politics. In the shadow of such events, the Marxist cry 'Workers of the world, unite', must sound hollow. "But perhaps the first object of your IFPCW, if less revolutionary, is worth soldiering on for: To support national and international action in the struggle against any kind of exploitation and oppression and to make international working class solidarity effective."

XXII

In November, the Prime Minister of Malaysia, Tun Abdul Razak, visited Singapore. Lee welcomed him at a dinner in his honour on 14 November. Lee recalled that it was one and a half years since his last visit to Kuala Lumpur. So many things had happened in the intervening period to make Razak's visit more than just a courtesy exchange of views. International events had moved at a dizzy speed, leaving the background, against which assessments were made more than a little uncertain and confused. "From détente, one would have expected a period of international tranquility and economic co-operation. Instead, we suddenly discovered that the world has had another round of conflict, with both super-powers supplying arms to the warring states of the Middle-East. Even after two cease-fire resolutions in the Security Council, there was an alert of American forces. And, as the repercussions of the oil embargo hit Japan and Western Europe, and, to a lesser extent, America, all the developing world will also be affected, as production goes down, prices go up, and trade recession sets in."

Nearer Southeast Asia, in Indo-China, the problem surrounding the American President, arising out of Watergate, had left their shadow on the otherwise relatively fair picture which emerged after the Paris peace agreement in February 1973. But one turn for the better was the rise in commodity prices by two to two and a half times, giving Malaysia a boost in foreign exchange earnings. Even if commodity prices were later to level back, the substantial increase in the price of crude oil would ensure that rubber was kept well above the prices that prevailed when Lee last visited Kuala Lumpur. "We rejoice that Malaysia is prospering, and that her economy has now a buoyancy which will ensure a period of economic well-being and hence greater political stability." Lee recalled that the year before in Kuala Lumpur, he said that the Singapore-Malaysia working relationship was brisk and businesslike. It was just as well. For, had it been charged with emotions, there would have been unnecessary heat generated over the termination of currency interchangeability, the break-up in the Rubber Exchange, and of other links which had survived separation. Lee said he was extremely sorry that he and Razak had been unable to have discussions whilst they were in Ottawa last August. Tun Ismail had been one of the most valuable links which had survived to their mutual benefit. His passing was a loss for Malaysia and for Singapore. But it made necessary the forging of new links. Lee was happy that during this visit, they had been able to talk easily, and with candour. It had taken some time to establish such an equable relationship. "I do not remember any discussion we have had when you were more related, undisturbed by the irritations which officers of our two governments from time to time involve themselves in. Given a little more time we shall have less of such problems as officers on both sides hoist in the mood which prevailed in our discussions. Some already recognise that there are no marks for scoring points or being one-up. The matter-of-fact way in which you reduced our bilateral problems into their proper proportions against the broader canvas of our common regional future will not fail to influence relationship and abstract the emotional and superfluous in dealings between our two governments. It will be necessary for both ourselves and our ministers to keep in touch, for great events are taking place, and the future appears laden with surprises."

XXIII

The following month, the Prime Minister of New Zealand, Mr. Norman E. Kirk, visited Singapore. At a dinner in his honour on 22 December, Lee said that "we in Singapore have a special regard and respect for New Zealanders. We have found your government sincere in its approach and forthcoming in its policies. These make for warm personal and inter-government relations." The inter-governmental understanding and ties had been built up from the early years of empire. But they were nevertheless real. And they formed a useful credit item to carry forward as a new page was turned into an era where, under vastly changed world conditions, they had to seek new links for economic co-operation and for continued stability and security.

The relatively simple world that they knew for many years after the end of the Second World War, when American supremacy and Britain's special relationship with America were fixed reference points, was no more. The world picture had grown increasingly complex. The emergence of the Soviet Union as a super power, equal to the United States in military terms, had been demonstrated in Europe and the Middle East. The Soviet Union's new position might be felt in other parts of the world. In Southeast Asia, there was the growing strength of China which must be taken into account for the medium term. No one relished the prospect of being caught in a new cold war between two communist giants, the Soviet Union and China. Instead, Singapore would like good relations with all the super powers and the great powers. "We want to stay non-aligned and avoid involvement in their conflicts."

The question was how was this to be achieved? American dominance in Asia could no longer be what it was. The naval presence of the Soviet Union was increasing. The renewed presence of China in the international community was actively felt. And what course would Japan follow to ensure economic well-being? These were factors which would determine the shape of the future, "and our responses in anticipation of their probable developments". However, whatever the picture that would emerge as a result of altered circumstances of the great powers, Lee hoped to keep much of the old links, as these links would help ease adjustment into the more complicated multi-polar world.

"We appreciate these old ties, all the more because regionalism has come to Southeast Asia. And New Zealand is part of our wider region. Regional economic strength has been demonstrated by the EEC. In Africa, in the OAU and the Arab world, regionalism has emerged as a potent political force. For Southeast Asia, perhaps also the Pacific, we must try to achieve whatever regionalism can yield in economic co-operation and political stability. And if we can gear these regional arrangements into the economic dynamos of America, Japan and Western Europe, then development will enhance peace and prosperity. For these industrial countries can furnish the capital, technology and the markets to make better standards of living possible.''

Since Britain first declared her intention to join Europe in 1962, multifold new economic nets had been woven across the Pacific, especially between Southeast Asia and Japan, and Southeast Asia and America. "We have increased our ties with Australasia. We have benefitted from the generosity of successive New Zealand governments in providing us with technical expertise, training for economic and defence needs and university education. For Singapore, the past ten years have been momentous. Great changes had taken place all over Southeast Asia without overwhelming them. It was in good measure because of Singapore's Commonwealth friends. They helped Singapore to safely bridge the period of instability and insecurity to the present tranquil and economically rewarding state of Southeast Asia. So it was more than just ordinary courtesies of protocol when he expressed his appreciation for the contribution made by New Zealand — a contribution much larger than the proportion of either numbers or GNP, because of the stalwart and robust qualities of the New Zealanders.

In his response, Mr. Kirk said that his purpose in coming to Singapore was to convey personally to Lee and his colleagues the thinking behind New Zealand's new independent approach to the region in which they lived. "This is not a passing vogue. It will not be undone or reversed." New Zealand was willing — whenever it would be welcome and helpful — to become more directly associated with the various regional groups which were working to promote political and economic developments. "Our contribution to the Commonwealth Five Power defence arrangements is consistent with that spirit. We are maintaining our participation in full and will keep our forces in the area for so long as they are wanted by the governments concerned. We will however be placing greater emphasis on the strictly New Zealand character of our contribution to the Five Power arrangements."

THE YEAR 1974

I

Singapore's worst fears were not realised in 1974: the economy kept in good shape though there was a lower rate of growth. In his New Year Message, Lee spoke of the uncertainty following the Arab oil embargo. Amidst this uncertainty, two factors were certain. First, the price of oil had gone up about threefold since October 1973. This increase in oil price was expected to put up price levels of other goods by about 2 per cent. Second, for several months of 1974, oil production would be down to between 85 per cent – 87 per cent of levels for September 1973. This short-age of oil meant that industrial production might be lower in 1974 than in 1973, unless people could save energy through domestic economies for industrial production. In the industrial countries of Western Europe and America, for a 3 per cent – 4 per cent economic growth, the consumption of oil went up by about 10 per cent. And it would be some time after the embargo was lifted before oil production went up 10 per cent over 1973 production. And when it did, there would be enormous problems of balance of payments deficits for the oil-importing countries. The whole international monetary system would be put to severe strains as the world adjusted to high oil prices. An era of relatively cheap oil for industrialisa-tion had come to an end. Those countries with oil, or alternative energy sources, like coal or hydro-electric power, would enjoy a decidedly eco-nomic advantage over countries without such resources. This advantage would last till the 1980s until new sources of energy were discovered, or present energy technology, like nuclear power, perfected.

Singapore had neither oil nor coal. Nor did Singapore produce commodities which could take advantage of dearer petro-chemicals. "This is why we cannot afford to go soft. We have to depend on our organisational ability, our skills, our competitiveness. Preliminary figures show that we have done well for 1973, comfortably over 10 per cent growth in our GDP over 1972. But for 1974, we must wait to know when the oil embargo will be lifted. Meanwhile, we must cut down domestic use of energy to keep our industries going. And let us not forget that, every few months, several new factories are ready to start production and need additional energy."

There was one item of good news. The food shortage of 1973 seemed over, as good harvests were reported everywhere. If the oil embargo did not continue too long to cut down the producton of fertilisers, then good harvests were also possible in 1974, and food prices would keep going down. But they might never go back to what they were in 1972, before the world-wide food shortages. This was because most of the major industrial countries of the world had been inflating, issuing more paper money than making the goods or producing the services which the paper money could buy, in order to generate full employment for political reasons. "Although we have not issued money without foreign exchange backing, we have been caught by the inflow of more foreign exchange, and by the higher prices of imported foodstuff and machinery. However, we have always earned our keep and paid for our needs. The world will continue to need the goods we produce and the services we render. Our wages will go up if productivity goes up. This principle holds true whatever the uncertainties of 1974."

II

Japan's Prime Minister, Mr. Kakuei Tanaka, paid a visit to Singapore early in the year. Welcoming him on 11 January at a State dinner, Lee remarked that Mr. Tanaka's visit took place at a time when the world was suddenly faced with more baffling problems than in the past. High oil prices would trigger off predictable problems like higher costs and slower economic growth. They would also set off unpredictable problems, including the effect of the flow of vast reserves of currency which the oil producers would accumulate. Conventional wisdom derived from experience of nearly three decades since the end of the war was that the industrial countries would grow richer and stronger, and the gap between them and the less developed countries would widen. This order of things had been reversed for oil producers and, for the time being, for the commodity producers also. 1973 saw this sharp rise in commodity prices, the result of growing scarcity and increasing demands from the booming economies of the industrial countries. Now, the boom in the industrial countries was

184

cooling off with high oil prices. But commodity prices had not yet shown any decline to more moderate levels.

The familiar guidelines which helped shape policies of government, both of industrial and less developed countries, had now become unsafe to rely on. Confusion caused by the energy crises prevented most countries from establishing new reference points and drawing new guidelines. It might take many months before new sign-posts and guidelines were established to help governments find their way forward. "Meantime, we have to go back to proven basic principles, that social discipline, hard work and thrift are the attributes which will lead a people safely out of a confused economic situation. The take-it-for-granted attitude of expecting more economic benefits each year, and with less effort, cannot survive the changed economic conditions." Lee said he was therefore impressed by reports that Mr. Tanaka and his Ministers had urged the Japanese people to go back to their traditional virtues, to abjure extravagant and often unnecessary consumption of material goods. This advice to return to simpler ways of life before material affluence became fashionable, applied also to Singapore, "even though we are not as wealthy or as industrialised as Japan." There was a period of trial and testing in store for peoples whose economies were without the advantage of natural resources, and instead depended on efficient production and servicing. Such peoples had to show that they had not lost their will to strive and their capacity to survive. "I have no doubts that under your dynamic and capable leadership the Japanese people will overcome the difficulties that have suddenly arisen with the huge increases in the price of oil. And this time the goals achieved may well be all the more satisfying by the creation of a healthy and gracious environment for the industrious, disciplined and artistic people of Japan. Let us hope that despite the setbacks of 1973, the world will continue to move forward towards a freer interchange of ideas, goods and services, stimulating the world into thinking in global, and not in narrow, nationalistic, terms. For it is under such conditions that there could be greater economic benefits for all."

In his response, Mr. Tanaka said he had been most impressed to see at first-hand the vigour and dynamism of Singapore advancing steadily towards prosperity in an atmosphere of stability and comfort. He paid "sincere tribute" to Lee "for the superb leadership which has brought about the Singapore of today. We in Japan have long admired your fifteen years of continued devotion to nation-building through industrial development and improvement of the life of the people, since this valuable task was entrusted to you as Prime Minister at the remarkably young age of thirty-five back in 1959." Mr. Tanaka said he had come to Singapore to convey to Lee personally the ardent desire of Japan to build and strengthen further the friendly relations between the peoples of Japan and Singapore as good neighbours sharing the benefits of peace and prosperity. Both Japan and Singapore made it the basis of their national policies to seek to improve the welfare of their peoples through industrialisation. They also both depended on trade with the outside world for the bulk of their economic life. "I have no doubt whatsoever that, upon such common grounds, Japan and Singapore can prosper together in their co-operative endeavours as good partners in the years to come."

III

Shortly after Mr. Tanaka's visit, Lee left for an official visit to Manila. At a dinner given in his honour by President Marcos on 15 January, the Prime Minister said that while over the past few years relations between Singapore and the Philippines had been more than cordial, he hoped that after this visit, with greater understanding between them there would be more trade and co-operation in economic projects. Lee said his visit took place at a time when the course of events in this part of the world had altered dramatically. The future was uncharted and might be fraught with surprises. Old maps were unreliable guides. Issues which had preoccupied them for some three decades — anti-colonialism, the Cold War and Third World solidarity — had been displaced by more formidable issues. The energy crisis was indicative of the new type of problems that were likely to be encountered in the coming years. Here, the conflict between the haves and have-nots made for a different kind of division between nations. The established divisions between communist and non-communist systems, between developed and developing nations, between coloured and non-coloured peoples, between agricultural and industrial societies, had become less relevant than the division between say oil producers and oil consumers. These new problems did not lend themselves to solution by individual national initiatives in view of understandable limitations. Highly industrialised countries were therefore unable to meet these global problems through their separate national endeavours. There were no purely American, Russian, Chinese, or even comprehensively Asian, solutions to such problems, which threaten the inter-dependent world.

"In Southeast Asia, we should strive to avoid the deleterious consequences of old fashioned nationalist economic policies through co-operative endeavour. A start has already been made through ASEAN. The pace of co-operation in the ASEAN region has perforce been slow in its initial years. It may well be that the changes which have taken place in East and Southeast Asia will give added impetus to ASEAN's search for more substantial economic progress. The ASEAN countries hold the promise of rapid and dynamic growth. It would be a pity not to realise this promise. The question is whether we collectively have the imagination to discern the possibilities and the boldness to take the steps to realise our potential in joint enterprise."

Lee said he was privileged to be in Manila to meet President Marcos at an important juncture in the history of Southeast Asia, and to hear his views on how Southeast Asian nations could respond to the changed circumstances surrounding them. He looked forward to the opportunity to be briefed on the economic and political outlook of the Philippines. He hoped to get an insight on how the Philippines was grappling with the tasks of social and economic changes.

The joint communique revealed that the President and the Prime Minister "had a comprehensive and fruitful exchange of views on a wide variety of subjects of mutual interest. The President and the Prime Minister reaffirmed their support of, and reliance upon, ASEAN as a principal viable organ for close co-operation among its members.

"Encouraged by the trend of expanding trade relations between Singapore and the Philippines, the President and the Prime Minister agreed that further steps should be taken to substantially increase the volume of trade between the two countries."

IV

The Prime Minister, in his Chinese New Year Message, felt that the "Year of the Tiger" looked a shade less grim than it did on January 1. "With the agreement on Egyptian-Israeli disengagement, oil will probably continue to flow without new outbacks. The problem of very high oil prices remains. This will cause prices of other things to go up. So the 'Year of the Tiger' will see higher prices and slower economic growth. But this is better than recession and unemployment. A happy new year to all, and let us resolve to make the best of a difficult year."

V

Declared Lee, when opening the Pulau Brani Naval Base on 26 January: "Singapore has one of the biggest harbours in the world. It is the fourth largest in the world in tonnage of ships calling. It is our intention to develop a flotilla of patrol craft and MGB (missile gun-boats) to help patrol the approaches to our harbour. This base in Pulau Brani is ideally situated. It is sited right opposite our harbour. It is an agreeable site, with excellent facilities for the stationing and training of the personnel in Maritime Command."

In December 1973, 150 Higher School Certificate students enlisted for national service were posted to the navy to assess their suitability for the Midshipman School which was being set up with help from the Royal New Zealand Navy. Some of the better students would be encouraged to become regular officers in Maritime Command. However, the government was aware that SAF officers and regulars were very conscious of opportunities for promotion and comparable rewards between all branches of the SAF and the private sector. Up till now, those serving in

Maritime Command believed they had been at a slight disadvantage compared to those in the army and the air force, where expansion had been faster. Lee took the opportunity to assure those in the navy that their interests would advance in step with those of the army and the air force. In fact, for the immediate future, it would be necessary to select and train high calibre officers for senior staff and command appointments of Maritime Command for it to take its rightful place among the other services of the SAF.

Those who did not make it to senior staff and command positions would have alternative sea careers in ships engaged in regional or world trade. SADC (Singapore Air Defence Command) pilots would have a choice in mid-career to convert to civilian work in Singapore Airlines. For Maritime Command officers, arrangements could likewise be made for them to get their Foreign-going Master's Certificate, Home Trade Master's Certificate, or Local Trade Master's Certificate, to work on ships belonging to Neptune Orient Lines and other Singapore shipping lines. Singapore made more than half its living by the sea. "The Maritime Command must reflect the importance of the sea to our livelihood. In co-operation with our neighbours, we must play our part to keep down unlawful activities like smuggling and piracy."

VI

The world economic situation continued to concern the Prime Minister. He told a meeting of representatives of the Citizens' Consultative Committees and Management Committees of Community Centres, on 5 February, that what happened in 1974 depended on how the major industrial nations of the world reacted to the energy crisis. Assuming that the Arab oil embargo was lifted as progress was made towards a settlement for the Middle East, the twenty major industrial nations of the world, members of the OECD, would try to make up for production lost because of the oil embargo and pay the price of much higher oil prices. In that case, production might increase between two to four per cent over 1973 production, assuming the embargo was lifted in the first half of the year. Then the volume of world trade would increase. "We shall also benefit from the increased production and trade." On the other hand, the major industrialised countries might become very concerned over their huge balance of payments deficits because of the high oil prices. Each might try to restrict imports and expand exports. At the same time, each would vie for the reaching of bilateral agreements separately with the oil producers, to get oil in return for industrial equipment, technology, arms and know-how, so cutting down on foreign exchange losses. In this case, balance of payments deficits for the countries succeeding in reaching such agreements would be less. But those not able to barter industrial technology, arms and know-how for oil would be affected by the bigger deficits. "We are in this unfortunate group." However, if there were no lifting of the Arab oil embargo, because progress towards a settlement was slow, and there were deadlocks from time to time, then the world might face lower production, because of shortage of energy supplies, lower volume of world trade, and lowered standards of living. "These things are beyond our control. In a world so closely inter-dependent and inter-related, it is not possible to isolate ourselves from conflicts in which we are really spectators. It is like the two 'Red Army' Japanese and two Arabs who have hijacked the *Laju* after letting off plastic explosives in Bukom. We are the third largest oil refining centre in the world, after Houston and Rotterdam. If the Bukom raid had been successful, the considerable refining capacity would have been knocked out for several years, affecting not only Singapore, but also the countries in the wider region which got their supplies from Singapore. Then even if the oil embargo were lifted, and limitless supplies of crude oil were available, there would still be a shortage of oil in the region because there would have been a shortage of refining capacity. These other countries are also bystanders in the Middle East and Vietnam conflicts, but they have nevertheless suffered through the oil cuts and may have suffered more if the refinery had been destroyed." Singapore's duty was clear — to take every precaution to prevent sabotage to property or industrial production or danger to lives. "The reasons of any group to pick any quarrel with us, must be minimised."

In any case, 1974 looked an unpromising year. From February, all those earning less than $1,000 would get $25 more per month. In July, there would be a review. But it was impossible to expect more money in wages would mean more things could be bought. In the industrial West, prices rose at 8 per cent to 12 per cent a year. Because of oil shortages, compounding industrial strikes and business uncertainty, the economies of most western countries were slowing down. So they were having increasing unemployment and inflation. That was the fearful meaning of stagflation, stagnation and inflation, low economic growth, plus increases in prices. The only silver lining was the possibility of good harvests in 1974, despite the higher costs of fertilisers derived from oil. This would bring food prices down. "Most of these things again are beyond our control. But it is in our control not to make the inflation in Singapore worse than it already is because of rising costs of imports. Wage increases must be matched by increased productivity and exports at better prices. We are not blessed with oil or minerals or agricultural commodities. But we have got a strategic economic position, a sound infrastructure for industrial production, and efficient services, from repairing ships, aircraft, and replenishing their oil and stores, to providing expertise in engineering and management problems, and an ever more efficient financial centre and money market. If everybody works his best and his hardest, real standards of living may not go up very much, but they will not go down."

VII

On 31 January, two Japanese and two Arab terrorists had attacked an oil refinery causing minor damage to three storage tanks. They hijacked a ferry boat, *Laju*, and held its crew hostages. They claimed to represent the PFLP (Party of the Liberation of Palestine) and the Japanese Red Army. The Japanese authorities, who had been reluctant to arrange their safe departure from Singapore, were brought to agree when the Japanese Embassy in Kuwait was seized by terrorists. They demanded that a Japanese aircraft should bring the terrorists from Singapore to Kuwait. A Singapore Government request to the Government of North Korea to accept the terrorists was refused. When negotiations were completed without loss of life, thirteen Singapore Government officials accompanied the terrorists to Kuwait.

Negotiations were still going on when Australia's Prime Minister, Mr. Gough Whitlam, arrived on an official visit. At a dinner in his honour on 7 February, Lee said it was his privilege to welcome to Singapore for the first time a Labour Prime Minister of Australia. Lee added that despite considerable foreknowledge of both Whitlam's thinking and the Australian Labour Party's published policies, he still found the first few months of Labour government in Australia stirring with the drama of fundamental changes carried out with great panache. "I must take this occasion to mention a few changes your Government has introduced in the field of foreign policy which are imaginative and bold. I venture to suggest that they are unlikely to be altered. For example, your decisive break with the White Australia policy and on related issues of race and colour, not just with regard to Asia, but also with regard to Africa, is a stand on principle which no successor Australian government can find it easy to publicly go back on. Of course, when you changed your immigration policy there have been some unexpected difficulties for Singapore. It is not that we disapprove of your principle of racial non-discrimination. Like other countries of the Third World we need trained manpower for our development. And the prospect of losing such people by emigration to a wealthy country, where rewards are so much greater, was one my colleagues and I found most disturbing. But I do not doubt that you are against racial discrimination, and your deep concern for the Australian Aborigines and their future in Australia is well-known. You have waved away the aura of racial superiority of the white peoples, a belief which the passage of time has made not only untenable, but unnecessarily offensive. Further, your generous responses to calamities in Asia were gestures reflecting a generous spirit and conscience, those of an Australian leader confident and self-assured in dealings with big and small countries, but compassionate and sensitive to the travail of poorer neighbours in Asia. You had no hesitation in committing Australia to pay for the repatriation of people by the UN High Commissioner for Refugees to and from Bangladesh and Pakistan. Even the restoring of ancient monuments in Southeast Asian countries struck a sympathetic chord in you."

In the meantime, startling events had shaken the economic order of the world. Since October 1973, Lee said, his colleagues and he had been hard-pressed to find their bearings in a new energy situation. The outlook for growth and development for those countries without energy resources of their own had suddenly become more daunting. And, of course, Singapore was unfortunate to be one of those without such energy resources. Once again, Australians found themselves amongst those blessed by nature, bountiful in coal, natural gas and oil, except for the heavier fractions, ample assurance of a comfortable and prosperous future in a world of increasing energy costs. And Australia's abundant mineral resources in a world conscious of growing scarcity of exhaustible stocks, assured her of increasing wealth and a greater voice in world affairs. "Indeed your pre-election resources policies to harness and husband Australia's resources for greater Australian participation demonstrated foresight before the cards fell on the commodity exchanges of the world. The impression your policies have given abroad is one of vigour. The optimism and enthusiasm in your dynamic approach to both domestic and external events and forces are widely known. I sometimes felt that perhaps I have been looking at some of those problems with eyes grown jaundiced, perhaps because I saw too much of their negative and intractable side thereby losing the zest and gusto, which you have exuded both at home in Australia and wherever you have travelled abroad. I appreciated the opportunity I had this afternoon to share your thoughts, and to learn how you see the future for East and Southeast Asia, and how Australia and the South Pacific can help in the economic and social development of this region."

In his reply, Mr. Whitlam gave an assurance of "Australia's strong and continuing interest in maintaining a substantial and enduring relationship with Singapore" in fulfillment of a "long history of past and friendly co-operation". The withdrawal of Australian forces from Singapore was not, he said, a gesture of isolationism, but a "reconstruction and redefinition and re-orientation of defence policy". The grant in military aid to Singapore was increased substantially.

VIII

Lee was in a philosophical mood when, on 3 March, he addressed the Annual Scientific Meeting of the Royal Australasian College of Physicians. Technological break-throughs, he said, often brought about unexpected results. These consequences were not intended by the scientists who made the discoveries, nor contemplated by those who financed the research. Modern medicine, both in public health and in personal care, had made tremendous progress in the three decades since the last War. But it had created new enormous problems in the process. In poor countries, populations had increased. In rich countries, geriatrics had created more pressures to care for large numbers of older people who led lonely lives, without enough social participation that made life rewarding. Medical science had helped many with hereditary defects to live. It had increased the numbers who could transmit these defects to the next generation, and so increased the numbers needing special care and treatment. Compassion within nations had led to more and more social and health services being paid by the better able and the more productive, to try and achieve more equality for the less able and the less productive. The wealthier a society become, the more they could afford to, and usually did, spend on such welfare. As the world got wealthier, so compassion had led to international social and health projects. The strong and wealthy nations had tried to redress the balance by helping the weak and the poor. WHO (World Health Organisation), based in Geneva, helped to improve standards of public health and medical care. FAO (Food and Agriculture Organisation, based in Rome, helped to alleviate the terrifying effects of drought and famine, disasters which periodically struck poor and undeveloped parts of the world, where agriculture was wholly dependent on rainfall, and there was no fall-back on dams and irrigation. UNCTAD (United Nations Conference on Trade and Development) had met regularly to get two decades, the sixties and the seventies, dedicated to development. The results, so far, had not been up to expectations. The developed countries had been asked to pledge to give 1 per cent of their GNP in aid for development for the under-developed. But this target had not been achieved, and few countries had even attempted to achieve this 1 per cent.

The spread of modern science and technology to the less developed countries had not been an unmixed blessing. In most countries, population growth had been faster than the rate of economic development. Now, with the oil crisis, the United States had cut down on aid. Neither Western Europe nor Japan was expected to increase their aid. The oil-producing countries were now going to have huge surpluses. But why should they give more aid than 1 per cent of their GNP, which was a level developed countries had not reached? As a consequence, countries which had come to depend upon this aid, estimated at some US$10 billion a year, were not faced with large needs which could not be met.

If the international community, through UN agencies like WHO, FAO and the World Bank, had not, in the first place, injected medicine and food into large areas of the under-developed world, the peoples in these areas might have taken some other path for their own advancement. If only education and expertise had been transmitted, and machinery and equipment given or loaned, but not food, they might not have become so heavily populated. Indeed, they might have become self-reliant and found a social and economic equilibrium which was not dependent on annual aid of food grains. But then, once upon a time, America, Canada and Australia had huge food surpluses. And it seemed only humane to help feed the hungry peoples. Now it was doubtful if the consequences of these humanitarian policies had added to the sum total of human happiness. These were baffling problems. And they had accumulated and grown in magnitude over the past two decades.

Nature had always favoured the survival of the ones most capable of adapting to changing circumstances. Biologically, it had led to the dominance of man over all other living creatures. From time immemorial, the more aggressive groups had moved into the more fertile valleys. Agriculture was the first technological breakthrough that enabled civilisation to flourish. So the less agressive were pushed into the less fertile areas. Now, in a curious way, through the discoveries and needs of the advanced technological societies, some of those dispossessed had come into great fortunes.

Technological breakthroughs by advanced peoples had conferred benefits in unexpected ways to peoples living in poorer parts of the world. For instance, once upon a time, the kingdom of Brunei included the whole of Sarawak and the whole of North Borneo. But the White Rajahs, the Brookes, pushed the Brunei Malays northwards out of Sarawak. Alas, from the north, the British North Borneo Company pushed the Brunei Malays southwards. So they were squeezed into the most infertile part of the west coast of Borneo. Many decades later, it was discovered that the reason for the poor agriculture was that there was oil in the earth. And so the wronged and the long suffering were now flourishing. Similarly, the aggressive tribes had occupied all the fertile river valleys and highlands in East and Central Africa. They had pushed other tribes into the barren scrub-land, once known as Northern Rhodesia. But, meanwhile, the industrial nations had developed a demand for copper. They also developed the means to prospect and mine this copper. Northern Rhodesia was scrub-land and infertile but it was also in the copper belt. Today, Zambia had one of the highest per capita incomes in Central Africa.

So it had been with the Arab world. The Arabs who straddled the Euphrates, the Nile, and the Mediterranean Coast, thought that with rainfall, they were the fortunate ones. The Arab peoples of the deserts, particularly those in the Arabian peninsula were thought to be the less fortunate. Meanwhile, the industrial world had developed a growing demand for oil. It had also developed the technological capacity to drill for it both on land and offshore. Oil exploration had now established that two-thirds of the world's proven oil deposits were in this arid and agriculturally unproductive area of the Gulf. So all this while, there had been great wealth under the desert sands for those who were thought to be the less fortunate of the Arab peoples. Some of these Gulf States were, until recently, protected by Western powers like Britain. Western concepts of national sovereignty developed in four hundred years of dealings between the nation states of Western Europe had now become applicable in dealings between the technologically advanced nations and the new countries which inherited these colonial boundaries. So the advantage had now shifted to a fortunate few with oil.

A question being asked was whether these wealthy oil states would show a compassion for the plight of the less developed world. Would they show much more consideration to the poor countries than the consideration advanced countries once showed to them? Some hopes were raised, but did not materialise, at a recent meeting in Lahore. But, compassion and sentiment aside, something had to be done about the huge sums of money which the advanced countries would issue to pay for the oil, or the world economic and monetary system would be wrecked by inflation and instability on a scale unknown before. It has always been the technologically strong who have laid down the rules of the game. Under these rules, they, the technologically strong, must pay vast sums for the oil they need to keep their economies going. They must pay either in kind or in money, but mostly in money. So what else besides gold would go up as people lost confidence in paper currency? The rules of the game could not be changed so long as the two super-powers neatly balanced each other. So the world security system, based on a balance of nuclear terror, allowed all countries, including the oil producers, to make the most of their natural resources.

The major oil-consuming countries had met in Washington. "One must hope there will be rational decisions arising out of these discussions amongst the big consumers, and that then the big oil consumers and the big oil producers can, through understanding of their common interests to keep the world economy growing, make such accommodations as will enable them to prevent economic instability and chaos. The eventual outcome of these recent developments on the restriction of oil production and the sharp increases in oil prices will be as intriguing as it will be momentous for the future of all nations, the developed, the developing and the less developed. The crux of the matter is: can the strong alone inherit the earth? Was there not a biblical reference to the meek coming into some inheritance?"

But who could predict what was ahead? Further technological discoveries in new energy sources and in other fields might open up new vistas for mankind. Inevitably, these innovations would bring in their train new problems for mankind. But, having opened Pandora's box, and all desires released, only hope remained. Man's irrepressible curiosity would lead him to new discoveries. Up till now, these discoveries had solved more problems than they created. For never had mankind been so successful in taming the forces of the physical world. Never before had man become so numerous, so long-lived, so mobile, and so materially well-off. The question now was whether optimism about the future was justified when the world's population was expected to double to over seven billion by the year 2000, in spite of the efforts of UN agencies and governments to encourage birth control. Worse, many conservationists, scientists and economists feared that technologically advanced states were damaging the environment, and exhausting the non-renewable resources of the earth, leaving future generations worse off in a hundred years' time. But perhaps because these alarms had been sounded, the future was not without optimism for most of mankind.

IX

On 27 April, the Prime Minister spoke at the 5th anniversary dinner of the Sembawang Shipyard Employees' Union. He recalled that the Sembawang British naval dockyards had been handed to Singapore in December 1968. Earlier, in 1967, the Government had brought Swan Hunter into Keppel Shipyard to modernise the management and facilities at Keppel, and to acquaint themselves with the potentials of ship-repairing in Singapore. "We expected then that we would have to take over the naval base by the mid-seventies. But it happened much sooner than that." In 1969, the first year of operation of Sembawang Shipyard, the turnover was $30 million — $9 million for commercial repairs and $21 million for naval repairs. Two years later, 1971, it was $55 million — $40 million commercial, $15 million naval repairs. Four years later, 1973, it was $81 million, all commercial repairs. The work force had grown from 3,452 at the end of 1968 to 3,680 at the end of 1973, plus 850 contract employees for Sembawang Shipyard Ltd. and Sembawang Engineering (P) Ltd. More significantly, local management, nil in 1967, was now 184. Naval expatriates, now nil, was 152 in 1968. Swan Hunter personnel reached a peak of thirty-eight in 1970. It went down to twenty-four in 1973. By 1978, local management should be able to run Sembawang Shipyard.

But it was only in fairy tales that stories end happily ever after. One phase had been completed successfully. The oil crisis in 1973 threatened the world's economy, in particular shipping and ship-repairing. With the lifting of the oil embargo, this threat had been removed. However, a change had taken place in the rate of increase of consumption of energy. All countries had cut down waste and economised on the use of oil. This, the reopening of the Suez Canal, and the Egyptian oil pipeline between the Red Sea and the Mediterranean, had led shipping experts to forecast a surplus of tankers. Large numbers were already on order when consumption was increasing at the old rates. One suggestion to overcome this expected surplus of tanker capacity was to have them travel more slowly, conserving fuel and acting as floating storage tankers. But the economics of this had not been worked out; particularly with increased seamen's wages, including those of Japanese crews. Fortunately, this slow-down in tanker traffic would be mainly on the Gulf to Europe route, rather than the Gulf to Japan. In fact, with the reopening of the Suez Canal, there might be an increase in non-oil cargo ships, as the trade routes between Europe and the Far East was shortened by nearly 8,000 miles by not having to go around the Cape.

"Meanwhile, your wages have steadily gone up. For over a year, we have been hit by high food prices. So a NWC $25 interim award was made from February this year. Ship-repairing is an international business and highly competitive. However, the cost of living and wages have gone up as much, if not more, in Hong Kong and Japan. So long as we remain competitive, our economy can afford the wage increases. In other words, management must be efficient, labour relations healthy, and the work force keen and hardworking, always ready to learn and increase their skills.''

The story of Sembawang Shipyard was part of the story of how Singapore overcame the economic problems of British military withdrawal. The quotations for Sembawang Shipyard shares on the stock exchange reflected its solid economic base. It was not one of those shares which shot up to the sky on speculative euphoria and then crashed down to the bottom in a gambler's bout of overgloom. Right now, depression enveloped all stock exchanges throughout the world. High interest rates and tight credits were part of the cause. But the depression was particularly exaggerated in Singapore and Hong Kong. "I call it the casino syndrome. When shares go up, more and more buyers rush in, believing that their winning streak has set in, and push prices well beyond realistic limits. When shares go down, as the small dabblers scramble out, other operators sell short to push prices further down. In early 1973, there was manipulated boosting of the share market by professional syndicates. We checked this in February 1973 in Singapore. But in Hong Kong, some groups played the market till March and were reported in the British financial papers to have cleaned up some £500 million of poor people's savings.'' Sembawang Shipyard's shares were not a speculative counter. "We cannot afford to gamble in a casino, relying on winning streaks. Our lives and our children's future must be built on a solid infrastructure of education and skills, tuned to high performance by efficient management, always able to respond quickly to sudden changes in the world.''

One emerging problem was the trend amongst workers to spend freely and save less. Singapore was caught in the meshes of the consumer society. A plethora of advertisements urged people to buy what they did not really need, as finance companies and other mechanisms encouraged people to buy now and pay later. So it was necessary that savings should be enforced through CPF contributions. The Government was considering increasing the interest rates for CPF deposits. This had to be done gradually because it meant increasing interest rates paid by HDB and JTC. But it was a fairer way of sorting the burdens, since those who bought houses or rented HDB or JTC flats should not be subsidised too much by using the low-interest capital, obtained from CPF contributions of those who could not buy, or were unable to rent these low-cost homes.

"Finally, let me congratulate the Sembawang Shipyard Employees' Union. It is four years since I was at your annual dinner. From 1,474 members in 1969, you now have 2,438 members, out of a total work force of 3,680. Pragmatic union leadership has been an important contribution to the progress of Sembawang Shipyard.''

In a message for the NTUC's May Day 1974 Souvenir Programme, Lee observed that never had the economic outlook been more uncertain in the world. Inflation had become endemic amongst the industrial countries. Besides the steep rise in food prices, because of shortages of grains and meats in the past fifteen months, there had been political and industrial unrest in countries as far apart as Britain and Japan. 1973 recorded a steep rise in Singapore's consumer price index, mainly the result of rice going up by over 100 per cent, and high price increases in other basic commodities. For the present, the trend was for rice prices to go down. But it was not possible for them to go back to the levels of 1972. However, this trend towards lower prices might not be sustained if the next harvests were poor. "We face a dilemma. We have got six months' stocks of rice. If prices go up, we can temper the increase in rice prices with these stocks in hand. If prices go down, we should not complain if the price of rice we buy does not go down as fast as the international market prices, because we have to use up this stockpile. But the trouble is, people will complain. In fact, many Singaporeans are becoming very good at grumbling."

Meanwhile, the National Wages Council had to watch developments closely in the next few months in order to make the right recommendations for wage adjustments in July. But whatever those recommendations might be, it was not realistic to expect an increase in real wages as high as those enjoyed in the past few years, before the oil prices quadrupled. "Our trade is worldwide. So it is not possible to insulate ourselves from global economic forces. And the worldwide trends are towards chronic inflation, with slower rates of economic growth. In other words, there will be a lower rate of increase in real wages. This is a fact of life. We must face up to it. But if we keep the management-worker relations good, and productivity higher, then there will be increases in real wages, however small compared to those between 1970 – 73."

XI

At a reception given by the NTUC in honour of participants in the ICFTU-ARO seminar on Trade Union Research, on 6 May, the Prime Minister said that trade union research into the problems of the labour movement in the context of developing societies of Asia had before it an immense and unexplored field. But the areas on which research must concentrate depended on the conditions in each specific country: what the political and economic objectives were, what level of development they had reached, and what the pressing problems were. Then again, on objectives, there was the question of priorities. It did not need research to convince most political leaders in office, whatever they might have believed in opposition, that the overriding objective must be to increase the GNP, and that this came before a more equal sharing of that GNP. Japan was the Asian model where education, modernisation and industrialisation had been placed over and above a more equal distribution of GNP, and with conspicuous success.

Unfortunately for most countries in Asia, political leaderships had not got strong trade union leaderships to underwrite that priority. This was because trade unions were still in their early stages of organisation. And the leaderships of unions, seeking to enlarge their following, found that it was easier to increase membership by pressing for immediate and more equal sharing of the GNP. For, giving increased GNP priority demanded a postponement of immediate benefits for members. So, the end-result had often been a conscious policy by the political leaderships to downgrade the importance of the role of trade unions. Singapore was fortunate in having a trade union leadership that shared the same priorities as its political leadership. The emphasis was on development, to increase GNP through better education, training, acquisition of higher skills, induction of more sophisticated manufacture and technology from developed countries. There was an appreciation by the unions and the government that this meant the widening of differentials in rewards between the unskilled and skilled, between technicians and engineers. But, though these parameters were agreed upon, research work by unions was difficult. Collection and publication of statistics by government agencies and departments were slow. Nor did they have the accuracy and reliability of figures compiled and issued by governments in developed countries. Further, in developed countries, such statistics could be corroborated by non-government institutions devoted to the study of national economies, and by international organisations like the OECD.

Because statistical measurements were inadequate and slow to come by, it was all the more necessary that trade unions should conduct their own research. Then they could get a better assessment of the state of the economy. A hard assessment of the domestic situation, viewed in the context of the international economic trends, gave union leaders the confidence to press their views and policies on employers and the government. Trade unions themselves, however, were hampered by the same shortage of trained manpower in data collection and analysis as the government. "For instance, in Singapore, we have not yet worked out, with any confident accuracy, a formula to determine the GNP deflator to determine annual growth at constant prices, as distinct from current prices. So figures, based on current prices, are used by management and unions. The government's formula of what the deflator ought to be is used, but it is not conclusively accepted that this was in fact the rate of inflation for the past year. When, as for the past fifteen months, we are faced with hyper-inflation, as a result of rocketing food prices and double-figure inflation rates imported from the developed countries, it becomes extremely difficult to determine what is a fair sharing of the real increase in GNP between management and unions, between shareholders and workers. In the end, it must be a compromise which will compensate workers for their loss of real earnings through inflation, whilst maintaining the edge in our export

The Shah of Iran visited
Singapore in 1974.

Japan's Prime Minister Tanaka
paid an official visit to
Singapore in 1974.

Lee with President Sadat
in Cairo in 1975

Lee with Marshall Tito and the Yugoslav Prime Minister, Dzemal Bijedic,
(extreme left) in Yugoslavia

In the White House with President Ford and Dr Henry Kissinger

Australia's Prime Minister, Gough Whitlam, paid an official visit to Singapore in 1974.

prices, and also continue to encourage further foreign investments in skill-intensive middle technology manufacture."

1973 – 74 were years not likely to be forgotten by fixed-income workers, or by their union leaders. Before people could get over the problems of scarce food and soaring prices, oil prices were quadrupled as from the beginning of 1974. The special session of the United Nations, which discussed problems of the raw material producing countries, had shown how frustration and emotion could make dispassionate discussions, rational analyses and co-operative solutions difficult. The fact that the developed industrial nations had for so long fixed the terms of trade in their favour, against the raw material producers, made it difficult for the non-oil commodity producers not to want to get their own back on the industrial countries. They also hoped to form cartels, like the oil producers, contrive scarcity and jack up prices. That it was doubtful such moves would succeed in non-oil commodities did not alter their emotional desire for such solutions. If it was any consolation for poor and rich countries who had to pay the higher oil prices, the recent embargo on oil had demonstrated beyond doubt that the world was already closely inter-dependent and inter-related.

If there was to be hope of greater success in future development programmes, there must be a more realistic appraisal of what could be achieved in each given country within a development decade. A decade was less than half a generation. And it took at least two generations to produce an educated and trained industrial work force, plus the management and engineering expertise to run an industrial economy.

The oil-producing countries would now demonstrate to an excessive degree how keen and willing the developed countries were to transfer capital, machinery and know-how in exchange for vital supplies of energy to fuel their own economy. But there might be limits on the speed with which each oil-producing country could absorb this transfer of capital machinery, know-how, discipline and skills. "Let us hope that out of all these traumatic events, the developed and developing countries will both recognise that their interests are best advanced by co-operation, not conflict." A willingness of the developed countries to transfer capital, know-how and skills for offshore manufacture, either through multinational companies or in joint ventures, would increase the willingness of the developing countries to open up their exhaustible resources to feed the industries of the developed countries. And even if commodity prices went down from the heights they reached in the period of scarcity and speculative demand of the past year, they might still be well above the levels they were down at for years. This should enable the developing countries to have more foreign exchange to pay for machinery and know-how and give a boost to trade and development. It might not be too late for trade union leaders in developed and developing countries to learn that greater co-operation tended to greater prosperity, and helped to maintain peace and orderly progress for peoples throughout the world.

"For economic reasons, the English language is vital. It has helped our economic development. But for our multi-racial, multi-cultural people to learn only English would be folly. For this will detach them from their cultural roots. After fifteen years of grappling with this basic problem, we have settled for bilingualism — the mother tongue and English." The Prime Minister restated Government language policy in an address at the presentation of the Prime Minister Book Prize on 29 May. For those who did not speak one of the four languages taught, Chinese students who spoke a dialect at home, for example, bilingualism really meant more speaking a dialect at home and learning two other languages in school. A Chinese dialect and Mandarin were not different languages. They were more different pronunciations of the same basic language. But it nevertheless increased the difficulties of bilingualism. If the family spoke English, or Malay, or Mandarin, or Tamil at home, the child had only one other language to learn in school. And the home helped the learning of the other language. But it might take one generation to achieve this position.

Languages were best and easiest learned early in life. If they could not start in a home, they should be started early in kindergartens. If learning was kept up until the late teens, they were mastered for life. A language learnt late in life was never fully mastered. Effort was always required to be fluent. It might be that for average or below average students, the studying of two languages resulted in lowered standards than if only one language was studied. "But it is better to know your mother tongue and English, both imperfectly, than to know well only one." The learning of a language did not stop at school. Speaking, reading, watching TV and the cinema and writing reports or letters were a life-long experience. What was crucial was to achieve a minimum proficiency in the language before that part of the mind which facilitated speech and the learning of languages lost this capability. Neuro-surgeons believed that this capacity was considerably diminished after maturity, usually after twenty. "If I were a student again, I would first go to a Chinese school. That would be the easiest and surest way to master Chinese. I would also want to learn English in school, especially to write it correctly. I would have no difficulty in speaking English, since that I can do at home. If I had the teachers in school, I would also learn Malay. It is very close to Bahasa Indonesia, and would help me understand our neighbours, and their culture. Because I did not learn enough Chinese and Malay in school, it has taken much effort for me to use Chinese and Malay, and with less facility than if I had acquired at least fluency in conversation."

It was the English-speaking parents who sent their children to English schools who were worried about the increase in the teaching of the second language. There had been no complaints by Chinese-speaking parents in the Chinese press. Those of them with children in the English schools were happy that their children would learn more Chinese. Those of them with children in Chinese schools had always been happy to have them learn more English. The same was true of Malay and Tamil parents, whatever schools their children were in. The crux of the problem was that many English-educated Chinese parents, with children in English schools, believed there were no economic benefits in learning Chinese, especially if it was at the expense of English. They were wrong. They had only given this matter superficial thought. If they wanted to give their children the best guarantee of survival, whatever the future held, they should send their children first to Chinese schools. There, the atmosphere and environment were such that given six years of primary education, their children would be effective in Chinese for life, provided they continued learning it in an English secondary school. The Education Ministry allowed this switch from a Chinese primary school to an English secondary school. Not many parents took this course, probably because not many knew of it. Whilst in a Chinese primary school, there was no fear that children would not master English, for they would be taught it in school, and would use it at home. Chinese is a difficult language. It is monosyllabic, tonal, written in characters and not phonetic script. But it could be learned easiest when young, preferably at four years old, whilst playing at kindergarten. But the grudging attitude of some parents and the scepticism of some principals and teachers in English schools made the learning of Chinese more difficult in English schools.

"I am convinced that if the price for knowing enough Chinese is a lower standard of English, at Primary Six or Secondary Four, it is still worth it. The children's English will improve with further reading and writing after schooling. What will help bilingualism is a positive attitude from parents, principals and teachers. This is more important than methodology or exposure time. We want to give our children the best combination of languages for their future — Chinese, or mother tongue, for the ethics, values on work and discipline in an orderly society, and English for access to new knowledge, and for jobs. Our children, especially those now in primary schools, will live to see a different world, and a very different Asia. One day they will be thankful that they were not trapped by the short-sightedness of their parents, or their government, which left them monolingual and unable to cope with the needs of their time. Bilingualism is the minimum. And, for those above average, a third language is valuable."

The Prime Minister congratulated the prize winners for having done well in their examinations in their mother tongue and English. A language lived in the lives of those who spoke it and used it. "Keep it alive in your lives by using it everyday at home, in school, with your family or friends, reading or writing."

XIII

In his opening address at the Conference on Southeast Asian Security on 31 May, the Prime Minister wondered whether searching discussions on problems of security and defence by conferences "like this one organised by the Institute of Southeast Asian Studies and the International Institute for Strategic Studies" could affect the decisions of major powers and the course of events that flowed from them. Had there been such a conference in Singapore twenty years ago, in 1954, immediately after Dien Bien Phu, could it have foreseen that guerilla insurgencies in Indo-China could not be defused by the deployment of conventional forces not indigenous to the countries? If foreseen, would it have changed the course of events? But, in 1954, a conference on the security of Southeast Asia held in Singapore might well have concluded that the psychological boost to the Malayan Communist Party after Dien Bien Phu would be so great that, unless a firm stand was taken to draw the line somewhere, communism was going to triumph. But, with the benefit of hindsight, this line should have been the Mekong, which divided the Sinicised East Asian Vietnamese from Laos and Cambodia, the Hindu-influenced Southeast Asia. The results could have been much more satisfactory.

A conference in 1974 found governments in the region adjusting their policies to the radical change in America's policy of containment of China. "We all had first notice of this in July 1971, when President Nixon announced his visit to Peking. The communique after his visit in February 1972 set in motion a flurry of adjustments. By October 1972, the Japanese Prime Minister, in Peking, had agreed to diplomatic representation. In early 1973, exchange of diplomatic missions were agreed with Australia and New Zealand. And now Malaysia. If there are no untoward developments in the next few years, the People's Republic of China (PRC) will be represented in all the other countries of Southeast Asia." China's immediate interest in Southeast Asia was to check Soviet influence increasing at her expense. As American and Western presence, up till now so dominant, began to decrease, the Soviet Union might get an advantage. China facilitated an end to American presence in Indo-China by the agreement signed in Paris in February 1973. In the immediate future, to ensure diplomatic representation in other ASEAN countries, the PRC's relations with Kuala Lumpur would probably be impeccable. China could afford to wait before she widened her activities, from limiting Russian influence to increasing her own.

It was worth remembering that Indonesia was one of the first countries in Southeast Asia to have diplomatic relations with the PRC. Relations lasted for seventeen years, from 1950 till 1967, two years after the abortive coup of "Gestapu" in 1965, when relations were suspended. That episode in China's diplomacy turned on the fortunes of Dr. Sukarno and could not be rated a success. A few hundred thousand Indonesians were killed. A considerable percentage of them were ethnic Chinese, believed to have aided or abetted the PKI. The "Overseas Chinese" of Indonesia were the first to learn their lesson on the limitations of Beijing's power and influence. Even those who had remained Chinese nationals were not spared from the tribulations. Partly because of this traumatic experience, other countries in Southeast Asia had been hesitant in exchanging diplomatic representation with Beijing. Malaysia's step marked a new phase.

China was re-entering this region with the benefits of her experience in Indonesia. She had seen the dangers in encouraging subversion and insurgency. She had learnt the limits of using Chinese ethnic and cultural sentiments to spur these purposes. Of course, there were many differences between Indonesia and Malaysia. One of them was that, although Malaysia had no experience of diplomatic exchange with the PRC, she had had more than twenty years' experience of communist guerilla insurgency. But, whatever the problems, in the long run, Southeast Asia had to learn to live with China. Assuming that there was no war between major powers, and no catastrophe involving the use of nuclear weapons, what would Southeast Asia be like in 1994, two decades from now? China would have a second strike capability, and might be working towards nuclear parity with USA and USSR. There could be a Chinese naval presence in the South China Sea and the Indian Ocean, perhaps not as sophisticated or as numerous as that of the Soviets or the Americans. "What we have seen from the past two decades is the gradual decline of the overwhelming supremacy of America and the West in Southeast Asia. What is surprising is not that a decline in a dominant presence should have happened, but that this presence should have lasted so long, and then declined in so climacteric a manner. From 1965 to 1973, there was a painful demonstration in Vietnam of the limits of American power, when a small and determined people, with Soviet Union and PRC weapons and economic assistance, made the application of such prodigious power so wasteful and in the end, for various reasons, so indecisive."

But an America freed from the morass of guerilla insurgency on continental Asia would recover self-confidence and re-assert policies with a much more powerful economy than either the Soviet Union or the PRC could hope to match. "One must assume the steady growth of a Soviet naval presence in aid of her economic and political interests. The riddle to which nobody knows the answer is: where does the powerful economic dynamo of Japan fit? For, in another twenty years, it will not be enough for Japan just to remain equidistant from the USSR and the PRC, with close security and economic links with America, though one hopes that the Japanese will still be using the American nuclear umbrella."

Twenty years was a whole generation away. Meanwhile, the countries of Southeast Asia had to attend to the immediate changes that followed a dismantling of the barriers of containment, with an eye to, and the eventual establishment of, a PRC presence and influence in Southeast Asia. It was not improbable that détente involved an America conceding that the establishment of a PRC influence might be a counterpoise to a greater Soviet influence in a region, which must be the case if the PRC were not present to join in the contest. "A point worth remembering is that we are not going back to the early 15th century, when Admiral Cheng Ho of the Ming Dynasty sailed the waters of Southeast Asia, nor to an earlier era between the 7th and 12th centuries when the Chinese went to Cambodia on elephants, as depicted on the bas-relief of the temples in Angkor. We are not going back to the era when transport and communications made her the Middle Kingdom for all around her, which could be reached by horses or elephants, or sailing ships. Twenty years from now, China may become more like a sun than a moon, radiating heat and influence. But she will only be one of three such suns. And there will probably be another two planets with considerable gravitational pull in economic fields, Western Europe and Japan."

The central question for the countries of Southeast Asia was how to maximise their freedom of choice in this multi-polar world, the right to choose their political systems, and their partners in economic progress. How did they avoid having constraints clamped on them, so that they would be freer to act independently than, say, Finland, or less economically isolated than, say, Cuba? For success, much depended upon America's political nerve and diplomatic skill in not reducing her influence faster than she needed to, thereby triggering impelling reactions on the part of the Soviet Union and the PRC to move in faster than they needed, or were ready, to.

Next, much depended on the capacity of the governments in Southeast Asia, particularly those in ASEAN, to perceive and acknowledge that they had certain interests in common, and adjust their policies so as not to harm these common interests. Each government must specifically avoid policies which might be bilaterally advantageous, but regionally deleterious. An example was in the situation that had arisen in the southern Philippines as a result of the flow of arms which it had been alleged were procured with funds from outside the region. Any dissident group, whether in non Muslim-majority countries, as in the Philippines or Thailand, or even in a Muslim-majority country, as in the case of Indonesia, that received a boost through contacts within the region with such common-cause funds from outside the region would sooner or later set off a chain reaction for similar inflows from other funds, for other common causes. In the end, such interventions were a grave disservice to the collective interests of all. For if forces extraneous to the region were allowed, through connivance or abetement, to advance their influence for ideological, religious, irredentist reasons, through the supply of money and arms, then the great powers would soon get into the act, and get into it much more effectively. If the countries of Southeast Asia, whatever the differences and conflicts between themselves, can place their group interests beyond such interventions, they would have a fair chance of preserving the maximum of freedom of choice provided by a balance between the great powers.

Perhaps the events of the last few months reflected the beginnings of such an awareness. Hence the elaborate round of official contacts in ASEAN before Malaysia's initiative on China. Even more significant might be the efforts being made to cool off the misunderstandings over the Sulu problems of the Philippines. If such trends continued, the future was not without promise of stability and security.

XIV

In mid-June, the Prime Minister went to London to see British Ministers about defence matters. The election of a Labour Government in February 1974 had given warning of the withdrawal of British forces, though the timing and extent were not immediately clear. In London, Mr. Harold Wilson told Lee that his government had not yet decided about the future of the British forces in Singapore. The final announcement was made six months later by Mr. Mason, the British Secretary of Defence. He said, on 3 December, that Britain would withdraw their forces under the Five Power Defence Agreement with the exception of a small group which would contribute to the integrated air defence system. The consultative provisions of the defence agreement would however, remain in force.

XV

Back in Singapore, Lee, on 31 July, addressed the 23rd World Assembly of the World Confederation of Organisations of The Teaching Profession. Education was of importance to Singapore — the accelerating speed of technological change was continuing to have profound effects on society. A developing country, said Lee, aspiring to join the ranks of the developed, must educate its total population. There must be universal education to ensure a more or less completely literate work force, easily trainable to fulfil all the multi-fold jobs of an industrial society. When education came to be treated as one sector of governmental planning for social and economic development, however, attitudes to teaching as a profession underwent a change, and not for the better. It had affected the reasons why people wanted to become teachers. Since education was a component part of the development process, to produce manpower needs, teaching was no longer regarded as a calling which required dedication in those entrusted with the nurturing of the young. It was increasingly viewed and openly discussed as just another career. Its attractiveness depended upon the effort demanded of the job, measured against material rewards, perks and holidays. These were compared to other jobs open to those demanding ability and qualifications equivalent to those for teaching.

True, technological progress had improved the aids for teaching, sophisticated audio visual techniques, close-circuit television, and so on. But, however ingenious and useful teaching aids were, they were not able to displace the teacher-pupil relationship as the single most important factor to bring out the best in a student. Teachers were placed in moral charge of children in their most formative years. They moulded the as yet unformed characters of their pupils, they helped shape the attitudes and values of the next generation. Unfortunately, the changing values in most contemporary societies seemed to produce less of the dedicated types. Even the Catholic Church, which, as an establishment, had nearly 2000 years of continuity, found it difficult to recruit young people into their holy orders. This was one of the side effects of growing materialism. When teachers in developed countries of the West went on strike for more pay and perks, there could be little doubt that the temper of the times had changed, and a more acute sectional and individual selfishness had infected whole societies. And by the time teachers felt this way, such social attitudes would be reflected in a more acute way in the younger generation. But, somehow, these trends must be reversed.

The immediate question was: would one make up for the loss of dedication, or the absence of personal commitment to the future of pupils, by a higher standard of professional competence? "I would be cheered if, in your deliberations, you could point the way to higher teaching skills and techniques which can make up for this absence of personal interest by teachers in the welfare and future of their wards. Now let me refer to a problem which complicates education in developing countries. The reverse side to teaching is learning. Learning depends on language. In developing countries, self-respect and cultural continuity favour the mother tongue. But for access to new knowledge, and ease in communicating with managers and technocrats coming from the developed world, English, or one of the other languages of the developed countries, is of immense advantage in rapid social and economic transformation."

Faced with three major mother tongues, and nearly a dozen dialects amongst the population, Singapore had settled for bilingualism, the mother tongue and English. To teach the English language effectively meant allocating time judiciously between the mother tongue and English. It also meant recruiting student-teachers whose mother tongue was not English, but whose command of the English language was good enough to teach English to students whose mother tongue was also not English. The core of teachers who had mastered the English language during the colonial period was small. At that time, education was for a small portion of the population. With self-government, the speed of expansion of schools was phenomenal. All parents sought a place in school for every one of their children. So the government could not be demanding in choosing recruit teachers. It was the chicken and the egg problem. Was it possible to produce, if not in this then by the second generation, people who could speak, read and write English fluently and effectively when their parents did not speak it at home and their teachers did not have complete mastery over the language? Yet, somehow this must be adequately achieved. "When it is achieved, then our teachers and their pupils will get even more infected by the attitude of the developed English-speaking world, including their growing selfishness and self-indulgence. This is a conundrum many countries in the Third World have to solve. Perhaps, in your deliberations, you may help me solve this riddle."

"Not since the great depression in 1929, has there been such upheavals in the world," noted the Prime Minister in his National Day Message. Double-figure inflation rates, with rising prices of food and manufactured goods, were straining the social fabric of even highly-developed societies, like Italy. For the first half of 1974, America's GNP fell by 2.75 per cent. Japan's fell by 6.5 per cent. America and Japan were Singapore's two largest trading partners in the industrial world. When their economies went down, Singapore's was pushed down also. "In 1973, Singapore made 12 per cent real growth. In 1974, for the first half, it was estimated that growth would be 6.7 per cent in real terms; that is after adjusting for inflation."

Because governments of industrial countries were facing galloping inflation, they had tightened credit, putting up prime rates of interest to 12 per cent. Italy's was up at 20 per cent. Singapore was forced to follow this "liquidity squeeze". Prime interest rate was 11¼ per cent. Otherwise, Singapore money would flow out. But high interest rates slowed down investment. And without investment there would be no increase in production. And because production had slowed down over the whole industrial world, demand for raw materials had gone down and commodity prices had come considerably down. The world had become so inter-dependent and interlocked that it was impossible to insulate from developments in the industrial giants, in the oil-producing countries, and in the food-producing countries.

The quadrupling of oil prices had changed the outlook for all the world. "We were planning for 12 per cent growth. Now, we may have to settle for 6 – 8 per cent, depending on how the industrial countries recover in the second half of the year. Our biggest problem has been the sharp increase in prices of food and essentials. We cannot look for soft options, like subsidising food, absorbing the rise in oil prices, and keeping down electricity charges. We do not have oil wells. Nor do we grow rice, corn, or soya beans. The feedstuff for our pigs and chickens is imported at world market prices."

To subsidise consumption was to pour money down a bottomless pit. Once the government raised taxes to subsidise and sell rice cheap, it would have embarked on an exercise in self-deception, in deficit budgeting, that must end up in bankruptcy.

But import tariffs had been removed or lowered for food and other essentials, to lower prices and counter profiteering. Wages had been increased by a higher percentage for the lower paid than for the better paid. Each worker had the responsibility of deciding how to spend his money. If he chose to burden himself with many children, when family planning and abortion facilities were easily available, he must carry his own burden. "If we subsidise, in effect, we take money from the prudent worker, with a small family, to subsidise those who choose to have large families. However, we subsidise all activities which will improve our capacity to produce. We spend revenue, from taxes you pay, on better educaton and industrial training, for better health and housing, and a cleaner environment. The guiding principle is to spend on areas which will increase our ability to increase our earnings."

Nine years of rapid growth had got people used to expect more each year for the same work. The young had never known the uncertainties of unemployment and hardship. Many did not make a habit of saving a part of their earnings. In 1973, the percentage of earnings saved dropped. So in 1974 CPF rates have been increased. This would help to keep inflation down. It would also finance housing, urban redevelopment and other public works. More people had been sucked into the consumer society, buying more and more things on hire purchase. Their monthly commitments had become heavier. So when the economy slowed down, they got worried. A longer-term view of life had to be cultivated. "We need a philosophical compass, not to lose sight of the fundamentals of life in Singapore, in Southeast Asia."

The present economic difficulties were world-wide. The prospects for 1975 were still unclear. Some countries were solving their problems better than others. The Germans and the Swiss had stronger and healthier economies than most others in Europe. Amongst the factors that made a country better at overcoming economic problems were: first, the cohesiveness of the society; second, industrious and competent workers proud of their better finished products; and, third, most important of all, the ability of the people and their government together to take tough decisions, and stick to them. "I believe the Japanese also have these qualities and so will overcome their present difficulties." Political stability and an industrious and skilled work force were the foundations of Singapore's economic growth. There was no law of nature which said that every year standards of living must rise and the quality of life must improve. "But if we keep raising our technical skills and professional standards, we can make a better living each year."

For the future, birth rates must be kept low. "Then we can afford more on education and training, and so increase our earning power. This is our way forward as a competitive and efficient centre for industry and services. Geography and history decided this for us. Whilst we have no vast hinterland to open up for plantations or mines, we have the location, the social and economic infrastructure, the discipline and skills to keep us competitive. Singapore has always had to face competiton in a tough world. Our young are ambitious and energetic. They must also acquire those qualities which enabled their parents to make Singapore what it is today — the grit and determination to stay the course, the strength and stamina to ride over rough patches. We must take in our stride today's upsets, making adjustments as conditions change, whilst keeping our eyes on targets for next year, for the years after, working and planning into the next decade and beyond."

"Our 9th anniversary sees a very different Singapore," said Lee at the National Day Rally on 18 August. "The prospects were of an entirely different world since the quadrupling in the price of oil January 1974 and the growing double-digit inflation rates in Europe, in Japan and even in America and alas, in Singapore, too. Last year, in money terms, Singapore made 22, 23 per cent, but half of it, was inflation. So in 1972 prices, Singapore only made 11½ per cent. For the first six months of 1974, 6¾ per cent, after adjusting for inflation. You know we were hoping for 12 per cent."

Lee reviewed the world's economic picture. The American economy, he said, was the world's largest, with GNP at over $1,000 billion, or American one trillion dollars. So between them and the Germans who were also anti-inflation, squeezing credit, there would be an anti-inflation emphasis in the next few months. If inflation was brought under control by next year, the OECD estimates might be right. They said plus 3¾ per cent growth for the seven big industrial countries for the first half of 1975.

This would have repercussions for all countries. Booming economies demanded more raw materials, more steel, copper, zinc, rubber and palm-oil. When they slowed down, they needed less iron ore, copper, even less crude oil. People were calculating that there was a surplus of production over consumption of about somewhere between three to four billion barrels a day, 10 per cent. All the storage tanks were filled because everybody was slowing down to fight inflation. And so the Australians were getting less. They were booming last year. They were getting less now for their iron ore and other minerals. And the Malaysians had advised their rubber growers to hold back 10 per cent of their rubber production in order not to let the price go down. This had a multiplier effect. The whole world was interlocked, which meant that unless tough measures were taken and discipline enforced, Singapore would get roaring inflation and reserves would be depleted.

Lee said that people, particularly foreigners, in their newspapers, said "we are an authoritarian lot because we are prepared to discipline ourselves". There was a style about writing articles as there was with clothes. The West set the style. "When we discipline ourselves, the Western journalists say authoritarian government, dictatorial, no freedom. When Bangladesh gets into trouble, let me read to you the kind of sympathy they show. I am reading from a reputable newspaper, the *London Times*, 14 August. And they sign themselves. Mr. Nicholas Ashford writes: 'Bangladesh lives continuously on the brink of disaster, and it is hardly surprising that many foreign aid officials have become fatalistic. Some believe Bangladesh can never become economically viable, and will always have to be supported by massive injections of foreign assistance. Even optimists expect that the country will require sustained large-scale aid for many years ... and that self-sufficiency will only be possible if the high population growth rate can be curbed.' When you cannot put your house in order, they say, 'Well, there you are — hopeless case, non-viable.' The sympathy you get are just words."

Another correspondent, the same newspaper — three articles on a human tragedy. Michael Hornsby from Dacca was more sympathetic because he was right there on the spot: "So far, the only international response to the Bangladesh Government's appeal for help has been a trifling contribution of $20,000 from the United Nations Disaster Relief Office in Dacca, and an aircraft load of supplies from Britain." And the ending was, Michael Hornsby from Dacca: "There is probably also a feeling that the floods do not represent a compelling case for a special international relief effort in as much as they are an annual phenomenon with which Bangladesh must learn to cope with its own resources if it is to be a viable country." "If we don't cope with our problems, that's the sympathy we will get."

There were other problems. And they had to be faced. The world was changing rapidly. The international background was changing. It was only a matter of time before the People's Republic of China would be represented in all of Southeast Asia. "We have made our position clear. When our immediate neighbours, Malaysia, Indonesia have diplomatic relations, we will have diplomatic relations. Just like China, we calculate what is in our interest. And our interest is best served by not taking first or second place. There are many reasons. First, the long-standing suspicion that we are 75 plus per cent — actually 78 per cent by the 1970 census — ethnic Chinese. American, Australian, British scholars, they call us Overseas Chinese. There is a very subtle difference in the term. They don't call Australians and New Zealanders Overseas British: they are Australians, they are New Zealanders. But they call us Overseas Chinese. I think there is a sub-conscious question mark. When I tell them I am a Singaporean, sometimes they say, 'Yes, perhaps you are': they concede that. But they want to know whether the 78 per cent minus me are Singaporeans. I am convinced that the majority, the overwhelming majority, are. Otherwise, they would not have voted for this government so decisively in 1968 and again in 1972. But there is no harm in letting others take first and second places." There was no question of recognition. "We recognise China; China recognises us. We carry a dialogue in the UN, wherever they are represented— in London, Tokyo, if we like, in Hong Kong. In Singapore, there are two banks. The Bank of China and the Kwangtung Provincial Bank are owned by the Government of the PRC. And two insurance companies. No problems about trade. In fact, they buy very little and we buy a lot. The balance of trade is immensely in their favour. Of course, we don't object to this so long as over-all, there is a credit balance."

Lee said that the ultimate question that must be measured against every policy was: "Was this in our interest? As of now, I say no. And I am prepared to say that the majority of the people will support this. When the time comes and it is in our interest, we will do so."

The Prime Minister spoke about rumours which had been spread, that he was about to resign, that there was a row in the Cabinet, that he and Dr. Goh were quarrelling. All this was a lot of mad nonsense, but he warned that these were not the last of the rumours. "You are going to hear more. Always ask yourself: What's this aimed at? To shake your confidence. Who benefits if Singapore is shaken? Not Singaporeans. And what proximity to truth? Singapore must grow in sophistication, in their ability to take things in their stride. Never get carried away with too much success, never be downcast when you haven't made the targets you aimed for because intervening circumstances have changed the situation. But there is one fundamental quality we have, which nothing can change, and that is the verve, the vitality, the drive in our people. Call it what you will — the DNA, double helix — whatever you like to call it, is in us. That is the most precious asset we've got — but it can only be used if there is organisation, there is cohesion, there is unity of purpose and objective between government, people, between unions and employers."

XVII

Another batch of infantry officers were commissioned on 31 August. "People learn at different speeds," Lee told them. "We have found that some of our best NSF recruits can, with special instruction, be taken through from raw recruit to 2nd Lieutenant between December of one year, after their 'A' levels, and September of the next — under nine months. The average SAF training time span is thirteen and a half months — twelve weeks basic military training, seventeen weeks section leader training, and six months' officer cadet training." Selectivity, whether in schools or in the SAF, presented the classic dilemma. Selectivity or streaming increased the pace of learning, and minimised frustrations for the fast learner at having to go at the speed of the slower in the class. But it was very necessary, as officers, that they knew what the capability of the average soldier was, and how much allowance must be made for the slowest of them all.

The orthodox view of the teaching profession had always been against streaming and selectivity. The argument against selectivity was that more than half of life consisted of learning to live with, and having to work through, ordinary people, most of whom learnt and worked at ordinary pace. The argument for selectivity was that it brought the best out of a student in the shortest time, for he was kept on his toes by others who could more than match him.

There were merits in both approaches. The argument would go on. For this was a human problem, and a balance must be struck between maximum results and long-term human considerations. "However, we must judiciously use selective group training whenever there are specific objectives to be achieved with dispatch. You are the fourth batch of his special officers' frame. This year, we have added a variant. Instead of leaving only the potential SAF Scholars in this frame after the basic training, the Overseas Merit Scholars are also taken through this special frame. The Overseas Merit Scholars will do another two and a half years when they return. So we will have a group of people, well above average in ability, who would have done more in the SAF, doing a further two and a half years' National Service as commissioned officers after their graduation. They will go into the reserves with much more specialised training in specific jobs. This reservoir of ability and experience will come in useful for the many reservist roles in the SAF.''

Lee recalled that the first SIR battalion was formed nearly twenty years ago, in 1957. In 1962, the SIR expanded into a second battalion. ''If we had known that they would be the nucleus of the officer cadre of the SAF, how much more could have been achieved! Even so, quite a number of the original officers have risen to the challenge. Without them, it would not have been possible to cope with the task of building up a national service SAF so rapidly.'' Every year, some six to twelve promising young men were selected as SAF Scholars. After they graduated they would have to tackle multifold problems of training and exercising troops and reservists. They would have to build up systems for the maintenance and logistics of ever more sophisticated systems. The more complex the system, the more necessary it was to simplify instruction for the average soldier. Officers expected to do this could not be simple people. Of the first batch of five SAF Scholars who went overseas three years ago, four took First Class honours and one an Upper Second. Keen and fresh minds, grappling with apparently intractable problems, must come up with the answers. In 1974 six SAF Scholars would join this task force of hard digits. When they finished their studies, they could expect to be asked to do the difficult jobs, to solve the apparently insoluble problems. Much had been achieved by officers, without whose experience and reliability the expansion of the SAF could not have been so rapid. Much more remained to be done and would be done. ''We will not be satisfied until performance levels in the SAF match the best we have achieved in the public sector.''

XVIII

New Zealand's Prime Minister, Norman Kirk, died suddenly on 1 September and Lee sent a message of condolence to Hugh Watt, Deputy Prime Minister of New Zealand. Lee said he was grieved to hear of Kirk's death. ''He was a man of principle. What he said he followed up by what he did. At the Commonwealth Conference in Ottawa last August, he impressed all who met him for the first time by his sincerity and his convictions. His death is a loss to New Zealand and all those in the Commonwealth who knew and respected him. The countries of South East Asia, which he visited so often whilst in Opposition, have lost a good and dependable friend."

XIX

Lee's efforts at heavy sarcasm were unfortunately misunderstood, no doubt deliberately, by some reporters of his speech to the Commonwealth Press Union on 30 September. The Union was meeting in conference in Hong Kong on the subject of pressures on the Press. He said he had not been asked to speak on this subject, but he knew they would be curious about how he pressurised pressmen. In heavy sarcasm, unsmiling Lee said: "Well, in addition to all the conventional pressures we learnt from the West, we also have special inquisitional instruments, ancient modes of torture, specially graduated to inflict pain, more excruciatingly than that the journalist inflicts on the politician, plus of course, interest added for grave injury done to the public good. We have also modernised these ancient forms with the addition of electrical and electronic gadgetry, stereophonic sounds to amplify the terror, and low sound waves to give sensations of an earthquake. In this way, we can transform a bold and fearless critic, into a willing and compliant sycophant." Lee added that to get the lurid details, he would leave the subject "for quiet discussion between you and your Singapore colleagues, who I know will be only too happy to tell you all about it when I am not present. I hope that there are representatives from other parts of Asia, Africa, or South America, who can compare notes with your less fortunate colleagues in Singapore." Amazingly, extracts from this speech were later quoted by writers anxious to "prove" that Lee tortured pressmen in Singapore.

In his speech, Lee turned to "less serious subjects" like the Commonwealth and the changing world. The Commonwealth, like all living associations, was itself changing, at least as fast as the rest of the world. Britain's membership of the EEC was the most significant event in the past two years. The economic bonds of Commonwealth preferences had given way to discussions for trade agreements, or association, or commercial co-operation agreements with the EEC. The aftermath of British empire was different from that of any other empire. Britain's first overseas colonies were in North America. After these colonies fought for and obtained their independence in 1776, they went on to take over all the Dutch, French and other European colonies in North America and developed into the world's greatest industrial and technological power. That they made this an English-speaking people had had, and would continue to have, a profound impact on the Commonwealth and the rest of the world.

It was said that Harold Macmillan saw Britain's role as the cultivated Greek to the newly arrived Roman. But the analogy of the Greek-Roman symbiosis did not do justice to the heritage Britain left behind in America.

The Greek language was reduced to insignificance, while Latin became the *lingua franca* of the then civilised world. In the British-American relationship, it was as if the Greeks made the Romans and their empire Greek-speaking. True, Webster's was different from the Oxford English dictionary. New inventions, new ideas, had added new words, expressions and idioms. But there was sufficient feed-back to make the English language essentially similar and understandable, not only as between Englishmen and Americans, but also between them and Canadians, Australians, New Zealanders and the non-native English-speaking Commonwealth. Many of the new Commonwealth countries had found that it was an asset to keep the learning and use of English. It was now a language of the educated in large and important centres of the new and the old world. De Gaulle could have been pardoned for an "expletive deleted" in his other world if he could have heard the recently elected French President meeting the new German Chancellor conversing without an interpreter in English!

"And so it is in Southeast Asia. The British gave us their language. When Ministers and officials of the five ASEAN countries meet, they speak English. The Thais have always learnt it with the British accent before the last War, and the American, since then. The Filipinos speak Spanish-American. The Indonesians, with their facility for picking up languages, speak English fluently with a Dutch accent. Malaysians, like Singaporeans, speak it with a Malaysian-Singaporean accent, or rather several sub-accents depending on their dialect groups. In truth, the British created a world audience which the Americans took over and expanded. Today, the sheer volume of American publications, from dailies to weeklies, to monthlies and books for recreation and education, they pour out broad as the Mississippi, compared to the River Thames. The impact is pervasive."

The facility of understanding each other in the Commonwealth was likely to continue. But it would be unrealistic to ignore America's economic weight, scientific lead and technological ascendancy. This wealth had its repercussions on the mass media. Ten years ago, the British quality newspapers had more experts on Southeast Asia than the Americans. Today, after US$130 billion spent on Vietnam, the Americans had more experts. Even the best of British quality papers were unable to maintain correspondents in each of the major areas of Southeast Asia. They had to use stringers. "And recently I read an interview given by President Giscard d'Estaing in a British newspaper. It was an interview given by the French President to an American, James Reston, printed in the *London Times* by arrangement with the *New York Times*. There was a finality in this symbolic acknowledgement of the overwhelming weight of American resources."

With the world changing so fast, it was dangerous to predict trends even up till 1980, let alone the year 2000. If present trends continued, experts said that all the industrial world's reserves of some US$400 – 500 billion would belong to a few Arab oil producers. And this was just the beginning. Could it be that the Americans and Russians had created a new "Pax Soviet-Americana", the condominium M. Jobert quite rightly resented? Had their nuclear missiles formed the neat balance of the new Roman Arch beneath which the oil producers were disporting themselves with their fabulous wealth? "For days, weeks and months after the oil embargo last year I watched, incredulous and in awe. An oil sheikh had only to leak good news to the press, for instance that the embargo was likely to be lifted, and Dow Jones and *Financial Times* indices would go up. Then, when another oil sheikh announced the price of oil would double from 1 January 1974, Dow Jones and the *Financial Times* indices slipped down, as did other stock markets in Frankfurt, Tokyo and Paris, and, alas Singapore." All this had a most fantastic impact on floating exchange rates. Young money brokers, presumably bright and sprightly, calculating that the oil burdens on the balance of payments would be least on America, decided that the US$ must be worth more than the £, Yen, the French Franc, and the Deutsche Mark. And they made the $ go up within a matter of hours by more than 10 per cent.

"I watched this buffeting of the financial and currency systems of the world, wondering whether some super wizard had decided to punish the strong industrial nations for the cavalier way they had treated the long-suffering Arabs. But alas, many more longer-suffering masses in India, Bangladesh, and Africa were punished as well. Day by day I watch stocks and shares, short-term deposits and gold bullion, like so much *Monopoly* money or plastic chips in a casino, go up and down, and eventually end up in a heap in front of a few fortunate enough to have oil and to take advantage of the modern-day Roman Arch — a neat balance of nuclear missiles between America and the Soviet Union. It is a breathtaking pastime, this new sport, which we in the still poor Third World watch in bewildered amazement as the Fourth World punishes the first no doubt for the vicarious satisfaction of the Third. But I cannot help wondering what would happen if somewhat, somehow, someone moves one little unclear keystone from the 'Roman Arch' of the new 'Pax Soviet Americana'. Or indeed what if the two policemen in this condominium decided they should stop all this gambling in the interests of an orderly world?"

Meanwhile, the world scene kept changing like a kaleidoscope. The world's greatest boxing contest would take place, not in America, but in Kinshasa. The contestants would get at least US$5 million each. Indeed one of them was already demanding more, even though both their purses were tax-free in Zaire. "Last week I read that BBC TV was going to run, for two years, a trial newspaper on television *Ceefax*. Press the button and you can have the sports or business page, home, European or overseas news. IBA, Independent Broadcasting Authority, will run a similar experimental programme called *Oracle*. This was good news indeed. It was giving back to the printed word via the electronic media, the importance it should always have, over the picture and the spoken word. I could not help wondering whether this is not once again the Briton playing the

Greek in the Roman Empire. Let us hope this will not be like what the Comet was for the Boeings and the DC8s. But even if it is, it proves that the British are still an imaginative, inventive and creative people, reaching out for the frontiers of knowledge despite a smaller economic base. And the British contribution to contemporary literature not least because it's in elegant prose is still considerable. And I consider myself fortunate to have learned the classical version of the language to my continuing joy and advantage.''

XX

In his Hari Raya Puasa Message, the Prime Minister, on 16 October, said that the world was facing grave economic crisis and inflation. "All people, Muslims or non-Muslims, in countries which do not produce oil, face a decline in their real living standards. Bangladesh, still having a bad time trying to recover from the ravages of war, was hit by new floods and natural disasters. On the other hand, non-Muslim countries like Germany and Venezuela are doing well, the first because of a well-developed economy and a highly trained and disciplined work force, the second because they have oil.'' Singaporeans, Muslims, Christians, and others, had been fortunate. They had been celebrating their traditional festivals with money to spare. Political stability, higher skills and greater effort, had been the basis of their progress. "As the international situation now shows no signs of improving, we shall have to be ready for harder times. There may have to be adjustments to changing conditions. Only in this way can we ride out, without too much hardship, the economic troubles besetting the world. We must all pull together. We must stay efficient and competitive in wages and costs.'' Lee wished all Muslims in Singapore Selamat Hari Raya Aidil Fitri.

XXI

In Parliament on 6 November, the Prime Minister formally proposed that President Sheares be re-elected President of the Republic. The motion was carried unanimously. Lee said that as President, Dr. Sheares had undertaken his duties with a conscientiousness which had characterised his whole working life. Unfortunately, in December 1971, his health suffered a setback, whilst under examination in hospital at Houston, Texas. "Those of us who know how gravely ill he was before and after he had his operation in December 1971 were deeply concerned. However, he overcame the setback. Slowly and steadily, he pulled himself up from the aftermath of such a major operation. Courage and tenacity summed up the spirit in the man. He never treated himself as an invalid and, as a con-

216

sequence, his doctors were surprised and delighted, within less than a year of the operation, to report that he could resume his normal duties." Firmly, but surely, he adjusted life to his new condition and settled a format for an active intellectual life. He resumed his regular protocol and social duties. He also resumed his teaching and demonstration classes at Kandang Kerbau Hospital, imparting his considerable experience and expertise to young doctors aspiring to be gynaecologists. He had carried his office with unassuming dignity, application and self-discipline. He had won the respect of all who came to know him. He took his official and social duties seriously. He had a keen and lively interest in his work. He read up the background to all the papers that constitutionally had to go to him, and thus was abreast with what was going on in government. "In moving his re-election, my colleagues and I have every confidence that he will continue to discharge his duties ably. He has now gained wider experience, and a greater understanding of the ways of men and nations. Every dignitary who has had to call on him has received unfailing courtesy. To every one of them, he has paid the deepest compliment any Head of State can pay, namely to take a real interest in the man, learn about him and about the country or causes he represents."

XXII

Economic matters continued to concern the Prime Minister. In his Deepavali Message on 12 November, Lee again referred to the economic recession and food shortages facing all except the oil producers. Deepavali celebrated the victory of light over darkness. "Let us hope that the forces of light and reason will prevail in our closely interdependent world. The danger caused by quadrupled oil prices is that each major industrial country may try to reduce its balance of payments deficits by exporting more and importing less, thus defeating each other, making the recession worse. Within the limits of international constraints, we can activate and accelerate economic development. We shall speed up construction in development projects of various ministries and statutory boards. We shall stimulate private building. By judicious incentives, we shall speed up implementation of investments already in the pipeline, especially those based on the by-products of our refineries. We shall ease the way for expansion of oil rigging, shipbuilding and ship-repairing industries. For in these sectors, petrochemicals and in oil rigging and ship repairing, we are in a favourable position. We must use up funds and workers otherwise idle. This will mitigate the effects of recession and increase our productive capacity, ready to take off when the world economy picks up." He wished all a Happy Deepavali.

XXIII

For the first time in nineteen years a Colombo Plan ministerial meeting was held in Singapore, on 2 December. Lee recalled that it was twenty-four years, since January 1950, when a meeting of Commonwealth Foreign Ministers in Colombo initiated "this imaginative plan for technical assistance". Since then, the Colombo Plan had expanded to include non-Commonwealth countries, both as donors and recipients, making a total of twenty-seven. Since 1950, US$2 billion had been expended on technical assistance alone, half of it, just over US$1 billion, for exports, one-third, over US$600 million, for equipment, and one-fifth, nearly US$400 million, for trainees and students. These were money values, spread over twenty-four years. Adjusted for inflation, this could be something nearer US$4 billion in current money values. This might not seem a very large sum. But the transfer of technology, knowledge and skills, which was the primary function of the Colombo Plan, made it the most worthwhile US$4 billion ever expended on a project where a group of advanced countries set out to help the technologically more backward.

Singapore was grateful for the help received under the Plan. In money terms, it had been some US$3 million. But the multiplier effects of the professional personnel trained in management and technology could not be so simply quantified. Over five hundred professors and teachers had come to Singapore and trained hundreds of engineers and technicians. Over two thousand Singapore students had been trained in British, Australian, New Zealand, Canadian, Japanese and Indian universities. They had made the Singapore of 1974 very different from that of 1950. "Without this trained manpower, we could not have made the transition from a centre dependent so largely on entrepot to one primarily based on manufacturing, and repair and servicing of ships and aircraft, and the provision and maintenance of present communications, from underwater-cables, to microwave, to earth satellite receiving stations." The world had just been buffeted by high commodity prices, and had become conscious of the constraints, if not the limits, on growth by exhaustible raw materials and recent volatile prices. It was useful not to forget that technology, knowledge and skills were fundamental to the creation of wealth. For thousands of years, without the knowledge and the technology, all these raw materials had been of no use to man. Without the combustion engine, and later electricity, oil would never have become the critical resource for energy. Without further R and D into petrochemicals, it would never have been transformed into fertilisers, pharmaceuticals and man-made fibres. Now that the world had got used to consuming such large quantities of oil, unless vast new oil-fields were discovered, the wealth of the world would increasingly flow to the oil producers, especially the Gulf States.

But it was significant that, after twenty-four years, the donor-countries in the Colombo Plan, whatever their present economic and political difficulties, were still the technologically advanced. It is they, the

Americans, the West Europeans, the Japanese, who had the knowledge and skills, the social discipline and political organisation who were capable of undertaking the research and development which might, within one to two decades, provide the world with additional new sources of energy. Meanwhile, developing countries not endowed with abundant natural resources, like Singapore, would be in for a more stringent time. "The best means to a decent life for our people is the acquisition of more knowledge and higher skills."

After over twenty-five years of experience in aid to developing countries, results had not been such as to encourage more aid. This, plus the oil balance of payments crisis, had brought aid programmes to a watershed. Developed countries were reassessing what more could, and what should, be done. Lee believed that aid which increases dependency had been counter-productive. It became an annually recurrent obligation which became increasingly burdensome. On the other hand, aid which made the donee capable of doing things for himself had been more than worth the cost and effort. Assistance in the transfer of skills and technology, when successful, had freed the donor from continuing obligations and won him a friend and trading partner. It also freed the donee from the embarrassment, if not the humiliation, of perenially having to look for more aid.

Helping the developing world had now become intertwined with oil politics. In Rome, at the recent FAO meeting, the food-producing countries generously pledged millions of tons of grain. Unfortunately, several more million tons were needed to feed hungry millions in Asia and Africa. Some of the oil producers, notably the Shah of Iran, had risen to the role enabled by the greatly increased wealth of his country. Both in multilateral aid, through the IMF and other UN agencies, and in bilateral agreements, he had set a good example. "Let us hope that in the coming months and years, arrangements can be worked out whereby the wealthy oil producers can help finance the training and the expertise needed by the Third World, now dropping further behind into fourth place." The Colombo Plan's technical assistance concept was sound. It imparted skills, transferred knowledge and technology, in order that the backward could become more capable of looking after their needs. Some have learned to modernise their agriculture and feed themselves. Some have learned to produce industrial goods and to provide services which would earn them the foreign exchange with which to pay for what they needed. The donor had not let himself into an arrangement which got the donee accustomed to living off charity. Instead, the donee had learned to make a better living for himself, sooner than he could have if he had to learn it all from scratch, without help. The Colombo Plan had done just this. It has cut down the learning time and also made the process less painful, for many also had still a long way to go to catch up with the advanced technology of the post-industrial societies.

XXIV

Appropriately enough, the Prime Minister's final speech in 1974 concerned the absorbing subject of energy. Addressing the Pacific Basin Energy Conference on 9 December, Lee said that since the oil crisis in October 1973, millions of words had been published on the subject. Innumerable conferences had been held. This one justified itself by concentrating on the Pacific area. He said he was not an oil expert. Nor was he knowledgeable about potential oil-fields, on-shore or off-shore, in Southeast Asia, the South China Sea and off the China coast. "However, in a moment of rashness, I committed myself to a speech." A coup by OPEC in converting the price from under US$2 per barrel in 1972 to over US$10 per barrel from January 1974 had totally altered the outlook for the world. Unless massive new oil-fields were discovered, equal to those in the Gulf, an unlikely prospect, the end of 1973 was a turning-point in the history of the world. "I used turning-point after the definition Arnold Toynbee gives it — a decisive event affecting the course of history." For months, the American Congress and Administration made growling noises about lions and gazelles. Later, the line was that with progress towards an Arab-Israeli settlement, Saudi Arabian oil would continue to flow, and prices would automatically go down. The Europeans, particularly the British, were not so sanguine. They were more concerned with the immediate need to borrow, or to use the current euphemism, to re-cycle petrodollars. Americans were not impressed. They said the private banking and financial institutions could handle these surplus petrodollars. They were concerned with getting the price of oil down. President Ford, at the United Nations, spoke in harsh terms about the world being held to ransom. The Arabs were unmoved. So the mountain moved to Mohammed. On November 15, Dr. Kissinger spoke of creating a US$25 billion facility for industrial countries to finance their oil deficits, conditional on their cutting down oil consumption by 10 per cent, and so gradually bring oil prices down by controlling increases in demand. This was American acknowledgement that what had been put up by political act, the Americans were unable to put down by a political act.

Historians might one day note the irony of how a group of deeply religious and anti-communist Arab countries took up the oil weapon, prohibiting oil exports to America, to force the Americans to force the Israelis to withdraw to their 1967 frontiers, and strengthened the communists. That was October 1973. By December, OPEC had delivered a *coup de grace*. OPEC agreed to quadrupling the price of January 1973. Thereby, the whole non-communist industrial world was weakened *vis-a-vis* the communist countries, both the Soviet Union and People's Republic of China. For neither communist bloc was a nett oil importer. Their economies would not suffer disruption because of this sudden increase in the oil price. In fact, for the Soviet Union, Rumania and China, their oil resources became infinitely more valuable. Now, they could trade their oil on the free world markets, for more hard currency, perhaps convertible currency was now a more appropriate description, since no currency appeared hard, bobbing up and down violently in floating currency exchanges. Now, communist countries had more to pay for more western technology.

For twenty-eight years, since the end of World War II, the Americans were able to demonstrate that free, private enterprise, plus democratic forms of government, provided greater material well-being, plus greater individual liberties than communism. As the primary victor of the last war, America, with Britain's support, imposed on the vanquished, Germans, Italians and Japanese, various forms of representative government. The Cold War led to the Marshall Plan. The Korean War led to the rapid industrial rehabilitation of Japan. Plus GATT and ample oil supplies, seemingly limitless as new fields were being discovered the world over, the Americans were able to demonstrate through Western Europe and Japan that the free world, private enterprise plus democratic, representative government, was infinitely superior to the drab, tightly controlled and planned communist societies. One Soviet counter was to weaken the West by encouraging anti-colonialism, and stoking fire in liberation movements. The Americans countered by urging their West European allies to decolonise quickly while continuing trade and investments. This tactic worked for over a decade. In fact, it worked too well. Prices of raw materials went down, as prices of manufactured goods went up.

In the competition between democracy and communism for the hearts and minds of the Third World, the West relied heavily on their greater material well-being, more food, more cars and consumer durables, and more and better homes. It was the consumer society, fueled by cheap oil, helped by abundant, cheap raw materials, free trade flows regulated by GATT, and stable currencies with exchange rates regulated by IMF rules. Now, all these factors were in disarray. Out of an estimated total noncommunist world's GDP of US$4,000 billion per annum, 4 per cent, or US$160 billion, would go to the oil producers. The effects of this transfer of real wealth would be several multiples of this 4 per cent, especially since at least half of this sum could not be spent on investments or consumption in the oil-producing countries.

Some British writers doubted whether democratic forms of government could survive under these conditions, lower GNP and reduced living standards. One man one vote had worked in Germany and Japan since World War II because economic recovery was rapid, and economic growth equal to rising expectations. Political parties could promise and deliver more each year. Now, conditions had changed. Despite borrowing of surplus petrodollars, there had been smaller GDP or minus growth rates for 1974 for most OECD countries, including America and Japan. Even if the OECD estimate of 1 per cent growth for 1975 was fulfilled, it was still 3 per cent short of the capital transfer of 4 per cent that must be made, assuming that there were no further increases in the price of oil. If oil prices were adjusted for inflation, the position would be worse. A British political-economist, affected by the grim, almost despondent, mood over Britain, doubted if democracy, as it was known in the West, could survive other than in the United States. Only the Americans would have enough for their own needs — over 70 per cent of energy and over 8 per cent of essential mineral resources, to survive the consequences of the vastly altered terms of trade.

Even before this oil crisis, democracy did not provide Italy with stable governments. Now, Italy's credit-worthiness was in doubt. Italian gold reserves had to be transferred to Frankfurt as collateral for a US$2 billion credit in Deutsche Marks. Britain and France had their own share of political and industrial problems. Only Germany's economy was still sound, with a 2 – 3 per cent growth expected for 1974 and only 7 per cent inflation. The Japanese had had a political spasm caused by a 25 per cent inflation rate and a 4 – 5 per cent drop in GDP for 1974. If this crisis could be expected to have such ill-effects on the political democracies of the industrialised world, how much more adverse must it be on the less-developed world? Even during periods of high economic growth, from 1950 to mid-1973, many new, developing countries, with no broad economic infrastructure, nor traditions of democratic government, had passed, from the more or less representative governments set up by Britain, France and Belgium to take over independence, into army rule. Sri Lanka had to invoke martial law to counter a "Che Guevarist" uprising. In the Philippines, after twenty-seven years of independence based on a constitution modelled on the American original, lawlessness, corruption and insurgency appeared so intractable that martial law had to be proclaimed.

With Western Europe and Japan less prosperous, now that they had to face staggering balance of payments deficits, the western democracies would appear less superior to the communist system — either that of the Soviet Union, or Eastern Europe, or that of China and North Korea. "These views I advance are more to stimulate thought and discussion than as a prophesy of inevitable decline. The Third World countries, which found one-man-one-vote difficult to operate, even under the best of economic circumstances before the oil and financial crisis, may increasingly experiment with new forms of government and other systems of organising society. Most do not want the communist system. Indeed, nearly all have neither the capacity nor the desire for the rigorous discipline that communism requires. Communist countries, both the Soviet Union and China, have now however given up proselytising." They still believed that history was on their respective sides. And to help the inevitability of the collapse of the capitalising system of the West, in Bucharest, during the UN World Population Conference, both the Soviet Union and China opposed the need for population control. They, the godless, teamed up with the Pope and his God-fearing disciples in Latin America, in urging the wealthy countries to be less selfish and to help feed even bigger populations of the poorer world. With more mouths to feed, less resources to go round, the greater was the likelihood of social breakdown, and revolutions headed by Marxist-Leninist groups.

But it was not only in those poor countries that Marxist-Leninist groups might succeed. Even in the Middle East, Marxist-Leninist groups amongst the Palestinians, might well gain ascendency. And as the Arab oil states spend their increased wealth on faster and greater industrialisation, they would have need for more Palestinian technicians and engineers, amongst whom there would be quite a few Marxist-Leninists. The structure and nature of their traditional societies would be transformed by this and by universal education. It would open them to influences from the West and the Soviet and Maoist ideologies. It might be that many thinking men in the governments of these Arab oil producers were aware of these dangers and preparing to counter them. So they might not use their present overwhelming cartel strength to break the free-world economic system of which they form a part. But some western historians, specialists in Arabic studies, doubted if this would be their response. In short, no one knew how the world would be altered in ten years or less. Everyone knew the world was going through an anxious, troubled and confused period. All of a sudden, many of the fixed terms of reference had disappeared, or become less relevant. And it was extremely difficult to get used to the consequences of the new dispensations of wealth, though not yet of power in the world.

"All I can take comfort in is that Southeast Asia is less stricken than other parts of the developing world. Indonesia exports more than 1.5 million barrels of oil a day and expects US$6 billion in foreign exchange, guaranteeing an ample balance of payments surplus. Malaysia, self-sufficient in oil, with a diversity of products from palm oil and tin, is doing well, with rubber recovering, and timber awaiting a revival of demand in America and Japan. Thailand is sound in a world of high rice and food prices. The Philippines is doing splendidly with teeming Japanese tourists, high sugar prices, and, who knows, maybe off-shore oil. Singapore is bearing up. Growth rates will be less than half those of last year's. How we shall do next year depends on whether the West Europeans and the Japanese succeed in persuading the Americans that recession is more dangerous than inflation. But strong and decisive leadership, crucial in a crises-stricken world, is not self-evident in America, nor so evident either in Western Europe or Japan."

223

THE YEAR 1975

I

Lee travelled extensively again this year, visiting New Zealand, Jamaica (for the Commonwealth Conference), the United States, Japan, Indonesia, Egypt, Yugoslavia, Iran and Malaysia. Everywhere he went the Prime Minister gave interviews, made speeches. He continued to be Singapore's best roving ambassador . Even when no formal speeches were made, no interviews given, as when Lee informally visited Kuala Lumpur from 14 – 16 January, valuable personal contact was made with leaders and officials.

In his New Year Message, Lee predicted that there would be considerable fervour in the traditional greeting of a happy and prosperous new year. Everybody was agreed that the outlook was poor for the first half of 1975. Some economists and bankers believed that things would pick up in the fourth quarter of '75. Others thought this would not be till 1976. The major forces that would determine the course of events in 1975 were beyond Singapore's control. "We have to take them in our stride. There will be more retrenchments before the economy picks up. Neither breaking of heads in riots, nor the wringing of hands in despair, is of help. What is helpful is a mature understanding of the interactions of world political and economic forces, and for us, as a cohesive people, to demonstrate that we can maintain social poise and discipline despite economic upsets."

Singapore had no oil. Preliminary figures showed real growth at slightly half that of 1974's. Fortunately, the balance of payments was in

224

healthy surplus. Being well-placed geographically was an advantage. This advantage had been enhanced by a well-developed infrastructure for air and sea transportation and communications, banking, insurance and finance.

Imports and exports for the twelve months, December 1973 to November 1974, increased by 65 per cent, from $21 billion, for the same period the year before, to $34 billion. But of this $13 billion increase, about $5 billion was the increase in oil imports and exports, up $7.2 billion from $2.3 billion, because of the increased oil prices. In volume (cargo discharged and loaded), the increase was only 1.4 per cent, from 61 million to 62 million freight tonnes. Unfortunately, as 1974 went on, the position weakened. "We did much better in the first half of 1974 than in the second half. We did better in the third quarter, July-September, than the fourth quarter, October-December." As the economy of the world slowed down, prices of all commodities tumbled, except oil and food which depended upon the weather and fertilisers. "Nobody knows what 1975 has in store for us. There are too many imponderables. Nobody knows how the American economy will perform — not even the Americans themselves." The US economy would affect the West European and Japanese economies. Together, they would influence the rest of the non-communist world. "It is best that we prepare ourselves for lean times ahead, and be ready to seize our opportunities when international trade picks up. We should be ready to spring back to full production, to use up the excess capacity, now under-utilised because of lowered demands, leaving some machines idle and thousands of workers retrenched."

Fortunately, the region as a whole was better off than most other parts of the developing world. Singapore's neighbours had oil. "So long as we are prepared to adjust and change to changing circumstances, however unpleasant and difficult these changes may be, we shall progress, though not at the high growth rates as the past few years."

II

At a constituency dinner on 25 January, Lee referred to measures which the Americans and Germans had announced to reflate their economies. He said Singapore had taken steps to ease credits and re-stimulate production. Suddenly, the Stock Exchange had gone up by nearly 30 points, from 146 to 174. Singapore had, as always, over-reacted. "We must be careful not to over-react to the euphoria of economic recovery, for there can be no rapid return to what was. The high cost of oil is with us for many years." It would be at least ten to fifteen years before any probable breakthough in technology for energy. Reflation in America, Western Europe and, later, Japan, was only a partial solution. It reversed the 1974 policy of credit squeeze to contain inflation, because the squeeze was threatening a worldwide depression. Perhaps America had hoped that leaders of the big oil countries would relent in the face of an imminent collapse of the Western economic system. "It did not work. Instead, the Americans have now agreed to re-cycling of petro-dollars, or more borrowing, of oil producers' monies, to keep the Western industrial system going for the time being, and avoid whole countries in the industrial West going broke as no one will lend them more money which they cannot repay."

High oil prices had changed the distribution of world wealth and so the pattern of consumption. Now the pattern of production must change to meet the new pattern of demands. But the suddenness of the rise had led to a dislocation between demand and supply for all kinds of products. It took time to re-deploy capital and labour to manufacture products in demand in the new economic circumstances and wind down production of goods in excess supply. Reflation did not bring about this re-deployment. It only lessened the pain of adjusting so suddenly by stretching out the time. But reflation carried the risk of very high inflation rates in a few years' time, unless it was carefully monitored and controlled. But the American system of government called for a presidential election every four years. The next election was due in November 1976. So long-term plans would probably be after the elections.

Lee spoke of the repercussion in the car industry, and in shipping. "We must face up to the realities of these sudden, but fundamental, changes. We have to revise our development plans and scale down our expectations of rapid growth. Our ship-repairing, ship-building and oil-rigging industries have increased their contribution to our GDP last year. But it is only fools or knaves who believe the world owes pleasure-craft builders a living. The first items people save on in lean times are luxury goods, particularly when they not only cost more to buy but, worse, cost more to run. Stylish pleasure boats which American Marines made come in this category. Workers in pleasure-craft industries, instead of protesting, could do better for themselves to persuade their employers to keep the assembly line going by working less days a week at less pay, in the expectation of a partial recovery of demand by end of 1975 or 1976. Perhaps enough Arabs, Iranians, Venezuelans and Indonesians may take to fishing and water-skiing to make up for the number of Americans who have decided they can no longer afford to do so." Except for the rich oil producers, the period of rapid economic growth, based on ever higher consumption, and so higher production, particularly in the industrialised societies of the West, was over. "We must expect to see much less unnecessary consumption, like second and third family cars."

Singaporeans must return to the virtues of long and thorough training to acquire high skills. For example, the finish on building construction had been deplorable. Every year it got worse. Whether it was HDB low-cost housing or so-called luxury private development, work was slipshod. It was the couldn't-care-less sloppy slapping on of tiles, blobs of cement and colour-wash carelessly dropped on expensive tiled floors, badly fitted locks, ill-fitting windows and doors, and poor electrical fittings. More money amongst workers who wanted homes quickly led to workers who built homes wanting more money for less effort. As experienced workers become rare, contractors and architects had put up with lower standards from apprentices who thought that the world owed them a living. One good side-effect of this slowing down in growth was more people sticking to their jobs. They had to develop pride in work done well.

In 1974, 17,000 workers were retrenched. About three-quarters were women and girls. It was Government policy to give preference to women and girls in all the physically lighter jobs. The boys should be employed in physically more demanding jobs. That went for government ministries and statutory boards, and even the Police and the SAF. The private sector would also be urged to do this. If population planning was to succeed, so that Singapore did not become unbearably overcrowded, the bias in favour of boys had to be cancelled. Parents must see that it made no difference whether their children were boys or girls.

Summing up, the Prime Minister said the present reflation in America, Western Europe and, later, Japan, would prevent worldwide depression. It re-stimulated demand for products which would continue to be produced because capital and labour had already been invested and specialised to produce them. It gave more time to re-deploy resources from areas which higher energy cost had now made uneconomic. The problem now was how to redeploy capital and labour to meet the new consumption needs of a changed world. "This world of the middle 70's and 80's cannot afford the lifestyle of high consumption and waste which have characterised the West. Unless and until there is a breakthrough to cheap energy, the world cannot afford to use and throw away ever scarcer materials, requiring expensive energy to mine, transport and process into finished products. And this change is not going to be painless."

III

On 29 January, the government announced its proposal to get the Central Provident Fund (CPF) to collect 50 cents per Muslim per month, starting from the middle of 1975, for building one mosque in each new town. In the course of the next three to eight years, four new mosques, each varying between $500,000 to $800,000 in costs, would be built in Toa Payoh, Queenstown, Jurong and Chai Chee. Two other mosques would also be built, one in Woodlands or Ama Keng, another in Telok Blangah or Pasir Panjang. Each Muslim employee would have the right to opt out of the contribution of 50 cents a month if he or she did not wish to contribute. The Majlis Ugama Islam Singapura (MUIS) would use their tithe-collecting system to collect contributions from those who did not have CPF accounts, either because they were employers or self-employed.

The Prime Minister and the Minister for Social Affairs and Malay MPs met eight leading members of MUIS on 10 December, 1974. All eight

227

members — Haji Buang bin Haji Siraj @ Haji Abdul Rahman, Syed Isa bin Mohd bin Smith @ Syed Isa bin Mohd Smith, Karikakam Mahamood Shahi Hamid @ K.M. Shahul Hamid, Dr. Yusof Ahmad Talib, Ahmad Elahi bin Mohamed, Mohamed Javad Namazie @ M.J. Namazie, Othman Jantan and Haji Muhtar bin Aziz — acknowledged that with the redevelopment of Singapore, it was inevitable that places of worship, among other buildings, would have to give way to high rise buildings. The few exceptions would be those of historic value. They agreed that the building of one new mosque for each new town was the most practical way to meet the needs of the Muslims as they resettled in the new towns. The MUIS had formally taken a vote on this matter and written to the Minister for Social Affairs supporting the policy of the government.

IV

"In the Year of the Hare, no mishaps are expected," declared Lee in his Chinese New Year Message on 10 February. He said that with the world facing its gravest economic crisis since reconstruction after World War II, this was reassuring. "Let us hope that recession can be reversed without too much inflation, and that costs of oil will not be compounded by more troubles in the Middle East. A Happy New Year to all."

V

Opening the first centre in Toa Payoh of the SAF Reservists' Association (SAFRA) on 19 February, the Prime Minister said that SAFRA membership was nearing 10,000. Until recently, it had been operating in temporary premises belonging formerly to the Norwegian Seamen's Mission in Prince Edward Lane. So the response was encouraging. National Service had become part of Singaporean's way of life. SAFRA would have more centres in other areas of high population. These centres would provide convenient meeting places for reservists and their families. They would all have sporting, social, cultural and educational facilities for men and their wives and children. Membership fees were $2 per annum for other ranks and $5 for officers. For this centre in Toa Payoh, two and a half acres of land had been provided. The clubhouse cost nearly $2 million. But the capital expenditure and annual grants to pay for the costs of running the centre was money well-spent if it maintained camaraderie amongst SAF reservists and provided facilities to help city dwellers keep fit and healthy. However, just as important were the facilities which would be available for wives and children. The well-being of the SAF reservist included the well-being of his family. "From the experience of this Toa Payoh centre, we hope subsequent SAFRA centres will be better designed to meet the needs of our reservists and their families."

VI

On the Fifth Anniversary of the Singapore Industrial Labour Organisation (SILO), Lee on 22 March, stated that in the past three years, wages in Singapore had gone up by more than 30 per cent, faster than wages in Hong Kong, Taiwan and South Korea — countries in more or less similar stages of industrialisation. Fortunately, because Singapore had a more diversified economy, the Republic came out of 1974 with less pain than Hong Kong. Meanwhile, Hong Kong workers, because of unemployment and recession, had willingly taken wage cuts of between 15 – 30 per cent. "At the same time, because we had a comfortable balance of payment surplus, our $ has floated up against the US$ by as much as 20.17 per cent over Smithsonian parity. One year ago it was only 13.04 per cent over par. In one year, it has become 7 per cent dearer to buy with US$. MAS (Monetary Authority of Singapore) percentage change in parities showed the US$ down − 3.8 per cent since we floated in June 1973, and − 11.3 per cent last Friday, 21 March 1975, — a difference of − 7.5 per cent. The strength of our $ is a virtue in developing our Asian Dollar market and banking and financial sector. But this strong $ means that Singapore wages cost more to foreign investors. It also makes the costs of our ship-repairing, aircraft maintenance and other services more expensive, and so less competitive." In fact, to attract industrial investments, to make exports easier, and to make services cheaper to foreign users, it was better to have the Singapore $ float downwards. But when exchange rates were floating, the verdict of the foreign exchange markets had to be accepted.

Representatives of unions, employers and government in the National Wages Council should take this higher exchange value of the Singapore dollar into account when considering the National Wages Council recommendations for 1975. "Every year, to reach the right wage adjustment, we must judge (1) how we have performed in the past year, (2) how we are likely to perform in the current year, and (3) how our competitors and customers will fare." At present, the most important factor was the prospect that this was a year of slow recovery from recession in the industrial countries. Therefore, it would be a year of slow growth for Singapore. The substantial adjustments that were made in 1973 and 1974 could not be expected. Singapore wages, translated into US$, compared to wages in Hong Kong, Taiwan or South Korea, must not over-price Singapore goods and services, "If our economic activity is not to diminish, and unemployment not to increase, this year any wage increase must be very modest and moderate compared to 1974."

229

VII

In Parliament on 27 March, the Prime Minister moved the Second Reading of the Bill to amend parliamentary pensions. The Bill dealt with the withholding of MPs' pensions. Lee said there could be no question that if any Minister, Parliamentary Secretary, Political Secretary or MP had been convicted under the Prevention of Corruption Act, or of any crime involving corruption under any other written law, even if he had only been fined and not imprisoned, this warranted the withholding of the pension. The President, after consideration of the record of the proceedings of the court, would decide whether the whole or a part of any pension should be withheld. "Every Honourable Member knows that nothing is more likely to lower standards of integrity in the conduct of government than to have a member of the political leadership setting a bad example. All those who hold office must abide by strict standards of public and private conduct. It is not possible to enforce high standards of integrity in the civil service if the political leadership tolerates any corrupt behaviour amongst its own ranks. An MP or a Minister must take the consequences of any corrupt act. Losing his pension is one of the least of the sanctions."

VIII

In April, the Prime Minister visited New Zealand. He addressed a parliamentary luncheon in Wellington on 4 April. He said he was deeply honoured by the gathering of New Zealand Members of Parliament from both sides of the House. It was just over ten years since he had previously visited New Zealand. It was a vastly different world. Perhaps it was worth recalling that the world appeared as fraught with danger then, as it did now. The only difference was that, then, it felt a cosier world. The divisions of the good and the bad guys, within and between countries, were simpler. Friends and foes were easily identifiable. And the USA was the strong sheet anchor for the non-communist world. A recent poll commissioned by the Chicago Council on Foreign Relations, and carried out by the Harris organisation in America, disclosed that 77 per cent believed the United States should intervene if Canada were attacked. But only 39 per cent of Americans favoured sending troops to rescue Europe from a Soviet attack. 41 per cent opposed sending troops, despite NATO commitments. However, of those considered in "leadership" groups (politicians, academics, journalists), 71 per cent would fight if the Soviet Union attacked Europe. These were just poll figures, and probably bore no reflection on the responses of the American government or people if those events actually occurred. But they did reflect the mood of the American people at that point of time.

It served no purpose to speculate how much the disasters of Vietnam had to do with Americans turning inwards, how much arose from preoccupations with unemployment and recession resulting from the oil embargo, and how much was aggravated by worries over the still unresolved problems of the Middle East. There was little anyone could do, except watch the tragedy in Indo-China work itself out to the bitter end. Thailand, now under civilian rule with popular elected leaders, might resolve her economic and social problems faster than communist subversion and insurgency could be fomented. Anyway, the secondary areas to the conflict in Indo-China - Malaysia, Singapore and Indonesia - had become more stable and viable in the past ten years. With Thailand and the Philippines, they were linked in a co-operative framework, ASEAN. The Philippines was beset by insurgency problems both in the south and the north. But with resolute leadership and imaginative solutions, these problems could be resolved in time. Students of politics were told that there were no abiding friendships between countries, but that there were only abiding national interests. As between persons, this was not so. There were many people in Singapore, and, he believed, in other parts of Southeast Asia, who had a great regard for New Zealand, and for New Zealanders, as a stout-hearted and generous people, who, in making their contribution to secure Southeast Asia against communist insurrection, did more than their fair share to help their neighbours. There were many young people in their twenties and thirties, who had been educated in New Zealand universities on Colombo Plan scholarships. They would always have a special place for New Zealanders.

New Zealand-Singapore relationships had changed with the passage of time. Britain's historic withdrawal from the Far East had ended the network of security co-operation. It was another piece of history, of a job well-done. The present regional balance and stability were the results of the stabilising influence the ANZUK forces had played. But other links could be strengthened, especially economic ones. Ties of friendship, respect and understanding could help expand trade and travel. They could facilitate the export of New Zealand products and disseminate New Zealand technology, particularly those based on the biological sciences — agriculture, animal husbandry and food processing — for which New Zealand was justly well-known.

What had happened was part of history. "It should teach us, if we can learn from experience at all, what should be avoided and what more can be done for a better tomorrow. The world is too inter-dependent for any country to insulate itself from the rest of the world." When recession struck after the oil crisis, Singapore felt it in a matter of weeks. And New Zealand's geographic distance from danger zones made no difference to the impact of recession on commodity prices and the balance of payments. "This is one inter-related world, especially for those not in the communist bloc. We are interlocked in our economic well-being. You have helped us get off the poverty line. However different future relationships of the past, future ties in trade and technology between New Zealand and Singapore, between Australasia and Southeast Asia, will be more equal and mutually rewarding."

Three days later, Lee spoke at a Press Club luncheon. He said he was not going to talk about dominoes. He had never played the game. Nor did he think it an appropriate figure of speech for the tragedy being witnessed in South Vietnam and Cambodia. What was happening there was having a profound effect on the minds of others in Southeast Asia, particularly Cambodia's immediate neighbour, the Thais. The Nixon doctrine, announced in Guam in 1969, that America would materially help those who were ready to help themselves, died with Watergate. Everyone knew that no American soldier would ever fight a guerilla in Asia after the Paris Agreement of January 1973 allowed them to disengage with honour. By August 1973, the American Congress had interdicted their President from using American bombers without Congressional approval in Southeast Asia. Nixon resigned in August 1974. There had been no time to spell out a Ford doctrine. But he did try to define his aid policy on South Vietnam, namely three more years of military and economic aid before a final cut-off. The American Congress did not agree with their President.

The new Thai Prime Minister had now publicly asked American forces to leave within a year. Since American forces could not help them on land or in the air, the Thais might as well make a virtue of requesting an American military withdrawal. From a symbol of power and security, they had become obstacles to a change in posture, which had to precede a change of relationships with the other great powers. Lee doubted if any Thai government, civilian or military, would want to be engaged in the kind of guerilla insurgency that had crushed Cambodia and South Vietnam. Rather than go through this mincing machine, it made more sense to seek political and diplomatic solutions. Adjustment and accommodation to changed circumstances were necessary. Thais and others in Southeast Asia knew that the patience and perseverance of Americans had not matched that of the communists, not simply communists in Vietnam, but also their suppliers, the PRC and the Soviet Union. Since the Thais were unlikely to be able to make amends to the North Vietnamese for the damage which the American B-52's, using air bases in Thailand, had caused, it would be easier for them to befriend the PRC than the North Vietnamese. After all, Thailand did no harm to China. In any case, the PRC had shown themselves to be more reliable friends, to judge from their support of what once looked the hopeless cause of Prince Sihanouk and the Khmer Rouge.

The rest of Southeast Asia would have to live with whatever political accommodation the Thais made. Fortunately, Thailand had ample time to work out what was in her best interests. For the North Vietnamese would take many years to mend a war-shattered Vietnam before undertaking further adventure in helping Thai insurgents. And the Khmer Rouge or GRUNK, the acronym for Prince Sihanouk's government, would be busy·

not only repairing the shattered economy of Cambodia and her displaced people, but also preventing the Vietnamese communists from becoming the dominant influence over their country. In fact, Prince Sihanouk took elaborate pains to state that Cambodia's number one friend would always be the PRC. If Khieu Samphan and other Khmer Rouge leaders shared this view, then Hanoi's capacity for aiding and abetting insurgency might not reach Thailand other than through Laos to the northeast of Thailand. Thailand's southern neighbour, Peninsular Malaysia, had a completely different situation. Malaysia's guerilla movement had always been, and still was, led by ethnic Chinese. For a communist insurgency to succeed, the rebels must throw up Malay leaders to have a better ethnic balance in the leadership. Only in this way could they get more representative support from the ground. Whilst this was not impossible, it would take a very long time, if it could be done at all.

"An era has come to an end. America had been the dominant power in Southeast Asia for thirty years since the end of World War II. Once America acknowledged that she could no longer intervene in Southeast Asia, it is fair to assume that the contest for influence over the peoples in the region will be mainly between the PRC and the Soviet Union, both of whom openly avow their duty to help communists everywhere and to promote revolution." The fear of Southeast Asian countries was to be caught in a competitive clash between these two. China had the advantage of historic associations with the region. Memories of past tributes paid and an awareness of geographical proximity made all in Southeast Asia anxious not to take sides with the Soviet Union against the PRC even though the Soviet Union was ahead on military technology. Most hoped to maintain equable relations with both the PRC and the Soviet Union. But this might not be possible unless these two communist centres ceased to compete for ideological and nationalist supremacy — a prospect which appeared remote. Meanwhile, a continuing American naval presence and increased economic relations would help the rest of Southeast Asia to adjust less abruptly, and to make the task of learning to live with a communist Indo-China less painful.

In a television interview in Christchurch, Lee was asked if, following events in Indo-China, Singapore felt secure, and required overseas military aid, Lee replied: "When you have been living next to a volcano and you know that it erupts from time to time — many of them false alarms, but every now and again real hot molten lava begins to flow — you develop a degree of equanimity which must never allow you to be lulled into a sense of placid indifference, because that is fatal. Nor can you afford this high tension all the time — every rumble and you are on your toes — or you become neurotic. I think you have got to see it in its perspective."

"You said about five years ago, that by the middle '70s, you should have enough men trained to dissuade anyone from believing that capturing Singapore was a walkover. We are now in the middle '70s. Have you reached that stage?"

Prime Minister: I would like to believe that I have not failed in achieving what we knew we had to achieve.

"From this position of internal strength and in view of what has happened in Vietnam, how do you see your foreign policy developing in the new situation? Will you, for instance, be recognising Peking?"

Prime Minister: We have always recognised Peking. I think right from 1949 ... I mean, the Bank of China was transferred from the KMT in Taiwan to the People's Republic of China or the PRC in Peking. And they have owned and operated it, thanks to the wisdom of the British in the first place, and we continued it, despite a slight risk of its being shut down in 1965 just before we were asked to leave the Federation of Malaysia.

"Given the fact of your new-found military strength and the presence of ... "

Prime Minister: No, no. Never use such words like 'military strength'. Given our capacity to make it impossible to walk over Singapore. I think it is very important that we strike the right note in order that we can achieve the relationships, psychological and diplomatic, which makes economic and social goals the targets on which men's minds are focused."

"Are you saying that you have now achieved that capacity?"

Prime Minister: I think we have, yes.

"Given the fact that you have, does the idea of neutrality appeal to you at all?"

Prime Minister: That is a very ambiguous word. Can you be neutral if you are going to be eaten up? You can be neutral if two big powers are fighting and you don't have to join because you cannot influence the outcome. You have got to live with whatever emerges. Can you be neutral if local powers, regional powers, are involved, and the outcome affects you? Is it possible to be involved with the maximum of chances of success and the minimum damage in case of failure?

"What is your answer to these questions?"

Prime Minister: Well, I think we get to wait first and let the dust settle in Indo-China, in Vietnam, Cambodia. I think there is a lot of heat and sweat and other things which go with the end of an era. In Thailand, they need some time and they have quite some time to decide how they are going to resolve their insurgency, incipient insurgency problems. And I am quite sure that they are not going to slog it out like the Vietnamese have. Nor are they likely to want a Khmer Rouge situation.

"In this new era that is obviously opening in Southeast Asia, does Singapore have a problem of identity as a Chinese, or largely Chinese, city-state set in a largely Malaysian area?"

Prime Minister: Well, yes and no. Yes, in the sense that in countries such as Malaysia and Indonesia, they have — Malaysia more than Indonesia — large ethnic Chinese in their population. And, partly because they are what they are — more hardworking and more striving,

234

or more of them being successful — there are those problems of you are different and why are you doing well. No, in the sense that we have been there for over 150 years. And I am less of a Chinese, a PRC Chinese, than say, you are less of an Englishman.

"Prime Minister, you used the term — when we were talking about a neutral stance — of 'being eaten up'. Who do you see as eating you up?"

Prime Minister: Well, there are several possible scenarios. It doesn't help to spell them out. I mean, of course, one thinks out the most horrendous.

"Which would that be?"

Prime Minister: It doesn't help to discuss and define them. But the most likely one, given the situation as it is today, is a Thailand that has accommodated, over-accommodated, as a result of what is happening or what has already happened ... The way Phnom Penh went down, the way in which the last Thai government so solidly and overwhelmingly backed the Lon Nol regime ... They couldn't get on with Prince Sihanouk ... It is very important for us that they should have time to weigh all the odds before they make an accommodation because to over-accommodate is to bring problems down into Peninsular Malaysia and Singapore.

"From my understanding of what you have said several times, you believe that the best answer to this encroachment is for the encroaching to come up against a fairly strong economy where central issues cannot be stirred up against the country itself."

Prime Minister: Well, it is not just a strong economy. You can have a strong economy and a very inequitable, unequal distribution of wealth and opportunities. And if you get lots of bright able men feeling frustrated, leading a lot of angry and dissatisfied and willing-to-die young men well, that is a typical insurgency situation.

"Do you have that situation?"

Prime Minister: I would think not.

"Prime Minister, I wonder if we could concentrate our attention on Singapore's internal situation? First of all, on the nature of the man currently leading Singapore. I am interested in the fact that you spent some very academically rewarding years at Cambridge. What influence or what degree of influence did years of Cambridge have in moulding your outlook?"

Prime Minister: I think the most single important event in my life was the Japanese entry into Singapore when the Imperial Guards set up sentry points at every bridge, chased me into a corner of my room whilst the officers and men took over the house and billeted themselves and I was generally knocked about. I wondered why it should be so. I think that was the most single traumatic experience and one I am unlikely to forget and one which I fear because the younger generation, the next generation of Singaporeans, have never gone through. It is very difficult to infuse into them the same degree of awareness that in certain situations you must be prepared, whatever the odds, to fight and die. And if the other chap knows

235

that you are prepared to fight and die then it may become unnecessary.''

"Did that experience do something traumatic to your view of the British — in that Singapore was a British colony in those days?''

Prime Minister: Yes and no. Yes, in the sense that the British had their priorities and they failed us, they failed to defend us. They evacuated British civilians and a few of the locals closely involved with the business of government with them. No, because I saw them fight. And, in defeat, they were an impressive if rather a sad and tragic spectacle of motley men but still with discipline, marching past my house into captivity for three days and nights. There were varying contingents. There were the Gurkhas who were almost as disciplined and as good as the British. They never broke ranks, right to the end, right into prison. There were others who did and they didn't cut such good figures as fighting men.

"Where does Singapore's next generation of leadership come from?''

Prime Minister: This is one of the biggest problems that we face. Because, from a situation of crisis which throws up a people who feel they must do it, we have now moved into a situation where going into politics becomes an alternative career and not a very attractive one, because the price is too great. You are under a magnifying glass. It is not just the press. It is what people say of you, your public, your private life, as against making a fairly comfortable living in the professions or in academic. And this is a real problem.

"Prime Minister, I think many people around the world admire very much what you have done for Singapore, you and your party. Yet there are some things in people's minds which appear to be to some degree dictatorial within your attitude. I'd like to know — how do you think the history books are going to see Lee Kuan Yew?''

Prime Minister: I don't think I worry too much about what people think. And when you say people here, you mean the people in the news media, people in academia, the so-called liberals with a small 'l'. I think I can put up with them. In fact, criticism or general debunking even stimulates me because I think it is foolish not to have your people read you being made fun of. And we have got books circulating in Singapore written specially for this purpose by foreigners. Fine! But I would like to believe — never mind, what historians say, but whoever wants to do a Ph.D. thesis — and perhaps there will be quite a few who might want to dig up the archives — they might come to the conclusion that here were a group of men who went through quite an unusual set of experience in a very momentous period of the world, beginning with the Second World War and decolonisation and the setting up of new countries, so many that the United Nations now has become quite unwieldy, and not many of which are likely to succeed. And perhaps if we don't fail, and we will not know that really for a very long time until we have stepped down from office, then obviously despite the criticisms, despite the doubts and queries of how Westerners would have done it, we had our feet on the ground, our heads fairly screwed to our shoulders and we did the right thing by those whose fate was temporarily entrusted in our hands and by our own convictions.

"Well, let us leave that to the history books."

IX

The Prime Minister attended the Commonwealth Heads of Government Meeting in Jamaica from 29 April to 6 May 1975.

In Kingston, Jamaica, on 30 April, Lee addressed the Commonwealth Conference. He said: "It is fortuitous, but I hope not unlucky for Southeast Asia, that I am asked to speak on the day the communists have taken Saigon. It marks in a dramatic way the decline of Western dominance vis-a-vis the communists, USSR and PRC. With the fall of Indo-China, some US dollars two to three billion worth of the latest in American weaponry may become a source of incalculable mischief, not just for the rest of Southeast Asia, but also for the rest of the world. Today, you can buy an M16, one of the best battle-tested rifles, for 2,000 bahts in Thailand, about 200 American dollars. It may well go down to about 1,000 bahts or US$100, now that Saigon has surrendered. It is in this context that I believe more strife in Southern Africa is inevitable. For the last white settlers in Africa will fight for their redoubt. The Soviet Union and now, with added spur, the PRC, are two steady suppliers of weapons and tactics which will see that this redoubt is liquidated, at very low cost to themselves. But it must be paid for in blood by the blacks themselves."

Lee continued: "If we look back, the genesis to the current world problems is in World War II, in 1944, at Yalta and Teheran. The unconditional surrender of Germany and Japan meant the emergence of a vast and powerful Soviet Union. It was inevitable. But Roosevelt believed that he could build this new world order on co-operation between him and Stalin. But Roosevelt was sick and ailing. As it turned out, Stalin was the man who got the mostest out of the war. For twenty-eight years, the Americans refurbished Europe with their enormous, undamaged economy — Bretton Woods and IMF fixed stable exchange rates, GATT and the Marshall Plan rebuilt industrial Europe. The war in Korea helped Japanese recovery. But it was later to lead to the affluent, consumer society, to the liberal attitudes and soft values, the permissiveness, which have eroded the stamina to put up with hardship, seemingly unending difficulties. I sometimes wonder whether it may not have eroded the moral fibre of the West to stand up, and take the punishment even if their own fundamental interests were at stake."

The old Cold War was over. It was now détent. Under the Cold War, the developing countries could plead misery and the danger of going communists, and aid would come. Since the Americans, West Europeans and Japanese were infinitely wealthier, more could be got from them than

237

the Soviets with their poorer equipment and much more demanding political terms. But the Soviets, and even more the PRC, were very wise in their choice of who they chose to support. They chose the tough and ruthless leaders, those most likely to win. To weaken the West, the Soviets and the PRC pressed hard and gave great support to anti-colonial movements. The American response was to urge rapid decolonisation. The tragedy was that in the competition between democracy and communism for the hearts and minds of the Third World, the West relied almost completely on greater material advantage, more food, more cars, fridges, television sets and other consumer durables. It was the consumer society, fuelled by cheap oil, helped by abundant raw materials at low prices, and free trade flows guaranteed by GATT, stable currencies under IMF rules. Now all those factors had gone, giving way to a new era, "detente minus" — minus real peace and co-operation in Third World countries. The Prime Minister of India had rightly pointed out that every time Europe and America had been in trouble in recent years, the Soviet Union had been considerate and understanding. The result was that the West was in total disarray, quarrelling and squabbling over apparently divergent interest, like the sharing of oil during the oil embargo on America or the consumers and producers conference. It was only the PRC that told Europe: "Get together, defend your collective interests."

There were limits to growth. Lee said he was not sure that people could be prevented from wanting growth — it was the easiest way to win votes. When America and Britain won the war, they imposed on the Germans, the Italians and Japanese, one man, one vote. That was supposed to be the model of perfection on how to govern human society — maximum individual liberty, accompanied by maximum material progress. But was it true for new developing countries? Permissiveness and social indiscipline led to disorder and decline in under-developed countries. "One man one vote" every five years, yes — but after that, "work hard" was necessary since nothing was for free, not even cheaper OPEC oil for developing countries.

The traditional classification of the three worlds was that the affluent world was first. So they, together with the West Europeans and Japanese, comprised the First World. If developing countries joined and adopted their system, they might eventually join this affluent First World. The Second World consisted of the Soviet Union and the East Europeans, less sophisticated technologically. The Third World, of course, was the rest. For over two decades, the First and Second worlds competed for converts. Now, more than one hard look had been given to this problem by strategic and economic policy planners in the West. "My colleague, Mr. Rajaratnam, the Foreign Minister, was in Peking recently. The PRC Foreign Minister explained that the First World consisted of the two super powers, USA and USSR. They are the ones competing for world hegemony. The Second World consisted of the middle powers, like the countries of Western Europe and Japan. And the Third World consists of all of us and them, the PRC. They had made the grade without external aids, and perhaps we can usefully learn from their methods and create our own models of how to do it ourselves."

On another subject, Lee suggested that there were limits to growth, but there were also limits on what national sovereignty could do for its people's well-being unless a country was as big as the USA or USSR. "We are strapped to an inter-dependent, inter-related world. All of us here are plugged into the same grid of course, but when there is a shortage of power, it is the supply to the Third World that gets cut. We get the black-outs first. Let us not forget it is 'detente minus'. In Bucharest last year, at the World Population Conference, the Pope must have been embarrass-ed. He found himself supported strongly by the USSR and the PRC. The Russians and the Chinese communists are in favour of more and more people. They agreed with the Pope that it was the selfish wealthy countries who were eating up too much of the world's resources. And only if they would give a little more. We are already heading for trouble. Even if we start aiming for zero population growth, vast areas of the world are going to die of famine and regimes will topple, like Ethiopia."

Lee continued: "Yesterday, we heard you, Mr. Chairman, speak elo-quently on how inequality of wealth and opportunity between nations were going to be a source of great trouble. There are vast American, British and Western investments in gold and diamond mines. Insurrection in South Africa will further weaken the West. It will happen sooner or later. I believe inequalities within nation states, particularly poor, devel-oping ones, is the greatest spur to revolution, with more and more of the Third World going communist. One of the sad phenomena I have noted is that in many cases the poorer the country, the richer the leader or leaders. But it's not just the poor Third World countries that face this danger of more and more revolution. In the Middle East, after twenty-eight years of 'diaspora' for the Palestinians, many have become Marxists, Leninists. They are the trained and well-educated. A number of them are doing the complex jobs in the Gulf States. And all these wealthy oil countries are now with more and more sophisticated minds to operate them. Hence all these new F16s, Mirage F1, nuclear power stations, must change the social order. Adjustments to make for less disparity in wealth and privilege must be made, so that revolution or insurgency, as in Oman, becomes unnecessary."

In conclusion, Lee quoted Sun Tze, who lived over 2,000 years before Clauswitz. He was a military strategist. He said: "Know yourself, know your enemy, a hundred battles, a hundred victories." Lee said he knew the other side, the communists and their backers. But he did not know that the bastions of democracy could not match the resolve of the communists. Now Indo-China had gone to the communists. Providing the rest of Southeast Asia understood that the priority was first to eradicate inequal-ities of wealth and opportunities, to reduce social injustices, and inculcate work-discipline, adjustments could be made to this new dispensation of power without insurgency and a new social order. "But both in the economic and in the political and military fields, it is 'detente minus'. The process of attrition goes on. Americans do not want to fight the Russians and vice-versa. The Chinese have enough nuclear capacity for the Russians not to want to fight the Chinese either. They do not want collision with each other. But collision will be through third parties, their proxies. Let us not be foolish proxies. I want to be myself, as I am sure all of us here would like to be our own men. That when we meet next time, we will have learnt to live with slower economic growth. We have to go through an anxious, troubled and confused period. It helps if we keep our cool. All of a sudden many of our fixed terms of reference have disappeared, or become irrelevant. And it is extremely uncomfortable to get used to the changed balance of power and wealth. But finally, it is power, and the use or non-use of power, that will decide the destiny of the world. It is the power of the Americans and the Russians, and later of the PRC, and how they restrain themselves and their allies, that will decide the framework of peace plus competition for influence. Within this context in Southeast Asia, we have to chart our future, especially after Vietnam."

In another Commonwealth Conference speech on 5 May, Lee said that every issue raised by each participant was of supreme importance to himself and his country. The world began with the home. But it cannot end there. There was a world priority of issues. First, the Middle East conflict, for it carried the dangers of another oil embargo, of the use of petrodollars to disrupt the world economy. The object was to push the Americans, and the West Europeans and Japanese, who, in turn, would pressure the Americans into getting the Israelis to settle. It must be a settlement with Egypt and Syria, and must include a solution to the Palestinian problem. Second was the problem of adjustments to the sudden shift in wealth to the oil producers, most of whom could not use their vast earnings. This had caused dislocations and was one of the causes of a decline in industrial production in the developed countries, and lowered commodity prices in the developing countries. Then came the dramatic events in Cambodia and South Vietnam. The immediate repercussions were felt in Asia. But they had wider implications. The relationships between the great powers, because of the leverage some of them might have on third countries where insurgencies could be intensified with their help, had changed to the advantage of those who could help insurgencies succeed. And Vietnam would be an inspiration to guerilla insurgencies all over the world, not least in Southern Africa, and in the developing countries with oppressed ethnic minorities, like the Eritreans in Ethiopia.

Referring to the collapse of South Vietnam, Lee said China helped in this victory with economic and military aid. So did the Soviet Union, with more sophisticated weaponry. But let the world never forget that it was the North Vietnamese and the Vietcong who paid the price. They fought and won on their own. "In some six to eighteen months, when the flush of victory has subsided, we shall know how swiftly China, Vietnam and the

Soviet Union have moved to consolidate their respective positions to increase their own influence, and diminish that of the other.''

There were 1,500 to 2,000 remnants of the Malayan Communist Party. They flitted in and out of the boundaries of Thailand and Northern Peninsular Malaysia. They had found secure supply lines extremely difficult to establish. Provided Malaysian policies did not increase Soviet influence, especially when China's interests were at stake, China might well be content to leave things as they were for a long time. In fact, it was generally believed that it might be in everyone's interests, including China's, to have the Americans withdraw more gradually from their military bases on the Asian Mainland. For, if this withdrawal took place precipitately, it could give the Soviet Union the chance to move into areas China considered vital to her, and force China's hand.

Lee thought that the best scenario, and one not improbable, given the right political and diplomatic responses, was that insurgencies in Thailand would slowly disintegrate into banditry in three to five years. But before then, the Thais would have effectively changed their foreign policies and diplomatic postures. This would help to stem the flow of weapons, instructors and volunteers. Thailand was the only country in Asia that successfully balanced the British pressing eastwards from Burma and the French pressing westwards from Laos and Cambodia, and acted as a buffer between two metropolitan European powers, thus maintaining their independence. But their greatest strength was in their resources to population ration. They were Asia's rice bowl, the only country in Southeast Asia, after the devastation of the Vietnamese Mekong Delta, and insurgency and other problems in Burma, to expand as an exporter of food — rice and maize, cattle and pigs. Every international aircraft that touched down in Bangkok took food, fruits and drinks on board. Bangkok was the busiest airport in Asia, outside Japan. The Thais could manage their situation, provided there were no dramatic statements from the American Congress or Administration that would intensify anxiety or increase alarm. The important thing at present was for everyone to keep their cool and let the dust of battle settle.

He was not saying that because Thailand held, therefore the other countries in Southeast Asia would not have acute problems. Malaysia and Singapore, the Philippines and Indonesia, all had, in varying degrees of intensity, rebellious groups. But so long as supply lines to insurgents in West Malaysia from Vietnam had to come across 600 to 700 miles of water from Vietnam, it was a problem the Malaysians could contain. It became acute only if commodity prices dropped precipitously. If rubber, tin and palm oil prices all dropped at the same time, it would cause unemployment and distress. This would increase support for the insurgents. Hence Malaysia's and Singapore's approach on commodities. They supported indexation to industrial products, in principle, especially if it meant a real transfer of wealth to the poorer developing parts of the world. But since any such scheme would take a long time, if it was all possible in a free

241

world market economy, then price stabilisation schemes, with minimum floor and ceiling levels, were more practicable and likely to be the sooner achieved. Producers were guaranteed a minimum price. Consumers were guaranteed supplies never beyond a maximum price, even in periods of relative scarcity. The problem was to muster adequate funds through the IMF-consumer countries/producing countries/petro-dollars, to finance an adequate stockpile.

Lee concluded: "We should, in reasoned terms, get Washington, Brussels and Tokyo to accept that it is in their interests for both the commodity producers and consumers, the developing and the developed, to have adequate, secure supplies at steady prices. We may even persuade them, the developed and industrialised, that to help the developing to industrialise is not to take the cake from the mouths of the workers of the industrial countries. Like Japan, as developing countries industrialise, they will add to the total wealth of the world, increase markets for the advanced products of the developed in the markets of the developing, if the developing can sell their simpler manufactures to the developed."

X

After the conference, Lee left for America for an unofficial visit. In Washington, on 8 May, he met and dined with President Ford. At the dinner, given in his honour by President Ford at the White House, Lee said it was two years since he had been there as a guest of Ford's predecessor. For America, her friends and allies, the world had been somewhat diminished since then. In the first years after the end of World War II, the great events were the Cold War, the Marshall Plan, the Berlin Blockade and the Korean War. In each one of these trials of will and strength, America and her allies in Western Europe and, later, Japan, came out strong and united. But the dramatic turn of events of the past two years, the war in the Middle East in October '73, followed by the oil embargo, and four-fold increase in oil prices, the partitioning of Cyprus in June '74, and more recently the loss of Cambodia to the Khmer Rouge and the capture of South Vietnam by the North Vietnamese army, had weakened America and her allies. The economic recession and increased unemployment, on top of the crisis of confidence over Watergate and other related issues, bequeathed a host of grave problems on the great office of the presidency. They had become the more difficult to resolve because of bitterness and animosities within America, and between America and her allies, over past policies and suspected future courses of action. Then, as the United States were near distraction, as a result of these problems, the North Vietnamese, who had been well-supplied with arms by her allies, struck with suddenness and boldness, and brought off a great political coup, routing the South Vietnamese army. They had judged the mood of America correctly. They got away with it. These events had grave implica-

242

tions for the rest of Asia and the world. "I hope you would not think it inappropriate for me to express more than just sympathy that so many Americans were killed and maimed, and so much resources expended by successive Democratic and Republic Administrations, to reach this result. It was an unmitigated tragedy. It was not inevitable that this should have happened, especially in this catastrophic manner, nor that the problems will end after communist control of Cambodia, South Vietnam and Laos, and their allegiance to competing communist power centres."

Now, much would depend upon President Ford's Administration getting problems back into perspective. An economically weakened America, with recession dampening the industrial economies of Western Europe and Japan, leading to falling commodity prices for the developing world, other than the oil producers, threatened to further weaken other non-communist governments the world over. Now it looked as if the worst might be over.

It might take some time, and no little effort, to sort out the complex problems of the Middle East, to remove the threat of a sudden cut in supplies of oil at reasonable prices. Then came the restoration of confidence in the capacity of the United States to act in unison in a crisis. But no better service could be done to non-communist governments, than to restore confidence that the American government could and would act swiftly, and in tandem between the Administration and Congress, in any case of open aggression, and where the USA had a treaty obligation to do so. If the President and Congress could speak in one voice on basic issues of foreign policy, and in clear and unmistakeable terms, then friends and allies would know where they stood, and others would not pretend to misunderstand when crossing the line from insurgency into open aggression. Then the world would see less adventurism.

When confusion reigned, it was more often because men's minds were confused than that the situation was confused. "I found considerable clarity of exposition on future policies, both here and in our discussions this morning, and in most of my discussions on Capitol Hill. Whilst there was no congruence of attitudes and policies, I believe there is enough common ground on major issues. If this common ground can form the foundation of a coherent, consistent policy between now and the next presidential elections, there would be relief around the world." Like the rest of the world, Asians had to get their people reconciled to slower rates of growth, now that the cost of energy had nearly quintupled. But growth, however slow, compared to what it used to be, would be of immense help in keeping the world peaceful and stable. Only then would great matters be accorded the priorities they deserved. And men's minds would be less confused. One such confusion was that since Vietnam and Cambodia were not America's to lose in the first place, nothing had been lost. It was this apologetic explaining away of a grave setback that worried many of America's friends. "Since we do not belong to you, then you have lost nothing, anyway, if we are lost." Added Lee: "I am happy to tell you, Mr.

President, that my immediate neighbours and I have not been lost. Indeed we have every intention to co-ordinate our actions and policies to ensure that we will not be lost. It is a euphemism for a takeover, often by force. It will help if Americans do not find this strange."

Lee told the Asia Society when he addressed them in New York on 12 May that one problem every Minister from Southeast Asia faced, when making a speech after the dramatic events of the past few weeks, was how to strike a balance between, first, maintaining confidence and stability, with investments uninterrupted and economic development, and second, the need to alert one's people, to galvanise them into unity of purpose and action, but not to alarm and paralyse them through exaggerated fear and unnecessary panic. A certain sense of urgency had to be injected, so that public opinion was mobilised and people prepared to make the sacrifices to make the economy hum, to generate revenues adequate to pay for security, with enough left for social advancement. It was important not to overdo the urgency or one might arouse an air of crisis at home, and consternation abroad. If this happened and confidence was shaken, there would be less economic growth, more unemployment, more discontent, adding to the numbers of potential insurgents bringing about the very evil one wished to avoid. "I believe my best course is to take an intermediate view of events. I have no apocalyptic predictions. Nor will my views tranquilise opinion that all is and will be well. For that way I shall surely lose my credibility and reputation."

When the dust had settled in six to twelve months, the nature of the regimes, in Saigon, Phnom Penh and Vientiane would be known. "We may know how much influence Hanoi, and the Soviet Union, have over them through military and economic aid, as compared to China." Meanwhile, it was as well to remember, when reading statements from Thai or Filipino ministers, made in anguish or anger, through the mass media, that the events of the past few weeks, in Cambodia and South Vietnam, took everyone by surprise, including the United States Administration. United States secretaries, when speaking publicly, took into account the temper of Congress, and the mood of Americans generally. Hence they were unable to publicly reassure ministers in Bangkok, who felt that they had been seduced to over-commit their government and people to the American side. Leading officials in Bangkok felt especially indignant that after twenty years of unquestioning support for American policies, they were now left in serious doubt whether, apart from moral support, they could rely on the United States against externally aided insurgency. A civilian Thai government needed time to carry out its programmes and policies to remove disaffection, the result of social injustices, imagined or real. Meanwhile, ministers and generals had just had the shattering experience of seeing close friends in Phnom Penh and Saigon fleeing into exile, with only a few, brave enough, like Long Boret, to go back to Phnom Penh to face the ultimate.

It was as well to discount 60 per cent of what was being said in press reports. Statements were being made, partly for internal consumption, and partly for international pride. The mass media did not help by putting difficult questions to the United States Secretary of Defence to elicit replies which were bound to be less than satisfactory to Southeast Asian allies, especially those who sent troops to Vietnam. So they got the Secretary of Defence to say that if there were an external attack on Thailand, then the United States government was morally bound to intervene. The news agencies then whipped around to Bangkok to ask for rejoiners. They got one, from the Thai Foreign Minister. He was normally a courteous and generous man. On this occasion, he was provoked into saying that Americans had no morals, so why talk of moral obligations? The best service the Western press could render was to report events calmly and objectively, and to help tempers cool. "I do not believe that, apart from that part of Thailand in the Northeast, where there are some four million Laotians, twice as many as there are people in Laos, insurgency is ever likely to succeed." By culture, the gentler Buddhist religious outlook, allegiance to the monarchy, and a long experience of shrewd and skilful diplomacy thereby keeping their independence, Thailand was in no danger of becoming either a Vietnam or a Cambodia. They had twenty years of American, West European and Japanese investments, a thriving tourist industry and a very strong agricultural base. They were the biggest food exporter in South and Southeast Asia, rice and corn, beef and pork. Disaffection was not in the countryside, but in the big towns, like Bangkok. It was the students, who, anxious to secure good jobs after graduation, were pressing for more equality of wealth and opportunity. They had been the leaders of political discontent, culminating in riots that overthrew the military government in October '73. In a crisis, of course, it was the King and his advisers who would temper the effect of any policies to which politicians campaigning for office might inadvertently have over-committed themselves.

Next, Malaysia. Malaysia was well-developed compared to the other countries of Southeast Asia. The insurgents, about 2,000, were the remnants on the Thai-North Peninsular Malaysia border. They were mostly ethnic Chinese in their leadership and their followers. They knew they could not win the revolution, unless they could get sufficient Malay peasant-worker support, and align themselves with radical Malay-Muslim intellectuals who, like the Thai students in the towns, might become affected with the disparities of wealth and opportunity for those not with good university degrees, or good connections. Malaysia had a sound economy, widely diversified, minerals, especially tin, and commodities — rubber, palm oil, timber. And there was a growing industrial sector. Their problems were manageable, certainly not so acute that only revolutionary means could resolve. This would be ever more so after the economies of the industrial countries picked up by the latter half of 1975, or early 1976. But a boom in commodity prices in '76 – '77, if followed by a precipitate drop, because the industrial countries were again caught in another bout of inflation in '77 – '78, could prove awkward. Insurgency or terrorism was improbable in Singapore. Most of the recent sporadic acts of terrorism had been committed by Malaysians — members of the MNLL, Malayan National Liberation League, or MNLA, Malayan National Liberation Army — again mostly ethnic Chinese who had infiltrated down into Singapore for the specific purpose of committing these acts of terrorism. They wished to demonstrate that their movement was "Pan-Malayan", that is to say Peninsular Malaysia plus Singapore. Their actual recruitment in Singapore had been disappointing.

Then Indonesia. It was completely different from the country under Sukarno. The four-fold increase in oil prices had given them a bonanza of four to five billion dollars a year, with one and a half million barrels per day export of sulphur-free crude at a price of over twelve dollars a barrel. True, Pertamina, the National Oil Corporation, was facing some liquidity problems. They had been borrowing on short-term money markets because of regulations preventing them from borrowing long-term without the permission of the Indonesian Ministry of Finance. But this was a temporary difficulty. Short of a worldwide prolonged recession, mass unemployment and deprivation, insurgency in Indonesia was not likely for the foreseeable future. Indonesia was over-mindful of Madiun in 1948, and Gestapu in 1965, with the Sukiman Razzia of 1951 in between. And the four billion dollars worth of oil exports was augmented by foreign exchange earnings from rubber, tin, copra, copper and bauxite exports. And they were getting self-sufficient in rice and cereals. When the benefits were spread and felt beyond Jakarta and Java, into the other urban centres and the other islands and into the countryside, with subsidised fertilisers, better seeds and increased production of food and commodities, chances of instability and revolution were slender.

Last, the Philippines. They enjoyed bouyant balance of payments surplus in 1973 and 1974. The economy bounced with vigour with the great increase in sugar and copper prices in 1973, '74 and early '75. They also plugged most of the leaks in foreign exchange. But the Sulu insurrection, externally fuelled by petro-dollars, appeared intractable. Since there was no limit to the funds available for more and more weapons of an ever more sophisticated vintage, this could become an unquenchable fire. The demand for autonomy by the Sulu rebels in the last negotiations in Saudi Arabia included a separate constabulary and armed forces, in fact, *de facto* independence — something which a government in Manila would not be able to concede. The problem was whether any government could survive a bleeding of resources in fighting an insurrection with ever more sophisticated weapons. Perhaps the best counter was some stalemate position, the holding of strategic positions, with a minimal drain of revenues for counter-insurgency, and a maximum concentration of resources on economic development. Relief would come when, sooner or later, the suppliers had to attend to their own problems, and would have neither the time nor the excess zeal to embark on a proselytising mission,

246

the eventual success of which was dubious.

But the future of all these five countries would be influenced most of all by the economic health of the industrial world, by their own capacities to attract capital and investment, their access to markets for commodities, agricultural and mineral, and exports of their simpler manufactured goods to America, Japan and Western Europe. Healthy economies, with decreasing unemployment, reducing birth-rates, and increasing per capita income, must be felt by the majority of the people, especially if there was a more equitable distribution of the GDP. These factors would determine whether insurgencies could succeed outside Indo-China. Communist insurrections had not succeeded in Pakistan, India, Bangladesh, Ceylon or Burma, though they had impoverished some of these countries. There was no reason why insurrections could damage the ASEAN countries. The resources-to-population ratio was better, and the economic and social infrastructure more developed. The negative factors were incipient rebellious groups, which now might come into possession of a part of the vast armoury of weapons which the communists captured in South Vietnam and Cambodia. If these weapons went into a "swords into ploughshares" programme, then peace and stability was almost guaranteed for Southeast Asia. However, it was doubtful if the new owners of these American-made weapons had these priorities, now that they had won their "war of national liberation". This arsenal could provide them with convertible currency to help their rehabilitation. At the same time, such sales to the right customes could justify their revolutionary dogma and prove their ideological purity by supporting revolutionary causes anywhere and everywhere in the world.

The future had become a shade grimmer as a result of the sudden collapse of nerve in the leadership of South Vietnam, and the complete collapse of will in the officer cadre South Vietnamese Armed Forces, shattering the morale, both of their troops and of the civilian population. The unbelievable speed at which everything happened, handed over almost intact, with little or no fighting, to the North Vietnamese army several billion dollars worth of military hardware. This was a contingency no one had planned for. "But, as your President said, this was not the end of the world, except for those who were trapped in Vietnam and Cambodia, and were committed to the American side."

This was the start of a new era. Political postures would change. Policies would be adjusted. They would take account of the relationship between the super-powers, with the strongest, the United States, in a curious deadlock on several issues between the Presidency and the Congress, at least until the next presidential elections. "I believe that after the next elections, whoever wins it, the Presidency and the Congress will recognise that for the security and stability of America and the world, the isosceles triangular balance of power in the Western Pacific must be kept. It is not an equilateral triangle, because Chinese military strength cannot yet match that of either the Soviets or the Americans. If America's naval presence and her economic contributions were to be diminished, more conflicts will take place, because China's answer to Soviet naval and economic power would be to intensify local insurgency. This clash must imperil the stability of America's allies in the Western Pacific, affecting the balance between the great powers, and affecting peace and stability in the rest of the Pacific Basin. My hope is that a modus vivendi between the Presidency and Congress can be reached before the next elections resolve their differences. Otherwise, there may be further major losses in Asia and elsewhere. And the pity would be that such losses could be made completely unnecessary, simply by America making her position clear beyond any pretence of misunderstanding, that any adventurism anywhere will be countered swiftly and with all the great power and resources that America, they knew, still possesses.''

During a question-and-answer session that followed the Prime Minister's talk, he was asked what his predictions might be with regard to the probable relationships between Hanoi and Moscow on the one hand and Hanoi and Peking on the other. Did he see either of the great communist powers exercising a special influence as against the other or whether Hanoi would continue to try to play one off against the other, in order to maintain the greatest possible economy?

The Prime Minister replied that he did not believe that history was all bunk. He thought it had some relevance to tell something about the nature of peoples and their cultures and their societies. This took a very long time to change; not that it did not change but it did take a long time. "I think Vietnam, with more than a thousand years of resistance to Sinic domination, in spite of absorbing a lot of the Sinic culture, is really a bigger Yugoslavia than Yugoslavia itself, in the sense that Vietnam fought longer, more tenaciously, more ferociously with more international involvement on the communist side than the Yugoslav. And they are now in Asia — using it in a very broad sense — what Albania in Europe is to China. The Vietnam-Soviet Union relationship and the Albania-PRC relationship is in that same category. So it is most complex, most interesting — and if I were not living in Southeast Asia — I would find it a fascinating and exciting problem to investigate. I think, first, we have to allow them to get over this period of great exhilaration, great exuberance and tremendous pride which is only natural after fighting for so many years and with conspicuous success in the end; not that the success was inevitable but it did happen. It was made inevitable by so many things like Watergate and related issues. But I have met them. They have a trade mission in Singapore. They are extremely polite. We talk through interpreters, the medium being Mandarin, not English. And in that sense I think they are extremely proud and some people may be unkind and uncharitable and call them arrogant, especially now that they have become triumphant. One must not forget, that as of today, there is nothing to stop the North Vietnamese army, if they so wished it, to march right down across Laos, across Cambodia, across Thailand into Malaysia right down to Singapore. It is the most experienced, it is the toughest, it has the best-equipped army and air force. And with that, of course, goes a certain elan. So we have got to allow people who are drunk of this hubris some time to subside. There is always the 'morning-after'. And as all traders know in Southeast Asia, just wait until the 'morning-after' when steel is needed or asbestos or corrugated sheets and piling and all the other necessities of life. And reconstruction as we have learnt in Southeast Asia, particularly in a war-ruined economy can be a very painful and prolonged business.''

Lee continued: "I would like to believe that we could establish, first, correct relationships. It must not be misunderstood that because we extended recognition to the victor, because we acknowledged the fact that he is the victor, therefore, we have thereby accepted a henpecking order. I think that is not something which we should mislead them over. And by all means, let us have them in co-operation, in collaboration, in peaceful reconstruction and commerce. But let us be correct. I mean, they run a different system. We wish them well. Maybe, with enormous help from the Soviet Union and her allies in Eastern Europe and the more she gets from that side, I think the less willing will be the People's Republic of China in wanting to contribute to a signed success in reconstruction. Because, whose credit was it?''

Lee predicted that this "sharpening of competition and patronage" was going to be a factor in Southeast Asia, and one of the ways out of the danger of being crushed in the competition was to maintain correct, if possible, cordial, relations. "If not, let's just have it correct. And sooner or later because we are what we are, well, we shall have to buy from each other, we shall exchange goods, we shall render services." And only that afternoon, the United Nations Secretary-General made discreet enquiries if Singapore would offer infrastructure in warehousing and wharfage and so on, for the relief effort he was mounting in South Vietnam. He had not yet got his $100 million, but he had got a part of it, and goods were already arriving. "And, of course, my answer must be to give it every sympathetic and every considerate assistance. But, you know, we do have other obligations to all kinds of container vessels, all kinds of freighters and so on. But it reminded me, immediately, of the fact that perhaps if we don't lose our nerve, we may learn to live with them. That I am sure we will. And what I hope is, they learn to live with us, warts and all.''

XI

Whilst Lee was in New York, he was interviewed by Japanese Television. The Prime Minister was asked whether he thought that the United States had lost credibility among Asian nations through Vietnam.

Lee replied: "America has not increased its prestige, has it? Credibility is a question of whether you believe that the enormous strength and power is matched by will and reserve. It's no use having strength and power if the will and resolve is not there ... I think the United States has suffered a serious setback in its prestige. But I don't think anybody believes that the United States has become weak and feeble ... At the same time we must remember that the Americans are a very resilient and resourceful people ... " They are ingenious, they've got vitality, they've got drive.

What about Japan's position? Lee's advice was that Japan should not "just keep on extracting raw materials and exporting more cameras, transistors, TV sets; then politically you become much more acceptable to the rest of the world. I think you have to learn what the Americans and the Europeans have done, namely to be willing to pass on the skills, the technology. You will always be three, four steps ahead of the rest of Asia. You know that. So why do you want to keep the lot?"

In reply to a further question, Lee said he did not suggest that Japan should become a considerable military power ... "I think what we would like to see you do is to treat Southeast Asia more as a partner and less as a hewer of wood and drawer of water ... You should make it simpler to get into your markets."

In Tokyo, on 22 May, after talking to the Japanese Prime Minister and other ministers and officials, Lee gave a press conference. He was questioned about ASEAN, especially about the Thais and the Filipinos who helped America in Vietnam. Lee thought that given time, everything could be sorted out peacefully. He wished the socialist countries of Indo-China well. Did he anticipate any increase in Sino-Soviet rivalry in Southeast Asia, and if so how it would affect other countries in the region?

The Prime Minister said that as he understood it, relations could not possibly be more different, or more difficult. Therefore, all the countries of Southeast Asia would like to avoid being caught in any competitive clash of interests between these two communist powers. "The realities, however, are that the Soviet Union has greater military, naval and economic strength than China. And any country that wishes to avoid intensified insurgency may well be advised not to give the balance of advantage to the Soviet Union as against the People's Republic of China." He thought that so long as the "long arm" of the United States was in the area to match the Soviet Union it would be "less uncomfortable, more convenient" for the countries of Southeast Asia to adapt to the changes that were taking place in the balance of power. He thought it would be many years before there was an equilateral triangle. He remembered that Zhou En-lai, China's Prime Minister, had said it would take China twenty-five years to become a front-rank nation.

Asked about the Law of the Sea, Lee said he felt sure that eventually a "reasonable and just set of rules" would be agreed upon. He was also confident that "whatever the territorial sea limits may be, traditional sea lanes which have been recognised as international highways for hundreds of years, will continue to be so." Lee argued that in that way, trade would be facilitated, and the whole world better off. In any case, he did not see

250

the superpowers agreeing to anything less than that.

Interviewed by *Chuo Koron*, the leading Japanese magazine of philosophy and politics for publication in the 10 June issue, Lee predicted that Cambodia and South Vietnam would have to settle down before anyone could tell if they were going to be closer to China or the Soviet Union.

He was asked if he thought that Singapore would be affected if Japan and China signed a peace treaty. The Prime Minister said the treaty would be a positive development because it would increase Japan's economy, and this would give Japan greater potential to help Southeast Asia to develop.

The interviewer recalled that when Prince Sihanouk was in power, Lee had a very good, close friendship with him. Would this close friendship now help improve the relationship between Cambodia and Singapore?

Lee replied: "The personal esteem I have for him of course will help my relationship with him. But whether this will be translated into government-to-government close relations will depend on his influence over the government, the socialist government of Cambodia. And I am sure that in the end it will depend on whether or not we can make a contribution to the reconstruction and rehabilitation of Cambodia, which I think is more important than personal relations."

XII

Opening Sembawang Shipyard's 400,000-ton new drydock on 25 May, Lee said that six-and-a-half years after the Sembawang Naval Dockyards were handed over by the British, workers in the companies which took over the property exceeded the workers in 1968. The income generated had risen five times. In the early '60s, Singapore had not made its mark in the world as a centre for shipbuilding or ship-repairing. Now, there were over four major ship-repair establishments and over fifty smaller repair yards. Over the past five years, the industry had grown at 30 per cent a year. Total revenues generated by all shipyards in Singapore in 1974 was $720 million, compared to $227 million four years ago, 1970, and compared to $24 million nine years ago, 1965.

"With this latest dock, we have three VLCC docks. Another is being built. Now, the largest tanker afloat can be repaired in our shipyards. A multitude of specialist companies have grown up to offer every specialist service in support of the industry. We are moving into third place as rig builders in the world. However, the oil crisis and the economic recession in the industrialised nations have created new problems. There has been massive, almost panic, stock-piling of crude oil all over the world. This has caused a glut in oil, as every country economizes in consumption at a time of a worldwide recession. Further, VLCCs are acting as more oil tanks by reducing speed, to save fuel, and because costs of chartering have plum-

251

metted down. There is now a surplus of VLCC tanker tonnage. Unless the decrease in oil consumption is overcome by the middle of next year, with the industries of the developed world recovering from recession, there will be a corresponding reduction in repairs of VLCCs. But if the recession continues, more VLCCs will be mothballed. Moreover, the development of oil resources in the North Sea and Alaska, nearer to the industrial nations, will reduce tanker demand. It will cut down distance tankers have to travel when the production begins. Next, the reopening of the Suez Canal this June will cut down shipping time. So unless more goods are exported, less ships will be required. The opening of the Suez Canal will also increase competition from shipyards in the Mediterranean. Fortunately, the VLCCs plying the Gulf to Japan route will not be affected. Hence we in Southeast Asia have a vested interest in Japan's economic recovery.''

These developments had changed projections of growth in various ship-repairing centres. Nearly thirty million deadweight tons of tankers were now mothballed. Many new orders for VLCC were being cancelled, through negotiations and compensation. Singapore workers and management were aware of this new situation. Ship-repairing was labour-intensive. It was because wages had gone up considerably in Japan that Japanese dockyards sited subsidiaries elsewhere, especially in Singapore. "We cannot afford to price ourselves out, or some other lower wage cost centre will be developed as a ship-repairing centre that will replace us."

Wages could go up, but they would have to be much less than those in Japan, Taiwan or Hong Kong. "Let us not forget that productivity in these centres is higher because of higher skills and hardier workers. We must, through government-sponsored training programmes, better management and greater worker effort, achieve the same high productivity. Only then can Singapore afford wages as high as its more advanced competitors. But ship-repairing costs in Singapore must always be lower than comparably located competitors. We overlook this fact of life at our peril.''

XIII

As a mark of friendship and esteem, the Prime Minister on 3 June sent the following message to Mr. Takeo Miki, Prime Minister of Japan on the death of the former Prime Minister, Mr. Eisaku Sato: "My colleagues and I read with sadness of the death of former Prime Minister Eisaku Sato. He will long be remembered and respected as a Japanese statesman who repaired and strengthened Japan's economy, and put her economic strength in support of foreign policies which could enhance peace and stability. Please convey our sympathy and condolences to the bereaved family.''

XIV

With five intakes of National Servicemen a year, from different language streams, communication in the Armed Forces was critical. With time, education in primary and secondary schools should lessen the problems. But, said Lee on 19 July, opening the first SAF training aids competition and exhibition, many from dialect-speaking homes, in English language schools, had not been able to learn English in the days before bilingualism. "Let us hope, with bilingualism, if they do not master English, they will have learnt enough Mandarin. Otherwise the SAF will have to continue its special Hokkien-speaking platoons. Fortunately, the problem is not as acute with Malay-speaking or Tamil-speaking homes."

No amount of words could describe a scene better than the picture. And no amount of still pictures or diagrams could be better than a scale model. And no model was as good as one which had moving parts to show how it worked. The American-Soviet space link-up, pictured with English words on one side and the Russian Cyrillic script on the other, dramatically illustrated this problem of communications. Millions of words had been used to describe it. However, diagrams and sketches of the spacecraft, depicting orbital paths, the final rendezvous, and the docking mechanisms, gave a more vivid idea of what took place than all the millions of words. The more training aids, and the better they were, the easier it was to get national service recruits to understand what they had to learn to do. Training aids were more important to the SAF than to other armed forces, because SAF had to teach those who did not make the primary school leaving certificate and those who were going to universities. They all had to be taught, albeit at different speeds, and in different groups.

XV

Mr. Kukrit Pramoj, Prime Minister of Thailand, accompanied by the Thai Foreign Minister, Mr. Chatichai Choonhaven, paid an official visit to Singapore later in the month, and at a State dinner in his honour, the Prime Minister, welcoming him, referred to a great many changes that had taken place in Southeast Asia, "some good and some not so good". Among the good tidings was the emergence in Thailand, after many years, of a democratically elected government which Mr. Pramoj led as Prime Minister. It was not just a change in form. It was a change of considerable substance. "A government responsive to the needs of the people, whose collective interests you so eloquently express, is one of the factors for success in rapid change, without violent revolution."

Lee said he had the advantage that afternoon of hearing the views of Mr. Pramoj after he had met delegations from Hanoi and Saigon, and of his meeting with Chairman Mao. Lee said he was struck by his philosophical frame of mind. It helped to keep historic events in human proportions. "You have a shrewd understanding of men and politics. So long as those in high office do not confuse the unavoidable drama of politics with the realities of life, then things should be well. With your wry sense of humour, it is my impression that your vision is firmly on the realities." The countries of ASEAN were at the crossroads. "If we make the right decisions separately and collectively, then we may adjust, with less turbulence, to the great changes the region is facing after those momentous events in Indo-China. The converse is equally true, that decisions, taken in haste, may turn out to be against long-term interests, and will accentuate the unsettling effects of these events."

One valuable result of these developments was that the other members of ASEAN were drawing closer together in co-operation in the economic, diplomatic and political fields. "We want to live in peace and amity with the new governments of the countries of Indo-China." The success of Thailand and the Thai people in adjusting and accommodating to these new realities, without having to change the Thai way of life, or Thailand's system of government, would be most reassuring to the other partners in ASEAN. "We wish the Thai Government and people success in finding the right balance between continuity of long established Thai institutions and traditions and change now necessary because of different external and internal circumstances."

Singapore had been more conscious that the future of ASEAN countries was so interwoven. "We should muster enough political will to take the decisions which will strengthen our cohesiveness as a group. This, in turn, will enable us to build a constructive and co-operative relationship with those countries in the region with different political and social systems. And perhaps the great powers, whose interests in the region are not always identical, may yet find it in their separate interests to let us go about our peaceful business, in amity with all of them."

The joint communique said that the two Prime Ministers noted the invaluable contribution that ASEAN could make towards the promotion of peace, prosperity and stability in Southeast Asia. "They reiterated the firm commitment of Singapore and Thailand to the goals and solidarity of ASEAN. In that light and, bearing in mind the changes in the region which had brought ASEAN to the crossroads, they felt that all possible measures must be taken to ensure that ASEAN moved in the right direction. They were convinced that the framework of ASEAN would continue to provide a sound basis for its members to intensify their co-operation on matters affecting their collective well-being ... The two Prime Ministers reviewed developments in Indo-China and expressed the hope that the end of hostilities would lead to harmony and co-operation in the region as a whole. They noted that the ASEAN states had shown their willingness to enter into friendly relations and to live in peace and amity with the countries of Indo-China on the basis of mutual respect for each other's sovereignty and

254

territorial integrity and non-interference in the internal affairs of one another. The Thai Prime Minister informed the Singapore Prime Minister of the recent developments in the conduct of the foreign and domestic affairs of Thailand. The two Prime Ministers agreed that the efforts being pursued by the Thai Government and people would be a significant contribution to the efforts of ASEAN to establish a firm foundation for the peace and well-being of the region as a whole. The two Prime Ministers discussed the role of the major powers in the region and were of the view that the major powers could by minimising or intensifying their rivalries affect prospects for peace, security and prosperity in the region. They agreed that the major powers, in the pursuit of their own interests, should take into serious account the interests of the smaller nations of Southeast Asia. They believed that the major powers could play a constructive role in the region and thus welcomed any genuine contribution that the major powers could make in this direction, particularly in the economic development of the ASEAN states. Nations in the region should, for their part, pay regard to the legitimate interests of outside powers in the region."

XVI

"1975 is the first time since 1965 that we experienced almost zero growth in our GDP," the Prime Minister stated in his National Day Message in August. The momentum in the economy carried through 1974 with a 6.8 per cent growth, whilst America, Japan and most of Western Europe suffered massive declines. But the recession had caught up with Singapore. From January to June 1975, the GDP barely grew at 0.2 per cent compared to the same period in 1974. Fortunately, America, Japan and most countries of Western Europe were slowly recovering. This recovery would pull up Singapore's economy. "We may end 1975 with 2 – 3 per cent growth."

Throughout 1974, the ship-repairing and oil-rig building industries enjoyed a boom. But now, Japanese shipyards were fighting for survival as orders for super-tankers were cancelled. Being quick to adapt and to adjust, the Japanese were doing ship-repairing and building of smaller ships and oil rigs. This would take away business from the other shipyards in Asia, especially those in South Korea, Taiwan and Singapore. Fortunately, most Singapore shipyards had work booked for the next one to two years. But in South Korea, Taiwan and Hong Kong, wages were lower, and workers worked harder under tougher conditions. So Singapore exporters of textiles and garments, woodwork and timber, and electronics would face stiff competition for new orders from these countries.

The oil crisis and world-wide recession were factors beyond Singapore's control. "We have to learn to live with these upsets. But some factors are within our control. For instance, we will improve our investment rate, if workers and unions are known to be hardworking, willing to learn and keen to make capital productive." The level of investments in industries had been affected by the recession. In 1974, with the momentum of ten years of high growth, Singapore promoted investments of nearly $900 million. For the first half of this year, there were only $150 million. Another $180 million was expected for the rest of the year. This would give a total for 1975 less than 40 per cent of 1974's. The world economy was not expected to boom like the years before October 1973. This affected Singapore's own prospects. The days when young workers and young graduates went hopping from job to job, seeking more comfortable working conditions and more pay, were over. "The sooner we realise this and shake ourselves out of our complacency, the better." It had been government policy to employ girls for all jobs which were physically less demanding, and which girls could do as well as boys. "We would ask private firms, wherever possible and practical, to do likewise. Most clerical jobs, service in shops, restaurants and hotels, and light manual work, should be done by girls." Over 70 per cent of the workers retrenched in the past eighteen months were girls. According to Labour Ministry registers, there was an increase in unemployment to 4½ per cent. But there had been no drop in the number of work permit applications for foreign workers. In other words, young Singaporeans were shying away from construction and other heavy jobs. That would not do. Singapore could not afford to have young men, including National Servicemen on ROD (Run-out-date, completion of National Service), looking for soft jobs all the time.

The most significant event in 1975 was the sudden collapse of Cambodia and South Vietnam, followed by a swift takeover of Laos by the Pathet Lao. For several years, the new governments in Vietnam, Cambodia and Laos would be busy with repairs and rehabilitation. "After a while, we may resume trade and buy agricultural products from them as we used to before the war disrupted supplies. We want a constructive relationship with these new governments of Indo-China." An era ended when the American Congress washed their hands of regimes dependent on American military and economic aid for survival. A new balance would gradually emerge. The shape of this regional balance would depend on the bigger framework between the big powers in this part of the world. No country wanted to be involved in a tussle between any two of the big powers. Greater co-operation and cohesion in ASEAN would be good for all member countries. "Then, separately and together, we must keep our valuable economic links with the industrialised countries of the West and Japan, and increase our trade and economic links with China and the Third World, with the Soviet Union and the Comecon countries." ASEAN countries could together create a better climate of confidence in the ASEAN region as a whole. "It should never be said that we did not learn from the lessons of Indo-China."

At the National Day Rally at the National Theatre on 17 August Lee described the past decade as "probably the most spectacular of all the ten years of Singapore's history". There had never been such rapid transformation in any ten years. The physical landscape changed with new buildings, new roads, fly-overs, traffic jams, homes, new factories. GDP went up, at factor cost, nearly three times between 1965 and 1975. When money was borrowed from the World Bank or from the Asian Development Bank, there were no more soft loans. "We are classified now as an intermediate country — not developed, not developing, but intermediate — and we pay the going market interest rate."

Every opportunity was seized to develop as fast as possible because ten years ago there was massive unemployment — at least over 12 per cent. "Ten years later, with the new standards of incomes, we have got ourselves into a different mood, the younger generation especially — people who were not old enough in 1965 to understand what hardship and unemployment meant. And they are truly a different generation. Expectations have gone up. Unconsciously, we have entered into the free-spending consumer society of the West. Parents spoil their children. There is better clothes, better food, better housing. All the time their expectation goes up and up, believing that it is always going to be up the escalator." Lee said that if there had been no oil crisis, the 1973 prices had not quadrupled, the developed world had not taken a nose-dive and GNPs weren't down by 12 per cent, 13 per cent, 14 per cent in America and Japan, "perhaps we could put up with this. But let me, by way of illustration, show you the changed attitudes which we cannot afford because the next five years will not be like the last five years — we are not going to get the 10 per cent to 14 per cent real growth which we made in the years 1968 to 1973."

Recently, an exercise was mounted to recruit drivers for the Singapore Bus Service. It was thought that the National Servicemen who had learned how to drive a three-ton truck should be offered the opportunity. So three recruitment exercises were mounted. Ten years ago, a man introduced into the STC or into a Chinese bus company as a driver, would have been happy to give one month's salary as commission. The posts were circularised. About eight hundred National Servicemen went on ROD between January and July. About five hundred turned up to listen to the opportunities offered them. SBS produced a coloured brochure, "The Bus Way to a Secure Future" — with diagrams and pictures. And on the face of the brochure it said: "This is not a sales brochure which you receive every day. This is a career prospectus which took us months to prepare just for you." How many applied? Seven the first batch, thirty-four the second batch, twenty the third batch. How many were still working? One driver and three temporary conductors training to be drivers. Remarkable! Whilst training, recruits were paid $11.60 per day, one year. Then $12.80. All this bewildered Lee. He said he inquired at the Central Manpower Base what jobs they were doing. What happened to these National Servicemen? They had a good education. Many of them were just sitting at home! Forty or fifty of them were still unemployed. This was the new generation Singaporean. "If there had been no oil crisis, no problems in the West, we could perhaps, put up with this. I ask parents whose instinctive response to their own hardship when they meet good times is to pamper their children, to remember that we are in for a less good time. It is always comfortable and easy to move into a higher standard of living. But I believe we are lucky if we make in the next five years — nobody can look beyond three to five years — somewhere between 3 per cent to 5 per cent, maybe with luck 6 per cent, growth in real terms.''

Now it was going to be different. It was going to take two years to know how the interaction of the world powers would be and, in particular, the contest for influence over the Indochinese states, which meant that co-operation in ASEAN on the economic and the political fields must become a sincere effort to try and accommodate each other, in order that by being a more cohesive group, ASEAN could deal with a group of countries with different political and economic systems on more or less equal terms.

"We have done as well as we could possibly have done in the past ten years. To do as well as we can in the next five years, let us have no scales on our eyes. Let us face the world as we find it — as we find the other countries, as we will find ourselves. And if we are to overcome these problems, many of them will depend on our own internal thrust, the drive that we have got, the capacity to face up to our problems before they become too big and too unmanageable — whether it is in cars, or in babies.'' Lee believed that the Singaporeans' response to the problems of population control or restriction of cars was an indication of a basically resilient and disciplined society. It could make it but it had to be told what the alternatives were. And the alternatives were truly unpleasant.

The past ten years had been almost too fast in its speed of change. "And, in a way, I sometimes regret that we did not get a harder knock in 1974 — which Hong Kong had with 30 per cent of its work force at least unemployed and most of it taking 30 per cent, 40 per cent reduction in wages, and real hardship. I am not saying it is a good thing. But I am saying that it is good for the soul. And employers, when they start looking for workers, like to have workers who know what hardship means. And if you can't have real hardship, then you have got to inculcate the right attitudes and values.'' The government would do all it could in the schools, in getting the jobs and training them. "But if you bring a child into this world and you don't bring it up right, then the ultimate responsibility must be yours.'' Lee hoped that together they would make the next five years at least not less successful than the past 1¾ years since running into the oil crisis. If it was no worse than what it had been and better than what it had actually been up till now, they would be alright at the end of another five years. But it required that constant drive and that willingness to learn, to achieve and to be proud of doing; not just minimum of effort, maximum of monetary rewards. That attitude would never take them into the industrial society.

XVII

Opening the Tenth Singapore-Malaysia Congress of Medicine on 21 August, Lee said that the standard of the medical profession in Singapore had always been high. In a period of rapid university expansion throughout the developed and developing world, standards had fallen in many universities. "We cannot let this happen in Singapore." It was because standards in some of the new Commonwealth countries had been allowed to slide down that Singapore had been forced to revoke the old reciprocity rules. Even the British had to do likewise.

The Academy of Medicine stood for "Standards of Excellence". This was not an easy aspiration to achieve. "We use the English language, and most of your members hold memberships or fellowships of the old Royal colleges in Britain or Australasia. In no profession is the brains drain bigger and easier than in the practice of medicine. For years, especially after the last war, the British have supplied the Americans with thousands of doctors every year, professional men who see no reason why they should be trapped in a national health service plus high personal income tax. This, in turn, had led to a flow of Indian and Pakistani doctors to Britain. It will be interesting to see how the British can maintain their national health service now that they have abolished reciprocity." Perhaps it would lead to a more selective brains drain of the more able Indian and Pakistani doctors, those who could make British medical standards and understand English as spoken by examiners in the major towns of London and the Midlands. Singapore's policy had been to avoid an over-supply of GPs or of specialists in any field. Over-supply would result in less rewards and a higher temptation to migrate. It was unrealistic to try to establish a higher doctor-population ratio than that in Australia and New Zealand or Canada and Britain, where standards of living were higher and the rewards to medical practitioners correspondingly bigger. Singapore's ratio of 1 to 1350 was fair. Singapore had succeeded in doing this because in the past fifteen years, many of the best students, who used to go into medicine, had been going into engineering and other applied sciences. It had been argued however that because of the many discoveries in the medical sciences, the practice of the GP had become much easier. When the GP was in doubt over diagnosis, or treatment, he could send the patients to hospital for specialist attention. But for over 98 per cent of cases, a wide spectrum of antibiotics and patented medicines catered for their needs. And because medicine had become relatively much easier to practice, more doctors had been freed to specialise.

As medical facilities improved with the new Singapore General Hospital and the Kent Ridge University Hospital, the range of medical specialities which hospitals could provide would be increased and improved. The inhibiting factor was the costs, whether Singapore could afford, not the new equipment, but the staff to support the specialists in using the latest equipment, without enough fee-paying patients to lessen the government subsidy on recurrent costs. Easy air travel had made it possible for patients to seek specialist treatment in world-renowned centres in America, Britain and Australasia. It should not be long before Singapore doctors could collect enough patients requiring such specialist treatment and, instead, bring out the leading world exponents of these operative techniques to Singapore. This could be done only if Singapore had the equipment and personnel to back up the specialist, and where treatment was not urgent.

Opportunities which the jet-travel age had opened up should be seized. Singapore should become a regional centre for specialist treatment, with resident specialists, backed by regular visits of outstanding practitioners. These men could be persuaded to travel to Singapore during their holiday or off-peak season, to demonstrate and pass on their skills and techniques. Paid air passages, and fees carrying only a 40 per cent income tax, had brought out eminent QCs to Singapore, mostly during the legal vacations. There was no reason why similar arrangements could not be made for physicians and surgeons. In time, research into cancer, heart diseases and other killers would produce partial or complete answers to those presently incurable diseases. But the discoveries that had already made a tremendous impact on society and politics, had been the basic ones, those which had eliminated plagues and pestilence. This had led to enormous expansion of population in all he developing countries. Formerly, incurable tropical diseases had kept population down. Now, the problem had to be resolved by family planning. But the question was whether the need for family planning was understood and the practice widespread enough to be sufficiently effective, or grave social and political unrest, leading to revolution, overtook more countries in the Third World. Nigeria, with oil, Bangladesh, without, were both afflicted by the same problem of populations increasing faster than wealth could be generated and distributed.

The world since 1945 had been experiencing change at a bewildering speed. Every medical discovery was a blessing for those who suffered from the diseases the discovery cured. But it also created new problems. In the developed world, the problems were related to the care and ailments of the old, since people lived longer and families preferred to leave the old to be cared for in state institutions. Next, widespread knowledge of contraception and dissemination of pills and contraceptive aids had wrought a revolution in social and sexual mores of the young. They had altered traditional attitudes to marriage, divorce, parenthood and responsibilities for children. Human civilisations of the past 4,000 to 6,000 years had rested on the fabric of the family relationship, with paternity conferring a responsibility to bring up one's offspring. If the present trend continued, some new social cement had to be found to supplement the basic family mechanism for civilised living and for the provision of the next generation. So much for the developed countries.

In the developing world, the grave problem was the population explosion. Because the social infrastructure of homes, schools, playing fields, hospitals could not be doubled with population doubling every twenty years, social and political unrest was inevitable. Many countries faced the threat of revolutions. Revolutions, in turn, made it even less likely that the problems of population control, education, economic development would take place. Somehow, a solution must be found. Singapore was at an intermediate stage. "We are damping down the rate of population growth. Better homes, and educated women holding jobs, have helped slow growth rates down to 1.4 per cent for last year compared to nearly 4 per cent in 1959. I hope we can avoid most of the problems that have troubled Western societies, of too many unmarried mothers and high rates of divorce, as the use of the pill became widespread. And we must, by income tax and Housing Board concessions for those with retired parents living with them, try to sustain the Asian tradition of caring for the old within the family, instead of sending them into state or welfare institutions, where the occasional family visit is the last vestige of filial obligation."

XVIII

The Prime Minister spoke about the role of women in industrial societies at the NTUC's International Women's Year Seminar on 1 September. He said this role had radically changed in the past hundred years. Industrialisation required women workers. This had led to the education of women. This, in turn, had led to demand for political equality, the right to vote, equal rights, before and after marriage, in the ownership of property. Now, the trend was to eliminate every bias, prejudice and discrimination in opportunities for education, jobs and promotions. The role of women in agricultural societies had been to work in the field, to bring up children and to perform the household duties. This still prevailed in large parts of Asia where the economy was based on agriculture. But it had changed with industrialisation, in Japan, China, India and the urbanised parts of Southeast Asia.

In Singapore, a quiet revolution had been taking place. In 1957, women formed 18 per cent of the work force. In 1974 they reached a peak of 32 per cent. In May 1975, because of retrenchment in the electronic, textiles and garments factories, it dropped to 30 per cent. In America, 46 per cent of the labour force were women. It was only a matter of time before women nearly equalled men in employment. The key was education. Old-fashioned attitudes of teaching women enough to be literate and useful wives had undergone profound changes in the past twenty years. This was reflected most in university education. In 1955, in the University of Singapore, 18.9 per cent of the students were women. In 1975, 44 per cent. In Nanyang University, 1956, 21.4 per cent; 1975, 43.4 per cent. The only differences between men and women workers were physical and biological. Women were equal to men in intellectual capacity. "With more jobs open to them, and separate income tax for married women, the status of women in our society has been changed. With economic independence, the dependent position of wives however must also change. This is reflected in higher divorce rates, and all the social problems of broken homes for children. On the whole, we have been fortunate in educating our women, opening up jobs for them, and having them more independent, without too great an upset in traditional family relationships."

There had been no vociferous women's liberation movement in Singapore. It had been government policy to encourage the education of women to their fullest ability and their employment commensurate with their abilities. Parents had also changed their attitudes and had sent their daughters for secondary and tertiary education as they would their sons. Singapore's problem, as they have found in the West, was that women had to break their careers, for four to six years, to bring up two or three children, and then resume their careers. This break in their careers could be minimised if new social institutions and organisations to help married women look after their children whilst they were at work, could be organised. Well-run creches and kindergartens, near factories or homes, staffed by well-trained workers, should be part of the new social institutions.

What had not yet taken place in traditional male-dominant Asian societies was the helping in household work by husbands — the marketing, cooking, cleaning up. This change in social attitudes could not come by legislation. Such adjustments should be allowed to develop naturally. The primary concern was to ensure that, whilst all women became equal to men in education, getting employment and promotions, the family framework in bringing up the next generation did not suffer as a result of high divorce rates, or, equally damaging, neglect of the children, with both parents working. But lower birth rates, with a two-child family as the norm, would help to make this less likely. Societies which faced up to problems of new social and family relationships and set up new social institutions to help working wives to bring up the next generation, were those most likely to provide better lives for their people. "We cannot not educate and use the energy and ability of our women."

XIX

Early in September, Lee left for Bali to have informal discussions with President Suharto on the developments since they last met in Singapore in August 1974. He was accompanied by Mr. K.C. Lee, Senior Minister of State for Foreign Affairs.

In a press statement put out by the Indonesian side, the two leaders were reported to have discussed various international and regional matters as well as subjects of bilateral interest to Indonesia and Singapore. The two leaders in particular discussed in depth matters relating to ASEAN. They considered ASEAN's achievements during its eight years of existence as satisfactory. They felt that there was a need to strengthen the organisation and intensify regional co-operation within ASEAN in the social, political and economic fields. This could be done by holding an ASEAN summit meeting. The objective was to strengthen national as well as regional resilience. It was necessary to intensify preparations so that the ASEAN Summit Meeting could be held at the end of this year with a maximum of success. On the question of economic co-operation, it was agreed that the most important objective was the realisation of concrete economic proposals which would directly benefit the people of the ASEAN countries.

XX

On 13 September, the Prime Minister left for official visits to Iran, the Arab Republic of Egypt and Yugoslavia.

At a dinner given in his honour by the Prime Minister of Iran, Mr. Amir Abbas Hoveyda, in Teheran on 15 September, Lee said he had looked forward to his visit. Iran was a country with a glorious and ancient civilisation, and now on the move, at an exciting pace, towards a great and illustrious future. He had the privilege of seeing it during an exciting period of transformation into a modern industrial nation. In the past few years, he had read and heard much of the Shahanshah Aryamehr, of the tremendous pace of economic and social progress taking place in Iran under his guidance, with the able support of his Prime Minister. The events of the past two years had been momentous. They had created a new centre of wealth and power in the Gulf. Iran had played a leading role in bringing this about. Iran was wisely transforming exhaustible resources into inexhaustible capital, in knowledge and skills in science and technology, in industrial capital and "know-how", and management. These would ensure the continued prosperity of Iran and her people. Few countries were blessed with such abundant resources as Iran, and even fewer had the good fortune of such formidable foresight and resolve in their leaders.

"Last year, we had the honour of having the Shahanshah and the Shahbanou, visit Singapore. It was a memorable occasion. It has made us more conscious of Iran. Iran's growing strength is a factor for stability and peace in the Gulf. My Cabinet colleagues and I found the Shahanshah's views most reassuring, that Iran's policy was to ensure the security of the Persian Gulf and the Indian Ocean, so that oil, which moves the world's economy, should flow uninterrupted and unhindered to all parts of the world. He also proposed regional co-operation to bring all the countries on the northern and eastern tier of the Indian Ocean together in economic co-operation. I am sure that increasing contacts, resulting in more trade and investments, will advance the well-being of all who participate in this plan. Iran by her considerable economic weight and burgeoning industries can stimulate more such bilateral and multilateral trading arrangements." The era ahead was so vastly different from the past. The progress in science and technology had resulted in one interdependent world. The meeting of the Non-Aligned countries at Lima in August, and the Special Session of the United Nations General Assembly which followed it in September, marked a fresh start towards a more equitable system in which the dominance of the economies of a few industrial nations was tempered by willingness for more stable terms of trade for the commodity producers, and the poorer countries of the Third World, and more generous conditions under which transfer of industrial capital and "know-how" could take place. Lee wished the people of Iran continued prosperity and progress.

The joint communique recorded that Singapore's Prime Minister was received in audience by the Shahanshah Aryamehr. Official talks between the Prime Minister and the Prime Minister of Iran, were conducted in a friendly atmosphere and spirit of mutual understanding. "The Singapore Prime Minister expressed admiration for the tremendous pace of economic and social progress taking place in Iran under the guidance of the Shahanshah Aryamehr. The two Prime Ministers exchanged views on current international issues including the concept of wide regional co-operation among the countries bordering the Indian Ocean. They expressed the view that increasing contacts resulting in more trade and investments would advance the well-being of all those who participate in the Indian Ocean community concept."

Both Prime Ministers appraised favourably the development of bilateral relations and noted that there existed conditions for the promotion of mutually beneficial relations in many spheres, particularly in the economic and commercial fields. They agreed that more positive and concrete efforts should be made to promote at all levels closer contacts between the two countries. Among the areas reviewed were the exchange of expertise in banking, port development and operations, shipbuilding and housing development. In that connection, the Iranian side agreed to send to Singapore in October 1975 an economic mission comprising representatives of the public and private sectors. To expedite the strengthening of economic relations priority would also be given to the development of direct transportation and communication links between the two countries. The two Prime Ministers agreed that direct air services between the two countries would serve to promote closer relations and understanding between the people of Iran and Singapore. They agreed to hold early consultations with a view to conclude an air services agreement.

XXI

At a dinner given by Mr. Dzemal Bijedic, Prime Minister of Yugoslavia, at Belgrade on 21 September, Lee remarked upon Yugoslavia's progress and development since his previous visit. Under the outstanding leadership of President Tito, Yugoslavia had played a signal role in gathering together the non-aligned countries of the world. This movement helped the many new and weak countries to find strength in a common cause for greater freedom of political choice and to choose their partners in economic co-operation in the period of the cold war. From this early phase, the non-aligned world had progressed and now sought a fairer and more just system of the world economic order. The avoidance of harsh language by both the industrial nations and developing nations and the more constructive proposals that the special meeting of the UN General Assembly had brought forth, was due in great measure to the realisation by most countries that this was too interdependent a world in which the issues of peace and an equitable economic order were directly inter-linked. This had created a more hopeful mood for the future.

During his stay, he looked forward to learning from the Yugoslav experience. Like Yugoslavia, Singapore had to keep an international perspective. "We in Southeast Asia are also working towards the maintenance of regional stability and economic prosperity, in co-operation with our neighbours."

Lee congratulated Mr. Bijedic on the marvellous progress Yugoslavia had made in the past, and in particular in 1974, when Yugoslavia was able to register a 11.6 per cent growth in GDP when most non-oil producing countries, including the most advanced countries, suffered minus growth rates. It was a great achievement for Yugoslavia's economic policies "implemented under your able leadership".

The joint communique stated that Lee's talks with President Tito and Mr. Bijedic took place in an atmosphere of friendship, mutual confidence and understanding. The two sides discussed a wide range of international political issues and economic problems as well as the bilateral relations between the two countries. During the discussions, similarity or identity of views on major issues of interest to the two non-aligned countries was manifest. It was noted with satisfaction that the bilateral relations between Yugoslavia and Singapore had been developing successfully, marked by a number of meetings of high-ranking officials of the two countries as well as by the co-operation on the international plane. The two sides pointed out their determination to continue to encourage all forms of co-operation, particularly in the economic field in which existed numerous possibilities for a closer and more effective linkage of the economies of the two countries.

In reviewing the international situation, the two sides noted the significantly increased importance of the policy of non-alignment which, by its principled positions and through the untiring activity of non-aligned countries on the international scene aimed at safeguarding peace and progress, had become one of the essential factors in international developments. The two sides hoped that the end of the war in Indo-China would contribute to strengthening the non-alignment policy in that part of the world as well as creating relations of co-operation, based on the principles of peaceful co-existence, non-interference and full equality.

The two sides pointed out that the danger of aggression and war, pressure and interference in the internal affairs of others, particularly the non-aligned countries, had not yet been eliminated. In this context, the two sides considered the main hotbeds of crisis in the world, extending their full support for the efforts towards establishing a just and lasting peace in the Middle East, based on UN Resolution 242, Israel's withdrawal from all the territories occupied in the 1967 war, and on the realisation of the legitimate rights of the Palestinians. "For it is the only way to ensure stable peace and security of all the states in that region."

Special attention was devoted to the economic problems and, in that context, the significant contribution of the Conference of Ministers for Foreign Affairs of the Non-Aligned Countries in Lima was accentuated. The two sides pointed out the great unity of action and stressed the importance of the solidarity manifested by the non-aligned countries in the struggle for changing the existing world economic system and inequitable economic relations. The two sides pointed, in particular, to the need for strengthening further the unity of action of the non-aligned and other developing countries and establishing a constructive dialogue with the developed countries, with a view to bringing to a successful completion the initiated process of establishing equitable international economic co-operation and more balanced economic development of all countries, and, in particular, a more rapid economic growth of the developing countries. Pointing out the great significance of the Seventh Special Session of the General Assembly of the United Nations, as well as of the regular session of the General Assembly, the two sides re-emphasized the great importance of the Organisation of the United Nations as an irreplaceable world forum for dealing with the acute problems of the contemporary world. In this context, the two sides pointed to the direct significance of the Fourth Session of UNCTAD and expressed their readiness to co-operate closely in the preparations for the session, so that it might yield the best possible results.

In appraising as successful the activity of the non-aligned countries so far in promoting mutual co-operation, which had been demonstrated in the high degree of unity and solidarity, as well as their entire engagement with regard to the other international issues, the two sides underscored the great importance of the forthcoming summit conference of the non-aligned countries in 1976 in Sri Lanka. Examining the successful activity of the non-aligned countries on the international plane, the two sides pointed out their readiness to intensify efforts and to co-ordinate their activities in the preparation for this important gathering in Colombo, as well as to continue, along these lines, their further exchange of views and contacts. Expressing their mutual desire for an even greater expansion of co-operation between Yugoslavia and Singapore, the two sides expressed their willingness to continue and reinforce their efforts with a view to utilizing the existing possibilities and open up new prospects for the all-round development of bilateral relations and promotion of friendship between the two countries.

XXII

Back in Singapore, Lee on 25 October received a group of visiting financial writers from seven European countries. He was asked about Mr. Jim Slater and Haw Par. Lee said briefly that the investigations into the affairs of Haw Par would continue even though Mr. Slater had resigned. Lee was questioned about the effects of the situation in Vietnam. Did he not think that, as the result of the communist victories in Indo-China, Europeans had lost confidence in the rest of Southeast Asia from an investment point of view? This, he said, was a question they had better ask the Europeans. "I have not lost confidence in my neighbours. In the intermediate future they are in no danger of going communist." As for the long-term future: "Well, I don't think there is anybody with the kind of telescope that can see that far."

Lee said that Singapore in the immediate future would remain a catalyst in the region for more rapid growth, "because we provide the infrastructure — finance, both banking and insurance, storage, harbour facilities — to enable development to take place in the region." In the intermediate future, anywhere up to ten to fifteen years, "provided we are not upset by more unforeseen catastrophies of the nature of Vietnam", it was likely there would be more gradual economic integration. "Not in a common market, because, as you have pointed out, the levels of development are different, and to have free mobility of capital, labour, within ASEAN is not achievable. But we can move towards adoption of several of the UN Agencies Studies and Recommendations, for a free-trade zone." The UN, Lee explained, had made recommendations along the lines of the Latin America Free Trade Area. Certain projects like steel and petro-chemicals (where parts of the whole complex were distributed between member states), had also been recommended. Lee saw that taking place "mainly because economies of scale demand that to make it viable there should be such an arrangement".

Did he see any use for a Commonwealth Club? Lee replied that this was a very wide question. As an economic club, it had ceased to exist. As a political clearing house of ideas, it was valuable, because more than thirty heads of governments met regularly to discuss problems using a common language. These meetings played a valuable role, supplementing, perhaps influencing, bigger deliberations in Paris or Washington.

Towards the end of the year, plans were being made for the Heads of Government of the five ASEAN countries to meet in Bali early in 1976. In November, 1975, Lee gave two separate interviews, one to an Australian journalist, the other to the chief editor of the Indonesian newsagency, ANTARA. In both, Lee was questioned about ASEAN. He told the Australian journalist, Michael Richardson, replying to a question: "We have never been at a more important moment than now to summon political will to expand economic collaboration. For eight years many assessments and recommendations have been made by UN agencies." Lee went on to say that everybody understood that the nature of modern industry and technology required wider markets because of economies of scale. Vast capital investments required vast consumption of the products of those investments. "If we are to improve the standard of life of our peoples we can do no better than by increasing the degree of integration of our economic activities. But it should be gradual in order not to upset existing patterns of trade and vested interests. I think the will exists in most of the ASEAN countries, though there will be a great deal of argument between economic planners and officials in charge of working out these details when they meet. If we do not do it this time ... then we have failed our people. It would mean we didn't rise to the occasion."

Asked about relations with the communist governments of Indo-China, Lee said there was no desire on the part of any of the ASEAN countries to have an antagonistic relationship with any of the Indo-China states. All the countries in ASEAN, with varying degrees of speed, warmth or intensity of expression, had made it clear that they wanted constructive economic and other relations with the countries of Indo-China.

Asked if ASEAN should be given a more active security and self-defence function, Lee replied: "The first pre-condition for solidarity between nation states is a reason for being and staying together, for example, mutual benefit. And this mutual benefit must be a continuing one: first in the field of economies, then it will go on to foreign political fields, then it will naturally develop into other areas. It is no secret that at present we exchange intelligence assessments on a bilateral and even a multilateral basis. But even countries of the European Economic Community can't adopt a common security position despite the fact that they are all members of NATO, because they still lack united and common economic interests. To put security and self-defence before you've got common economic interests to defend doesn't make sense."

Interviewed a couple of weeks later by Mr. Mohammad Nahar, chief editor of ANTARA, Lee said that the Bali conference would be the first meeting of all the leaders of ASEAN countries. It was important that the summit was not seen as an exercise of international co-operation without substance. Much depended upon the will of the political leaderships. "There can be concrete results which will show results, which will bring benefit within three to five years, if we make the right decisions." But this

268

meant a willingness to try something new. In the past, all major links had been with countries outside ASEAN. They had been growing faster than links within ASEAN. "Therefore, we have got to try to increase our attractiveness as trading partners, through closer co-operation and integration of our development plans and policies."

Asked for his views on a free trade zone, Lee said there were many steps towards closer economic collaboration and co-operation. The simplest first step would be to work for a tariff reduction to increase trade within the region. The hardest to achieve was economic union ... "We must set ourselves a target. Are we aiming for a free trade area or are we trying to have a Common Market?"

The Indonesian editor asked Lee whether he thought the Indochinese countries should be included in ASEAN. Lee replied: "The Indochinese countries are now communist in their systems. ASEAN countries believe in private enterprise. There are two different systems. This does not mean there is no scope for us to co-operate economically for mutual benefits. In fact, we welcome this co-operation. But we must recognise that the economic and political systems are different."

THE YEAR 1976

I

This was another eventful and very busy year, which culminated in general elections and the return of Lee's government for another five-year term in office. The year started on a sad note with the death in London of Tun Razak, Malaysia's Prime Minister. Fortunately for Singapore, he was succeeded by another old friend of the Republic, Datuk Hussein Onn. Within the space of a few weeks, Lee visited Thailand, President Marcos made a state visit to Singapore, and Datuk Hussein Onn paid an official visit shortly afterwards. All the ASEAN Heads of Government met in Bali in February, and there produced a Declaration of ASEAN Concord and a Treaty of Amity and Co-operation in Southeast Asia.

In March, Lee entertained Mr. Nelson Rockefeller, Vice-President of the United States, at a banquet at the Istana, and in May led a goodwill mission to the People's Republic of China. Faced by spurious charges (including one that Lee had ordered journalists in Singapore to be tortured), put up by small groups in the Dutch and British Labour Parties, the PAP resigned from the Socialist International, of which they had been members since 1966. Lee did not attend the Colombo conference of non-aligned nations, but the Foreign Minister, Mr. Rajaratnam, read a message from him. Australia elected a new Prime Minister and Lee flew to Canberra for talks.

In November, Jimmy Carter was elected President of the United States. Both President Suharto of Indonesia, and Mr. Thanin, Thailand's

270

new Prime Minister, visited Singapore informally and Lee made an unofficial visit to Malaysia to see Datuk Hussein Onn.

On 6 December, Parliament was dissolved and general elections held. The PAP won all sixty-nine seats (sixteen of them uncontested), securing 72.4 per cent of the votes cast.

II

In his traditional New Year Message, Lee reported that Singapore ended the full second year after the oil crisis, with the lowest GDP growth since 1965. After near zero growth for the first six months, the economy picked up in the last six months to give 4.2 per cent growth (preliminary estimates) for 1975. He predicted that if economic recovery in America, Japan and Western Europe continued, as most economists forecast, Singapore should do better in 1976. "That we have not been worse hit by the recession is because we anticipated many of the problems and we were willing, as a government and as a people, to take corrective measures, however unpleasant, to solve them. Responsible leadership in the unions, and the realisation on the part of workers that adverse circumstances demand greater effort, have been great assets. These, plus the ingenuity and drive of our administrators and entrepreneurs, have made positive growth possible, despite world-wide recession and a 10 per cent drop in world trade." 1976 marked the beginning of a new era. The countries of Southeast Asia were adjusting themselves to a new power balance around and within the region. "We have to seek stability and security under vastly different conditions." Each ASEAN country had its own set of economic, social and political problems. By co-operation in economic and other fields, they could help each other in increasing confidence in the region and thereby to increase investments and accelerate economic development. These, in turn, would mitigate economic and social problems and mute political unrest. In this way, ASEAN co-operation could blunt the thrust of guerilla insurgencies. Many Singaporeans in their teens and early twenties were too young to remember the troubles and hardships of the 1950s and '60s — the continuous political strikes, widespread unemployment, agitation and unrest, the uncertainty and despondency. The older generation must help to stiffen the moral fibre of the young ones. "We must be on our mettle and prepare ourselves psychologically for sudden difficulties. We must never be thrown off-balance by the shock of the unexpected and the seemingly insurmountable. We must always be able to respond swiftly to new political or economic difficulties." It might be that no amount of explanation could be a sufficient substitute for the personal experience of near-despair, enhanced by the deprivations and hardships of unemployment and a hungry family. Over a decade of rapid economic growth, a new generation had grown up, expecting life to be better each

271

year, almost as a matter of course. "To justify this expectation, let us make a habit of systematic application and high standards of competence."

III

Lee, on 9 January, sent the following message of condolence to Mr. Deng Xiaoping, Vice-Prime Minister of the People's Republic of China, on the death of Mr. Chou En-lai: "I learnt with deep regret of the death of His Excellency, the Prime Minister of the People's Republic of China, Mr. Chou En-lai. The People's Republic of China has lost a great leader. The world has lost an outstanding statesman. Please accept, Your Excellency, on behalf of the Government and people of Singapore and on my own behalf, our deepest sympathy. Please also convey our sincere condolence to Mrs. Chou En-lai and family."

Five days later, the Prime Minister sent the following condolence message to Datuk Hussein Onn, Acting Prime Minister of Malaysia on the death of Tun Abdul Razak: "My colleagues and I are deeply grieved to hear you announce the death of Tun Abdul Razak over the radio tonight. He was an outstanding and respected leader. His contributions to the inde- pendence and the development of Malaysia and her people is a significant part of Malaysian history. Several of my senior colleagues and I were his close friends from our student days. We all feel a sense of personal loss over his departure. Our deepest sympathies go to his wife, Toh Puan Rahah, and his family and to you and your Cabinet colleagues."

IV

On 19 January, the Prime Minister flew to Thailand for a short informal visit. Afterwards, he made a private visit to Hong Kong to be briefed on Hong Kong's MRT project. At the end of the Thailand visit, Lee issued a statement about his meeting with Prime Minister Kukrit and Foreign Minister Chatichai. He said that both sides had agreed and resolved that the strengthening of ties between ASEAN countries would make for more constructive relations with the big powers and with the other countries in the region. "ASEAN collective strength, with growing economic co- operation and increasing political solidarity, must be our prime objective. Such cohesion will reduce the dangers of manipulation by outside powers."

Lee said that during discussions with Prime Minister Kukrit, he became more aware of the realities which shaped Thailand's foreign policies. He now had a better understanding of the direction and thrust of Prime Minister Kukrit's policies and political philosophy underlying his

272

concepts of co-operation in ASEAN. "Needless to say, Mr. Kukrit expounded his views with a lucidity, elegance and humour which always arrest attention and concentration."

V

The President, Dr. Benjamin Sheares, spoke for Singapore at the state banquet in honour of President Ferdinand E. Marcos, President of the Republic of the Philippines, on 27 January. He said his visit came at a time of great changes in their part of the world. The era of complete Western dominance in Southeast Asia had ended. The phase when the great European powers and, later, the United States, ensured the security of the region and controlled the course of events, was now over. "However, we must keep our economic and cultural links with the Western industrial nations. Their economic strength and technological prowess can continue to have a beneficial effect on the development of the region. But more and more, it is what Southeast Asians themselves decide and do, in economic and diplomatic co-operation, that will ensure our security." For the first time in nearly two centuries of Southeast Asian history, it was possible for the peoples and governments of the region to take partial charge of their economic and political future. Whether this phase of history would be one marked by greater achievements would depend on how the peoples and the leaders of the region responded to the opportunities and the challenges before all in ASEAN. The future was never pre-ordained. No one nation in Southeast Asia could decide how Southeast Asia would respond to the opportunities and challenges which would shape the geo-political future of the region. However, ASEAN, if the five governments so agreed and decided, could enhance peace and prosperity in the region.

"You, Mr. President, are one of the great leaders of ASEAN. You have contributed much towards the growth of ASEAN, from a vague concept into an organisation now taken seriously by those who wish us well, and more significantly, by those who do not wish us well. Without leaders like you, President Suharto, the late Tun Razak, and Prime Minister Kukrit Pramoj, men able to see the great potentialities of ASEAN, this effort at regional co-operation will not have made it to this point when decisions await us at the first meeting of Heads of Government soon. We may not have moved as expeditiously towards our objectives as we could have. But we have moved faster during a comparable period than many other regional organisations far older than ours. Had there been no ASEAN collective will, following the United States' military withdrawal from the region, events would have developed very differently and unfavourably for us. We would not have been able to co-ordinate and co-operate to overcome the new problems, and to seize the fresh opportunities the sudden change in fortunes has brought about. Our respective economic and social programmes, pursued vigorously and strengthened by ASEAN cohesiveness, can reduce the threats from guerilla insurgencies, endemic in the region. Eventually, our co-operation can make security and stability a natural state of affairs for Southeast Asia. You, Mr. President, are an ASEAN leader with the capacity to rise above the trivia of everyday problems. You take a wider view of the future for the peace and progress and prosperity of the peoples of the region."

The ASEAN meeting in Bali next month could be a turning-point in the lives of their peoples. ASEAN Heads of State and Government would meet. They could decide to mobilise the considerable talents of their peoples, anchored in ancient cultures, but ready to move into the technological era the West had pioneered. "We are ready for economic development to the benefit of all. Increasing wealth and strength, dependent on the decisions ASEAN leaders will take in Bali, followed by systematic and thorough implementation of plans agreed, can transform slow progress into rapid development, dispel unemployment into bustling economic activity. Then disaffection and bitterness will be expunged and pride in performance instilled."

The joint communique recorded that at their meetings, President Marcos and Prime Minister Lee Kuan Yew exchanged views on a wide range of subjects of common interest and regional importance. Their discussions, which were held in an atmosphere of warmth, friendship and mutual understanding, reflected the close relations existing between Singapore and the Philippines. The President and the Prime Minister agreed that co-operation between the two countries should be further intensified, particularly in the fields of trade and industrial development, and in the sharing of knowledge and skills in urban development. They reaffirmed that bilateral co-operation should be pursued in the general context of ASEAN co-operation. The President and the Prime Minister noted with satisfaction that the two countries shared common aspirations and were committed to the promotion of peace, progress and prosperity in Southeast Asia.

The President and the Prime Minister agreed that the primary objective of ASEAN should be the enhancement of its collective strength, based on economic progress and political stability. They therefore agreed that ASEAN member countries should take decisive initiatives to develop fully their collective strength to make the region an area of peace and progress. They reaffirmed their confidence in ASEAN as the vehicle for regional economic co-operation and development. They also expressed their confidence that the forthcoming meeting of ASEAN Heads of Government in Bali would identify feasible areas for intensifying ASEAN co-operation to enhance prosperity and stability in the region. They agreed that the acceleration of economic development was a major solution to social problems and political unrest in the countries of the region. They also agreed that this would help to reduce threats of subversion within the individual countries and in the region as a whole. They shared the view that the great powers could play a positive and constructive role in the develop-

274

ment efforts of the countries in the region based on the principles of mutual benefits, non-interference and respect for sovereignty.

VI

"The 'Year of the Dragon' should bring us good fortunes," said Lee in his Chinese New Year Message on 29 January. He added that this traditional belief, fortunately, was reinforced by the leading indicators in the economies of America, Japan and Western Europe. The recovery of their economies was already showing through in higher commodity prices. More goods were being made. More people would have jobs and money to buy these goods. This greater economic activity would increase world trade. "It adds up to a little more prosperity for us. However, let us not simply wait for the dragon to work its magic for us. Instead, let us help the dragon by being more productive and more efficient. I wish you all good health and good fortune. May I ask that we all work harder to make sure that we have both. Work makes for good health. Work makes for progress."

VII

The Prime Minister of Malaysia, Datuk Hussein Onn, made an official visit to Singapore on 5 and 6 February. Datuk Hussein Onn was accompanied by the Minister of Foreign Affairs, Tengku Ahmad Rithauddeen, as well as senior government officials. While in Singapore, Datuk Hussein Onn had discussions with Mr. Lee Kuan Yew on matters of mutual interest. In view of the close relations between the two neighbouring countries, both governments agreed to continue to keep to a minimum the protocol formalities of such visits. No official statement was issued.

VIII

The Prime Minister led a strong delegation to Bali for the ASEAN Heads of Government Meeting, 23 – 24 February. On arrival in Bali, Lee stated that a successful conference would strengthen all the five countries of ASEAN in tackling common regional problems. It would also help improve relations between the members of ASEAN and those countries of Southeast Asia with different political and economic systems. Lee said he hoped with the other Heads of Government to make a contribution to making this conference the first and most significant step forward in ASEAN's journey towards closer economic, political and diplomatic cooperation. "In this way, we can ensure the continued stability and progress of our region."

275

Lee made two speeches, one at the opening session and the other at the closing session. At the first, he recalled that in August 1967, in Bangkok, the Foreign Ministers of the five ASEAN countries signed the ASEAN Declaration. The first objective of this Declaration "was and is" to accelerate economic growth. But all objectives rested on the premise of regional peace and stability. Over the years, regular meetings of officials and Ministers had made for greater understanding of each other's aspirations and problems. The basic question was how to ensure continuing stability by stimulating economic development to resolve social and political problems. Otherwise, increasing disaffection and discontent would fuel incipient insurgencies into full-scale revolutions. It was as well that the pace of co-operation was never forced. New nations needed time to realise that sovereignty did not mean self-sufficiency. The scientific and technological discoveries, which led to the age of jet travel and satellite communications, had welded one instant inter-dependent world. In a super-power world of missiles, rockets and orbiting space stations, independence could only be relative. Eight and a half years ago in Bangkok, most people assumed that America and the West had a vital interest in, and would help ensure, a non-communist Southeast Asia. Half a million American troops then in South Vietnam were proof that this was so. Today, America and the West were set on détente with the Soviet Union. They had also started a dialogue towards normalisation and cordial relations with the People's Republic of China. America and the West were prepared to live with the new governments of Vietnam, Cambodia and Laos, and for that matter, with the new Marxist government of Angola. As never before, the future of non-communist Southeast Asia rested in the hands of the leaders and peoples of non-communist Southeast Asia.

ASEAN was at a crossroad. It had developed into a potentially significant force in the region. Further impetus to realise this potential, to decide the direction and speed ASEAN was to go, could come only from Heads of Government. "The simple issue before us is whether we have the will and the vision to reconcile our short-term interests with long-term objectives." Extensive, at times intense, discussions had preceded this meeting. Agreements had not come about easily. Though all were agreed on ultimate objectives, it had been difficult to get agreements on the next few steps. Many domestic economic interests, and several different ideas of how to obtain constructive relations with new governments in the region, had temporarily clouded fundamental issues. There were two views of these arguments and disagreements. The first was that they revealed a lack of unity of purpose. This was not true. There was unity of purpose in greater regional co-operation. "We all seek stability and accelerated economic growth. An ASEAN framework can the better enable us to resolve our economic, social and political problems without outside interference."

The second view was that there were differences in methods and attitudes. This was partly true. Different systems had been inherited. Differ-

276

ent administrative machines had been developed. Different styles of political leadership had been evolved. Healthy arguments on ways and means to agreed goals were a sign of vigorous life in the ASEAN organisation. What was crucial was that out of arguments stemming from different perceptions of common problems must emerge agreements on the fundamentals of a solution. There had been arguments on whether ASEAN countries could now take one big step forward towards greater economic and political co-operation. Even the European nations of the EEC, nearly nineteen years after they signed the Treaty of Rome in 1957, continued to have strong disagreements from time to time. They could not agree on energy-sharing during the oil crisis of 1973. On monetary union, agreed to in principle, at least two of its major members, Britain and Italy, had to abandon it in practice. Perhaps the EEC was too advanced to be ASEAN's model. "But, in one respect, we have a situation vaguely analogous to theirs. What gave birth to the EEC was the pressure of a competing and different political and economic system, Comecon, the Soviet Union and the countries of Eastern Europe. Since April last year, the ASEAN countries have to face up to competition from the Marxist-Socialist systems of Vietnam, Laos and Cambodia. We must ensure that differences in political and economic systems between these countries and ASEAN are confined to peaceful competition."

In competition, one party did not seek the destruction of one's competitors. Indeed, competition meant the emulation of the strong points of a competitor. The countries of ASEAN had not been ravaged by war. For the present, they had the greater capacity to forge ahead. Economies were in various stages of dynamic growth. "If we are able to combine our individual fortes, whether it is national resilence in Indonesia, Rukunegara of Malaysia, the New Society of the Philippines, the traditions of monarchy and Buddhism of Thailand, or Singapore's matter-of-fact habit of facing up to the realities of life, together, we can do what we individually cannot do as well." As ASEAN, they could talk with the industrial nations of America, Japan and Western Europe on a more equal basis. With combined strength, they could get better results in long-term co-operation in trade and transfers of technology. They could work more closely and effectively with the countries of Australasia and the Pacific than if they were to go their own separate ways. In the nature of things, with many Ministers and even more officials, it was difficult to keep all the deliberations secret. It was the business of diplomats, and even more so of newsmen, to ferret out the areas of agreement and of differences. At the end of this meeting, the major capitals of the world would have a shrewd idea of whether ASEAN would crystallise, take definite form, and move ahead in economic, political and diplomatic co-operation.

"Let us seize our opportunities for co-operation, for continued security and stability as a more cohesive group, pursuing more coherent policies. Then we can establish more equable and friendly relationships with all the great powers, and their friends and allies in and around the region. Let us give our peoples cause to believe in our policies, that they have been forged to consolidate regional stability, co-operation and progress, and that these policies will eventually spread prosperity over the countries of ASEAN, and also bring benefits to all countries willing to trade and be friends with us." This meeting would be memorable for consolidating ASEAN as a regional force in the international community. There had been speculation whether the five governments would accord priority to common issues and interests, those which should bring them closer together, or whether they would pursue individual pet subjects. Over the past few months, differences of views' had been gradually narrowed. Energies had been concentrated on those subjects which were of importance to each and every one of them. However, on the eve of the meeting, before the Heads of Government arrived, full accord had not been reached. Addressing President Suharto, Lee said: "I had believed that the salubrious air in Bali would have a soothing effect on harassed officials and ruffled Ministers. But, when I arrived yesterday, I discovered it was you who infused your calm and wise counsel into the Meetings of our Ministers. Thus were the differences resolved before the Heads of Government arrived. This gives me good reason to believe that our deliberations in Bali will be positive and productive."

At the end of the Bali meeting, Lee on 24 February, said that up to the previous day, a favourite question posed by ASEAN-watchers was: "Has ASEAN a future?" When officials followed up on the Agreements that had been reached at this meeting, the question would then be: "What kind of future is it to be for ASEAN?" ASEAN's future was not in doubt. It might move slowly or swiftly; probably a moderate speed was best. From time to time, it might take wrong turnings but ASEAN had now made a permanent landmark on the political and economic landscape of Southeast Asia. From now on, ASEAN would merit more than a desk in respective Foreign Ministries. The Heads of State and Government had now given their imprimatur to ASEAN's wider role in economic planning and development. "We can also expect more concerted policies in international affairs." All five Heads of Government had given their Foreign and Economic Ministries and the ASEAN Secretariat a clear sense of purpose and direction. The documents signed and the setting up of an ASEAN Secretariat to co-ordinate activities, and to report separately to meetings of Foreign Ministers and meetings of Economic Ministers, were the first steps emphasising the substance of regional co-operation, not the forms. "We must aim, in the next three to five years, to give each and every partner such stake in ASEAN that it will be difficult for any partner to get out of ASEAN without creating problems far more unpleasant than any that member will face in ASEAN."

Lee said the meeting had succeeded because there had been considerable give and take, and common ASEAN sense. "So long as we do not insist that one partner should give more than he can economically or politically afford, for the present, or take more than is reasonable, disagreements can be overcome — as we have done in Bali. Mr. Chairman, you understood this, and you saw to it that there was fair give and take between us, both in the arguments and in the results, and that is why positive and significant decisions were reached." Before concluding, Lee, on behalf of his delegation and himself, extended his warm and sincere thanks for the infinite pains taken by Indonesian officials to ensure the expeditious work of the Conference, and "something not inconsequential, the comfort and convenience for our work and relaxation".

The full text of the Treaty of Amity and Co-operation in Southeast Asia, and the Declaration of ASEAN Concord, follows:—

TREATY OF AMITY AND CO-OPERATION IN SOUTHEAST ASIA

PREAMBLE

The High Contracting Parties: CONSCIOUS of the existing ties of history, geography and culture, which have bound their peoples together; ANXIOUS to promote regional peace and stability through abiding respect for justice and the rule of law and enhancing regional resilience in their relations; DESIRING to enhance peace, friendship and mutual co-operation on matters affecting Southeast Asia consistent with the spirit and principles of the Charter of the United Nations, the Ten Principles adopted by the Asian-African Conference in Bandung on 25 April 1955, the Declaration of the Association of Southeast Asian Nations signed in Bangkok on 8 August 1967, and the Declaration signed in Kuala Lumpur on 27 November 1971; CONVINCED that the settlement of differences or disputes between their countries should be regulated by national, effective and sufficiently flexible procedures, avoiding negative attitudes which might endanger or hinder co-operation; BELIEVING in the need for co-operation with all peace-loving nations, both within and outside Southeast Asia, in the furtherance of world peace, stability and harmony; SOLEMNLY AGREE to enter into a Treaty of Amity and Co-operation as follows:

CHAPTER I
PURPOSE AND PRINCIPLES
Article 1

The purpose of this Treaty is to promote perpetual peace, everlasting amity and co-operation among their peoples which would contribute to their strength, solidarity and closer relationship.

Article 2

In their relations with one another, the High Contracting Parties shall be guided by the following fundamental principles: a. Mutual respect for the independence, sovereignty, equality, territorial integrity and national identity of all nations; b. The right of every State to lead its national existence free from external interference, subversion or coercion; c. Non-interference in the internal affairs of one another; d. Settlement of differences or disputes by peaceful means; e. Renunciation of the threat or use of force; f. Effective co-operation among themselves.

CHAPTER II
AMITY
Article 3

In pursuance of the purpose of this Treaty the High Contracting Parties shall endeavour to develop and strengthen the traditional, cultural and historical ties of friendship, good neighbourliness and co-operation which bind them together and shall fulfill in good faith the obligations assumed under this Treaty. In order to promote closer understanding among them, the High Contracting Parties shall encourage and facilitate contact and intercourse among their peoples.

CHAPTER III
CO-OPERATION
Article 4

The High Contracting Parties shall promote active co-operation in the economic, social, cultural, technical, scientific and administrative fields as well as in matters of common ideas and aspirations of international peace and stability in the region and all the other matters of common interest.

Article 5

Pursuant to Article 4 the High Contracting Parties shall exert their maximum efforts multilaterally as well as bilaterally on the basis of equality, non-discrimination and mutual benefit.

Article 6

The High Contracting Parties shall collaborate for the acceleration of the economic growth in the region in order to strengthen the foundation for a prosperous and peaceful community of nations in Southeast Asia. To this end, they shall promote the greater utilization of their agriculture and industries, the expansion of their trade and the improvement of their economic infra-structure for the mutual benefit of their peoples. In this regard, they shall continue to explore all avenues for close and beneficial co-operation with other States as well as international and regional organisations outside the region.

Article 7

The High Contracting Parties, in order to achieve social justice and to raise the standards of living of the peoples of the region, shall intensify economic co-operation. For this purpose, they shall adopt appropriate regional strategies for economic development and mutual assistance.

Article 8

The High Contracting Parties shall strive to achieve the closest co-operation on the widest scale and shall seek to provide assistance to one another in the form of training and research facilities in the social, cultural, technical, scientific and administrative fields.

Article 9

The High Contracting Parties shall endeavour to foster co-operation in the furtherance of the·cause of peace, harmony and stability in the region. To this end, the High Contracting Parties shall maintain regular contacts and consultations with one another on international and regional matters with a view to co-ordinating their views, actions and policies.

Article 10

Each High Contracting Party shall not in any manner or form participate in any activity which shall constitute a threat to the political and economic stability, sovereignty, or territorial integrity of another High Contracting Party.

Article 11

The High Contracting Parties shall endeavour to strengthen their respective national resilience in their political, economic, socio-cultural as well as security fields in conformity with their respective ideas and aspirations, free from external interference as well as internal subversive activities in order to preserve their respective national identities.

Article 12

The High Contracting Parties in their efforts to achieve regional prosperity and security, shall endeavour to co-operate in all fields for the promotion of regional resilience, based on the principles of self-confidence, self-reliance, mutual respect, co-operation and solidarity which will constitute the foundation for a strong and viable community of nations in Southeast Asia.

CHAPTER IV
PACIFIC SETTLEMENT OF DISPUTES
Article 13

The High Contracting Parties shall have the determination and good faith to prevent disputes from arising. In case disputes on matters directly affecting them should arise, especially disputes likely to disturb regional peace and harmony, they shall refrain from the threat or use of force and shall at all times settle such disputes among themselves through friendly negotiations.

Article 14

To settle disputes through regional processes, the High Contracting Parties shall constitute, as a continuing body, a High Council comprising a Representative at ministerial level from each of the High Contracting Parties to take cognizance of the existence of disputes or situations likely to disturb regional peace and harmony.

Article 15

In the event no solution is reached through direct negotiations, the High Council shall take cognizance of the dispute or the situation and shall recommend to the parties in dispute appropriate means of settlement such as good offices, mediation, inquiry or conciliation. The High Council may however offer its good offices, or upon agreement of the parties in dispute, constitute itself into a committee of mediation, inquiry or conciliation. When deemed necessary, the High Council shall recommend appropriate measures for the prevention of a determination of the dispute or the situation.

Article 16

The foregoing provisions of this Chapter shall not apply to a dispute unless all the parties to the dispute agree to their application to that dispute. However, this shall not preclude the other High Contracting Parties not party to the dispute from offering all possible assistance to settle the said dispute. Parties to the dispute should be well disposed towards such offer of assistance.

Article 17

Nothing in this Treaty shall preclude recourse to the modes of peaceful settlement contained in Article 33 (1) of the Charter of the United Nations. The High Contracting Parties which are parties to a dispute should be encouraged to take initiatives to solve it by friendly negotiations before resorting to the other procedures provided for in the Charter of the United Nations.

CHAPTER V
GENERAL PROVISIONS
Article 18

This Treaty shall be signed by the Republic of Indonesia, Malaysia, the Republic of the Philippines, the Republic of Singapore and the Kingdom of Thailand. It shall be ratified in accordance with the constitutional procedures of each signatory States.

It shall be open for succession by other States in Southeast Asia.

Article 19

This Treaty shall enter into force on the date of the deposit of the fifth instrument of ratification with the Governments of the signatory States which are designated Depositories of this Treaty and of the instruments of ratification or accession.

Article 20

This Treaty is drawn up in the official languages of the High Contracting Parties, all of which are equally authoritative. There shall be an agreed common translation of the texts in the English language. Any divergent interpretation of the common text shall be settled by negotiation.

IN FAITH THEREOF the High Contracting Parties have signed the Treaty and have hereto affixed their seals. DONE IN Denpasar, Bali, on the Twenty-fourth day of February in the year one thousand nine hundred and seventy-six.

DECLARATION OF ASEAN CONCORD

A COMMON BOND EXISTING AMONG THE MEMBER STATES OF THE ASSOCIATION OF SOUTHEAST ASIAN NATIONS, The President of the Republic of Indonesia, the Prime Minister of Malaysia, the President of the Republic of the Philippines, the Prime Minister of the Republic of Singapore, and the Prime Minister of the Kingdom of Thailand, *REAFFIRM* their commitment to the Declarations of Bandung, Bangkok and Kuala Lumpur, and the Charter of the United Nations; *ENDEAVOUR* to promote peace, progress, prosperity and the welfare of the peoples of member states; *UNDERTAKE* to consolidate the achievements of ASEAN and expand ASEAN co-operation in the economic, social, cultural and political fields; *DO HEREBY DECLARE:*

ASEAN co-operation shall take into account, among others, the following objectives and principles in the pursuit of political stability:

1. The stability of each member state and of the ASEAN region is an essential contribution to international peace and security. Each member state resolves to eliminate threats posed by subversion to its stability, thus strengthening national and ASEAN resilience.

2. Member states, individually and collectively, shall take active steps for the early establishment of the Zone of Peace, Freedom and Neutrality.

3. The elimination of poverty, hunger, disease and illiteracy is a primary concern of member states. They shall therefore intensify co-operation in economic and social development, with particular emphasis on the promotion of social justice and on the improvement of the living standard of their peoples.

4. Natural disasters and other major calamities can retard the pace of development of member states. They shall extend, within their capabilities, assistance for relief of member states in distress.

5. Member states shall take co-operative action in their national and regional development progress, utilizing as far as possible the resources available in the ASEAN region to broaden the complementarity of their respective economies.

6. Member states, in the spirit of ASEAN solidarity, shall rely exclusively on peaceful processes in the settlement of intra-regional differences.

7. Member states shall strive, individually and collectively, to create conditions conducive to the promotion of peaceful co-operation among the nations of Southeast Asia on the basis of mutual respect and mutual benefits.

8. Member states shall vigorously develop an awareness of regional identity and exert all efforts to create a strong ASEAN community, respected by all, and respecting all nations on the basis of mutually advantageous relationships, and in accordance with the principles of self-determination, sovereign equality and non-interference in the internal affairs of nations.

AND DO HEREBY ADOPT

The following programme of action as a framework for ASEAN co-operation:

A. *Political*

1. Meeting of the Heads of Government of the member states as and when necessary;

2. Signing of Treaty of Amity and Co-operation in Southeast Asia;

3. Settlement of intra-regional disputes by peaceful means as soon as possible;

4. Immediate consideration of initial steps towards recognition of and respect for the Zone of Peace, Freedom and Neutrality wherever possible;

5. Improvement of ASEAN machinery to strengthen political co-operation;

6. Study on how to develop judicial co-operation including the possibility of an ASEAN Extradition Treaty;

7. Strengthening of political solidarity by promoting the harmonization of views, co-ordinating positions and, where possible and desirable, taking common actions.

B. *Economic*

1. *Co-operation on Basic Commodities, particularly Food and Energy.*

(i) Member states shall assist each other by according priority to the supply of the individual country's needs in critical circumstances, and priority to the acquisition of exports from member states, in respect of basic commodities, particularly food and energy. (ii) Member states shall also intensify co-operation in the production of basic commodities particularly food and energy in the individual member states of the region.

2. *Industrial Co-operation*

(i) Member states shall co-operate to establish large-scale ASEAN industrial plants, particularly to meet regional requirements of essential commodities. (ii) Priority shall be given to projects which utilize the available materials in the member states, contribute to the increase of food production, increase foreign exchange earnings or save foreign exchange and create employment.

3. *Co-operation in Trade*

(i) Member states shall co-operate in the fields of trade in order to promote development and growth of new production and trade and to improve the trade structures of individual states and among countries of ASEAN conducive to further development and to safeguard and increase their foreign exchange earnings and reserves. (ii) Member states shall progress towards the establishment of preferential trading arrangements as a long-term objective on a basis deemed to be at any particular time appropriate through rounds of negotiations subject to the unanimous agreement of member states. (iii) The expansion of trade among member states shall be facilitated through co-operation on basic commodities, particularly in food and energy and through co-operation in ASEAN industrial projects. (iv) Member states shall accelerate joint efforts to improve access to markets outside ASEAN for their raw materials and finished products by seeking the elimination of all trade barriers in those markets, developing new usage for these products and in adopting common approaches and actions in dealing with regional groupings and individual economic powers. (v) Such efforts shall also lead to co-operation in the field of technology and production methods in order to increase the production and to improve the quality of export products, as well as to develop new export products with a view to diversifying exports.

4. *Joint Approach to International Commodity Problems and Other World Economic Problems*

(i) The principle of ASEAN co-operation on trade shall also be reflected on a priority basis in joint approaches to international commodity problems and other world economic problems such as the reform of international trading system, the reform of international monetary system and transfer of real resources, in the United Nations and other relevant multilateral fora, with a view to contributing to the establishment of the New International Economic Order. (ii) Member states shall give priority to the stabilisation and increase of export earning of these commodities produced and exported by them through commodity agreements including bufferstock scheme and other means.

5. Machinery for Economic Co-operation

Ministerial meetings on economic matters shall be held regularly or as deemed necessary in order to: (i) formulate recommendations for the consideration of Government of member states for the strengthening of ASEAN economic co-operation; (ii) review the co-ordination and implementation of agreed ASEAN programmes and projects on economic co-operation; (iii) exchange views and consult on national development plans and policies as a step towards harmonizing regional development and (iv) perform such other relevant functions as agreed upon by the member Governments.

C. Social.

1. Co-operation in the field of social development, with emphasis on the well-being of the low-income group and of the rural population, through the expansion of opportunities for productive employment with fair remuneration;

2. Support for the active involvement of all sectors and levels of the ASEAN communities, particularly the women and youth, in development efforts;

3. Intensification and expansion of existing co-operation in meeting the problems of population growth in the ASEAN region, and where possible, formulation of new strategies in collaboration with appropriate international agencies.

4. Intensification of co-operation among member states as well as with the relevant international bodies in the prevention and eradication of the abuse of narcotics and the illegal trafficking of drugs.

D .*Cultural and Information.*

1 . Introduction of the study of ASEAN, its member states and their national languages as part of the curricula of schools, and other institutions of learning in the member states;

2 . Support of ASEAN scholars, writers, artists, and mass media representatives to enable them to play an active role in fostering a sense of regional identity and fellowship;

3 . Promotion of Southeast Asian Studies through closer collaboration among national institutes.

E .*Security.*

Continuation of co-operation on a non-ASEAN basis between the member states in security matters in accordance with their mutual needs and interests.

F .*Improvement of ASEAN machinery.*

1 . Signing of the Agreement on the Establishment of the ASEAN Secretariat;

2 . Regular review of the ASEAN organizational structure with a view to improving its effectiveness;

3 . Study of the desirability of a new constitutional framework for ASEAN.

Done at Denpasar, Bali, this Twenty Fourth Day of February in the year One Thousand Nine Hundred and Seventy Six.

In a joint press communique, the Heads of Government stated that the meeting was held in the traditional ASEAN spirit of friendship and cordiality. They reviewed the activities of ASEAN since its inception in 1967, and expressed satisfaction with its progress, especially in fostering the spirit of co-operation and solidarity among the member states. They discussed developments affecting the ASEAN region. They reaffirmed the determination of their respective Governments to continue to work for the promotion of peace, stability and progress in Southeast Asia, thus contributing towards world peace and international harmony. To this end, they expressed their readiness to develop fruitful relations and mutually bene-

288

ficial co-operation with other countries in the region. They expressed the hope that other powers would pursue policies which would contribute to the achievement of peace, stability and progress in Southeast Asia.

The meeting discussed ways and means of strengthening co-operation among member states. They believed that it was essential for the member states to move to higher levels of co-operation, especially in the political, economic, social, cultural, scientific and technological fields. On the Zone of Peace, Freedom and Neutrality, the Heads of Government expressed their satisfaction with the progress made in the efforts to draw up initially necessary steps to secure the recognition of and respect for the Zone. They directed that these efforts should be continued in order to realise its early establishment.

The Heads of Government signed the Treaty of Amity and Co-operation in Southeast Asia. They also signed the Declaration of ASEAN Concord. In pursuance of their determination to forge closer economic co-operation among member states, they agreed that a meeting of Economic Ministers be convened in Kuala Lumpur on 8 – 9 March 1976 to consider measures to be taken towards implementing the decisions of the ASEAN Heads of Government Meeting on matters of economic co-operation. They also agreed that the Meeting of Economic Ministers would discuss particularly the following questions:

(i). The mechanisms by which member States shall accord priority in critical circumstances, such as natural disasters, major calamities, and shortages due to artificial or natural causes, to the supply of the individual country's needs in food and energy and priority to the acquisition of exports from member States.

(ii). The measures to be taken for intensifying co-operation in the production of basic commodities particularly for food and energy.

(ii). The formulation of appropriate measures for initiating co-operative action towards establishing ASEAN large-scale industrial projects. Examples of some of the ASEAN industrial projects that could be considered by the Meeting of ASEAN Economic Ministers are urea, superphosphates, potash, petrochemicals, steel, soda ash, news-print and rubber products. The meeting will also give consideration to other projects.

(iv). The instruments to be employed in preferential trading arrangements to facilitate the expansion of trade among ASEAN member states in basic commodities, particularly in food and energy, and the products of ASEAN industrial projects. These instruments will include, but not be limited to, the following: (a) long-term quantity contracts, (b) purchase finance support at preferential interest rates, (c) preference in procurement by government entities, (d) extension of tariff preferences, and (e) other measures agreed upon.

(v). The formulation of joint approaches to international commodity and other economic problems, giving priority to stabilization and increase of export earnings of ASEAN commodities, through commodity agreements, including buffer-stock schemes and other means.

The Foreign Ministers signed the Agreement on the Establishments of the ASEAN Secretariat. The Heads of Government took note of the nomination of Mr. Hartono Rekso Dharsono as Secretary-General of the ASEAN Secretariat. The Heads of Government of Malaysia, Philippines, Singapore and Thailand were warmly appreciative of the exemplary chairmanship of their meeting by the President of the Republic of Indonesia and expressed their thanks for the traditional Indonesian hospitality extended to them and the excellent arrangements made for their meeting.

IX

In Parliament, on 16 March, Lee Kuan Yew replied to criticisms raised by back-benchers on discourtesy, indifferent attitude and bureaucratic approach of the civil servants. The Prime Minister said he did not want to stand as a defender of rude, arrogant, unfeeling and discourteous civil servants. Where they existed, where they could be pin-pointed, action would be taken. There was for senior civil servants a Civil Service Staff Development Institute which, amongst its other duties, tried to involve the civil servants in the wider aims of the Government and the duties of the Administration. The Civil Service, with the help of the Public Service Commission, had tried to define those areas where the public came into contact with the officials, whether it was the Immigration Department, the Registry of Vehicles, the hospitals, clinics, post offices, wherever there was a counter, and attempts would constantly be made to improve the way in which the public at large was being served.

Having said that, Lee picked up the points made by MPs. He was glad there was no charge of dishonourable, corrupt or other practices; "if MPs come here and complain of discourtesy, inadequate toilet or canteen facilities, tatty signboards, all this is in part a reflection of our relatively healthy state of affairs. In fact, there should be a conducted tour for MPs and some of their constituents who complain of the bureaucratic practices of parts of the Third World. When they come back they would be extremely grateful that they have Singapore and the Singapore Civil Service. That having been said and done, I think we have to take this in the context of our total society. Consideration for each other, courtesy or the lack thereof, comes out of a long cultivation of good habits. It is extremely difficult to be polite and courteous to a crude, obstreperous and ill-mannered person. It is a two-way process, whether it is the SBS bus drivers and conductors against passengers, whether it is motorists versus lorry drivers, or motorists versus motorists, or motorcyclists versus motorists; whether it is jostling at the National Stadium or in the schools; it is the general tenor of behaviour, the accepted standards of conduct of a society as a whole. In the past seventeen years, or perhaps I should go back to 1955 when we had the first elected Government and the pressures of elected representatives wanting less high-handed treatment for their illiterate, ill-educated constituents, things have improved. But they can improve only so far as the general level of conduct and courtesy between our citizens can improve. I have known of communities where people are elaborately courteous to each other because of the nature of long years of cultivated breeding, cultivated nurturing of good public behaviour. Words like 'I am sorry' or 'please' are not something one hears over the telephone. They are 'What?' 'Who are you?' And if you say, 'Sorry, it is the wrong number', they say 'Oh!', not 'I am sorry'. I have picked up the telephone and have had to deal with telephone operators who did not know who I was and treated me just like a member of the public. So I have a fair idea of the general level of public conduct ... ''

Lee continued: "Of course, you can have the very converse where you have all the manifestations of good behaviour but actually a crude vicious inner self. I have known of capitals in this world where, having nudged you out of the bus queue — this was twenty or thirty years ago when I was a student — they say, 'Pardon me'. They give you a sharp nudge and they are on, and you are off, the bus. They say, 'I am sorry'. They have all the external manifestations of a cultured, well-bred person. Which would you have? An honest straightforward Singaporean who says, 'No'. 'What'. 'Who is there?' or a hypocritical one who says, 'I am terribly sorry', when he is not?"

Lee said he agreed with the Member for Anson. He was not interested in whether an officer in the Civil Service has got a B.A., M.A., Ph.D., or D.Sc. Could he get a job done? Could he get a team to work with him? Was he a talker or a thinker, or a talker and a doer? The best, of course, was the man who thought before he expounded, and having expounded, then acted. But at the end of it all were the results. It had got nothing to do with whether he had got a Ph.D. or a School Certificate or even a Std. VI qualification. In the old days, Std. VI would have taken a person very far. It was whether they had it up there and whether they had drive. But the chances were, with the methods of universal education and selection all along the way, race after race, year after year, if one could not make a simple B.A., then it was hardly likely he could last the marathon. And that was what the government was looking for — people who could last the pace, not just one test but many. Every Minister could testify that when such a person was discovered, then a large section of a Ministry and its problems were taken off the Minister's shoulders and happy reports were made every month; and after a while, every three months, and after a longer while, once in six months.

Lee hoped he had made his position clear. "We are the political side of the Service. I do not defend rudeness. I do not defend arrogance. I do not defend mediocrity. I do not defend the desire to do the minimum and get by. But this is what we have got. This is after seventeen years of PAP government. I think it could have been better, but it may have been a lot worse. In fact, let us start off in the knowledge that it is better and let us make it better. But to make it better, let us not come here with any scales over our eyes. True, MPs must make some noise for querulous constituents. But it is extremely difficult when the answer is 'No' to make a member of the public go away happy." And as MPs knew and even Ministers knew, some fellow Ministers had the habit of passing on the buck. So the MP came to Parliament and passed on the buck to the Minister. "I have got a lot of experience with that. I got Ministers passing on the buck to each other and they land up on my plate." Finally, the answer is still "no" because if you say "yes" then you have changed the rules for everybody and an unworkable situation is created. So the man who knows how to say "no" and keep his constituents happy and have them voting for him at the next elections should quietly congratulate himself either at his innate good nature that God has endowed him with, or for his cultivated sense of self-discipline that keeps the face in relaxed and happy countenance, while he is really fed up to the teeth with troublesome constituents. "Whichever way it is, I hope all MPs will look after their constituents, keep them happy even when the answer is 'no' because, as you know, if the answer is 'yes' he would not be looking for the MP."

X

The practice of Ministers opening new factories continued. Lee gave an address at the official opening of Singapore Time (Pte.) Ltd. on 19 March. He said a factory to manufacture watches, tools and dies, and machine tools which Seiko had set up in Woodlands, was ideal for a new town. It was pollution-free. Workers could live within walking distance of the factory. Its products had high valued-added components — 80 per cent for stop-watches, 70 per cent for wrist watches and for machine tools. From basic materials like brass and stainless steel-bars and coils, machines and workers of this factory would produce fine precision watch-parts and assemble them into watches. Ninety of the present 307 workers were trained in Japan for periods from six to eighteen months. Daini-Seikosha was at present training Singaporeans as technicians, tool- and die-makers, skilled machinists and mechanical assemblers in Singapore and in Japan. Lee said he was relieved to learn that the performance of the first eighty Singapore trainees in Japan had been satisfactory enough for Mr. Hattori, Senior Managing Director, to bring Phase II of the operations forward by one year.

If the workers joining Singapore Time (Pte.) Ltd. kept up this promising start, in five years there would be nearly 1,200 workers, most of them highly skilled in the metal engineering trades, working automatic screw machines and cylindrical grinding machines. They would be an asset to the company, and to Singapore. After discovering the job-choosy attitudes of young workers, including National Servicemen, he was reassured by this evidence that for skilled jobs, young Singaporeans rose to the demands of high-precision work. "My tentative conclusion is that whilst every Singaporean hopes to be at least a skilled technician, those who cannot acquire the skills, at least initially, refuse to take on heavy jobs or those which dirty their hands. Unfortunately, many parents and working brothers and sisters are willing to support younger members of their family in their search for easy or soft jobs, preferably in air-conditioned hotels, restaurants or emporiums." When he was in Tokyo in May 1973, Lee visited Seiko's Takatsuka and Kameido factories near Tokyo. What impressed him was the intense concentration of the workers on their jobs, refusing to be distracted by a party of visitors going in and out of their production line. From the traditional coil spring watch of the quartz watch, research and development by scientists and inventors ensured progress. However, whatever the technology, only concentration on the job and consistently high standards could guarantee precision and high quality finish. Young men and women who joined Singapore Time (Pte.) Ltd. must show that they could achieve this international level of competence. The Singapore worker must prove that he was as good as Seiko workers in Japan. That was the crux of the problem.

XI

When Mr. Nelson A. Rockefeller, Vice-President of the United States visited Singapore, the Prime Minister, on 28 March, entertained him at a banquet at the Istana. Lee said one major preoccupation of governments in Southeast Asia was the kind of relationship they should and could establish with the major powers. All were aware that a new balance of power was emerging in the world with immense significance for the region. Some were uncertain whether in the intermediate and longer term, it would be a balance between two or three powers in Southeast Asia. "We know that the Soviet Union, a super power, formerly excluded from the region, has made its presence felt. We also know that China has become a major factor. She is a part of Asia, with abiding interests in this region. Southeast Asians have always assumed that the United States will continue to be a force in Asia. I hope it will not be long before Americans see Southeast Asia, not in terms of their memories of Vietnam, but in terms of the promise of a more positive and productive contribution to the economic and social development of the non-communist countries of Southeast Asia."

Lee revealed that in his discussions earlier in the day with the Vice-President, he had been struck by the vitality and clarity of Rockefeller's exposition of the stand of the United States towards Asia, and the Pacific and Indian Oceans, and of the major issues of the contemporary world. "You left me the impression that there were grounds for optimism, that Americans are an indomitable and resilient people, and will rise afresh to the new challenges in this increasingly interdependent world." The five

293

countries of ASEAN were all geared to the economies of the West. They had embarked on their first major co-operative effort. "We have also taken to heart the lesson of Vietnam, that communist subversion and insurrection cannot be defeated by force of arms alone. Force is necessary to counter guerillas using force. But what is also needed is fairly rapid economic development and a much fairer distribution of the wealth development generates. This will melt the disaffection and discontent on which communists depend for enrolling recruits for violent revolution." The recent meeting of ASEAN Heads of Government in Bali ended with a call to all developed countries to help ASEAN countries to help themselves in their plans for economic and social development. "There is urgency in our fight against poverty, compounded by unjust distribution of wealth." For this task, the United States was well-equipped to help. The USA had the financial and industrial resources. They had the scientific and technological resources. They had vast markets to stimulate the growth of developing economies. "Of course, the ASEAN countries must also accept the self-discipline and sustained effort that modernisation demands in the process of economic and social development."

Lee said Southeast Asia need not be an area of new conflicts or new problems for the United States, Japan or Australasia. "We want to be free to choose our form of government, our way of life and our partners in technological progress." The more the external pressures a country was under, the more the consideration it should receive from the United States and her allies in the Pacific and in Europe, in opportunities to expand trade and to attract investments. This was the most significant contribution the United States could make to friends in Southeast Asia. When the Presidential elections were over, Lee was sure that Rockefeller's wisdom and counsel, the result of long years of public office spread over a wide spectrum of responsibilities and interests, would carry great weight by those who had to make the big decisions to achieve a durable balance of power and peace in the Atlantic and Europe, in the Mediterranean and the Middle East, and last, but not least, in the Pacific and Indian Oceans, East and Southeast Asia, and Australasia.

XII

Lee spoke at the inaugural dinner of NTUC's Second Triennial Delegates Conference on 25 April. The prospects and problems Singapore faced in 1976, he said, were very different from those of 1965, after separation, or of 1968 when British military withdrawal started. "In '65 and '68, we faced acute crises. People knew our very survival was at stake. This realisation made everyone willing to bear hardship and to make sacrifices which enabled us to overcome our problems. We survived. Better still, we prospered." From a GDP in 1965 of $2.8 billion, or $1,474 per capita,

Singapore grew in 1975 to a GDP of $8.05 billion, or $3,578 per capita. This was not an accurate reflection of the increase in the wages of workers. Foreign investments, banks and financial institutions meant dividends were remitted for foreign corporations and shareholders. But, nevertheless, per capita incomes, grade for grade, of unskilled and skilled workers, clerical workers, and executives and professionals, showed nearly a three-fold increase in the past ten years in money terms. In real terms, the modal income per worker doubled from $190 per month. The internal factors were positive. A keen work force, prepared to learn and work. Unions, management and government knew what was at stake and went all out to resolve problems by expanding investments to create jobs. "We built factories, offices, hotels, homes, schools, hospitals, roads, flyovers, power-stations, reservoirs, parks, gardens, beaches, and all that make the Singapore of today." External factors were also favourable. The industrial nations had a most rapid expansion of their economies of 4 – 6 per cent per annum. World trade increased annually, by 8 – 9 per cent.

"Today, the outlook is completely different. The internal factors are not as good as they were. Rapid economic development had led to increased standards of living, and, unfortunately, to a reluctance to sacrifice personal and group interests for the sake of national interests. Our economy is more diversified and stronger. Our work force is better educated and trained in various industrial skills. However, that willingness to take on any job, however tough, heavy or dirty, has gone. A new mood has set in with the better life. At present, we have about 40,000 unemployed, approximately over 4 per cent of the work force, on the live register, nearly half of whom are looking for jobs for the first time. Sample quarterly surveys show these to be more or less accurate figures. If these 40,000 unemployed were prepared, as their elders were, 8 – 10 years ago, to do heavy jobs, under hard conditions, there would be no unemployment at all in Singapore. But to get these jobs done, we have to let in more than 40,000 on work permits. Fewer and fewer Singaporeans are going in for building and construction, and for ship-repairing and shipbuilding. Last month, March, as the economy recovered, we had to issue over 2,000 work permits, the majority for building and construction, and over 300 for ship-repairing and shipbuilding. These are well-paid jobs. But they demand hard work, often in the sun and rain. Young Singaporeans prefer to remain on the live register, looking for jobs even for less pay, preferably white-collar jobs in offices, otherwise in air-conditioned hotels, shopping complexes and factories."

People complained of the poor quality of workmanship in HDB flats, and rightly so. But how could the HDB be expected to improve the quality of work when over 50 per cent of its labour force were unskilled apprentices on work permits? Many of them, when they become skilled, left for home, to take jobs with their new skills near their homes. Although the pay was slightly less, they spent less because they lived with their families. So Singapore had become a training ground for building and construction

295

workers. Lee recognised that this trend was not peculiar to Singapore. The same pattern had been seen in Europe. As standards of living went up, citizens chose the cleaner and easier jobs, and left the tougher jobs for guest workers. "But let us remember, Japan has no guest workers. They do their own heavy and dirty jobs. And they are a better society for it." Fortunately, Singapore did not have the problem of class conflicts as in some older industrial countries of Europe. Singapore must be careful never to allow class divisions to be artificially created. Easy social mobility, the result of common-type schools for all, no special privileges because of the wealth or status of one's parents, a common duty and experience in national service, scholarships and promotions on merit, had been factors which prevented class stratifications. Every year, he was struck by the varied background of Singapore's scholars. They came from all levels of society. Their fathers ranged from hawkers, taxi and bus drivers, storekeepers, teachers to executives, and, strangely enough, few professionals. "We must keep our society based on equal educational opportunities for all, and jobs, promotions and rewards on merit."

In Germany, workers and unions participated with executives in management. The German government was prepared to take unpleasant measures to keep inflation down. So they had done much better than Britain. British workers and unions were still embroiled in old class antagonism against the bosses and the upper classes. "But we are starting to have the European problems of citizens avoiding heavy jobs. We have to reverse this preference for clean, preferably white collar jobs." It had to be fought at every level, in the schools, in the homes, in the mass media. Attitudes of parents must be changed. Everybody expected his or her children to rise in status, and earn more. A transformation had overtaken the whole society, unconsciously affected by rising incomes, television, the glossy advertisements, the tourists from wealthy countries. It was a side-effect of the consumer society.

If Singapore had suffered acute recession and unemployment, accompanied by cuts in pay in 1974 and 1975, as in Hong Kong, it would have jolted workers and shaken out their complacency. But it had been the government's duty to soften the blow of world recession. Through a combination of factors, Singapore got off lightly. As a result, many workers, and some union leaders, believed that all was well and more miracles could be expected out of the Singapore government. Unfortunately, this might not be possible the next time.

Lee announced that in June, for the mid-year school holidays, the government would mount a campaign. Ministers and Members of Parliament, together with principals, teachers and school students, would use their hands to improve school playing fields and gardens, and to clean up the buildings. "We must hold fast to the tried and trusted virtue of hard work. Dirtying one's hands, sweating, and soiling one's clothes are good for the body and soul, and for our economy."

Singapore's greatest achievement has been in family planning. The number of live births had dropped from nearly 62,500 in 1959 to just under 40,000 in 1975. This drop had been consistent and continuous. "So now we can afford to increase the minimum number of years for schooling and industrial training. Eight years of primary education with automatic promotions, with three fruitless attempts at the PSLE, made no sense. We are moving to nine years of teaching geared to the child's learning ability. And we look forward to the time when teachers will have classes of 30 – 35 students, not 40 – 45." But this was for the intermediate term, the 1980s. Within the next two years, 1976 – 1977, the government had to get some 84,000 jobs for people already born 17 – 19 years ago. This was a problem, as on present projections, there would be 44,000 jobless Singaporeans. "And if they shy away from the tougher jobs, even though they are better paid, the unemployment will be bigger." It would be worse if parents, brothers and sisters aided and abetted them by paying for their keep whilst waiting for the comfortable job to come along. "We must make a virtue out of more sober rates of growth. Our workers must develop high skills in precision technology. Everyone must realise that as long as we have not established a reputation for ourselves as hardworking and intensely proud workers, whose products are equal in quality and high finish to the Swiss or Japanese, we shall only be slightly better than assembly-line operators. And our products must be sold under the label of the well-established multinational company."

Lee said that a Japanese industrialist recently discussed this matter with him. "He put it aptly when he said that what we must do is what the Japanese have succeeded in doing, a complete turn-around from the 'cheap but inferior' image their products had before and just after the war. When it comes to concentration on skills and high standards, we have shown that we can do it. The problem is with those who cannot achieve these high skills, but shy away from work of lower skills under harder working conditions, even though the pay is good. We must change our internal factors for the better, all the more because we know that external factors are now less favourable."

Two events, with momentous long-term consequences, still cast shadows. First, the oil crisis. With high oil prices, the high growth rates of the '60s were over. Second, the new communist governments in Cambodia, Vietnam and Laos. It had taken two and a half years for the industrial world to get out of recession and inflation precipitated by the oil crisis. Growth rates of the industrial countries were expected to be down by more than half of what they were. Increase in world trade would be down, also by a half. Hence, getting exports of technology to Singapore would be more difficult. Before, the situation in the industrialised countries had been one of high demand for goods and labour shortage in the industrial countries, leading to export of factories rather than import of guest workers. Now, the conditions were the reverse. Under-used manufacturing capacity led to reluctance to start expansion of manufacturing capacity, either at home or abroad.

Next, the communist victories in Vietnam, Cambodia and Laos one year ago had not helped. Trade with the three countries had gone. Investors were still uncertain and apprehensive over the long-term security and stability of Southeast Asia. It might take some time for investors to make up their own minds as to the risks in Southeast Asia. It was a Southeast Asia which must resolve its own social and economic discontent and defeat insurgent terrorism on its own, with political, economic and social policies to back the police and armed forces. "The way we and our neighbours tackle our own economic and political problems, and how well we co-operate to strengthen each other, are critical factors." The five ASEAN governments could, by demonstrating better co-operation in the economic and political fields, re-establish confidence in non-communist Southeast Asia. This was the nub of the matter. "We must follow up the promising start made in Bali in February, and the small but practical step forward in Kuala Lumpur on five ASEAN projects. If we gather momentum, all will benefit. But we must proceed expeditiously or the impact of such co-operation will be frittered away."

XIII

In his May Day Message, the Prime Minister attributed Singapore's rapid progress up until the oil crisis in 1973, to workers who were hardworking, who had acquired skills quickly, who were positive and productive. The NTUC played a crucial role in channelling the energies of union activists into constructive pursuits, like INCOME, WELCOME, COMFORT and other co-operative ventures. Union leaders learnt the other side of any enterprise, namely the vital need for good management. "We can expect slower growth in the years ahead. It is always easier to go from a hard life to a good life than the other way around. After getting used to a better life, through the induction of higher-technology industries, it is going to be difficult to adjust to slower rates of growth. The input of higher-technology industries is slowing down. This will test the mettle of our workers, and the strength of leadership of the unions." Lee concluded: "Let us psychologically prepare ourselves for slower economic growth and for tougher competition and harder conditions. It we are realistic in our expectations, life will not be so bad in the end."

XIV

Late in April, Lee Kuan Yew, as Secretary-General of the People's Action Party, wrote to Bruno Pittermann, the Chairman of the Socialist International. Lee told him there were moves by a group in the Dutch Labour Party, supported by Miss Jenny Little, International Secretary of the

British Labour Party, to try to mobilise support to expel the PAP from the Socialist International. Lee said these moves had been going on for some months. He learnt of them after 4 March, when Hans Janitschek, the General Secretary of the Socialist International, saw Singapore's High Commissioner in London. Lee continued: "Since then, I have requested and got a copy of the Dutch Labour Party paper against the PAP. It is a distorted and absurd picture of the PAP painted by judicious excerpts. For example, it quotes, on page 14, from my speech to the Commonwealth Press Union to prove that we torture journalists in Singapore. (I enclose a copy of my speech, with the quote underlined.) It also quotes from (1) a book by a Marxist British lecturer, Iain Buchanan; (2) a book by an Indian journalist, Thayil Jacob Sony George, based in Hong Kong; (both these books are freely on sale in Singapore, and obtainable in our libraries); (3) a stencilled loose-leaf paper publication in January 1976 by a so-called 'Federation of United Kingdom and Eire Malaysian and Singaporean Student Organisations' (FUEMSSO). Some of the articles are scandalous, scurrilous and libellous. And the General Secretary, Hans Janitschek, was wise in not circulating the FUEMSSO publication even to the PAP. It includes the reprinting of statutory declarations in various *habeas corpus* proceedings in Singapore, taken out on behalf of political detainees by a Ceylonese lawyer, T.T. Rajah, a well-known fellow-traveller in Singapore, detained in 1974 for involvement with the Malayan National Liberation League (MNLL), a subsidiary organisation of the Malayan Communist Party (MCP), now released for reasons of health; (4) a report by Amnesty International, which, besides listing out communist detainees, highlights the so-called 'frame-up' of a former University of Singapore Students' Union President, Tan Wah Piow. Tan was convicted in open court, after a long hearing, protracted by his conduct of his own defence, for rioting, and sentenced. He did not appeal against conviction or sentence. The Singapore Government is aware that a communist-front group in Singapore has been feeding this distorted picture of the PAP to similarly inclined groups in Britain and Holland. These groups have got through into the Socialist International, working via Marxists and Liberal intellectuals. The main object of this campaign is to mount pressure on the PAP to get the release of some top, tough communist political detainees. Allegations of torture made in statutory declarations are patently false. Our law courts are open, with appeals going to the Privy Council in London. Yet no civil or criminal action has been brought by anyone for battery and assault, let alone torture. And there are quite a few pro-communist and even more anti-establishment lawyers ready to pick up cudgels on behalf of any aggrieved party. Detention without trial for political activities of communists and their supporters has been part of the laws of Malaya, now Malaysia, and Singapore, because of the armed insurrection by the MCP which began in 1948 against the British and has continued ever since. Since then, the MCP has been outlawed in Malaya, now Malaysia, and Singapore, and is an underground party. From time to time, they infiltrate and penetrate legal open parties, trade unions and student associations. They use them as their united front for mass agitation in support of their armed revolution.

"It may be difficult for West European socialists to understand that communists in Southeast Asia are different from their own communists. They think of communists as somewhat odd and eccentric people who, having moved close enough to get into government in coalition with socialist and even non-socialist parties, have now become so patently democratic as to renounce the dictatorship of the proletariat. In Singapore, it is difficult to persuade the communists whom we have arrested, so as we can release them, to denounce communist use of terror and armed violence to bring about their dictatorship of the proletariat. We do not try to persuade them to renounce the dictatorship of the proletariat as undemocratic in a multi-party system. Two of these detainees, Dr. Lim Hock Siew and Said Zahari, are personally known to me from our anti-colonial United Front days, from 1950 to '62, when the United Front broke up. They know that I know that they are communists. One may admire them for the tenacity of their convictions, even if they happen to be misguided. But it will be reckless for the Singapore Government to release them to work for those who are actively engaged in armed insurrection, unless they denounce the use of force to achieve power. Four years ago, we arrested Dr. Lim's younger brother, Lim Hock Koon. He is a district committee member of the MCP. He was instructed to move from his hiding place in Indonesia to return to Singapore to carry out underground activities under the name of the MNLL. When arrested, he was co-operative. He agreed to persuade his elder brother, Dr. Lim, to give up his communist pursuits. Instead, his doctor brother re-affirmed him in his communist cause. Now, we have two detainees instead of one. Meanwhile, with the communist victories in Indo-China, the MCP has stepped up its campaign of assassination and terror in Peninsular Malaysia, in preparation for another bid of power through armed insurrection. Fortunately, their organisation in Singapore does not receive the kind of support it once did. Nevertheless, two men carrying explosives in a car to blow up the home of the manager of the Nanyang Shoe Factory, blew themselves up instead on 22 December 1974. On 8 July 1975, at Loyang, in the northeast of Singapore, a cache of arms was found in earthen jars buried in the ground. They included 189 hand grenades, 210 detonators, one .38 revolver, one .25 Colt automatic pistol and fifteen rounds of ammunition. On 30 July 1975, at Jalan Tiga Ratus off Changi Road, in the east of Singapore, another cache of 109 hand grenades was discovered in two earthen jars buried in the ground. Booby traps with explosives are frequently put up for killing and maiming innocent people. They included a British RAF officer's daughter, Miss Katie Jane Salter, aged seven, killed on 23 April 1970, in Changi near her house.

"These communist groups are mustering support abroad, posing as democrats. Alas, they now appear to be able to enlist some groups in the

Socialist International to help their United-Front candidates in the next elections, due to be held before the end of 1977. Significantly, they are enlisting the aid of West European Marxists, not of Asian socialists. I know that in fact they despise West European Marxists as 'petit bourgeois intellectuals', but whose support would nevertheless add grist to the communist mill. One of their main issues in the coming elections will be the unconditional release of these communist detainees. This is a matter for Singaporeans to decide. In successive general elections, the communist-front groups have made the unconditional release of these political detainees a key issue. On each occasion, they have lost. The overwhelming majority of people in Singapore are not in favour of letting loose these men who are out to re-create an atmosphere of turmoil and tension conducive to communist agitation, chaos and terrorism. We were invited to join the International in good faith in the middle '60s. We believed then that the Socialist International was a clear-cut democratic socialist alternative to communism. It now appears to us that the Socialist International may, wittingly or unwittingly, become a vehicle to further the communist cause in Singapore. Perhaps the trend towards electoral united fronts between socialists and communist in France and Italy has had its wider effects and has changed the mood and attitudes of West European socialist parties.

"We shall be sending Mr. C.V. Devan Nair to attend the next Bureau meeting on 28 – 29 May in London to face our accusers. I hope that our accusers will not be tempted to ask for a postponement. At this next Bureau meeting, if the Socialist International does now throw out the spurious charges put up in the paper by the Dutch Labour Party, and supported by the International Secretary of the British Labour Party, the PAP would not want to remain a member of the Socialist International. Out detractors have so far chosen to conduct their campaign in a devious and surreptitious manner. I see no reason for subterfuge. I propose to make this letter public and bring the issue out into the open. The PAP has been in office for seventeen years. We have reduced poverty, unemployment and illiteracy. We have banished despair and instilled dignity and pride in our people. We have created a better, more just and equal society than the one we inherited from the British. Our people have increased their support for our policies from 54 per cent of the vote in May 1959, to 69 per cent of the vote in September 1972. In between, we won two other general elections. PAP's record of honesty and scrupulous government is not something my colleagues and I need apologise for."

The following letter from Lee to Janitschek, dated 8 May, was handed to him after the Dutch Labour Party failed to withdraw their charges: "Unless the charges made in the paper by the Dutch Labour Party are withdrawn, I have asked Devan Nair to hand this letter of resignation of the People's Action Party from the Socialist International. The Dutch Labour Party questions the right of the PAP to govern Singapore in a manner which has the overwhelming support of the majority of the people. By secret ballot in general elections, all seats returned PAP candidates in April 1968 and again in September 1972. What the Dutch Labour Party would wish us to do, namely release all communist detainees unconditionally, without first their denouncing the use of armed force by the Malayan Communist Party, is calculated to give solace and comfort to the communists. The PAP was invited to join the Socialist International in 1966. The Socialist International knew of the laws that provided for the detention of these local communists without trial. Indeed, they knew of these detainees. Now, this same situation has become reprehensible. Some West European parties, ignorant of the realities of the politics of Southeast Asia, and fed selective items by communist united front groups, have assumed the right to tell the PAP how to govern Singapore. Successive British Labour and Conservative governments had used these laws for detention without trial of communists and their active supporters from 1948 – 59. They had to use them more extensively than the PAP has had to do, as there was then a full-scale insurgency on. There were no protests in Britain or Europe. Now, some young socialists feel they have a civilising mission among the backward nations of Asia and seek to condemn the PAP. At least the old colonialists were honest in their attitudes of superiority. The new socialists hide their arrogance behind a smoke-screen of liberal intellectualism.''

XV

Accompanied by the Foreign Minister and the Minister for Finance, Lee arrived with a goodwill mission in Beijing on 10 May. At a banquet the following evening in the Prime Minister's honour, Mr. Hua Kuo-feng, the Prime Minister of China, said that on behalf of the Chinese Government and people, he expressed his warm welcome and took the opportunity to extend cordial greetings to the people of Singapore. ''Singapore is a young country in Southeast Asia. Her industrious and valiant people, working hard in a pioneering spirit, developed the country and waged a protracted and heroic struggle against colonial rule. Since the independence of the Republic of Singapore, they have carried on an unremitting effort to safeguard national independence and state sovereignty. In international affairs, Singapore opposes hegemonism and power politics, stands for peace and neutrality of Southeast Asia, actively develops relations with other Third World countries, and has contributed positively to promoting economic exchanges and trade among nations. We sincerely wish the people of Singapore greater achievements on their road of advance.''

Mr. Hua said that at present, the international situation was developing in a direction most favourable to the people of all countries but unfavourable to imperialism and hegemonism. The Third World countries and peoples, strengthening their unity and supporting each other, had scored one victory after another in the struggle against imperialism and hegemonism and were playing an ever greater role in international affairs. The superpowers were finding it more and more difficult to muddle along. Their intensified global rivalry for spheres of influence and world hegemony was the cause of world intranquility. But no matter how desperately they might struggle, they could not escape their ultimate doom. "The people are the matters of history. The future of the world belongs to them, and it is very bright." An excellent situation had emerged in Southeast Asia with the historic victories of the peoples of the Indo-Chinese countries. The struggle of the peoples in Southeast Asian countries to safeguard independence and sovereignty and combat big-power hegemonism had continued to develop vigorously. Relations between these countries and other Third World countries had witnessed a heartening growth and reinforcement. After the defeat of one superpower in Southeast Asia, the other superpower was trying to take the chance to squeeze in, to carry out infiltration and expansion there. But as facts had proven, where this superpower reached its claws, the people there would better perceive its expansionist features. It had been strongly condemned by the peoples of the Southeast Asian countries for its underhand activities in this area. "We are pleased to note that more and more countries in Southeast Asia have clearly stated their opposition to the practice of hegemony by any country in any part of the world. This is a far-sighted stand which conforms to the interest of the people of all countries." The first ASEAN summit conference held not long ago reaffirmed its positive proposal for the establishment of a zone of peace and neutrality in Southeast Asia and achieved significant results in strengthening regional economic co-operation. "We feel sure that so long as the peoples of the Southeast Asian countries uphold independence and strengthen their unity, they will steadily win new victories in the struggle against imperialism and hegemonism."

Mr. Hua said China was a developing socialist country belonging to the Third World. The Chinese Government and people had always maintained that all countries, big and small, should be equal. "We are firmly opposed to big nations bullying small ones and strong nations bullying weak ones. We hold that the Five Principles of Peaceful Co-existence should guide relations between nations and that each people have the right to decide as they wish the social system of their own country." No country had the right to carry aggression, subversion, control, interference or bullying against other countries. China would never be a superpower, now or in the future. "We will unswervingly stand by all oppressed people and oppressed nations of the world and fight together with them against imperialism, colonialism and hegemonism."

Mr. Hua said that the struggle initiated and led by Chairman Mao personally to repulse the Right deviationist attempt to reverse correct verdicts had already won great victories. Marching victoriously along Chairman's Mao's proletarian revolutionary line and in high spirits, the Chinese people were launching a new upsurge of in-depth criticism of

303

Deng Xiaoping to repulse the Right deviationist attempt to reverse correct verdicts and were persisting in grasping revolution and promoting production and other work and preparedness against war. "The situation in China is getting better and better. The victory of the current struggle will no doubt greatly raise our people's revolutionary awareness, further consolidate our dictatorship of the proletariat and promote our socialist construction, making China stronger and more prosperous. The people of all nationalities in our country are determined to unite and carry this great struggle through to the end."

Mr. Hua said there was a profound traditional friendship between the peoples of China and Singapore. "Sharing a similar historical experience, our two peoples have always sympathized with and supported each other in the struggle against imperialism and colonialism. Our friendship has made new progress in recent years. Our friendly contacts, cultural exchanges and economic and trade relations have steadily increased. The current visit to China by the good-will delegation led by Prime Minister Lee Kuan Yew personally provides an opportunity for a direct exchange of views between leaders of our two countries on matters of common interest. This will certainly help enhance the mutual understanding and friendly relations between our two countries." He proposed a toast to "the prosperity of the Republic of Singapore and the well-being of her people, to the continuous growth of the traditional friendship between the peoples of China and Singapore and the friendly relations between the two countries, to the health of Benjamin Henry Sheares, President of the Republic of Singapore, to the health of Prime Minister and Mrs. Lee Kuan Yew, to the health of the other distinguished guests from Singapore, and to the health of all friends and comrades present here!"

In his response, Lee thanked the Government of the People's Republic of China for the warm and friendly reception they had received from the moment they arrived in China. "Since the visit of my colleague, Mr. Rajaratnam, in March last year, a steady flow of cultural, sports, trade and industrial missions has led to better understanding. A wide cross-section of people from Singapore has visited China. These visits have left Singaporeans deeply impressed by China's many achievements. A once weak and divided China was treated with disdain by the industrialised powers. In less than three decades, China has been transformed by the efforts of her own people into a strong and unified nation which commands the respect of all. I hope the government of the People's Republic of China has now a better perception of the Republic of Singapore. History brought together Chinese, Malays and Indians in Singapore. All are proud of their own heritage. Sharing a common experience, we are developing a distinctive way of life. By geography, our future will be more closely inter-linked with those of our neighbours in Southeast Asia."

Lee said a new phase had begun for Southeast Asia, after the great changes that had taken place in the past few years. "Together with our neighbours, we are seeking to establish peaceful and stable conditions under these vastly changed circumstances. Singapore is associated with four other countries in Southeast Asia for economic and political co-operation in ASEAN to bring about orderly progress. The solidarity of ASEAN countries will increase our ability to avoid external personal pressure or manipulation. China has expressed her support for ASEAN. I hope others, inside and outside the region, will also understand the objectives of ASEAN and support it." For hundreds of years, China had had contacts with the peoples of Southeast Asia. These contacts were now being re-established in a vastly changed world. Communications were instantaneous and transportation of persons and goods rapid, reliable and regular. The ease and speed with which he and his colleagues travelled from Singapore to Beijing was a reminder, if any was needed, that of the big countries, China is the one nearest to Southeast Asia. Indeed, China was a part of Asia, and China's policies would be a major factor in the evolving situation in Southeast Asia.

Lee hoped after his visit, that Sino-Singapore relations would grow and broaden. On many international issues at the UN, Singapore have found themselves in agreement with China. However, it was to be expected that there would be differences of views in some areas because of different national interests or ideology. "These need not prevent us from improving our cultural, trade and other relations. For my colleagues and I have come bringing with us the goodwill and good wishes of our people for the People of China." He raised his glass to the prosperity of the People's Republic of China and the well-being of her people, to the continuous growth of the traditional friendship between the peoples of Singapore and China and the friendly relations between the two countries, "to the health of Mao Tse-tung, Chairman of the Central Committee of the Communist Party of China, to the health of Premier Hua Kuo-feng, and to the health of all friends present here."

At a return banquet two days later, the Prime Minister said that during the three days of formal and informal talks, he had had personal experience of how the views of the Government of the People's Republic of China were expounded on the international situation, the three worlds which China categorised countries under, and the principles which guided the policies of the Government of the People's Republic of China in dealing with the countries of Southeast Asia. Southeast Asian countries were classified in the Third World together with China, which Mr. Hua had modestly described as a developing socialist country. Lee said that the prospects for cordial relations between the two countries, "though we have different economic and political systems", were good. "I have become aware that whilst we use different terms, sometimes in fact we refer to the same things. I have become familiar with a whole series of concepts succinctly described by compressed phrases, full of meaning, not always possible of adequate translation into English." China and Singapore were agreed that they should conduct their bilateral relations by concentrating on those matters on which there was agreement and not those on which there were different views because of different basic assumptions.

Premier Hua said that being a socialist country, China supported the revolutionary struggle of all countries. But Premier Hua also stated that China did not interfere in the internal matters of other countries, "and that how the Singapore Government deals with its communists is a matter for the Singapore Government to decide. Based on non-interference, I believe that we can develop our relations. Both sides are agreed that it will take time to change the frozen ritualised attitudes and policies of the past."

Lee proposed a toast "to the prosperity of the People's Republic of China and the well-being of her people, to the continuous growth of the traditional friendship between the peoples of Singapore and China and the friendly relations between the two countries, to the health of Mao Tse-tung, Chairman of the Central Committee of the Communist Party of China, to the health of Premier Hua Kuo-feng, and to the health of all friends present here."

Premier Hua Kuo-feng, in reply, described the visit by Prime Minister Lee Kuan Yew at the head of the goodwill delegation as a "major event in the relations between China and Singapore". Chairman Mao had met and had a friendly conversation with Prime Minister Lee Kuan Yew. In the past few days, the two sides held talks and had a sincere exchange of views on matters of common interest. The Prime Minister and the other distinguished guests from Singapore visited places of interest in Beijing and had come into contact with the Chinese people. Mr. Lee's visit was of benefit to promoting the friendship between the peoples of China and Singapore and the mutual understanding between the two countries. "I am confident that through our joint efforts the friendly relations between our two countries will continue to develop on the basis of the Five Principles of Peaceful Co-existence."

He proposed a toast "to the prosperity of the Republic of Singapore and the well-being of her people, to the steady growth of the traditional friendship between the peoples of China and Singapore and the friendly relations between the two countries, to the health of Benjamin Henry Sheares, President of the Republic of Singapore, to the health of Prime Minister and Mrs. Lee Kuan Yew, to the health of the other friends from Singapore, and to the health of all friends and comrades!"

Entertained to dinner by the Guangdong Provincial and Canton Municipal Revolutionary Committees, Canton, on 22 May, shortly before returning to Singapore, Lee said that many Chinese had left China through Canton for Southeast Asia during the period of turmoil and disorder, when China was carved up and exploited by the industrialised nations, and again during the years of resistance to Japanese invasion. Hence his interest in Canton.

Of his two weeks in China, Lee said they had been most instructive and interesting. All members of the delegation were impressed by the tremendous hard work put in by the people. Peasants worked from dawn till 7 o'clock in the evening. Factories worked all seven days in the week. Workers took turns for their one-day off a week. The discipline of the people, and the uniformity with which policies were implemented throughout the country, were tributes to thorough organisation. Although there were variations in the temperament of the people, from the relatively dry, and less fertile north, like Tachai and Yenan, to the wet and fertile areas of Wusih, and to the sub-tropical regions of Kweilin and Canton, the drive and exhortation to greater achievement was always present. He expressed his admiration for the hardworking peasants and workers of China. The orderly way in which every community conducted itself reflected thorough organisation. "I return to Singapore, carrying back a great experience. China's problems, and the self-reliant methods of solving them, will always be vivid in my mind." As a result, he had become more conscious of Singapore's very different situation and different way of life. "Many of us remain ethnically Chinese. Many speak the same language, but without the new vocabulary that you have developed. But we have developed differently, because we have different ways of earning our living in a completely different environment. I must confess that all members of my delegation find it a completely different tempo and way of life."

He proposed a toast "to the progress and advancement of the people of China, to the friendship between the peoples of Singapore and China, to a better and more realistic understanding of each other, and to the health of the Vice-Chairman of the Kwangtung Provincial Revolutionary Committee and Chairman of the Canton Municipal Revolutionary Committee, and to our other Chinese hosts present tonight."

XVI

On 5 June, the Prime Minister launched the "Use Your Hands" campaign in a speech at the National Theatre. He said the campaign to get students, teachers and principals to use their hands was a start to reverse the process of the past eight years, "during which we went through a rapid change in social attitudes and life-styles". If the recession in the past two years had been accompanied by considerable unemployment, this campaign would not have been necessary. When people were jobless and hungry, they were not choosy about job status, comfort and convenience. But Singapore was spared heavy retrenchments and unemployment. Attitudes to jobs were formed partly in the schools. As important was the influence of parents, family and neighbours. It had been decided to start with the schools. Every child in Singapore went to school for a minimum of nine years from the age of six. The attitudes of principals and teachers could influence young minds.

When the economy was expanding, creating more jobs than there were suitable applicants, citizens had the first choice of jobs. Work permits were issued for vacancies which could not be filled.

Figures revealed the kind of jobs Singaporeans preferred. There were nearly 150,000 clerical and related workers. Only 2 per cent were work permit holders. There were about 25,000 service workers in the hotel and catering industries. Only 2 per cent were work permit holders. Of 21,000 domestic servants, 21 per cent were work permit holders. Of 5,200 hair-dressers and barbers, 40 per cent were work permit holders. For blue-collar jobs, of 27,800 in shipbuilding and repairing, 11 per cent were on work permits; of about 1,600 metal processors, 46 per cent were on work permits; over 4,700 wood workers, 56 per cent on work permits. "On building construction, I find the figures of the Ministry of Labour so unsettling, that I have asked for a re-check. Out of 55,000 workers, over 60 per cent are on work permits." Recently, a Labour Ministry study group interviewed at random 1,700 National Servicemen on ROD. They were young men who had gone through tough training. Over 77 per cent said they did not want jobs in the construction industry, and 55 per cent said they did not want jobs in shipbuilding and repairing, even though the jobs were well-paid. Their reasons were: high physical risks, strenuous work, lack of career prospects, uninteresting work.

Lee said that the one sector which showed rapid recovery from recession and promise of further growth was tourism, with a growth rate in 1975 of about 8 per cent when the overall GDP growth was 4 per cent. This would accentuate the drift towards comfortable jobs. "This is bad, as we have not yet established a solid industrial base, with highly skilled workers." He conceded that the next few days of publicity for this campaign would not suddenly change attitudes acquired over many years. But although it might take several years, "we must continuously strive to change attitudes to jobs and get our young into those jobs which are important to our economy. The mass media can help in this."

When Singapore's financial centre expanded rapidly, many foreign banks upgraded clerks to book-keepers, and accounts clerks to accounting assistants. Singaporean typists were upgraded as stenographers, while stenographers became personal secretaries. The higher income, resulting from economic growth, led to better clothes and shoes, motor-cycles and cars. Because they had clean and nice clothes, they sought clean and nice jobs. Students were reinforced in these attitudes by a younger generation of teachers. Those who became teachers, and what they expected of teaching, had changed with the times. There were very few men. Ninety per cent of the intake in recent years had been women. They were better dressed and spent more time and money on their clothes and appearance than their predecessors did. "This is not a rebuke. It is a statement of fact. As dress-styles and spending habits of the community changed, so did those of the younger teachers." If Singapore's economic future could depend solely on commerce, finance and servicing, Singapore could afford to let things be. "But prudence tells us that the hard core of workers in all the essential industries must be our own citizens, be it construction, metal processing or shipbuilding and repairing. There cannot be this disparity of 2 per cent work permit holders for clerical and service jobs, and 60 per cent for construction and metal processing. Even if it takes the next five to ten years to put this right, we must begin now."

A change in social values and priorities must, of course, be accompanied by adjustments to salaries for the different kinds of work. And the manpower policy must be one that seeks consciously to improve the quality of the working population. "If we have to import workers, then they should preferably be those with better skills and education."

Lee concluded with the observation that the campaign could only succeed if principals and teachers were seen to be proud to use their hands. Ministers and Members of Parliament were also joining to launch this campaign. But after the opening, the teachers and principals must be seen carrying it on. This might not be easy. But it was most important to Singapore's future. "So let us get on with it and keep at it."

XVII

On behalf of the Government, the people of Singapore and himself, President Sheares sent the following message to President Ford on the occasion of the bicentennial celebrations of the United States of America on 4 July: "On the occasion of the bicentennial celebrations, I convey to you and through you to the people of the United States of America heartiest congratulations on behalf of the Government and the people of the Republic of Singapore and on my own behalf. American science and technology, agricultural and industrial strength have given her power and influence to help shape the future. For half a century, the United States has consciously striven to discharge the world responsibilities that go with such great power. On balance, American power has been exercised with restraint and in a manner which does her people credit. I am confident that the American people will recover their poise and that the idealism and dynamism in American society will reassert itself and play its part in bringing about a more prosperous, more equitable and stable world. With abiding good wishes."

XVIII

"Our prospects for 1976 – 77 are good," declared Lee in his National Day Message. As the world recovered from recession, Singapore's own economy was picking up. Singapore had 7 per cent growth for the first half of 1976, compared to zero growth for the first half of 1975. For the whole of 1976, a growth of 6 – 8 per cent could be expected, compared to 4 per cent for 1975. Foreign investments were picking up. $155 million were committed for the first half of 1976, compared to $85 million for the second half of 1975. However, these investments were in small and medium projects. The big projects were still held up, partly because of excess manufacturing capacity in America, Japan and Western Europe, and partly because of investor's caution. They wanted to asses the stability of non-communist Southeast Asia after the communist takeover in Indo-China in 1975. Although there had been some increase in communist insurgent activities in Thailand and Peninsular Malaysia, the situation had remained stable.

"We have good relations with all our neighbours in ASEAN. They are based on growing confidence and understanding of each other gained over many years." There was now a beginning for long-term economic co-operation. But the pace was slow compared to what could be achieved in the ASEAN agreement for preferential trading arrangements. However, there was good co-ordination in matters of security.

A start had been made in normalising relations with Vietnam and Kampuchea. "We want peace in Southeast Asia." For eleven years, Singapore had broadened its economic base. Workers today earned more than three times their dollar incomes of 1965, more than doubling their purchasing power. All had better homes. Over 112,000 families owned their HDB (Housing and Development Board) and JTC (Jurong Town Corporation) homes. Everyone had equal opportunities of education and employment. Although things were going well, Singaporeans should always be prepared for the unexpected. National Service must be taken more seriously. Too many national servicemen. both full-time and reservists, took their duties casually. They did not believe they would ever be called upon to prove themselves. Hence they lacked the desire to excel, a characteristic Singaporeans displayed on nearly all occasions.

Lee insisted that regular officers and NCOs must demand high standards of performance during training sessions and exercises for NSF and reservists. Military skills in both individual and group action must be learnt until they became almost reflex responses. Then there would be no fumbling even in the heat of an emergency. The Singapore Armed Forces was relaxed because Singapore was relaxed. In an emergency, motivation would be high. However, unless military habits and skills had already become ingrained, high motivation then would not be enough.

The international situation was on the eve of changes. Whoever was elected the American President, there would still be new men in key positions to advise on policies in foreign affairs and defence. In China, succession to the original leaders of the Communist Party of China was being resolved. The interaction between America, the Soviet Union and China would be different under new leaders. "We shall know the shape of things to come by the end of next year." For over a decade, Singapore had done well. Problems which appeared insurmountable had been surmounted. In every crisis, people rallied behind the government and worked together to overcome problems, however tough. Now, different problems and challenges were on the horizon. Would Vietnam, Kampuchea and Laos concentrate on their reconstruction? Probably yes. Would there be rivalry between communist countries for the allegiance of underground communist parties in the countries of ASEAN? "We do not know." Whatever the answer may be, "let us get on with the work in hand. There are jobs that must be done. And whether they are in air-conditioned offices or factories or out in the sun and rain, the work has to be done, and done well. That is our way forward."

At the eleventh National Day Rally at the National Theatre on 15 August, Lee said Singapore had made eleven years of rapid progress, "the result of an intense, striving people determined to get things done". Sometimes he thought some parents were too demanding of their children. Hence, from time to time, even in school examinations, when they failed to meet their expectations or their parents' expectations, young people committed suicides. This was a strange phenomenon. In the university it was understandable, but when it happened in schools, Lee said he thought parents were pressurising their children too hard. No man nor woman could do more than his best, "and to do your best is the limit".

These eleven years had wrought great changes in Singapore's society: changes in dress-styles which were obvious, in spending habits, which were fairly obvious, but more importantly in attitudes towards the kind of jobs people wanted. So long as investments were flowing in at the rate they were in 1973, before the oil crisis — nearly a $1,000 million for that year — those rising aspirations could be met. But since that oil crisis, it had gone down — 1974, $800 million, 1975, $400 million, first half of 1976, slightly less than $200 million, but picking up, probably the same as 1975, which meant that in three, four, five years' time Singapore would feel the slow-down. Which meant it was absolutely essential to keep wages fairly stable — probably 5 per cent, 6 per cent, maybe 7 per cent if they did well, per year.

But there was another problem. Certain jobs were not considered desirable because workers preferred less pay and better conditions of work like air-conditioned hotels, shops, offices to climbing a multi-storey building under construction. "We've got to try and change these attitudes. It is not going to be easy." If this continued, then policies would have to be changed "because we just can't afford to be a training ground for work permit holders."

Turning to the question of education, Lee said this was an emotional and a political issue and also one which had tremendous economic consequences. Part of the problem why many of the skilled jobs had now to go to work permit holders was because they used to be performd by Chinese school graduates. They were the skilled workers. The Chinese primary school graduate became the skilled artisan. Now parents had decided that their children would also be technicians and engineers, and they had sent them into the English schools so fast that there was now a shortage of English language teachers in the schools for Malay children who used to go to Malay schools, Indian children who used to go to Tamil schools, and Chinese children who used to go to Chinese schools. How to tackle bilingualism? "You don't want to anglicise your population." For the Chinese, it was particularly hard because Chinese was a completely different language, a completely different script and worse, many spoke dialect at home. So, in fact, it was not bilingualism, but trilingualism or "two-and-a-half". Parents should try to minimise the burden, the load on their children, by switching or encouraging them to switch either into Mandarin or into English when they spoke to their friends and even to their parents at home.

Lee reckoned there were very few problems in Singapore which cannot be overcome, except the higher expectations of every year, life getting better, wages getting better. This could not be if there was a slow-down "in the kind of industries we get in".

Housing was entering a different phase — from one of quantity, there was now a problem of quality. Two hundred and twenty thousand units, half sold on the home-ownership plan. "From 1976 – 1980, we are building another 150,000 units, 80 per cent will be sold — 120,000. By then, 70 per cent of Singapore will be living in HDB towns, new towns. From 1981 – 1985, we will build another 100,000, we will have 80 per cent of the population, and 9/10 of that will be sold, making a total owned by people who live in them 320,000. Plus HUDC some 3,000, 4,000 units — anybody who is working will have a home and own his home." The problem was what to do with the one and two-room flats of poorer days. "We will convert the two-rooms into four-rooms and use the piling that's gone in, and the one-rooms into two-rooms."

Then, there were the problems of transportation. "We are solving it for the time being. I say this very guardedly. Because the ALS (Area Licensing Scheme) area can only take 250,000 jobs comfortably. After that, if it goes up to the maximum, if all the urban renewal projects, all the new offices sprout up, it goes up to 300,000, well, there will be a monumental jam. Even buses alone will jam. They have worked it out, they tell me there is not enough turning-round time. So we go into the underground, MRT. And let me tell you how much it costs. From Jurong to the town, from Bedok to the town, from Ang Mo Kio to the town, it will take ten years to build and will cost more than $4,000 million. I don't mind $4,000 million if at the end of it all it is going to make a good return, like we move the airport from Paya Lebar to Changi, we are going to spend about $1.8 billion, maybe two billion dollars, a thousand million dollars, before we are finished. Five hundred million dollars more than if we stayed in Paya Lebar and built the second runway one mile nearer town, and then you will have the aircraft zooming up and down, round the clock, hitting the town even during working hours. So we said, right, worth the $500 million because at the end of it, everybody benefits and it is going, I hope, to pay a return. But this underground having been built will cost, if you pay for the capital expended — amortization and the rest of it — we will lose $70 million a year in 1992 or 1995, whether you start building in 1982 or 1985. So I asked: How is it Hong Kong can make money; because obviously they can't lose money; their MRT is a private enterprise effort. Well, the answer is: We are not so densely packed as Hong Kong. So perhaps we should all live more densely packed, less green spaces and the underground can make money! But I think some of the MPs may lose a few votes. So this is a new problem concerned with the quality of life."

But when it came to not just a massive capital investment but an annual subsidy of $70 million and then add another 7 per cent for inflation each year, the problem had to be carefully considered. The decision had to be postponed. "That's all we can do — postpone it. But it must be taken because I do not see how you can have intense urban development without a mass rapid transit system."

The Prime Minister spoke about the work entailed in keeping Singapore clean and green. "I think this is the only city that has cleansing seven days a week. Your garbage is collected every day, including Sundays and public holidays. It is not done in many parts even of the developed world."

A whole generation had striven since the fifties to make Singapore what it was today. "A younger generation is taking this as norm and I hope will lift it further up the face of the cliff. And for that, you need to have people with determination, ambition, and high expectations and the will to work to achieve their expectations."

XIX

The Prime Minister, obviously for political reasons, did not attend the fifth non-aligned Heads of Government Conference held in Colombo later in August. He asked the Foreign Minister, Mr. S. Rajaratnam, to go instead to read a statement from him. In the statement, Lee said the question he asked himself, as he read through the draft resolutions submitted to the Conference was: "Who am I uniting with and for what objectives and purposes, and against whom? The inspiration of the non-aligned movement goes back to 1955, the Afro-Asian Solidarity Conference in Bandung. It was the solidarity of the Asian and African peoples seeking an end to colonialism and foreign domination and against the colonial powers — the Europeans. In 1961, when the non-aligned nations, met for the first time at Belgrade, the host was European, but one with impeccable credentials against foreign domination. The movement had become more sophisticated. It had moved from being anti-European, to being neutralist, or non-aligned between the contending power blocs of NATO and the Warsaw Pact. In Colombo, 1976, I have no doubts as to the credentials of my hosts. They are anti-colonial. Sri Lanka had also faced a 'Che Guevarist' revolt in 1971, which was soon resolved. I share this hall

313

with representatives from the Philippines, Portugal and Rumania, present as guests. Singapore is in close association with the Philippines in ASEAN, and I support her presence here as guest. I welcome the impartiality with which we have a member from NATO and a member from the Warsaw Pact. I know of the position of Rumania in the Warsaw Pact. I am not sure if Portugal has been accorded guest status because she wants a similar position in NATO. Perhaps it was the courageous, if belated, act of abjuring her colonial past that deserves acknowledgement." Significantly, Lee did not refer to the presence of Vietnam. He repeated: "For what purposes were they united?" Some issues were simple and clear-cut. "We are solidly against colonialism and racial discrimination and repression. There are remnants of white colonialism and racial discrimination and repression in Zimbabwe (Rhodesia), Namibia (Southeast Africa), and the appalling inhumanity of apartheid in Azania (South Africa). We are united to ensure that Arab lands occupied by the Israelis are returned, for a just and durable peace, in accordance with UN resolutions. If we are realistic, we must also seek a solution to the problem of the homeless Palestinians." It was only natural that, with so many countries freed from colonialism, the issues which now troubled them (85 member states) were the economic ones. The new international economic order, a phrase forged out of repeated failures of UNCTAD Conferences, was a request for international equity and justice between rich and poor nations. As the Declaration of the sixth Special Session of the UN General Assembly in 1975 pointed out, 70 per cent of the world's population had less than 30 per cent of the world's income.

But it was not completely true to say that the non-aligned were the poor versus the rich. Rumania was not a member of the poor group. Nor indeed were those amongst them who were oil producers. But they were with them against the rich of the Western world. Whether it was aid, trade, commodity, stockpile arrangements and the financing thereof, transfers of technology and MNCs or transnational corporations, the poor were seeking new arrangements in their economic relations with the industrialised countries of the West. The most successful of all commodity producers, OPEC, succeeded because their customers, the industrialised countries of the West, could not survive without their oil. The Soviet Union was not only self-sufficient, indeed she was an exporter of oil and natural gas, and supplied the needs of her Comecon members. The People's Republic of China was also an oil exporter. It was also the West who were the main buyers of the commodities of so many of them. And, naturally, it was the West that was in control of the IMF, the World Bank, IDA, GATT and a whole host of international regulatory agencies. "I am sure the distinguished delegates from Cuba, the Democratic People's Republic of Korea, the Socialist Republic of Vietnam, Lao People's Democratic Republic and Democratic Kampuchea are solidly united with us in our struggle against the West for a more equitable arrangement and a just sharing of the world's wealth. But I believe they are not depending on the IMF, or the World Bank, or in commodity stockpile financing, or transfers of technology through MNCs for their salvation. I respect their choice of the road to economic advancement. I hope they will reciprocate the sentiments. However, I was disappointed to read the draft amendments put in by the Laotian delegation in which they referred to the victories of the peoples of Vietnam, Laos and Kampuchea as an example for the revolutionary movements and struggles against non-colonialism in Southeast Asia, as an example for these countries to achieve genuine independence. It made me wonder which countries in Southeast Asia are not genuine in their independence and should be helped to become genuine. Is this a precursor of the kind of double definition of independence which will classify a Marxist state as genuinely independent and the others as being not genuine and so their peoples are to be supported to overthrow by violence established democratic governments? I had always believed Laos to be a genuinely independent country, at least since 1962 when at Geneva its neutrality and sovereignty were guaranteed in an International Agreement signed amongst others by the Soviet Union, the People's Republic of China and the USA."

But times had changed. Some communist countries like Yugoslavia had demonstrated that sincere independence and non-alignment by living in peace with the very different political and economic systems of its neighbours, Albania, Austria, Italy and Bulgaria. Lee hoped countries like Laos would get over their urge to proselytize and not help in the forced conversion of their neighbours. "If the non-aligned movement is to stay united, then we must be prepared to live with the different economic and political systems of our many members. We cannot tolerate interference in the internal affairs of any member, especially if help to revolutionary peoples means active assistance to insurgent groups to overthrow established governments in order to impose a Marxist system of government. We are all against economic domination by the West. We seek a better economic future in more equitable economic relationship with the developed countries." According to 1974 World Bank figures, the developed non-communist countries had a GNP of $2,500 billion, the communist countries a GNP of $686 billion, and the non-oil developing countries a GNP of $536 billion. A report of UNCTAD Secretariat, 19 September 1975, showed that in 1974, of the $37.5 billion in disbursements for international financial co-operation, $31.4 billion came from the DAC (Development Assistance Committee) countries of the West, compared to $0.55 billion from the communist countries. In effect, it was to the developed countries of the West that they had to address themselves for a better deal. The International Development Strategy had estimated that developing countries required a transfer of 1 per cent of the GNP of the developed countries to produce a 6 per cent growth each year. Unfortunately, a UNCTAD Secretariat report dated 15 April 1976, stated that in 1975, the amount transferred by way of official development assistance was only 0.36 per cent as against 0.7 per cent projected by the DAC of seventeen developed

315

countries.

"So when I ask myself the question: 'Who am I united with, for what objectives and purposes, and against whom?', I am unable to give a clear-cut answer when it concerns economic issues of a more equitable world system. Co-operation amongst developing countries alone cannot provide the inputs of industrial capital and technological know-how nor provide the markets for the commodities we produce or for the simple manufacture we hope to make. Our economic prospects are better in co-operation with the developed countries of the West. Our objective is, therefore, to exercise moral and economic pressure (with the help of the oil producers) against the West, so that they will co-operate with us on more equitable terms. In meetings such as this in Colombo which precede an UNGA, we can mobilise the opinions of the governments and of the peoples of the world. Of course we have to contend with a largely unsympathetic and cynical Western mass media. Whilst we may be able to bypass them in the developing countries through proposals such as those recently made in Delhi for co-operation in exchanging information between developing countries, we may not get our message through to the peoples of the developed countries of the West. Somehow, we must get through to them, like the Vietnamese got through to the American people and turned many Americans against their own government's policies in Vietnam."

Lee reminded them that "if we fail to get co-operation, there are always austere and formidable examples of self-discipline and self-help of the developing Marxist-Leninist countries. However, I presume most of us do not seek such a rigorous solution to our economic and social problems." Hence, this gathering in Colombo sought a rational set of proposals on which the West could engage them in a more equitable system of trade, commodity stockpile agreements and their financing, and the good behaviour of their MNCs for rapid transfers of technology on favourable terms. It could be a long and arduous struggle for those of them without abundant oil reserves.

XX

The Prime Minister, on 31 August, sent the following message to the Malaysian Prime Minister, Datuk Hussein Onn: "On the occasion of Malaysia Day my cabinet colleagues and I send you and your government our warmest congratulations. May Malaysia continue to advance and prosper under your firm leadership. Our close co-operation and solidarity in ASEAN will enhance peace and stability at a time when the region is adjusting to profound changes."

XXI

Chairman Mao died on 9 September. Lee sent the following condolence message to Hua Kuo-feng, Premier of the State Council of the People's Republic of China: "On behalf of the Government of Singapore, I extend my deep sympathy to the Government of the People's Republic of China on the death of Chairman Mao Tse-tung. He was one of the giants of this century. He transformed China and thereby changed the course of events in Asia and the world. His passing is a great loss to the people and Government of China."

XXII

Several communist cells were uncovered, and some were arrested. Lee was asked in an interview by Adrian Porter, a BBC reporter, on 14 September, how deep communist subversion really went into the fabric of Singapore society.

Prime Minister: You must remember the communists have been at it since 1923 when two agents of the Cominform or Comintern came from Shanghai to set up the first cell. And in certain segments of the population they had been entrenched as far back as 1923. But by and large they moved their activities during the Japanese Occupation of Singapore and Malaya into the Peninsula. And they have never quite put their eggs in the Singapore basket in the same way as they have in the Peninsula basket. I would say that the discoveries we have made are mostly in the lower social, economic groups or strata — not very deep. I would be surprised, of course, if they didn't keep their old faithfuls amongst the intellectuals who had been lying low. But on the whole I would fairly confidently predict that provided the economy doesn't go down — we have a world-wide recession, unemployment on a massive scale — that their recruitment would be patchy.

Adrian Porter: But you seem to have lately discovered that a very influential editor, for instance, was infiltrating as a communist. And you have, across the strata — ballet dancers and even members of your armed forces at one stage. Do you think it does stretch across the strata and in fact is getting deeper? Let's put it this way — you seem to have more arrests of prominent people lately.

Prime Minister: That may be in a short time-span that you have been observing Singapore but over a wider time frame, the editor, for instance — his activities went back to 1950s. And he has been detained once. He came off promising not to have anything more to do with it. He went back to it. So he was an old hand at it. Ballet teacher, well, you get the odd characters. The soldier — he was a National Serviceman and only a corporal.

317

Adrian Porter: Are you concerned perhaps there might be a growing body of opinion amongst your student population with these tendencies?

Prime Minister: Compared to what it was in the 1950s and the early '60s, this is a very small activity.

Adrian Porter: We also have the same type of infiltration in this sphere, in Malaysia as well. Now do you see infiltration like this by the communists into the influential parts of society more dangerous than the actual guerilla warfare in rural areas and urban guerillas for that matter?

Prime Minister: I think this is a very different subject for me to enlarge upon. Strictly forbidden territory, I am not competent to pass judgement on what is Malaysia's Special Branch responsibility.

Adrian Porter: Can we move over to relations with Indo-China. It does seem in the last few months that they have had a dichotomy of thinking. On one hand they sent out goodwill missions. They professed a desire of having a friendship with the ASEAN nations and on the other, there seemed to have been some criticisms as to whether the ASEAN countries are, as you put it yourself, 'genuinely independent'. And they have said that they would encourage revolution in the neighbouring countries. How do you view this approach by the Indo-China nations at the present moment?

Prime Minister: First, may I correct you on the supposed friendly approach to ASEAN countries. I think that is not the Vietnamese position. They want to establish normal relations with individual countries of Southeast Asia who may be members of ASEAN. But when they did this trip round Southeast Asia, the Vice-Foreign Minister made a point of visiting non-ASEAN countries as well. And each was approached on an individual basis, not ASEAN. It's very much like the approach, say, of the People's Republic of China, except that the People's Republic of China is much more open and candid about it. They said: party-to-party relations go on notwithstanding state-to-state relations or notwithstanding however friendly and warm the state-to-state relations may be. The Vietnamese made it quite clear in their broadcast that people-to-people relations they fully support the struggles of the peoples of Southeast Asia to 'genuine independence' so on and so on. We have to take them at their word, their printed word, their official word, and I think they mean it, that they intend as the latest torch-bearer of revolution, successful revolution, to pass the flame on. You would have noticed how they have taken this quite seriously. Whether their will to pass the flame on will be tempered by their desire to get good state-to-state trading relations, economic co-operation, which would help their rehabilitation, is another matter. That depends on how the various countries in Southeast Asia react at this dual approach or twin approach and whether we can collectively and individually make it more profitable for the Vietnamese to have good state-to-state relations in return for less people-to-people interference.

Adrian Porter: Don't you have the feeling that those people who believe in the domino theory do have some justification?

318

Prime Minister: The Americans, when they wanted to intervene in Vietnam, get the think-tanks to work out this analysis and when they want to opt out of Vietnam they demolished the analysis. I think there's some basis for their analysis. With this proviso: that each individual country, as it is taken over by liberation communist groups inevitably tends to want to convert its non-communist neighbour. But it's got to take into account the problems, the peculiarities of that neighbour. The only countries in Southeast Asia sharing common boundaries with communist countries are now Thailand, sharing a boundary with Cambodia, Laos, and Burma sharing a boundary with China. It is not likely that the Khmer Rouge will have the inclination or the resources to spark off revolution in Thailand. In fact, the history of the Thai Communist Party showed help has come from elsewhere. Now, whether from the Laotian border you can spread revolution beyond the Lao-inhabited provinces of Thailand, has to be seen. And whether, if revolution is spread in this way and thereby influence gained over revolutionary groups in Thailand in this manner, other sources of revolutionary fervour and strength will sit back and watch their supporters switch allegiance. That is another matter. So it's quite a complex situation.

Adrian Porter: How much do you think the subversion by communists in this area is affected by the conflict between Russia and China?

Prime Minister: Well, we have no evidence that the Laotians are acting on behalf of the Soviet Union, or anybody else on behalf of the Soviet Union. But it would make sense that if, for instance, China is finding it inconvenient at this time to step up revolutionary activities, that others would find it an attractive time to do so. I think that would be a fair inference.

XXIII

"This Hari Raya Puasa comes as Singapore is recovering from two years of recession. The outlook is fair, with a 6 – 8 per cent economic growth for 1976," Lee said in a Hari Raya message, on 24 September. In 1957, out of 87,000 women and girls of all races economically active, only 4.2 per cent or 3,600 were Malays. In 1976, out of 287,000 women and girls of all races economically active, 12.3 per cent or 35,000 were Malays. The dramatic increase showed how Malay women and girls had taken their places in proportion to the other races in the factories, hotels, shops and offices of Singapore. The speed with which Singapore Malays had adjusted to Singapore's changing way of life was a matter for satisfaction for all. Universal education, with children going to the same schools, and the interaction between the different ethnic groups living together in new housing estates had brought this about. He wished all Malays and Muslims Selamat Hari Raya Adil Fitri.

XXIV

Tourism had by now become an important factor in the nation's economy. "We had 1.3 million visitors to Singapore last year," said Lee at the opening of the Singapore Handicraft Centre on 25 September. During the first seven months of 1976, tourist arrivals showed a 12 per cent increase over the corresponding period of 1975. The Handicraft Centre had brought together traditional craftsmen from East, West, South and Southeast Asia, to display their wares and, more interesting, to demonstrate their skills, whether in carving jade, agate or ivory, or working on brass, copper, or silverware, weaving carpets or pottery and enamel ware. Of the thirty types of handicraft, thirteen were from Singapore. It was not easy to nurture and sustain craft skills in a highly urbanised centre that grew on trade, services and industry. Indeed, even in acquiring new industrial skills, Singaporeans seemed impatient. Several Japanese precision engineering factories often lamented that Singapore's skilled technicians believed they had reached perfection after two years, when their own Japanese technicians trained in Japan took an average of five years to reach top grade. It was, therefore, no surprise that for jade and ivory carving, requiring many years of painstaking apprenticeship, master craftsmen had not found it easy to recruit and train Singaporeans. It was easier to pass these skills from father to son, or master to apprentice, in the traditional agricultural societies of Asia. But the demand for tourist souvenirs, something to remind them of their visit to Singapore, might stimulate ingenuity and skills which might otherwise remain undiscovered. Those with a flair for designing something which caught the fancy of the visitor would not find his task unrewarding. This Centre, by its location and its attractive architectural style, would give the craftsmen and entrepreneurs who had set up business every chance of success. "They have a favourable setting to enthral and enthuse the visitor with all the ancient skills brought here from East, West, South and Southeast Asia."

XXV

Prior to his visit to Australia, the Prime Minister gave several interviews to New Zealand and Australian journalists. He was asked by Bruce Kohn of the New Zealand Press Association, on 25 September, how he saw the situation of the New Zealand forces in Singapore. Did he see them as a defence commitment?

Lee replied: "The decision to keep the battalion in Singapore a few years longer has nothing to do with any affirmation or reaffirmation of defence commitments. It's convenient for your Defence Ministry to have them based in Singapore for a little while longer. And as old friends, we are happy to be able to oblige. There is nothing more to it than that."

On 28 September, he was interviewed by Gerald Stone of Channel 9, Australia.

Gerald Stone: Several months ago, officials in Singapore had reason to express concern over the fact that certain radical elements from Singapore were using Australia as a base of operations against your government. Are you still concerned? What are you doing about it?

Prime Minister: Well, this is part of a pretty widespread net. The main thrust of the communists is from the border of Thailand and Malaysia, and to recruit enough for their main assault units and their guerilla forces for the thrust-down. And, of course, it's useful if you've got people who can make you appear to be reasonable social reformers and make the governments look fascist oppressors. And, also if you have intellectual elements in London, Brussels, Bonn, Paris and Sydney, Melbourne, Washington, New York to purvey this air of the social reform against dark forces. But the main thrust is with guerillas and main assault units down the Peninsula. And you don't recruit them from the relatively bourgeois intellectual types who go abroad for their studies.

Gerald Stone: Are you saying that what they're doing is propaganda, or are there actually more militant and aggressive activities that might be organised from Australia?

Prime Minister: I would think that the bulk of it would be directed at the West. It won't be directed so much at augmenting the fighting capability of the Malayan Communist Party or the Communist Party of Malaya. And, of course, money comes in useful. And you might get the odd intellectual who not only is intellectually convinced, but convinced enough to come back and join the guerilla army and be a combat engineer.

Gerald Stone: Well, this raises the question of the ballerina — Miss Goh, who wasn't exactly a combat engineer, but she apparently, according to information that your government released, fought against your government — actually entertained guerilla forces and did do some anti-government work in Sydney. Is that the type of activity we're talking about, or are there other Miss Gohs in Australia?

Prime Minister: I would imagine that she wasn't the first and wouldn't be the last of the arty-crafty types. It will go on, if only because this is an ever-shrinking world. It's easy to get to Australia, 7 – 8 hours. And they've got similar support in Europe, eventually America. It's this kind of activity which the Vietnamese communists had which helped them considerably in confusing Americans as to what it was all about, pretending that it was really a private civil war between Vietnamese and nothing to do with communism.

Gerald Stone: Do you think much money may be coming from what you called 'subversive elements' in Australia to help finance these activities against your government?

Prime Minister: In the context of their total resources — negligible, but still useful.

Gerald Stone: You raised the other question, the more important

321

question of actual guerilla activities. How do these stand now? Are you satisfied with the counter-measures against those activities?

Prime Minister: It's a very wide, broad question — one which encompasses the situation in Thailand, the border situation between Thailand and Malaysia and the internal situation in Malaysia itself. I think it will be beyond the scope of this interview if we go into the details of that.

Gerald Stone: Could we take, let's say, what has happened in the past five years? Are you finding that there is more intensified guerilla activity now on the Malay Peninsula or is there less?

Prime Minister: There is more, but that's partly because victories in Vietnam, Laos and Cambodia were a tremendous boost for insurgency in Malaysia and in Thailand. But whether they can sustain that thrust — will depend on the kind of external aid — sustained aid which they can get in weapons, resources, to take on an established government.

Gerald Stone: Is there enough concern at this moment to perhaps be talking to the Australian Government again, or thinking of talking to the Australian Government again about the renewal of a forward defence policy?

Prime Minister: No, no. We can't go backwards in time. What has happened to the Americans in Vietnam and to a lesser extent to all the others who were with the Americans in Vietnam, including Australia, is not something you can wash away and pretend it never happened. After Vietnam, I do not believe any external forces will ever get themselves involved in guerilla warfare. It's one of those myths which has been created out of this experience — and has brought about a tremendous change in thinking — strategic thinking. Of course, the Cubans proved in Angola that they can help one faction in a three-corner fight to get on top and so far keep down any guerilla activities. But then, they are not bothered by the mass media and having to explain how or why Cubans have to go to Angola to die and so on. And then, the anti-MPLA forces haven't got an outpost in Havana to put out propaganda on behalf of the other groups. So, in effect what's happened is — the West has found itself incapacitated in countering this type of penetration.

Gerald Stone: That almost sounds hopeless. What you are saying ...

Prime Minister: No. What I am saying is that the West as such can no longer do it. Hence we have got to do it ourselves. If we're going to survive as non-communist societies, then we've got to organise ourselves to meet this kind of challenge without Western soldiers getting involved.

Gerald Stone: Well, it sounds then, really what you want from Australia is just to be able to cool its own radical and militant elements, to make sure that it doesn't undermine its own confidence and its own belief in the destiny of a free country.

Prime Minister: Really, it's more than that. Let's assume the worst kind of scenario. Assume that you can theoretically repeat what's happened in Vietnam and Cambodia, in Thailand, in Malaysia, in Singapore, in Indonesia, in the Philippines. Then in twenty, thirty years or thereabout or less, you would have a fairly hostile belt to your north. I mean there won't be people like me whom you can talk to and ask this kind of questions of, so it would be a very different world and I think it's those issues which should exercise long-term strategic diagnosis in Australia.

Gerald Stone: And presumably the understanding of the Australian people towards some of the things that are happening in this area of the world.

Prime Minister: Yes, in the longer term.

Gerald Stone: You may recall that several years ago in an interview with me, you said that you sent some of your more radical students to Australia to sort of learn the niceties of the middle-class way of life. I wonder if you regret that now, in the sense that Singapore has developed a reputation as being amongst the most prosperous and hardest working people in the world. The Australians label themselves as lazy, too pampered. Do you think the Singapore students are learning the wrong values?

Prime Minister: No, I don't regret that. I think the situation then was different and even the situation now is not quite so bad; Australians can afford to go less hardworking because they don't have to work so hard. Maybe you learn how to do things with less effort, more efficiently. I would think when the student studying in Australia — 3 – 4 – 5 years gets back into a Singapore context, the spurs are stuck on his hinds and away he goes.

Gerald Stone: Even your critics admit you've been tremendously successful in motivating your people to work towards a given goal. Australia seems to have in a way lost its purpose — its sense of direction. What makes you successful, do you think, in that regard?

Prime Minister: First, I think we start off at a different level — the population here starts off with a very low base line. We started off poor and hungry plus the Confucian work ethic, plus the drive of the immigrants from India and Malaysia who wanted a better life. And you can't get a better life just by sitting back and doing nothing because there is no oil or nickel or uranium on the ground. You've got to get a better life by learning how to use your brain and your hands, by making things and making things better and more efficiently than other people.

Gerald Stone: What do you think then will happen to Singapore as you become more prosperous? Will the people slow down as they have appeared to slow down in the West? Will they become lazy as well? Or will they be motivated to keep working?

Prime Minister: I think there is a real problem here in that as we become less hungry, this syndrome is developed there, the people at the top work hard, probably because they want to strive, they want to succeed. And those in the lower brackets of society feel that it doesn't make sense — just driving harder and harder all the time. And one of the first problems that we have faced in this curious European, Western snobbery about jobs — certain jobs which the educated man or man who has been to school whether he is educated or not, spends some years and is literate more or less — doesn't want to do the heavy, the dirty jobs out in the sun and the rain — or the ones where there's social —

Gerald Stone: Stigma perhaps ...

Prime Minister: ... like having to clean the garbage. And we've already moved into that phase and we are getting people from outside coming in to do some of these jobs. And this is a real problem because it is now an inter-connected world and you've got the mass media spreading values, attitudes, and you've got over a million tourists coming through, showing people life-styles which they would only have seen in the cinema or in the glossy magazine, but now they see it in the flesh.

Gerald Stone: In Australia a great deal of our problems are to do with the militancy of a hard-core of very rigid militant trade unionists. Is this a problem with you, or how do you see the role of the trade unions?

Prime Minister: Well, it was a very serious problem here because at first we had the communists in charge of the unions and they were out to wreck the system. They were not out to improve the lot of the workers. Then, to counter that, the British TUC, the British unions, very kindly had started to train our unions — our non-communist unionists. But, fortunately, we moved early enough away from that model because we didn't think the British model, which is so bound up with their history of antagonism and class-bitterness, is a good model for us. So we got them to move towards the German model and the Japanese model — the house unions' people who participated with their employers in improving the lot of the irrelevant because we haven't got the same history. We haven't got the same bitterness or the stamp of accent from public schools as against council schools and all that goes with accents in a class-conscious Britain. And the desire to get even with the bosses — them and us, I mean it does not apply here. We all started poor — even the bosses.

Gerald Stone: Do you think that it applies in Australia? Do you see Australia following the British model?

Prime Minister: I don't think so because I would have thought that you didn't have the same class divisions. I am surprised that there is this export of British trade union shop-steward practice into Australia and New Zealand because the conditions are so completely different. You haven't got the same history of an upper crust that lives separate from the lower sections of society.

Gerald Stone: You seem to be saying that Britain is unique in the type of militant trade unionism; it's suffered within its own country and exported to some of the Commonwealth countries.

Prime Minister: Yes. I think that's right. I think they were the first country to industrialize and they were the first country that went through the kind of deprivations of Birmingham, Manchester, and all the slums and all the sweated labour. And they fought back — the working classes in the kind of unions that they built up — craft unions. And one employer having to reach agreement with a multitude of unions before he has got peace in his factory.

Gerald Stone: Well, you broke out of that mould by sending labour officials to study a different system — you said the German system ...

Prime Minister: And structuring our unions differently and working out our arbitration and legal systems differently.

Gerald Stone: Of course, in Australia, the unionists — particularly radical unionists would say: Well, what happens in Singapore has nothing to do with unionism, it is against the interest of the workers, not for the interest of the workers.

Prime Minister: If it were against the interest of the workers, we would have been out in some election ten, fifteen years ago.

Gerald Stone: I think you were suggesting a moment ago that a communist leadership in trade unions can't really legitimately represent the interests of the workers because they try to bring down the society. Now, we have, of course, some communist leaders in Australian unions. So, this question is very important. Do you really think they can't represent the interest of the workers?

Prime Minister: Well, they can, in the sense that they want to get more out of the bosses for workers. But the ultimate objective, as I understand, communist working within non-communist system, is not in order that they will help the system to work better but in order that they can bring the system down. This is a basic contradiction.

Gerald Stone: Yet, they would say — these communist union leaders — I think, the same, very much to the answer you gave me a little while ago — that if the workers didn't like it, they would have voted these communists out of power.

Prime Minister: Not quite. One, because they do get some benefits for the workers. And secondly, there is no compulsory voting of the total union membership. And with all organisations, an activist within the union, you need a few activists, a lot of passive members, and the activist-communists remain in charge.

Gerald Stone: Australia, as you know, is going through a great deal of economic difficulty at the present time and has taken certain steps including import controls to try to set this right. Has this affected Singapore adversely?

Prime Minister: Yes, it has and others besides us. I think the last Labour government under Mr. Whitlam started off with the right attitudes that they should lower these protectionist barriers and allow the simple manufactures from the countries of Asia to get into the Australian market. And then when unemployment started with the recession and with inflation, the barriers were put up and quotas were slammed down and we were hit in footwear, shoes, knitted garments and so on. And they are now, I think, it's some percentage, some fraction of the quota or the export levels before the tariffs were lowered.

Gerald Stone: Would you say that Singapore was seriously affected or considerably affected?

Prime Minister: No. Our trade with Australia is relatively small in percentage of our overall trade. So, it didn't really hurt us so much but the expectations of being able to develop trade with Australia, well that has been snuffed out for many years now.

Gerald Stone: For many years?

Prime Minister: It's going to take several years to get back to what it was and to get another Prime Minister feeling sufficiently confident that his population, especially his unions, will understand that it is in Australia's long-term interest to have good relations with the poorer parts of the world and allow them to export their products into Australia and not have Australians put up these tariff walls and have everything that Australians require produced by Australians at about six, seven times the cost of what is going to be if there were not the tariff barriers.

Gerald Stone: So you are saying that, perhaps, it is better for a country — a country like Australia to suffer some short-term economic dislocation including increased unemployment and allow itself to compete more fairly with its neighbours?

Prime Minister: No. I don't think I am saying that. All I am saying is that you've got to live with the rest of the world just as we have to. And these are the realities of life. And you are an extremely desirable market because you have got a wealthy purchasing community. But when you seal yourself behind this wall, then you have got all your neighbours and trading partners put off because you are giving nothing away.

Gerald Stone: Do you think that you are expressing the sentiment of the ASEAN nations?

Prime Minister: I think some move was made to get dialogue going between ASEAN and Australia on trade. And I hope it gets going at some time, but the idea of an immediate discussion on liberalising trade, well that was just laughed at by the ASEAN countries as a result of their experiences.

Gerald Stone: You are going to Australia, you'll be in Australia next week. Is this one of the points you want to discuss with Mr. Fraser?

Prime Minister: Mr. Fraser has got immediate problems — to contain inflation and diminish unemployment. I don't think I want to add to his problems.

Gerald Stone: I certainly don't expect you to interfere in any way in internal Australian politics, but the circumstances regarding Mr. Whitlam's dismissal were certainly unusual. As a serious student of constitutional law and Commonwealth history, what did you think about that?

Prime Minister: Well, I read the papers like everybody else and I would hope that some formula can be worked out whereby the stability of Australian Constitutional Government is reassured. All those who wish Australia well would like constitutional certainty and stability to be a way of life for the Australian people.

Gerald Stone: Do you think that was an unusual solution in terms of what you know about Commonwealth Law?

Lee speaking at the 1976 ASEAN Summit Meeting

Lee and his delegation during talks in Beijing in 1976 with Prime Minister Hua and the Chinese delegation

Lee in Beijing in 1976 with ailing Mao Se-dong.

In Beijing in 1976—toast with Prime Minister Hua

A welcomed visitor— President Suharto of Indonesia

Prime Minister: Well, I can hardly add anything to what very well-qualified constitutional lawyers have advised on the matter.

Gerald Stone: Do you think you can get along with Mr. Whitlam? There were some reports that you and Mr. Whitlam had your differences.

Prime Minister: Well, my job is to get along with anybody and everybody who has business to transact with me. And if I also like the person I am dealing with, well, that is a bonus.

Lee was asked by another Australian journalist, Michael Richardson on 6 October whether, if the Malayan Communist Movement disavowed use of force to work within the established political system he would permit them to function as a legally constituted party?

Prime Minister: If we were sure that this is not just a superficial tactical disavow of the use of force, but there will be sufficient guarantees that if they win an election, there will be an election after that. Yes, we would allow them to operate.

Richardson: Based on their past behaviour, do you think it's likely that you could get from them those kinds of guarantees that you would seek?

Prime Minister: No. You have put me a hypothetical question, and I am saying it's purely hypothetical. My answer is based on a hypothetical question.

Richardson: The case where a number of Singaporeans and Malaysians alleged to be communists, who trained or worked in Australia was widely publicised a few months ago. Do you think Australia is still a seabed for a significant number of budding Singaporean and Malaysian communists?

Prime Minister: Yes, one of them, next to Britain, another place where we have large numbers of students. I doubt if they will make the hard-core of the communist movement. They will be useful adjuncts in softening up Western opinion whether in Europe, Britain or Australia, New Zealand, and, perhaps, even America. But they are largely what the communist termed 'bourgeois intellectuals' to be used, not really to be the hard-core of the communist movement. They will be sympathisers, fellow-travellers, useful for the presentation of communist objectives as nationalistic rather than communistic.

Richardson: Does that worry you? And is there anything that can be done to ensure that this problem is minimised?

Prime Minister: Well, it bothers us because it means you have got to make sure first, that the art engineer or computer programmer who's being converted doesn't slip through into sensitive positions, and that is the first concern: That we shouldn't be unaware of high level manpower converts to the communist cause. Second, that we should not allow them to mislead the European or American or Australian public opinion.

Richardson: Are these people trained in Australia and elsewhere by committed Australian communists or do they merely use the more liberal atmosphere prevailing in those countries to study Marxism or whatever it

327

is that makes them join the communist movement?

Prime Minister: I think the main recruitment is by a central group consisting primarily of Malaysians and, of course, the environment in Australia which used to be inhospitable to such groups has become, over the years of student protest and unrest in the universities, most sympathetic to them. And they have linked up with, I understand, Australian Trotskyite groups and radicals generally.

Richardson: Singapore's opposition parties claim that the political system is loaded against them. Do you feel that it would be a good thing for Singapore to have a non-communist opposition, represented in Parliament after the next election?

Prime Minister: Now, first, you have made certain statements which are contentious. People can strike here and they do strike. The right to strike is part of our trade union movement and it is embodied in the laws, but part of the law requires that there be a strike ballot taken, that's all. You've said opposition parties, said that the dice is loaded against them. Well, they keep on fighting. They lose. So, they said the dice is loaded. You've spent a lot of your time in Singapore and I think you should do more than just repeat what they said. You ought to give your assessment. If you are a Singaporean, would you vote for any of the opposition leaders or their followers? I would like an answer to that question.

Richardson: You have turned the table round.

Prime Minister: And frankly, the opposition as it is — opposition groups as they are, comprised at the moment, are not people who are likely to pose a serious alternative government. They are not men of serious intent. I think you've got to understand the history of this place — what happened before, to understand the situation today. When the British faced an insurrection in 1948, as a counter to that insurrection, they encouraged one man one vote. And the communists boycotted these elections as bogus. The only people the British were able to draw into their arena until the PAP came were the softies — the people who thrived under British protection, compradores if you like, people who depended on British patronage and nobody took them seriously — not the mass of the electorate and in any case there was no universal franchise. Then came 1957 when constitutional reforms were seriously embarked upon and universal franchise was introduced and the general elections followed in 1959. Then the communists came in with the PAP in the united front to contest what was fairly substantial political power. And we won. Then, of course, came the break between the non-communists in the PAP and the communists, contrived by the British in 1961, 1962. Then thereafter there has been a ding-dong between the communists and the non-communists. And the people in their late thirties and forties and fifties remember all this and know that politics is not just another ball game. It's a very serious matter of life and death because if the communist win, well, that's life for them and maybe very unpleasant life for those who have lost, who have opposed them. And even for the PAP, I mean, we have been trying all

328

these years to build up an able, competent second generation leadership if not with the same experience and emotional commitments that was the product of the last war and the Japanese Occupation and the communist struggles, then at least with a commitment to society, and it has not been easy. The able ones, the honest ones, are doing very well in the professions, in industry, in banking and finance partly because of the PAP. So, they say: Fine, you are doing fine, carry on. I think this is a very grave problem of finding able men of high integrity and a sense of purpose — commitment to society, to do something other than for themselves.

Richardson: What sort of society is the PAP Government trying to mould?

Prime Minister: Again, to understand this you must understand the past — what we inherited from the British. A disparate group of immigrants who came to Singapore and Malaya to make their fortune and many didn't and left their progeny behind. And we've got to weld a certain sense of common destiny out of disparate, originally disparate groups. So, there must be, first, certain basic ingredients of racial tolerance, religious tolerance and a placing of certain common denominators as paramount, that you must have this tolerance of different racial groups, religious groups, language groups and within that find common denominators because we share common destiny whether we like it or not, whether we share common ethnic and linguistic or religious loyalties. And so, you've got to forge these common denominators and we found it up to a point by voluntary choice, for instance, for education. You can go to any school you like and learn your own language be it Chinese, Malay or Tamil, and you will learn English. That becomes a common cement ... We have a chance to prove that if certain adjustments are made to prejudices, whether it's against race or religion or culture, you can still have a reasonably tolerant, give and take society. And it's going to take continuing effort but we haven't done so badly so far. During Malaysia we had two communal riots. There has been none since separation. I hope there won't be anymore. And it's got to be a society which is sufficiently on the ball to adjust and to adapt to new technology, to new ways of earning a living, of living itself, because this is an era of rapid change not just in technology but the consequences of technology on the ways of life. The pill has made society and relationships between men and women completely different. Are we going to lose everything of the kind of families which Asian societies have centred upon? The nucleus of all Asian society is the sanctity of the family. Can we preserve some of that despite (1) the pill; (2) independent mothers with jobs of their own, with education of their own, with training of their own? And, therefore, not having to put up with difficult or erring husbands? Are we going to go just like other western societies, particularly in America, where marriage is no longer a sacred institution? A new style of life emerged. I think it would be a pity if that took place. So, some people must be thinking about these problems and seeing how we can learn to absorb this technology, to absorb the results of discoveries without necessarily destroying or abandoning what was good of the past. I don't think you can say what kind of society we want to mould. It's what kind of society we can achieve despite the destructive consequences of modern science and technology which includes mass air travel and the exposure of large numbers of people to other civilisations, other cultures. Are we just/going to be another urban centre, part of the free-wheeling Western world and bereft of any trace of the values, norms which thousands of years of very difficult histories have found to be necessary to maintain civilised living? I don't know. I think we tried. And I hope those who take over from us will keep on trying.

Richardson: Singapore stops well-short of being a welfare state unlike Great Britain. Is this because you can't afford the financial outlay or because you feel that the government that gives too much to the people destroys their will to work?

Prime Minister: Well, for the present it's something which we cannot contemplate, because it's crippling financially, and because the work ethic, whether it's Confucian or Puritan or Calvinistic, well, that's destroyed and we haven't got North Sea oil like the British or the North Sea gas like the Dutch. You see the Dutch used to be considered frugal, hardworking — a very clean and thrifty people. I remember my vacation there, when I was a student over a generation ago — a Spartan clean seaside resort, very well-starched white aprons for the Dutch ladies, but now I read that the younger Dutch ladies help Palestinian guerillas and print pamphlets for the IRA. Perhaps, an absence of a challenge of a sense of purpose in life is going to be more and more of a problem in many societies which become so secure in meeting the basic necessities of life, that they lose their sense of direction.

Richardson: To what extent does Singapore's racial harmony and political stability depend on continued economic growth?

Prime Minister: If you mean by that, that unemployment leads to racial animosities and friction, I don't think that's true because bosses or the government hires and fires not on the basis of race, but on the basis of performance on the job. It could be that certain areas would be more adversely affected in a recession and you could have more of a certain racial group employed in that particular sector. But I don't really believe that we have gone through all that we have done in the past seventeen years without having moved away from that. I mean, do people really believe in an unemployment situation, with recession the order of the day, that a person is unemployed because of his race? I hope not, anyway.

Richardson: Based on evidence so far, do you think the terms set by Vietnam and Laos for good relations with ASEAN and its five constituent states are acceptable?

Prime Minister: I think I must correct you there; the terms that Vietnam has set are not for relations with ASEAN. It's for relations with individual countries of Southeast Asia. They have no relations with ASEAN

As far as they are concerned, it's countries, A, B, C, D, E, and others in Southeast Asia. If you read their statements you will find that there is a preamble and then the four conditions. The 'preamble' states their stand, that they have a duty to fully support the struggles of other peoples in Southeast Asia. The Vietnamese people support the struggles of other people, that is, the so-called liberation movements or guerilla groups striving to overthrow legitimately elected governments by force of arms. Then they said on the basis of the following four conditions we will establish relations. Well, the four conditions are not objectionable, it's their way of saying non-interference and equality and so on. But whether the 'preamble' is intended seriously and will be implemented, is another matter. We'll have to wait and see. If it is, then, of course, it will be very difficult for relations between the countries of ASEAN and Vietnam and Laos.

Richardson: Do you agree with those who said that in recent years, China has substantially reduced the level of its ideological and material support for insurgency in the ASEAN region? Is China a long-term factor for regional stability, do you think?

Prime Minister: First, China has not reduced her ideological support. She makes a point of it. You can see it in the reporting, even of condolence messages to the Chinese Government by the communist parties of South East Asia. They are carried prominently in *Ren Min Jih Pao*, *The People's Daily*, and also on the radio. So, the ideological support has never weakened. I think we ought to take them seriously at their word, that they are a Marxist-Leninist party that will help other Marxist-Leninist parties. The material support may have been kept relatively not at critical level, because of their policy for good government-to-government relations. For as long as that policy continues, that is a factor for stability. How long it will continue I do not know. For, I think, as long as it is necessary to counter the dangers that China sees of Soviet replacement of American presence in Southeast Asia, or what is called by China as 'hegemonism'.

Richardson: Against the background of the USSR's growing military might, does the Soviet naval presence in the Indian Ocean give you any cause for concern?

Prime Minister: So long as the American naval presence matches the Soviet naval presence in size or quality of fleet, no. But if the Soviet naval presence is the only one, or the overwhelming one, then I think life could become a little more uncomfortable.

Richardson: Do you see any danger of a further reduction in US strategic interest in eastern Southeast Asia after the November presidential election?

Prime Minister: Yes, I think there is a distinct possibility that in the short term, in the first few years of a newly elected President, the mood of the American people would be to get away from their troubles in Southeast Asia which have caused so much travail in America. And the attitudes for policies that have been spelt out about American troops in

331

Korea and their withdrawal, eventually, must mean a dimunition of interest. But whether in the medium term, it is possible to reconcile American policies which include Japan as a critical part of the trilateral alliance — America, Western Europe, Japan — without taking into consideration other parts of East or Southeast Asia, well, is another matter. We will have to wait and see because Japan can't live and thrive and prosper just as Japan in conjunction with the United States. It's got to be Japan as Japan's security interest and Japan's economic interest.

Richardson: But if there is a significant reduction, whether in East or in Southeast Asia of this American interest will that have an unsettling effect?

Prime Minister: For the first year or two, I think no, because by and large, people will expect this response to American sentiment which is a fact of life. They have gone through a very painful period. But if it persists — that means, if that is the policy even after considering dispassionately the various policy choices, then, of course, a profound reassessment would have to be made by all the non-communist countries of Eastern Southeast Asia as to what their policies, foreign policies and defence attitudes have to be.

Richardson: What is the purpose of your visit to Australia?

Prime Minister: I was supposed to have made this visit to Australia and New Zealand in April last year but Mr. Whitlam's legislative programme at that time made it impossible for the visit to take place. Now it takes place under a different Prime Minister, and naturally — nearly a year and a half has passed and the subjects we will be discussing, in both foreign affairs and regional affairs and our bilateral interest, will be different. The world has moved. But knowing the thinking, which is not necessarily spelt out in speeches, does help in understanding what is spelt out in speeches. And I hope that at least would be achieved.

Richardson: You and the former Australian Prime Minister, Mr. Whitlam, engaged in some verbal jostling from time to time. Selective immigration and the brain drain of talented Singaporeans to Australia was one issue. Is this still a problem?

Prime Minister: We sorted it out whilst Mr. Whitlam was still in office. And so far as I know, the solutions we agreed upon are enforced. Namely, we will sponsor our students to Australia for university education and those whom we sponsor, we can request their return. We can't make a doctor or an engineer whatever he is, work and stay in Singapore if he doesn't like it. He'll leave. But we do say that at the end of a stay in Australia — be it four, five years, he should be made to return because you get into a way of life. I have been a foreign student after all and I know they get into different ways of life. They just stay on because it requires the least effort — it's inertia. One gets used to a different way of life and readjusting is not attractive. But having readjusted into Singapore and they find it still doesn't give them the satisfaction or the rewards, then they are free to go.

Richardson: There has been criticism by ASEAN senior officials of barriers to trade with Australia, ranging from high tariffs on manufactured goods, to inadequate shipping services and trade union action. In the next five or ten years, are terms of trade going to be a more important factor shaping ASEAN's relations with Australia, than, say, continued Australian aid to the region?

Prime Minister: I would like to believe that Australian policies can change in this respect and that your industries can stand the influx of simple manufactures from the ASEAN countries. But maybe it can't. Maybe both your unions and your manufacturers cannot put up with this inflow of simple manufactures. Mr. Whitlam tried it. He scrapped quotas on garments, knitwear, and then there was a howl about Australian shirts not being sold and so on. And with it came the oil embargo and recession and the step forward had to be reversed. Well, if it can't be made, then there will always be this resentment because Australia is an attractive market and one which is denied them by trade union policy and by manufacturers who see no reason why they should share their market. Now, if you can't do this, maybe you can't, then I think some other fields must be explored because the countries of ASEAN are the receiving end of the trade imbalance. With the Japanese they are, by and large, exporters of raw materials to Japan — importers of machinery and finished products. In other words, they don't like it. It's a role they don't like to have to stay in and Australia can help to get them out of this role. The Japanese are trying to help — not very successfully. The Europeans, the Americans are helping more by their GSP concessions — General Specialised Preferences. And if the Australians can't do that, then you must find some way other than aid, which is always demeaning to the recipient, to increase economic interchange. I don't know how it can be done. It's probably not easy, but you can help stimulate economic growth, investments, technical transfer of technology and technical expertise. It is a very broad subject.

Richardson: Would action, though in that area, the latter areas, that you've mentioned — technological input, training be an acceptable alternative, do you think?

Prime Minister: It'll be accepted as better than nothing, but the resentment, (I think, if we are to speak frankly, the Australians have got to know what Southeast Asia thinks, will be there. Because to find Europeans, 8,000 miles away or Americans equally far away, more willing to import simple manufactures from ASEAN countries than Australia just a block away, is going to be very difficult to live down, particularly, when it is aggravated every now and again by Australia's Seamen's Union, you know, championing the rights of local seamen to pay equal to Australian seamen or if that's not possible, then to pay of a measure which Australian Seamen's Unions consider to be humane and right and proper. Well, it just compounds that problem. It shows a lack of sympathy for aspirations of relatively backward people in the industrial world to try and catch up with the ways of industrial countries, the ways of life of making a living of industrial states.

Richardson: What useful purpose, if any, do the five-power consultative defence arrangements serve now? Do they need to be modified?

Prime Minister: Well, I think we ought to leave them as they are.

Richardson: They are still a useful stabilising factor?

Prime Minister: In certain circumstances; it's no longer what it was. But there is no point in scrapping them since it doesn't incur grave risk for any of the five. I think just leave them alone. They may turn up to be useful in certain situations.

Richardson: You mean — like what?

Prime Minister: If you want to invoke it for various exercises.

Richardson: Training exercises.

Prime Minister: Amongst other things.

Richardson: Could you be more specific than that?

Prime Minister: Well, we don't know what the future holds and what common interest may make us want to do.

XXVI

Before the Prime Minister left for Australia he made a speech at the commissioning parade of the Third Standard Military Course of SAFTI and Third Midshipman Course of Midshipman School, Queenstown Athletic Centre, on 15 October. He said the parade marked the end of their basic training as officers. They had been taught the fundamentals. No one could teach each of them how to be a leader of men. They would have to learn how to earn the respect and confidence of other men placed under their charge, what moved them, and why some officers were better than others in getting their men to do better. From now, they could, generally speaking, be told what to do. How they do it will be their individual responsibility. "You will be responsible not only for what you yourself do, but also for your subordinates, what they do, or fail to do." They had another year and nine months of national service. The most of them would go on to university. Some might treat this period as a distraction from their academic career. Later in life, they would realise that how to get on with other men and how to get them to do things to the best of their ability, were amongst the most important things in life. "Whatever your future profession or vocation, men management is a common factor of all top jobs. The SAF gives you the format within which you can learn the basic motivations of human beings, their needs, their drives." If they did well in the SAF, it was likely that they could also handle men when they were not in uniform and still get them to give of their best.

XXVII

In Australia on 18 October, the Prime Minister took part in the "Monday Conference" television feature. The moderator was Robert Moore, and the panel consisted of Ken Randall, journalist, and Dr. Fedor Mediansky, a lecturer in political science at the University of New South Wales.

Robert Moore: Good evening, and welcome to Monday Conference again. The Prime Minister of Singapore is making his third official visit to Australia. He arrived yesterday and he will be here for twelve days. Mr. Lee's first visit was in 1965 and to show that in a changing world there are still some strains of continuity, I recall that I interviewed him then eleven years ago. Lee Kuan Yew became the first Prime Minister of Singapore in 1959. He has remained so ever since. At present his People's Action Party (PAP) holds all sixty-five seats in the Singapore Parliament. Singapore is, of course, one of the smallest independent states in the world, made up of one larger island and fifty-four smaller ones. Its population is about two and a quarter million. In 1974, 3.6 per cent of Singapore's total trade was with Australia which made us then Singapore's sixth biggest trading partner. Singapore is, of course, a favoured country with Australian tourists. Prime Minister, I mentioned our earlier meeting eleven years ago, because one of the things that struck me is that in 1965 there were no demonstrators in the street against your visit. What has changed — with either you or Singapore or the demonstrators?

Prime Minister: Well, quite frankly, Australia has changed. There were then Australian students, probably not as numerous. They probably paid fees and therefore took their work a little more seriously and took demonstrations less seriously. The world has moved on. There are more university students, all for free, and there are more Malaysians. And I am told some Singaporeans, one-fourth Malaysians, and they have gone with the times.

Moore: You have been reported as saying that Australia was now a more hospitable place for dissident Singaporean students who came here. Why is that so?

Prime Minister: I don't think I said dissident Singaporean students alone, I mean dissidents of all kinds. I don't really know. I think a different mood, anti-establishment. This is part of the American trend. The Americans have snapped out of it and undoubtedly sometime, some place, the Australians also will.

Moore: Do you think the time might come when you may prohibit Singaporean students from coming here on scholarships?

Prime Minister: (Laughter) No, what for? I don't think the average Singaporean who comes here is a liability either to Australia or to Singapore. He is, by and large, a fairly serious-minded sort of person. He probably wants to blend whilst he is in Australia. But he knows he has got a job

335

waiting for him and he wants to climb up that ladder. And I would be surprised if there is any benefit in preventing him from climbing up that ladder either via a university in Australia or in Britain or in America.

Moore: Can we look at some of the things that the students, in their publications, and I've seen one or two of them, I don't know how valid their statements are, but what they are saying, they are demonstrating against in your Singapore, the kind of things like political detention, detention of political prisoners without trial, some of whom have been detained since 1963, the licensing of newspapers and printing presses; what is alleged to be a suitability certificate for students — again, I don't know the technicalities of that — and suggestion that the trade union movement in Singapore is a tame cat movement and is more concerned with keeping wages down to be attractive to foreign entrepreneurs.

Prime Minister: Well, I think they ought to have paid you for a free advertisement.

Moore: No, be fair, that's not an advertisement. You know as well as I do that those things are commonly said about Singapore. Whether they are true or not is for you to say.

Prime Minister: Well, I don't subscribe to this view that repeating a whole host of irresponsible things is responsible television media work. If you want to go through that in a serious way, then we have to sit down and spend about at least half-an-hour to trace the history of it. You mustn't assume that the world is like you. Singapore is a very different place and if you had visited it eleven years ago, it was a pretty scruffy place and revolution was round the corner. You could have a riot at the drop of your hat. Taxis were burnt up, so were buses, and the communists were in charge of the unions. And we spent the last, not just eleven, really seventeen years fighting them in the open argument and the people that you mentioned who were arrested thirteen years ago were arrested not by me and my colleages in the Cabinet alone. We then had a security committee comprising the British, the Malaysian Ministers and ourselves. And all they need do is to say: I will not use violence, I will not help the Communist Party of Malaya, and we release them. That's all we ask of them. And if they refuse to say that, partly because they think they shouldn't unhelp the Communist Party of Malaya, then we say: Look, you can leave, and some of them, two of them, are doctors, they could leave for any country they like in the world and practise. One of them I defended for sedition some twenty years ago. I know him, he knows me. I know what he stands for: he knows what I stood for. We were in a united front. And because he has lost, I have to feed him and look after him and have people like Mr. Robert Moore ask questions publicly. But if I lose I don't think you will have the opportunity of asking my captors about what has happened to me.

Moore: No, but I think there is an unstated compliment almost in these criticisms that are made of your running of Singapore, in a sense that people, perhaps, expect more of you than they do a number of other heads of state.

336

Prime Minister: Well, you've got to understand that our communists — I don't know whether yours are like the Europeans, you know,
they have become very domesticated. They don't believe in the dictatorship of the proletariat. They believe in multi-party rule. They have that
soft gentle approach to life. And they assure everybody if they win, there
will be another election in which their popularity will be put to the test. But
our communists make no such pretentions, they make no such concessions. They believe in the violent overthrow by use of guns, of the government elected, or otherwise, and the establishment of a people's democracy
like, by way of example, Vietnam, Laos, Cambodia. I think you won't
have the opportunity to ask what has happened to, say, Prince Souvanna
Phouma, who is a very gentle, polished, educated Laotian. Nor would you
be able to ask whoever is in charge in Cambodia what's happened to
Prince Norodom Sihanouk. I don't think we can do better than what we
have done. If these people would say: I am against the use of violence, I do
not support the Communist Party of Malaya, fine!

Moore: Outside this obviously illegal form of opposition in Singapore, what are the parameters of the political debate within Singapore? On
what issues does the legitimate opposition differ with you? What sort of
things do they differ?

Prime Minister: Well, you must not forget that there was only one
political opposition and that was us against the communists. They really
were the first political party. In 1923, the year that I was born, two
members of the Comintern were sent from Shanghai and they set up the
first underground cells. There were no other political parties. They spread
into Peninsular Malaysia, and, with the War, the British provided them
with weapons to fight the Japanese, and they became the Marque, the
Resistance. At the end of the War, they nearly took over from the British
and a lot of British, Fijians, Australians and New Zealanders died in order
that they would not take over by force. And it was partly luck, that the
world boom was on our side, and partly the force of the argument, that the
country didn't go communist.

Moore: But Prime Minister, referring to what you said earlier, you are
not suggesting in Singapore you are either PAP or you are communist?

Prime Minister: No, what I am suggesting is that you need literally to
have sufficient conviction to say, well, if I lose and I die, so be it, before
you take on the communists. And therefore there were very few who
were prepared to do that. We did that. Fortunately, not without success,
and in the process they became the minority, we became the majority. But
our problem now is how to find successors — young men in their thirties
or early forties who would carry on the work. And the bright ones know
what is in the pack of cards and many of them say: Thank you, you are
doing an excellent job and I would like to do my research or do my accountancy or my banking, my law or medicine, you carry on.

Moore: Could I just ask you one last thing and I'll leave it for a while.
In your own case, do you have at this stage — not that presumably you'll

337

be retiring from politics for a long while yet — but do you have marked out a successor for yourself? Do you see someone coming up?

Prime Minister: No, I don't believe that is possible, not in the kind of world we live in. It hasn't worked out that way for Australia. If you remember, you cast your mind back to 1966, and I don't think it is going to work that way in Singapore. All you can do is to expose a fair number of able men with convictions to difficult situations and then let them contend amongst themselves.

Ken Randall: You are fairly relaxed about your attitude towards the demonstrators against you here, Prime Minister. But isn't it true that — just going back to something else you said earlier — that there are in fact no new scholarship students out here, all the students that have come here since your raising of the issue two years ago are now effectively bonded to the Singapore Government and can be returned. Do you really think in those circumstances that it's such a breeding ground of communists and subversives as you suggested in the interview you gave last week before you left for this visit?

Prime Minister: No, I don't think I suggested that at all. I consider the Australian environment completely different from the kind of harsh dedication required of guerilla insurgents. I don't know what was published, but ...

Randall: Well let's take another point of it. It's most unusual, quite bizarre, in Australian experience, to see demonstrations of this sort which are really quite quiet, moderate, political demonstrations, where the people are masked because they claim that their family associations could be jeopardised at home.

Prime Minister: (Laughter) Oh, come off it! Do you really believe that we waste our resources on trying to find out ...

Randall: But you obviously wasted or used, a great deal of resources this year, sir, on the ballet dancer incident which was laughed out of court in Australia and yet it obviously had a big impact in Singapore.

Prime Minister: Well, I don't know whether Australians laughed at that, but that wasn't a laughing matter because that led to a little pattern of how things are done — the recruitment of party's respectable people to support a terrorist movement. And it was important that that should be exposed. But comic students who put on these Klu Klux Klan type of garment. I know of no returned student from Australia who has become an active dissident, let alone a terrorist. So I see no reason why they shouldn't continue to come to Australia. The communists would like to be able to develop, not just in Australia but in Europe and America, sympathisers, supporters who would peddle the line that they are very gentle, social, democratic reformers. But if they are going to win, then they got to find hard tough men who will go with them to the jungle, fight, die, in order that others may win.

Randall: You don't think they're being produced out here?

Prime Minister: No, no, not possible.

338

Randall: Have you actually taken up this sort of issue with the Australian Government on an official level? This was raised several times during the incident we mentioned earlier. Why haven't there been an official complaint if you took it so seriously?

Prime Minister: Not at all, not at all.

Randall: What is the point, then, of making such big issues of it if you don't take it seriously?

Prime Minister: No, no, we take it seriously as a demonstration of how the pattern works, of what they try to establish overseas — involve ballet dancers and engineers, doctors, to subscribe to their cause and give it respectability. But the cause will win or lose depending on how good their generals are, how good their tacticians are in fermenting unrest, in spreading what are small guerilla groups right throughout the countryside until finally they become rampant and then they have a main strike force like the North Vietnamese Army — twenty divisions — and over went the South Vietnamese forces, just keeled over.

Moore: Prime Minister, Singapore resigned from the Socialist International this year, under a degree of pressure, I suppose. Do you still regard yourself a socialist? What were the circumstances?

Prime Minister: When a party in the Socialist International begins to raise the kind of issues you have done, you know, just reading out from student pamphlets, then I say to them, either you withdraw that or I don't think we are in the right company. I mean you ought to be asking the people who published those pamphlets to be members of the International.

Moore: Do you still regard yourself as a socialist, Prime Minister?

Prime Minister: The word has many meanings now — I mean, the Eastern bloc countries call themselves socialists. There's the socialist Republic of Vietnam. So in that, I am not a socialist. If you ask me whether I am a believer in equal opportunities, that man should not be judged by his birth or property or religion, then I say, yes. I believe that, and I believe the economic system should provide equal opportunities to all to exercise their talents. To that extent, I am an old-fashioned socialist — like probably Gaitskell was, or the older generation — British Labour Party types. But the new generation, so-called radical types, well, I am not completely in sympathy with them.

Moore: Would you identify at all with the Australian Labour Party, sir?

Prime Minister: That's coming a bit near the bone. I don't think it's wise of you to ask me such difficult questions.

Dr. Mediansky: Prime Minister, you mentioned that the accusations and criticisms of your Government have been from disreputable organisations, and I have a quote in front of me from one of your own political scientists in the University of Singapore who, in commenting about your political system which is described as a one-party Parliament, said that the most significant development has been the steady and systematic

339

depoliticization of a politically active and aggressive citizenry. Now, this implies all sorts of things about the freedom and ability of alternative viewpoints to be put forward within your political system. Would you agree with this and if so why has this happened?

Prime Minister: I profoundly disagree with this statement made. If whoever wrote that believes that a one-party Parliament that won all the seats in the last election in 1972, September, with seven seats uncontested and fifty-eight contested but won by us, the party in government, is unpopular, he should set up a party. There are about seven or eight parties and I am quite sure they are going to contest the next elections and I have every reason to believe that the electorate would return us; if they don't, well, they will have their choice of the seven or eight parties.

Mediansky: I have no doubts in my own mind that you would be returned at a subsequent election. The question is that ...

Prime Minister: Well, thank you. You are making a statement based on, if I may say so, hearsay, just as you made at first . . . you repeated the first statement which was completely spurious, so you have repeated the statements by other political commentators who say that we will win the next election. I find this one of the less attractive features of the contemporary media men. The purveying of statements made by others regardless of whether they are sound or unsound and I think ...

Randall: But isn't that what the whole interplay of opinion is about, Prime Minister? I mean you did seem to have objected to it in Singapore.

Prime Minister: No, no, I think the mindless repeating of statements ...

Randall: What makes them mindless? What's the judgement about that?

Prime Minister: Well, because Dr. Mediansky has not taken the time to go through and say: "Is this so, why should it be so?"

Moore: He was asking you.

Mediansky: But sir, how can you say that? You've suggested in the first place that these are mindless media men. I'm not a media man, I quoted a Singapore academic and a political scientist ...

Prime Minister: No, let's not, let's not mix it up ..

Mediansky: ... but sir, this is the second time ...

Prime Minister: ... I said ... you said, I have no doubts that you will win, other people have said so. Well ...

Mediansky: No, I didn't add the last part, sorry.

Prime Minister: Well, then how did you know that we would win?

Mediansky: I said I've had little doubts that you would win, that was my own personal opinion of it. I was about to ask whether it was a normal situation in a pluralistic society in the past to have merely one political party monopolising all the seats in the Parliament. This, to my notion of democratic procedure, seems a little unorthodox.

Prime Minister: (Laughter) You mean to tell me that it is undemocratic and unorthodox for a people to choose one party?

Randall: Well, it certainly restricts it on the interplay of viewpoints you were talking about.

Prime Minister: Have you got a textbook on political science or political economy which says that this becomes undemocratic?

Mediansky: It's highly unorthodox, as I put it.

Prime Minister: No, it's highly un-Australian, un-British, un-Western, yes, but you know that doesn't mean that it's unorthodox. This is one of the assumptions that the West makes — and I don't really mean so much the Australians as the Americans and the West Europeans who set these standards — that the world must conform to their norms. Now, would you be happy if we scrapped the first-past-the-post system as our opponents would have us do and adopted the Australian system of transferred votes, or better still, copied the Italian system and then end up with an ungovernable Parliament? Well, here is a system which allows a party, every five years, or within five years, to renew its mandate and it works, to my great surprise, because I doubted at the very beginning whether it would work in the first place and in large parts of the world, and not just Africa, or Latin America, in large parts of Europe it looks as if it may not be working, and I mean Western Europe, physical Western Europe; in Portugal, they're having a difficult time; in Spain, its doubtful whether it will work, in Italy ...

Randall: They've been a long time without the experience, Prime Minister. Don't you think that one of the things that stands out in the way that Dr. Mediansky is talking about is that you do have a system with just about all the trappings of Westminster and yet you keep on denying the similarities.

Prime Minister: Well, I did not choose the system, the system was imposed on me. The British imposed the system and I had to make amendments to the system in order that it would suit local circumstances and work, and perhaps, if a group of men who take over from us do not constantly remember that we are not Britain, we are not Westminster nor are we Australia or Canberra, then the whole system will break down and I have not the slightest doubts that if it does, if will be out of the window and you'll never go back to one-man, one-vote ever again.

Randall: Could we just change tack a bit, and could I ask you something about recent experience in a slightly different field? You've probably had, in the past couple of years, the worst economic shock that you've had for quite a while and you seem to be pulling out of it now quite reasonably, judged on the figures of the past few months ...

Prime Minister: That's kind.

Moore: (Laughter) You can quote him on that.

Randall: Other people's figures of the past few months. How seriously did you regard the economic recession in political terms while it was at its peak when you had record unemployment, and obvious signs of industrial unrest, was that a political threat?

Prime Minister: No, you see ... may I be quite frank? It's a mis-

341

statement of fact.

Randall: Which?

Prime Minister: First of all, we never had record unemployment because we had a buffer of what the Germans call guest workers. Secondly ...

Randall: Does that alter the fact that you had more people out of work than since you have been Prime Minister before?

Prime Minister: No, but we had ... no, on the contrary, when I took over office in 1959, unemployment was about 10 per cent. At its worst in 1974, one year after the oil crisis, it went up from 4 per cent to 5 per cent, so we were better off, so that's a mis-statement of fact. Secondly, the worst recession ever. Yes, it was a recession, we were making 10 per cent, 11 per cent, 12 per cent a year. In 1974, we made 7 per cent. In 1975, we made 6 per cent growth at constant prices. So, you see, you can't base all these questions on really unverified facts and it so happens in the case it's incorrect.

Randall: But Prime Minister, isn't the point that it was your party and your Government which adopted the policy of accelerated growth, industrial growth, manufacturing growth which led to an expansion of the work force, which led to the vulnerability to the sort of recession that you had and to the sort of unrest that went with it in the end? My point, whether or not you dispute the figures, was simply, how did it affect the social fabric of Singapore and how you're coming out of it?

Prime Minister: Well, if I may say so, Mr. Randall, I'll let you off the hook lightly. Please remember, don't make these statements which are not true. Yes, we did go for rapid growth; yes, we made it for about ten years, and then it tailed down in 1974 to 7 per cent, in 1975 to 4 per cent, this year with some luck we will make 7 per cent, but ...

Mediansky: Sir, on ...

Prime Minister: May I answer his question first. It did not end with social unrest or he wouldn't be reading what other political commentators, Dr. Mediansky's statement, that he thinks I'll win the next election. We'll win the next election because we have done relatively well despite the world recession. I'm not very proud of it because it wasn't as good as it could have been, but I think by and large, I'm greatly relieved and so is the rest of Singapore.

Mediansky: Sir, on the question of your economic success story which is widely recognised, some of your critics ...

Prime Minister: Widely read you mean, by other ... written up by other media men and repeated.

Mediansky: Sir, most of us rely for our information on the printed word. I must apologise for that. But there has been another element to this — the notion that your economic success story has been based on certain degree of deprivation of some of the weaker elements of your labour force. In support of this charge, it has been argued that the labour laws in Singapore discriminate against women. There is an argument that

342

even one-third of the labour force is composed of women and yet their wages compose about 15 per cent of the total wage bill. Similar charges have been made about the ...

Prime Minister: That is completely untrue. I don't know why these untruths are pervaded. And I think someone who goes on the mass media like television has a responsibility to make sure that what is uttered does not add to the confusion. We are one of the few governments in the developing world, and indeed I would say one of not very many governments in the world, that give our women completely equal rewards plus maternity benefits.

Mediansky: Are the figures wrong, sir?

Prime Minister: I don't know where you got those figures from. But I will tell you that first, the public sector. No woman is paid less than a man — all on the same salary scales, promotions, the lot, plus maternity benefits. The private sector I would imagine is fairly flexible. But I would imagine in the upper reaches, there might be some prejudice about sending a woman for advanced training and then she may give up her career halfway and so on. But I can't answer for that. I would dispute strenuously your claim that they comprise 30 per cent of the work force and get 15 per cent of the wage bill. That is something I find completely absurd.

Moore: Could I move on, if we may for a while, please, to economic relations between Singapore and Australia, which is obviously of considerable interest to all sides. You have recently — you have been quoted — as saying, understandably, that you would like a lowering of tariffs, Australian tariffs, against goods that your country produces along with other countries.

Prime Minister: If I remember rightly, the question that was put to me was trade between the countries of ASEAN, or the South East Asian Association of countries and Australia and I said yes, the Association wants it, but being a realist, knowing that Australia is going through a difficult time with employment, and inflation, it's not on, so I'm not raising the matter, but you see a journalist comes along and puts the question. I have to respond just as I have to respond to you, and then it's quoted back to me as saying I am asking for it at a most difficult time in Australian economic history.

Moore: Ah, that wasn't going to be my question. My question was going to acknowledge that, but then go on to ask you what are going to be the long-term political consequences, in the long-term ...

Prime Minister: What of?

Moore: ... of Australia maintaining its present tariff level against goods produced by the ASEAN countries. I'm asking you to project, if you wouldn't mind. I don't know, ten, twenty years from now, when hopefully economic conditions are changed within Australia.

Prime Minister: Well, you will have a higher cost of living and you are going to have neighbours who feel that here is a wealthy enclave all fenced in and not only that, when their ships go there, a whole lot of very caring conscionable Australian seamen tie up the ships because either the ships are not repaired in Australia or the seamen are not paid wages which Australian seamen feel are humane and reasonable enough to put them out of business and you are going to have resentment.

Moore: Are you speaking of Singapore specifically at this stage?

Prime Minister: No, I'm speaking of the ASEAN countries because there was a meeting of the Secretariat recently to respond to a request for a dialogue on trade and the possibility of some trade contract or agreement and it was almost laughed out of court because each one of the members has gone through this process.

Moore: I'm sorry, my point was a new one. Speaking now specifically of Singapore, are you in a position to offer Australian businessmen concessions such as would encourage them to take their resources and capital from Australia and set up again in Singapore?

Prime Minister: You are inciting me now on this television programme to say something which will enrage your unions and cause a great deal of flurry ...

Moore: No, I'm not, I am asking you a fair question.

Prime Minister: Just as I am beginning a visit, a friendly one which I hope will leave friendship in the nook of mercy and friendliness all round, but you are asking me now to say yes, indeed, I'll give Australian industrialists all these benefits, they will move their capital, they will manufacture in Singapore and send it back, all the finished products in Australia and I will have the unions right down my throat.

Moore: But what is the answer?

Randall: This is one case where we don't have to quote another journalist. Just reading your statutes it's obvious that you do offer very great incentives to foreign investors, including Australians. What sort of corporate citizens do you find Australian companies to be in Singapore? Could I just put one thing to you that's been reported occasionally? Occasionally Australian companies complain that they have run into difficulties with your public authorities of being over-generous on their payment of wage rates, for example.

Prime Minister: Are they?

Randall: Over generous in the payment of wage rates. Getting above the general level of ...

Prime Minister: I complain that my voters are getting more than they ought to get?

Randall: So we're told.

Prime Minister: I'd be delighted. You know, I am really amazed that there I have three supposedly intellectual TV types with, you know, well-read backgrounds and in-depth study, and I am getting thrown back at me a lot of spurious stuff, some of which I find too ludicrous for comment.

Randall: Well, we are telling you things that are said about your country in this country and some businessmen who operate in Singapore have said that the public authorities there have told them it is not in the public interests of Singapore to get ahead of the general level of wage increases.

Prime Minister: Oh no! And I stop him from paying his workers more?

Randall: I don't know that anybody's going to be stopped.

Prime Minister: You know, I am all in favour of wage restraints and so on in a time of crisis or inflation, but anybody who wants to give his wealth away is welcome to do so.

Moore: Prime Minister, what is the attitude of your country now towards East Timor? Is that a settled issue as far as you are concerned or what? I mean, as you well know, it's a topic of some debate in Australia at present and I wondered what your view was.

Prime Minister: Well, our view was expressed I think very eloquently by a colleague of mine at the United Nations, and I would hate to paraphrase him — if you had given me notice, I would have brought a piece of paper along like you have. When I read it at the time I thought, well, how very diplomatically and tactfully put, but if I try and do a paraphrase and I put the wrong word in, you know, Chinese proverb says, (Mr. Lee speaks in Chinese), one word goes out, four horses can't pull it back. So I am not going to put one wrong word out, if I may, on East Timor or for that matter on any other subject.

Mediansky: Sir, on Timor, let me give my paraphrased version of what I understand your policy to be.

Prime Minister: Thank you. I knew that you would have something up your sleeve.

Mediansky: Well, thank you sir, I keep cards there. I understand that of the ASEAN group of countries, your policy on Timor is the most similar to that of Australia. Have your relations, as a result of that policy, with Indonesia been affected by this issue, by the Timor issue at all?

Prime Minister: I wouldn't think so at all. First of all, let me — before all this leads to cables flying back and forth to Singapore and elsewhere in Southeast Asia — let me explain that I don't know whether it is similar or dissimilar. We have a stand and we have defended that stand. It is not as welcomed and forthcoming as the Indonesian Government would wish us to be, but in the circumstances of the case it is understood, not with great warmth of — or rather, not the way they think we should have understood it, but it has been accepted and is a position which we take, which we think, in the circumstances, is not only honest to ourselves but honest to them and to the world and I think that it is very difficult to maintain a long-term relationship of friendship and understanding if we begin to misunderstand each other, particularly if we begin to think that we can expect unquestioning support when that support has not been sought beforehand.

Moore: Could I ask you, Prime Minister, what does the current shuffle in the higher reaches of the hierarchy in China mean, if anything, to Singapore, the region, Australia? I am asking you obviously to chance your arm a little there, but do you have any thoughts on that?

Prime Minister: Well, I am chancing my arm much less now than say two weeks ago. I would think a lot of people in Southeast Asia would have sighed with considerable relief that there are men in charge who would be continuing this policy of good government-to-government relations and relatively muted ideological and other party-to-party support, from communist party to communist parties in Southeast Asia, and we hope that this would continue to the advantage of peace in the region.

Moore: And what about the new government in Thailand? Is that a pointer in the same direction or quite unconnected or what?

Prime Minister: No, I think that is a completely unconnected issue ...

Moore: I don't mean casually connected, but I mean, does it suggest a movement in the same direction of a presumably less ...

Prime Minister: No, no, my goodness me, I mean that is an entirely different proposition altogether. This is after the event. Nobody in Southeast Asia expected the kind of civilian representative government that went before it to last, but I must say that whilst we all wish it a more effective government, we also hope — or I hope — that effective government does not necessarily have to be accompanied by a show of effectiveness, that once it has established itself, then the more traditional Thai characteristics of gentleness will reappear.

Randall: Prime Minister, given what has happened in Thailand, given the Timor problem in Indonesia, President Marcos' current referendum on the affirmation of his own present form of government there, what sort of prospects would you give ASEAN at the moment as an effective co-ordination force in any field, but particularly, I suppose the economic one for its member countries in Southeat Asia?

Prime Minister: First, I don't see the nexus between the three events you have related — the new Government in Thailand, the position in East Timor and President Marcos' referendum, I think they are three unrelated facts. That having been said, I would go on to say that never before — and I speak as one who has been sceptical of ASEAN for a long while because it didn't get moving, there was a lot of talk, but there were very few decisions, hard decisions, but I must say that in Bali, earlier this year, in February, some hard decisions were taken — small steps — and maybe it was because every Government knew, after April 1975, both Cambodia and South Vietnam, and Laos, subsequently, that we are on our own; nobody's going to fight any battles for us other than ourselves. If we believe that it is worth fighting for, then we start doing things now and the will is there — never been there in the same manner before. The problem now is whether the organisational capacity to translate decisions into policies, into facts, into factories, into living preferential trading arrangements which is what they have called the system which we have agreed as the initial steps towards economic co-operation, will be implemented fast enough. This is the problem.

Randall: Why do you think that the rather diffused approach that Australia made earlier this year for some form of association, really didn't get beyond that, was laughed out of court? Do you think that the new one, which apparently had been launched now as a result of President Suharto's and Mr. Fraser's talks, will get any further. Is there any room for it to go any further?

Prime Minister: I am not so sure. I think if ASEAN governments are convinced that Australians are prepared to be serious about it and not just make token concessions, then it will be seriously looked at. It is a question of good faith and ...

Randall: That's not there at the moment?

Prime Minister: Well, it's not so much not there. I mean from past experience trade has been extremely difficult. There was a brief moment, before the oil crisis and inflation and unemployment when your former Prime Minister, Mr. Whitlam, brought the fences down and for nine to twelve months trade blossomed. Then came the recession and up went the barriers.

Mediansky: Sir, another question on ASEAN from a different point of view. When you were in Peking last May, you said in part in your major speech that "the solidarity of ASEAN countries will increase our ability to avoid external pressure or manipulation". What were you trying to convey to the Chinese Government with that statement?

Prime Minister: I wasn't trying to convey anything to the Chinese Government other than the simple words of that statement, that I believe if there is more co-operation and co-ordination between the ASEAN countries, it is less likely that anybody can play the ASEAN countries one at a time to the disadvantage of the others. And I would have thought that that statement was self-evident.

Randall: You probably noticed, also in April, before you went to Peking, the argument published by the Asian Defence Journal suggesting the case for a combined defence force of the ASEAN countries. Do you think that's ... ?

Prime Minister: Which Defence Journal?

Randall: The ASEAN Defence Journal.

Prime Minister: Where was it published? You mean the one by the Institute of Strategic Studies in ... sorry, I mustn't put it to you, I am trying to pull you out of your little ...

Randall: Well, let's ignore the source. The suggestion has been put in more than one place that one of the manifestations of ASEAN solidarity in the sense that your quote in Peking could have been construed as was in a combined defence force for whatever defined purpose.

Prime Minister: No, I think before we get to a combined defence force, we've got to get first into some kind of economic harmonization. You don't get into NATO without first some agreement about trade between the West Europeans and between the West Europeans and the Americans. What is defence in aid of? In aid of your freedom, of your liberty, of your physical well-being and your material well-being. Well, we've got to put that first. When that comes about, the next step is political

347

co-ordination so that you identify common political problems to the region, common threats to the stability and security of the region. Only after that do you come to a common defence position or a security position. I think first the economics, then the foreign affairs side, then the defence side.

Moore: Where does Australia come into this thinking then? From your point of view? Do you see ...

Prime Minister: I don't think Australia comes into the ASEAN concept at all. Australia, like Japan or other countries who would wish ASEAN well, could help in several fields: one in getting the economic side going, by, for instance, (when your recession is over and your unemployment is resolved and your inflation has been beaten), loosening up on trade and allowing ASEAN products to come in. Then some political consultation and identifying common political problems and on the security side, perhaps if you manufacture defensive weapons like surface-to-air missiles and so on, well, you might be able to supply the countries of Southeast Asia with the wherewithal to defend their independence and sovereignty with weapons which are not prohibitive to ...

Moore: But there is no specific strategic or defence policy that, if Australia only had, would fit in very nicely, to put in mildly, with the ASEAN grouping?

Prime Minister: I would have thought that the very fact that there were five non-communist countries in Southeast Asia — not as democratic as the Australians would wish, but not democratic in the People's Democracy sense of the word, would be a very great security plus to you, wouldn't it?

Randall: Is the Five Power Defence Agreement based on Malaysia and Singapore any sort of bar to your own Government and Malaysia advancing the sort of ideas you've talked about with ASEAN?

Prime Minister: I think we are anticipating too many things. It will take us several years to get to that stage and discussing it in public in this way will only retard that process.

Randall: Well, perhaps, in broader terms, do you think that the assessment of the Australian Prime Minister in June this year, and his foreign policy statement, that reasonable people could reasonably conclude that the Soviet Union still sought to expand its influence throughout the world in order to achieve what he called, Soviet primacy, is a view that you would share or that your colleagues in ASEAN would share?

Prime Minister: I didn't read that very carefully and I wouldn't like to put it in that way. My colleagues and I, and I think the governments of the ASEAN countries, from our experience of the Soviet Union, find them very unlike the Americans. The Americans are apologetic, a little bit hesitant, explaining things away why the Secretary of State had promised this, but Congress had done the other, and dealing with the Soviet Union and their Ministers and their Ambassadors, it is a vast difference because here is a power that's completely self-confident. It has been slightly the underdog in the early years after 1945, it's now accepted as an equal superpower with equivalents or rough equivalents in missiles, in everything, and it's now forging ahead and it is completely self-confident, not apologetic, and if one could choose an emotively neutral word, quite determined that the Soviet Union should be respected and should have its views heard and properly considered in all parts of the globe.

XXVIII

Two days later, Lee spoke at a parliamentary luncheon in Canberra. Both Mr. Fraser and the previous Prime Minister were present. Lee said there were very few countries he went to where he knew the Prime Minister and the Leader of the Opposition so well, and how each had achieved and deserved high office. Australians had a reputation in Southeast Asia for being an open, frank and uninhibited people. And, as befits the people, so the political leaders, and their style of political contest. There was that robust spirit of a vigorous people, often bubbling over to rumbustiousness. Behind all the political skirmishing and sniping, there used to be a great deal of common ground between the Government and the Opposition. He had been told that in recent months, some bitterness had crept into the political debate and that party partisanship had spread beyond the political parties into once traditionally neutral areas. But he had also been told that the tough fabric of Australian politics could take these temporary aberrations and pressures without much harm. Moreover, those who knew Australia well had told him there was really little that the politicians could do to prevent it from being a wealthy and happy country. It was only in poor developing countries like Singapore, with slender resources, that politics had to be taken seriously, and politicians carried a heavier responsibility for the miseries which were so often the common lot of their people. There were enormous resources in Australia which, as they were extracted, would lubricate any social or political friction. It was almost impossible to be angry and spiteful for long in a country where there were so many of the good things of life, and most of them nearly for free.

In 1973, the future promised an increasingly wealthy and abundant Australia. With the commodity boom, the industrial nations scrambled to stock up essential minerals. Even in early 1974, after the oil crisis, no one could have foretold that unemployment would become an Australian malady although by then there were some nagging signs of inflation. Now, it seems that the world's industrial countries were not going to rush in to grab Australia's natural resources. "I have read that some have to be persuaded to invest heavily to get the minerals extracted. But these are ephemeral problems. Given a strong and vigorous people, intelligent enough to know that they need not work so hard since nature has endowed them with so much, Australians are bound to prosper in a world where population pressures on finite resources must increase in the long run." And as political parties competed for votes, Australians were bound to get an ever greater spread of wealth. Eventually, even the pursuit of happiness might become the business of politicians who might promise this when all the material wealth and comfort had not brought happiness. Perhaps new drug therapies might help to redeem such pledges of politicians. Such was the problem of the biological and chemical sciences.

"I have had several references made to the problem of durability, and I feel that amongst friends I must share the secrets. First, one has got to start very young. It has a great advantage. Second, one has got to get over the temptation of the news media capturing one's soul. Third, never mind what the news media says, just keep the people well-fed, well-educated, well-housed, and promise them that little bit more over the horizons, provided they work. But that is only for Singapore. I do not know why it is or how it is, but my friend Gough always arouses that something in me. He enthuses me. He referred to Papua New Guinea. And I thought to myself, how kind of him to have thought of the new economic order, and to remind Australians, because if I were to do it, it would be so churlish of a guest, that this new economic order means that all the wealthy of the world please chip in and give to the poor of the world like me. I feel a little embarrassed everytime mention is made to me and my leadership. I believe I often look around to see if there is somebody else that they were talking about. Perhaps he has the secret. But the simple way is to speak the truth, and describe it as you see it. Finally, to you, Mr. Prime Minister, and the Leader of the Opposition, and to Mr. Sinclair, and to all Parliamentarians present, who are competing and thereby contributing to the well-being of this continental island paradise of the South Pacific, may I express my thanks to you all for this warm welcome."

The following day, the Prime Minister lunched with the National Press Club in Canberra. What would Southeast Asia be like by 1980? Lee said that four years ago, he had not foreseen that the Paris Agreement would be signed in January 1973, allowing American forces to leave without undue haste, and that after two years the North Vietnamese divisions would demolish the South. But then, no one could have foreseen Watergate. Nor did he foresee the Arab-Israeli war in October 1973, the oil embargo, followed by two years of world recession. On 2 November they would know whether the polls had not been misleading them over the past few months. But every Southeast Asian was conscious of the limits on policies of any American President, placed by both the Congress and the mass media, on any military involvement in Southeast Asia. On the other hand, every Southeast Asian would blanch at the prospect of having American influence displaced by the dominance of another great power. They assumed that an American naval task force would continue to be in the region, a factor for regional stability, balancing the strength of the Soviet fleet in the Pacific and Indian Oceans, and safeguarding free access to the Gulf.

Then the question of China's leadership after Chairman Mao. New situations had to be met. New problems would have to be resolved. A younger generation of leaders would have the thoughts of Chairman Mao to guide their policies. Southeast Asians had grounds for hope, that in the next four years, foreign policy would not change, and that good government-to-government relations would be maintained, with party-to-party ideological support for communist groups in Southeast Asia kept at the current relatively low levels. ''As for the Soviet Union, I presume there will be little change in the nature of the leadership and its policies, whatever changes there may be due to age or retirement. Soviet policy has been active and outward-going. Soviet underwriting of Cuba's intervention in Angola last year was an enormous boost to her prestige in the Third World because, unlike the American intervention in Vietnam, it succeeded. The implications were grave enough for Dr. Kissinger to go to Southern Africa to defuse Southwest Africa and Rhodesia. But when and how is South Africa itself to be defused?''

Against this background, Lee said his guess was that by 1980, the domino theory would not have been proved or disproved. The travail of successive Thai civilian governments since October 1973, after more than twenty years of military government, was to have been expected. Thailand's security depended as much upon whether the communist powers and Vietnam increased aid to Thai insurgents, as upon how the Thai Government responded to insurgency threats in its social, economic and military policies. China had a special interest in the extent of other great-power influence in Thailand, so near her southern boundaries. The Vietnamese had the Soviet Union as their main source of supplies for reconstruction. For some years it might not suit the Soviet Union to intensify Sino-Soviet conflicts in the post-Mao era. Furthermore, the Vietnamese might decide that their priorities should be the consolidation of their administration, and reconstruction of their economy. So, despite the rhetoric of people-to-people help for so-called liberation wars, they might not give substantial aid to neighbouring guerilla groups.

If external pressure was not intensified, the Thais would have time to adjust themselves, to mobilise their resources to tackle their problems. They were nett food exporters. One cause for concern was a slow-down in new investments, which was adding to unemployment, especially in Bangkok. Whatever the form of government in Thailand, it must increase returns to their farmers, and it must attract investments and create more jobs, especially in Bangkok. Public support was necessary for social, economic and security policies. The military leaders had to contain insurgency. But the government must rally political support for such security operations. If the Thai government could do this, it would become clear, if not by 1980 then by the middle '80s, that Thailand was not a domino. Moreover, no Thai government could contemplate neutralism as a serious policy choice. The Thais had seen what Laotian neutralism meant, for ordinary Laotians, for the neutralist leaders, for the monarch and for

Buddhism. It was not a solution any government with a feel for Thai history could consider, other than as a prelude to total submission.

Lee turned to Peninsular Malaysia. Since the communist armed revolt in 1948, which ended in 1960, Peninsular Malaysia had made considerable economic strides. The economy had been diversified. The GNP more than doubled from 1960 to 1975. Rural areas benefitted as much as the urban area. Some foreign correspondents had asked if there should not be more positive support for the government from the non-Malays in the fight against subversion and insurgency. Recent Malaysian Government shift in emphasis, from attacking Malay poverty, to attacking poverty as such, regardless of race, was a sign that the government was alive to this problem, and was seeking to broaden its policies for multi-racial support. Furthermore, an insurgency led by a mainly ethnic Chinese leadership of the CPM (Communist Party of Malaya), however conceived in class struggle, could easily turn into race conflicts. Also, the Maoist concept of the countryside surrounding the towns meant that the communist would have to mobilise the Muslim Malays, who were the bulk of the country-side, to surround the towns, predominantly Chinese. These problems must long have troubled the Communist Party of Malaya. Indeed, communist attempts to widen support, both by recruiting Thai Malays into their assault units, and Malay writers and journalists in the mass media, showed a lively awareness of this problem.

They must also be acutely aware that before they could make a serious bid for power, they must be able to present themselves as a multi-racial group, including a credible Malay component, in a united-front leader-ship. They might not be able to do this for many years.

As for Indonesia, the country should be secure from communist insurgency for a long time. It was not easy to rebuild the North Kali-mantan communists along the Borneo border between Sarawak and Kali-mantan. Nor was it likely that there could be a revival of separatist groups in Sumatra. And whatever resistance was left of Fretilin in Timor appeared manageable. This tranquil state of affairs would prevail up to and probably well beyond 1980. However, if and when insurgency increased in Peninsular Malaysia, communist groups in Singapore would have got active in support of the effort there. They were still recruiting amongst students in some Chinese secondary schools and in tertiary insti-tutions. Their recruitment was from groups as broad and diverse as construction workers to journalists and editorial writers, both in the Malay and the Chinese press. But the scale was modest, compared to the overwhelming and intimidating thoroughness of control they exercised in the fifties and sixties. Their long-established cells had always sought to re-establish their united front of workers, students and intellectuals.

Recent disclosures of their revival in new recruiting had caused surprise rather than alarm. It was a reflection of the different circum-stances of Singapore in the mid-seventies. Communism no longer had that Messianic appeal. It used to appear as an irresistible revolutionary force, attracting enough activists who took to arson, assassination and riots, and nearly succeeded in making the majority acquiesce in their methods and goals. The economic and social circumstances were now different. Economic development helped, especially where the benefits of this development had been widely spread. And more equal opportunities and social mobility had loosened up conflicts generated by unequal opportunities based on wealth, race, language or religion. Perhaps more important had been the widespread awareness of the realities of communist societies in other parts of Asia, that communism meant for Singapore a loss of freedom of choice in their personal lives, and a much reduced standard of living.

After Vietnam, there was a greater sense of unity and urgency for co-operation in the countries of ASEAN. There were hopes of normal and beneficial economic relations with Vietnam in June 1976. The Vietnamese Vice-Foreign Minister visited Southeast Asia, assuring all governments that they wanted normalised relations on the basis of non-interference, equality, and mutual benefit, spelt out under four conditions. But these hopes were dampened after the Colombo Non-Aligned Conference in August when Vietnam supported a move by Laos to reject the Kuala Lumpur declaration for a Zone of Peace, Freedom and Neutrality, which had been accepted in the Non-Aligned Summit of 1973 in Algiers. ASEAN countries were reminded of the different nature and objectives of the Indo-Chinese governments.

ASEAN countries have never been more conscious of their common interests in regional peace and stability. The spirit of co-operation had never been stronger. The problem was that the organisational capacity to give substance to this desire for regional solidarity was not adequate for the job. It was taking too many months to get broad agreements, already settled by ASEAN heads of government, implemented at official levels. "If ASEAN is to be an effective foreign policy instrument for the five countries, then great effort must be made to build up the organisational muscle, so that plans can get implemented with greater expedition. This is the immediate challenge to ASEAN."

Australians had shown a friendly interest in the future of ASEAN. The question some Australians must have asked was whether it was possible to spread insurgency in the islands of Southeast Asia ... as it had spread in the Indo-Chinese states of Southeast Asia. Parts of the Philippines showed that this may be the case. If so, then Australians would watch with more than ordinary interest the developments in the countries of ASEAN, as they strived for greater co-operation and strength for a stable and secure Southeast Asia.

In a question and answer session after the luncheon, Lee was asked about the boycott of the previous day's luncheon by sixteen members of the Labour Opposition. They had asked for an explanation on five points. A questioner asked Lee about two of the matters on "the detention without trial of many opponents of your government, including well-

353

known journalists and the poet, Said Zahari, for periods up to thirteen years. And, secondly, the curtailment of trade union rights in Singapore such as the Trade Union Amendment Act of 1966''.

Prime Minister: Well, in 1963 when Said Zahari and a few others were detained, the powers of detention were exercised by a Security Committee, in then self-governing Singapore which included a British Chairmañ, a Singapore Minister and a Malaysian Minister. And after the uprising in Brunei and subsequent disorders in Singapore and Malaysia, a group of people were detained — I think somewhere around sixty or seventy. Two of them have not been released because they refused to give a simple undertaking: one, not to use force to overthrow a government, two, not to support the Communist Party of Malaya. I think they are relatively simple undertakings to give for all peace-loving citizens, and I would sincerely hope that the sixteen members of Parliament will write to these two gentlemen and ask them to give these two simple undertakings so that they can have all the freedom they desire. And I think that may have a much more beneficial effect then asking me the same questions over and over again. The second point — the curtailment of trade union rights. I think you may have got the dates wrong. These 16 obviously have been misled by whoever gave them the data. The amendment of the trade union legislation was in 1968 after the British withdrawal took place. We then faced a cut of some 20 per cent of our GNP in less than three years and an increase in unemployment estimated at between seventy thousand to one hundred thousand people, both directly employed by the British and servicing British forces then in Singapore. And if you recall Singapore of the 1950s and the early '60s, it was quite a riotous and boisterous place, where riots and strikes and civil commotion were part of the order of the day. And we introduced certain amendments like no strikes or no union leaders being able to call a strike without a secret ballot being first taken to make it lawful. I think it was a very considerate and a reasonable proposition because the proof is really in the much more healthy trade union situation which now exists in Singapore, in the blossoming industries and the fact that unemployment is marginal.

Question: I'm a member of the Amnesty International local branch ... they reported that political detainees in Singapore were subjected to various forms of physical and mental torture. In a speech to the Commonwealth Press Union on 30 September 1974, you gave your reasons why torture was used when you said: In this way, we can transform a bold and fearless critic into a willing and complying sychophant. Is this reason still valid and, Mr. Prime Minister, is the practice of torture still widely used in Singapore?

Prime Minister: I think you border on the comic. I am very pleased that you put them all together because you make my job so much simpler. I'll send you a copy of the speech I made at the Commonwealth Press Union. They included very sober people who would find considerable embarrassment in your quoting what I said somewhat out of context. I

354

assured the pressmen that all the Singaporean journalists present there knew just what a panoply.of instruments we had, both ancient and modern electronic, by which we transformed fearless critics to spineless sychophants ... We have such things called writs for assault. Civil suits can be brought and appeals can go right up to the Privy Council. And we have urged both Socialist International and Amnesty International to finance these suits so that adequate publicity can be given as to our methods of interrogation and torture, if any, and the world will be that much the more knowledgeable about how we do things in Singapore.

May I explain that every five years at the outside, I have to submit myself to a secret ballot and for every individual you detain, you antagonise his family, his friends and you give a stick to your political opponents to beat you with. And I have not the slightest doubts that my political opponents will take these sticks and beat me at the next election. If you want to help them, there is nothing to prevent you when election time comes to turn up in Singapore and watch the fun and games.

Question: Prime Minister, is the Soviet Union still trying to have access in Singapore for naval repair facilities or any other facilities for that matter and if so, what is your current attitude?

Prime Minister: Well, I have said on two occasions since I arrived that the Soviet Union is uninhibited to any sense of guilt or constraint in acting other than as the great power that she is, and she seeks no reason why she shouldn't repair her ships in Singapore, whether they are trawlers or cargo vessels or even tourist vessels. But I do not know what exactly is the reason they have, as yet, not sent in naval vessels. They did send a naval tender — it is one of these feeding vessels, a mother ship, I think way back in 1972. If I remember rightly, that was as a result of some provocation given, that Singapore would be scared to repair Soviet vessels because other people might get angry with us. So they sent in a mothership and we repaired it. But they haven't sent in anything with more sophisticated gear on board and they wouldn't like anybody else other than trusted Russians to go prowling around these ships.

In a statement released as he was leaving Australia on 29 October, Lee said his discussions with Mr. Malcolm Fraser on international and regional matters had given him a better insight into his thinking and policies. "He is a realist. Our frank exchange on present trends was valuable because it gave me a three-dimensional perspective of the Australian government's view of the contemporary world." On major issues they were in broad agreement. With continuing American interest in the stability of the West Pacific area, a new security balance could be established by the contending, and sometimes complementary, interests of America, China and the Soviet Union. It would now require greater co-operation amongst the countries of the region. In particular, non-communist Southeast Asia must be more self-reliant and united in meeting their common problems. An era of dominant Western influence in Asia was over. And American intervention in guerilla wars was unthinkable.

However, co-operation in investments and trade between Japan, the countries of ASEAN, Australia and New Zealand would make Congressional support more likely for whoever was elected as American President and wanted to maintain a continuing American naval and economic presence in these regions.

"I believe relations between Australia and the countries of ASEAN have improved. It is becoming a more mature relationship, one between adults. The donor-donee relationship does not engender that mutual respect which is essential for long-term co-operation." There were difficulties in making any move "at present" on easing imports into Australia from the countries of ASEAN. But, in about twelve to eighteen months, when the Australian economy recovered, Lee hoped there would be a gradual and graduated lowering of tariff and non-tariff barriers to trade between the ASEAN countries and Australia. This was the best way to guarantee better relations between Australia and her immediate neighbours to the north. The connections between Australia and Singapore, dating back to the days of empire, had made for a hard-headed understanding of each other. Realistic and sympathetic understanding had been maintained, despite the vast changes in respective circumstances. "My government welcomes the promise of continuing co-operation with Australia in improving Singapore's defence capability. The significant emphasis is that any training is to help Singaporeans to look after themselves."

XXIX

On 4 November, back in Singapore, Lee was able to send a congratulatory message to Mr. Jimmy Carter, the President Elect of the United States: "On behalf of the Government of Singapore, may I extend my congratulations to you on your election to the high office of President of the United States. Under your leadership, I am confident that the United States will help maintain a balance of great power interests in the Indian and Pacific Oceans, and thereby contribute to the stability and development of the countries in the region."

XXX

The Prime Minister spoke about the Republic's problems of pollution when he attended the horticulture and aquarium fish show at the National Stadium on 5 November. "Many people in Singapore keep orchid plants in their homes or compounds. Some have colourful fishes in their living rooms. By tending to these orchids or fishes, they get relaxation better than any tranquiliser." Over the years, much expertise and knowledge had

356

been built up. In this show, the best flowers and fishes were in competition. The results of experiments of the orchid hybridiser and the aquarium fancier were on display for recognition. Continuing improvement and the development of new orchid types and aquarium fishes would result from competition. Those who scientific curiosity and tender care succeeded in bringing out new and colourful crosses of plants or fishes, would be rewarded. New hybrids found attractive and popular would have to be stabilised into stable new types. Many enthusiasts had turned their hobbies into profitable enterprises. In 1975, export of orchids from Singapore reached $7.5 million, an increase of 1600 per cent in ten years. The export of aquarium fishes was $14 million, 640 per cent increase in ten years. This trade grew with the increase in air freight capacity mainly from Singapore to Europe. Opportunities in the Japanese, Australasian and American markets could be seized when air freight to these areas become regular, more frequent and cheaper.

Flowers and fishes added to the gracious living in the home. Unlike loud stereo and TV, they did not disturb neighbours. Outside, in the streets and parks, the government was creating a pleasant and attractive environment, especially for pedestrians. "After six years of intense work, planting roadside trees and shrubs, covering concrete retaining walls with ivy and creepers, fences with hedges, and landscaping more parks and green spaces, we are making Singapore a more gracious and cooler city for everyone. We are now expanding the walkways linking shopping areas and parks." For more than twenty years, roads were widened to take take more cars. Parking lots were tarmaced. Pedestrian sidewalks were narrowed or abolished. The pedestrian had been squeezed in on to the roadsides. "We have now reversed this trend. There will be wider and safer walkways. The first pedestrian mall was at Raffles Place. The Orchard Mall has been a success. This Mall has now been extended from Ellis Road to the Handicraft Centre, from where it will reach the Botanic Gardens."

The Parks and Recreation Department was planning walkways for other centres of population besides the central area. They would widen existing five-foot-ways and place slabs over drains. Uneven levels of five-foot-ways would be graded for more uniform levels Non-slip tiles of different colours would be used, trees and shrubs planted. "In two years, we shall see a more attractive city." The next problem to tackle was roadside pollution from smoky exhausts, especially from buses, lorries and diesel taxis. There was inadequate preventive maintenance. The present practice was to repair a vehicle only after a breakdown or a summons for smoky exhaust. This would not do. SBS was building enough repair facilities to regularly check and service engines and keep them in good condition, whether or not faults appeared. Lorries and taxis must also have regular maintenance and preventive repairs.

A graduation parade was held at the Police Academy on 13 November to mark the first intake of officer cadets, and the fifth intake of full-time national servicemen, into the police force. The officers had been trained for nine months. Lee told them that they would have to lead police national servicemen who had done three months' training, followed by another three months of on-the-job training with experienced policemen. In the sixteen months since July 1975, when the first batch of two hundred and eleven started training, the Police National Servicemen had dealt with 1,630 cases. They made 2,314 arrests, leading to 437 convictions for criminal offences. "But policing does not mean merely arrests and convictions. It is upholding orderly life, a situation where people can go about their business and pleasure in peace and safety." Each year two thousand Police National Servicemen would join the force in four intakes of five hundred each. They would serve two years. Each year a hundred graduates were selected as Officer Cadets. They would serve two and half years. "By January 1978, we shall have 4,000 Police National Servicemen (36 per cent as Special Constables and 64 per cent as Vigilantes) and three hundred Officers." Each year two thousand Police National Servicemen (Special Constables and Vigilantes), one hundred Officers, would go into the reserves. They would do reserve duties, thus adding to Police manpower. "It is the impact of these men with Police Force training, discipline and powers spread all over Singapore that will be most significant. Grouped in areas where they live, they will be a natural security force for each housing estate, for each residential high-rise block, and for the office, shopping and warehousing areas near their homes. Their crime prevention capacity, the deterrent effect of their presence, will be considerable."

XXXI

Speaking at a gathering to celebrate the twenty-first anniversary of the PAP Thomson Branch on 17 November, the Prime Minister said that decisive events in settling the leadership of China, the election of Jimmy Carter as President of America, and the apparently unchanging Soviet leadership ("these three centres of power") set the new framework for international developments. In China, the developments seemed to favour a continuation of stable government-to-government relations between China and Southeast Asia. "In America, we shall have to wait several months to know the mettle of the new President and the men he will appoint as his principal Secretaries especially Secretary of State (foreign affairs) and Secretary for the Treasury (financial and economic affairs). But already we know that economic recovery in America is not as good as we forecast." Led by consumer spending, the recovery had not been followed by American investments in new industrial machinery. Political uncertainties, like the policies of a president then awaiting election, and the prospect of another increase in the price of oil, had not helped business of confidence. When industrial countries like America slowed down their economic recovery, when still facing heavy unemployment of more than 7½ per cent , the government would slow down overseas investments to keep more jobs at home. The momentum of Singapore's economic recovery would carry on into the middle of 1977. But unless American economic recovery got over "this stickiness", the effects on Japan and Western Europe would be bad. And this would also be bad for Singapore.

There was a danger of protectionist policies in trade to protect jobs. Some countries of Western Europe, especially Britain, faced balance of payments deficits against Japan. So the EEC had got the Japanese to agree to voluntary restraints on exports to EEC under threat of tariffs and quotas. In the five years before the oil crisis, ending in 1973, Singapore's rate of growth had been between 12-14 per cent per annum. Since 1973, it had been between 8 per cent for 1974, 4 per cent for 1975 and probably over 7 per cent for 1976. "We must hope that the present climate of unemployment and protectionism in America and Western Europe will pass with a return of business confidence under a new Carter Administration in America. Otherwise we may not be able to sustain an economic growth rate of 6-8 per cent".

Lee warned that they must be realistic in assessing the future. "We must prepare ourselves for the worst that can happen, lower our expectations, and gear ourselves for that extra effort." A recent survey by EBD and Ministry of Finance officers with a cross-section of manufacturers had revealed some interesting facts. Where employers were also manufacturing in Hong Kong, like textiles and garments, they complained that the Singaporean had not that same drive which the Hong Kong worker brought to his job. Japanese employers said that after 2-3 years' training, Singaporeans believed they were fully skilled when the truth was the Singaporean's productivity was only 75 per cent that of the Japanese skilled worker. American and West European employers reported that although Singaporeans had only 75 per cent the level of productivity of their workers in Western Europe and America, the Americans and Europeans believed that after several more years' experience under proper supervision, spurred on by appropriate incentive bonus schemes, Singaporeans could reach 95 per cent of the productivity of American or European workers.

"We cannot do much to change the external situation. It may become less favourable or more favourable for investments. We shall know within one to two years. But we can improve our internal situation. Our workers have to strive to reach the competence and skills and the productivity of the Japanese, Western European or American worker." Parents could not expect, and must not encourage, their children to select jobs which they and their friends considered socially desirable. "In these years of slower economic growth, we must consolidate our workers' skills. We must improve our education system and produce more trained workers and technicians and less students expecting jobs as clerks. Most important, we must dispel the belief that our sons and daughters can wait for better paid, cleaner and easier jobs, preferably in air-conditioned offices or hotels." To be hard-headed was to avoid disappointment. Singaporeans had always been quick to react to changed circumstances. That is why Singapore had done better than most in meeting the problems of the oil crisis with less recession and unemployment than Hong Kong or Taiwan. "We can continue to do better than most. But the Government must adjust its policies to encourage investments, to increase economic co-operation in ASEAN countries. Our traders and entrepreneurs must seek new markets, especially in the oil-producing countries. And our workers must respond to these changed conditions by increasing effort, resulting in higher skills and productivity."

XXXII

President Suharto of Indonesia paid an informal one-day visit to Singapore on 29 November. He was accompanied by Professor Widjojo Nitisastro, State Minister for Economy, Finance and Industry, Mr. Sudharmono, State Minister/Cabinet Secretary and several other officials. The Indonesian President had discussions with the Prime Minister before proceeding to Pulau Batam, Indonesia, in the afternoon.

XXXIII

The seventh WELCOME supermarket was opened by the Prime Minister on 25 November. Lee said: "We now have a network to check on the cost and profit margins of all essential commodities, like rice, noddles, bee hoon, milk powder, cooking oils, and detergents. We also know the cost and profit margins of the semi-essential items." In 1976, prices of food had fallen 6.4 per cent compared to 1975. So there was no excitement and little interest in food prices. But only three years ago in 1973, prices of food had been sky-rocketing. They went up about 49 per cent between 1972 and 1973. This was mainly because of bad harvests around the world. And with shortages, some wholesalers and retailers began hoarding and pushing prices up further. WELCOME supermarkets and the consumer clubs in the various constituencies must keep going. They had become a useful defence mechanism against profiteering when supplies for essential items, like rice, became scarce and prices shot up. Once in several years, world harvests would be poor either because of drought or flood. Then prices would go up, and shortages would be made worse by hoarding, speculating and profiteering.

For two years (1974 and 1975), those who brought from the WELCOME supermarkets had a rebate of 5 per cent on all purchases and a 6 per cent dividend on fully paid-up shares. There was every prospect of a similar rebate and dividend for 1976. For the year ending June 1976, WELCOME had 14,282 members and a turnover of $20.5 million. WELCOME supermarkets had kept prices of essentials low by cutting profit margins. So, other supermarkets and shops had to do likewise. The trend favoured the supermarkets because of bulk purchasing and lower overhead costs. "In all cities the world over, small shopkeepers have had to combine to form bigger shops or lose out to supermarkets. And that is the only way to lower costs and to offer variety."

XXXIV

International affairs were discussed by Lee in an interview by Mr. Motoo Kaede, a prominent Japanese journalist on 27 November.

Motto Kaede: After the war in Indo-China, the situation in Asia, particularly in ASEAN and its neighbouring countries facing the Indian Ocean, has changed. May I have your assessment on the current situation and your views on what will be necessary for ensuring stability in Southeast Asia?

Prime Minister: First, we must know what are the threats before we know what are the measures to counter these threats. We really are not in the position to say, as of now, what are the immediate threats. I do not believe that there will be an absence of American influence because if that was so, then there will be problems for the region. But the American influence will be more and more matched by influence from the Soviet Union. But in the economic field, the Soviet Union cannot match the combination of American economic influence and Japanese economic influence. And therefore, there will be some continuation of this kind of economic system which has prevailed before. The country facing the most difficult period of economic growth is Thailand because it had three years of relatively uncertain political situation in Thailand, with the result that investments have slowed down. And we must hope that confidence can be restored — confidence of Thai investors, and of American, Japanese and European investors in Thailand. Of course, once confidence is restored, investments will resume. The unemployment in Bangkok can be reduced and the country will face much less trouble from insurgents than if there is economic distress and unemployment. I think this is a very critical factor. This is one of the major concerns for the whole region. It's not just a Thai problem because when the problems of insurgency become magnified, it is bad for Thailand and other countries in Southeast Asia.

Motoo Kaede: May I have your comment on how ASEAN countries and Japan should develop their co-operation?

Prime Minister: This is a very tired question because so many people

361

have asked this question and there have been so many replies. I think it would be very unproductive for me to give a new variation of old replies. I think, by and large, Japan and the Japanese Government — Japanese industrialists and Mr. Miki, in particular, know what the problem is. And it is quite simple to establish in the minds of the people and the governments of ASEAN a confidence that Japanese intentions are not just to extract raw materials and to sell industrial manufactured products to the region; that in fact Japan intends to transfer skills, technology, capital into the region, however slowly it may be, to help the region develop so that they can, over several decades, become more industrialised. That is a very simple explanation of the problems. It cannot be solved by words. It cannot be solved by communiques. It must be solved by a series of actions which will make people in Southeast Asia believe that this is not just a public relations exercise.

Motoo Kaede: In China, after the death of Chairman Mao Tse-tung, there has been political turmoil. How does this affect the situation in Southeast Asia, particularly Chinese merchants living in the area?

Prime Minister: I think there has been very little turmoil since the death of Chairman Mao. In fact, it's remarkable how the situation has been resolved in such a decisive way without bloodshed. I believe that this means that the policies which were recommended by the "Gang of Four" will be pushed aside and sound government-to-government relations, including trade relations, will continue to develop and improve for everybody's benefit. But, of course, we must also recognise that this is a government which is based on Marxist-Leninist-Maoist principles, and therefore they must, in accordance with those principles, give moral support to Marxist-Leninist parties and Maoist parties in the region. So we must expect that.

Motoo Kaede: Recently, you went to Peking. You met Premier Hua. I would like to have your view on the future course of the Premier Hua's Administration. Do you think it will last long. Will there be another struggle among the leadership for power?

Prime Minister: I am not able to answer that question.

Motoo Kaede: Now, in the United States, Governor Carter was elected President and he will make some new approach to PRC. Recently, Senator Mansfield made some reports on the US policy towards PRC. What do you think of the future relationship between the United States and PRC?

Prime Minister: The statement made by Senator Mansfield was, at the same time, refuted by another Congressional group that had visited China. I do not believe that the situation between the United States and the PRC can remain static. I think moves must be made to take further steps in accordance with the Shanghai Communique. Either moves must be made to show further developments or there may be a loss of momentum in the normalisation of relations which people like Senator Mansfield obviously feels is undesirable. But what those moves are, I don't think we are in a position to say because I am quite sure President-elect Mr. Carter having stated all the things that he stood for during the election campaign and in their much publicised debates, is not likely to vary his position too much, too quickly. It is not possible. It would not be in keeping with what we know of Mr. Carter.

XXXV

Thong Chai Medical Institution treated 24,240 outpatients in the first six months of 1976. The land was given by the government in exchange for the old site. The building, furniture and equipment cost $3.8 million. Not taking the interests on this capital outlay, each patient-visit costs $3.20. This was also made possible because four Chinese physicians working to help Thong Chai were paid only an average of $400 per month each. "The government values the free medical services given by Thong Chai, Kwong Wai Shui and Chung Hwa hospitals," said the Prime Minister at the opening of Thong Chai Medical Institution Building, at Chin Swee Road, on 28 November. However, the statistics showed a clear trend from Chinese medicine towards western medical treatment in outpatient dispensaries and government hospitals. In 1955, the outpatient attendance rate per thousand of population was 1,230, that meant more visits than one person per year. In 1975, it rose to 1,680. Admissions to hospitals in 1955 were 52 per thousand; in 1975, 73 per thousand. Deliveries of babies in 1955, 40 per cent in the government hospitals; in 1975, 84 per cent. Another trend which would become more pronounced was the need for more medical care for more old people. In 1975, 6.6 per cent of population were over sixty years. They were 15.5 per cent for all hospital admissions but 27.4 per cent of long-staying patients. The percentage of over sixty years old was expected to increase from 6.6 per cent in 1975 to 9 per cent in twenty-five years. A practical solution had to be found by treating more patients without their having to be in hospitals. A compelling reason to find new solutions was the increasing costs of new hospitals and the annual increase in running costs. The new Singapore General Hospital, to be completed by 1980, would cost $200 million ($148 million for construction, $52 million for equipment). It would have 1,612 beds, or $125,000 per bed. "We do not know what the recurrent yearly costs will be. But it cannot be cheaper than the costs in the present Singapore General Hospital."

Excluding capital costs and equipment, cost per bed was $49 in the old Singapore General Hospital. 'A' class patients paid $60 per day plus service charges. 'B' class patients paid $30 per day plus service charges. 'A' class patients were paying slightly above cost to the government. 'B' class patients were paying about the actual cost. 'C' class patients paid a nominal $4 a day. It was not enough to pay for the cost of food, bedsheets and pyjamas. The medical treatment, drugs, nurses and doctors were for free. This nominal charge ($1 per day for the long-staying patients like the chronic sick) had to be made to check the drift towards unnecessary hospitalisation for illnesses which could be treated as outpatients. "We have been raising our standards of medical and health facilities, and the professionalism of our specialists. Only by realistic policies, anticipating and solving new problems can we increase the range and sophistication of our medical facilities, with more specialists using more costly, specialised equipment and the trained staff to support them. And for the past three years, cost of drugs, vaccines, medical and surgical supplies have been growing at 12 per cent per annum." Quite rightly Singaporeans expected with lower birth rates, with two-child family as the target, the best medical services for their children. This must be provided. By 1985, Kent Ridge University would be ready with 752 beds. It would cost $135 million, or $182,000 per bed. Further expansion would depend on how the economy grew. It was the increasing numbers of older people who lived longer because of better standards of living and better medical treatment, who would be the largest group the health services would have to look after.

XXXVI

At the invitation of the Prime Minister, the President of Indonesia, Mr. Suharto, paid another informal visit to Singapore on 29 November. President Suharto was accompanied by Professor Widjojo Nitisastro, Minister of State for Economics, Financial and Industrial Affairs; Mr. Sudharmono, Minister/State Secretary, and other senior officials. President Suharto paid a courtesy call on President Sheares. President Suharto and Prime Minister Lee Kuan Yew held discussions on bilateral and ASEAN co-operation as well as international developments. Their Ministers and senior officials also held similar discussions. President Suharto and Prime Minister Lee Kuan Yew agreed that to strengthen bilateral economic relations, Indonesia and Singapore would co-operate closely in the development of Batam Island. It was also agreed that both countries would promote further co-operation in trade, the establishment of a submarine telecommunication link and the provision of financial and procurement support for purchase of ships.

President Suharto and Prime Minister Lee Kuan Yew emphasised the urgency to accelerate ASEAN co-operation agreed upon at the Bali Summit. In furtherance of this, they agreed on measures to expand intra-ASEAN trade through preferential trading arrangements, expedite regional industrial development by establishing more ASEAN industrial projects through more regular co-ordination and consultations among member states, and to encourage greater investments among member states by concluding investment guarantee and the avoidance of double taxation agreements. President Suharto and Prime Minister Lee Kuan Yew reiterated the desire of ASEAN to promote co-operative relations with other countries and international organisations and called on the developed countries to adopt policies which would encourage the flow of investments into ASEAN and expansion of trade between ASEAN and the developed countries. It was agreed that ASEAN should make a joint approach to the United States to preserve the present system of tax deferral for American investments in ASEAN.

President Suharto and Prime Minister Lee Kuan Yew exchanged views on regional and international developments and agreed that a stable and prosperous Southeast Asia would be a positive contribution to world peace. They called on member states in Southeast Asia and other states to develop mutually beneficial relations in the spirit of mutual respect and understanding. The talks were held in a frank and friendly atmosphere. President Suharto expressed his thanks and appreciation for the warm and cordial reception by the people and the Government of Singapore.

XXXVII

At the NTUC Seminar on "The Family and the Trade Union" on 5 December, Lee said that the economic outlook for 1977 appeared more troublesome. OPEC Ministers were meeting to consider price increase. The increase would come at a time when economic recovery in America, Europe, and Japan had shown signs of slowing down. There were also political uncertainties in the years ahead. If there was no progress in the Arab-Israeli problem after the new American President took over on 20 January 1977, there would be another political crisis in one to two years. And if it included an Arab oil embargo, the world would spin again into recession.

Of the industrial countries, two countries (West Germany and Japan) had done better than others in overcoming the economic problems of high oil prices. Both in Germany and in Japan, workers and management took pride in the quality of their products, the productivity of their workers and the efficiency of management. Workers and management did not see themselves in hostile camps, in constant conflict. In both countries, communist influence in the unions was negligible. Both lost the last war. Both had intense national unity to rebuild their devastated countries. "We must learn from the Germans and Japanese. The Managing Director of Jurong Shipyard, Mr. Sakurai, has been working in Singapore for over twelve years. What he has said recently, other Japanese employers will confirm. The Singapore worker is intelligent and quick to learn. But the Singaporean soon believes that he has learnt all there is to learn, when in fact he has not reached the standards of the Japanese skilled worker or technician. Mr. Sakurai said some home truths about the differences between the Singaporean and the Japanese. The Japanese worker goes out of his way to attend to work not strictly his. He attends to another worker's telephone when his fellow worker is absent. A skilled worker will clean up his machine and polish up the floor around it, whilst the Singaporean expects the floor to be cleaned by somebody else because it is not his duty. The Singaporean's attention is confined to his own job and his promotion prospects. He is not keen to widen his responsibilities. That, together, he and his fellow workers can make the company more efficient and productive, and therefore make more profits, bringing more wages for everyone, is too vague a vision and does not move him. Too many workers do not identify themselves with their companies like the Japanese workers do." One sympton of this lack of identification and loyalty was the habit of job-hopping. The government's representatives would ask the National Wages Council to consider a recommendation to discourage job-hopping for frivolous reasons by making NWC benefits applicable in proportion to the number of months they worked with the same employer in the past year, that was to say, the number of months worked divided by twelve.

"This eagerness to get on personally and individually is also to be found in young Singaporeans in the professions. Engineers in the ship-yards expect rapid promotion to higher positions. When they do not get promotions, they resign and move into other shipyards for slightly more pay. The same attitudes are found in our accountants, architects, lawyers, doctors and others. Rapid economic growth has made the young apprentice and the young professional in Singapore impatient for rapid promotions, anxious not to lose out on the economic boom. They want to rise quickly, often at the expense of thorough competence." With the world economic outlook less promising, Singapore had little hope of repeating the 12-14 per cent real growth per annum for 1970-73. Investments had slowed down. They might not pick up for quite some time because of excess of manufacturing capacity in America, Japan, and Western Europe. Unemployment was very high at 8 per cent in America. In the EEC, some five million workers were unemployed. World trade had slowed down from the growth rate of over 10 per cent in pre-recession years to a decline of 6 per cent in 1975. Fortunately, world trade was expected to rise to 8-10 per cent this year. "We must try to achieve an average of 5-7 per cent growth per annum in the next three years. To do this under adverse world economic conditions, we must change our work attitudes. The Singaporean must constantly improve his skills and be prepared to do work outside his specific duties." This was a period of consolidation as Singapore strived for higher skills and greater profes-sionalism. The chase for higher rewards and rapid promotions would sober down with more sober growth rates.

Lee said that part of the secret of German and Japanese strength was the ceaseless drive for higher standards and greater perfection. Germans and Japanese took pride in their national performance, as much as in their company's performance. It was when the people lost pride in their collective performance, and, worse, when they became selfish in pursuing sectional trade union interests, that a whole people suffered as their collective performance went down. "We have to learn from other systems that work. We must identify and select those factors in successful systems which are relevant to us and modify and adapt them to fit our cultural and social conditions."

XXXVIII

On 6 December, the Prime Minister, at the invitation of Datuk Hussein Onn, made an unofficial two-day visit to Malaysia. A joint statement on 7 December stated that the visit was made in context of exchange of informal visits between the Heads of Government of the two countries. The visit provided the two Prime Ministers and their Cabinet colleagues with the opportunity to exchange views on, and discuss developments in, the region in particular, and the world in general. The two Prime Ministers reaffirmed their full commitment to ASEAN and agreed to accelerate the implementation of the decisions taken at Bali by the ASEAN Heads of State and Government, especially in matters relating to the establishment of preferential trading arrangements and ASEAN industrial development. They also called for the establishment of additional ASEAN industrial projects, and the conclusion of investment guarantee agreements among member countries.

The two Prime Ministers agreed that ASEAN should continue to further develop co-operation with other countries and regional and international organisations. They also agreed that the developed countries had a role to play by adopting policies which would increase the flow of investments into ASEAN countries and promote the growth of trade between ASEAN and the developed countries. On economic co-operation, the two Prime Ministers reaffirmed the need for continued bilateral consultations to promote bilateral and regional co-operation especially on matters of mutual interest in trade and industry. They also agreed that the spirit of co-operation evidenced in the conclusion of the international agreement on natural rubber price stabilisation would also be extended towards the development and expansion of trade and investments within the region. On bilateral matters, the two Prime Ministers agreed to continue with the close co-operation in all fields, "and are determined to strengthen further the already good and close relationship existing between two countries."

XXXIX

While Lee was in Malaysia, a statement was issued to the effect that the Cabinet had advised the President to dissolve Parliament on 6 December and to name Monday, 13 December, 1976 as the date for nomination of candidates in the General Election. Voting would take place on Thursday, 23 December, 1976 which would automatically become a public holiday. Voting, the statement reminded, was compulsory.

XXXX

Speaking at the thirteenth anniversary celebration of Sim San Loke Hup Athletic Association, at Keong Saik Road, on 11 December, the Prime Minister noted that new high-rise buildings had sprouted around Keong Saik Road. "We are rebuilding the old city. In spite of these new buildings, the population in the central area has been decreasing. Most of them are office blocks, with banks and shipping in the podium floors. In the past seventeen years, many young people have moved out to set up their own homes in the new towns. So we have had to reduce fourteen central area constituencies into eight. The reason why few residential high-rise have been built is the higher land prices. In the past ten years, only about 16,000 units have been built by HDB and about 1,7000 units by the private sector under URA sales, and another 500 units on private land. Unless this trend is reversed, in another ten years, the present eight constituencies may be reduced to two. This should not happen, for if it does, we will have a city which is used only from 8.00 a.m. to 6 p.m. At night, there will be no life in the city."

To prevent this, some tough decisions had to be made. First, that land which was presently used for residential purposes should remain zoned as residential. There would be a few exceptions. Second, that all green spaces for recreation would be kept green, like Pearl's Hill, Fort Canning Central Park, Hong Lim Park. "Around them we shall build residential high-rise with offices and shopping on the podium blocks. However, we must lower the price of flats in the city centre so that they cost not much more than in the new towns." Amenities for sports like table-tennis, squash, netball, badminton and basketball, would be built in or near the high-rise. Swimming pools and gardens, though on a small scale, would be part of the central city housing. Car parking, at present $60 per month for covered parking in the city, might be reduced for residents to be more like the $15 per month charged for uncovered parking in the new towns.

There was considerable discussion planning on how to keep the population in the central city area. "We should have a city centre most of whose parks, shops and restaurants will be used beyond office hours. There will have to be a balance between expensive middle income and low income housing. For instance, on the Marina land being reclaimed in front of Telok Ayer Basin, most will have to be high quality residences to match the high quality buildings already along Shenton Way and Collyer Quay. But without the lower middle income and low cost housing for the lower paid workers, there will not be the social relationships that naturally exist in the new towns with mix of HUDC, five-room point blocks, four-rooms,

368

three-rooms, and so on."

Five senior Ministers had remained to look after their city constituencies now expanded — Goh Keng Swee, Toh Chin Chye, Rajaratnam, Ong Pang Boon and Lee himself. "We do not intend to let the population drift away from the city centre because of the high price of land. It would be wasteful to such a city. We must retain that unique feature of the Singapore that we have known so long, a city bustling with life from the crack of dawn to past midnight, one which throbs with life and vitality." So we shall have more areas like Tanjong Pagar Plaza, with a swimming pool (Yat Kit) nearby, a garden and green space (like Duxton Plain Parkway) and a community centre (Tanjong Pagar). Perhaps we have learned how to improve on this." After four and a half years of resettlement, demolition, rebuilding, Tanjong Pagar Plaza had about the same number of families, but all better housed in healthier surroundings. Those who resided in them would have all the amenities of a Queenstown, but with the advantage of being able to walk to school or walk to office, if they wanted to, or use their car if they had parking space at the office, or a wife to drive the car away, for they were already inside the ALS.

XXXXI

Soon after the nominations closed for the 1976 general elections on 13 December, the Prime Minister held a press conference. He summed up the nominations with the opening remark: "Sixteen seats are not contested, the rest, by a multitude of parties. A common denominator of these parties is that they like to be elected into office, a creditable ambition. Another common denominator, which isn't as creditable, is that they don't seem to know what is it they want to get into Parliament for. Most of them want to give away everything — lower taxes, lower rents, lower Public Utilities rates. Abolish National Service — says Barisan Socialis; or change it into a community service, says Workers Party. Dismantle the Internal Security Act and release all detainees. We stand for the security of Singapore which unfortunately demands that hard-core detainees who refuse to abjure the use of violence will have to be detained. If they denounce the use of force to take office, or just to live peacefully — even if they don't support a government, we are happy to save expense in having to feed them and care for them. We believe that National Service has built up a small, but in our circumstances, a credible defence capability. We intend to fight on these issues. We don't believe that the public will go in for these give-aways; unfortunately none of these people who say they are going to give them away, have either, by management of their own parties of their own personal fortunes, shown that they are able to accumulate anything. They can give it away, but they don't know how to make it. The PAP has built up over $8,000 million worth of foreign exchange. And I think if we start giving things away, we'll end up paupers — a broken-back state, like so many who are now not only classified as the Third World but as the Fourth World. We intend to stay as we are. Moving up gradually, slowly painfully through hard work, from the Third World — reaching out to a transition stage into the top half of the Third World.

Question: Do you consider this coming elections much easier compared to the last?

Prime Minister: My own assessment is that some of the grouses — not all — of the previous elections which accounted for 30 per cent votes, ought to be satisfied. We have taken some care to ensure that where resettlement has to take place, people are fairly adequately compensated and the social ecology is not too abruptly upset. In other words, not only are they compensated, by and large, they are also able to make a livelihood under new conditions. It is always a problem when you knock down a block of old buildings. They are usually rent-controlled, extremely cheap. Then you put shopkeepers into a new building, the rents are prohibitive or they find them prohibitive, because they've got to compete against the supermarkets. So we have found a way whereby we either give them an alternative occupation, or if they still think they can be in the grocery business, then they pay half the normal rent — going up by 10 per cent to the normal rent over a period of five years. We will be careful not to have too much disruption in the process of building or rebuilding the city.

Question: You expect to win all the seats?

Prime Minister: We fight to win. When we field a candidate, we field him seriously as a man who can look after his constituency and make an intelligent contribution to the national debate.

Question: Would you yourself not personally tend to favour some kind of an opposition in Parliment?

Prime Minister: The pity of it is, that nobody in the Opposition has got it in him to pose a rational alternative on how to make Singapore more viable, more secure, more prosperous, on how to give the people a better life. None of them has come up with any proposals for that. They haven't got either political sense or substance. They want to do what they think are the popular things, or what the Malayan Communist Party's followers believe are the popular things — like the abolition of the Internal Security Act and no detention without trial, dismantling of National Service, reunification of Singapore and Peninsular Malaysia into Malaya under 'genuine' terms. I believe the people are entitled to something better. We've got to be our own monitors, our own conscience keepers. That has been our difficult job over the past eleven years since 1965 when the Barisan Socialis, on instructions from higher-up, walked out of Parliment and decided to take the battle into the streets. Now, of course, they are left high and dry, because the people don't believe in them. The communists just write off another united front as worthless. But, of course, had we not been active earlier this year — Mr. Rajaratnam just hinted at it — the communists would have been in a position to mount a new united front.

370

Question: Prime Minister, why are you calling the elections now, instead of nearer the end of your party mandate?

Prime Minister: I have always believed in clearing the decks before I run into a rough weather. The OPEC Ministers are meeting on the 15 of December and if we are lucky, we may have an increase that the world can live with. I hope it will be so, in which case all will be well. It may be that they will have the increase in two bites as has been reported from Qatar — a small one for January and another one for January and another one for June-July. The second one is that the economic recovery of the industrial economies both in America and in Europe, with exception of Germany and probably Holland, has not been as predicted. There is a great deal of talk about tax cuts in America when the new Carter Administration takes over, with a budget deficit of something between US$15 billion up to US$30 billion. Maybe this can get the US economy going, and at the same time, control inflation. I don't know. But I believe before running into rough weather, any sensible captain battens down his hatches. I need hardly mention what may happen between the Arabs and the Israelis if there is no move towards a settlement in the Middle East. Things will happen in 1977 and not all of them may be favourable. So we have decided that we will forego the nine months that we are entitled to. I might also add that the Japanese election results mean that one of our major trading partners and investors is in a state of flux for some time. Their economic recovery is also not likely to be as sustained as we have hoped it will be. All this is not helpful.

Question: Do you expect that the protest votes in this election will be lower than the 30 per cent in the last election?

Prime Minister: I would not be surprised, if it were lower than the last time. But, of course, the opposition must believe otherwise or they wouldn't be trying, would they? Mind you, less are trying this time than last time, which seems to me a pity because they have steered clear of the good seats. This means the percentage of protest votes from my point of view will not be complete and may not be accurate. It's an irrational opposition. Dr. Lee Siew Choh decided to go back to Rochore because he thinks it is the same old Rochore of 1963. He doesn't know the world has changed. The Workers Party, I think, are rather simplistic in their approach. They just looked up the election results the last time and they worked out all those areas where they thought the margin was very small for the PAP. So they have chosen Kampong Chai Chee where in the last elections we won against the combined opposition by six hundred votes. They have gone to Changi because they believe the margin the last time was not very big and perhaps with the building of the airport, the resettlement has disrupted people and made them unhappy. They are rather simple-minded in their approach, because first, it is a very different Chai Chee from 1972. We made it very different. We developed it — factories, new homes and a new town centre. I think they are going to get a surprise on 23 December. I am sorry if they won't be enjoying their Christmas. As

371

for Changi, they are also in for a surprise because this time we made sure that a resettlement takes place not only with better compensation, because we have enabled them to be sited in places where they can make a living. The protest will not be the same. Furthermore, the whole of Changi knows, including Changi New Village, that we have put a lot of effort into regenerating life in Changi since the British pulled out in 1971 — rebuilt the New Village, and putting up an airport which, when the workers move to from Paya Lebar, will give it a great deal of business.

Question: After the last elections, you were thinking of allocating some seats to the university?

Prime Minister: Well, the university dons unfortunately shied away from that. I was quite prepared to let them have two. One for Nanyang and one for University of Singapore. But somehow they felt a little shy. They thought the academic shouldn't be sullied by the rough and tumble of political debate in Parliament. And they would have had a rough and tumble because you can't expect to slosh ministers without being sloshed back. They didn't like the prospect. I am prepared to consider the proposal again. They may rotate their representatives until they can find some people who can take the rough and tumble.

Mr. J.B. Jeyaretnam, the Secretary-General of the Workers Party, wrote to the Prime Minister on 17 December about the secrecy of the ballot. He said: "I am writing to you on a matter which underpins the whole democratic system, the secret ballot. You have stated on a number of occasions that your government has been elected on the free vote of the people given without fear and you held that out as a complete answer to any suggestion that you and your government are undemocratic. I wish to bring to your attention something of which however I am quite sure you must be aware, that once again, as in the 1972 elections, fear stalks the minds of our electorate. Many people have telephoned me or spoken to me on receiving their polling cards. The fear, however irrational it may seem, is in the minds of our electors, particularly the uneducated, that your government will discover how he or she has voted in the elections, and they are terrified of the consequences. You must be the first to agree that a vote given under these circumstances, under this fear, cannot by any stretch of the imagination be called a free vote. You have often stated your belief in democracy and I now appeal to you in the name of democracy, and in the sacred right of every man and woman to vote without fear his or her representative into Parliament, to make a public announcement that the ballot in Singapore is absolutely secret and to give your own and the Cabinet's assurance that your government has no intention whatsoever of finding out how any single voter has voted and that your government would never even attempt to do this. I am not suggesting that your government has done this but there is the fear. If your government, as you wish others to believe, would not do this, then I can see no harm in your making this statement. By making this statement you will be striking a blow for democracy and I believe, Mr. Prime Minister, your stature will increase tremendously. I shall be pleased if you will let me have a reply to this letter by the 20th of this month. I am copying this letter to the Secretary-General of the United Nations and to the High Commissioners of all the Commonwealth countries represented in Singapore."

Lee replied on 18 December: "I have received your letter dated 17 December. The ballot has always been and is secret. You have my reassurance on this. However, I must remind you that it has been members of some opposition parties who have sought to cast doubts on the secrecy of the ballot. Unfortunately, you and your Party have not been free from blame. I propose to release your letter and my reply."

XXXXII

During the election campaign, Lee spoke twice at Fullerton Square, and also gave an eve-of-poll broadcast. This summarized much of what he had said at the two rallies. Lee reminded his television audience that up until 1975, Singapore had a security safety net. "We had British and Commonwealth forces in Singapore, first symbols and later tokens of our security. Now, we are on our own, and so are Malaysia and Thailand. After separation in 1965, we immediately built up our arm forces. Security is crucial to the survival of any people. Without SAF, all that we have is at risk. Anyone, even random terrorists, can hold us up to ransom. Opposition parties want to abolish national service, or reduce it to a community service. Are they out of their minds? We have built the SAF into a factor for stability. And it was because there was the SAF that there was no panic or even unease as the British and Commonwealth troops withdrew. Now, our survival depends, first, on ourselves, and it will be decided by a balance between the great powers, and second, on regional understanding that will enable the countries of ASEAN to co-operate with each other to prevent communist manipulation to knock us down one by one."

Singapore and her neighbours knew that they must work together as they faced the same threats. Thailand, Malaysia and Indonesia, had similar perceptions of these common threats. It was the danger of guerilla insurgency spreading, with external aid, beyond the areas that were now contained in, in Northeast Thailand, and on the Thai border with Malaysia. Furthermore, opposition parties proposed the abolition of detention without trial. One party, to sound moderate, said detention of communists was necessary, but that they should be brought to trial. "They know we cannot get witnesses to go to court to give evidence and face communist vengeance. British colonial governments since 1948, when the Communist Party insurrection began, witeir military might, could not get witnesses to do this. And even now the British Government itself in Northern Ireland has to use these powers of detention without trial." If the opposition were a serious alternative, and their policy were to be implemented, Singapore would slide back to the chaos and riots, the arson and assassinations of the fifties and sixties. With disorder, investments would dry up, the economy would stagnate, and many thousands would be out of work. "We ask you to endorse our policy on pro-communist detainees, namely that all detainees who denounce the use of force to seize power, as the Communist Party of Malaya is doing, will be released. Or they can leave for any country willing to receive them."

Lee said the communist problem would not just go away. But in a more fair and just society, they had not made much headway. "We have given every student, regardless of language, race, religion, equal opportunities for education and employment. Hundreds get scholarships every year, over a hundred and fifty go to universities abroad. All are judged and rewarded according to their performance, not their fathers' wealth or status. Economic progress has resulted from this and made life better for all. This has checked communist subversion and recruitment, especially of good cadres."

Turning to economic prospects, Lee said that the end of 1973, when the Arabs placed oil embargo, followed by a quadrupling of oil prices, was the turning-point in the course of world history. Suddenly, the rich and powerful countries of America, Western Europe and Japan found that they were at the mercy of a few non-industrial countries with vast oil-fields. "For some time, we will have to live with high oil prices. This means slower economic growth." Eleven OPEC countries during the past week had decided to raise the price of oil by 10 per cent. But the Saudi's and United Arab Emirates would raise theirs by only 5 per cent. What the overall price would be for Singapore and the rest of the world had yet to be worked out. Provided there were no further massive increases in the price of oil, the industrial countries expected 4-5 per cent economic growth in the next three years. They could not look further than that. If the industrial countries did make 4-5 per cent growth, Singapore could work for a 6-8 per cent growth. It would be more difficult than before the oil crisis. But it could be done.

"In the next five years, we will build 150,000 flats, 120,000 for sale. They will be better designed flats. They will be in well-planned and land-scaped new towns. Waiting time will be shortened from two to three years to one to two years. In ten years, we expect to rehouse every family. There need to be no more slums. But you must have the jobs and CPF to pay for these homes." The crux of the problem was new investments and jobs and the CPF. Then each citizen could own his home and have his family brought up in healthy and gracious surroundings. "We shall have more green parks and gardens, swimming pools, recreational facilities like the East Coast Lagoon with chalets and picnic areas, the beaches of the Southern Islands and the holiday camps at St. John's Island. Few cities in Asia have such recreational outlets for their people." Today, Singaporeans were better fed, better clothed, better housed, and better paid than seventeen years ago. "And you have also got the extra annual

374

wage supplement since 1973." Singapore schools and hospitals had attracted thousands of people from the region, seeking better education and medical treatment. They willingly paid admission fees of $4,000 per student to get into Singapore schools and full school fees of $30 per month for primary schools and more for secondary schools. They paid full hospital charges in private and government hospitals, "not the token charges you and I pay".

This has been achieved because "we set out to help ourselves. We have not gone around with the begging bowl, looking for aid, a euphemism for charity. We are a realistic people seeking realistic answers to our problems" However, as old problems were solved, new ones emerged. "As we solve our unemployment, we face another oil price increase, making recovery from world-wide economic recession more difficult. In a future full of uncertainties, one factor is certain. The PAP does not run away from problems. We solve them for you and with you. We analyse our difficulties, explain them and propose practical solutions. Then together, we set out to resolve them. After seventeen years in which we have gone through and successfully overcome crisis after crisis, you know you can depend on the PAP."

As expected, the PAP won all the seats. In a statement on 24 December, after the results of the general elections were announced, Lee said: "My Cabinet colleagues and I and all our PAP MPs are deeply moved by this massive vote of confidence you have given us. This will enhance our stability. Now you have given solid endorsement to our policies on national service and detention of pro-communist detainees, both vital to our security. We shall do our best to justify your faith in us and support for our policies. I am particularly happy that in the poorer and rural and urban areas, where people were troubled by low incomes or disturbed by resettlement, you have increased your support for us. We will continue our policies and do more in these poorer areas. We shall lessen the disruption and disturbance in your lives as we rebuild Singapore. We shall also find ways to lessen the problems for those who, as a result of changes in Singapore, have to change their occupation and find a new way of making a living. We face uncertain times ahead. But with your solid backing and co-operation, we shall resolve these difficult problems ahead, as we have done in the past."

In the early morning of 24 December, Lee gave a Press Conference. He said that the PAP vote worked out at 72.4 per cent or 72.5 per cent roughly for the PAP this time, as against 69 per cent the last time. In his own constituency, Lee got 89 per cent as against 84 per cent in 1977. "This time, we gave notice of early elections in September when we announced that we will not hold a by-election in Sepoy Lines because we are going to hold general elections in a matter of months. We had all the election registers open for inspection. They had the assurances they wanted as the vote was secret. So there are no alibis. I take this as an endorsement of our policy on National Service, on our policy of pro-communist detainees, on our policies for economic and social adjustments in Singapore. One thing which was significant was that those constituencies which are less privileged are the ones that have increased their votes for us. Some commentators indicated that we have represented the employers. It is not reflected in the votes. It is the underprivileged who have given us more solid support and accounted for the increase in the overall percentage of votes."

Later in the day, Lee Kuan Yew put out his traditional Christmas Day message. He said: "I wish all a Merry Christmas."

The Prime Minister advised the President to make the following appointments with effect from 31 December:

Dr. Goh Keng Swee	—	Deputy Prime Minister and Minister of Defence
Dr. Toh Chin Chye Senior Minister	—	Minister for Health
Mr. S. Rajaratnam Senior Minister	—	Minister for Foreign Affairs
Mr. Ong Pang Boon Senior Minister	—	Minister for Labour
Mr. Lim Kim San	—	Minister for National Development and Communications
Mr. Jek Yuen Thong	—	Minister for Culture and Science and Technology
Encik Othman bin Wok	—	Minister for Social Affairs
Mr. E. W. Barker	—	Minister for Law and the Environment
Mr. Chua Sian Chin	—	Minister for Home Affairs and Education
Mr. Hon Sui Sen	—	Minister for Finance

The swearing-in ceremony was held in the Istana in the afternoon of 31 December.

So ended an eventful year.

THE YEAR 1977

I

"The year 1976 was a moderately good year," said Lee in his New Year Message. "Considering the economic and political surprises and upsets in America, Japan and Western Europe, we can look back at 1976 with relief. We had almost no unemployment, and a growth rate of 7 per cent. For the first half of 1977, we expect to continue at the same 7 per cent growth rate. For the present, we cannot see beyond the middle of 1977."

The economic forecasts for 1977 tended to be less optimistic for Western Europe. The Japanese were deliberately cautious in forecasting Japan's prospects for 1977. Both Europe and Japan hoped that the new President in America could revive business confidence, that he could re-stimulate the American economy, despite the increase in oil prices and still avoid high inflation. The greatest imponderable was what was to happen in the Middle East. If there was no movement towards a settlement between the Arabs and the Israelis, then the Saudi Arabians and the United Arab Emirates might not be so resolute to restrain and moderate the periodic increases in the price of oil at future OPEC meetings.

1977 marked the beginning of a new era with a new President in America, and a new Chairman in China. A new great power set of relationships would settle the framework for the region and the prospects for stability and prosperity. The countries of ASEAN must be prepared for pressures on each of them, and for political attacks on ASEAN as a group. The aim of these attacks would be to weaken solidarity and "make it easier for those opposed to the political and economic system of the ASEAN group to deal with us one by one''. Hence, they must gear themselves up for greater co-operation, so that with a broader ballast they can move forward together with more strength. For Singapore, if the investments already committed for 1975 and 1976 proceeded, despite the economic uncertainties, there should be no unemployment in 1977. But if there was a slowdown in new factories or extension of existing ones, then new jobs would be less easy to get by the end of 1977. "However, in any case, we shall do more for the poorer urban and rural areas. The HDB will build over 30,000 units for 1977 as part of the 150,000 units in the present five-year plan. In addition to this, the URA, HUDC and HDB are drawing up plans to build 10,000 units in the next five years in the central city area, for shops and homes. 80 per cent will be sold on the CPF home ownership plan. 20 per cent will be for rent. We must check this trend of people moving away from the city centre to the new towns. We must try to keep Singapore a lively city, throbbing with life day and night. We shall minimise the dislocation to the lives of the people who live in the dilapidated areas of the central city area. We shall also lessen the problems of change in making a living in a new and different physical environment. But this needs co-operation from all involved. And we must hope the economy does not slow down, for if it does, the adjustments will become more difficult.''

Lee hoped that 1977, despite the uncertainties, could still be a fair, if not a good year. "I wish you all a Happy New Year.''

II

On 4 January, the Prime Minister issued the following statement: "Nearly all Ministers of State and Parliamentary Secretaries were re-appointed to their respective Ministries. Tuan Haji Sha'ari bin Tadin will not be in the Government. Dr. Augustine Tan will relinquish his post as Political Secretary to the Prime Minister's Office. In eighteen months, the Prime Minister expects to be able to decide on major new appointments in the Government. The new MPs would have had sufficient experience of politics at both grass-roots level and in Parliament where they should have demonstrated their debating capacity. The three Ministers of State, now in day-to-day charge of the Ministries of Education, National Development, and Communication, would have had time to demonstrate their judgement and their administrative capabilities.''

III

Interviewed by Dr. Winfred Sharlau of the German National Television, at the Istana, on 8 January, the Prime Minister was asked about a system of checks and balances in a situation in which in the general elections the PAP had won all the seats.

Prime Minister: Well, we faced this problem in 1965 when the communist united front, who had one-third of the seats, walked out of Parliament and boycotted Parliament. And the system that we had to devise in order to maintain public confidence and also to keep our own bureaucrats and ministers in check is a complete publication of all major policies and figures. Disclosures of all financial accountings are available to every member of the public, every press. And, I think most important of all, we have learned how to allow free and complete debate and even opposition within the party. In other words, so long as a Member of Parliament is not in the Cabinet, he can criticise and oppose any government policy. In this way we have ensured that every policy which is being opposed or discussed or causing anxiety or discomfort to the public — and it's being discussed in the restaurants, in the cafés — are brought into Parliament and debated.

Sharlau: Why did the opposition parties fail even to gain a single seat?

Prime Minister: Their fundamental error was to try to capture or win over the communist support, which the communists gave up when they boycotted Parliament and said that they would take the battle into the streets and into the jungles. So they have adopted the major planks of the communist programme: Singapore's independence is bogus, no National Service, free all communist prisoners. And then, of course, very simplistic and simple-minded welfare programmes of free bus rides, free hospitals, free everything. But I think their major error — which I hope they will continue to make — is to believe that they can capture the one-third of the seats which the communists held, up till the time they boycotted Parliament and resigned by adopting the main communist programmes. They have got some communist followers to support them, but they alienated the majority of the population who do not support these communist programmes.

Sharlau: Stability and confidence of the foreign investors have proven essential to the welfare of Singapore. But the degree of stability seems to be in dispute between you, your administration, on the one hand, and some news media — foreign. Do you think that a lot of foreigners tend to minimise the internal sweat?

Prime Minister: If the foreign newspapermen and correspondents were believable or credible to the people of Singapore who live here and know, then I would have lost the elections. I believe the younger generation of the anti-establishment libertarian type of reporting, which takes place in some parts of Western Europe, find absolutely no relevance in the minds of people here. Whatever they are reporting and what they are saying have been gleaned from the bars of hotels, talking to old hands or established local newspapermen, who are frustrated, angry or otherwise dissatisfied; and they build up a good story.

379

Sharlau: But when it gets difficult to get the success story of Singapore through to the Western public, then it seems to be evident that the gap between West and East is widening.

Prime Minister: It does not worry me.

Sharlau: Do you think the West has changed or the East?

Prime Minister: Well, maybe both have changed. I think we are not talking about peoples alone; we are talking primarily of media men. The West European media man has become very libertarian. He is in favour of Euro-communism, he thinks Berlinguer (Secretary, Communist Party) in Italy will make a good democrat and will run a multi-party democratic system. He thinks the Portuguese communists are good although it is regrettable they did not win more votes. He thinks the Spanish communists should be given the full run of civil liberties. He thinks the Greek communists will never make a come-back and should be allowed to create a fuss. But we live in Southeast Asia where the story has been fundamentally different. Where 150,000 Americans were killed, a quarter million injured, two million Vietnamese died, and things have not got better, either in Vietnam or in Laos or in Cambodia. And the people in Thailand know, the people in Malaysia know, the people in Singapore know, what is the meaning of communism. It is not a joke. It is not a public relations exercise of Mr. Mitterrand (First Secretary of the Socialist Party, France) being able to take away support from M. Michel (French Minister of State, Interior). This is a very serious business with guns — subversion and terrorism and guerilla communism and finally, large-scale forces to overwhelm government troops and take over by force. So long as the communists do not give up force they cannot play it both ways. You can't, on the one hand, say, my right hand has the gun, my left hand, I have the propaganda pamphlet, and I will make a speech in Parliament, or in the Bundestag or whatever it is. They have to choose, and they have chosen to play both ways, and we just can't allow it and the people support us in this.

Sharlau: Mr. Prime Minister, you have recently been asked whether you regard yourself as a socialist and you replied: Yes, an old-fashioned one. What kind of personalities come to your mind when you think of an old-fashioned socialist?

Prime Minister: Well, if we exclude living socialists so that we will not offend anybody, I would say I would understand Hugh Gaitskell, I would understand Attlee, Ernest Bevin or Guy Mollet. They were men who believed that communism and socialism are different: that if you try and blur the lines then the communists will slowly dominate your organisation. And secondly, they believed, and I still believe, that the fundamental premise of socialism is equality of opportunity for every individual regardless of your father or your mother's status or wealth. You should have the same opportunities for good health, good education, a full life. Modern Euro-socialism believes in cooperation with the communists, or Euro-communism, multi-party systems, coalition between socialists and com-

380

munists. But there is another aspect of it. Modern socialism or the new Left believes in equality of rewards, not in equality of opportunities. I believe the human being — anyway in the developing part of Asia — wants equal opportunities in order to strive, to show how good they are and, in the process, create wealth for everybody. But they will only do so if rewards are equated to performance and not rewards are equal regardless of performance. You know, even in China, the slogans on the walls that I saw, when I was there a few months ago, read: From each his best. According to work, it is distributed. So it is not from each his best to each his needs. That doesn't work. Of course, if it works in Europe, and Europe becomes more prosperous as a result of the new Left ideas, then I will revise my opinion and I will go new Left.

IV

From 4 – 18 January, the Prime Minister was in the Philippines on an unofficial visit. He exchanged views with President Marcos on developments in the regional and international scene. They discussed greater co-operation among ASEAN partners. The Prime Minister was accompanied by the Minister for Foreign Affairs, the Minister for National Development and Communications, the Minister for Finance and senior officials from the Ministries of Foreign Affairs and Finance.

Lee and President Marcos gave a joint press conference at Baguio City, on 19 January.

President Marcos: My friends, this press conference, jointly held by our distinguished visitor, the Prime Minister from Singapore and the Head of State of the Philippines, has been called primarily to emphasise the formal initialling of the joint press statement on the occasion of the unofficial visit of the Prime Minister, Mr. Lee Kuan Yew. The copies of this joint statement have been distributed to you. It refers primarily to the procedural efficiencies we have instituted in ASEAN to overcome some of the obstacles that have delayed implementation of the cooperative industrialisation programme as well as other projects of ASEAN. Thus, you will note that it now authorises the economic ministers to make economic decisions, although the arrangements and agreements of the different ASEAN member states will be promulgated by the Foreign Ministers.

"There are some projects that pertain to economic cooperation which have been agreed upon between Singapore and the Philippines. The most important would probably be the 10½ across-the-board tariff cut. The next would probably be the private sector industrial complementation agreement. Then, of course, with respect to relations with countries outside the ASEAN, we have this matter of now working out more clearly the joint approaches of the ASEAN member states — us, ASEAN — to the United States as well as the joint position of the two countries — Singapore and the Philippines — to maintain or preserve the present system of

381

tax deferral for American investments in ASEAN. The other matter, of course, would be to now open economic dialogue with such areas and regions like the United States. We are presently engaged in economic dialogue with the EEC and it is proposed we expand the economic dialogue between ASEAN and Japan. We are, of course, gratified that the new Prime Minister of Japan has indicated that one of his first overseas visits will be°to the ASEAN nations. We welcome such initiative on the part of the Prime Minister, Mr. Fukuda. We, of course, reiterate our position with respect to the great powers which is that we share the view: the constructive balance of power amongst them. Those powers who have legitimate interest in the region would contribute to the stability of Southeast Asia and Asia as a whole. And the peaceful and constructive competition among the great powers in the region would be beneficial to all concerned. I will now request Prime Minister, Mr. Lee Kuan Yew, to open the Press Conference with a statement."

Prime Minister: Mr. President, ladies and gentlemen of the press, I am not good as an opener. I usually find it easier to round off a press conference, particularly, if the pressmen are friendly. So, all I want to say is, that these various pages of the document have been the result of considerable, leisurely effort in the salubrious atmosphere of Baguio. The air in Baguio, as it was in Bali, where the former Thai Prime Minister made a memorable remark: All things are possible in heaven. We have tried in Baguio to do all things which are possible in the immediate future.

A reporter asked Lee about the attitude of the Western press.

Prime Minister: I was asked this question recently by a serious German television correspondent, immediately after my elections in Singapore. He asked me why the Western press took a very critical view of what Singaporeans were being made to do. My answer to him was: If the Singaporean believed they ought to be doing what the Western press were telling them to do, then I would have lost the elections. Since I didn't lose the elections, the conclusion I came to was that I had no cause for concern and really very little cause for even interest in the gratuitous advice that the press lords or TV anchormen proffer from time to time as to how I should suck the Singapore banana. They will, after a while, discover that their magical influence which has been so tremendous in America with Watergate and indeed in other parts of Western Europe, does not work in Asia — different cultures, different values, different standards of economic development demanding different priorities. It didn't work even in Japan. If the Western press carried the Japanese electorate, the LDP, with Mʀ. Fukuda as Prime Minister, would not be in office. So it really doesn't matter. At the end of the day, it's what we do for our people that counts. And the more they exaggerate our warts and moles and other deficiencies, of which I admit I have many, and I don't try cosmetic techniques to make myself look more presentable than I am, I think the less credible will they become. This is because in a world of very rapid mass communications and mass travel, people are beginning to rely not just on what they read in

382

the newspapers and on what they see on television screen, but what they actually see for themselves; what their friends whom they trust tell them. So far as investors are concerned — they are more important to me than the Western press and pressmen — it is what the banker and the Ambassador who lives in the country say that makes him decide whether he is going to screw down machinery worth hundreds of millions, sometimes a few billion dollars, to the ground. So perhaps I would like to believe that the Western press would continue to do me the service of using me as a whipping boy. These pressmen have very large expense accounts. They drop in for a week, sometimes, a week-end and have a marvellous time chatting up with knowledgeable people. They want a good story which they know the editor likes, presented in a certain way. And as for the moment, the fashion is whip and lash the governments of those who do not accept their standards. Of course, they are very discriminating. The editors and the TV anchormen have a very keen sense of where they can be heard. They have a job to do as I have, but the sycophancy, the supine paean of praise for the oil sheikdoms and kingdoms makes me wish that I were a sheik or a king of large tracts of deserts with oil underneath. But, of course, if you are a king or a sheik, like the one in South Yemen, without oil underneath, then you get it very hard. So, you see, after a while, it becomes rather obvious. But we mustn't be too harsh on them.

"The Western correspondents who travel out to this part of the world sometimes do understand. They do even try to present a fair picture. However, the man in his head office, whether it be New York, London, Paris, Bonn or even Rome, wants to present to his readers the Third World which he has decided is what it should be. I don't think we should grudge them the privilege of consoling themselves with the fact that by comparison with what they present us to be, they are doing marvellously. Look at Italy. Sixteen to seventeen inflation rate is considered a great improvement from the twenty plus per cent they had one and a half years ago. They were able to hold three elections that has led to a minority government of the Christian Democrats, with the Italians dependent completely on the goodwill, and good behaviour of the Italian Communist Party. The pound has gone up from $3.97 a few weeks ago, to $4.20 as a result of a loan of some $3.9 billion, or technically called 'Standby Credit'. But there is a social contract between unions and the British Government due for renewal in June. I am not a speculator. But I am going to sell pounds forward, round about May. I think it's going to be a realisation that the unions, particularly those key ones, can terrorise the economy. I have no less an authority than the previous British Prime Minister, Sir Harold Wilson, that there are very powerful men in the Labour Party who do not subscribe to the democratic principle of British socialism. They are Marxists. They have become asset strippers. They have moved into his Party, which has got assets, because they can't build up a Communist Party by themselves. And they are literally stripping off all the good men from the Labour Party and putting in the Trotskyists, Marxists and Maoists. We mustn't be too harsh on the Western press and their TV commentators. They have their problems. If they can say: Look at President Idi Amin! They have even compared what has been going on in Uganda, with what's going on in parts of Asia. It gives them what the Germans called *schandenfroh* — somebody doing worse than you; you feel happier. I expect them to say: Well, so many more millions of Indians are born every year only to be starved to death. And there they were, Englishmen borrowing £12,000 million a year to balance their budget. They live very comfortably and happily. I say good luck to them. Since they got North Sea oil, they don't need my good wishes. I haven't got North Sea oil and I am not going to follow any of their policies."

The Prime Minister was questioned about the across-the-board 10 per cent tariff reduction. Was this seen as an initiative which might, perhaps, be followed by other ASEAN countries, or throughout the ASEAN region, on a similar basis, and perhaps with a view to some sort of a common market of ASEAN countries in the same way as the EEC has formed their own common market?

Prime Minister: This was a proposal made by the President of the Philippines and we found the proposal realistic. It's a very small step forward, but it's a genuine step forward. It's a 10 per cent across-the-board between the two of us. But it means we have expressed in actual revenue terms or excise duty terms, our intentions that trade between us should be promoted and increased. It comes to very little. Let us assume there is a tax on Singapore-made or foreign-made cameras and there is a tax of 50 per cent. All it means is that the Singapore cameras can get into the Philippines at 50 per cent minus 10 per cent of 50 per cent which is minus 5 per cent. So it's really competing against the Japanese with an advantage of 5 per cent less than the Japanese, which is pretty tough-going. But the intention is there. I would believe that by the results of this first step forward, (as the Chinese proverb says, the longest journey begins with the first step) it will be proved successful enough to persuade some others to join us in this.

The Prime Minister was questioned about a speech he had made the previous day at the Philippines Military Academy.

Lee said: "First, at the Academy yesterday, I stated a general principle which has been enunciated by my government. I am no military expert and I am told that with greater sophistication and greater technology, one could bring about a presence in an area rapidly from the rear. From time to time, the Americans mount exercises, carry whole divisions of troops from America across the Altantic to the borders of the Alps which divide Eastern and Western Europe. It could be that with more sophisticated weaponry, missiles, radar systems, satellites, they would require less men on the ground. If men on the ground became necessary, there would be advance warning. That's what the British used to tell me when they were withdrawing. They said: Don't worry, we will come either west-about or east-about. We got so many aircraft. There is always a lead time of about anywhere between six weeks to six months, before a crisis

384

erupts. We could get going, and get our troops and their armaments out in a matter of days either flying east-about through Cyprus, Gan to Singapore or west-about to Ottawa, British Columbia, Vancouver, maybe, some islands in mid-Pacific, Hong Kong and Singapore. And they did mount some exercises. Unfortunately, the economy didn't hold up. So, now it will never be tested in a real crisis. But they demonstrated I think, in 1968, as they were withdrawing, that they could bring men out quickly, acclimatise them to different temperatures, humidities, terrain, within a matter of days. Whether the Americans can do better than that and put them in spacecraft and be out in the Philippines, I wouldn't know. But I would like to see a balance which would not give any major power or any super-power a dominance which leaves me with less leeway. At the moment, I have considerable leeway in choosing my partners in progress. That's a phrase I borrowed from Lester Pearson in his book — he wrote a report with a team of experts on how to develop countries, and it was called: *Partners in Progress*. My partners in progress are primarily the industrial countries of the Western world — the Americans, because they have the largest industrial capacity; the Japanese, because they are nearby, and they have reached the limits of what their people will tolerate (more factories despite the highest anti-pollution measures) and the West Europeans, who have, up till recently, lost the impetus to go overseas and return to their former fields of activity. At the moment, they have something like five to six million unemployed in Western Europe — over a million in Britain; over a million in Italy; about that in France and not far from a million in Western Germany, although a lot of them are guest workers. So I can choose my partners in progress. Let us assume that a great power that does not believe in the free enterprise system becomes the dominant power and influence in the region; that could become very difficult. It is part of their ritual to say: All countries, big or small, are equal, and we want friendship, peace, co-operation. When they say that to me — and they have said that to me often at varying levels of authority — I try and look behind their eyes. I have no doubts whatsoever that all countries — the greater they are, the softer they can afford to speak because there is a man walking behind them with a very big stick. I like to have another soft-speaking gentleman with a man walking behind him with an equally big stick. That will cancel them out and we could live peacefully, at least for the immediate and intermediate future."

Lee was asked to comment on the concern of the Western press "and even in the United States Congress" over human rights in the Asian countries.

Lee replied: "I think it is a phase they are going through, probably a sense of guilt of what had happened and what they did in Vietnam ... Again, I say this, more in sorrow, than in anger ... I am all for civil liberties and human rights. But the way they are going for Mrs. Indira Gandhi and India is questionable. I know India has enormous problems. When India had full democratic freedom, it meant that at any one time, there were twelve to fifteen Members of Parliament standing up and speaking in their Lower House. She has put a stop to that. She has brought — I don't know whether it is right or wrong — a whole group of newspapermen, whose great capacity is to learn how to be malicious and to torment a government from their Western counterparts, to a more sane and sober and constructive way of thinking. I find talking to Indian newspapermen outside India — particularly those who don't intend to return for a long while — that they have somehow developed the Western newspapermen's pattern of thinking. They believe whoever is in authority is fair target. They treat Presidents, or even lowly Prime Ministers as clay-pigeons — throw him up, shoot him down. Somebody will have to stick him back all over again or find a new clay-pigeon, a new Prime Minister. Well, maybe that is good democracy. It has led, I know, to near calamity in India. If a developing country is to develop, there must be social cohesion, work discipline and an order of priorities. From time to time I visit my counterpart in Kuala Lumpur. Whilst the Western press do not approve, I find the people reasonably clothed, definitely well-fed and perhaps not as free to raise divisive issues of race, language, culture and religion. I am sure that the present Prime Minister of Malaysia intends eventually when the economy develops, and the social cohesion and ethnic differences are blurred as a result of mutual accommodation, to let his people talk about differences in race, culture, language and religion without taking up sticks and stones, and later on, pistols and automatics to destroy each other. Let us remember that it was race, language and religion that led to the fragmentation of India and Pakistan. And with the same religion it led to the fragmentation between East and West Pakistan. My hope is that this particular phase of particular fashion fetish or fancy of the Western press would find a sufficient repose from their own libertarians. They will learn that there are limits to fundamental human rights and civil liberties. Otherwise, they themselves will be destroyed. That will sadden me because like them, I love all men all over the world, regardless of however developed or underdeveloped they may be.''

A reporter asked about the economic relationship between ASEAN and Japan. President Marcos first replied, then Lee added a few "footnotes''. He said of the three major industrial blocs of the Western world — America, Japan, Western Europe — Japan was the one closest to ASEAN. So transportation costs made it an advantage that trade should improve and increase as against Japan and Brazil or Japan and other parts of Latin America or Africa. "We however, find that it is almost impossible to get into the Japanese market for even relatively low priced intermediate stage manufactured products. Even the West Europeans can't get through the remarkable set of customs, excise and anti-pollution rules. They have threatened retaliation. We believe that trade is a two-way process. We accept the fact that the balance of payment has been, and has always been against us. But a little less patriotism on the part of the Japanese in buying only things Japanese would help to make the Japanese

386

more accepted as fellow Asians, with some, if not sympathy, at least empathy and understanding of the desire of the people to try and achieve the Meiji transformation from a feudal agricultural society to a modern industrial nation. But we can't do that if Japan won't buy our products. We can't get through because there are such complicated rules. Even when we do get through, under the General Rules of Preferences, we can't market them in Japan because the distributors are Japanese. I earnestly hope that there will be some soul-searching."

V

In a joint press statement issued in Baguio by the Prime Minister and President Ferdinand Marcos on 19 January, the opening paragraph stated that they had held a cordial and candid exchange of views on bilateral and regional co-operation and on recent international developments. Reviewing the progress of bilateral relations since their meeting in Singapore in 1976, the two Heads of Government expressed satisfaction over the acceleration in the flow of trade, exchanges in tourism and in the increasing contacts between their governments, as well as between business, technical and cultural groups of the two countries. Prime Minister Lee and President Marcos explored other areas of economic co-operation which would utilize their countries' resources and skills to mutual advantage. They noted that an auspicious start had already been made in establishing joint ventures. In support thereof, they agreed to hold immediate negotiations on an agreement for the avoidance of double taxation. They also agreed to consider the early conclusion of an investment guarantee agreement. They agreed to expand the existing exchange by the Philippines and Singapore, of air traffic rights in order to promote tourism, trade and communications. The two leaders discussed possible co-operation in the fields of public housing and agreed, as an initial step, for a Philippines Technical Mission to visit Singapore as soon as possible to define the areas of co-operation in this field. They agreed to work out co-operation in the processing of crude oil from the Philippines in Singapore refineries.

On ASEAN co-operation, they reaffirmed their commitment to the objectives and programmes of the Bali Declaration of ASEAN Concord. They reaffirmed their determination to co-operate with other ASEAN member states in accelerating regional development and the growth of intra-ASEAN trade. They set out details.

The two leaders also agreed to establish a bilateral Singapore-Philippines Commission to work out ways and means of increasing the economic and technical contacts between the two countries.

The two Heads of Government agreed to continue to co-operate on the exchanges of intelligence and consultations on ways of combating subversion and infiltration. They shared the belief that economic stability and social justice are important factors in countering subversion and

387

insurgency. The Prime Minister and the President stressed the importance of closer ASEAN relations with other developing states. At the same time, they reaffirmed the importance of increasing trade and economic relations with the developed countries on the basis of equality and mutual advantage. The two Heads of Government stressed the desirability of promoting and developing ASEAN co-operation with other countries, regardless of differences in political or economic systems, and with regional and international organisations.

The two leaders called on the developed countries to adopt policies which would increase the flow of investments into ASEAN countries and expand trade between ASEAN and the developed states. In this regard, they agreed that ASEAN should make joint approaches to the United States to preserve the present system of tax deferral for American investments in ASEAN. The two leaders expressed the hope that the countries now co-operating with ASEAN intensify such mutually beneficial relations as this would contribute to the stability and peace of the region. The two leaders supported the early establishment of an economic dialogue between ASEAN and the United States, and the expansion of the economic dialogue between ASEAN and Japan. They shared the view that a constructive balance of power among the great powers with legitimate interests in the region would contribute to the stability of Southeast Asia and of Asia as a whole. They also expressed the belief that peaceful and constructive competition among the great powers in the region would benefit both Southeast Asia and the great powers. The two leaders reaffirmed, in respect of the relations of their two countries with other powers, their adherence to the principles of equality, sovereignty, respect for the independence and territorial integrity of states, non-interference in each other's internal affairs, non-recourse to force or the threat of force, and the settlement of disputes through peaceful means.

VI

On President Carter's inauguration on 20 January, the Prime Minister sent a message of congratulations: "On this auspicious occasion of your inauguration as President of the United States of America, my Government and I extend to you our warmest congratulations and good wishes. Singapore and America's other friends in the region depend on your leadership in charting new directions for America to contribute to world peace, stability and economic prosperity."

VII

Lee made an unofficial visit to Thailand from 30 January to 2 February. It was in return of the Thai Prime Minister's visit to Singapore in December, 1976. Lee met the Thai Prime Minister and other Thai leaders and discussed regional issues and the promotion of greater economic co-operation among ASEAN countries on the basis of the Bali accord. The Prime Minister was accompanied by the Minister for Foreign Affairs, the Minister for Finance and senior officials.

A joint press statement issued during the visit stated the Prime Minister and Mrs. Lee Kuan Yew were granted an audience by the King and Queen of Thailand at Bhubping Palace, Chiengmai. Prime Minister Lee Kuan Yew and Prime Minister Tanin Kraivixien held a cordial and friendly exchange of views on bilateral and regional co-operation and on recent international developments. The two Prime Ministers reaffirmed the mutual interest of their countries in each other's well-being and reiterated their confidence that co-operation between the two countries would make even further progress. The two Prime Ministers noted with satisfaction the increasing bilateral co-operation between the two countries, particularly in the economic field. In this connection, they agreed to proceed with the implementation of a joint project on cattle-raising in Southern Thailand for export to Singapore. Their senior officials would meet to finalise details. The two leaders also noted with satisfaction the progress towards the implementation of the joint venture proposals for the production and marketing of agricultural products, particularly maize, as exemplified by the establishment of Sin-Thai Grain Pte. Ltd., to undertake the marketing of these products in Singapore.

The Prime Minister of Thailand expressed his Government's sincere appreciation for the readiness of the Government of Singapore to render co-operation in the fields of public housing, transportation, planning, traffic control and urban planning and development. Singapore also offered fellowships in various fields to Thailand. Prime Minister Lee Kuan Yew warmly welcomed the offer of the Government of Thailand to provide fellowships for special agricultural and industrial training programmes to the Government of Singapore. To facilitate and promote the flow of investment into their countries, they agreed to conclude an investment guarantee agreement. The two leaders further agreed to co-operate actively in the establishment of industrial complementation projects in order to encourage the promotion of manufacturing investments with skilled technology and labour-generating projects in Singapore and Thailand for the benefit of developing priority industries in both countries. They also agreed to take measures to promote closer customs co-operation.

To promote ASEAN co-operation, the two Prime Ministers reaffirmed their commitment to the objectives and programmes of the Bali Declaration of ASEAN Concord, in order to strengthen national resilience, thus enhancing the resilience of ASEAN as a whole. They reiterated their determination to co-operate with other ASEAN States in accelerating regional development and the growth of intra-ASEAN trade. To these

389

ends, the two Prime Ministers agreed on an across-the-board preferential tariff reduction of 10 per cent of existing tariffs on all products of their two countries traded between them within the framework of ASEAN economic co-operation. They agreed to take necessary measures, in accordance with the respective constitutional processes in their countries, to implement this preferential tariff reduction. In order to expedite the implementation of their assigned ASEAN industrial projects, the two Prime Ministers agreed that efforts should also be made to give full market support for the products of these projects — diesel engines for Singapore and soda-ash for Thailand. The two Prime Ministers reiterated their agreement for the early development of the Submarine Telecommunication Cable between Thailand and Singapore which would also facilitate linkages with other ASEAN countries.

The two leaders called on the developed countries to adopt policies which would increase the flow of investments into ASEAN countries and expand trade between ASEAN and the developed states. In this regard, they agreed that ASEAN should take joint actions to prevent measures being taken by developed countries, such as an alteration in the present tax deferral arrangements that would have adverse effects on investments in the ASEAN countries. Prime Minister Tanin Kraivixien and Prime Minister Lee Kuan Yew expressed their support for the early establishment of an economic dialogue between ASEAN and the United States, and the expansion of economic dialogue between ASEAN and Japan, and between ASEAN and other developed countries. The two leaders reaffirmed the desire common to all ASEAN members to promote friendly relations with all countries, irrespective of political and economic differences, on the basis of mutual respect for each other's sovereignty and territorial integrity and non-interference in the internal affairs of one another. They also expressed their desire to develop further co-operation with other countries, as well as regional and international organisations.

Lee gave a press conference at Bangkok Airport before his departure. He was asked about President Carter's decision to pull out US troops from South Korea. Would it have any effect on the ASEAN countries, especially Singapore?

Prime Minister: Indirectly, the policy is going to affect the position of the Japanese and our own position viz-a-vis the new defence situation in Northeast Asia. If you take the steps three or four stages forward, there may come a time when the Japanese self-defence force may have to be a real self-defence force, and, to that effect, it will affect the whole of the Western side of the Pacific.

Question: We have a new Administration in Washington. I would like to ask you if you share the concern of some people in Southeast Asia that the Carter Administration may ignore this area and possibly give too much attention to Vietnam?

Prime Minister: Give attention to Vietnam! I read Zbigniew Brzezinski's speech in Foreign Policy. He mentioned NATO, Japan, the Middle East, Southern Africa, the Soviet Union, China. He did not men-

In London with the Queen in 1977 during a Commonwealth Conference (Lee is in the back row)

In Singapore for an ASEAN meeting, President Marcos of the Philippines

Dato Hussein Onn, Prime Minister of Malaysia, paid an official visit ▶
to Singapore in 1976

Lee with Australia's Prime Minister, Malcolm Fraser

Japan's Prime Minister Fukuda, explaining a point during a visit to Singapore in 1977

British Prime Minister, James Callaghan, greeting Lee at the 1977 Commonwealth Conference, London

tion Vietnam or Southeast Asia. So that's the score.

Question: Would you have any comment, Prime Minister, on the statement made by the new US Ambassador to the UN and the new Secretary of State on their hopes for normalising relations with Vietnam? What effect would that have on Southeast Asia?

Prime Minister: I would hope that their expectations of rational, co-operative, constructive relationships will be fulfilled.

Question: Would you say that ASEAN has finally taken off?

Prime Minister: What has taken off is the rapport, the friendship which I think we have established between the new government in Thailand and ourselves and between the Prime Minister, Mr. Thanin and myself. ASEAN took off in Bali in February last year. You musn't be an agent *provocateur*.

VIII

President Sheares opened the fourth Parliament on 8 February. He said it would be idle to pretend that the security and economic prospects were better now than when they met in October 1972. Then, the Americans were still in Vietnam and backing the Thieu regime. Now, they had departed even from Thailand. 1972 was before the oil crisis, and more rapid growth was in the offing. Now, there was uncertainty and anxiety amongst the major industrial nations of the West. It was an open question whether they could co-ordinate their economic policies, especially America, Japan and Germany, to stimulate recovery from recession without another bout of high inflation. "We have now to be prepared for slower growth rates, and adjust accordingly our spending habits, both as a government and as individuals. My government has again been returned to office. The PAP won in all constituencies. This government has the highest number of votes, and the highest percentage of votes (72.4 per cent) cast in the six general elections held since representative government in 1955. This vote of confidence imposes a heavy responsibility on my Ministers to act fairly but firmly. My government will exercise its authority to govern with circumspection and moderation. It also placed on all Honourable Members, especially those not holding office, the duty to ensure that all shades of opinion out in the constituencies are vigorously voiced in Parliamentary questions and debates. No major policy or legislation should be passed without the closest scrutiny, and passed only after the most thorough debate."

President Sheares said that the mandate on which the government was elected was clear-cut. The issues were fought for months, indeed years, before the elections. Many of the opposition political parties, both those which took part in the elections and those which did not, repeated the demands of the CPM (Communist Party of Malaya — Malaya including Singapore), regularly voiced over its clandestine radio. These demands

391

included the unconditional release of all communist and pro-communist detainees, abolition of the Internal Security Act and National Service. The people rejected these and supported the government. But it would be naive to believe that the Communist Party of Malaya, in their armed struggle for a communist Malaya, would not try to abuse the opportunities of the democratic processes, and the mass media, to help camouflage their armed struggle to grab power. They would continue to rebuild amongst small misguided student groups, like the Malayan New Democratic Youth League (MNDYL). Student groups in the Polytechnic and in other tertiary institutions had been and would be their recruiting areas. Small groups of activists would continue to manipulate student organisations abroad in Britain and Australia, in active collaboration with British or Australian Marxists and Trotskyites, as the case might be. They now styled themselves the New Left. But their techniques of oft-repeated lies, and their exploitation of innocent soft-hearted or soft-headed liberals, were long-established techniques and tactics of the communists, learned by the CPM from other communist parties in Europe and Asia, repeated with minor variations on new audiences in different places. And there was always the younger, politically innocent, if not naive, generation.

The vote was also a renewed mandate not to be beguiled away from a most necessary law, which the British themselves drafted and promulgated when faced with communist insurgency in 1948, namely, detention of communist and pro-communist elements without going through the processes of a public trial accorded to ordinary criminals. "My government, in accord with humane sentiment, will release them if they will denounce the CPM's use of force to seize power, and themselves forswear the use of force to unseat a constitutionally elected government." Lest it be forgotten, it was a mandate also to reject the soft-headed, pernicious policies that all the good things in life, from bus rides to PUB (Public Utilities Board) charges, could be given for free, or otherwise to reduce the fares or charges when the costs were going up. Only education, medical treatment and housing would be subsidised, in order to help everyone to be educated and healthy as well as to be able to look after himself. But nominal charges must be paid even for schools, to pay for extra-curricular activities, and for hospitals, to prevent unnecessary pressure on medical facilities.

"Before us are some terrifying examples of what can happen to those who go in for soft options and subsidised living, a temptation in any one-man-one-vote election campaign. Some once-great nations have been beguiled by this illusion that somebody else will pay, that all people had to do was to elect a government that would take money from those who have and give it to those who have not. Indeed, the British Prime Minister lamented a few weeks ago that the most hateful slogan he had heard was made at a recent protest march of Marxist and Trotskyite infiltrators of his Labour Party: What do we want? Everything! When do we want it?

Now!" A great people had been temporarily reduced to straitened circumstances by this excessive cushioning of life by state subsidies. When the Prime Minister visited China in 1976, his realistic communist hosts described such sad situations as "teachers by negative example".

President Sheares said the government held firm to this simple truth: that to get from each his best, rewards and recognition must go to those who excelled in consistently high performance. Between the soft solutions of some West European socialists of equal rewards, and the hard realities of Asian conditions, the government had no doubts that the people of Singapore unequivocally upheld Asian precepts — "From each his best; To each his worth". The communists in China have a variation of this in their aphorism: *Ge jin suo neng, an lao fen pei* — from each according to his ability, to each according to his labour. "However, we are different from China. We have access to modern science and technology. We have rapid economic and material transformation that comes from these modern management methods, capital inputs and marketing know-how. But we must not abandon the cardinal precepts of our long-proven culture systems, precepts which enabled some Asian civilisations to survive, and without a break in continuity, floods, famines, pestilence, wars, disasters and foreign conquests. Whilst we admire, and must learn and acquire their science and technology, their management skills and marketing know-how, we do not seek to model our lives on Western social mores and their contemporary life-styles. We must learn the experience of the Japanese — how, in less than a hundred years since the Meiji Restoration of 1868, they have become a modern industrial state, without abandoning their own cultural traditions. Their experience is more relevant to us than those of the countries of Western Europe. The exceptions are perhaps West Germany and Switzerland."

The President said Singapore had to formulate its own way of life, taking what was best from the West and fitting it into the Singapore context. "We must not allow our values and our philosophy of what is good government to be overwhelmed by the standards and norms of the contemporary West, regardless of their relevance to our social, economic and political conditions, simply because, for the time being the West have the material abundance and technological superiority. Let us select the relevant factors in their societies, factors which have made them strong and have been proven by the test of time. Then we can incorporate these factors into our system without damage to ourselves."

IX

"VC Today" was the name of a display at the National Stadium on 13 February. Lee described the performance as recognition of the new role of the Vigilante Corps. The Vigilante Corps started in 1964 as a voluntary organisation. Because it was voluntary, members were keen. When it became a national service force in 1967, it took many years to overcome problems of morale and discipline. These were not solved until just a few years ago when the men found that what they were doing had a purpose. With the Community Security Force, the Fire Brigade and Civil Defence, the Vigilante Corps found a new sense of purpose. Morale had improved. Absenteeism had been reduced to a negligible problem, for the men knew they were engaged in work valued by the community.

The Police were faced with new types of crimes and criminals as Singapore changed from attap and zinc houses to high-rise new towns. Where the Community Security Force had been deployed, the crime rate had fallen dramatically. In 1974, the areas they patrolled had on the average twenty-one crime-free nights per month. For December 1976, in 188 of the 242 sectors they patrolled, they were able to keep all thirty-one nights crime-free, and in another thirty-six sectors, thirty nights crime-free.

Lee said: "We are determined and have the capacity to check the crime rate, whether it is drug trafficking, drug addiction, petty thieving, extortion or molesting of young women in lifts. Many crimes arise from problems of anonymity and difficulty of geographic control in high-rise living. With the full use of national servicemen in the Police, the Vigilante Corps, plus the SAF reservists spread all over the new high-rise buildings, and through the computer, we have the capacity to marshall these resources, plan and provide security, and prevent crime." Several schemes were being considered. There might have to be a period of trial and error before they could achieve a practical maximum security solution varying with each neighbourhood. He was confident that patrolling and policing could be made thorough. With manpower at their disposal, the active national servicemen both in the Police and in the VC, the SAF Reservists, they should be able to do so. "And if we succeed in setting up block committees for each high-rise, or groups of two or three high-rises, then crime in these high-rise buildings can be dramatically checked."

X

"Nothing more dramatically showed how different Singaporeans are from the West than last year's birth figures," declared Lee in his Chinese New Year Message. In 1976, the "Year of the Dragon", the most auspicious of all the twelve mythical animals of the Chinese almanac, total births shot up to 42,230, an increase of 5.71 per cent over 39,948 for 1975, the "Year of the Rabbit". Lee said he had called for a detailed breakdown of the figures. "Staring me in the face was: Malay births decreased by 3.39 per cent (from 5,647 to 5,456). Indian births decreased by 1.5 per cent (from 2,389 to 2,304). Others, besides Chinese, increased by 2.78 per cent (from 1,327 to 1,364). Chinese birth increase was a phenomenal 8.06 per cent (from 30,635 to 33,106). Yet in 1975, Chinese births decreased by 7.5 per cent from 33,128 in 1974 to 30,635 in 1975. Many Chinese families had decided to postpone their children from the 'Year of the Rabbit' to the 'Year of the Dragon'. Some decided to have their babies earlier, preferring a 'Dragon' child to a 'Snake'. I wish their children well. All the traditional omens are on their side. After all, I have a 'Dragon' son.''

No amount of work by the Ministries of Education or Culture could change these deeply ingrained cultural beliefs. Perhaps over one or two generations, some of these traditional attitudes, or articles of faith, might alter. Many years of experience had taught him that on crucial, emotional issues of language, culture and religion, the Singaporean, however Western-educated or modernised, had deep abiding values, faiths, and myths, handed down from mother to child, and reinforced by the father and members of the family and society. In 1976, the auspicious "Year of the Dragon", Singapore made a 7 per cent growth in real terms — 9 per cent in money terms, minus 2 per cent for inflation. The "Year of the Snake" begins under less auspicious circumstances. There was not the same buoyancy of expectations as at the last Chinese New Year. There were problems about oil prices and the Arab-Israeli problems. The American economy would be stimulated by more than US$30 billion, about US$15 billion through tax rebates, and the rest by deficit budgetting, deliberately to create jobs. "Let us hope it works without re-creating troublesome inflation again. The EEC countries are going through a difficult phase with unemployment at high levels, especially in Italy and Britain. The Japanese, hardworking, united, shrewd and pushful, are finding the Europeans increasingly difficult. They have been threatened by the EEC over shipbuilding, for taking too many new orders because European shipyards cannot compete. And Japan's US$5 billion balance of trade surplus against America for 1976 may have to be scaled down if the Japanese are to help President Carter resolve American unemployment. This means hard times ahead for all, including us, Singaporeans. Our expectations of rapidly rising standards of living must be scaled down. Management and workers must be more efficient and productive. And our entrepreneurs must seek new markets for their products, especially in the oil-producing countries of the Middle East.''

Lee said: "We must also increase regional co-operation. Then with greater solidarity, our bargaining position with America, Japan, Western Europe and Australasia will improve to the benefit of every ASEAN country. We must think in terms of ASEAN. Enlightened self-interest requires that we have thriving and prosperous neighbours. Indeed, in 1974 and 1975, when Hong Kong suffered minus growth rates, one of several reasons why Singapore did better than Hong Kong, with 6.7 per cent growth for 1974 and 4 per cent for 1975, was that our ASEAN neighbours were prospering, helped partly by the boom in commodity prices, oil, rubber, tin, copper, palm, rice, sugar, maize, besides also importing industrial machinery for their industries." But more important than prosperity was security. The better economic conditions were in ASEAN, the greater the resistance to communist infiltration and subversion. "We must help each other to help ourselves, the non-communist countries of the region."

XI

Nobody in Singapore has been an elected Member of Parliament longer than Lee Kuan Yew. He is one of the original three PAP members who fought the 1955 elections. They won easily. By 1977, Lee had been an elected MP for twenty-two years. On 23 February, he made a long and rambling speech in Parliament during which he welcomed eleven new Members to the House. He said that while, over the previous days, he had not always been physically in the House, "with the aid of modern electronics" he had, with considerable ease, been able to follow the proceedings. He urged the new Members to take themselves seriously, for "upon us", he said, "was the burden of finding a successor government worthy of its responsibilities". It was not an easy job. Very few countries had been able, through the one-man-one-vote system, "to produce a group of men who could provide a continuity in good government, change of policies, flexibility, to reflect the changing moods of an electorate. You need a wide spread, a wide variety representing all types, selective and representative of the population. That is why we are here."

Lee said he was a little disappointed that some new Members were questioning the policies of the government, especially on language and education. "May I explain briefly and simply for new Members. Language, culture and religion in a multi-racial, multi-lingual, multi-religious and multi-ethnic society, with one-man, one-vote can lead to great tragedy, as it has in India and Pakistan. And in Canada, after nearly two hundred years of British conquest of Quebec, the Quebeconis are talking of separate independence." Lee recalled early difficulties in Singapore over the language problem. "I believe that we are beginning to become one people, very slowly, very gradually ... but until today the Chinese Chamber of Commerce votes along clan lines ... there is weighted representation ... Hokkiens, Teochews, Cantonese, Hainanese, Shanghainese, Hakkas."

Turning to education, the Prime Minister said this politically had been a "red-hot potato. It was dynamite". He paid a tribute to the former Education Minister, Mr. Yong Nyuk Lin. "He took the job where angels feared to tread." He held office for four years and four months. Then Mr. Ong Pang Boon took over. He was in charge for seven years. "Education was still a hot potato." Mr. Lim Kim San took over for two years. He was followed by Dr. Lee Chiaw Meng, who was Minister of Education for nearly two years. So, until June, 1975 there were only four Ministers in sixteen years. Not only that: there was continuity in Permanent Secretaries. Altogether there had been only six changes.

There had been two ways to bring about bilingualism — by edict or by voluntary choice. "Had we done the stupid thing by edict and said to the people 'You will learn two languages and you will learn English as one of them', I think Singapore would have gone a different way. We would be speaking Chinese in this Chamber!"

Having dealt in some detail with the happenings in the State during the development of the education policy, Lee claimed that in political terms, the education policy had been a resounding success.

In passing, Lee mentioned the family planning policy "which had worked", though it had not been popular with the seven Catholic MPs. Fifteen of the sixty-nine MPs were Christians. "Fifteen but of sixty-nine is 21.79 per cent of the population of this House. I congratulate the Christians. The missionaries did a good job in producing leader-men. In total population, the Christians are only about 9 per cent: 21 per cent in this House representing 9 per cent. Ah! But that is not the whole story. We have seven Catholics, more than 10 per cent of the House, and Catholics make up less than 4 per cent of the population."

Speaking again about the importance of bilingualism, Lee said: "If you lose that Chinese education and you go completely English-educated, you will lose that drive, that self-confidence. That is what is wrong. The danger is, if you are Chinese-educated and only Chinese-educated, you are monolingual; then your source of literature will be communist. That means big trouble. But if you are bilingual, you will have binocular vision; then you see the world in 3-D. I will confirm that. We went to China last year in May. Many members of the party spoke Chinese, were Chinese. There was no problem of language. We understood what was being said and what was being written. There is a new diction. Completely different. Of course, the Member for Katong is right, no culture, no civilisation, stands still. Or it dies, or it is mummified. The difference between the Chinese in Peking or Canton and the Chinese in Singapore is so great as to make it a difference of kind. And when the Chinese in Singapore is trilingual and he knows of another different world, a vast world reaching out to Mars and beyond, he listens to all this exposition, understands it, but he says to himself, well, that is one way of doing it. But in Singapore we had better do it the simpler way. For us, the easier way is just plug it into the grid. We stand other risks, of course, because the grid is already there. You tap Western science, Western technology, trade with the West. But when they have a depression, recession and unemployment, we get the rigor. We cannot avoid that. Whether America is in recession, or Europe has got five or six million unemployed, it makes not the slightest difference to China. Therefore, a critical decision was made. And I say the decision is right and must be pursued vigorously — for if we become a monolingual society, deculturised from our roots, we are in deep trouble. Have we got a total complete value system to replace the Confucian system, to replace Malay culture and values and Islam?"

Lee continued: "We do not know what is going to happen. The end product has got to be partly the decisions we make, but also mainly what the interaction will be between English and a whole world of literature, science, technology, arts, culture, music, the mass media and the lot, and the basic values of your own self. It is critical." Bilingualism had its advantages. It had its dangers. "Because if the boy is monolingual, then the literature that he has will be more and more only from China. And whether you read the most innocent book on the beauty of Kwei Lin and its stalagmites and stalactites, in between you will get the *Thoughts*. Yes, it is part of the new evolving value system. But it is a risk we must take. For another reason, that those who are at a disadvantage, who live in a completely dialect-speaking village or home, who are not particularly fast in learning, when they go to school they are learning two foreign, or two new languages, neither of which is their mother tongue. Mandarin and English. What are we? Is it growth, more growth, more materialism? Just what are we doing? What do we try to be? Does man live by bread alone? Well, we are trying to make a nation, a people — tolerant, considerate, compassionate but rugged or we will not survive. Because it was never the intention of the British that Singapore should ever be independent. Let me assure all Hon.Members that each time I swear the oath of allegience to the Republic of Singapore, my mind goes back to 9 August, 1965. I did not want it. We had independence thrust upon us. And the expectation was that in two to three years we would be so down on our knees and crawling, that we would have to go back on any terms. No autonomy in Education, Labour, and all the other subjects. Different terms. Maybe if they were kind, like Penang and Malacca. But we resolved to make this work. Never forget that it was the will, not just of a few men. That was necessary. But the will was in the people. Otherwise it would not have worked. They went through the biggest education Singapore ever got. It was from September 1963 to 9 August, 1965. We learnt what life was about. It also caused two riots — June 1964, late September 1964. During the second one I was away in Brussels as the guest speaker at the centenary of the Socialist International. Then they wanted me to explain how bad communism was — the communists were winning in Southeast Asia except Singapore. But alas, the world has changed. Now the Socialist International has got new activists. They will not invite me to address them. What is the point of addressing them anyway? They want to dress me down. They have no use for us."

"We want to try, very simply, to allow each individual ethnic, cultural, lingusitic, religious group to keep what it can of its past and to acquire what is necessary to make Singapore an industrialised society, or we will never get off the ground. If we go back to a farming community with the *cangkul* or the spade, and to fishing, I do not think we can support a population of thirty thousand on three meals a day."

Lee said he wanted to touch on a few other items before he completed his induction into both mass politics and parliamentary politics for the new Members. "The way we conduct ourselves in this Chamber and outside as MPs, as Parliamentary Secretaries, as Ministers, will decide whether in 1981, beginning middle, end, depending on when we think we will get the maximum votes, the elections are fought from now, not in 1981. We did not fight the elections on 23 December. We fought it as from September 1972. We made sure that no MP, no Parliamentary Secretary, no Minister misbehaved or abused his power. Because if you do, it is a very tight and swift compact society, it spreads like wildfire. Dr. Ong, the Member for Kim Seng, his generation does not go to coffee-shops. But let me tell him that he would be surprised to know what is being discussed and debated with very great candour and vehemence and the very frank language with which it is discussed of the weaknesses and follies of MPs, Ministers and others. And when the CP mounts a smear campaign, I have seen sane rational men, Ministers, suddenly turn pale because the branch secretary came and said: By God, the whole kampong has switched allegience. Rumour has it that you've got four wives. The Minister collects a whole bundle of pamphlets, brings his biography and personally distributes it to counter the smear. It took us the best part of thirteen years from 1952, before we even founded the party, to 1965, to establish ourselves as people who can be trusted and relied upon regardless of smears. That is why we could allow a deliberate smear campaign of corruption during the campaign and took action only after. We ran the risk that if we took action during the campaign, they would say: Unfair. But after the campaign — you utter all these falsehoods, knowing that there was no other way in which to shake the confidence the people have in the Government, than alleging corruption, well, matters have got to be resolved. We have to make changes in the election laws. Because if a man is bankrupt it is no use suing him."

Lee had something to say about gambling. "*Big Sweep* and *Toto*, it is a problem we face. They face it in Moscow. If you do not run the *Big Sweep* and *Toto*, the *chap-ji-kee* man who has always swindled the people of their money is still there. Gambling is the history of Singapore. The Chinese who travelled overseas are the biggest gamblers you can find in the world. To leave China was to gamble. In Manchu China, if you returned you were beheaded. Because you were bringing in dangerous foreign ideas. So to leave China for Nanyang was a gamble. We are an open, exposed society. You want to stop the tourists? You want your hotels empty? There is no other way than to implant the values in. Let us not kid ourselves. No society is static, it either adjusts, adapts, learns how to protect itself, or it is debased, corrupted, and brought down. You face up to it by implanting basic values. That is why, however different the various religions, this government is in favour of a man believing in something than believing in nothing. I would rather have a Muslim, a devout Hindu, than a permissive atheist. It is because of the problems of atheism in the West that they are in trouble. Fortunately the Chinese never believed in heaven and hell for rational behaviour. Man must behave, says Confucius, long before Mao, in a certain way in order that orderly civilised living is possible. Not that you will go to hell if you do bad, or you will go to heaven if you do good. But if you do not do that, civilised living is not possible for anybody ... There are certain values which have preserved us. This is much the oldest civilisation in the world. It is one of the great civilisations. Civilisations existed in the Mesopotamian valley, in Mohenjo Daro, and lots of other places. But the Chinese is the only one which had a continuous history and survived, more or less with definite links to the past. It is different from what you see in Greece (the ruins) and the people now in Greece. The first principle of any civilisation is orderly living and the rearing of the young. Maternity is a matter of fact, provable fact. Paternity is a matter of opinion. You can have blood tests and so on. Maybe they can find a test to establish it. Yes, the child is yours. Nobody else's. How do you know it is not my brother's? And so the Jews accept this fact. And the Jews say, Never mind who the father was. Is the mother a Jewess? If she is a Jewess, then the child is a Jew. I am not saying, No, let us be celibate. I am not even thinking let us all be faithful to our wives; let us have no divorces. I do not ask that. All I ask is, please do not misbehave yourself. Anybody who has a paternity suit against him is out and there will be a by-election. That is all I say. Let us have none of this.''

Lee continued: ''The mass media of the West believes that we ought to be like them. Why? Because we are human beings and they are civilised. They are advanced and, therefore, we must be like them. We are not like them. We are not civilised. But you see, here is my authority. Ours is the oldest civilisation in the world. It goes back 5,000 years, provable 4,000 years. The fifth thousand is mythology ... You say, Look, you touch my wife, I kill you. Then there is a pool in which everybody can forage. It may be hypocritical. Maybe it is bad. But it preserved the civilisation for 5,000 years and it had nothing to do with God, heaven and hell. And I say, you lose that, we lose all. I use the language of the West but the inside, my value system, is different. I understand the Englishman. He knows deep in his heart that he is superior to the Welshman and the Scotsman. Deep here, I am a Chinaman. Yes, an uprooted Chinaman, transformed into a Singaporean. Because when I went to China, I discovered that I was not a Chinaman ... You know, I often meet great statesmen, my privilege. They told me wondrous tales before I went to China. Of course, a lot of it was true. It is a marvellous society compared to what it was. But in Singapore any time, every time, you can damn the Prime Minister and so long as it is not a lie and a criminal lie, nothing happens to you. You can say a lot of things. You can write books about him, damning him. So long as it is not a libel, go ahead ... I have the rare distinction of having two Ministerial colleagues with brothers in China. I have a perception, and I think they have a perception (they have been there), of China, and the great sacrifices being made to turn China into a modern industrial state by the end of this century. SIA does not yet go to Peking, but one day, we will when we establish relations. And I am absolutely certain that this can be done, given appreciation that we share a common destiny. Without that appreciation, of course, we are in trouble.''

400

"Finally, Mr. Speaker, Sir, may I pose the real basic problem facing Singapore, and indeed, the world — the answer to communism and its spread. Here in Southeast Asia, it is by insurgency, subversion, input of ideology, infusion of weapons and insurgency. If we just take Singapore alone, we would have solved the problem. But we know that it has not been solved, because it is not just Singapore. They say Malaya — Malayan Communist Party — including Singapore. So what is the answer? The answer of the West — this was the answer of Europe and America of the Dulles era — was that if you are not anti-communist, you are immoral. Dulles said the Indians were non-aligned and so they were immoral. How do they prevent their people from going communist? Their counter ideology was then anti-communism. And in America a witch-hunt, the McCarthy era; if you are a communist, you are out. So if you want to be a naturalised American, you swear that you have never been a member of the communist party at all, ever in your life. But in Britain — and they used to tell me with great pride and I listened to them and I almost believed them — they said, All you have got to do really is to develop. Then you would be like us, where we can have communists running around and they cannot cause any trouble. You see, they have got no followers because we give the good life to the people. So they are treated as cranks, idiots, half-wits. Those were the 1940s when I was a student. Then came the 1950s when I was a politician and a member of the Singapore Government All-Party Delegation. The government then was a very weak one, not independent, and used to go to London every year to negotiate a new constitution. And I met my old friends. They said, Yes, that is the way. Morgan Philips, now dead, general secretary of the British Labour Party, said: Don't worry at all. The communists are cranks. Look at them, at every election they lose. The TUC said: Ah, no problem at all. Just a few cranks. Their counter was materialism. I give you the good life which means: With one-man one-vote I seduce you away from the ideology by the good soft life. Did it work? I do not think it has worked. The communists have now got into powerful positions in the unions because they work harder. To be a communist, you must have very active glands. If you want a good life, you go into the city and make money like Slater Walker. Or you do it the honest hard way — be a doctor on National Health or a dentist on National Health. This is also a good way. Or if you have really got active glands, you think the society is wrong, you are deprived, you never went through a good school that taught you to speak English like an English gentleman, but you spoke English like a working class person whose home was poor, then with active glands you work like a beaver, because your glands are pouring out adrenalin. So now they are in charge of very powerful critical unions and they are setting the pace. They are calling the shots.

"What happened here in the forties, fifties and sixties? I think we have very happy memories of the Middle Road unions. Every day they ate there and they slept there. They showed the workers how hardworking they were. They denigrated me. They said I had an air-conditioned office

401

and I slept in an air-conditioned room. I was a bourgeois. So were all my friends bourgeois men. They thought we were chicken. We learnt how they operated. It is the same modus operandi. They are active. They are working with social democrats or democratic socialists. The social democrat likes his glass of beer, likes to have fun, so he leaves the meeting early. When all the chaps have left, they take the vote at two o'clock in the morning and carry the union. So, in the PAP, we used to squat till three or four o'clock in the morning, and in this Parliament. For those who were then not here, we used to have marathon sessions that began at two o'clock in the afternoon and ended up the next morning at seven o'clock. On one memorable occasion, the failed candidate for Rochore made a seven and a half hour speech. Marvellous. He had ghost writers there, scribbling away. As he finished a whole sheaf, more sheaves came in, seven and a half hours — to intimidate us. They made a very grave error of judgement. He gambled, and he is a great gambler, and he lost. We learnt how they operated. We knew how the magician worked. We were not in the audience. We were actually at the back stage, watching the magician and, in fact, helping him from time to time. The tricks are quite skilful. So when it came to our turn and they wanted to operate on us, we said, Ah, yes. We were not there when they pulled the trigger. We were somewhere else. And what was more important, we never gave hostages to fortune. Keep your hands clean, gentlemen. If we allow you to put your hand in anybody's till, then we are all dead, politically. That is the first lesson.

"That is why it was with great sorrow that we had to prosecute Mr. Wee Toon Boon. I had no choice. He was my friend. He was my comrade, going back to 1957 in the City Council elections. He fought the communists with us. But as Singapore developed and with rapid development, people got rich quickly. His CCC member was a contractor, building the people all sorts of buildings. He lent him Mercedes cars. You start off, first, by lending the man. Any time you like to use my car, it is there. Why sit in a Ford? You are a Minister. But Ministers use cars only on official functions from the pool. He said, use my Mercedes. It started off that way. Then your appetite is whetted. Then step by step you are seduced until finally, why not ...? Once you have given a hostage to fortune, it is finished. So please, gentlemen, learn this. There are many more lessons which, I hope, I will have the pleasure of imparting in time, by which I mean, in time before you are put to the test. That is really the crunch.

"There are some other debating points. The Member for Nee Soon said, we rush through Bills in the House and so on. Wrong. We have had an impeccable record. In the Third Parliament from 12 October 1972 to 24 November 1976 there were only five Certificates of Urgency. It is a good debating point that we rushed through the House, all three readings, without adequate time for study and debate. A common occurrence? Five times in four and a half years, and every one of them was very urgent, technical one. Do better next time.

"Somebody else wanted the Parliamentary Pensions Act to be

amended because, quite rightly, we all feel very sad. I think the Member for Nee Soon also said: "... the Parliamentary Pensions Act should be amended to see whether our late MP is due for any entitlement under this Act. We all feel and, I feel, I have lost a good friend. But we cannot. We can pass it, but it would be wrong. Because the next step is that the civil servant will say, me too. What is your answer? What is our answer? Yes, for me, sixty-nine heroes of Singapore defenders of freedom, but not for you, the sixty thousand civil servants, plus the statutory boards. A hundred thousand-plus people? We have to pay all the widows? The law says, and we follow the law, that if a man dies before he has retired, although he has qualified for a pension, his dependants get one full year's pay without paying estate duty or income tax. That we shall do. And the rest is up to you and me. And I am glad to say that quite a few have written to give more than I have suggested. I am quite prepared for some shocks. Some may write in and say, please can I, in view of the harsh circumstances I am in, give less than what you have suggested? Well, that is our responsibility. We discharge it. And in 1980/81 we can face the people."

Lee went on to deal with other matters, PUB bills among them. He said: "You know the Singaporean. He is a hardworking, industrious, rugged individual. Or we would not have made the grade. But let us also recognise that he is a champion gambler ... We will sort out all the problems. But one major and decisive problem is how do we produce, before the crunch comes, a group of men who will survive the crunch? The last time in 1959, very fortunately, if my memory is right, we won forty-three out of fifty-one seats. In 1961, when the crunch came and they thought the other side was winning, it became 16 – 25. It was quite an experience, and of course, the British were quite worried too. So they said: Look, keep the communists out at all costs. Have an alliance with — never mind, whether they are corrupt or not — the Labour Front, socialists, whatever it was. Have an alliance with them. If we had, we would have died. Finally it became 26 – 25 with the death of Ahmad Ibrahim. If Singapore wants excitement that is real excitement. That is real drama and a real test of nerves. We had to bring in a sick Member here to vote at all odd hours of the day and night. From mid-1962, when Ahmad Ibrahim died, till September 1963, over one year, it was a test of nerves. So we knew what the melting point was, at what degree of temperature. It was a process of elimination.

"Among the gentlemen of that generation, there are only ten left in this House. Of the 1955 generation, when I was sitting in the Opposition debating with first, Mr. David Marshall, and then Mr. Lim Yew Hock, there were four of us — three PAP and one Independent. Ahmad Ibrahim is dead. Goh Chew Chua is dead. Lim Chin Siong is in Britain, I hope living comfortably and happily. He also made the wrong choice, but at least he was courageous enough to say: Well, I call it quits. And I respect him. I am the sole survivor of the 1955 generation. There are nine others from 1959. Harrowing days they were! Let me read their names. I go back to 1955. Mr. Chan Chee Seng (Jalan Besar) 1959; Mr. Chor Yeok Eng (Bukit Timah) 1959. He will bear witness that Barisan went to look for him in the middle of the night. He lived in Bukit Timah in a lonely place, and they were going to fix him. If he crossed over, then it would become 26 – 26. If I had to go to battle and I had to choose one other, I will pick him. (Applause). Goh Keng Swee, Lee Khoon Choy, Ong Pang Boon, S. Rajaratnam, Toh Chin Chye, Haji Ya'acob and Yong Nyuk Lin. I am not a Muslim. I do not know where Haji Ya'acob got his strength from, maybe from Islam. But if I am in a tight corner, I think I would like to have Haji Ya'acob around because together we had gone through some very tough times. (Applause). The real test was when there were race clashes and the police were not in our hands from 1963 to 1965. It was so easy for the Malays just to flip over and fix Ya'acob. He was offered a vast sum of money. Ten years' salary and allowances just to switch over. You can buy, you can fix, you can threaten, you can do all kinds of things. We have gone through all that.

"Now, I give you the 1963 generation that went to the elections with us, not knowing whether we were going to get hammered or not. The communists were running around. Rahim Ishak, E.W. Barker, Fong Sip Chee, P. Govindaswamy — may I pause here? Congratulations! He made Mr. David Marshall lose his deposit in Anson (Applause). When the communists backed Mr. David Marshall in the by-election in 1962, Mr. Marshall won. When the communists fielded their own candidate, Mr. Marshall lost his deposit. You beat Barisan. We want to make sure that we have got men like him, Ho Cheng Choon, Ho See Beng, Jek Yeun Thong, who was my Political Secretary in 1959. I am glad that I lose only my Parliamentary Secretary and not my Political Secretary. My Parliamentary Secretary, who Mr. Jek had guaranteed had given up communism, suddenly walked over to the other side. I woke up one morning to find he was anti-Malaysia, anti-merger. You know this was a very deep conspiracy. Jek (I give no secrets away) was the leader of the cell under which was Chan Sun Wing, my former Parliamentary Secretary. But Jek did not know that his former superior turned up and told Chan Sun Wing to switch. So Jek's order was countermanded. Chan Sun Wing thought that the other side was going to win, so better take the other side's orders. God bless Chan Sun Wing. I hope, if he is alive somewhere in the Rhio Islands or in Indonesia or some place, that he is living peacefully and happily because if he comes back the police would like to ask him a few questions. 1963 — Lim Kim San, Ng Kah Ting (Punggol), my congratulations. We did not expect to win. The Member was then twenty-three, a very young man. He probably also did not expect to win, but fought and won. Ng Yeow Chong — I am sorry to say, Mr. Speaker, Sir, he has not been able yet to attend our sittings because he is receiving treatment in hospital for his eye. Othman Wok and Rahmat Kenap. He has not got a Ph.D. He has not got a B.A. Nor even a School Certificate. But I tell you what he has got: courage, loyalty and steadfastness in a crisis. After the

404

riots in Geylang Serai, it was like that, each time I went down to face the mob. It was easier for me but tougher for him because he was then treated as a traitor, *kafir*.

"Sia Kah Hui, Teong Eng Siong — 1963 generation: 24 out of 69 — just one over one-third. If we can pass to you, the other two-thirds, an idea of what it was like, then maybe we will be all right. I am not saying that you (the two-thirds) are not all right. All I am saying is that you would not know until the guns open fire. You can put soldiers through: what they call, the fireworks — where they know that they are firing blanks and thunder flashes, and there is so much smoke and so on. But when an army goes in, like the American army landing in North Africa in 1943 for the first time, they got really slaughtered. It was only after that first shock that they got over the combat shock, and became warriors. You can stimulate it but it is not the same. When he knows it is a real live bullet, because it goes *zing* and is meant for him, that is the time when you know — you look at his pants and you know whether he is a man or he is not. Then we have the 1966 generation — the by-elections when Barisan Sosialis walked out. Ho Kah Leong, Lim Guan Hoo. He went to fight Bukit Merah, which was first won by Barisan. Well, he won. But we shall miss him. I hope he can recover but the chances are very slender, and his wife and family are facing a tremendous ordeal. Mr. Tang See Chim, Dr. Yeoh Ghim Seng. Then the 1967 generation. Mr. Ang Nam Piau, Mr. B. Selvadurai. I think the 1967 generation is not quite the same, because then they knew they were winners. In 1966, maybe we could still have lost. But in 1963 when we fought we knew that we could not only lose our pants, but we could lose our lives. And those who were at the counting centres at Bukit Timah, where they lost — Mr. K.C. Lee for Bukit Panjang and Mr. Chor Yeok Eng for Bukit Timah — if we had lost and Barisan had won, I think they would have come out of the counting centre pretty bashed up ...

"One last word of advice, if you like to call it, or just plain fact. If you want to be popular, do not try to be popular all the time. Popular government does not mean that you do popular things all the time. We do not want to be unpopular or to do unpopular things. But when they are necessary, they will be done. Popular representative government means that within each five-year period, your policies have demonstrably worked and won popular support. That is what it means. And if we flinch from the unpopular, we are in deep trouble. Of course, the Area Licensing Scheme (ALS) was unpopular. Of course, car taxes were unpopular. But, gentlemen, which would you have? A jammed-up Singapore with car owners exasperated, bus passengers exasperated, or 20,000 to 30,000 car owners having to lay up their cars and hundreds of thousands going through in buses or in shared cars? We made that decision, and it was right. Of course, if we had an election period, like the New Zealanders and the Australians have for three years instead of five years, that is more difficult. But Sir Robert Menzies, in spite of three-year periods, won and stayed in office for twelve years. But he knew that popular representative government means that sometimes even when 15 per cent (he once told me up till 55 per cent) are against you, if it is right, proceed. When it works out all right, they will swing back. But if you flinch, then that 55 per cent becomes 65 per cent and you are out. The way to enjoy your pension is to ensure good stable, fair, just, government which commands the trust and respect of the people. No more, no less. Singaporeans have been accustomed to high standards of effective government. They deserve nothing but the best. And it is our duty to ensure that they continue to receive the best. Thank you, Mr. Speaker."

XII

Ludovic Kennedy of the BBC interviewed Lee on 5 March.

Kennedy: Prime Minister, how worried are you by recent reports of the growing communist guerilla activity in Thailand, not only in the north of Thailand but also on the Thailand-Malaysia border, which isn't so very far from here?

Prime Minister: Actually, the situation is better now than it was, say, six months ago when there was almost no effective government in Bangkok, and the border between Malaysia and Thailand was no man's land. In other words, it's free-for-all for the communists. Now they have a government in Bangkok, a civilian one backed by the military and they are co-operating with the Malaysian Government in not eliminating, but at least keeping the communists on the move instead of consolidating from platoons to companies, to battalions, and finally, to brigades and divisions.

Kennedy: Do you think in the long-term it is only a matter of time before Thailand goes the way of Vietnam and Cambodia?

Prime Minister: I do not believe that it's a simple business of dominoes falling. But Thailand has got a problem or many problems. One of the problems is how to ensure that her border areas which had never had much government, even in the best of times, are now not turned into areas where organised groups begin to build up military strongholds and from whence they sally forth and knock down police posts, soldiers doing sentry duties and gradually spread terror of fear and with fear comes obedience from the farmers and the peasantry generally, and then recruitment of more sons of peasants into their ranks.

Kennedy: You are not worried about things in the foreseeable future. Is that right?

Prime Minister: Foreseeable? This depends whether you are long-sighted or short-sighted. If you say I am not worried for the security of Singapore for the next five to ten years, I think you are absolutely right.

Kennedy: But you can't see beyond that?

Prime Minister: I would not like to put on a pair of binoculars and go beyond say, ten. In ten years, if the Western position, which really means the American position in Asia, and in Africa for that matter, and God knows what would happen in the Middle East, goes down and eroded in the way it has been in the past ten years, then we have to live with the realities of a very pervasive, completely uninhibited and forward-going, forward-looking Soviet presence ...

Kennedy: Yes, you said at the Commonwealth Conference in 1975: If the United States were to withdraw from Southeast Asia, the Russians might move in, or words to that effect. Do you still ...?

Prime Minister: ... Since then, they have moved in, in a big way.

Kennedy: To the Indian Ocean?

Prime Minister: And the waters of the South Pacific and the Western Pacific, and they have one of the largest fishing fleets in Southeast Asia. You can see them with all the latest of anything in American gadgetry that you can think of, for sounding out fish, depth of shoal and all the rest of it. I think you will find two or three very modern vessels under repair in our dockyards. But that is not the only problem. The problem then will be growing conflict, competition, between them and the People's Republic of China.

Kennedy: Well, I was going to ask you that, Prime Minister. Do you have any misgivings about the intention of the People's Republic of China, so far as Singapore is concerned and Southeast Asia generally?

Prime Minister: You are asking me to say publicy that I have misgivings about the intentions of a government, which we are on correct and gradually cordial and probably in the future, friendly relations. It's hardly the kind of question one puts on television. If you ask me privately, I'll say they are extremely courteous, congenial hosts, very candid in the way in which they expound the philosophy of life and that philosophy includes the belief that the east wind must triumph.

Kennedy: That the east . . .?

Prime Minister: That the east wind must triumph. The east is red and so eventually all Marxist-Leninist parties throughout the world, genuinely Marxist-Leninist parties, not revisionist ones, they will triumph because that is the course of history. But having been brainwashed in bourgeois British institutions about civilization and the theories thereof — rise and fall of Rome, Bertrand Russell and Western Civilization — I am hoping it is not pre-determined ... I am not really sold on the inevitability of the evolution of man and society. I think Darwin, maybe, can explain how we became homo sapiens, but what will be, having got here, nobody really knows. And I don't think even Rand Corporation, having taken a beating in what they thought would happen in Vietnam, would stick their necks out.

Kennedy: Prime Minister, I believe that you are coming to the next Commonwealth Conference in London this summer. Do you believe that these Commonwealth Conferences, which are a relic of empire, really serve any useful purpose now?

Prime Minister: I don't first of all, subscribe to your aside, relic of

407

empire. I don't think the Conference in any way represents the past. It's what we are groping for into the future. The past is behind us. But as a result of the past, we have certain common doctrines or common denominators — language, terms of reference, methods of administration, thought processes, saving-grams, telegrams, ministers who hold political responsibilities and permanent civil servants who carry on whatever the ministers do. And we live in a completely different world from what was empire. And this is a world of instant communications and instant transportation — almost instant with the supersonic. People are meeting and conferencing and persuading either for or against, at any one time, any number of propositions — whether it is the Arab-Israeli thing or Rhodesia on which very few are on the side of the whites in Rhodesia — I am sorry to say or rather I am happy to say, depending on whether you think the whites in Rhodesia have been wise or unwise. I am sorry because I think they have been unwise — they have left it too late. So you've got to mobilise opinion ...

Kennedy: I thought you were going to say which side you are on, Prime Minister, just then, in Rhodesia.

Prime Minister: Yes, I am on the side of the winners, the blacks. They must win.

Kennedy: Do you think in Africa, where you have travelled extensively, that they can ever achieve the same kind of multi-racialist society which you've achieved so successfully here in Singapore?

Prime Minister: Here again, you are asking me publicly to pass judgement on an ideal which African leaders of great eminence have passionately espoused, and I must wish them well and hope that the ideals can be achieved. I think the odds against such an ideal being established in the immediate future are extremely great; because of the black-white dichotomy, tied-up with history of exploitation, tied-up with problems of slavery and what the blacks underwent in America and the present black-white problem still unsolved in America, tied-up with Britain's black-white growing conflicts and that in France. So I think it is one of the most difficult problems of race integration or co-existence ever posed on man.

Kennedy: What is your view about President Amin coming to the Conference, Prime Minister?

Prime Minister: I need notice of that question. I don't know whether he is coming. I would be surprised if he did. And I am not sure whether I'll be agreeably surprised. I'll be hard put to go through the motions of protocol or what protocol requires on such occasion.

Kennedy: You will find it embarrassing. That's what you are saying?

Prime Minister: That is what you are saying.

Kennedy: Prime Minister, you had some quite harsh things to say about Britain recently. At the opening of your Parliament the other day, you said of us, "A great people have been temporarily reduced to straitened circumstances by excessive cushioning of life by state subsidies." Do you think that was quite fair?

Prime Minister: It is only one of the reasons for the economic and the social problems in Britain. It's a vast subject, which you know more about than I do. But the part that I am concerned with, is that one-man-one-vote means that at every election time, it's an auction of, really, wealth that has not yet been created. So if I do not effectively debunk the theory that the government will provide — there is always more and more for less and less, there is no need really to try because we are doing all right now — we will be a broken-backed state like so many of the others in the Third World. We've just got off the ground. We nearly fell flat on our faces with the problems of confrontation during Dr. Sukarno's Indonesia, British withdrawal and with it the bases were closed and so on. And now just the first touch of comfort — we are above the rice-line. There are any number of aspiring Wedgewood Benns who think we ought to be giving things for free, that we should not have prescription charges; that it is wicked to make people pay for their medicine; that it is wicked to make them pay for the extras the children have in school, like going out on outings and so on. It is a very attractive election programme.

Kennedy: You also said, Prime Minister, that "If we had British-style trade unions we would be bankrupt." Now, what did you mean by that?

Prime Minister: Now, please! Some of the union leaders are good old friends of mine and I hope they will remain good old friends. In fact, they taught me a lot about labour and the labour movement and so on. But the way things have gone in Britain over the past ten years — well, really from 1964 onwards, thirteen years — it's not the kind of labour movement that I knew in Britain when I was a student there watching it, watching socialism — the democratic way — that the will of the majority is expressed periodically, within a period of five years, and once expressed, that will must be respected. Well, it's a different Britain. That was old-fashioned constitutional theory. The new theory now which I am seeing evolved is: never mind what the majority will is. We, the union leaders who have been elected by a small group of very important people — the shop stewards and the people who stayed late into the early hours of the morning to make the crucial decisions when the others have got tired and gone home — have decided that this will be so. And quite rightly, Mr. Denis Healey, as Chancellor of the Exchequer, tells the House of Commons what he hopes the budget should be and then says: "I will discuss it with the trade unions." Well, if my colleague, the Minister of Finance, is caught or trapped in that position, I think we are bankrupt. Yes, because they would want the moon, the stars and beyond and why not? We have got some reserves, our credit is good, we could go on for five, maybe, seven years. Then what? Without North Sea oil?

Kennedy: How can we put our house in order?

Prime Minister: Why do you want to put your house in order? You've got North Sea oil that lubricates and will smooth out every friction. You will be as happy and as relaxed as the Arabs.

Kennedy: I thought you were going to say the same as you are.

Prime Minister: No, I have got to work. Every grain of rice that we consume is paid for in foreign exchange. Nature did not intend that Singapore be an agricultural country. That's why it was uninhabited. It was intended to be discovered or re-discovered — if you want to be sensitive to the feelings of people who believe in myths and mythology of the region — by one called Stamford Raffles, later made a knight, 1819 — turned into an emporium, a base, a manufacturing centre, a financial centre, an independent republic. And it's a fine mechanism, which, if we tamper around with the kind of screwdrivers and spanners that we have along the picket lines, when they squatted in front of the gate and don't allow lorries carrying coal or oil to pass into the power stations, well, the clock stops ticking.

Kennedy: Do you think that the recent Haw Par affair is a symptom of declining standards in British life?

Prime Minister: No, I think it is a sympton of this craze for easy money. Only a fool works hard to get to the top. The bright will work out some clever scheme all within the law. You juggle the books, prices of stocks go up and down and in accordance with your profits that you disclosed or chose not to disclose. The moment you say you are taking over a company — the magic, the touch of Midas or the belief that there is a touch of Midas makes it go up — people who are in the know buy before the take-over is announced. It's an episode in the life of the British people, in fact, in the life of the Western European peoples or Americans, too.

Kennedy: Have you any complaints in the decision of the Metropolitan Magistrate that Mr. Slater had no case to answer?

Prime Minister: Mr. Kennedy, I spent four years of life trained in the intricacies of the laws of the England. I was called to the bar as barrister at the Middle Temple. I was subsequently made an honourary bencher which entitles me to certain privileges without fee. I have absolutely no comment whatever.

Kennedy: If I could just ask you this: In view of the fact that the Magistrate decided that there wasn't a case to answer, was it right and correct of the Singapore Government to bring extradition proceedings against Mr. Slater?

Prime Minister: You may find this difficult to believe. But, you know, I have so many things on my plate that, really, Mr. Slater and his activities occupy only a minor part of that plate. These decisions were taken by the Attorney-General, who, in this particular case, was, I think, careful enough not to risk his own reputation and, therefore, had the opinion or opinions of two separate eminent silks at the English Bar, and they advised that there was a case.

Kennedy: I only asked the question, Prime Minister, because the whole case has stirred up a lot of interest in Britain. *The Times* of London did express some concern in a leading article that if any of these people were extradited here they might not get a fair trial. What is your comment on that?

410

Prime Minister: I don't know who wrote that article. But I think it was so funny. It isn't true. Once a upon a time, the London *Times* carried a certain aura which was a reflection of the patina of empire. It had solemn columns on its front page. It reports news, straight. It does not crusade. It does not sensationalise. I think that editorial is a piece of good sensational writing, worthy of the best of the Express-types. We allow British silks especially during the summer vacation, which is, I think June till October, to come out here and lead our own advocates. So there are hundreds of British QCs who know what the truth is. And I think I can go to the Middle Temple and they will still provide me with free port after dinner.

Kennedy: And yet, Prime Minister, when one talks about justice in Singapore — you have in fact abolished trial by jury.

Prime Minister: Yes. Since 1969, and we've had far better administration of the criminal law and justice. You see, the Anglo-Saxon tradition of trial by jury may be good for Anglo-Saxons or the descendants thereof. It never really worked for non Anglo-Saxons.

Kennedy: Why not?

Prime Minister: I don't know — many reasons. The French don't have it. They are Latin. I think the idea of twelve random jurors sitting there and deciding whether you ought to go to jail or whether you ought to pay damages, or not, it's completely alien. And I never forget my first case when I was assigned to defend four murderers. Remember the famous jungle girl case in Singapore in 1950-51?

Kennedy: I just remember the name.

Prime Minister: Well, a Dutch woman who was running away from the Japanese, gave her daughter to a Malay woman to look after. She came back after the War, reclaimed the daughter. The Chief Justice, then an Englishman, pending hearing of the case, sent the girl back who had been converted into Islam to a convent to be looked after, and hell broke loose. The police force mutinied. Malays and Muslims took out their knives and a lot of white men, just because they were white, nothing to do with the case, were killed. These four were accused of killing an RAF officer and his wife and child. They were travelling on a bus from RAF Changi down to town. I was assigned — I had no choice. My job was not to ask them whether they were guilty or not because I knew what the position was and so did they. All I did — and it was my first case — was to work on the weaknesses of the jury — their biases, their prejudices, their reluctance really to find four Mussulmen guilty of killing in cold blood or in a heat of great passion, religious passion, an RAF officer, his wife and his child. I did the simple tricks of advocacy — contradictions between one witness and, his previous statement to the police and the preliminary enquiry — and a long submission to the judge the four were acquitted. The judge was thoroughly disgusted. I went home feeling quite sick because I knew I'd discharged my duty as required of me, but I knew I had done wrong. I decided when we became the government, we will not allow this foolish, completely incongruous system which will never take root

411

here, because no juror will take upon himself the onus of saying: Yes, he will go to jail.

Kennedy: Prime Minister, what do you say to the fact that some people have been detained in prison here for something like thirteen years without trial. Is that justice?

Prime Minister: It is outside the laws of the courts. It's legislation which the British passed when they were faced with a communist insurgency — a revolt. Same laws, the same ones, I suspect, are now in operation in Ulster. There are three of them — you are right — thirteen years, 1963, really coming on to fourteen. Two of them are doctors. I defended them for sedition when we were fighting the British together. I brought out the most ferocious sedition trial QC then at the British Bar — Dennis Pritt. We became great friends. He was a communist or sympathiser — a Marxist; I wasn't. I learnt a lot of the tricks-of-the-trade, including how to lose in a controlled manner one's temper or to pretend to. How to put up a spacious argument — a sound, solid law, and we got them off, between him and us. And the two doctors know that all they have to do is to say, I denounce the use of armed force to overthrow the government and therefore do not support the Malayan Communist Party in their attempt to do so, and they will be released.

Kennedy: Are you saying that in ...?

Prime Minister: And they refused to do that.

Kennedy: But are you saying, Prime Minister, in a strong and prosperous society that you have here now in Singapore — the last election you won the biggest victory ever, you got all the seats in Parliament — that if you release these three people that you couldn't contain them?

Prime Minister: No, that's not the point. We can release these three people. We released one — Dr. Poh Soo Kai, as a trial to see what would happen. We released him in 1972 after we won the last elections with nearly as good a majority — 69 per cent of the electorate. And what did he do? He gave medicine and treated a known, wanted, injured terrorist. There is now evidence by a lawyer, at present under interrogation, who has gone to a magistrate and made a confession, on his own. Now, we have to get him struck off the rolls. But that's not all. He also gave large quantities of antibiotics and other essential medical supplies to couriers, to send them to terrorist forces in the jungle, all in the course of the four years he was out — from 1972 to 1976.

Kennedy: So these other two will have to stay there, forever?

Prime Minister: No.

Kennedy: Until they sign your document?

Prime Minister: No, they don't have to sign a document. All they need say is: I denounce the use of force. I do not support the Malayan Communist Party in their use of force to overthrow the government. But if they believe, as I think they do, that this is inevitable, that there will one day be a great victory parade and they will be on the rostrum where all the

412

local Lenins and Maos will be — well, then they stand firm on principle and wait for tomorrow. I am offering them another alternative: go to any country that's willing to accept you. I am not trading. I am not doing a Chilean exchange with the Russians. You are free to go. They are good doctors, well-trained. You need them for your medical help. I would let them go and help you relieve your shortage of doctors with no conditions whatsoever. But if I allow them here to go out and feed medicine, treat injured terrorists, slip supplies into the jungle — apart from the trouble I am creating for myself, I think the Malaysian Government will take a very dim view of my co-operation in joint security problems.

Kennedy: I am also told, Prime Minister, that there are other people who have been put in prison because you personally brought charges against them for saying libellous things about you during the elections. Is that so?

Prime Minister: No, no, no.

Kennedy: I have got it wrong?

Prime Minister: You have got it wrong. I can't bring a criminal charge against anybody. The Attorney-General does that. There are two forms of libel — criminal libel, civil libel. These men during an election campaign went around saying that I have made through my wife and my brother, who are practising law, $500 per conveyance per flat. And as we have already sold 150,000 flats — public housing, I am therefore worth somewhere between $50 to $70 million.

Kennedy: He said all that?

Prime Minister: Yes. Well, the Attorney-General — and I thank him for it — did not act during the elections or that would have lost me votes. But after the elections, with modern tape recorders, you can't deny what you have said. So they pleaded guilty.

Kennedy: Did the Attorney-General ask you? Did he have your permission to do this?

Prime Minister: No, he doesn't have to ask me.

Kennedy: So you didn't know anything about it?

Prime Minister: No, I knew that he must act. If he knows his job, he must act. I am a lawyer, he is a lawyer. In fact, I am more senior a lawyer than he is. I was called to the Bar earlier than he was. Then, you see, what's the point of suing them in civil libel because they are men-of-straw. But I still got to sue them because some of them, whilst they may be men-of-straw have the capacity to make a really rousing speech. And corruption in a developing country — sad to say — is very often a way of life for those in office.

Kennedy: Wouldn't it be more generous of you, Prime Minister, to have said about these people, if they will withdraw what they said, if they will make an apology, then you will forget about it?

Prime Minister: That's for the civil side. I have offered that. However, I will not forget about it because I think we must still enter judgement so that they cannot interfere in the next elections. If you get bankrupts

413

turning up and uttering more and reckless falsehoods in the next round, I am in trouble, because some fool one day may light a prairie fire. But when a man — and I've got one, unfortunately — who is a lawyer and therefore must be presumed by the public to be a person who knows the law, says words to the effect which he contests as defamatory, which my lawyers advised me it is defamatory. Well, let the case be argued whether I am corrupt or not. Because if they can make this corruption stigma stick, then I have had it. Then all the good that you have done is wiped off because there is one thing, which a Singaporean voter expects and has been made to expect: absolute integrity on the part of those in office. We may make mistakes. They will forgive me. But they know that they were honest mistakes, not one where there was a 5 per cent kickback.

Kennedy: Can I go back to something that you were reported to have said in 1955 when you first entered Parliament? At that time , when your party, the People's Action Party, spoke out against arbitrary arrest, of detention-without-trial and you yourself are reported to have said, "We either believe in democracy or we do not. If you believe that men should be free then they should have the right of free association, of free publication. No law should permit those democratic processes to be set at naught." Prime Minister, do you do that, today?

Prime Minister: Yes. I believed that in the circumstances of that time. I mean, I could, you know, quote you, Churchill ... That was what I believed then.

Kennedy: But that was a worse time than now, was it not?

Prime Minister: Yes, of course. That was against a British colonial government responsible to nobody other than Whitehall. This is 1977. I am twenty-two years older. I hope more mellow. I hope more charitable. I hope more magnanimous. But I am also a realist. The magnitude of what one terms 'licence' or 'civil liberties' or 'personal freedom' has got to be adjusted to the circumstances. And as far as the communists are concerned, they wanted both ways — both the ballot and the bullet. They can't. They want the ballot and the processes that go before the ballot, to aid them both internally and internationally in the use of the bullet. They learnt it from the Vietnamese: the battle was not fought in Vietnam alone; it was fought in Washington, it was fought in the streets of Stockholm, it was fought in Sydney, in Melbourne, in Paris, in London. 'Vietnam' became a dirty word. They are trying to do to me — which they must try and they are trying to do to all the other non-communist governments in the region — what they did to Thieu. If they can portray me as corrupt, fatuous, dictatorial, capricious, wicked, vicious, then half the battle is won because when the fight begins, I've got to get the arms. I have got to buy them ...

Kennedy: Can I interrupt you here for a moment. It seems to me that you are saying that these things that I read out to you, you believed in at that time ...

Prime Minister: Yes, of course. And I still believe in them.

414

Kennedy: But ... qualify them today because of changed circumstances.

Prime Minister: No, because you can't have the ballot and the bullet at the same time.

Kennedy: Well, you say you believe in free publication? But isn't it true that newspapers here have to be licenced, that some have been closed, some journalists have been put in jail ...?

Prime Minister: No, just a moment. You are mixing them all up. It has always been the case that a newspaper in Singapore and in Malaya, where the British governed, must have a licence. And there has been only one newspaper that had its licence withdrawn, and that was when it could not prove where the money came from, besides a former Chief Minister of the State of Sabah.

Kennedy: And have journalists been put in jail?

Prime Minister: There is one at the moment, and he is, as a good journalist, writing this time a real true story of what he has been doing. And I hope by the end of this week, the composition would have gone before a proper magistrate with no police officers. At least that's what I hope they have the sense to do, because it really is a very interesting story of how a non-communist began associating with communists and slowly began to imbibe communist views and interpolated communist views in his interpretation of Singapore.

Kennedy: Would it be fair to try and sum up what you have been saying about this loss of civil liberties, have been sacrificed in order to make sure that you have greater liberty? Would it be fair assessment?

Prime Minister: One way of putting it. If you ask me to put it, I would simply say: The people of Singapore have a government which they can kick out of office freely, without hindrance by just crossing them off the ballot.

Kennedy: But did you ever feel, Prime Minister, it's often been said in the West that a good democracy, a good democratic society is one in which you have a good government but you have a good opposition to match that government. Do you ever feel the lack of that?

Prime Minister: As a Western-educated, trained Singaporean, I understand what you are saying. And perhaps if I could get a nice sparring partner, it will provide me with a backdrop — that contrasts. But I often wonder whether the foreign journalists or the casual visitor like you, has fathomed or can fathom the mind of an Oriental. And I am having to look after Orientals, whether they are of Chinese descent or Malays or Indians or Eurasians or Ceylonese and so on. What's inside is completely different: Is this a good government I can trust to look after me and my family and see that my children are educated and have a job better than mine and have a home better than mine? Is this fair or is it unfair, unjust, favouring its relatives, its friends? Looting the public purse for its relatives, for itself so that ministers live in luxury whilst the masses live in squalor? Those are the crucial issues, because those are the issues that have toppled governments in the Third World. You can ask any taxi driver — he is the most uninhibited Singaporean you can think of. You can ask a bartender in any hotel. He'll let off a bellyache. But at the end of the day, when he puts his cross, when election comes, he had given me and my colleagues over the seventeen and half years — come June, eighteen years of office. In five successive elections, the percentage of votes has gone up from a first-time high of 53 per cent to an all-time low of about 47 per cent, to all-time high, last December, of 72½ per cent, which I think is cause for some satisfaction.

Kennedy: I was going to say to you, Prime Minister: Isn't it a fact that there seems to be little radical criticism in the newspapers. . . . in the newspapers of the government . Does that mean that everybody is so . . .?

Prime Minister: The newspapers are not owned by the government.

Kennedy: I am saying that isn't it a fact that there is so little radical criticism of the government?

Prime Minister: The radical criticisms are in pamphlets. So you can't sue any printer.

Kennedy: You mean, to sue for radical criticism?

Prime Minister: No, no.

Kennedy: What is wrong with that?

Prime Minister: You see the difference in wavelengths. When you say 'radical criticism' you mean criticisms of policies — that the government is too right-wing or right-minded, it hasn't got the same compassion for the poor and the starving and the underprivileged. That's not the argument. When they hit you, they hit you with the poisoned dart: that this is a corrupt, capricious, wicked, vicious fascist system. Now, you tell me whether a newspaper with assets — printing presses, goodwill, office which it owns — will publish that. They are free to do so and my party funds will improve.

Kennedy: Prime Minister, could I just say this: You were once asked by my colleague, Lord Chalfont, if it would be fair to sum you up as being an 'enlightened dictator'. And you replied to him, no, you weren't a dictator because your poster or pictures of you weren't all over the town. But would it be true that you are nevertheless a kind of 'enlightened dictator' behind the scenes?

Prime Minister: I am on the scene all the time under the glare of footlights. My public behaviour and my private behaviour cannot be compartmentalised. I am on parade all the time. Why need I be a dictator? They come to violent ends. And like all men I like a quiet and quick end, not a violent one.

Kennedy: In one of your election speeches you said this — you said: The real issue you faced — you were talking to your electors — is what happens when the present leadership is gone. We are not immortal. Does that mean that you have it in mind that, Prime Minister, to step down in the near future?

Prime Minister: If I said yes to that question, I know, a lot of big

416

companies will be extremely unhappy and whose shareholders will be saying : Look, is this true? And the Stock Market will not react favourably. My duty is to aknowlege the fact that there comes a time when my collegues and I, who are now in our early fifties — I am fifty three — to late fifties — just will not have the sheer physical vitality of reacting in a crisis. The mental vitality may be there. But the pressure and the speed with which events are taking place — the changes, the geopolitical upsets that have been going on in the past ten years — I don't think we can react in ten years' time the way reacted to one, being booted out of Malaysia in three readings in the Malaysian Parliment in one day and find a new way of how to make a a living, how to feed our people. Nor could we have reacted to the British Government having to say we can't afford the bases.

Kennedy: Very briefly, you see yourself going on for the time being but not for the indefinite period.

Prime Minister: That is an understatement! I would like to be able to hand the torch over and hope it will burn brighter and better.

XIII

Two days later, Lee was interviewed by Ali Hamdi El Gamal, Chief Editor of the Egyptian newspaper, *Al-Ahram*.

Question: How do you assess the role of Southeast Asia in world affairs in the future?

Prime Minister: I believe we are in a completely different era after Vietnam, Watergate and on top of that, in between there was the Arab victory against Israel in 1973, the oil embargo and the oil crisis — a new situation has been created. How the great powers will find accommodation to take advantage of this new situation as against each other is difficult and too early to forsee. So much depends upon whether the Americans, despite their reverses psychologically — Watergate, Vietnam, Angola, will have the resilience and the will to exercise the kind of balancing influence which only they can exercise against the strength of the Soviet Union on the oceans of the world, including the Indian and Pacific Oceans. And if they do not, then we will have to adjust our policies accordingly. I don't think in a world of instant communication and instant destruction, any group of nations, however industrialised, like Western Europe, can really play a decisive role. The decisive roles are played by the superpowers. There may be more than two superpowers later on. As of now, there are only two. So for Southeast Asia, what we are trying to do in ASEAN is to find greater strength in preventing manipulation of one country against the other within the region by outside powers to the disadvantage of the region. That is the first most important objective of ASEAN. The second objective is to accelerate and enhance the speed of economic progress in each country through economic co-operation amongst ourselves and with the industrial nations having interest in the region, like Japan, America, Australia and New Zealand. Trade with the wealthy countries of Western Europe. And we hope increasingly — because of the geography and the proximity, ease of transportation — with the Arabs in West Asia. After all, it was the Arabs who came here first, not Vasco da Gama. They came here hundreds of years before the Europeans and brought Islam and the Arabic scripts to the region. With the new-found or rediscovered wealth and strength of the Arab world — initially oil but eventually in industrial capacity — I can see mutual advantages in closer trading links between the countries of West Asia — all the way from Egypt, Saudi Arabia, the countries with ports in the Red Sea and the Gulf, Iran, Pakistan, and India — and us because we will complement each other. It may take fifteen, twenty or thirty years, but it will happen.

El Gamal: What about the communist threat in the area — you know, Vietnam and Cambodia? Now we hear about Thailand?

Prime Minister: It depends upon whether there is active aggression, intervention from outside. If it is just the Thai communists being supplied by sympathetic governments with arms, with instruction manuals, I think there is no problem. The Thais can handle the problem. The problem will arise when having given arms and the instruction manuals, it's not successful or not as successful as to be able to establish liberated areas, then you send instructors. Then the number of instructors increase and from instructors they become participators. I think that is the danger. We all recognise the capacity for protracted guerilla war which the Vietnamese demonstrated to the whole world over a period of thirty years — from before the fall of Japan in 1945, till they finally moved into Saigon in April 1975. That's fighting for Vietnam. Whether the Thai Communists represent the mainstream of Thai nationalism, that's another matter. We will have to wait and see.

El Gamal: Don't you think it will be too late to find out because you see what has happened in Angola, for example, what's happening in Somalia now and Ethiopia, what's happening in the Middle East, too, and in Southeast Asia? International communism is ...

Prime Minister: In this particular case, I am a little bit hopeful in that there is not one communist power interested. There are two communist powers interested, and their interests do not coincide. In fact, there are three communist powers, if you take Vietnam as a communist power in its own right, as I think they are. And each has its own long-term interest to protect. If one tries to pre-empt on the territory of or the area of influence of the other — what the other considers to be its own natural area of influence, it will be interesting. I would be surprised if there is no reaction. Therefore, I think there are grounds for believing that, it is not as simple as Angola. There, it's black versus white, and so the Cubans supported the blacks and drove out the few South Africans and others who supported minority groups in Angola. I don't think it's so easy to find Cubans in Southeast Asia.

El Gamal: You find somebody else. The Cubans were not representing themselves. They were representing a superpower. They were pushed by a superpower group to play this role in Angola. This superpower can find another Cuba in Southeast Asia?

Prime Minister: I believe that Vietnam is a communist power in its own right. It is not a Cuba. And I don't think the Russians believe that their relationship with Vietnam is the relationship of Moscow to Havana. Moscow-Havana is different from Moscow-Hanoi. And I don't think Peking-Havana is the same as Peking-Hanoi.

El Gamal: Both Peking and Moscow you think — could not influence Hanoi?

Prime Minister: I think they will try to influence Hanoi. You have seen over the past twenty-one years — from 1954, the Geneva Accord till 1975 — they both helped Hanoi, trying to influence her. But, in the end, Hanoi got help from both sides in order to achieve the aims and objectives of Hanoi, not the aims and objectives of either Moscow or Peking. This is a different proposition.

El Gamal: Sir, we move to another point — the ASEAN group. Is it a kind of common market?

Prime Minister: It is too early at this stage to talk of a common market because a common market in terms of the European example means economic union. I don't think we are ready for that yet. Various countries of ASEAN are in different stages of economic development and have different five-year plans. But the movement towards closer co-operation is there. And I think it is accompanied by a political awareness that unless we are together we will be used against each other and we will be destroyed by one another, which will be silly of us. All are aware of this. So maybe economic union in the year 2000 and 2100. But I think we get together and take practical steps each year, each time.

El Gamal: But what about the idea, the main idea of this group together? What were the initiatives?

Prime Minister: The idea is, very simply, to prevent ourselves from being converted to some other system which we do not want. It's so simple as that. We are what we are. We are quite happy to be what we are.

El Gamal: Is it open for any other Asian countries?

Prime Minister: Yes, of course — those who subscribe to our objectives.

El Gamal: What about the Middle East, Sir? How do you see the situation?

Prime Minister: I hope after his visit to the Arab countries and to Israel, the Secretary of State of the United States has a better picture of the gravity of the situation and of the urgency to make a move forward towards peace. I think it is inconcievable that the United States does not realise that they cannot find a better situation for a settlement in the

419

Middle East because, delay, procrastination, inaction, for whatever reason, may lead or must lead to less favourable conditions. It is in the interest of the United States whilst they have governments in office in Egypt, Syria, Jordan, and in Saudi Arabia which are all in favour of peace, that they should seize this moment to make progress towards a durable and just peace. I don't know if it is possible to have it in one final conference, or maybe a series of conferences. But there must be movement forward. The world cannot afford a stalemate, or there will be a change in the total geo-political picture in the Middle East, which, as I have said, will be a change unfavourable to America and the West. They must recognise that and we hope because they recognise that, therefore, they must seize the historic opportunity this situation presents them to bring peace to the area.

El Gamal: As Prime Minister, what is your biggest problem?

Prime Minister: I have so many problems. It is difficult to say which is the biggest problem of them all. They are all big. They are big, bigger, biggest. So it is very difficult to say.

El Gamal: Which one takes most of your time, Prime Minister?

Prime Minister: I think that is not a fair measure of the size of the problem. A lot of time is wasted on matters which are of no great consequence because meetings have to be attended and decisions have to be taken or approved. But it doesn't mean that they are important or they are big in the sense that they are decisive. I think the biggest single problem is really to be able to react quickly with great flexibility to sudden crisis and sudden new situations because we are living through an era of great uncertainty — economic and political uncertainty — and if the leadership of any government is slow in reacting or facing up to new problems which arise like the oil embargo and the oil crisis and all that followed, then we will find ourselves in grave economic and political difficulties straight away. I think this is very important. In other words, a capacity to anticipate, and if the unanticipated takes place, to have enough resilience to overcome the 'unanticipated'. That's the most difficult. We never anticipated the oil embargo. We never anticipated the oil price going up. But once it happened we anticipated all the consequences and so we took measures to mitigate the economic consequences, we were relatively successful. So we did not suffer any minus growth or recession. 1973 was a boom year; 1974 we went down from about 14 per cent in 1973 to 6 per cent growth. 1975 was a bad year, but we still made 4 per cent growth, and last year 1976 we recovered — we made 7 per cent. But that was only possible because we then shifted our emphasis from some sectors to other sectors and redeployed our resources. And it is this capacity to meet changing circumstances which is critical. Life is not static for governments or for individuals.

XIV

Haji Ya'acob bin Mohamed, Minister of State in the Prime Minister's Office, put out the following statement on 9 March: "Mr. R. Murugason has appealed for contributions to a Save Democracy Fund on behalf of Mr. J.B. Jeyaretnam. Mr. Jeyaretnam, in his speech at Fullerton Square, on Saturday, 18 December 1976, made certain statements about Mr. Lee Kuan Yew as Prime Minister, his wife, Mrs. Lee, and brother, Lee Kim Yew, and their law practice in the firm of Lee & Lee. Mr. Lee Kuan Yew's personal lawyers have advised him that the statements were and are defamatory. A writ for an injunction against repetition of the words in dispute, and damages for defamation was taken out. Mr. Jeyaretnam can seek public financial support to fight this case from the High Court, to the Court of Appeal, and on to the Privy Council in London. But let us avoid the hypocrisy of a Save Democracy Fund. The fund is to save Mr. Jeyaretnam from the possible legal consequences of his action, if they are held to be wrong in law. If the courts find his words were not defamatory, Mr. Lee personally, and not the Singapore Government, will have to pay Mr. Jeyaretnam's legal costs. Mr. Lee is not seeking public financial support for defending the right of a Prime Minister to have recourse to the law in regard to statements which he has been advised were and are defamatory of him."

XV

"There are many reasons why the parliamentary system has failed in many new countries. I propose to touch on one of the factors," said the Prime Minister at the annual dinner of the Law Society of Singapore, on 26 March. "Democratic government requires, *inter alia*, that the government alone should not have to carry the responsibility of influencing public attitudes and opinion. To work with democratic system, leadership at all levels, in particular non-political functional or professional group leaderships, should play their part in educating the people. They should help create a climate in which difficult problems arising from changing circumstances can be met with new solutions." Lee continued: "Perhaps, you can take comfort from the fact that lawyers are not the only ones lacking the will for self-discipline and the strength to shoulder the responsibilities not only for their members but for society as a whole. The Singapore Stock Exchange Committee is the saddest example of the weakness of functional group leadership. They have shown a singular lack of discipline, responsibility or strength. They have used the authority the government has allowed them to exercise, to protect their own sectional interests at the expense of the public investor. The result is that the government may have to intervene. Half the problems stem from our past. For a hundred and forty years, a paternal colonial administration governed Singapore entirely on its own. The responsibility for the well-being of society was not that of the individual Singaporean. We've had just over ten years of representative government. Unless we learn very quickly as individuals and as functional and professional groups to take the wider view and uphold first, the public interests and only next our sectional interests, the democratic system cannot endure, let alone flourish. I said all this (word for word) on 11 March, 1970. It is as valid today as it was then. As for the Stock Exchange, it was prophetic. What went wrong? Many things. First, we have not had time enough for people to adjust and adapt themselves to a new situation, where we are in charge of our own destiny. To be in charge means to exercise authority, and, from time to time, it means having to do the unpleasant, but the unavoidable. I want to discuss some problems which we face as a new nation."

The political and economic prospects for a people had a profound influence on the young especially the brightest and the best, in their choice of jobs. Figures showed the kind of people who opted to study law in the past seventeen years since 1959. They reflected the changing prospects of Singapore. Entrance to the university was based mainly on the points system. It was fair, without bias, without favour. The maximum number of points that could be scored for an 'A' level was 64. Medicine had always been the top choice. The lowest cut-off point in 1959 for medicine was 36. For the arts faculty, 24 points, law, 19 points; law went down in 1961 and 1962 to an all-time low of 15 points, against 37 for medicine, 25 for dentistry, 22 for arts. 1961 and 1962 were years of riots, arson and assassinations. Few parents in Singapore and their bright children believed that the rule of law would continue in an orderly society in which lawyers would play a role between the legislature, the executive and the people. But the political, economic and social conditions turned for the better. By 1969 the cut-off was 32 points for law, 47 for medicine and 40 for engineering. "I am happy to tell you that the cut-off points for law, last year, went up to 44 points, against 49 points for medicine, 40 for engineering and 40 for dentistry."

Lee said: "We are mature enough to talk about these things without causing alarm or distress. If you take up medicine, you get a universal profession. You can practise anywhere, in Britain, in Australia, New Zealand, Canada. You can take the American examinations they conduct from time to time, and the whole English-speaking world is open to you. This is a fact of life. There are today in Singapore, nearly 600 lawyers with practising certificates in a population of 2¼ million. This compares to about 1,000 lawyers for a population of 10 million in West Malaysia. We have many lawyers, but not enough good ones. The reasons are in our recent history. In 1964, we had 235 lawyers. The numbers have gone up nearly three-fold in a space of twelve years. But the great increase was in the 1970's. In 1968, we started the Asian Dollar market. Between 1970 and 1973, the number of banks and financial institutions proliferated. Com-

422

panies were incorporated, debentures, loans, mortgages and corporate business boomed for lawyers and accountants as we developed as a financial centre handling nearly US$20 billion, known as the Asian Dollar. Much as I would like to believe that more bright students and their fond parents have decided that they ought to take the law because the future promises stability and the continuance of the rule of law, the figures tell me a different story. Unexpectedly, despite our manpower planning, we found ourselves short of lawyers. The dimmest, dullest wit can make a living at the Bar and did so comfortably. The attractions of high rewards quickly brought about this switch!''

These figures did not give a complete picture. Every year, an average of about a hundred of the best students went on scholarships overseas to universities in Britain, English-speaking North America, Australia, New Zealand, and now West Germany, France, Japan and even Russia. Because Asian parents were careful over their daughters' upbringing, those sent abroad were mostly men. In another five to ten years, whoever occupied the office of Minister for Law would discover that his best lawyers were young women and not young men. Of the bright young men sent abroad over the past fifteen years, only eight opted for the law. Three of these eight were in the past two years. So there was a curious situation. Because people were conscious that the law was tied more than any other profession to language and to the political system, bright students had opted out of the profession, until the banking boom in 1970 – 73. ''Hence I do not share, Mr. Chairman, your optimism that we will produce the legal experts in all relevant fields of the law Singapore is concerned with, like shipping and banking. With few exceptions the bright ones have opted otherwise, especially the men.''

Singapore children were already going to schools where more than 75 per cent of the teachers were women. In another five years, 90 per cent of teachers would be women. This would be so even in the secondary schools. The 10 per cent man were the brawny, not brainy ones. They would take the boys out to the playing fields for rugger, soccer, hockey or what had you. The brainy ones who had to run the schools as headmasters and senior teachers would be women. That would nearly be the position of the lawyers, unless the trend changed. The practice of the law was believed to be a tranquil profession, with regular office hours. It was nearly as good as the schools, from 8 to 1; a meal break in between; with long annually, predetermined school holidays. This meant that in an emergency, if the Minister for Law was not a trained lawyer, he would have to look directly to an Attorney-General, who in ten years' time might well be a lady. ''And she may not like to be summoned at awkward hours of the night. And crises have a strange way of happening at awkward times. I have no answer to this problem. We have tried several solutions over the past ten years, including an offer of special scholarships to the best universities that any student chooses, provided he or she can score three distinctions at 'A' levels. There were no takers, even with less qualifications.''

This problem was noted ten years ago. Perhaps the corner was being turned. In 1976, two scholars took up this offer, in 1975, one scholar did law. But perhaps they were bright enough to calculate that there would be ten to fifteen years in which they would have qualified in time to make good within this time-frame. And they would take their chances after that in management, or other cognate professions, if the political situation became adverse. It was a sobering thought that bright young minds might be calculating in this way. Another reason for this development was the school system. Streaming took place and still did, as early as fifteen plus. Students went into the science or arts stream. The traditional cultural attitudes of parents and students had made many girls believe they ought to be doing Arts. This meant that they studied English language and literature — and so they went on with greater ease and facility to the study of the law. The boys had gone into sciences and on to engineering, architecture, and the hard sciences. But this was changing, albeit too slowly.

"Finally, some matters nearer the bone. Yours is the one professional body that has the dubious distinction of having a confessed communist, on its governing body. He has admitted he helped a wounded terrorist escape. For some time I have questioned this premise of self-regulating professional bodies. We inherited a system of self-governing guilds and professions from the British. They arose out of British historic experience which the British exported to their empire. It worked with British lawyers and doctors in charge. It was a closed system controlled by British lawyers, engineers, architects and so on. The Freemason's Lodge in Hill Street saw to it. It was a secret society of the ruling elite; membership means a dedication to helping each other. Freemasonry demanded, however, amongst its positive aspects, a certain minimum standard of decorum and propriety for the system to work. In the past few years, from time to time, I have read in the newspapers of advocates and solicitors who were being sought by the police — their names were not mentioned, even when their clients' accounts were found to be short. It is unbelievable. I have wondered why you, Mr. Attorney, have not told the press that they should publish the picture of the man who is being sought, with his name and his address and the last known place he was found frequenting, not necessarily the same thing as his last known address." All this added up to the necessity to amend this self-regulation mechanism. Voting should be compulsory. "This was what we did for general elections in 1959. We had seen how the communists operated. We decided, rightly as it turned out, that compulsory voting would lead to more representative government. The activist requires no encouragement to exercise his right. It is the passive majority who must be told they have got to exercise their rights, or these rights will be usurped by a minority up to no good. That will cure half the problem."

The second amendment that would have to be passed was what had already been done in the case of the architects and the engineers. The Minister would have the right to appoint a senior government architect or engineer to sit on the governing board, amongst other things, to determine admission and to decide whether a person was fit to continue to practise the profession. "There is with lawyers — as with jurors, which we have had to abolish — an unwillingness to do the unpleasant. If we are to maintain standards of integrity it means axing those who do not measure up to these standards. You know as I do, Mr. Chairman, that when it came to several crunches in the past few years, what the Council did was to flinch from the unpleasant. Instead of seeking to strike a member off the Rolls and pressing for it, it has allowed members to be suspended for six months, or for a year, or for two years. This is not the way to maintain standards of honourable conduct. Who is to say it is not honourable enough if the lawyers will not? My colleague, the Minister for Law — an honourable and fair gentleman. Since you have shown no wish to exercise your right to punish the erring, my minister in charge will nominate a senior legal officer who understands the necessity of having to be firm in insisting on high professional standards."

Lee said that the Law Society had one consolation. "Whoever succeeds me is not likely to be a lawyer, and to know you and the legal profession and its shortcomings so intimately. If I fail, you have seen what has happened elsewhere in Asia and in Africa. Only foolish students believe that their riots change governments. The generals and the soldiers know better. Worse, sometimes, it is not even a general, but only a half-colonel. If I succeed, then the next Prime Minister will inherit a sophisticated economy. Without a sound grounding in the theories of economics and practice of finance, he will not be qualified to direct the government policies."

XVI

What is the secret of Singapore's economic and political stability? Lee was asked this question during an interview on 15 April by Guenther Scholz, Head of the Bonn Office of the German Radio Service, *Deutsche Welle*.

Prime Minister: Well, we had very great political upheavals — revolutionary fervour, riots, assassinations, demonstrations for many years in the 1940s and in the 1950s and right into 1961, 1962, 1963, and it was after continuous political battles with the communists who were in charge of the students' organisations, the teachers' unions and the workers' unions, that we were able slowly to convince the people that the communist movement and its leadership were leading the country to ruin and leading the lives of the people down the cesspit. So after that traumatic experience, we were able, slowly from 1963 onwards when they lost the elections, to build gradually a non-communist trade union movement, which today has more followers than the communists ever had. We have been able to minimise the influence of the communists amongst the teachers and the students. And, of course, with economic development, the thinking and expectations of the young have changed and they no longer feel that the situation is so desperate that we must have a communist revolution to put it right, but that we can make things better year by year provided we work, provided there is social discipline and provided productivity goes up. In other words, the workers, together with the government and the management, increase the total gross domestic product.

Scholz: Would you name the system in Singapore as socialistic or capitalistic?

Prime Minister: We have a mixed economy. There are certain sectors of the economy which are run by the State, like the public utilities, transport, shipping, the airlines and so on. To that extent, the factors of production are in the hands of the State, but we do not believe that we have either the management capacity or the technical know-how or the marketing to be able to run the many industries which we have brought into Singapore. So they are in the private enterprise sector. So it is a mixed economy, but the bias of our social policies is towards equal opportunities in health and education for everybody. So the duty of the government, as we see it, is to give everybody as good a chance as everybody else in health and education, so that despite the disadvantage of poor parents, poor homes, they can advance themselves.

Scholz: Do you think your experience in your work in Singapore could be of use to developing countries or the experience is more to be seen in connection with the Chinese character of your country?

Prime Minister: No, I don't think the latter part is completely correct. There are elements of our experience which could be of universal application. Of course, it will have to be amended to suit the circumstances or meet the different circumstances of other developing countries, but in order to develop, you must first have a leadership that is able to mobilise the support, the determination and the efforts of the population towards certain definite goals which it has defined beforehand. It must be able to provide an honest and effective government so that if mistakes are made, as they are bound to be made, the people will know they have been made in good faith, not because somebody got 2 per cent or 3 per cent kickbacks for contracts and so on, because, once that situation arises, there is no confidence between the workers and the leadership — and programmes and projects fail. So these are elements of universal application. Then there must be the capacity for change in the formulation of policies and programmes to meet changed circumstances partly because the international situation has changed, partly because the domestic opinion or priorities have changed. This means always a capacity to have a feedback on policies, the reaction of the people to policies and the adjustment of policies by the leadership or the government to meet the changed attitudes of the people. I think these are of universal application, but, mind you, it is not easy to establish these conditions because each country inherits what the colonial power left behind. And we were fortunate in that the British left behind an honest civil service, working institutions, working infrastructure. There are places where the departing power did not leave these things behind. Therefore, the job is more difficult.

Scholz: How do you judge, Prime Minister, the influence of the Chinese policy in Southeast Asia after the death of Mao? Do you see a competition between China and the Soviet Union in this area?

Prime Minister: I would think in the longer run, yes. There must be competition. As of now, there is probably a muted competition because the Soviet leadership would like to assess the nature, the character and the stand of the new leadership in China and to see whether perhaps an accommodation can be reached. So the competition is muted. But after a while, it is in the nature of the two systems — one run by the Soviet Union and the other by China — the People's Republic of China — to compete for followers: to compete for more parties to be installed as governments of neighbouring countries — to be loyal to, and to be supporters of either Moscow or Peking. So the competition I think is inevitable.

Scholz: Do you think the danger of war in the area has diminished since the retreat of the United States from Vietnam?

Prime Minister: I think the danger of more communist guerilla insurgency spreading from Laos and occasionally, we hear reports even of clashes between Cambodia and Thailand, not just of Laotians and Thais, but Cambodians and Thais — that has increased. How it will develop, we do not yet know. We must hope that this can be contained and that correct and friendly relations between governments of different systems — of communist systems in Laos and in Cambodia and the free enterprise system under a monarchy in Thailand — can co-exist. But, of course, we must expect the communist government to help communists in Thailand to create revolution, but as long as that is done without sending foreign troops into Thailand, I believe the situation is containable by the Thais themselves.

Scholz: What part does Singapore play in the so-called north-south dialogue between industrial countries and developing countries? On what side do you stand yourself?

Prime Minister: We are anxious that there should be reasonable, practical solutions to this desire for greater sharing out of the world's wealth, which the developing countries feel today, is being monopolised by the industrial countries. It is true that in the past there has been exploitation of the natural resources of the developing countries to feed the industries of the European and American and Japanese economies and they have been the buyers of manufactured goods and the terms of trade have been unequal. But we are not convinced that this can be resolved just by changing the system overnight and saying we have a new economic world order, and we index raw materials to the rate of inflation or to some Common Fund, which will buy raw materials at minimum prices, whatever the market demand may be for them because, unless the solutions are practical, we will only lead ourselves into high hopes in order to collapse again. So they must be practical and we would support a commodity-by-commodity approach. Each commodity has its problems whether it is rubber, tin, copper, zinc, bauxite; whether it is perishable, how it is to be stored, what are the fluctuations in demands, what should be the minimum bottom price, what should be the top price beyond which a stockpile is used to control the price, what should be the amount of soft loans from developed countries to the very poor developing countries. I think a practical approach to specific problems is more likely to bring results than a grand comprehensive plan like a Common Fund which everybody contributes to — everybody meaning everybody with money. And then this will buy up anything which is produced by the developing countries whether or not it has any relevance to the market demand and the market price. It will only compound things. Supposing, for instance, we start buying, by way of example, coffee or tea at certain fixed prices, then the demand falls so the price goes down, but the Fund keeps on buying. So the world will have store-houses full of tea and coffee which cannot be consumed for five, ten years. Then what happens? Then people will one day come to the conclusion that this is madness, and the Fund will collapse, so that we will be in a worse position.

We sympathise — first of all, beause we have been a poor country — we sympathise with all the countries facing these difficulties of trying to diversify their economy, of trying to industrialise, but there is no magic solution in just one or two ideas — like calling it the new world economic order and the Common Fund. If it were that simple, the World Bank would have thought about it, the IBRD — the International Bank for Reconstruction and Development — would have thought about it ten years ago and today, there would have been no developing countries. All would have developed. It is a complex problem and many solutions will have to be tried for the many problems that exist.

Scholz: You know, the German approach is very similar to your own.

Prime Minister: Perhaps because the Germans are also practical people. We have to be practical because that is the only way we can survive.

Scholz: Prime Minister, what do you think about the Socialist International movement of which Willy Brandt is President?

Prime Minister: Well, this is a tribute to Willy Brandt's stature and status; his contribution to democratic socialism as a great German Social Democrat who played the role in recognising the realities of the consequences of the World War Two. He won a Nobel Peace Prize for his efforts in trying to make peace durable. But, the Bureau of the Socialist International is attended by international secretaries of the various parties, and they have not changed. They have over the years become more and more Marxist in their approach — some of these member parties — and I hope Willy Brandt will have a good influence in making them go back to the social democratic path.

XVII

"May Day 1977 is a time for rejoicing and also thoughtful concern," declared Lee in his May Day Message. "We can rejoice because we got through three difficult years after the oil crisis, from 1973 to 1976, without damage to the economy. Our workers did not suffer in lower wages, and there was only slight unemployment. The future however gives cause for thoughtful concern." New governments in America, Japan and West Germany were trying to co-ordinate their economic policies to prevent the world economy from stagnating or going protectionist. "We hope they will succeed in re-stimulating the world economy, but without excessive inflation. Then we shall all be the beneficiaries." If the stimulation did not work, then Singapore might be in for some very hard times. Or, if the stimulation was overdone, there might be high inflation by 1978. "So we must be prepared for whatever may be the outcome of their policies, and adjust our own policies accordingly, as we did during the three difficult years 1973 – 76. May next May Day, 1978, see the world in better shape."

XVIII

Singapore Airlines celebrated its thirtieth aniversary, and at a dinner on 1 May, Lee claimed that Singapore's willingness and ability to recognise and accept the work done by the British in the colonial era, and to build upon it, had been one of its strengths. This had been so with SIA. SIA had the courage to admit that it really started in May 1947, when Malayan Airways started with three Airspeed Consul aircraft, flying from Kallang Airport to Kuala Lumpur. In 1976, SIA carried 1.9 million passengers to Europe, Asia and Australasia. In 1976, there were 4.5 million passenger movements in and out of Singapore Airport, of which one-third was carried by SIA. Transit passengers were 0.9 million, leaving 3.6 million passenger movements in and out. Divided by two, it means 1.8 million passengers. Of these, 1.5 million were tourists and 0.3 million Singaporeans and foreigners resident in Singapore. By 1981, conservative projections showed passenger movements of 8.8 million. 1.6 million would be in transit. The balance of 7.2 million movements meant 3.6 million passengers — 2.8 million tourists and 0.8 million Singaporeans and foreigners resident in Singapore.

Lee said the government made a major decision when it decided to move the new international airport with two runways to Changi, an investment of $1,500 million. It was on schedule, the first runway operational by the end of 1980. "We have constantly to further develop and improve our infrastructure, especially in transport and communications. Thereby, we make Singapore an air and sea junction for people and goods. We do not have, nor do we want, a big population. Strategic location is not enough.

429

It is the infrastructure facilities and our operational efficiency as a distributing centre for people and goods that ensure our role as the centre of transportation and communications. And as science and technology advance, so we must move with these innovations, first, cables, then microwave, now satellite, all supplementing each other, providing an almost fail-safe communications system. For our part, it means coaling for steamships, to oil bunkering, to tankers and containers and bulk ore carriers.''

When investment was made in a major international airport, the primary objective was to succeed as an air junction. If SIA could thereby benefit by getting more traffic rights from other countries, because more airlines want to come to Singapore more frequently, it was a valuable subsidiary benefit. It was important that SIA management and workers recognised this — that the primary objective was the success of the air junction. Tourism contributed 4 per cent of the GDP in 1976, in hotels, shopping, entertainment and so on.

Lee congratulated the airline on having lived up to his expectations, after he spelt out to them on 16 July 1972 the challenge before them. ''I said then that SIA's future depended more on the reality SIA leaves behind on its passengers than any PR job. That has been so. Of course, good advertisement has helped. But it is the reality that counts. Reputations are made and lost. We have enhanced ours by what travellers have had to say of SIA. But have a care. We can just as easily slide downwards if SIA workers believe they can act like their European, Australian or Japanese counterparts. We will face ever stiffer competition from other Asian airlines, like CPA, or Thai Airways, or PAL. They have lower wage costs with hungrier and keener workers.''

All airlines used similar, if not identical, aircraft. But the Europeans, Australians and Japanese had larger fleets. So their maintenance cost per unit was lower. Moreover, SIA had always to overcome the prejudices of the travelling public against what they suspect were less than 100 per cent standards of high maintenance air safety. Too often, Asian airlines and, worse, disasters in Asian airports, like those in Delhi, left passengers with the impression of sloppiness in the maintenance of equipment on aircraft and in airports. Passengers were disturbed when they saw poor standards of cleanliness and, worse, slovenly service in the aircraft — no smartness in the bearing, dress and behaviour of aircrew and cabin crew. They wondered if these were not also the standards of the maintenance staff and ground crew. ''As a traveller, I have had these thoughts. I have stressed again and again on the constant need to ensure that what passengers can see of SIA aircraft and aircrew and cabin crew, and Singapore Airport, reassures them of our attitude of mind, our zeal for tip-top standards of safety, efficiency and courtesy, which prevails over all sectors, including the maintenance and ground crew. Maintaining these high standards is not a favour SIA workers are doing to management or the government. It is what you have to do to keep your jobs in a very competitive industry. In the airline and airport business, to stay still is to stagnate, and to stagnate is to be overtaken. We must press forward to ever higher performance.''

Five years of progress and expansion, despite the oil crisis, and with it higher wages and rewards, were cause for congratulations. But a note of caution. ''Never let your European, Australian or Japanese counterparts persuade or delude you into believing that you can be paid like them or, worse, work as lightly as they do. If your unions set out to model SATU (Singapore Air Transport-workers Union) or SIAPA (Singapore Airlines Pilots Association) or European or Australian unions, then SIA and you are doomed. Remember, our success as an air junction, is our primary objective, and SIA must and can help us achieve this. My Cabinet colleagues and I will have no doubts that we must have a busy and thriving airport to have a successful airline.''

The majority of the passengers using Singapore Airport were non-Singaporeans. In fact, the ratio in 1976 was five non-Singaporeans for every Singaporean. And these five would never had flown into Singapore, to be flown out again, but for the fact that Singapore was their destination for business or pleasure. Singapore was not a terminal point like London, Tokyo or Sydney. ''We do not have their massive population base, nor the high standards of living, which their advanced industrial economy can give their workers. Our advantages are lower wage costs, a willingness to learn and work, to serve efficiently and cheerfully and keep passengers comfortable and happy and, most important of all, get them safely and punctually to their destinations. In other words, for SIA management and headquarters staff, for engineering workers on the ground, to the pilots and navigators on the flight deck, and the stewards and stewardesses, the key is work discipline. Slacken on discipline, and SIA will begin to lose out. Passengers will still come to Singapore, via other airlines. And you can be sure that Singapore Airport will be run efficiently and courteously — modern facilities, well-maintained and immaculately clean, quick clearance by Customs, Health and Immigration.''

That, added Lee, was firm government policy. Having decided to invest $1½ billion in Changi, the government was out to ensure full use. SIA management must set out to win passengers by competition, not protection. SIA must take full advantage of the fact that the more people came to, and through, Singapore, the greater was their leverage for more traffic rights elsewhere. For Singapore workers, the more attractive Singapore was as a place to come to for business or pleasure, the better it was for Singapore taxi-drivers and workers in hotels, restaurants, shops and the airport, and not only for a small proportion of the workers in SIA (8,900, or 0.97 per cent of the total workforce). One constant in the history of Singapore's development was free and open competition. This principle had served Singapore well.

''Finally, let me express the hope that when I get on board an SIA aircraft, I shall see and feel a representative flavour of Singapore. It is important that our multi-racial society be fairly reflected, not just on the ground

431

staff, but also in the cabin crew, and eventually in the flight deck. There are certain imbalances, which are the result of RSAF recruitment policies. There were distortions in recruitment that took place in the past few years. My advice is not to try to put these distortions right immediately, or we will do ourselves harm. However, gradually and consistently, you should set out to make SIA representative of what Singapore is, a society based on a man or woman's worth and performance, qualities which have nothing to do with a person's race, language, religion, or family status, or connections."

XIX

The Asian Labour Summit was held on 5 May and Lee addressed it. He said it was not easy to define the role of trade unions in developing countries. Nearly all developing countries were mainly agricultural, with their cities bulging with people drifting in from the countryside. Most cities had more people than they could provide for in jobs, food, clean water and sanitation, homes, schools and other necessities of modern life. However, whether it was in the industrial countries of Western Europe and America, or the Soviet Union and Eastern Europe, or in developing countries like China or India, trade unions were part of the social outgrowth of industrialisation.

Lee said he believed that in the earlier stages of industrialisation, trade unionism modelled on European or American practices, tended to hinder rather than help the process of industrialisation. But despite this, if workers were not unionised and industrialisation succeeded, then management-labour relations might have become so poor that combative and confrontation type unions, often led by communists, would be the result. So most developing countries had trade unions even though they had to work under severe constraints. In most cities of developing countries, the biggest group that could be mobilised or unionised was the unemployed. Indeed, this was the situation in Singapore in the 1950s and early 1960s. Fortunately, both the political and trade union leaderships recognised this. Both agreed that their common objective must be the creation of conditions which would encourage the expansion of industries to create jobs for the unemployed. And because Singapore's industries had to be export-oriented, a broad framework was built for co-operation between unions, management and government. For only in this way could Singapore products compete with the products of very hardworking and hard-driving people in the developing countries of East Asia, where manufacturers were not fettered by problems of Western-style unionised labour. Perhaps this was the reason for Singapore's salvation: "the realisation that there were limits beyond which if we had gone we would have priced our goods out of the export markets, inhibited the expansion of existing industries, and discouraged new investments, and so ending up with more unemployed. The end result would have been disastrous."

The question might well be asked: What do Singapore trade unions do? Workers needed to have an organisation so that they could protect their legitimate interests against any arrogant or high-handed methods of management, capricious hiring and firing — in short, workers had a right to their dignity as workers, as citizens, as human beings. Unions in developing countries must concentrate their activities not only on bargaining for better terms and conditions or service and fringe benefits, but also enlarge their activities to cover a wide range of social, educational and economic fields. They must supplement what their governments should be doing for their citizens and perhaps bring specific benefits and improved services to their workers and union members. Schemes for adult education or workers' colleges, housing and consumer co-operatives, co-operative insurance for life, medical and dental treatment, and later, as the economy progressed, even holiday, recreational and educational tours. These were functions which unions could undertake and so improve the services and facilities available to their members over and above what their government could do for the ordinary population. Because in a developing country situation it might take a long time to provide the level of such services which would compare with those of industrial countries. In the process, they would educate some of their members in the running of these co-operative enterprises and services. Such collective self-help educated a whole generation of the more active and intelligent unionists into the facts of contemporary society and the economics of the system upon which the lives of their workers and their families depended.

Lee turned to another subject. "I understand amongst your midst are representatives of unions from industrial countries. May I take this opportunity to point out that each time unions in industrial countries demand protection from imports, either by tariffs or quotas, they keep out goods from developing countries. They are in fact transferring relatively minor hardships their members are undergoing, with the buffer of ample unemployment benefits, nearly making up for what they were getting when in employment, to workers in developing countries. These hardships, when transferred, are multiplied many times over because workers in developing countries do not have governments which have economies which can afford to give them adequate unemployment relief, adequate to keep their families fed, housed and educated until economic recovery makes jobs available again."

Lee said it had been his sad experience to discover that he had suffered from such problems more from socialist governments in industrial countries than from liberal or conservative governments. The reason simply was that socialist governments were more closely allied to, and dependent upon, their trade union support. Therefore, it was most important for trade unionists in developing countries to impress upon their counterparts in the industrial countries that they owed them this modicum of humanity.

As a corollary to this, since the economic slow-down after the oil crisis, European and American trade unions had been most vociferous against the transfer of capital, technology and jobs by their multi-national corporations (MNCs) setting up factories in developing countries where wage costs were lower. Here again, sound economic principles of division of labour, and high principles of the brotherhood of workers of the world, were breached, if not abandoned, whenever there was the slightest hint that the observance of these principles would adversely affect the jobs of union members of industrial countries. So the industrial countries, whose level of wages had become too high to support labour-intensive production of goods, continued to have factories for textiles, garments and shoes, and other labour-intensive manufacture.

"Again I have faced this paradox, that socialist governments in the industrial countries, ideologically sympathetic and committed to the cause of an egalitarian world, have been less inhibited in putting obstacles in the way of MNC exporting factories and jobs, and so transferring technology and capital to the less-developed countries. Again, trade unionists from the developing countries must make plain to their brothers in the industrial countries that we are not likely to ever achieve any comaraderie if this is how we treat each other in practice." Developing and industrialised countries must together face up to these problems. Trade unionists from the industrial countries had their obligations to their own workers. Those delegates from developing countries must and could convince them that their long-term interests lie in a more peaceful and co-operative world. For the alternative was a world split into blocs, the wealthy, the intermediate and the poor, at odds and in confrontation with each other. Unionists and workers in industrial countries must understand that to transfer unemployment to the less developed to protect labour-intensive industries meant more hardship for more workers in developing countries and their families. Over the longer term, it was in everyone's interests to forego short-term selfish interests by shutting out imports. "By all means let us seek temporary adjustments by voluntary restraint of levels of exports. But a gradual phasing out of factories producing goods with a high labour-content in countries where wages are high makes economic sense in a world of cheap and reliable transportation. The world is more likely to survive without strife and wars if we recognise and honour our obligations to each other in this one inter-dependent world. Modern science and technology have made this a more integrated and more inter-related world than ever before. Our interests are in freer trade, more countries becoming developed, exchanging more goods and services to the benefit of all. And there is no way of turning the clock back, without causing unnecessary hardship and bitterness."

On the other side of the coin, the unions and the governments of the developing countries must set out to put their own countries in order — not least the horrendous problems of rapid population growth. The President of the World Bank, Mr. Robert McNamara, had been

434

reported as predicting the present world population of four billion would stabilise itself at 11 billion by the year 2000 (according to a UPI report). The bulk of the population explosion would take place in South Asia and in Africa south of the Sahara. "I was shocked to read this projection of eleven billion, for I had mentally accustomed myself to a doubling to eight billion." The world could not solve the population problem by plagues and famines, through droughts and floods or pestilence. The isolated societies of the sailing ship, each living their own separate and unrelated lives, was over. WHO and FAO came to the rescue, to salve the world's conscience. Leaders were discussing and conferencing all the time, "as we are tonight". Passions and frustrations of such huge masses of hungry and deprived people could only lead to tragedy, for themselves, and for the world, if ever the poor got their hands on atomic weapons.

"The moral rights are not all on the side of the developing and the downtrodden. Nor are the wealthy and technologically advanced blameless. I suggest the way forward is for the developing countries, their governments, unions and management, to mobilise their people, to demonstrate that they intend to and can help themselves. They must have the will and the discipline to put their countries in order. Then the industrial countries will find it worth their while to help them. And such help will be put to effective use. The more a developing country puts its house in order, the more it deserves support from the industrial countries. It is not only morally right. It is the best way to encourage similar responsible attitudes and responses in other developing countries. Then all will be nudged into more self-help and discipline, and effective use of aid and trade. Then the world may find salvation."

XX

"Why do the ASEAN leaders want to invite the Prime Ministers of Japan, Australia and New Zealand to a summit in Kuala Lumpur in August?" Michael Richardson, an Australian journalist, asked the Prime Minister on 6 May.

Prime Minister: What happened was that the ASEAN leaders decided upon a working summit in August, and it was decided that the time had come to start a dialogue at a very high level with the Japanese Prime Minister to see if it was possible to define the complementary relationship between the countries of ASEAN and Japan in greater economic cooperation. Arising out of that, the Australian and New Zealand governments made known their interest that their Prime Ministers would also be happy to associate themselves with such a dialogue along similar lines. That's how it came about.

Richardson: In what ways can Japan, Australia and New Zealand — individually and collectively — help intensify the tempo of economic

435

development within the ASEAN region?

Prime Minister: Well, first Japan. It has the third largest economy in the world, next to America and the Soviet Union. Its industrial capacity is tremendous and it has already reached saturation, the industrial overflow into South Korea, and to a lesser extent, to Taiwan. Therefore, there is great potential for this overflow to go into the non-communist countries of Southeast Asia, particularly in the more polluting industries — those industries where you are processing minerals or ores into minerals, or concentrates, before you go on to metals and finished products. The imbalance in trade, of course, is very much strongly against the ASEAN countries and Japan may find that it is useful and in her longer term interests to develop this complementary economic relationship with the countries of ASEAN, Burma and the other non-communist countries of Southeast Asia willing to co-operate with her. The industrial capacity of Australia and New Zealand is not quite as great as that of Japan. But they have a different contribution to make. First, the decision will have to be made by the Australians and the New Zealanders, as to whether they want to be in this grouping. It's not just a one-sided arrangement. Nor is it for short-term economic advantage. This is a long-term, long-range programme which, if it succeeds over the next ten or fifteen years, would lead to a kind of association which can be loosely compared to the association which the EEC has with the ACP (African, Caribbean and Pacific) countries. It will enable both the developed countries within the group, and the developing countries associated with the developed group, to exercise a greater influence over the policies of the great economic powers when they meet as they do from time to time. For instance, this weekend in London, only Japan is representing the Western Pacific. If we are in constant consultation and association with each other, then there are certain interests which would be germane for the Japanese to press, not only on their behalf, but also on our behalf, and on behalf of Australia and New Zealand. The trend has been towards a regional grouping for a greater say in international global decisions.

Richardson: Is there any likelihood of pressure being applied to Japan by ASEAN states if Tokyo is reluctant to liberalise terms of trade and development assistance to ASEAN?

Prime Minister: I don't think that's the right approach at all. If we begin to think in terms of retaliation, pressure or leverage even before we being to talk, then we are off on the wrong foot. This is a co-operative effort in which each side must have appraised itself beforehand and decided it's worth giving it a go, making it work. So there's no merit in saying: if they don't give us this, then we shall do that. I think that approach is just fatal.

Richardson: The interest you expressed in having, over the long term, some kind of arrangement akin to the Lome Convention, is that interest fully shared by your ASEAN partners?

Prime Minister: Yes, we have discussed this at various levels over the past six months or more. We are in the process of defining what kind of relationship we can start off with.

Richardson: Will that process of definition continue between now and the summit?

Prime Minister: And during the summit. Because it's not just how we see it. It will depend on how Mr. Fukuda and his team see it.

Richardson: At the end of your visit to Australia in October, you expressed the hope that in about twelve to eighteen months, when the Australian economy recovered, there would be a gradual and graduated lowering of tariff and non-tariff barriers to trade between the ASEAN countries and Australia?

Prime Minister: No, I disagree with that profoundly. I think the balance of trade between Australia and ASEAN today is very much against the ASEAN countries. The latest figures available, July 1974 to June 1975, showed that the balance of trade favoured Australia to the tune of some $480 million. If you take away from that imports of petroleum and petroleum products which Australia has to buy from refineries in Singapore — she's got to buy anyway if it's not from Singapore, from the Arabian Gulf — then the trade deficit is even higher. So what's been happening is that the ASEAN countries have been selling some transport equipment, wood, palm oil, cork, crude rubber, yarn, textiles, and garment products. But the Australians have been selling much more in machinery and equipment, wheat, sugar, chemicals, motor vehicles and parts, tin ores and other ore concentrates. So the liberalisation may not even balance the trade. But it will remove a source of considerable frustration and bitterness on the part of countries like the Philippines, Indonesia and us, and Malaysia too, who feel this is a one-sided business; of a very wealthy continent, sparsely populated, with enormous natural resources, not yet fully developed with an industrial capacity commensurate with those resources, and wanting to do all the little things, the labour intensive products like shirts and garments, knitwear, shoes and socks — all for itself, behind high tariff walls. Buying little and selling more. Hardly the kind of good neighbourly policy which will generate understanding, goodwill, stability and sound relations over a long period. Of course, let me add that successive Australian governments have been conscious of this and have made up with aid, which are giveaways, once and for all. It's like giving toffees and chocolates away. That's not the kind of relationship which generates mutual esteem, respect and an adult, continuing interdependence which in the long term is the only sound relationship we can develop.

Richardson: Latest reports from Canberra indicate that the Government, under pressure from protectionist lobbies, is going to extend quotas for textiles and footwear in Australia, the kind of labour-intensive industries you mentioned. Do you feel it would make sounder economic sense, leaving aside the foreign policy argument you mentioned, for Australia to bite the bullet and start the process of adjustment in those industries now, sooner rather than later?

Prime Minister: I don't want to say anything which will impinge on the internal politics of Australia. But in the long run, I don't see how we can live peacefully, amicably and at ease with each other, when you are going to be a very wealthy community, with very high wages because you are a wealthy economy, making all these simple products with a very high labour content and, because of your high wages, therefore very expensive. To make it viable, you then put up very high tariff walls and quotas to keep goods out from countries which have meagre natural resources, a lot of manpower and cheap wages. It doesn't make sense. And if that's the way the world is going to be — if the relationship between the countries of ASEAN and Australia is the relationship between the developed and the underdeveloped world, then I see strife.

Richardson: If the economic relationship between ASEAN, Japan and Australasia can be broadened over the next five or ten years in the way ASEAN leaders want, what impact would it have on regional development and stability?

Prime Minister: To make that kind of an impact it's ten to fifteen years, not five to ten years. The first few years we just define what are the initial areas we can move on. Then we have a declaration of intent. Then we find a mechanism to fulfil these declarations of intent. Then slowly you may decide that in your longer term interests fot both economic and political and geopolitical considerations, you need stable, sound, healthy neighbours. So you may say in that case you shouldn't be making shirts, socks and shoes for yourself because that's got high labour content. If we can develop that kind of relationship, first as a group of non-communist nations in the Western Pacific, we'll have more say in world forums — and the world is getting smaller; Ministers are meeting whether it's in the UN the OECD, or seven in London and thereafter four of them are meeting privately — it means that in a regional group like this we can get *entrée*, because collectively we'd carry more weight and whoever attends the meeting would ensure that the interests of the countries within this group are not overlooked, which at present is the case.

Richardson: Would this kind of regional development strengthen the position of ASEAN countries in withstanding the pressures of communism?

Prime Minister: It definitely will generate more economic progress, more stability, and the capacity to withstand subversion and insurgency. It's a plus factor, not a minus factor.

Richardson: Would it be useful to have some kind of formal arrangement between ASEAN, Japan, Australia and New Zealand — possibly a trade treaty offering mutual advantage?

Prime Minister: It's too early to start talking in terms of a trade treaty. When you say mutual advantage please remember that the EEC-ACP relationship underwent a subtle change from the Yaounde Convention to the Lome Convention, because the Americans raised extremely serious objections to what is known as reverse preferences — preferences from the underdeveloped to the industrial countries in that relationship. And if we are not to be trapped within that same bind, we must be extremely cautious how we go about this. Otherwise, we're going to get not just the Americans upset, but also the Europeans upset because the Europeans made the concession to American opinion by foregoing reverse preferences in the Lome Convention. Therefore, I do not think we should lightly toss around an exclusive Western Pacific group or club, in which we'll have special arrangements with each other and exclude or put the Americans and West Europeans to disadvantage. I think that would be the wrong basis on which to start up the group. But there must be some kind of *quid pro quo* worked out in which, in return for transfers of technology and capital in the lower and middle technology ranges of manufacture, and also access to markets, there'll be more purchases of machinery and food from countries like Japan, Australia and New Zealand. And there are advantages anyway of freight — the distances are so much shorter between ASEAN countries and Japan, ASEAN and Australasia, than say ASEAN and Western Europe through Suez, or America through the Panama Canal.

Richardson: So you see such arrangements greatly increasing the two-way volume of trade?

Prime Minister: It should, provided of course you don't have freight cartels which make short distances become more expensive than long distances, which is one of the dangers of the Australian Freight Conference.

Richardson: Mr. Prime Minister, are you confident the Carter Administration in the United States will maintain sufficient American interest in the stability of the West Pacific area so that a new security balance can be established by the contending, and sometimes complementary, interests of the United States, China and the Soviet Union?

Prime Minister: I have been told by a high official of the Carter Administration that the American position is one of continuing interests, but that they have not yet defined their specific policies. They are in the midst of studying specific areas and issues, and decisions will probably be made in the course of this year or next. We'll have to wait and see. This is a different America. After Vietnam and after Watergate, America shows no inclination to be involved in conflicts anywhere in the world unless major strategic interests are involved. We've got to wait to know what Americans decide is in their major strategic interests in this part of the world and adjust our positions and policies accordingly.

Richardson: I see, though, that Mr. Holbrooke in an interview on Voice of America recently, said that he personally felt America's contribution to East and Southeast Asian region in the future could be more of an economic nature — economic inputs. Do you feel the Americans are sufficiently conscious that that's going to be wasted unless there is an adequate contribution from them towards maintaining a balance of power?

Prime Minister: Again we'll have to wait to know. It is not just what

Mr. Holbrooke feels as of now, but what the American Government, the President and his National Security Council, will feel and decide after they've gone through their several rounds of negotiations with the Soviet Union on SALT II, on demilitarisation of the Indian Ocean, and so on. When the new American Administration has got a fair measure of the Soviet responses to their proposals, they will have a much sharper perceptive of the kind of problems they will have to face up to. And unless huge oil reserves are found in Antarctica or elsewhere equivalent to those in the Gulf area, the Gulf and the routes to the Indian Ocean from Western Europe, from America and from Japan are critical strategic routes. If, however, there is militarisation agreed to and all nuclear submarines of all nations surface in the Indian Ocean, or promise to do so and then, naturally, we can all live in a more peaceful and relaxed world. If that is not to be the case, then the Americans will have to make up their minds what they must do to ensure that these sea routes are not vulnerable to harrassment or interdiction.

Richardson: Are you concerned at the prominent publicity in the United States and the Western press about corruption and human rights violations in Asia, and of the possible impact these issues may have in the application of American foreign policy towards East and Southeast Asia?

Prime Minister: Yes, I was because I was not sure how it was going to be interpreted and implemented in practice. In South Korea, there has been a curious turn of events. President Carter met Mr. Fukuda and said that he would withdraw all their troops from South Korea. The American House of Representatives have said no, they would not withdraw — the human rights issue notwithstanding. In the case of Southeast Asia, in a presentation to Congress, Mr. Richard Holbrooke has asked for continued military assistance to countries like the Philippines, Indonesia and Thailand as being necessary for strategic reasons. It is an important and an interesting factor in the American policy. America is not going just for small countries like Korea or Thailand or the Philippines. She is raising this issue with the Soviet Union and thus raising the moral prestige and moral righteousness of the American people and the American President. It is how she pursues the human rights issue, *vis-a-vis* countries like the Soviet Union, the East Europeans, and other big communist powers — that's going to raise her standing in the world — then the world will sit up and take note of America's moral stand. However, if for strategic or other big-power considerations, the issue is not pursued against the Soviet Union and other big countries, but is continued against the small non-communist countries to make up for not squaring up with the big ones, then the human rights issue may become counter-productive.

Again, when we talk about human rights, we are really talking about different things in developing countries. I once went to a national dress — black tie dinner given by Her Majesty the Queen — the idea of black tie on a formal occasion is that everybody accords full respect to each other. The alternative to black tie was national dress. And a chief, who was also the

President of one of the countries in Africa, turned up that evening with a skirt, no shoes, no shirt, and two feathers in his hair — the two feathers denoting to his people that he is the Chief. We are entering an interesting new age where isolated societies which have developed different concepts of human dignity and patterns of human behaviour, resulting in different systems regulating human relationships, of right or wrong conduct, because of the jet, satellite and television, are suddenly brought together. Their leaders are meeting and meeting frequently. Now the American and some Western leaders are suddenly saying: "Well, you ought to behave like me. If you do not you fall short of civilised standards." Can we and must we all accept the same moral standards, or human rights? Or like varying dress-styles they have really evolved over different historic, cultural, climatic and technological circumstances?

Over time, the Americans, I believe, will grasp the fundamentals of what comprises the common fundamentals of civilised society. That whilst we may be at different stages of economic, political and social development, and though we have different histories and evolved different ways of life, they may wish to encourage people towards a democratic-type open society, where there is greater free-play — where the dissenter is not executed or sent to a psychiatric asylum.

The communists have already found these different backgrounds of different peoples a fact of life. So they stress the fact that there are different roads to socialism. In other words, not everybody has to have big five-year plans for steel mills, hydro-electric projects or thermo-nuclear generating plants. Each will work out its own way to the communist millenia. But the basic objectives — no private capital, complete state control of all the factors of production — all in the hands of the state, and the state represented by the dictatorship of the proletariat, which means the politburo of cadres of the Communist Party, these are the essentials. How these essentials are arranged in each particular society can vary. Similarly, the Americans, I believe, over the next 12 to 18 months, may also discover that there must be many and different roads towards a democratic society. Peoples may differ from the Americans, British or Australians. But so long as there's freedom of access to information about what is going on in the world and you can read more than what the government puts out, that is an essential part of the ingredient to the open society. The essense of it is that because we have been so different, if we are going to have fewer countries in the world going Marxist and communist, then we must make adjustments for their different cultural and historic past and let different peoples find their way towards that relatively free, liberal give-and-take society, where dissent, so long as it does not express itself in violence against the established society, is allowed free airing because no harm results from a difference of views which does not lead to physical clashes as in post-election Pakistan.

XXI

Tom Elliott died. He was a Professor of Chemistry at the University of Singapore, with a keen interest in the trade union movement. The Prime Minister paid tribute to him in a statement released on 9 May. Lee said that the death of Professor Tom Elliott was a loss to the NTUC, "and to all of us who have worked with him in the past. As early as in 1952–53, he identified himself with the cause of the workers of Singapore. He helped me in the work of arguing the case of the unions in several arbitration tribunals, including those of the Naval Base Labour Union. He became a Singapore citizen, and played an active part in building up a non-communist trade union movement."

A by-election, in Radin Mas constituency, to fill the vacancy caused by the death of N. Govindasamy, an old PAP stalwart and friend of the Prime Minister, was held on 14 May. The contest was between Bernard Chen Tien Lap, a 35-year old high-ranking civil servant, and J.B. Jeyaretnam, the secretary-general of the Workers Party. Bernard Chen was returned with 12,053 votes against Jeyaretnam's 5,021. Ten days after becoming an MP, Bernard Chen was appointed Minister of State in the Ministry of Defence.

XXII

Late in May, the Prime Minister left Singapore for the Philippines (where he had informal talks with President Marcos), Tokyo (where he had discussions with the Japanese Prime Minister and other Ministers), and London, where on 8 June, he spoke at the Commonwealth Conference. He discussed changing power relations. In 1945, Lee said, the United States had emerged from the war as the strongest military and economic power in the world. She had more than half the GNP of the non-communist world, and the monopoly of atomic weapons. By 1971, America, in SALT I, conceded to the Soviet Union rough equivalence, in other words, equality in nuclear strength or status. In several other respects, the communist side had enjoyed added privileges, like its theory of socialist sovereignty, exercised in Czechoslovakia in 1968. By this theory, the Soviet Union reserved the right to rescue another socialist country, in this case Czechoslovakia, which had been in danger of losing its socialist character through internal aberrations of the communist leadership. So the East European states were inviolate allies of the Soviet Union. Further, the communist powers could influence the internal affairs of non-communist countries, through aiding communist parties in these countries, or encouraging, funding and feeding whatever fad, fetish or fancy of the day

442

that might weaken the fabric of non-communist societies.

On the other hand, other than through radio broadcasts which could, and were, frequently effectively jammed, the West was not able to influence events within communist societies, like the Soviet Union, Eastern Europe, Cuba, China, North Korea, Vietnam, Laos or Cambodia. And so it might prove to be the case in Angola and Mozambique. "The rule is, once gone communist, it stays communist."

Lee described the first decade after the war, 1945 – 55, as optimistic years. Western Europe had been successfully rehabilitated by the Marshall Plan, West Berlin held by an air-lift in 1948. The invasion of South Korea by North Korea in 1950 had been repulsed by UN troops. And this war helped the rebuilding of Japan's now powerful economy, the third largest in the world, after the USA and USSR. The second decade, 1955 – 65, witnessed increasing prosperity, the beginnings of the affluent society. Economic growth seemed unlimited. Even as the empires were dismantled, Europe, including Britain, became more prosperous. America led the way, followed by Western Europe and Japan, into the consumer society. The third decade, 1965 – 75, was a decade of decline, marked by political turmoil and periodic economic crises. American forces intervened in Vietnam. It was to be a most divisive war, both within America and between America and her allies in Western Europe. It meant the end of President Johnson's "Great Society". All the hopes of the civil rights programme, giving the black American equal opportunities in a great society, were shelved as blood and treasure went into war. Americans demonstrated and rioted in their cities. The war accelerated world inflation rates. It led to a crisis of confidence in American constitutional institutions. By 1971, the non-convertibility of the US$ into gold became a fact. Then came floating exchange rates. And in October, 1973, after the fourth Arab-Israeli war, when an oil embargo was imposed, the West went through an unprecedented crisis, and a recession from which it had not quite recovered. In the fourth decade, America, Western Europe and Japan found their economies in a state of malaise. All the basic assumptions of the past could no longer be taken for granted. Uncertainty prevailed over large areas of both the strategic and economic fields. The post-Keynesian era had not produced a post-Keynesian formula which could get sluggish economies moving, to reduce unemployment without unacceptably high inflation. There was no magic formula for the problems of excess industrial capacity, unemployment and inflation in the industrial countries, and low commodity prices for the exports of developing non-oil countries.

"For me, a vivid example of the changed power relations is to imagine what Southeast Asia would have been like if the Americans had succeeded in Vietnam, and prevented the communists from taking over South Vietnam, or Laos and Cambodia. Behind this security shield, the other non-communist countries of Southeast Asia could have indulged in their quarrels over territorial claims — the Philippines over Sabah in East

443

Malaysia, or problems of minorities, like the Muslim Malays in South Thailand. But the communists have won. The Vietnamese have become a formidable military power in Southeast Asia, and the third largest communist country in the world.''

The Western media had lost their crusading interest in the future of Vietnam, Laos and Cambodia. The war had ended, regimes were changed, flags were different, and national anthems were new. The Western media, which covered every horror and atrocity during the war in colour TV and in many billions of vivid words, were completely excluded. What was taking place in these three countries had occasionally been pieced together and published in some newspapers in the West. The press reported the horrors of communist rule with resignation. Gone was the fire of missionary reform which marked their attacks on the old non-communist regimes. The workings of the communist system after victory made for fascinating, if sometimes terrifying, reading for the rest of non-communist Southeast Asia. Two years after the war, every day refugees still fled across the borders of Laos and Cambodia into Thailand. And whole Vietnamese families risked a watery grave, as they made out for the open seas in coastal fishing boats, then dashed for freedom. And this, despite the knowledge that all coastal states within reach were no longer able or willing to absorb them. For the United Nations Refugee Commission, after the first burst of humanitarian activity, had become less active, with low funds and less countries willing to take the refugees. But the stories the refugees had to tell were horrendous. They had been confirmed by Roman Catholic priests of Canadian and French origin. Many stayed behind after the communist victory. Recently they had been asked to leave. Some kept diaries of their last eighteen to twenty-four months in Saigon. They made fearful reading. But the Western media wanted to forget these issues.

However, it had made the non-communist countries of Southeast Asia determined to preserve themselves from similar catastrophe if their communist guerillas took over. "Without this shock, I doubt if the organisation which five countries had formed in 1967, ten years ago, Indonesia, Malaysia, the Philippines, Singapore and Thailand, for economic and regional co-operation, could have been more than just another organisation for Ministers and other officials to go conferencing. The seriousness of purpose came only with the shock of the terrible alternatives. There is urgency for greater economic co-operation, to accelerate growth, to reduce poverty and lessen recruits for communist guerilla bands. The political will has been found to get together to meet the new problems. The question is how to make the pace of co-operation grow faster." And it had to go faster if co-operation between the ASEAN five in Southeast Asia and Japan, and perhaps Australia and New Zealand, was to produce a significant uplift to counteract the slowing down in new investments and jobs — a slowdown which reflected a world-wide overcapacity in the industrial nations, plus a lurking fear that Thailand, now a front-line state, could face a crisis of confidence in the longer term.

Domestic capital had left Thailand, and Thai Ministers had to make appeals to their fellow countrymen to bring these funds back to get the economy going.

An era of optimism in increasing growth and prosperity had ended in October 1973, with the oil crisis. It showed up the vulnerability of all countries in this inter-linked and inter-dependent world. Only the communist bloc of the Soviet Union and Eastern Europe, and China, both systems more geared to the high cost of economic autarchy, were left unaffected by the climacteric of the world's economy. The Soviet Union had not been slow in increasing the prices of Soviet oil and gas for her communist allies. In 1973, when the embargo was imposed, the United States imported only 9 per cent of her total oil consumption. In 1976, the United States imported 29 per cent of her total oil consumption. For countries of Western Europe and Japan, the position reflected varying degrees of precariousness. The old world order had changed to the advantage of the oil producers, and of the Soviet Union and China, both nett oil exporters. The problems of the Arab-Israeli conflict had to be resolved, however intractable they might have been until then. "If there is no solution, then we all face the danger of the economic system to which we are linked disintegrating, if oil is used as a weapon to force a solution." Meanwhile, after a decade of apparent stalemate, revolutionary changes in Southern Africa were in the offing. The collapse of the right-wing dictatorship in Portugal led to the emergence of Marxist-inclined governments in Angola and Mozambique. Now southern Africa, including South Africa, was on the threshold of a classic guerilla struggle, different from, but still akin to Vietnam. The question was no longer whether there would be majority rule in Rhodesia by 1978. The question was whether, even after a black majority rule government was installed, it was possible to dissuade Marxist-trained guerillas and their leaders from going on with their guerilla insurgency from sanctuaries in neighbouring Marxist states, until Marxists had installed themselves in power in Rhodesia even after it had become Zimbabwe? It was fortuitous that at this eleventh hour, an American from the deep south had been elected President. He had uttered the hitherto unutterable, that majority rule must prevail in South Africa itself. "Let us hope there is time to save South Africa (Azania), Zimbabwe, and Namibia from Marxist-trained guerillas. But the saving will have to be by the Africans themselves as in Zaire, not by Americans."

One unmistakable trend in the changing relations between the great powers had been the dedication of the Soviet Union to military strength, coupled with the inability of the West to spend more than the minimum on defence. It was the result of the one-man one-vote system in the consumer society. The electorate was promised full employment, better wages, and more expenditure on social services. Political parties, after election, in order to fulfil their election pledges inevitably have to cut down on defence. By 1975, the Soviet Union had exceeded the United States in absolute expenditure on defence, although her GNP was less than two-thirds that of the United States. Japan spent least of all the industrial countries on defence. But the new American President had announced that there would be a total withdrawal of all US forces from South Korea in five years. Japan had been put on notice that there would be a new security situation in seven years' time. She faced a difficult decision, whether she could continue to spend less than 1 per cent of her GNP on defence, or whether she had to have a defence capability, even if it meant amending an American-imposed constitution, which prohibited rearmament.

Military strength derived from industrial and technological, capacity and total economic capacity. If the West were so minded, and had spent anything comparable to the Soviet 11 – 13 per cent of their GNP on defence, it would have presented the Soviet Union with completely different military prospects, and the world outlook would be different. This had not been the case. One-man one-vote made it impossible for any of the industrial countries to go in for increased defence expenditure, especially when the atmosphere was one of détente.

The argument against vast expenditure on conventional arms in an age of nuclear tactical and strategic weapons was attractive. Why waste money on conventional arms, when in any clash, eventually one side or the other must use tactical nuclear weapons, and if the aggressor persisted, he must be prepared for MAD (Mutually Assured Destruction)? But was this so? Had the Soviet Union made her people endure great deprivation, sacrifice the better life to become a great military world power, but remained unable to put into use her vast arsenals? Or was it possible that the possession of nuclear weaponry, plus overwhelming conventional arms, could lead to a more neutral and friendly Western Europe, not unlike Finland, with or without the softener of friendly Euro-Communists? This trend made a communist government in China warn the Europeans of the dangers of the "Munich spirit", and chided the West over their faith in détente. A communist power openly urged the capitalist West Europeans to unite and build up their defences. China's own experience with her communist neighbour had aroused deep suspicions of long-term Soviet intentions. China's ability to counter Soviet initiatives was limited by her smaller industrial capacity and lack of technological sophistication. Therefore she had had to stand by and watch as the Russians gained influence over neighbouring Laos. For it was the Russians who had produced the airplanes and helicopters to run the internal transportation of Laos, amongst other essential services previously provided by the Americans. So too, she had to stand by to watch Angola link her defences with Cuba and Russia. But for Southeast Asia, proximity gave China capacity to react. And there was no need for direct intervention. Any country considered crucial or vital to her interests that became pro-Soviet faced the penalty of increased support for its communist insurgents. "Whether we are in Asia, Africa, the Caribbean or in the South Pacific, the sources for our economic progress and our weaponry are either America, Western Europe and Japan, or the Soviet Union or, to a lesser extent, China." The Soviet Union might have less than two-thirds of the GNP of the United States of America. Soviet agriculture might not be sufficient to ensure that she could feed her own people after every harvest. But her capacity to make arms in vast quantities, and in quality equal to, if not better than, the West, had been demonstrated.

The Soviet Union was probably sincere in wanting détente between herself and America in order to avoid any situation in which accidental conflict could occur directly between them. But the contest between the two systems went on. Marxist-Leninist dogma asserted that the Western capitalist system was doomed for the dustbin of history. "But the Soviet Union sets out to help history all the same. Every issue which offers a chance to weaken the West, whether it is blacks versus whites in southern Africa, or Arabs and their oil versus Israel in the Middle East, is exploited to the utmost. Of course, their greatest triumph was in Vietnam, where American self-confidence took a beating."

But, however strong the Soviet Union might be militarily, Southeast Asia had learned that if it was to make economic progress, it must work with America, Western Europe and Japan. The Soviet Union's record in accelerating economic development had been poor. Two billion roubles were spent in Indonesia with nothing to show for it. Even more went to waste in Egypt. The Soviet Union had been a great supplier of powerful weapons. But she had not provided a good generator for economic transformation. And it might not be for want of good intentions. After all, the Soviet bloc owed the West over US$40 billion in credits for Western technology and machinery. And China, given the choice of American or British civilian aircraft, as against Russian ones, had chosen the Boeing 707 and the Trident. China had also chosen to buy American computers for weather forecasting. Experts said they were also useful for military purposes.

Perhaps the most significant tribute to western technology had come from the Vietnamese. To fight a war, Soviet hardware was more than adequate. To rebuild the economy, the Vietnamese had used South Vietnam's membership of the IMF and the World Bank, and the Asian Development Bank. The Socialist Republic of Vietnam had retained the membership. They had invited investments from the West and Japan to facilitate reconstruction. The terms for such investments appeared generous and were negotiable. And it was not just for propaganda that Vietnam was pressing hard for the US$4.5 billion which Mr. Nixon promised in a letter signed when he was President in 1973. Of all communists, the Vietnamese were best placed to know and compare the standards of technology of both sides. After the communist victory, many secret or "hidden" communists in the old government of South Vietnam were now serving the government of the Socialist Republic of Vietnam. They had seen the efficacy of American, Japanese and West European technology and machinery, especially for civilian purposes.

A disturbing consequence of Soviet effectiveness in the instruments of war, as compared to the implements of peace, was that her interests were better served in crises than in peace. Peaceful economic competition, to which Western leaders, including the British Prime Minister, had invited the Soviet Union, held out little attraction to them. It was a contest they were not likely to win. The Soviet Union's aid record in 1976 had been half that of West Germany. But competition in the supply of arms, in exploiting animosities between different ethnic, religious and ideological groups and class divisions, promised greater returns. Exploitation of these conflicts might not add to the economic strength of the Soviet bloc. But it weakened the economic resources available to the Western side. Hence the opportunities for strife in southern Africa would not be passed over. Of course, the stakes were highest in the Middle East. "The oil states of the Gulf need not go communist. They need only go radical Muslims like Libya under President Gaddafi, and the whole world may be altered beyond recognition." But the industrial countries of the West faced increasing animosity and resentment from the developing countries, aggravated because there was no alternative better economic grid for the developing countries to plug themselves into. Frustration over fluctuating commodity prices, ever higher prices of imports of manufactured goods from the industrial countries, and the failure to get substantial changes after innumerable conferences, culminating in the North-South talks in Paris, was mounting. Developing countries were convinced that the present system was loaded against them. The danger was that, denied a more equitable economic relationship, developing countries would take measures to inflict damage on the developed, even though they would hurt themselves even more.

Recently, the American President stated in unequivocal terms that the Cold War was over. He made clear that American policies were not guided by blind anti-communist reflex mechanism, hitting back wherever the communists were seeking expansion, and making allies of morally unworthy regimes. The curious thing was that the Soviet Union had never admitted to the existence of Cold War, let alone starting it. However, when the French President, Giscard d'Estaing, sought from Mr. Brezhnev in 1976, after the Helsinki Conference in 1975, an assurance that "détente" extended over the ideological arena, the response was sharp. Communist interpretation of history required that the class struggle went on. "So we can expect continuing pressure on weak spots, continuous probing for opportunities to expand communist influence. An example is West Berlin. Despite the *Oestpolitik* policies of the Federal Republic of Germany, and the acceptance of East Germany and her new boundaries by the West German Government, pressures continue. The population of West Berlin is declining. Subsidies to keep the industries buoyant have not prevented the young from drifting away." At the end of President Carter's visit to London, there was a solemn re-affirmation of the American, British and French position on West Berlin. But would the communists ever cease their pressure on Berlin, or elsewhere in the world?

Perhaps the question they should ask themselves was: Is the non-communist world worth saving? In economic performance, scientific and technological dynamism and cultural creativeness, it was the more productive and abundant world, one which held out promise for the deprived and the poor, the vast majority of mankind. Every time people were given the choice, the flow of refugees was always from communist to non-communist areas, never the other way round. What then, was an intelligent and rational response to the communist challenge, "this attrition, this constant eroding of the non-communist sectors of the world?" Lee suggested they begin by remembering that, despite conflicting interests, the non-communist countries shared a common interest in not wrecking the existing system, however inadequate it might be in serving their economic and security needs. There had to be changes to the system, one settled before the end of the last world war, now more than thirty years old. These changes must take into greater account the interests of over seventy-five nations that had become independent since 1945. But it would be silly to risk a breakdown of the system by too much pressure for too many changes in too short a time.

For example, if the oil producers pressed too hard, not only would the non-oil countries of the Third World be pushed against the wall, even the industrial economies of the West take such a beating that the balance of power between the communist and non-communist nations be upset. Once upset, the security and survival of the oil producers themselves would be in jeopardy. "So one must hope that they will not destabilise a situation which has enabled them to exploit their cartel position." Next, industrial countries, particularly those with large balance of payment deficits on top of heavy unemployment and inflation, must resist protectionism. The strong ones, like the Germans and the Japanese, must allow their currencies to float up, to take in more imports, lessening the trade deficits of the weaker economies. The alternative was a retreat into protective trading blocs, not unlike what happened after the Great Depression of 1929 – 33. This protectionism was the genesis of the Second World War — something that the Japanese Prime Minister, Mr. Fukuda, then a commercial attache in London, and now under pressure to cut back exports, had pointed out. The next time the results would be even more catastrophic.

Protectionism hurt not only Japan. When Japan was pushed, she in turn pushed against those down the line. In 1976, when the Japanese were told to cut down their new orders for shipping from nearly 80 per cent to 50 per cent of total world orders, so that European shipyards could survive, or to face retaliation in other areas unconnected with shipping, they had to back off. The Japanese kept their shipyard workers on. They re-deployed this labour force into the areas hitherto the business of the smaller shipyards in East and Southeast Asia. These smaller shipyards, including those in South Korea, Taiwan, Malaysia and Singapore, were squeezed for business as the Japanese moved into the building of smaller ships, oil rigs and ship-repairing. With their system of no-retrenchment, it was inevitable that they had to use these workers, and they under-priced and undercut the smaller shipyards of Asia.

The large issues contained in the title "New International Economic Order" did not lend 'themselves to solution in one gala conference. A serious study of each commodity and its special characteristic was a prerequisite to any practical price stabilisation scheme. A fund, or several funds under a common fund, would have to be raised to pay for stockpiles, which might check wild fluctuations in commodity prices. But, however dressed up, fairer terms of trade meant that governments in the industrial democracies, based on one-man one-vote, must be persuaded, either with or without pressure from the oil producers, that their longer term interests demanded a gradual conceding of their present dominant trading position, and the opening up of their domestic markets to the simple manufacture of the developing countries, before people in the poorer countries could get a fair share of the world's resources.

But it would be simplistic to believe that developing countries would become developed, just by getting the developed to give more equitable terms of trade, and bigger transfers of capital and technology. There could be no self-sustaining growth without strong political leaderships which could imbue their peoples with social and work disciplines. And the most fundamental of all disciplines was to desist from large families, so that populations would not expand faster than any economic development could hope to cope with. The present 2½ per cent increase per annum in developing countries meant that schools, hospitals, jobs and homes must double every twenty years. Without this political will, these spiky problems would never be grasped, let alone resolved.

"We are engaged in a test of stamina and will between the communist and the competitive non-communist systems. The communists have gone in for military strength. They have mobilised their human resources and scientific research for military purposes. This has left their economies distorted. It is difficult to keep political discontent from surfacing, however comprehensive their control of men's minds. Sooner or later their peoples will realise the awful price they have had to pay to achieve military dominance. And with growing person to person contacts, an awareness of the real world outside their controlled societies is unavoidable. Communist societies may face greater contradictions within their societies, and between the Soviet Union and her East European allies, than anyone in the West may imagine. And Soviet failure to gain adherents after such vast investments in countries like India, Egypt and Indonesia may well be repeated in Africa and Latin America, despite their Cuban allies." The future was not pre-determined. "It is what we make of it." Leaders in industrial and developing countries must face up to the new problems that had sprouted in a world brought into close contact and constant interaction by rapid transportation and instant communications. It was a world where diverse peoples and their leaders were in ceaseless competi-

450

tion to get more of the apparently finite resources for their own constituents. However, the world needed more than selfish, self-serving policies to survive, and to overcome the problems of "this one interlinked, inter-dependent world that Western sciences and technology, trade and industry have brought about." To succeed, there must be faith, will, stamina and patience in governments of the industrial and developing countries, so that, in co-operation, not confrontation, they could modify the present system, and make it work equitably in the changed circumstances of the last quarter of the twentieth century.

XXIII

Back in Singapore on 27 June, the Prime Minister spoke at the official opening of the Fourth Meeting of the ASEAN Economic Ministers. He said that since the formation of ASEAN in 1967, ASEAN countries had gained a closer understanding of each other's problems and aspirations. In Bali, in February 1976, the Heads of Government emphasised the importance of regional economic co-operation when they assigned to ASEAN Economic Ministers the vital task of accelerating this co-operation. "This Fourth Meeting of the ASEAN Economic Ministers in Singapore must review the progress made, and propose further action for the Heads of Government meeting in August. More remains to be done." Trade within ASEAN as a percentage of total ASEAN trade with the world had dropped from 15.5 per cent in 1970 to 12.6 per cent in 1975. Powerful economic factors had caused this. ASEAN had been a traditional supplier of primary commodities and processed products to the rest of the world. Because of similar resources and levels of development, member countries had not been able to achieve a greater exchange of goods among themselves. "We can, and must, make trade between ASEAN countries grow as fast as ASEAN trade with the rest of the world." An important step to expand intra-ASEAN trade was taken when the Economic Ministers signed the Agreement on Preferential Trading Arrangements in Manila in February, 1977. "This Agreement must be implemented with a sense of urgency to match that which moved Heads of Government at their first meeting in Bali last year."

In 1975, ASEAN countries together imported more than US$23.84 billion worth of goods. Less than US$2.47 billion of these total imports were supplied by ASEAN countries themselves. There was therefore some US$21 billion worth of imports into ASEAN countries from the rest of the world. Some of these imports could, by preferential trading arrangements, patterned on that reached for the first five ASEAN projects, be made and exported from ASEAN countries themselves. Products at present imported in substantial quantities from non-ASEAN countries, and within the industrial capacity of ASEAN countries, could be studied

451

for manufacture in ASEAN, and included in an extension of the preferential trading arrangements agreed to at Bali in February 1975, and elaborated upon at Manila in February 1977. ASEAN Economic Ministers could consider whether their officials should not focus their efforts in this area. ASEAN Economic Ministers could draw up a programme to identify these products, and set a time-table to agree upon an exchange of preferential trading arrangements. This concentration on areas where there were no vested interests of any already-established industry, would be more productive. "For there need be no existing obstacles to check the pace of regional economic co-operation."

Lee said that in recent months, ASEAN member countries had suffered from a proliferation of non-tariff barriers in industrial countries. Despite the agreement among the seven at the London Summit in early May rejecting protectionism, such problems persisted. Industrial countries continued to transfer their problems of unemployment by keeping uneconomic industries going, producing goods with high labour content. The burden was transferred to developing countries. In fact, unemployment was greater in the developing countries of ASEAN, and such unemployment caused greater hardships because developing countries could not afford to cushion their workers from the rigours of unemployment in the same way as the industrial countries. "In our dialogue with the EEC, Japan, Australia, New Zealand and Canada, and later the United States, ASEAN countries must press home the disruptive consequences of their protectionist policies on our peoples. For such representations to be effective, we in ASEAN must avoid trade policies which adversely affect each other. Further, our bargaining position will be strengthened if we can co-ordinate our import policies collectively to close our consolidated markets to those who unreasonably and unilaterally shut off our exports."

Of special concern was ASEAN's relationship with Japan. Japan had been an active partner in trade with ASEAN. The exchange of goods had expanded rapidly, from US$3,349.3 million in 1970, to US$11,352.5 million in 1975. Japan was an advanced industrial society. Japan was also a big market of 112 million people, with a per capita GNP of nearly US$5,000, at 1976 current prices. Japan was geographically well-placed to be a good partner of ASEAN for trade and economic co-operation. ASEAN was a rapidly growing market for Japanese consumer and capital goods. ASEAN also supplied Japan's need for raw materials. More of such raw materials could be semi-processed in ASEAN countries before exported to Japan and elsewhere. This was in the interests of the Japanese, who had become very conscious of the pollution of their environment. There was much mutual advantage in a constructive long-term relationship. ASEAN sought preferential access to the Japanese markets for ASEAN primary products and simple manufacture. And in the nature of such relationships between industrial and developing countries, reverse preferences must be avoided. The EEC had abandoned them in the Lome

452

Convention. "But we must work out arrangements which will give Japan compensating advantages."

Australia and New Zealand were also important industrial countries geographically close to ASEAN. ASEAN trade in 1975 amounted to US$1,375.0 million with Australia, and US$234.3 million with New Zealand. Their present problems with domestic unemployment might limit the possibilities of trade expansion in the immediate future. But this problems should not side-track them, or ASEAN, from examining and deciding on longer term relationships. "Much will depend on our respective perceptions of our geo-political relationships. Has Australasia a stake in a stable Southeast Asia, in particular those parts of Southeast Asia which have economic systems compatible and complementary to theirs? Can we in ASEAN be patient enough to look ahead to what is possible in the intermediate future, and see what is possible in spite of the long-standing practice of high protectionism in Australia and New Zealand for their industries?"

Lee believed there were enough men in positions of leadership who could see the advantage of developing a complementary economic relationship between countries adjacent to each other, one group with low wage costs and, for the time being, low industrial capacity, another group with very high wage costs and high industrial capacity. There were obvious advantages in complementary relations. Otherwise the EEC would not have thrived, nor its relationships flourished with its associated countries, Greece, Portugal and Spain, besides its world-wide ties with the African, Caribbean and Pacific countries of the Lome Convention. At this meeting, ASEAN Economic Ministers must reach maximum common ground among themselves. "If we take a wider view of the economic and political development of the region, we cannot but find ourselves coming to similar conclusions, particularly on the need to strengthen our leverage by pooling our markets for collaboration with industrial partners, or retaliation against selfish protectionism of our trading partners." Co-ordination and co-operation would widen economic opportunities. On that note, Lee formally declared open the Fourth Meeting of the ASEAN Economic Ministers. He hoped the deliberations would chart out the steps forward towards closer co-operation in ASEAN.

XXIV

On 29 June, Lee was questioned in Parliament about his discussion with the Japanese Prime Minister on the proposed $2 billion petro-chemical project in the Republic. Lee replied: "When I met Mr. Fukuda, the Prime Minister of Japan, on 30 May this year, all issues regarding the Singapore-Japan petrochemical project in Singapore had already been resolved by officials of both Governments. Mr. Fukuda confirmed that the project has been agreed to by, and will receive the support of, the Japanese

Government. This endorsement and support was repeated by all the Japanese Ministers concerned, for instance, the Ministers for International Trade and Industry, Foreign Affairs and Finance. The following are the main points of the Agreement. The joint venture "upstream" company of the project will be owned on an equal basis by the Singapore Government and Japanese participants. Japanese participation in the "upstream" company will be through an investment company being set up in Japan. The Overseas Economic Co-operation Fund (OECF), which is a Japanese Government institution for overseas development assistance, will invest three billion yen (about $27 million), equivalent to 30 per cent of the equity of the investment company. The remaining 70 per cent equity will be taken up by private Japanese companies, including Sumitomo Chemical, Mitsubishi Petrochemical, Mitsui Petrochemical, Asahi Chemical, Showa Denko, Idemitsu and other Japanese petrochemical companies. In addition, long-term loans for the project would be provided by the Export-Import Bank of Japan both for equity participation by Japanese companies as well as for the purchase of machinery and equipment from Japan.

"The Singapore project will be the first petrochemical complex to receive OECF equity participation. The project has the support of both the Japanese Government and the Japanese petrochemical industry. It goes without saying that continuing co-operation between Singapore and Japan is a key factor in the success of the project. The petrochemical complex when completed in 1981 will consist of an 'upstream' company and initially three 'downstream' companies. The 'upstream' company will own the naptha/gas oil cracker, which is the core of the complex and other common-user facilities. The 'downstream' companies will purchase ethylene and propylene from the 'upstream' company for conversion into plastic resins and other end-products. The project will make a significant contribution to our economy, both during construction and during operation. Much of the engineering, plant fabrication and construction work will be done locally. The project will require about 4,000 direct workers during the peak of the construction period and about 2,000 employees for the operation of the complex. Engineering companies, plant manufacturers, plastic fabricators and other end-product users are likely to be attracted to set up in Singapore. The multiplier effects of this project will therefore be considerable."

XXV

Lee opened another important ASEAN meeting, the Tenth ASEAN Ministerial Meeting, held in Singapore on 5 July. He reminded the delegates that in a month's time, the ASEAN Heads of Government would meet in Kuala Lumpur. "This ASEAN Foreign Ministers' meeting will

454

have to sort out the issues, and decide the agenda between important and more important matters which the Heads of Government must resolve since they met seventeen months ago in Bali.'' Amongst the items with a claim to a place on the agenda were those which the ASEAN Economic Ministers discussed the previous week. They reached some degree of understanding on the first five ASEAN industrial projects, and also agreed upon seventy-one product items which would enjoy tariff preferences and other forms of preferential trading. ''You may well decide that these, as well as those areas which require consultations and discussions at the highest level, should be placed before the Heads of Government.''

Ten years after its formation, ASEAN had to grapple with difficult geo-political problems of a world in a state of transition. The simple fact was that ASEAN's future now depended primarily more on what they did than what others would, or could, do for them. ''We have to take the initiative, through co-operation among ourselves, especially in the economic and political fields. Together, we must establish closer, more constructive and complementary relationships with Japan, and perhaps also with Australia and New Zealand. These closer economic ties will increase the chances for a stable and thriving Southeast Asia. Unlike the conditions prevailing ten years ago, today this stability depends more on our own efforts. However, we may be helped by the major powers creating conditions favourable for a stable and peaceful East Asia and Pacific.''

Lee said that in their deliberations, they would have to take into account the vastly changed power relationships, not least of them the fact that, like the Japanese, ASEAN had to live with a continuous land-mass which was communist, all the way from Siberia, China, down to Vietnam, Laos and Kampuchea. Fortunately, it was no longer a monolithic communist bloc. ''We have each sought varying degrees of equidistance from the Soviet Union and China. As important, we must build our relations with our new communist neighbours in Vietnam, Laos and Kampuchea on a constructive and productive basis. We must emphasise in our relations with them our desire for peaceful relations, however different our systems of government. They have our full assurance that we do not wish to interfere with their internal affairs. And, naturally, we expect them to respect our sovereign right to decide our own economic and political systems, matters for our own governments and peoples to decide. And we intend to counter and dissolve incipient guerilla insurgencies that are trying to expand, and will seek outside aid. We have begun to address these problems on our own.''

A strong, vigorous and thriving ASEAN became a desirable economic and trading partner. ''Then we are friends who are desirable assets to be more closely associated with, not embarrassing liabilities to be shied away from. This is our best contribution to the stability and security of this part of the world. The converse is just as stark in its implications. The future of ASEAN depends largely upon what we choose to make out of it. The stronger ASEAN is, the better it is for each of us. This is not rhetoric. It is the simple truth." Lee referred to a statement of America's role in Asia, made by the US Secretary of State, Mr. Cyrus Vance, on 29 June in New York. "You will have noted how he spelt out the interests of America in East Asia. His emphasis was on the economic relationships, that America's trade with East Asia and the Pacific is now one-fourth of her world trade, more than that with any other region, including the European Economic Community. He stated that the United States sold US$22 billion worth of products in the region. Of this US$22 billion, US$3.7 billion, or 16.82 per cent, were sold to ASEAN. He pointed out that from ASEAN, America bought one-tenth of her crude oil, and a higher percentage of her rubber, tin, cocoa, bauxite and other important raw material imports." Mr. Vance then expressed the hope that out of US-ASEAN consultations, expected within a few months, there would be a basis for stronger American support of Southeast Asian regional efforts. It was a speech totally devoid of rhetoric, and free from any ideological overtones. The emphasis of the speech was on the economics of America's relationship with East Asia and the Pacific. The speech recognised the importance of overcoming the difficulties that were ahead. With industrial countries plagued by inflation and unemployment, the countries of East Asia and the Pacific would go through a difficult period. "And we all have experienced how under these adverse conditions, governments in industrial countries talk bravely of the importance of liberal trade, whilst quietly putting the pressure on for voluntary restraints, or erecting more tariff and non-tariff barriers."

In August, ASEAN Heads of Government would be meeting the Prime Ministers of Japan, Australia and New Zealand. ASEAN had serious issues to discuss with them about immediate and long-term economic relationships, both collectively as a group in ASEAN, and bilaterally. The question before the Foreign Ministers of ASEAN was not whether it could help enhance the development, progress and stability of member states. "We all know ASEAN co-operation will make that difference. But will this be done in good time? The answer to this question depends on how long we take to work out the implications of the new situation, make the political adjustments, and take substantive steps to give regional co-operation substance rather than form. We have to cultivate new habits of accepting the responsibilities of working together in order to enjoy the benefits stemming from greater co-operation and cohesion. How willing are we to adopt new economic strategies to make it worthwhile for industrial countries, like Japan, the United States and the EEC, to invest in ASEAN and speed up our industrialisation? For before we can ask the industrial countries for the best terms possible, we must decide among ourselves how much we are prepared to do to make ASEAN worthwhile for industrial investments. For ASEAN is no more and no less than what its partners are prepared to make it, by expanding the list of ASEAN industrial projects, by agreeing on more preferential trading arrangements, by expanding the list of product items for preferential tariffs, and in other ways tried and found successful in other economic groupings.'' Industrial countries would want to broaden their economic links with ASEAN if steps were taken which would benefit them and ASEAN. ''Thus we can the more surely increase our economic strength. And with economic strength, all other social and political problems will become that much easier of solution.''

XXVI

On 1 July, the Government declared the parliamentary seat occupied by Mr. Lim Guan Hoo to be vacant. Mr. Lim had been in a coma for five months and was not expected to recover (in fact, he died shortly afterwards). A by-election was called for 23 July and the PAP nominated Lim Chee Onn, another civil servant. Lee, in a statement, said: ''Lim Chee Onn started to act as Deputy Secretary, Ministry of Communications, two years ago, when he was only thirty-one. Like Bernard Chen, now MP for Radin Mas, he was one of a group of outstanding officers in the civil service in their early thirties. The PAP Central Executive Committee decided to field Lim Chee Onn because he has proved his ability and capacity as an administrator, and because we believe he can take the rough and tumble of politics, and is young enough to develop political sense. He will learn, and learn quickly, how Singaporeans think and feel, and how to get policies settled and people mobilised behind them in their implementation. That he has been prepared to resign his job, give up the security of the civil service and go into politics, speaks for itself. We believe he can be more than an MP. We have now taken out two promising officers in the Administrative Service, talent-spotted by the Establishment Unit which I set up under the Head of the Civil Service, Mr. Howe Yoon Chong. We were most reluctant to do this. But the unexpected vacancies of two seats in Radin Mas and Bukit Merah made this a rational decision. I commend Lim Chee Onn to Bukit Merah. I have no doubts that he can keep up the work of Lim Guan Hoo.'' As expected, Lim won easily, beating Dr. Lee Siew Choh, leader of the Barisan Sosialis by 11,625 votes to Dr. Lee's 4,473.

XXVII

The Prime Minister on 6 July sent the following message of condolence to His Grace, Monsignor Gregory Yong, on the death of Archbishop Olcomendy: 'I have asked Mr. Ng Kah Ting, MP for Punggol, to represent me at the funeral service of the late Archbishop Olcomendy. I received news of his death with sadness. He had, for many years, been a

457

staunch pillar supporting inter-religious peace and harmony in Singapore. He served on the Presidential Council for Minority Rights for three years. May I record the Government's appreciation for his valuable services. He was a religious leader of the Catholic community whose understanding for the problems of our multi-racial and multi-religious community helped to keep the social climate relaxed and tolerant. My condolences go to you and the Catholic community in Singapore."

XXVIII

Lee repeated some of the arguments he'd already made about ASEAN, when he spoke at the opening of the ASEAN Heads of Government Meeting in Kuala Lumpur, on 4 August. He said that in Bali, eighteen months earlier, ASEAN had taken a big step forward. "We signed the Treaty of Amity and Co-operation in Southeast Asia, the Declaration of ASEAN Concord, and agreed to five ASEAN industrial projects and preferential trading arrangements. We gave substance to regional economic co-operation. In Kuala Lumpur now, we have to decide whether we move forward, step sideways, or move backwards. For we cannot stand still." That ASEAN had the potential to increase stability and economic progress for all of them was recognised by those who wished them well. Otherwise serious-minded people in high office, not only in Japan, Australia and New Zealand, but also in the EEC and America, would not spend their time and energy conducting dialogues with them to discover how trade and economic co-operation could be further developed between them and ASEAN. West Europeans who had travelled their own long and arduous road to economic co-operation and political cohesion in the EEC, had accorded ASEAN concessions as a group. They had indirectly encouraged ASEAN to make more progress together, by agreeing to cumulative rule of origin to enable products with local content from more than one ASEAN country to qualify for preference in their GSP. Lee reminded the meeting that on Sunday, they would together discuss ways of increasing economic co-operation with the Prime Minister of Japan. It could be an important landmark on a road that could take them to a mutually productive relationship. But it could just as easily become a ceremonial ritual along an inconsequential road that would lead them nowhere. It depended upon whether the Japanese took a long-term view of their interests in Southeast Asia. Equally, it depended upon whether the countries in ASEAN were able and willing to create the conditions which would make it advantageous for the Japanese to expand their processing and manufacturing industries in ASEAN countries, to lower the barriers which were blocking ASEAN exports to Japan, and to join in schemes for stabilising foreign exchange earnings from commodity exports of ASEAN countries.

"The Australian and New Zealand Prime Ministers will also join us after our meeting. Our meetings with them could eventually lead to better trade and closer co-operation and understanding between them and the ASEAN countries." In Manila in September, the ASEAN-United States dialogue would begin. We have had the assurance of the US Secretary of State that the United States would wish these talks to form the basis for stronger support of Southeast Asian regional efforts." A new American President and his Administration had shown in the past six months a different spirit and approach to world issues. For Southeast Asia, the US Secretary of State had spelt out simply that Americans saw things in terms of their economic interests. The security considerations of the past two decades were no longer relevant. Their only major strategic consideration in Asia was Japan, with whom America had a mutual security treaty. America considered this treaty to be a cornerstone of peace in East Asia. But this had not inhibited American plans for the withdrawal of all US forces in Korea in five years, despite a distinct lack of Japanese enthusiasm for this step.

"In an era when Americans have shown how allergic they are to military involvement in any place in the world which does not directly threaten their strategic interests, ASEAN, it has been said, is conspiring to become a military grouping for the advancement of American interests. We should take it as a backhanded compliment that ASEAN has the basic ingredients for success. So even those who do not approve of our efforts have not found it possible to ignore our getting together, for no one wastes his breath on an organisation which is on its way out." People would take ASEAN as seriously as ASEAN took themselves. "Our Economic Ministers have not been able to resolve the five ASEAN industrial projects which were agreed to in principle. For preferential trading arrangements, only seventy-one items have been agreed. Surely we can do better than this."

Lee continued: "We have to overcome the habit of thinking in terms of the previous framework of our own national economic plans. They were drawn up in an era when we thought the Americans and the West would provide us with the necessary security umbrella to carry on modernisation and industrialisation within our own national frontiers, some kind of semi-economic self-sufficiency through industrialisation by import substitution. The world was not to be thus. At the end of this conference, our success will be judged not by the speeches made, but the agreements on concrete items, the bolts and nuts of economic co-operation. To reach such agreements, we must be prepared to ask our economic advisers to overcome the habit of thinking only of our respective national economic plans. We have real problems. Let us formulate real solutions. Our real solution is stronger economic co-operation and better development rates. The immediate step we can take is to press on with the five ASEAN industrial projects, and increase the items for preferential trading arrangements."

There was a clear correlation between close trade and economic ties, and long-term political interests. In the middle of 1977, to underline their long-term common political interests, the EEC of nine countries abolished all tariffs on most industrial goods between themselves and the seven countries of EFTA (Austria, Finland, Iceland, Norway, Portugal, Sweden, Switzerland). The closer the economic links a country had with an economic grouping, the more it must stay together with the foreign policies and political orientation of the group. The big powers knew this. So to preserve their neutrality, Finland, Sweden and Austria had scrupulously stayed out of any association with EEC, although their interests were infinitely more with the EEC than with Eastern Europe. "We in ASEAN share vital common political interests and objectives. We will not achieve these vital objectives if we do not, besides other measures, expand and strengthen the economic ties between us. This is why we are here today."

At the closing session of the meeting, Lee said that the Kuala Lumpur meeting would perhaps be remembered for the realistic assessment of ASEAN's progress and potential. The free and informal discussions among Heads of Government had made them realise why certain objectives of ASEAN could not be achieved as quickly as some of them would have wished them to be. There were difficulties which, for a variety of reasons, could not be overcome as simply as they would wish. As a result, they had to accept a pace of intra-ASEAN economic co-operation which was more congenial to all, even though it might be less than what was achievable if they all set their sights higher. However, the progress which ASEAN had made in the past eighteen months was not insignificant. The agreement on the five ASEAN industrial projects was upheld. And the seventy-one items for the preferential trading arrangement would be added to as and when the Economic Ministers felt they could make further advances, even before their annual meetings. "So whatever the pace, we are agreed upon the direction we should go."

In the next few days, they would find their work less vexatious. "In our external relations, we share common views. So we have no major adjustments to make in our basic assumptions when discussing economic relations with Japan, Australia and New Zealand. Similar experiences have left us with similar attitudes. It is psychologically easier to deal with ASEAN's external partners, then to sort out the intra-regional arrangements between the partners themselves." But this was only in the initial phases. In the intermediate stage, they would discover that to quicken the pace of economic co-operation with industrial countries, they must increase the pace at which they moved in adjusting intra-ASEAN relationships, in order to facilitate and absorb a larger transfer of capital, technology, know-how and skills. "But in the spirit of ASEAN consensus, we have agreed that we shall tackle these problems when we come to them."

"It has been fair so far this year," said Lee in his eve of National Day Message. "For the first half of the year, we made 8 per cent growth. However, the indicators show a slowing down. For the whole of 1977, we may make between 7 – 8 per cent growth."

Because the economy had been diversified, Singapore had not been too badly hit by the oil crisis. Those countries which depended on textiles and garments for a high portion of their exports had been badly hit by protectionism of the industrial countries. And there were signals of greater protectionism because unemployment was still high in Western Europe and America. Singapore's unemployment figures also showed a slight trend for the worse: in the middle of 1976, there were about 4.5 per cent unemployed. By the end of 1976, it had improved to 3.7 per cent; in the middle of 1977, it had worsened to 3.9 per cent. What all this added up to was that expectations must be lowered. Slow growth and high unemployment would plague the world's industries and economies for the next two to three years. "And we cannot escape the effects of this. In fact, we must be grateful that unemployment has not been worse, otherwise our school leavers and university graduates cannot afford to be so selective over jobs, as some still are today. For we have many more work-permit workers than the thirty-seven thousand Singaporeans registered as unemployed."

Lee said that the government had tried to make up for a sluggish world economy by large increases in construction in the public sector. But there was a limit to pump-priming. "We have also tried to increase regional co-operation. But progress will be slow. Moreover, it is not easy to increase regional co-operation when international trade is not on the expansion." The government would try harder. "And so must you, both as workers and entrepreneurs. We have not adjusted to the shift of purchasing power to the oil-producing countries. We must increase our efforts to export more to these wealthy countries." Some countries, like South Korea, had moved quickly into these new markets. There were over a hundred thousand Koreans working in the oil-producing countries of West Asia on construction projects. They were tough and hardworking. When Singaporeans were sent into this area, they found the climate too hot and too cold. They often packed up, although they were paid two to three times what they were paid in Singapore. And Korean businessmen had been active. Their exports to the oil-producing countries had gone up. They had been out in force getting contracts for construction, and selling their products. "Our businessmen must try harder, to get to know who wants what. I know we have quadrupled our exports to the oil states of the Gulf. However, it is the quadrupling of a very small base. More can be done. But it will not be done by correspondence. Businessmen must get out, make contacts, sweat it out to sell our goods and our services. There is no easy way. So long as we are prepared to adjust to changes in the world, and work hard to overcome new difficulties, we shall stay on top of our problems. "Today, one of the problems was that many young people believed that prosperity and growth were part of the nature of Singapore. It was necessary to remind them that prosperity and growth did not come naturally in a place without natural resources. They were the result of man's effort and ingenuity. Because we avoided massive retrenchments and pay cuts the oil crisis caused in places like Hong Kong, young Singaporeans have not been tempered by hardship. We can see a clear change in their spending habits. Shops and supermarkets, including the NTUC ones, are crowded for several days after pay-day, at the end and middle of the month. Then sales drop. People no longer budget and save like they used to. Whatever they have, they spend. Even their CPF they often use up completely to pay for instalments on their flats. We must save and invest for our future. The Japanese private domestic saving and investment rates were over 34 per cent of their wages for the 1960s and '70s. This was a key factor in their economic success."

There were many uncertainties ahead. But one thing was certain. To stay on top of their problems, Singaporean must have the will to work, and the will to succeed. "And I believe we, including our young, have the will, and that we can succeed."

Lee elaborated this theme at the National Day Rally at the National Theatre on 13 August. He said: "This is the twelfth occasion since 1965 and every year we have been lucky. I touch wood each time. I say that because each time it looks as if it's going to get much tougher, much harder." He believed that Singapore had a population that kept on trying. "We will strive and we will make 4 per cent, 5 per cent, 6 per cent, 7 per cent, maybe 8 per cent growth. Then in five years, we are going to clear the US$3,000 per capita mark." This would bring problems. The World Bank had a simple rule of thumb. "Below US$1,000 you are a developing country. Beyond or above US$1,000 per capita you are in transition towards developed ... Let me explain some of the consequences of this. First, neither the World Bank nor the Asian Development Bank is going to give us any concessions whether we are going to develop an MRT or an airport, whatever it is. We will borrow at the going rate. No concessions. Recently, the IMF wants to promote us from a donee country in receipt of special concessions to a donor country to join the industrial countries and help the developing countries. So we said: Look, please be careful. We are not really in that class. The problem has not been solved."

Singapore's argument was that their per capita per annum was calculated on borrowed capital, borrowed technology, foreign marketing, and export of dividends. "They say: All right, we will knock off 20 per cent for that. That's not a very great help. But when we clear US$3,000 in real value, then the real problem will start." So, Lee continued, he wanted to alert them "it's going to get tougher. It is like mountaineering — the higher you climb the more exhilerating it is, but the tougher it is to climb up higher because there is less oxygen in the air. This makes me come to my next point, namely, the expectations of our young, expectations which parents encourage. It is alright to set your sights high. Work hard, get a good education, reach out for the stars. But settle for what you can be. Not everybody is going to be an astronaut. And what's more, settle for the jobs that are going and not the jobs that you think ought to be there.''

Lee explained why he believed it was safer to lower expectations. There was unemployment in the industrial countries — Western Europe, America, Australia, New Zealand. So they took protective measures. When there was unemployment, pressures were on. These were governments running one-man one-vote system. The pressures were on to cut out imports. It was a vicious cycle because it meant a slow-down in world trade. So, instead of getting cheap shoes, garments, raincoats, pocket calculators, television sets, they were expensive. The world was poorer off. It did not lead to more capital investment, more production, more consumption. It stalled.

"Well, in this kind of a climate just lower our expectations when it comes to the kind of jobs we are doing. This year, the government's representative on the Wages Council pressed this point of view — that in this period of uncertainty when we are not getting the input of new investments that keeps on raising or bringing up the level of technology, and, therefore, the value-added per worker within each factory, we better go slow on wages. It's expansion of existing technology and existing factories that we must depend on for jobs. Even if we can get more factories, they don't give many jobs like Sumitomo Petrochemicals. It will create 4,000 jobs when the factory is being built. After it is built, it will employ only 2,000 people, but all highly-skilled technicians and chemists. That's what you call high-value-added — a capital investment which can go for as much as nearly $2,000 million, employing only 2,000 people. So it can pay high wages.

"I am not at all sure that we can have more of this, because there is excess capacity in so many areas, including, at the moment, petrochemicals.

"The Japanese factories are working at slightly under 70 per cent of capacity. We hope, by the time the one in Singapore is in production in 1981, world recovery plus normal expansion of demand, they would have reached a 100 per cent capacity. Therefore, when looking for jobs, let's not be too difficult.''

A pattern was emerging. "We are becoming a little bit like what's happened in Western Europe, including Britain, where people don't want to do what they consider jobs not equal to their status — socially not desirable jobs — even though they pay well. And, therefore, the work permit phenomenon is not a temporary one. The British brought in about a million West Indians, Indians and Pakistanis. The Germans have about two million Turks and Yugoslavs. The strange part is, in spite of recession and unemployment, the West Indians, and the Pakistanis are still doing certain jobs in Britain, and the Turks and the Yugoslavs doing certain jobs in Germany. Maybe we are already trapped in that kind of a bind. I refuse to admit that the Singaporean can get snobbish so quickly. But the signs

463

are that he has gone that way. It's a combination of the soft line plus a little bit of shrewdness or low cunning. When a building is going up, the outdoor work is done by work permit holders except for the old workers. When the building is completed, then our boys, who have been trained in our Ponggol Vocational Institute and other training centres, will come in and put in the wiring, the wash basin, the tiles, the plumbing. He is already covered, not subject to sun and rain. He is more comfortable. Never mind how much the other fellow gets because he is not really that hungry any more. It is quite a combination of creature-comfort plus, of course, the inconvenience of either working with a safety belt on or risking falling off the scaffolding. So he waits till that's all over and he goes into the solid structure. We've got that kind of a situation. If the permit phenomenon was to be permanent, there would have to be an annual intake, which would be permanent, of so many thousands of healthy, striving, often because they are hungry, types. They, having stayed for five years, could be expected to marry a Singaporean and add to the population. There was, logically, no other way. At the same time, we must also lower our birth rate in order to absorb foreign workers on a permanent basis. "This was a tentative conclusion. We will watch the figures over the next three to four years. And if they show this persistent pattern — the choice of work, then the adjustments have to be made.'' Lee concluded: "Finally, may I say that one redeeming feature of Singapore is that it responds. It responds to the challenge, it responds to the exhortation. And it takes note, it makes adjustments. As we begin to change the priorities and the incentives, people change in their choices. I am convinced that more than half the reason why we have succeeded, why we continue to succeed, in spite of the oil crisis, is that we have got basically a rational thinking population. If they can get away with it, they will. You give them half a chance, they will. On the whole, they understand. People understand certain things have to be done. And firm, stable, just and orderly government is the first requisite for our continued survival and our continued prosperity. And on that note, I wish you another happy, prosperous and successful year.''

XXX

Japan's Prime Minister, Mr. Takeo Fukuda, visited Singapore. At a banquet, the Prime Minister, in a speech of welcome on 14 August, recalled that it was ten years earlier, in 1967, that a Japanese Prime Minister, the later Mr. Eisaku Sato, first visited Singapore and other countries in Southeast Asia. His visit had been made at a time when the world order appeared relatively certain and likely to endure. Japan had been set on very high growth rates. Energy and resources seemed limitless. Pollution and other environmental problems had not become matters of acute public concern they have now become. "Our guest tonight was Prime Minister Sato's close colleague. He belongs to that generation of outstanding men in politics, the civil service, finance, industry and commerce. They are men of rare distinction. Their courage in the face of defeat and adversity, their ability, dedication and team work brought about the miracle of Japan's rebirth after the utter destruction and devastation of the last war."

When after the Japanese elections in December, 1976 Mr. Fukuda became Prime Minister, leaders in ASEAN countries were greatly relieved. He was a tried and tested leader, a known and reliable factor, in a world of change and uncertainty. "Many of us knew him personally for many years. His wide-ranging intellect and thorough grasp of world problems, his expertise in matters of economics and finance, his capacity to anticipate problems and the need for change long before they became conventional wisdom, these qualities made his assumption of the Prime Ministership of Japan a reassuring and welcome development. As far back as 1972 – 73, before the oil crisis, he had spoken up for more moderate Japanese growth rates, and the dangers of headlong growth in a world of finite resources. He was one of the few men who was wise before the event." Mr. Fukuda had assumed leadership at an age when most non-Japanese were set and inflexible in their ways. But even by Japanese standards, he was out of the ordinary. "His is a lively mind, and an active disposition. By temperament and character, he is ever ready to respond to new challenges, whatever the economic and political circumstances, but without over-reacting to them."

It was fortunate that Japan had a tried and proven leadership at a most difficult period in the economic history of the world. This leadership had charted the Japanese recovery from the shock of the oil crisis in 1973 and negative growth rates in 1974 to a healthy real growth of 6.3 per cent in 1976, and a balance of payments surplus. However dramatically the world situation might change and become more adverse, the Japanese people had risen to the challenge and overcome these new problems, given wise and able leadership. Japan's remarkable record of high economic performance through the last thirty years was a tribute to her peoples' industrious nature, their sense of national unity and the quality of her leadership in government and in enterprise.

The response of the countries of ASEAN to these adverse external developments was to seek greater stability in regional co-operation, co-operation in economic, political, social and cultural fields. Japan had, by the visit of Prime Minister Fukuda to Kuala Lumpur to meet the ASEAN Heads of Government, and by his individual journeys to each one of the ASEAN countries, signalled her willingness to co-operate, and to help in creating stable and prosperous conditions. This was the most significant visit made by a Japanese Prime Minister. The Japanese Government had been cautious but realistic and practical in their positive approach to proposals for greater economic co-operation. "We in Singapore will try to match this realistic, practical and positive approach. Both bilaterally, and in the context of ASEAN, we look forward to expanding ties between

Japan and us." Mr. Fukuda had proposed an additional factor in their relationship. He had deplored the emphasis on money and material factors in their dealings and stressed the need to establish heart-to-heart communications. "We shall respond in like spirit." Lee said that in this, he was encouraged by the understanding they already had of each other. Both between people in government and in industry and commerce, Japanese and Singaporeans had established a sensible working relationship. "If we can sustain mutual respect, although the Singapore-Japan relationship is basically not an equal one, then we would have achieved this heart-to-heart rapport. I hope Prime Minister Fukuda's visit will encourage these developments. Japan and all the countries of ASEAN desire and can contribute to the peace, stability and prosperity of the whole region."

In his response, Japan's Prime Minister said their two countries shared a common base in that they were both seafaring nations, blessed with few natural resources, which must depend on industrialisation and trade for economic development. A strong nationalistic trend had appeared of late in various problems related to the international economy. "I am concerned that should we leave this state of affairs unattended it will have profound political and social consequences in the whole world. It is my conviction that, in such circumstances, our two countries should jointly exert their utmost efforts for the maintenance of free trade and the freedom of the seas. I feel greatly encouraged to find that Prime Minister Lee shares my concern in these regards."

XXXI

Wishing all Muslims in Singapore "Selamat Hari Raya Aidil Fitri" on 14 September, the Prime Minister reminded them that the rebuilding of Singapore had brought changes for the better — better homes, better jobs, a different and, on the whole, better way of life, in high-rise buildings in new towns. However, new homes meant acquiring new habits, such as tight budgetting for rents or instalments, conservancy charges and PUB bills. HDB figures showed that the few who got into arrears and did not pay their rents or instalments on time were spread more or less proportionately amongst all racial and religious groups in Singapore. Singapore Malays had been as successful in budget-conscious spending as other Singaporeans. Indeed, Malays now living in old kampong areas wanted to move out more quickly into the new towns, as they saw their friends and relatives do better in their new houses, with their daughters as well as their sons, working in the new factories, and adding to the family income.

Lee promised that every new town would have a representative cross-section of Singaporeans of all races and religions. One important benefit was that there would be fewer MPs who would not understand and support policies necessary for a multi-racial, multi-religious Singapore.

So, whether it was Telok Blangah, Clementi, Bedok or Ang Mo Kio new town, "we will ensure that there will be a new mosque to cater for the average range of 10 – 20 per cent Muslim inhabitants." Malays being resettled chose the new town nearest their present homes. Lee was confident that they would see the need to take the next logical step, that was, to choose the town nearest their place of work.

XXXII

On 1 September, Mr. Goh Chok Tong was appointed Senior Minister of State in the Ministry of Finance. Four days later, Dr. Ahmad Mattar became Minister of State in the Ministry of Social Affairs, acting as Minister for Social Affairs in the absence of Inche Othman Wok, now Ambassador to Indonesia.

Mr. Ong Teng Cheong, Senior Minister of State for Communications, was appointed to act as Minister for Culture during the absence of Mr. Jek Yeun Thong (Ambassador to London).

On 1 October, Dr. Ow Chin Hock became Parliamentary Secretary to the Minister for Culture. The Ministry of Science and Technology, which had been looked after by Mr. Jek Yeun Thong, then came under the charge of Mr. E.W. Barker, Minister for Law and the Environment. The Permanent Secretary (Environment) would service this Ministry.

On 29 September, the Prime Minister, accompanied by the Foreign Minister and Mr. Goh Chok Tong, left Singapore for Canada (for discussions with Mr. Trudeau on current international economic and political issues) and for Washington to meet President Carter, Vice-President Walter Mondale, Mr. Cyrus Vance, Secretary of State, and other American officials.

An official statement was put out on behalf of the Prime Minister in Washington, on 7 October, to the effect that the Prime Minister had explained to President Carter how a continuing US presence would ensure a climate of confidence, and enhance stability in the region. Confidence and stability were two essentials for continuing investments, increased trade and sustained economic development of the ASEAN countries. It was the even spread of the benefits of economic development that would ensure that democratic societies in ASEAN would grow and thrive. "The President's grasp of the problems of the region and his positive position on a continuing US presence in the Western Pacific, the Prime Minister believes, augurs well for the future."

Interviewed three days later by the US *News and World Report*, in Washington, Lee was asked if he thought America's concentration on problems of Europe, the Middle East and Africa, was taken in his part of the world as abandonment of Asia?

Prime Minister: No. It's an inevitable shift in the areas of crisis. Vietnam is over. The Middle East has become a problem that affects the whole world. And Southern Africa, long neglected, now demands attention. So as long as somebody is tending to the back burner and keeping watch on Asia, all may be well.

Question: Is there a feeling that someone here in the US is on watch? For instance, do past and projected withdrawals of American forces from Asia raise concern?

Prime Minister: Whether it raises concern has nothing to do with whether somebody is watching. The withdrawal order came as a surprise, more so for its abruptness. But things have calmed down and the speed of events made more palatable. But I hope somebody is watching developments, not just in the Northeast, but in the whole of Asia.

Question: Are US forces being reduced to a dangerous level?

Prime Minister: As of now, no. I am assuming that American discussions with the Philippines will lead to a long-term stay at Clark and Subic Bay and that the Army division being withdrawn from South Korea will stay as a strategic force somewhere in the Western Pacific.

Question: How large a military force must the US keep in Asia to maintain the military balance and retain its influence?

Prime Minister: The naval balance must be rough US equivalent to Soviet naval power in the area. There must be sufficient American forces to influence the thinking of governments, to assure them that outside intervention against them would not be permitted and to caution them that they themselves should not embark on ventures.

Question: How strong is the Soviet Union in Southeast Asia?

Prime Minister: It's not just Southeast Asia. The Soviet Union has a naval capacity today in the Indian Ocean and in the Western Pacific which did not exist in the early sixties. This power developed in the late sixties; it's a reality in the seventies. And as new ships are launched, whether in the Black Sea or in Baltic ports, they have more and more to spread over the oceans.

Question: Are you concerned primarily with the Russian threat? What about China — and Vietnam?

Prime Minister: The first priority is to maintain a balance in the naval capacity of the US and the Soviet Union. The Chinese are not able to match this naval capacity. They are anxious not to upset any of the countries in Asia by trying to stretch themselves uncomfortably beyond their borders. That will continue for a long time. Therefore, the Chinese would like somebody else — the Japanese and the Americans or whoever else — to fill the spaces until such time as the situation alters in China's favour. The Chinese do have the capacity, using their links with the guerilla insurgent movements in various Asian countries, to react on land to any move made by the Soviets — or, for that matter, by the Vietnamese, on their own or together with the Soviets — against any move which will exclude them from influence in areas they consider critical.

Question: Can the Association of Southeast Asian Nations — Singapore, Thailand, Malaysia, Indonesia and the Philippines — play a military role in Asia?

Prime Minister: In a limited regional context in border-clearing operations to flush out communists from their base areas, yes.

Question: But not as a replacement for American forces?

Prime Minister: There is no substitute to a Soviet naval vessel other than a US naval vessel.

Question: Would you welcome a greater military effort by Japan to take up some of the slack in Asia?

Prime Minister: That's a difficult question to answer. Increased effort by the Japanese to take up the slack left behind by diminished American defence expenditure in North East Asia would enable American resources to be spread over the rest of the Pacific. But a Japanese force playing a wider role outside their home waters would be contrary to the Japanese Constitution, as Japanese leaders repeatedly point out. And I'm not certain a wider Japanese role would be all that reassuring to the rest of Asia.

Question: Aside from military matters, do nations of Asia look to the Japanese for leadership in achieving economic stability?

Prime Minster: Until very recently, there has been no declared policy by Japan on her own to assume a role in helping development of the economies of the LDCs (lesser-developed countries) in Asia or Africa or elsewhere. It's not a burden Japan has taken up. But Japan now has shown increased awareness of the problems of countries in Southeast Asia. She gets a considerable part of her raw materials, including oil, and she markets a considerable amount of her manufacture — capital goods and consumer durables.

Question: Would greater participation in development lead to Japanese economic domination?

Prime Minister: We can't have it both ways. Although Japan did not undertake an active role in the economic development of Southeast Asia, she is the No. 1 trading partner of the five countries of ASEAN. So why not have the Japanese take on the responsibilities of being our major economic partner?

Question: There seems to be a growing trend in world trade towards protectionism. Is this affecting Singapore's economy?

Prime Minister: Yes, indeed. And we see an unexpected meanness and pettiness from people who had behaved generously until they ran into high unemployment over a prolonged period. When cut orchids from Singapore flown into Europe in the summer season are considered a threat to tulip growers in Holland, it shows how sensitive West European Governments become when faced with unexpectedly high unemployment.

Question: Do you see any danger of a trade war?

Prime Minister: A lot will depend upon the leadership of the United States. You must set a good example.

Question: You stated that the Chinese, at least for the time being, want to maintain stability in Asia. Does this mean Peking has withdrawn its support and encouragement for communist guerillas operating in Thailand, Malaysia and Burma?

Prime Minister: Well, it was explained clearly and simply to me last year by Premier Hua Kuo-feng that it was the duty of the Communist Party of China to support the Marxist-Leninist parties anywhere in the world. This they have done and proposed to do. But it's moral support.

Question: Just moral support? No weapons?

Prime Minister: I did not ask about specifics of aid.

Question: What about the vast quantities of American arms North Vietnam captured in South Vietnam? Are these weapons being sold or given to communist insurgents in other Asian nations?

Prime Minister: The Vietnamese have been meticulous in letting everybody know that these weapons are not for sale and have not been passed on to mischief makers. Whether that will continue, we don't know. As of now, the evidence shows that Hanoi has been correct.

Question: If China, as you say, is giving only moral support to the insurgents and Vietnam is not supplying weapons, where are the rebels getting arms and money?

Prime Minister: I didn't say the Vietnamese were not supplying weapons. I said they were not using captured American weapons for these purposes. There are other weapons which have always been used in this kind of running battle — rifles, mortars, hand-launched rockets and so on. There's no shortage of supplies.

Question: Are these arms mostly Soviet?

Prime Minister: Some are and others, I would think, are of Chinese manufacture. Money? The insurgents run tax-collecting systems in the areas where they are the primary authority. There is some form of revenue collection. Where else they get further subsidies you can guess as easily as anyone else.

Question: Are insurgencies in Thailand and Malaysia making headway?

Prime Minister: As of now, it's marginal. Post-war events in Cambodia and Laos diminished support for Marxist and communist guerillas. The flood of refugees and their stories of horror served as an antidote against communist propaganda. It will take years before there can be an upsurge of antipathy against the government and sympathy for the objectives of the guerillas in the adjacent countries. Thailand has a curious situation. In the border regions of the north-east with Laos, east with Cambodia, the Thais have vividly seen how harsh life can be under the communists. On the other hand, the military in Bangkok used what was reported to be excessive force against Marxist and radical students. As a result, several hundred students fled to join the guerillas. These articulate recruits, if they can take the hardships, will provide the largely peasant guerillas with a sharp cutting edge.

Question: What is actually going on in Cambodia? Is the blood-letting there as massive as reported?

Prime Minister: It is an enigma. We do not know what will happen. All we know is that the Kampuchean Government, through Deputy Prime Minister Ieng Sary, has repeatedly assured us that they want good relations with us. I met him six months ago when he was in Singapore. I was surprised to find how soft-spoken and mild-mannered a person he was.

Question: When South Vietnam collapsed in April 1975, there was widespread speculation about the repercussions throughout Southeast Asia. Has the effect been as severe as was feared?

Prime Minister: In retrospect, the position today is one or two shades better than what I had expected. There are two main reasons. First, there was the impact of the atrocity reports carried out by refugees from Vietnam, Laos and Cambodia — particularly to Thailand. Second, the newly-established communist governments in Vietnam, Cambodia and Laos have been preoccupied with the problems of restoring their devastated economies. Feeding peoples at a time of drought absorbs considerable resources. A great deal of energy and attention has had to be devoted to domestic problems. What the situation will be five or seven years from now, will depend upon how quickly and effectively they can overcome those domestic difficulties.

Question: Once Vietnam repairs the war damage, would you expect Hanoi to turn aggressive and create trouble for its neighbours?

Prime Minister: Five to seven years is a long time. A lot will depend upon what kind of a nation it becomes. We must hope that in the process of rehabilitation, the Vietnamese will discover — as indeed there are signs that they are discovering — how much easier it is to destroy than to build. And the more they rebuild, the more they become linked with sources of development capital like the World Bank and the Asian Development Bank, which must require minimum standards of peaceful and co-operative conduct. Therefore, if a cycle is established in which Vietnam gets more credits, more help from Western sources for her reconstruction, the desire to rebuild and develop could make her behave in a more rational and peaceful way than if she were making little progress in peaceful reconstruction of the economies both in the north and south.

Question: Has the rivalry between Russia and China contributed to the higher-than-expected level of stability in Southeast Asia? Will it continue to do so?

Prime Minister: That is a difficult question to answer. The outcome of the Vietnam War — in which the Soviet Union clearly gained more influence than China — has made it necessary for the present policy to be maintained, a policy of not alarming the countries in Southeast Asia. But if the conflict is intensified between the Soviet Union and China, either directly between themselves or through third countries, then, far from being a stabilising factor, this rivalry could become a factor for intensifying guerilla insurgency. Moscow and Peking could end up competing for influence with different factions within the same guerilla movement. It's not an easily predictable situation.

In Boston, an Honorary Degree in Law was conferred upon Lee by the University of Massachusetts in Amherst, on 15 October. In his address, Lee said the degree was due to the drive and efforts of the people of Singapore for which he had been credited. "They translated into reality plans drawn up by experts and specialists from the World Bank and other international agencies. These plans were designed to create an industrial and servicing sector for an economy based largely on agriculture, trade and British military bases spending, and which was, by 1960, unable to cope with an unemployment rate of 12½ per cent in a population of two million growing at 4 per cent per annum. A group of practical and dedicated administrators reshaped these plans to make the best of local material and conditions. It was fortunate that there were enough trained indigenous manpower to put ideas into action and bring about rapid growth."

Per capita income, which reflected, if broadly, material progress for Singaporeans, went up from US$450 in 1965 to US$2,500 in 1975, measured at market prices. If adjustments were made for inflation, the per capita income went up by about four times in ten years. This could not have been done without the booming economies of the industrial nations of America, Western Europe and Japan throughout this period, It was an unprecedented period of sustained expansion. Singapore's external trade expanded at more than 15 per cent per annum through the 1960s up to 1973 with the energy crisis. Since 1973, further economic development in Singapore had been at modest rates, averaging 6 per cent in real terms. Much of this was provided by the momentum of what had been achieved before the oil crisis.

In per capita terms, Singapore, with a population now of 2.2 million, was only slightly better off than the population of the main cities of developing East and Southeast Asia. But in per capita terms compared to a total country, Singapore had been uncomfortably placed with middle-income countries of the Mediterranean with a large percentage of workers in the agricultural sector, like Spain, Greece and Israel. This was a dubious distinction. It was this absence of a sizeable agricultural population which had distorted the comparative per capita picture. However, the price for this progress had been change in the attitudes of Singaporeans as they entered the consumer society. Amongst the more unexpected changes was the adoption of contemporary Western attitudes to work by the young. There was the same desire to avoid taking jobs which were considered demeaning or were dirty or heavy. However adequately compensated these jobs might be, young workers preferred less pay for easier, more pleasant conditions of work. So domestic service, garbage removal, road making and construction work exposed to the weather, were now to be done by guest workers, though there was 4 per cent unemployment. "Perhaps if we had not made the learning of the English Language compulsory in all schools, exposing a whole generation to the mass media of the English-speaking world, television, newspapers and magazines, these values and attitudes may not have been absorbed. But without the English language, we might not have succeeded in teaching so quickly a whole generation the knowledge and skills which made them able to work the machines brought in from the industrial countries of the West."

Singapore had not succeeded as well as the Japanese in preserving the ethics and values of their traditional elders. Perhaps, in some other place, another people were succeeding in making the transition without the widespread introduction of a foreign language. And if they then fended off foreign attitudes and life-styles, they would be an infinitely superior model for rapid development and modernisation.

Lee was back in Singapore in time to send all Hindus a Deepavali Message. The "Hindu Festival of Lights", he said, was a reminder that tolerance and respect for each other's religion and customs had contributed to the stability and progress in which all Singaporeans benefitted.

XXXIII

Two loyal civil servants passed away and Lee sent messages of condolence to the widows. To Mrs. Pang Tee Pow he wrote on 16 November: "I cannot find words equal to my sorrow at the death of Pang Tee Pow. The day after a meeting on 28 July in the Cabinet Office, I heard he was taken ill. A few days later, I was told it was cancer of the lung. I found it painful to see him decline so rapidly on the several occasions I visited him. It must have been a harrowing experience for your children and you. I first knew him some fifteen years ago. He was my secretary. He was dependable and unflappable. The last seven years he spent in the Ministry of Defence. His competence, hard work and judgement, stemming from long experience handling men, these qualities made him a pillar of strength in Mindef. He never evaded his responsibilities nor shirked unpleasant decisions — qualities essential for the management of a large disciplined force. We shall all miss him. I understand how grievous your loss is for I feel the gap that has been left in the top ranks. This gap is not easy to fill. My deepest sympathies to you and your children."

To Mrs. Li Vei-Chen, Lee sent the following letter two days later: "I was sad to learn this morning that your husband, Li Vei-chen, had died at the age of seventy-four. I first knew him in the early 1950s, when he was Chief Editor of the *Nanyang Siang Pau* and I was a member of the Legislative Assembly. In 1965, he became my Press Secretary. I got to know him well. His grasp of both the Chinese-speaking and English-speaking worlds was invaluable. He helped me put across government policies to the people. It was then a most difficult and delicate task, for the schism between the two worlds was so much more pronounced in the 1960s than it is today. I am deeply grateful to him for the ten years of loyal and effective

473

service he rendered to the government and to me personally. He was, by nature, reserved. This was a valuable trait. He spoke only when it was necessary and no more than enough. All those who knew him liked and respected his quiet and dignified demeanour. May I send you and your daughter my sincere condolence.''

XXXIV

Jurong continued to play an important part in the modernisation and industrialisation of the Republic. Lee spoke at the official opening of the Jurong Town Community Centre on 26 November. It was an example of Lee's keen interest and thorough attention to domestic matters, as well as to international affairs. He described Jurong as the most dramatically transformed part of Singapore. In the September 1963 elections, Barisan Sosialis won Jurong constituency with 55 per cent of the votes. The PAP lost, getting 31 per cent of the votes. In September 1972, the PAP won 74 per cent of the votes cast. In 1976, the MP was returned unopposed. However, Boon Lay, which was part of Jurong constituency, gave the PAP 78 per cent of the votes cast. In 1963, Jurong was a rural constituency of poor farmers, who grew vegetables and reared pigs, and subsistence fishermen, mostly Malays. It now had the largest number of factories and factory workers of any constituency. 80 per cent of them were living in JTC or Housing Board flats. There were still patches left of the old rural Jurong. So the Gek Poh and Juboon Community Centres still catered to rural residents.

"I congratulate the MC of Jurong Town CC for raising $550,000. With a government subsidy of $160,000 to make up $710,000, they have built and furnished one of our best-equipped community centres. It started with four converted flats, with a build-up area of 200 square metres. This new Centre has 1,450 square metres. There is a well-furnished air-conditioned reading/library room. There is a book loan service twice a week, with staff from the National Library. It has a squash court. The children's playground has equipment supplied by the Bernard Van Leer Foundation. On weekdays, an average of three hundred residents use the Centre. It is a lively Centre because it has an active Management Committee and an attentive MP. It provides kindergarten, sports, vocational and cultural activities. The Chairman of the MC is a doctor, the Secretary, a legal manager, the Treasurer, a businessman. Committee Members include hawkers, a provision shop owner, accountant and Port Safety Officer. A Youth Executive Committee was formed in August last year. The Chairman, a Nanyang University graduate, is a translator. The Secretary is a National Service 2nd lieutenant. The Committee comprise foremen, welders and production operators.''

However, there were some special problems in Jurong. There were complaints of dust pollution. Investigations by the Ministry of Environment showed that the dust came mainly from the burning of wood-chips from plywood factories, of which there were twenty-five. It was not a problem during the northeast monsoon, when the winds blew the smoke into the sea. The Ministry of Environment was studying ways of more efficient burning of wood-wastes to minimise this problem during the southwest monsoon. Other problems were the traffic jams and the long delays for workers travelling to work. Several companies had complained that their workers arrived late and tired for work. The best solution was to get Jurong workers to move into the housing estates nearer Jurong, like Teban Garden, Clementi and Ghim Moh. "We are trying to encourage people to opt for estates nearest their place of work. The problem of commuting to work and to schools can be considerably reduced if workers live in estates nearest their place of work, and their children in primary schools within the new towns." Also, the roads to Jurong would be improved. The Pan Island Expressway, from Jalan Anak Bukit to Jalan Boon Lay, would be completed in 1981. There would also be a new road extension from Commonwealth Avenue to Jurong Town Hall.

It was unfortunate that up to three to four years ago, the HDB had been too busy with their own developments. They could not help the JTC with the planning and developing of Jurong Town. Now, the Chairman of JTC was also the Chief Executive Officer of HDB. He could draw on the accumulated experience and expertise of HDB to help fit facilities into Jurong Town, so that those who lived in Jurong and in the adjoining HDB estates could have the advantage of the amenities of HDB new towns.

Lee concluded: "We have broken the back of our early problems — unemployment, squatter slums, poor health and education. Now, we are faced with new problems, traffic jams, pollution, inadequate technical education. And we have to keep our wages competitive and workers productive in a world where growth has become slow and at a time when the major industrialised countries are becoming more protectionist, thereby further slowing down trade and hurting the economies of developing countries, like Singapore."

XXXV

In December, the Prime Minister made another unofficial visit to Thailand at the invitation of the Thai Prime Minister, General Kriangsak Chomanan. Lee discussed bilateral, regional and international issues and continued to promote economic co-operation between ASEAN countries.

On 14 December, speaking at the centenary dinner of the Hongkong & Shanghai Banking Corporation, Lee admitted that once in a while, he departed from his normal practice. "I accepted your invitation to dinner to celebrate the hundredth year of the Hongkong & Shanghai Banking

Corporation in Singapore. Then I feared I was setting a time-consuming precedent. I checked and was told the next centenary will be that of the Citibank N.A. (formerly FNCB). I asked when that would be. I was told in July 2002. I had looked forward to a quiet dinner. A fortnight ago I found a draft speech and notes on the HSBC in my tray. I queried the need. I did not remember having promised to speak. The answer was reassuring. My memory was not failing. I had not promised to speak. However, my host intended to say a few words. Would I respond? Well, I should have known better. I do not get free dinners. I read the draft speech and the notes. Compulsively I asked for facts not in the notes. If MAS has done my homework for me, then the first bank established in Singapore in 1846 was called the Oriental Bank. But it folded up in 1884 — obviously bad management, for the great crash came only fifty years later. The second bank was Mercantile Bank in 1854 — now merged into HSBC. The third was the Netherlands Trading Society or NTS Bank in 1858, now renamed Algemene Bank Nederland N.V. The fourth was the Chartered Bank in 1859. Yours was the fifth when you set up business in 1877. You must have saturated the banking market, for there were no new banks till the next century, 1902, with the FNCB. Then the Banque De L'Indochine Et De Suez, 1905. The first non-imperial bank was allowed in 1907, the Four Seas Communication Bank, a modest effort by the Chinese community in Singapore. It could not have posed any threat to the British banks. Over the next two decades, five more Singapore Chinese banks were allowed: Lee Wah Bank (1920), Kwong Lee Bank (1926), Oversea-Chinese Banking Corporation (1932), United Overseas Bank (1935), and Ban Hin Lee Bank (1936)."

Lee said they must have been good for Singapore's trade with China and probably added to the business of British banks. Otherwise the Straits Settlements government would not have allowed the Bank of China and the Guangdong Provincial Bank both to be set up in 1939. As if to be fair, the Governor, probably with the concurrence of Whitehall, balanced them with two from India — the Indian Bank and the Indian Overseas Bank in 1941. Then came war. It took four years of rehabilitation before the Overseas Union Bank, in 1949, started a new expansion of post-war banks which was to make Singapore a banking and financial centre. The breaking of new ground came when a Dutchman, employed in an American bank, in 1968, proposed to Goh Keng Swee, then Minister for Finance, that Singapore could be a home to the Asian Dollar, as London was to the Euro-dollar. "Van Oenen's was a perceptive mind. Goh seized the idea, refined it and tested it out. It worked with remarkable progress as the world money markets bounced with confidence at what was to be another five years of boom before the oil crisis. In nine years, the Asian Dollar (ACU) has come up to $20 billion."

Singapore now had seventy-six banks. Only thirteen were local. There were also forty-two banks which had representative offices, twenty-three merchant banks, thirty-four finance companies and a number of discount houses, money brokers and investment houses. Singapore's policy had been liberal, if selective, admitting freely banks of international standing to improve both internal banking services and to expand links with other financial centres throughout the continents. "As I studied the list of banks established in Singapore over the past hundred and thirty-one years, I was struck by the thought that they must have been the precursors of the multi-national corporations. It was their world-wide network which enabled Singapore to build up its entrepot trade, financing the clearing of forests for plantations, collecting raw produce, now called commodities, for export to Europe, America, and later Japan, and importing British manufactured goods for distribution in the Far East. They gingerly stepped down the footpaths which were to become well-trodden and in time be converted into the motorways for the big multi-nationals. Without these early footpaths, it would not have been possible to have accomplished so swiftly, in just over a decade. This spread of capital, technology, management, marketing, from the industrialised countries of America, Europe and Japan to the developing countries of East and Southeast Asia, and imparting of skills in handling complex machines to workers who only recently handled nothing more complicated than a bicycle, the widest imagination could not have foreseen the pace of change."

The expansion of the HSBC since it was first established in 1865 in Hong Kong, with an office in Shanghai and London, reflected the vagaries of fortune, the ups and downs of nations. Their branches were chronologically: (1) Yokohama, 1866, (2) Calcutta, 1867, (3) Bahamas, 1869, (4) San Francisco, 1875, (5) Manila, 1875, (6) Singapore, 1877, (7) New York, 1880, (8) Lyons, 1881, (9) Jakarta, 1884, (10) Penang, 1884, (11) Bangkok, 1888, and (12) Hamburg, 1889. A few were no longer in banking centres of any consequence. One had overtaken London in importance — New York. Politics and economics were not separable. Between Adam Smith and John Maynard Keynes, Marx and Lenin changed the geopolitical balance of Europe. Between Keynes and Milton Friedman or Arthur Burns, Stalin, Mao and Ho Chi Minh changed the geopolitical balance of the world.

But the HSBC had adapted and adjusted. The present state of the world economy was troubling the finance ministries of all non-oil exporting nations. Their Ministers and economists were baffled. They were not able to lead their peoples out of "this morass of high unemployment and inflation". Could it not be that President Carter's team lacked the vision and girth that President Roosevelt's team must have had? Why could there not be another "New Deal" to get people working again, resuming the journey to further progress and prosperity? Alas, the infuriating ineffectiveness of successive reflationary efforts seemed to provide no clues to a magic formula. "Perhaps our present malady, though less painfully acute, is more deep-seated and more difficult to cure than that of the 1930s! Perhaps also, even had there been no oil crisis, the present stalling of the world's economy after the most prolonged spell of economic expansion the world has enjoyed, was coming in any case, though it might have been less sudden and the dislocation less painful. The maturing of the new growth industries and no new frontiers to open up made a slow-down inevitable." Singapore, like Hong Kong, was unable to influence the big political and economic decisions which would be taken by the industrialised countries to reduce unemployment and contain inflation. "But we will have a better chance of reducing the hardships these decisions may inflict upon us if we stay trim, alert and adjust our policies to meet harsher circumstances." Small trading outposts of colonial empires like Hong Kong and Singapore were supposed to have faded away as their roles disappeared with empire. This had not been so. For different political and economic reasons, both Hong Kong and Singapore had developed new outlets for the drive of their entrepreneurs and the energies of their peoples. They had both carved out new rules for themselves as the countries around them went through revolutionary changes.

For the foreseeable future, Singapore and Hong Kong had complementary and competitive roles. Activities of corporations like the HSBC would keep this relationship healthy and beneficial to both. The British Empire had gone. But London was still one of the great financial centres of Europe and the world. Both Singapore and Hong Kong had forged links beyond London, with New York, Frankfurt, Zurich, Paris, Tokyo, and every major national or provincial centre in Europe, North America and Australasia. And a web of personal and institutional contacts with traders, executives of private and state corporations, government officers and Ministers, would facilitate the spread of capital and technology, knowledge and skills, into vast areas where they were needed and would be productive. Billions of potential GDP were waiting to be generated by matching untapped resources with unemployed or underemployed workers, a magic which enterprise could bring about.

XXXVI

On 23 December, Lee addressed the Political Association of the University of Singapore on "Higher Education and Singapore's Future". He remarked upon the fact that since he last spoke in that lecture theatre, the temper and composition of the University had changed. First, nearly all the male students had now done two and a half years' National Service. Second, the prospect was of a less buoyant employment market for graduates. He believed the mood was more sober and less boisterous. One way to keep a population on its toes was high unemployment, a salutary method of social discipline. "We have been fortunate, particularly in not having had significant unemployment in the years since the oil crisis. Therefore, social discipline and work discipline have to be achieved by other means — management controls, cultural habits and social pressure.

From Labour Ministry statistics, graduate unemployment is zero. By not having been born earlier to catch the economic boom before October 1973, what you will miss is the prospect of rapid promotions and increments.''

For any government, high graduate unemployment was one of the key indicators of political disorder. The more trained and educated people a country had, who were unemployed, the greater the potential for social and political unrest. Therefore, oil-producing countries who had come into fabulous wealth since 1973, had been cautious — having seen what had happened in India, in Pakistan, in Ceylon — in substantially and rapidly increasing number of students who went to universities. Singapore's graduate unemployment rate was zero for two reasons. First, rapid economic development. Second, a university enrolment policy that ensured that only those who were clear potential passes were admitted, and that the pass standard was never lowered. "We have from 1970 to 1977 between 7 – 9 per cent of those who made Secondary 1 going to university. This compares with 9.5 per cent for England and Wales. However, if we take the percentage on the base of entrance into Primary 1, then although for England and Wales the figure is still 9.5 per cent, for Singapore, the figures range from 4 – 5 per cent. The reason is that some 35 – 40 per cent of Primary 1 students did not pass the primary school leaving examinations. I hope, with the abolition of automatic promotions, we shall reduce the failure percentage rate to between 20 – 25 per cent. From 1970 – 75 in Japan, the figure was 31 per cent. In America, 48 per cent. These are not comparable figures because the Japanese and American education systems are different from ours which was built on the British norm. Japanese and American figures will include all those who made Pre-U 2 of our school system. However, the Japanese percentage of 31 per cent is impressive because a large slice of that figure is in technical education.''

If the Polytechnic and Ngee Ann students were added to the percentage who made up the tertiary-educated, against Secondary 1 as the base, there was an additional 6 – 9 per cent. But placed against a Primary 1 base, the figures went down between 4 – 5 per cent. Those in the apex of this pyramid, the universities, might be reassured to know that there were in 1976, 4,730 employment passes issued to professionals. Engineers were the largest group (2,552), next, teachers (1,191), then doctors and dentists (338), accountants (278), and architects (210). In addition, there were 920 university-trained who were on work permits. They were starting their careers with salaries below $750. Again, the largest group was for engineering (188), and next science graduates (171), most probably as trainee teachers.

"A significant part of our economic growth has been contributed to by these professionals. Another set of figures will give you an idea of the magnitude of the seats you will have to fill if we were to attempt a policy of Singaporeanisation. There are 15,155 employment pass holders and foreign investors. Together, they earned, in 1974, from the latest figures

479

available, $420 million. This is income for themselves, not for the companies. It is from their income tax returns in Singapore. It does not include the arrangements they may have for incomes to be paid in the Bahamas or Bermuda or other tax-free havens. Remove these 15,000 and I venture the guess that we have within twelve months about 300,000 unemployment (30 per cent of our work force)." It would take twelve months because economic activity would go on until new decisions were not made, or wrong ones taken, and production and sales came to a halt. Lee asserted that when the Government embarked energetically on this economic policy of global economic links after 1965, "we did so with our eyes wide open". This economic strategy had linked Singapore more closely and directly to the major centres of industrial strength — trade, manufacture, communications, finance, the lot. There was no way to embark on Singaporeanisation without irreparable damage. "I do not see us producing the number of engineers, management consultants and decision-markers with the experience and judgement to fill these jobs, even if all the firms wanted us to, for at least twenty years. Before then, new advances in business and industry will bring in a new generation of exports and expertise. Therefore the urgent need is to get more of our students educated better, to cut down the wastage. We have to improve our education from kindergarten upwards to post-university training."

Singapore's wastage rates were terrifying. In 1964, nearly 64,000 students entered Primary I, the peak years. They were born in 1958. The PAP took office in 1959. "So I can disclaim responsibility. But the PAP was saddled with the burden." In 1977, the Primary I admissions were down to 47,000. For 1976, and again in 1977, they were below the 40,000 mark. "Had we left population trends alone, we would have had shot beyond the 80,000 babies per annum mark by 1977. Then this great opportunity to transform the educational quality of the population would never have been. All these years, since 1959, we have just been mass-producing schools and teachers, and juggling with languages of instruction. It was a messy, massive exercise as much in education as in politics. And it was and is highly-sensitive politics because language and culture arouse great passions. The wastage is unbelievable. Can it be that we are more stupid than other people?"

Each year, some hundred top scholars went abroad on scholarships. Formerly, they were nearly all men. Now, there were gradually more women. Nearly half of these scholars each year were in the first class honours list of their universities, in Britain, Canada, Australia and New Zealand. Even those in Japan, France and Germany did very well, despite having to learn a new language. "Yet until last year, we could not get more than 55 or 60 per cent to pass their PSLE after six years of schooling at the first attempt. It was amazing. We should have had the feedback within the Education Ministry. We did not. The feedback came through only National Service. We discovered it when we had to get Hokkien-speaking platoons formed and to teach officers to speak Hokkien in order to

480

command the men. Only then did the Education Ministry know what had gone wrong. Once a student misses language comprehension, he or she has missed the bus with automatic promotions."

When a Singapore child went to school he was exposed to bilingualism, in 75 per cent — maybe 72 per cent of the cases — to two new alien languages. At home he spoke Hokkien, Hainanese, Teochew, Hakka, Cantonese, Hindi, or Bengali — "name the dialect and we have got it". He went to school and was immediately confounded by a barrage of two verbal artillery systems. He was subjected to two percussion bangs. Into one ear he got English, into the other Mandarin. He spoke neither at home. No two languages were more different and diverse. Chinese was monosyllabic, tonal, idiographic, no phonetics, without inflexions, and a unique syntax. But after a while, he discovered how the sounds were related to his dialect at home. But, the English his teacher spoke, he did not quite understand at all. And when he was about to make sense out of it, he was further confused when he watched television. Between the Singapore announcer and the whole range of American, British and Australian accents, many a student got lost. So he retreated into Hokkien, Singapore Hokkien, not Amoy-standard Hokkien. "He is what, if I were a doctor, I would call a linguistic autistic — he withdraws into himself, the patois of his home and his friends. Education is a very gradual process. We will not know our errors until some eight to ten years. And we will not see the success of corrective policies until another eight to ten years."

Lee said he would be surprised if the PSLE wastage could not be reduced to 25 per cent. 25 per cent was still very high. But this might be the price they had to pay to produce bilingualists. In most monolingual societies like America, the illiteracy rate was about 10 per cent. "But we cannot have monolingual education." However, he was cheered by the drop in total births. With the number of teachers already recruited, classrooms would go down from forty-four to about thirty pupils. "We can have more individual attention and correction of all compositions. We have too many gradings of compositions with no corrections of grammar and style. We have too many 'tikam-tikam' multiple choice questions. Gradually, we shall have a population which will react instantaneously, laugh, cry, and be angry together at the same time. We will share a common language — nearly."

But for their life-times, whether as supervisors or executives, they would be faced, "and those of you who have done National Service know this well", with having to repeat their instructions in one other language besides English. And it was absolutely wrong that one other language should be a dialect. It meant that because of the structure of the society, for a long while, those who wanted to be effective in supervisory positions must be bilingual, preferably trilingual — a tremendous imposition. Every word, from "A" for apple had to be learned in three languages. That was the price they had to pay for at least another generation. "Because I learned my Mandarin and dialect in adult life, I have had to keep new phrases in practice so that they will roll trippingly off my tongue. So, I used to carry a multi-purpose plug for my tape-recorder when I travel. When I had to switch between English, Mandarin, Hokkien, and Malay — never mind Tamil — the mental transformers had even more work to do than the multi-purpose plug. These transformers, physically and mentally, that I have to lug around are an encumbrance. Unfortunately, they are not excess luggage I can afford to jettison.''

Lee said his final point was that most of the acute problems were of a very special nature, and they could be solved only by those who understood the complexities of Singapore and Singaporeans. "If most of this meagre 4 per cent of Primary Is, who get to the top of the educational pyramid are without that sense of commitment to the community that carried them and paid for them to get up to the upper reaches of the education ladder, then Singapore will falter and fail." Wastage there always would be. But a clear majority must have an abiding commitment to the joint interests of their fellow citizens and themselves or Singapore would fall apart into the disparate racial, clan, dialect and religious groups from whence they sprang. "It is this sense of responsibility, this unavoidable obligation to keep Singaporeans together, to protect their lives and livelihood, which cannot be imported. We can afford to import the professional expertise and entrepreneur flair in the 15,000 employment pass holders. But we cannot import this feel for Singapore, and what makes Singaporeans tick. Only we can do this for ourselves."

And one unpleasant decision which the University of Nanyang had taken, a most necessary decision, was that from 1978 their undergraduates in Accountancy and Business Administration would sit for the same joint examinations with students of the University of Singapore. They would attend the same lectures in the English language given by the same lecturers. They would probably be supervised or tutored by their own respective staff. The target date to get this done for all faculties was 1981. This was the measure of the totally different political climate of Singapore. It had taken over twenty turbulent years to have economic imperatives work through the passions of language and culture. Only in 1977 — twenty-one years after Nanyang University was founded, had the self-governing Chinese-educated Council of Nanyang University reached an unanimous decision to teach in English. Only the older Ministers understood and sympathised with the dilemma of this group of men. "I share their desire to preserve as much of the traditions of Confucian scholarship, values and culture as is possible in Singapore. English has provided a neutral instrument all racial and dialect groups can learn to use with no unfair bias. English has given us direct access to the knowledge and technology of the industrialised West. Without the continued use of English, Singapore would not have secured a new base for her economy, and brought up-to-date her role in the international and regional economy. It is the duty of the government to ensure that Nanyang University's reorganisation succeeds. For to do nothing is to see more years of wastage in Nanyang University.''

Lee told his listeners that their responsibility was not simply to pass examinations and get a job. ''In order that you can do your job and discharge your debt to the community you must have a second and third language capacity. You must feel for your people — those who could not make it to the top. Only that sense of commitment will enable you to carry them with you in the difficult decisions your generation must take before Singapore becomes a totally homogenous people. Singapore may never be homogenous in its ethnic composition, perhaps not even in its language use. But we can share one language and one national ethos. We share the same future, and we may as well make the best of it.''

After his speech, Lee answered questions from the audience. He was asked about an interview in which he told *Newsweek* that he had found two to three persons with the right sort of leadership qualities required for Singapore. ''What special qualities do these three persons have and why do we have only three persons?''

Prime Minister: Why indeed? I have often asked myself. Well, we have been having too good a time of rapid growth up to recently. That is one reason. It is very difficult to size up a man and predict how he will react under crisis. He may have all the necessary attributes and qualities. But the most important quality is how a man reacts and performs under grave pressure, under crisis, when his physical, intellectual and emotional being is under extreme stress. The Americans partly fathomed this unknown when selecting their astronauts. They put them through psycho-motor stresses and simulated space crisis conditions. When the *Apollo 13* had a malfunction and a real crisis occurred, three men would have gone into space for ever and ever, never to return, if even one had lost his nerve. Their intellects told them that they were in danger. Their instincts and emotions were to flee from danger. Where to? Their intellects took hold. They obeyed ground control, went to sleep, breathed slowly, consumed less oxygen, lowered cabin temperature, to save energy. They had one chance to make one loop round the moon and come back safely. And they did. We can measure a man's ability and output, gauge form his social habits, his emotional make-up, his balance and character. We can only guess what his motivations, his convictions are. His courage in the face of danger, and his capacity to communicate his thinking and feelings, to inspire confidence in people to work and fight to overcome these dangers — these are imponderables. His responses and his performance under prolonged stress, we only know when a major crisis develops. All we need is a skipper — a captain, with first mate and second mate, all with qualifications to be captain. Then let us hope that one at least will not melt under heat, however intense.

Question: Singapore has been striving as an independent Republic for the past twelve years without a constitution of its own. We still depend on borrowed provisions of the Malaysian Constitution. I think this is the best opportunity to ask the Prime Minister the reason.

Prime Minister: Every opportunity is a good opportunity. The reason is simple. To draw up a constitution we need a skilled parliamentary draftsman — a rare creature. Parliamentary draftsmanship is more than craftsmanship with words and phrases. It is infinitely more difficult than ghost writing for political leaders. From the first draft produced, I am convinced that we cannot hire such a draftsman. He may be a good draftsman. But he does not know Singapore's conditions and the contingencies that may arise. I dread adopting a draft which would lead to endless litigation all the way up to the Privy Council. As I watched the amendments that have been made by the Government of Malaysia and by the Government of Singapore to the Malaysian Constitution from which we derived a part of our Constitution, I became more convinced that we will have less pitfalls if we reformulate, recast, and restore into coherent form what we have now got and have worked successfully, instead of making a brand new constitution. It may be that I am becoming more careful and cautious. But I am not in favour of exchanging old lamps for new ones. Brand new constitutions have been torn up by nearly as many colonels and generals. We have got a working constitution, even though it does not look neat and tidy. Its framework has ensured you a university education and the prospect of a fairly lucrative career. Constitutions are drawn up by experts. But they have to be made to work by political leaders for the benefit of the people. And this can only succeed if the political leaderships have a grasp of the realities of the country, get the people to understand the limits of choice, and together, political leaders and voters, adapt, adjust, amend and accommodate to changing realities within the agreed constitutional framework.

Question: Singaporeans have every now and then been accused of being highly commercialised and preoccupied with the rat race of getting a good certificate and getting a job that pays well. I would like the Prime Minister's view on this.

Prime Minister: I would not be put off by these accusations, so long as I am making a success of life, earning an honest living. If I am poor, desperate and hungry, it is no use getting praise. That's no help. If that is what they say you are, but in fact doing rather well, nevertheless, reply, "Well, I will try harder and remove my blemishes." The criticism of a lack of balance, and of roundedness, is something which has been made of many young migrant societies. I have pondered over this for years, wondering whether we could improve ourselves. Watching the Australians — another young society, not much older than we are — I believe a certain brashness, a certain preoccupation with self and survival, with over-striving for achievement, a common trait is found in all new migrant societies. They have not spread their roots deep and wide. One day, if we flourish long enough we will get into the other extreme of being preoccupied with traditional values and practice of getting root-bound. Then we will need pruning or we shall go through a revolution to shake off the dead weight of tradition, of ancient but outmoded customs and orthodoxy. One sure way of improving ourselves is to be able to openly and honestly acknowledge our weaknesses for what they are. Recognise these faults, but do not undermine our strength, because it is that desire to achieve success, that will to succeed, that has been the Singapore story. Without this drive, we would have been flat on our faces. Whilst we must strive to succeed, let us acknowledge that it has left us with a certain jaggedness in our make-up. What will give our society a polish? An appreciation of the arts, and support for the writers, musicians, dancers, painters. A lot of time and sustained progress and we can develop the arts and cultivate those charitable humane responses which have been the hallmarks of civilised societies in the history of man. If we stay successful long enough, and rear the next generation better than we were brought up, we can eventually acquire these attributes.

Question: Sociologists and anthropologists agree that to build a successful political society you need a strong nuclear family. I don't know whether this applies to Singapore. However, the divorce rates in Singapore are on the increase. When such divorces are carried out by educated people who use the law as a weapon for extra-marital relations, it is going to affect the children, the future leaders of the society. How are we going to reconcile this factor?

Prime Minister: It is a problem which is as old as the first man and woman. Even when they lived together in tribes, proximity led to infidelity. No society remains static in ordering its human relationships. But there are certain norms or patterns for procreation which long-established societies share in common. It had arisen out of necessity to bring up the young ... We could not continue preserving the customs and practices of the first migrants. They were polygamous. We made polygamy illegal when we passed the Women's Charter in 1960 to make marriages monogamous. The woman is now in a stronger economic and social position. What we are witnessing in Singapore is something more drastic and fundamental a transformation. By the physical geography of our environment, we are breaking up the extended family. We are finding it extremely difficult to assist the extended family in establishing theirs in new forms of high-rise living. We have offered joint balloting for HDB flats for parents and their married children. Because parents have already bought their flats and they have got, by HDB rules, to resell it at the old price, and the new flats cost more, they have not been keen to move with their children into the same blocks in the new towns. We have to overcome this by internal price adjustments when old flats are given up for new. The second problem is even graver, for the next generation — the working mother. Your generation, I believe, was brought up with mothers who are housewives, who looked after you. In Germany, they have got what are called "key" children. And we are going to have them soon. Father and mother are out the whole day at work. Children big enough to go to school are given the door key, hung around the neck. He or she lets himself or herself in after school. Probably, he will eat in a hawker centre or fry an egg, and go out to play the whole day. There will be no parental control. I believe this cannot be good for the children. It is an irreversible step we have taken. We cannot now say, no, now we are going to get the women out of the factories and go back into the homes. We have got to find new answers to new forms of earning a living.

"For the younger children, we are experimenting with creches. Later, we must try play-schools. We will have to do this on a large scale. We tried to get factories to absorb them as part of the facilities in a factory. Mother goes to work, leaves child in the factory creche. The government, employer and union together carry the capital cost of the creche or play-school near or in the factory. Mother pays for recurrent costs, nurses, helpers, etc. She can see the child during her lunch break or in between her coffee breaks. When they are big enough for school, what then? One answer is full-day school and a meal in school. Mother goes to work, child in school under supervision, mother goes home, child goes home. The cost is phenomenal. We have to have twice the school buildings. And how do we cope with food? And more teachers will be needed for a full-day school.

"I am so concerned about the break-up of old patterns of matrimonial relationships. But I am more concerned with this drastic change in bringing up children. Asian customs and cultures have a child mollycoddled in the warm cocoon of the family. We are suddenly moving into a different pattern of life in a society of working fathers and mothers. For the professionally qualified, we have allowed work permit holders for domestic help. But think of all the mothers who work in factories. How do we give their children adequate human care? We have given some creches over to the NTUC to work out some experimental programmes. But this has got to be done on a massive scale. Forty thousand are born a year. They are going to have a chance of better education than their elders. We have got more resources now. But we are depriving them of care. What do we substitute for mothers' care in those working hours? Life means change. And we are living in a period of rapid change. As rapidly, we must evolve practical arrangements to meet new needs that have arisen because ways of earning a living have changed."

Visitor to Singapore in 1978—Prime Minister of Vietnam, Pham Van Dong

Sir Harold Wilson, former British Prime Minister (left), an old socialist friend of Lee, was entertained to dinner in Singapore in 1978. Next to Wilson is Dr. Goh Keng Swee and next to Lee is Dr. Toh Chin Chye.

Lee addresses the Tenth ASEAN
Ministerial Meeting held in Singapore
in 1977.

In the White House with President
Jimmy Carter in 1977

The Thai Prime Minister, General Kriangsak Chomanan, with Lee in Bangkok in 1978

Lee at the airport in 1978 to welcome the Deputy Prime Minister of the Peoples Republic of China, Deng Xiao-ping (above)

Lee in happy mood with Chancellor Helmut Schmidt of the Federal Republic of Germany at the Istana in 1978 (below)

THE YEAR 1978

I

Looking back, the Prime Minister considered 1977 to have been a difficult year. "I would not like to repeat 1977 again," he said in his 1978 New Year Message. "As economic recovery in the industrialised countries stalled, protectionists became vociferous. Despite a firm and resounding reaffirmation of free trade principles at the London Summit in May, governments of several of the seven leaders took a very tough stand on textiles exports from the developing countries, and coerced agreements which were contrary to the spirit and letter of GATT. The protectionist phobia spread beyond the export of goods. Even SIA came under harassment at some foreign airports, presumably because SIA had slumberettes and were offering services which other national airlines did not give free. Domestic unemployment under a one-man one-vote system makes governments selfish and mean. In the circumstances, we can count these our blessings, at least provisionally: 7.8 per cent growth, 2.9 per cent inflation (mostly increased food prices), 3.9 per cent unemployment. Thus, it looks as if the Singapore *bomoh* has pulled off another miracle cure, or was it sleight-of-hand?" Prudent planning, realistic policy adjustments made as and when the situation altered, these were more dependable. Co-operation of workers and unions was as significant a contribution as ever. A cautious wage policy, with a NWC increase of 6 per cent last June, was carefully discussed and agreed upon with union leaders and employers' federations.

Confidence in Singapore's stability and in the rational and predictable behaviour of workers, unions and the government made for a higher investment commitment in 1977, $388 million from January to November, an increase of 11 per cent over 1976. A major part of this was from existing industries expanding production in Singapore. "They were investors and managers who know us well."

On tourism, Lee said: "Much as it was unsatisfying to our ego and our moral scruples for a rugged, clean living society, we nevertheless welcome the contribution made by tourism, the highest increase of any single item, nearly 14 per cent. Tourist spending contributed to a record of 9.7 per cent increase for trade, restaurants and hotels. We are beginning to get blase and blatantly indifferent to tourists. Those who have to look after their needs in the airport, customs, immigration, taxi drivers, coach drivers, hotels and shops, have to make these visitors feel welcome. Some tourists have complained in our newspapers that our salesgirls appear bored and indifferent to customers. The long-term tourist flow depends as much upon recommendations from friends by word of mouth as from expensive advertisements for tourist promotion. If the word goes out that Singaporeans are honest, efficient and polite, and that Singapore is an interesting and unusual place, which it is, they will continue to come. Otherwise, we have only ourselves to blame if they go elsewhere for their holidays and their purchases."

Lee said that Singapore's standard method of countering recession, pump-priming the economy with big construction projects, had been worked almost to its limits. He warned that the private construction sector might not be able to keep it up. So the public sector would have to take up the slack. OECD forecasts for 1978 were gloomy, predicting a reduced growth rate of 3½ per cent for twenty-four industrialised countries who were their members. They were urging the Japanese, Americans and West Germans to reflate their economies. There was the underlying threat of more protectionism. As a slowdown in world trade took place, there might be a slowing down in demand for commodities. This might affect the overall buoyancy of the economies of ASEAN. All five members did well in 1977.

Some developments had been promising. A war in the Middle East and an oil embargo were unlikely, as long as there was hope of a peaceful settlement arising out of the momentous peace initiative taken by President Sadat. "He deserves to succeed as much as the Middle East deserves peace, after three decades of crises and wars." If nothing untoward happened, and the OECD countries made 3½ per cent, Singapore might achieve a growth of 6 – 7 per cent for 1978. "We cannot hope to achieve as much material progress as before the oil crisis. That is all the more reason why we must now concentrate on the character of our society. We must have more courtesy and give more consideration for others, not only on the roads as pedestrians or drivers, but in our human contacts in the shops, offices and public places, and neighbours in the new towns. Some grace and poise in our lives will give more polish to the ruggedness of our society."

Every citizen has a stake in Singapore's future, a share in Singapore's progress. Every citizen has a duty to strive and give his best to make Singapore a thriving society, to make that extra effort to meet changing world conditions. "If we do this, then I am confident I can wish you all a happy new year. We are our own *bomohs*. The *Singapore Girl* has worked wonders because others in SIA helped her. The Singapore man can work miracles if we, the *bomohs*, help him."

II

Lee Kuan Yew's personal friendship with the former British Prime Minister, Harold Wilson, goes back many years. On 10 January, 1978, Lee entertained Sir Harold to dinner at the Istana, where the Prime Minister acknowledged his debt to the British statesman. Lee said: "It is seldom that politicians get the opportunity or the occasion personally to express their appreciation for a good turn done to them. And when they do, their expressions of gratitude are often suspect. Cynical observers inevitably impute ulterior motives. Hence I treasure the occasion this evening, an occasion to recount, albeit briefly, how I came to be placed in the debt of Sir Harold Wilson. When Harold Wilson won the elections on 16 October 1964, Singapore was a state in Malaysia. I was in Temasek, Kuala Lumpur, listening to the BBC World Service. It was a narrow majority. But it was enough. It changed the course of events in Malaysia and Singapore. Less than ten months later, in August 1965, Singapore was peremptorily separated from Malaysia. It was not the best way for me to reciprocate his quiet support for rational and conciliatory policies within the newly formed Federation, which was then under attack by the late President Sukarno of Indonesia. And it was costing the British Government some £200 million a year to fend off confrontation.

"I have sometimes wondered what would have happened if Harold Wilson and the Labour Party had lost. I believe that, almost certainly, there would not be an independent Singapore. My Cabinet colleagues and I would still have grown older, but probably most of us would have become tougher, if not bloodier, minded. Perhaps some of us might not have the temperament or the psyche to have survived the rougher and more rigorous regimen that would have been required of us. So, perhaps it was as well that it turned out as it did. Put simply, if obliquely, I was saved from martyrdom by Harold Wilson."

Singapore was fortunate a second time in January 1968. The British Government's decision to withdraw from East of Suez could have been ruinous. Confidence would have evaporated, and the economy, with nearly 20 per cent of GDP then dependent on British military spending, could have been shattered. That Singapore was not another broken-back country was due in no small measure to the considerate manner and measured pace of the military withdrawal. All military base installations were handed over in working order, and as quickly as they could be converted to civilian use. This was not always the case when a metropolitan power departed from other parts of Asia or Africa. There was also an aid package of £50 million, one quarter grant, three quarters soft loans. It was not a vast sum in the Singapore of 1978. But in 1968, it was enough to make for a boost in morale — a key factor in making a successful leap from a colonial military and trading beachhead, towards self-reliant and secure nationhood.

"It was a hazardous task to evaluate the importance of recent events. Those historians who leave instant judgements to those in charge of the media best protect the reputation of their discipline. I am not a historian. I am a practitioner, and I believe I am not far wrong to state that, but for the understanding and support I received from Harold Wilson and his government, the history of Singapore would have been different. And I was fortunate to have enjoyed his friendship from the days when he was not yet the Leader of the Opposition. I can take this opportunity of recording my debt to him under circumstances which make it unnecessary to rebut any ulterior motives. He has retired from office. I do not seek, nor can he dispense, any favours. However, let me confess that my wife and I hope to continue to be beneficiaries of Mary Wilson's generous and bountiful good nature. She has always made us feel most welcome. Graciousness from the wives of those I have to deal with is a blessing, especially to my wife. And it is a blessing that is not guaranteed by the warmth of my personal relationship with their husbands. It is my pleasure and my privilege to be able to welcome both Harold and Mary Wilson to Singapore, and to ask you to drink to their health and happiness."

III

In February, the government set free Lee Eu Seng, former owner of *Nanyang Siang Pau*, detained since January 28, 1973 for using his newspaper to incite people against the government over issues of culture. A Home Affairs Ministry statement said that Lee had been divested of his control over *Nanyang Siang Pau*.

A week later, the government announced its decision to suspend the need for a student to possess a certificate of suitability before entering any institution of higher learning. The certificate was introduced in 1964 to prevent communists from infiltrating these institutions through their extensive network of cells in the Chinese middle schools.

When a Congressional delegation came from the United States to Singapore about this time, Lee told them in his opinion there was no absolute on human rights. He was commenting on President Carter's human rights campaign. Lee suggested that the United States use as its measuring stick the question: "Is the human rights situation getting better or is it getting worse? Is there a movement towards a freer society?" Lee pointed out that many nations which had oppressive regimes had become democracies. But no communist nation had ever been converted into a democracy. The BBC in February featured Singapore in the documentary television series, "The Age of Uncertainty". John Kenneth Galbraith, the commentator, described Lee as "the all-purpose politician, one of the more remarkable and durable people of our time."

In an interview with *The Australian*, Lee was asked how he felt when reporters referred to him as dictator, oppressor etc? Lee said it was "part of the caricature of the mass media — it's simplified. If I were all those things I wouldn't be getting more votes at each general election, would I?"

IV

A regional meeting of Commonwealth Heads of Government and their Foreign Ministers was announced early in the year to be held in Australia in mid-February. Lee was asked by Michael Richardson, an Australian journalist, what topics he thought could usefully be discussed at such a forum. The Prime Minister said they hoped to achieve a meeting of minds on subjects, economic and political, of concern and interest for the Asian and Pacific countries. "As you know, at biennial Heads of Government Conference of over thirty Commonwealth countries, the foci of discussions have inevitably tended to concentrate on urgent issues like the Black-White conflicts in Zimbabwe, Namibia and South Africa. On economic issues, we have by and large reiterated our arguments in the North-South Dialogue in Paris, Geneva and the United Nations. At a regional conference, we shall concentrate on matters concerning the Indian and Pacific Ocean countries. Because these concerns are less headline-catching, they have tended to be passed over rather quickly when we met in London. And when we discuss economic issues, we can speak more informally, passing over reassertions of positions we all have taken at the United Nations, in Geneva, in Paris, and instead make an earnest search of areas in which we can make practical progress, trade, investments, and economic co-operation. Whilst the New International Economic Order and the Common Fund are in the throes of creation, let us generate a little more trade and economic co-operation."

Richardson asked him if he thought the five-power arrangements between Singapore, Malaysia, Australia, New Zealand and Britain helped maintain confidence in regional stability and helped sustain US and Western interests in non-Communist Southeast Asia's economic development?

The Prime Minister replied that it had fulfilled such a function.

Whether it would continue to have any relevance depended not simply on Australia and New Zealand, but on the United States, her policies and posture in the Pacific and Indian Oceans. The Americans had said they intended to stay in Subic Bay and Clark Airfield in the Philippines. So long as United States was seen clearly to be a force in the region, these residual token forces were not irrelevant as tokens.

Lee was questioned about the conflict between Vietnam and Kampuchea. Did it have implications for non-communist Southeast Asia? Lee: "It has ominous implications. After more than thirty years of conflict, we have more armed conflicts now between communist states. If two communist states cannot live peacefully and settle their differences peacefully, what happens when there are border differences between communist and non-communist countries? I hope this is a passing madness and that sanity will prevail to bring the partners back to the negotiating table."

Does he think the conflict had overtones of great-power rivalry between the USSR and China? Lee: "Only in a very indirect way, perhaps. It is generally accepted that the Soviet Union is the closest ally and supporter of Vietnam and China that of Kampuchea. I am not convinced, however, that this is a proxy war between the two great powers. Too much is at stake for the two great powers for them to choose two such unequal proxies to slog their differences through."

Richardson told Lee that Amnesty International had that day issued a second edition of a booklet on people detained without trial in Singapore by the government. "It appears to refer to about forty cases of men and women allegedly being imprisoned in Singapore for non-violent expression of their political beliefs. But it only mentions five by name. They are Said Zahari, Lim Hock Siew, Ho Toon Chin, Lee Tse Tong and Poh Soo Kai. Amnesty calls on the Singapore Government to present any evidence it has against these and other 'prisoners of conscience' in open court or to release them immediately and unconditionally. Do you have any comments?" Lee: "Amnesty International officers who compiled this report on Singapore are either wilfully ignorant or dishonest. Amnesty's Charter says that a 'prisoner of conscience' is one who does not support or use or advocate violence to change a political system. They must know that these five detained are people who have been active supporters of the Communist Party of Malaya or are members of the party and its many auxiliary organisations. The CPM has set out on an armed overthrow of the governments of Singapore and Malaysia by armed force and terrorism. The five gentlemen named can walk out of detention at any time — and the others, too — by signing a simple undertaking that they will not in future, either directly or indirectly, help the CPM or any of its auxiliary organisations to overthrow the constitutionally elected government of Singapore. If they refuse to sign such an undertaking because they believe they will deprive themselves of a place of honour on the rostrum at a victory parade to celebrate the armed overthrow of the governments of Malaysia and

Singapore, I am willing to let them leave for Australia or any other country they wish to leave for that will give them sanctuary. Some countries may like to give refuge to would-be Ho Chi Minh's."

One of the five, Dr. Poh, was released in 1973 without giving an undertaking not to give support to those who used violence. In 1974, on two occasions, he supplied medicines — including anti-biotics and syringes — to treat a terrorist who had been injured by a bomb which exploded on him and whose injuries were widely broadcast. Doctors had been especially alerted to report such a patient. The man who got the medicines from Dr. Poh had publicly admitted his role. He explained on television the circumstances in which he got the medicines from Dr. Poh and the instructions given by Dr. Poh on how the medicines were to be administered. Dr. Poh had not denied this. "We know from evidence we have unearthed that the terrorist has slipped into peninsular Malaysia. Amnesty International would want us to prosecute Dr. Poh. We could not persuade the witness even to face the Medical Council to get Dr. Poh removed from the medical register for unprofessional conduct. Such is the terror of retribution in the minds of those who are enmeshed in the communist conspiracy."

Richardson said that the Amnesty Report alleged that confessions made by detainees implicating themselves and others in pro-communist activity were often induced by interrogation techniques that included some cases of physical assault but more often involved psychological softening-up like questioning naked or lightly clothed suspects in very cold air-conditioned rooms for long periods, keeping them in solitary confinement, denying them adequate sleep, and dousing them in cold water. Did security authorities in Singapore use such techniques?

Lee retorted that two years before, when similar allegations were made by a Marxist group in the Socialist International, he had invited them to help those persons who claimed to have been assaulted to sue the officers who had done violence to their persons. Under the legal system, appeals went to the Privy Council in London who reviewed the evidence recorded. Their ruling on a case was final. Any officer who assaulted a person under interrogation was liable to civil as well as criminal actions against him. All interrogations must wear down resistance of these persons by sustained psychological pressure, including physical fatigue, to get them to give leads to the next links in a well-established underground movement that first started with two Comintern agents from Shanghai coming to Singapore to build up the first cells in 1923, "the year I was born".

In his Chinese New Year Message, Lee said the horse was an auspicious symbol of great strength and high spirits. Many new year cards had paintings of the horse, with epigrams and proverbs of dragon and horse spirit and success. In 1977, no card depicted the creature that reigned. It was the serpent. Singapore had had a fair measure of modernisation and, alas, also Westernisation. However, traditional beliefs died hard. In the year of the dragon (1976), Chinese births went up by 9.8 per cent from 30,635 the year before (rabbit), to 33,627. For 1977 (serpent), Chinese births went down by 11.5 per cent to 29,758. Such was the curious result when old beliefs found expression through modern biological controls of fertility. Government planners would have to take these preferences into account to interpret trends, and to anticipate demands for hospital services, schools and universities. Further, the Ministry of Defence would have to make adjustments for their manpower intake, depending on the animal year it was eighteen years ago!

Lee added: "So long as these fluctuations in our new citizens are not more than 10 per cent, no great harm will come to the economy. We made creditable growth of 8 per cent, in spite of the serpent. With the horse, things should go well, despite protectionist tendencies in the industrialised countries. Faith helps overcome adversity. The horse will help us if we determine that it should be so, and by working to make it so. A very Happy New Year."

On 8 February, the Prime Minister sent a congratulatory message to Malaysia's former Prime Minister, Tengku Abdul Rahman Putra Al-Haj Ibni Al-Mahrum Sultan Abdul Hamid Halim Shah, on the occasion of his birthday: "Your old friends in Singapore and I send you our warmest congratulations on your 75th Birthday. Few leaders in the world have been so blessed as you. Your many years in office and since you relinquished your Prime Ministership were long and happy ones. May you have many more active and rewarding years giving the future the benefit of your vast experience."

V

Lee discussed "Bilingualism and Higher Education in Singapore" in an address to the Historical Society, Nanyang University, on 10 February. From 1956 to 1967, two years after separation of Singapore from Malaysia, Nantah had good students from all the best Chinese middle schools, not only in Singapore, but also from Malaysia and Indonesia. The early batches were probably the best. From 1960, PSC (Public Service Commission) started giving scholarships to Chinese middle school graduates to universities abroad. They were the top twenty students each year from the Chinese stream. From 1960 also, the University of Singapore started to admit Chinese middle school graduates. They were invariably the better students. The result was that Nanyang University lost the best Singapore students from the Chinese stream. By 1963, a hundred good Chinese middle school HSC graduates went abroad and to the University of Singapore. By 1977, 343 had gone abroad or to University of Singapore.

Meanwhile, the number of good students who came from Malaysia and Indonesia diminished. These countries had changed their educational policies, and their students did not have sufficient command of the Chinese language to enter Nanyang University. Perhaps even those who had enough command of the Chinese language had decided to seek university education in English abroad. Nanyang University's fatal error in adjusting to this drop in students was to lower standards in order to keep up the size of student population. It became so bad that for Malay Studies, students who had been rejected by University of Singapore, with as low as 20 points for HSC, were admitted into Nanyang University in 1969 – 72 when the minimum for other Arts subjects was 32 points. And they all graduated with Nanyang University degrees! When the government drew the attention of the University Council to this deplorable practice, the Malay Studies Department was allowed to phase out in the academic year 1972/73. Had Nanyang University responded differently, and kept at least the same minimum entry requirements as University of Singapore, Nanyang University would have become smaller by one-quarter to one-third. But its standing and reputation in Singapore and abroad would have remained high. By admitting and passing sub-standard students, Nanyang University lowered the standing and the employment prospects of its good students and so accelerated the flow of good students into University of Singapore.

In 1974, a Joint Universities Admissions Selection Committee was established for University of Singapore and Nanyang University to maintain minimum standards for admission. Even so, in order that Nanyang University would not have too few students too suddenly, minimum points for admission were slightly lower in Nanyang University than in University of Singapore. In April 1977, according to the Government Central Pay Office, there were 1,306 Nanyang University graduates with first degrees, and 7 with second degrees, as against 2,187 University of Singapore graduates with first degrees and 96 second degrees (Masters and Phds). All these Nanyang University graduates were working in an administration using English. There had been few difficulties. After the first three years in government service, with continuous and constant usage, Nanyang University graduates had had no difficulties in using English. However, only the better Nanyang University graduates were recruited.

"From my working experience," continued the Prime Minister, "I draw three conclusions. First, that the more able an officer, the more bilingual he is. A good Chinese-educated officer will master the English language even though his sentence structure and grammar may not be elegant. A good University of Singapore graduate has little difficulty in mastering spoken Mandarin and passing his Government Standard II Chinese written examinations. But because he does not write Chinese often, his written Chinese is poor. In other words, where other factors of the learning landscape are equal, the ability to learn a subject or discipline is the same as the ability to master a language. This is confirmed by the

495

Chinese stream scholars sent to Canada, Australia and New Zealand. Their results have been outstanding, and certainly not inferior to those of English stream scholars sent to these countries."

They were not sent to Britain, because the British universities did not accept the Government Chinese 'A' level certificates. In 1972, five SAF scholars were sent to Britain. They were admitted to Aston University, a new university, not yet under the jurisdiction of the Joint Matriculation Board in UK, and prepared to accept Singapore's 'A' level Chinese stream results not jointly conducted with Cambridge. Three years later, all five came out with First Class Honours in Engineering and Computer Sciences. They also were able to speak fluent English. Their written English had improved enormously, although not grammatically perfect and the sentence structure read awkwardly because they never got out of the Chinese sentence mould. Complete immersion in a total native English-speaking environment exposed their total working life to English, not only in the university, but also in the college halls of residence, the shops, buses, cinema, TV, etc. Their ability was high. The results were what had been expected.

Lee's second conclusion was that the greater and more frequent the usage of English, after a Chinese stream education, the more effective the English. The converse was also valid, after an English stream education, the more the usage of Mandarin (not dialect), the more the effectiveness of Chinese. This was confirmed by the ability of the Chinese middle school students in University of Singapore. Their immersion into an English-speaking environment was not as total as those students sent to Britain. But it was considerable. After difficulties in the first year, they all made the grade. The percentage of failures of University of Singapore students in science subjects was not higher than that amongst English stream students. The English-speaking environment in University of Singapore was a decisive factor.

In University of Singapore, the language used between students, between students and staff, was English. The immersion into the English language would not be as total and complete as that of a student in Britain or Australia for he still spoke Mandarin or dialect outside the university. Nevertheless, after painful difficulties in the first few months, all Chinese stream students broke through the language barrier by the end of the first year, and became part of the English usage community by the second. But these were the students with the better results in 'A' levels. Chinese stream students, although making up less than 40 per cent of the engineering faculty of the University of Singapore, got the following proportions of Class I Honours of total University of Singapore graduates:

	ENROLMENT Ch/Total	NO. SITTING FINAL EXAM Ch/Total	CLASS I HONOURS Ch/Total
1977	383/975 39.3 per cent	90/250 36.0 per cent	11/29 37.9 per cent

1976 352/980 35.9 per cent 55/245 22.4 per cent 2/19 10.5 per cent

1975 323/1002 32.2 per cent 71/237 29.9 per cent 12/26 46.1 per cent

1974 327/1104 29.6 per cent 87/283 30.7 per cent 11/26 42.3 per cent

That the environment was a critical factor in the learning of English was corroborated by the performance of those who became SAF officers in their two and a half years of national service. In the SAF, the immersion into English-speaking environment was not as high as in University of Singapore, for the SAF used Mandarin, Hokkien and Malay. Nevertheless, put into an environment where the usage of English was high, where they were compelled as officers to use English, they overcame the psychological problems of breaking into a second language, and learned quickly. Again, their grammar and sentence structure might not be as elegant as English stream students. But they were effective and articulate. "We have found that primary and lower secondary Chinese stream national servicemen, and even 'A' level students who only become NCOs or section leaders, do not improve as much as the Chinese 'A' level graduates who become commissioned officers. This is because they use more Hokkien working and talking with the 'privates'. Because the majority of national servicemen have only primary and lower secondary school education, from both the English and Chinese streams, Hokkien has emerged as the common language of the Chinese in the SAF."

Lee's third conclusion was that the earlier one started learning a language, whether it was Mandarin or English, the more grammatically correct and fluently one could speak and master a language. It was a mistake to believe that the second langauge should be learned only in secondary school. Neurologists had confirmed that there was a special part of the mind which was specially used in mastering language, listening and speaking, which was different for reading and writing. A child who was not taught to listen and to speak any language before seven might never learn to speak at all. And up to the age of fifteen, it was easier for a person to learn to hear, comprehend and speak a language. For reading and writing, learning later in adult life did not seem to be so much a disadvantage.

From 1959 to 1977, the percentage of Singapore students registering for Chinese language schools dropped from 45.9 per cent to 10.8 per cent. By 1975, it was clear that if Nanyang University continued to teach in Chinese, most faculties would close down in ten years. So in 1975, the government, with the agreement of the Nanyang University Council, tried to get Nanyang University to gradually use more English as the medium of instruction. It was an effort to reform Nanyang University from within. But the problems were many and difficult. The main obstacle to reforming Nanyang University from within into an English-medium university was that the Nanyang University campus was an established Chinese-speaking environment. The usage of English could not be easily established in this

497

environment. Whilst many teachers could speak and teach in English, they were much more comfortable and fluent in Chinese. But more important and decisive, students in Nanyang University, in an environment where the usage was Chinese, inevitably spoke to each other in Chinese.

Lee said that the way Singapore's economy had developed made it necessary for those who wanted to reach executive or professional grades to master English, spoken and written. The earlier in life this was done, the easier and the better the mastery. "From our experience with Nanyang University graduates in the government and from my personal observation of Nanyang University MPs, the mastery of written English is achieved by the abler graduates even where they start learning it years after graduation from Nanyang University. The mastery of spoken English is more difficult the older a person is. Hence, it is easier to do it during your university days than after you graduate. And it is easier for our students in Pre-U classes and junior colleges than at university. Of course it is easier to learn English in Chinese Sec 1 than at Pre-U 1."

That was the secret of the difference between the success in mastering English of Chinese stream students in universities in Britain, Canada, Australia, New Zealand and in University of Singapore, and the difficulties faced by Chinese stream students in Nanyang University. With increasing preference of Chinese stream students for University of Singapore, it was obvious that Nanyang University would be left with few students unless changes were made in Nanyang University. These facts were known to the Nanyang University Executive Council and Senate. Hence, in 1977, the Nanyang University Executive Council decided to have joint courses with University of Singapore. Unless this exercise succeeded, more and more Chinese stream students would opt for University of Singapore. Then University of Singapore would have had to keep its Bukit Timah campus to absorb all the Chinese school students who qualified for admission. The Kent Ridge campus could not accommodate them all.

A critical decision the government had to make in 1972 was whether Singapore should have one or two universities. "If it were in the national interests to have all students in one big university, then we would have planned Kent Ridge for 15,000 – 18,000 students. We decided to build Kent Ridge for 8,000 – 9,000 students. Singapore will be better off with two universities, one at Kent Ridge, the other at Jurong, competing with and complementing each other. It makes for more manageable size of university students, intimacy between staff and students. And we know from the examples of other countries that healthy competition for both staff and students improves overall performance in each. Whether it is Oxford and Cambridge, or Harvard and Yale, or Peking and Nanking, it is better to have two than one. But it is also clear that both our universities will teach in English other than for the Chinese language and literature departments. This conclusion was the result of our economic development and because parents choose the English stream for their children in increasing numbers.''

Nanyang University Executive Council proposed to start with Accountancy and Business Administration. In 1975, the first year of joint admissions, minimum entrance points were:

SU Accountancy 40; Business Administration 38
NU Accountancy 35; Business Administration 35

Those male students admitted to Nanyang University in 1975 were in national service. They would join University of Singapore students, and compete and cope with girls admitted in 1978, (with minimum entrance points for Accountancy, 43 and Commerce, 38) if 1977's minimum entrance points for Nanyang University and University of Singapore prevailed.

Some unequal results could therefore be expected for the first few years. The Chinese stream female students faced a difficult change into total English language learning. "My view is that they will learn and adjust faster if the lectures, tutorials and seminars are held outside Nanyang University, because we have found it difficult to establish this English-speaking environment in Nanyang University. Between 200 to 300 students from Nanyang University will join 400 to 500 students in University of Singapore for Accountancy and Business Administration, but in fact they will join an English-speaking environment of 12,000 students in University of Singapore. Some of the less able students may not cope with learning both the language and the subject. If Chinese stream students fail, they should be allowed to repeat the first year. If any student finds difficulty in following the course, he should be encouraged to postpone his course for a year, to concentrate on mastering the English language before rejoining the course."

Every year, less purely Chinese stream students would be coming into Nanyang University and University of Singapore. Once Nanyang University decided on joint courses with University of Singapore, and English as the medium of instruction, the teaching of English for those already in Chinese stream secondary schools had to be increased. Those in 'A' levels, and in Sec 4 likely to make 'A' levels, should be gathered in special classes for intensive English language instruction.

Despite all the difficulties of converting from Chinese to English as the language of instruction and examinations, the results in University of Singapore, Polytechnic and Ngee Ann showed that there were few or no failures because they came from the Chinese stream. Lee believed this was because the students admitted to University of Singapore, Polytechnic and Ngee Ann were those with ability, and higher scores in 'A' and 'O' level examinations. In other words, they were the abler students, who were also able to master the second language, English, despite initial difficulties.

This raised grave questions over the kind of people and society Singapore would become. If economics were the only consideration, then there should be no need for concern that nearly all parents were choosing English schooling for their children. "But with the study and use of a language, one understands and absorbs its culture, its value systems and the philosophy of life of the peoples who speak and write or wrote in that language. We have developed and progressed not because we were a Western-Occidental-type society, but because we were an Asian-Oriental-type society, hardworking, thrifty and disciplined, a people with Asian values, strong family ties and responsibility for the extended family which is a common feature of Asian cultures, whether Chinese, Malay or Indian. That we also can and do use English is an added advantage."

However, with the widespread use of English, television, the cinema, magazines, books and tourists, Western values, culture and attitudes to life have permeated the Singapore society, particularly the young. "We cannot isolate ourselves from the changing moods and thoughts of the world and the no-marriage family relationships Americans and some Europeans are experimenting with. But we can innoculate ourselves from fashionable but passing fads and fancies. We can do this by retaining the core of our own basic cultural values, a keen sense of our own identity, our different inheritance and history and the self-confidence this awareness gives. Therefore, we must continue the study of our mother tongues. It is in our long-term interests as a people, with undiminished vigour, to work and endure hardship, to have the self-confidence and drive to maintain traditional value systems."

In this connection, Singapore Chinese must decide whether they wanted Hokkien or Mandarin to be the *lingua franca*. If active steps were not taken to ensure the younger generation used Mandarin between themselves and used dialects only with the older generation who could not speak Mandarin, then, not only in the Army, but also in the markets, buses, taxis and shops, Singapore Hokkien would become the *lingua franca* of the Singapore Chinese. This would be sad, not because Hokkien was an inferior dialect, but because it was a dialect. It was not congruent with the written Chinese script. Present-day written Chinese was Mandarin reduced into script. Spoken Hokkien could not be put into *baihua*. If Hokkien prevailed, then the standard of written Chinese would go down. For the older generation, those over fifty, who did not study Mandarin in school, it might be too heavy a task for them to learn Mandarin. For them, the use of dialects would go on. Dialect films could be screened later at night for the older generation. But for the under-30s, there was absolutely no excuse for them not to use Mandarin. It was absurd that so many who had been to Chinese school gave up using Mandarin and were more fluent in Hokkien. To watch RTS features showing Singapore workers, who obviously had gone to Chinese schools, speaking halting Mandarin was painful. It was a grave loss to themselves and to society. "If in the factories and workshops the usage had been Mandarin between the workers, we would be a better, more united, a more cultivated and educated people."

Lee did not see Singapore becoming a monolingual society, with everybody speaking English. About 40 per cent at present could not pass

English in Primary 6 to enter Sec 1. The failure rate was 10 per cent less in the Chinese stream — about 30 per cent. The present practice was for such people to drift back into dialect. "Now with over 30 per cent teaching in Mandarin in English primary schools, we can and must ensure that those who do not make the PSLE (Primary School Leaving Certificate) will at least master Mandarin and enough of a written vocabulary to read a simple Chinese newspaper. With yearly examinations and no more automatic promotions, we can reduce the failure rate to below 25 per cent. They will always be literate, but perhaps only in Chinese and not English. The question: Is it to be Hokkien or Mandarin. Surely it must be Mandarin. If it is to be Mandarin, then Mandarin must be the language in workshops, in hotels, in restaurants, in buses and on television at prime viewing time when the young are watching."

VI

At the Commonwealth Heads of Government Regional Meeting in Sydney on 14 February, the Prime Minister spoke on trade and development. He called for an act of political will by the leaders of the twelve countries to foster closer economic co-operation, and improve intra-regional trade. Such political will was essential to overcome the obstacles in the way of intra-regional trade posed by the legacy of past imperial trading patterns, geographical expanse and problems of transportation and communication. Lee said that without political will, even geographical proximity and economic complementarity were of no use for trade. He proposed the following measures which, given the political will, would help generate trade within the region: (1) Allow and facilitate greater travel and contact between the people; facilitate instant communications between traders; ensure that shipping conference lines do not distort trade flows because of artificially high freight levels. (2) The industrially developed, namely, Australia and New Zealand should, on the basis of the political priorities they accord to the region, make GSP available to the members of each group; there should be deeper cuts and wider spread. (3) Between members of the region to direct commodity purchases through long-term or medium-term contracts from each other.

He suggested that these measures be implemented in the region in three overlapping sub-groups: (a) Australia, New Zealand, India, Bangladesh, Sri Lanka, Malaysia, Singapore, (b) Australia, New Zealand, Papua New Guinea, Malaysia, Singapore, (c) Australia, New Zealand, Papua New Guinea and the Pacific Islands. He said they were more likely to make more progress if at all, if the region was sub-divided in the above way.

Singapore's Prime Minister said that the reality of the region's trade was that the people with the leverage on them were outside (meaning North America, Western Europe and Japan). They were also the people whose markets were sought by countries in the region. By the proposed method of rafting with each other, the countries in the region could increase their bargaining position *vis-a-vis* the big three economic powers. Earlier, the Prime Minister presented figures to show the insignificant proportion of intra-regional trade of the participating countries compared to their world trade. Their exports to each other amounted to only 15 per cent of their total world exports. Imports from each other in the region were equally insignificant, apart from the Pacific countries' trade with Australia and New Zealand. This pattern of trade was the result of British Imperial preferences which tied the economies of the regional countries to Britain. Since Britain's entry into the EEC, its trade with the twelve countries had gone down from 8.2 per cent in 1970 to 5.1 per cent in 1976.

Lee also pointed out that the regional countries' trade with the three industrial giants — US, EEC and Japan — accounted for more than half their total trade, e.g. Australia's trade with the big three amounted to 60 per cent of its total trade; New Zealand's was 57 per cent and Singapore's 50 per cent. The reason for this was to be found in the GNPs of the giants. In contrast, the GNPs of the regional countries ranged from US$92 billion for India, US$76 billion for Australia, to US$5.6 billion for Singapore. While it was unlikely that regional trade could be increased in the immediate future, it was possible to do so in the intermediate term, provided there was a political will to exploit the advantages of geographical proximity and complementarity of products. Lee said the regional countries attending had to decide whether they met to advance mutual economic interests or whether they met like members of a caucus in the UN to advance *ad hoc* political interests. It would be more valuable for the regional Commonwealth leaders to see the sum total figure of intra-regional exports going up from 15 per cent to 25 per cent — a modest target — over a period of fifteen to twenty years. Trade lines took time to change but they had to make a start, quoting a Chinese saying, "the longest journey begins with the first step".

During a subsequent Press Conference on 17 February, Lee said he was leaving Sydney agreeably surprised that more was achieved than he thought would have been; that difficult as it was to bring eleven countries so far apart as Delhi and Nauru and Tonga and Western Samoa with such disparate interests, "we did manage to find sufficient common ground to agree that we shall meet again in 1980. I think that is quite an achievement."

Lee was questioned about the refugee problem. He said: "I think this is a world issue. It is not an issue connected with Southeast Asia or the Indian Ocean, Pacific Ocean countries. President Carter has made human rights and human needs and the equality of all mankind a major assumption of his political beliefs and political policies and I think we ought to take him seriously and spell out the consequences of those major assumptions in its application to this one very cruel outcome of a conflict that went on for many years and has not resolved itself. By the time you have

502

tens of thousands of people willing to risk worse than death for themselves and their families into the watery unknown, then if we are civilised human beings living up to our beliefs, we ought to do something about it and not just say this is a matter for the countries of Southeast Asia. Perhaps Australia feeling either geographic proximity or other moral obligations should talk about it. I think something has to be done and it has got to be done by the world community. Or again, we are embarked on an exercise that is sanctimonious humbug. One standard, when I talk about refugees, and what Southeast Asian countries are doing for them, and another standard when I talk about the rights of man and the equality of human beings in relation to southern Africa then you say — well, that is a long way off. But they are the same problem and we have got to face up to them."

VII

In Singapore, later in the month, the Prime Minister spoke at the Asia-Pacific Council of American Chambers of Commerce. "Six weeks ago," he said, "I was persuaded to speak to this distinguished gathering of top American executives in the Asia-Pacific region on the assurance that it would help improve the investment climate. Since then, the US$ has weakened to nearly 2.02 D-Mark or 1.79 Swiss Franc. Dow Jones industrial averages, having broken through the 800 psychological floor, is now 750. Last Wednesday, I was cheered to read a news agency report that AFL-CIO believed that their support for the Burke-Hartke bill for comprehensive trade legislation was a mistake. On Thursday, the *Asian Wall Street Journal* of Wednesday, February 22, disabused me of the illusion that they have had a change of heart. It was a change of tactics. Mr. Meany was still against the export of jobs and wanted, amongst other things, (1) import duties on the full value of products which have been assembled abroad from parts manufactured in the US, instead of the present tax restricted only to the value added by the assembly work, (2) elimination of DISCs (Domestic International Sales Corporations) which allow corporations to defer payment of income tax on part of their export sales profits, (3) termination of OPIC (Overseas Private Investment Corporation) which insures corporations against expropriation, revolution and other acts of god or demi-gods of foreign governments, (4) an end to foreign tax credit and tax deferral on foreign profits.

"These items are before your Congress. So too is Section 911 of the Tax Reform Act of 1976 and related sections of the Internal Revenue Code which will reduce the earned income after tax of Americans working overseas. Foreigners, like myself, have been heard by the Carter Administration before the tax package went before Congress. Now it is up to the lobbies to fight it out in Congress. Assuming that the labour supporters win, do these changes comprise the solution to America's problems of

503

high inflation of 6 per cent and high unemployment of 7 per cent? If no more jobs are exported by American industries, and if Americans, instead of shining each other's shoes, are making each other's shoes at three to four times the cost they now pay for shoes made in Korea and Taiwan, worse if Americans begin to make and assemble each other's electronic products, with much larger and more expensive but not necessary more nimble fingers, will American unemployment and inflation go down, the GNP go up and balance of payments less in deficit? Will they import less oil? Will they sell these products Americans made at American labour costs abroad — in Europe, in Japan, in the OECD countries?

"If the AFL-CIO succeeds in limiting imports to levels during a five-year period in the late 1960s, and allowing them to rise only as the US markets grow, will this not encourage the West European and Japanese unions to press for similar measures? Then what happens to the economies of the non-communist world? Does everyone get better off because there is no more free flow of capital and technology and goods, which are now produced at the lowest cost with the most efficient labour? Then what happens to the whole geo-political balance between the West and the East? What happens if the North-South dialogue ends not in sensible agreement but in their reappraisal of political identification and a realignment of policies?

"Is there much sense arguing about withdrawal of troops from Korea and promising some $8 billion worth of military aid in place of the security of these troops, if the South Korean Government were to be undermined economically by a squeeze of their exports to the US? And if the West Europeans and Japanese, who have also gone multinational, were also persuaded by their unions not to export their jobs, would it be the end of the world? Well, it may be the end of the world we have known and grown comfortable in for the last twenty-five years. But it is not the end. It will probably be the beginning of a meaner and more dangerous world. If the time of trade and investments that link the non-communist free-trade bloc were to be incapable of holding the system together, then we are going to be worse off; all of us."

Lee said that naturally, all this talk of organised and orderly free trade was disconcerting. People in the industrial countries were confused. Their governments had promised them low unemployment, moderate inflation, and fair economic growth. For growth alone would make possible an increase in real consumption of their lower-income workers, without a corresponding decrease in consumption in the upper-income brackets. Instead, they found themselves trapped with persistently high inflation, intractable unemployment and sluggish growth. What went wrong since the London Summit in May 1977? Some said the Germans and the Japanese did not live up to their commitments. They were asked to be locomotives, to join the US engine in pulling the sputtering engines of the rest of the industrialised world. What was clear was that both Germans and Japanese were never convinced that reflation was the remedy to the world's present economic plight. The trade-off between high inflation and lower unemployment was already not working before the oil crisis. Like drug addiction, it was requiring bigger and bigger reflation to produce smaller and smaller decreases of unemployment, in countries like Britain, before the oil crisis.

The Prime Minister said that on a recent visit to America, he learned that several leading American bankers and industrialists also doubted if there was a trade-off between 4 – 6 per cent inflation for fuller employment. This trade-off was known as the Phillips' Curve (named after a British economist who demonstrated in 1958 the nexus working on British inflation and unemployment figures between 1861 – 1913). Now, Mr. William Miller, next Chairman of the Federal Reserve, was reported to have said that the Phillips' Curve was not applicable because the nature of unemployment had changed as a result of high welfare benefits for the unemployed. "I suspect that there is some trade-off possible between some reflation and some unemployment. But only if reflation is financed from the existing supply of money, by borrowing from the commercial institutions, banks, insurance companies and others, not by borrowing from the Central Bank which prints new money to meet government deficits. What the peoples of the developed world may have to learn to live with is that their governments can no longer make the kind of high and steady growth of 6 – 8 per cent for over twenty years up to 1973. The era of new scientific discoveries leading to fast growth sectors in petrochemicals, electronics and aviation have now reached saturation point. The energy crisis in October 1973 simply aggravated the shock of this painful change to slower growth."

American industrialists who exported capital equipment to restore the war-ravaged economies of Europe and Japan were now finding the Europeans and Japanese fast on their heels, producing and exporting similar products with ever keener competitive edge — steel, cars, TV sets, computers and even some aircraft, like the European Airbus. The Japanese in turn were finding themselves pressed in steel, shipbuilding and petrochemicals by South Korea and Taiwan. Possible new frontiers for the industrial economies of the West, in the Soviet Union and the East European countries had not materialised. Partly, it was because of political conditions related to Jewish emigration and people-to-people contact which were never acceptable to the Soviet Union. China, which could have been a vast new frontier for spurting sales of industrial equipment, had turned out, for Chinese domestic reasons, to be a slow market until China's political priorities were settled and production of exportable items increased. Despite this, the OECD was forecasting 3.5 per cent to 4 per cent growth for 1978 for its twenty-four members. The OECD had been wrong several times before since the oil crisis and always erring on the optimistic side. Their forecast might turn out to be 3 per cent to 3.5 per cent.

Economic ministers in Germany and Japan might speak as if they were using neo-Keynesian language. But their policies were heavily influenced by Friedman's writing on monetary aggregates. In short, unemployment in the industrial countries, especially those with high welfare benefits for the unemployed, might continue to be high, inflation might be moderate, varying from a low of 2 per cent to 4 per cent in Germany, 4 per cent to 6 per cent in the US, and 7 per cent to 10 per cent in Japan, with 9 per cent to 11 per cent in Britain, and Italy, plagued by political and social instability, the highest scorer in the OECD league. However, sometime in the next few weeks, the Carter Administration would get an energy bill through Congress. The US$ must stabilise. But at what level? Some Europeans and Japanese suspected the US$ would be at a suspiciously new low to help boost US exports. Then with the prospects of an export-led expansion, Dow Jones industrial averages would rise.

But so long as the policy of a non-communist free-trading bloc was not fractured, and there was free transfer of capital and technology to countries where there was stability, countries which had governments whose commitments were dependable and whose policies were predictable, developing countries like Singapore would get by. "We will still grow, but like the developed, at half the pace we used to." From 1960 to 1973, Singapore's average growth rate in 1960 terms was 10 per cent to 11 per cent. Since the oil crisis, Singapore's growth for 1974 was 6.8 per cent, for 1975 4 per cent, for 1976 7 per cent, and for 1977 7.8 per cent. On average, it was half what it was before the oil crisis. Despite adverse international factors, the ASEAN countries had done well. Two of the members, Indonesia and Malaysia, were oil exporters. All had made more than 6 per cent growth each year since 1973. Japan and the US were the two main locomotives for the ASEAN countries. And they were still pulling the economies along. "Therein probably lies one lesson worth drawing."

Twenty years ago, in the late fifties, the French, preoccupied with the Algerian Revolution and their own internal political troubles, allowed their economic presence in Southeast Asia to decline. Ten years ago, Britain, gearing for a future in Europe, allowed their priorities to tilt towards Europe. Inevitably, there was a diminution of her economic thrust in Southeast Asia. In these twenty years, the Americans, the Japanese and the West Germans had increased their share of Southeast Asia trade, not only in percentage of imports and exports of the region, but also in terms of percentage of capital investment. Neither the British nor the French gained a commensurate advantage in Europe, or else-where, by not maintaining and sustaining their commercial and industrial presence in the region. If American legislators chose to hobble their managers and industrialists, the Japanese and Germans would press ahead. Maybe even the British and French could recover lost ground. For the ASEAN region had the advantage of political stability and cohesion, was dependable in the commitments of their governments, and was predictable in responding to change.

506

Singapore had learned by the negative examples of some Third World countries to cut down bureaucratic controls. "We have proved in the past eighteen years that the open competitive system, which rewards good performance, and enables men with talent to rise to the top without depending on family or political ties, can work to the benefit of all the people, giving better standards of life, education, health and housing. We have abjured vexatious licensing and government controls so that entrepreneurs can seize economic opportunities without having to wait for bureaucrats to grant multi-million bonanzas by issuing permits or licences." In Singapore, both with the government and with the workers, "profits" was a clean and wholesome word. When an enterprise makes large profits, government and workers were pleased, for the government got 40 per cent of corporate profits in the form of taxes and the worker could look forward to a bigger annual wage increase, which was determined by a National Wages Council in which the government, the unions and the employers conferred to reach consensus. "We are mindful of the dangers of high welfare and unemployment benefits, watching the consequences of this compassionate policy on the job-seeking habits of the unemployed. Visiting the major cities of the industrial countries, I am struck by this curious phenomena of high unemployment and yet a shortage of waiters, cab drivers, nurses and garbage collectors. Some jobs are not worth doing, as a result of welfare benefits. Whatever principles may be applicable in highly developed industrial countries, for a resource-poor country like Singapore, hard work and high performance amply rewarded, is the best way to attract capital and technology into the country to generate wealth."

Lee said that recently, he had four days of meeting and talking to Mr. Morarji Desai, India's Prime Minister. He was eighty-two. He emerged after one and a half years in prison to form a coalition government. "I found him serene and in good spirits. He told me he carries no worries. I was profoundly shaken. I have only 2.3 million people to look after. He has 650 million, 300 times my burden. He is thirty years my senior. I had to console myself. So I hoped that the rest of 2.3 million Singaporeans have been infected by my restlessness, and my incurable habit of seeking solutions to problems before they come upon me. Then perhaps I can be justifiably optimistic. But this thought does not make me serene. It makes me go out of my way to make doubly sure that the other 2.3 million Singaporeans do their work and do it well. I was fated not to achieve serenity yet."

VIII

On 26 February, the Prime Minister of Thailand, General Kriangsak Chomanan, visited Singapore. At a dinner in his honour, Lee, on behalf of the Government and people of Singapore, extended to him, his wife (Mrs.

Virat Chomanan), his distinguished Ministers and their wives, and other members of his delegation, a very warm welcome to Singapore. "We are confident that you will expand and deepen the good relations that have developed between Thailand and Singapore over the past decade. Your first journey abroad as Prime Minister is to your ASEAN partners. Let me assure you that if ASEAN is important to Thailand, Thailand is even more important to ASEAN." Lee said that since General Kriangsak had assumed office, Thailand's policies had been guided by the golden mean. "Whilst underscoring Thailand's deep commitment to ASEAN, you have, at the same time, made progress in pragmatic accommodation with the new governments of Laos, Cambodia and Vietnam. Again you have followed the golden mean between the policies of Prime Minister Kukrit in 1975 and those of Prime Minister Tanin in 1977. Your policies should bring peace along the long common borders you share with Laos and Cambodia, without sacrificing your security and integrity as a non-communist nation. Internally, you have brought about national reconciliation, with the intention of bringing together opposing political groups and factions. Your policies have brought many Thai leaders of greater ability and experience to serve the Thai people, preserve the Thai monarchy and uphold the Buddhist religion. My colleagues and I look forward to our discussions tomorrow to hear your assessments of events since we last met in Bangkok at the end of 1977. We look forward to discussing with you and your colleagues on how we can improve and expand our trade and economic co-operation within the framework of ASEAN. We have many interests in common. Our task is to advance those interests by practical steps which will increase the cohesiveness and coherence of ASEAN in the economic and political fields. The stronger and more vigorous ASEAN is, the more the chances of peace and constructive co-operation between the countries of Southeast Asia."

IX

In speeches later combined and edited, Lee dealt once again, late in February and early in March, with the problem of education. He said that one great strength in Singapore's society was the strong support for education. It sprang from the conviction of the people that the children's future depended on education. "The generous support from wide sections of the community for education springs from our tradition, founded on our history and culture. Whether we are ethnic Chinese or Indian or Malay, history tells us that through education we can improve our children's future. The history of the Chinese Imperial Examination System, which produced a meritocratic Mandarinate, has left its imprint on the Chinese who have great respect for scholarship. The Indian Civil Service Entrance Examinations System the British instituted allowed poor but able Indians to climb up to the top through education. The Malayan Civil Service started before the war was based on merit, following the Indian Civil Service pattern.

"Our task is to create an enduring society. It must have some essential common features. One of these is at least ability and ease in communicating with one another through the use of one common language in our multi-lingual, multi-cultural society. Hence our bilingual policy in education. But, in fact, for most Chinese students, bilingualism in school means trilingualism in practice. Ninety per cent of parents have chosen the English stream schools. Chinese students spend 30 – 40 per cent of instruction time learning or being taught in Mandarin. Except for a few, it is not their mother tongue. At home, mothers speak to children in one out of over a dozen Chinese dialects. The result is that when a boy meets friends from an English school, he speaks to them in English. Or he may speak Singapore Hokkien if his own English, or his friends' English, is not good enough."

The average student found it difficult to master three languages — dialect, Mandarin and English. It was not easy to master even two languages well. Americans had spent about twenty years, and many millions of dollars, trying to get computers to translate from Russian to English and vice versa. They could use this for their Washington-Moscow hot line. Whole teams of computer scientists and language experts in English and Russian had not yet succeeded. It had not proved possible to translate from one language to another with satisfactory results. The fault was not in the computer, but in the failure to provide it with sufficiently accurate instructions. No team of computer scientists had yet been able to think out the formulae how to teach, or to "programme", the computer to convert or translate from one language into another.

First, they had not yet been able to teach the computer the complex rules of grammar, or syntax, or how to make accurate sense of anything but a very short and simple sentence. Each language had its own way of using pronouns, adverbs, prepositions, and so on. Secondly, to "programme" the computer, one must teach, not one, but two languages with vastly different, complex systems of grammar and syntax. There was no one-to-one relation between sound and meaning. That was why languages differed. And they differed most of all in their grammatical structure. Thirdly, whilst they could teach the computer to translate individual words — "dog" and "cat" — "dog eats dog" had a meaning deeper than the literal. There was a story of one computer that translated "out of sight, out of mind" as "invisible, idiot" — doubtless apocryphal. Maybe one day they could teach or "programme" thousands of such deeper meanings of combinations of words to the computer.

"But let me reassure all parents: your child has a brain bigger than the biggest computer man has ever built. Whilst the world's biggest computer cannot handle two languages, most human beings can, especially if they are taught when young. Every human brain, unlike the computer, has an innate sense of language and syntax. The brain has been 'pre-programmed' to understand language. Some brain and linguistic experts have concluded that all languages have common 'deep structures' because of the structure of the human brain. Others believe that communicating human thoughts is so elaborate that only one solution is possible, and that this one solution has been independently reached by all societies speaking all languages through cultural transmission, and not through inherited genes or brain characteristics. Whichever is the explanation, the fact is that your child has a brain which can use two languages, whilst the computer as yet cannot. If you expect your children to go to school, spend 70 per cent time on English, and 30 per cent time on Mandarin, and then use dialect at home and with their friends and neighbours, their time and effort learning Mandarin will be wasted. If they can get through the day without speaking Mandarin, then it is not relevant to their lives. They will end up using English and dialect. So Mandarin, especially in English schools, will become a classroom and examination language. It will not become part of their lives, something they use at home with the family, at play with their friends, in the shops, cinemas, swimming pools and playing fields. Mandarin will become like Latin which I learned in school. I had to study it because I wanted to study law. I passed my Latin examinations. I have forgotten nearly all I had learned, because I did not use it once I had passed my Roman Law examinations. Then they will forget it."

Lee said that if the Singapore parent really wanted their son or daughter to speak their own dialect, then the government would seriously reconsider and re-examine the whole education policy. "If you sincerely want your son to speak good Hokkien, Teochew, Hakka or Hainanese between members of the family, then perhaps the schools should teach him through good Hokkien, Teochew, Hakka or Hainanese teachers. Then, by Sec 4, he will speak better Hokkien, Teochew, Hakka or Hainanese than his parents or grandparents. But is that what you want your son to do?"

Going back to teaching dialect was not as absurd as it sounded. It was done in Hong Kong, where Cantonese was taught in the schools and the Hongkong Chinese University. The British left dialects alone. The result was that the overwhelming majority spoke Cantonese, as they had done from 1840 when Hong kong became a colony. Chinese from Shanghai, Beijing, Fujien and Swatow, all spoke Cantonese, in the shops and markets. Otherwise they got no service. Television used only Cantonese or English. The choice for Singapore was simple — continue with dialects, and end up using only dialects and English. "We will continue to have a fractured multi-lingual society. Some 30 per cent in our primary schools, including the Chinese-stream schools, fail the PSLE. Those who fail have not been able to master English." But if they continued to use Mandarin, they would soon become literate. Language lived by daily use. "The more we use twelve or more dialects, the less we use Mandarin. This is the choice parents must make for their children."

In Taiwan, 80 per cent of the radio and television programmes were in

Mandarin. Hokkien was still used by the older generation when speaking to the younger generation. But young people had bigger vocabularies in Mandarin, over 3,000 words, and were fluent in it. To speak to their parents, the young needed a small vocabulary.

The government had a responsibility to solve this problem. But the government could not solve it without parents helping to encourage their children to use Mandarin. This decision every parent must take for his or her child. There were 365 days in a year. A child went to school for two hundred days. Of twenty-four hours in each of the two hundred school days, the child spent only five hours in school. The school could not compete against the home, if parents encouraged the use of dialect.

These problems derived from the past. Their forefathers came to Singapore speaking different dialects, because they came from different provinces, and from different districts in a province. The British left all dialects alone. The problem of many dialects could not be solved in four to five years. It would take ten to twenty years or longer. If a start was made now, those in the primary and lower secondary schools had a better chance of effective bilingualism.

Parents who were able to speak Mandarin should use it with their children. Those who could not speak Mandarin, but could speak English, should use English. Parents who could not speak Mandarin or English had to converse with their children in dialect. But they would be wise to actively encourage their children to speak to their friends in either English or Mandarin, and not use dialect to other school friends, or in shops, buses, taxis and markets. "Why weigh your child down with three languages? He will lose the Mandarin he is learning in school. Why cut him off from the wider world of Mandarin speakers and workers beyond Singapore?"

Lee was confident the problem could be solved without throwing any dialect away. But the vocabulary of dialect for only home needs must be limited and used only in homes where parent could not speak Mandarin or English. He was certain the child would pick up enough dialect to satisfy his grandparents. But he was equally sure that learning Mandarin was an unproductive exercise, unless the younger-generation Chinese Singaporeans were made to use it outside the schools, in the shops, markets and playing fields. "Our Chinese-educated are using less Mandarin in their daily lives and more dialects. They are gradually speaking more Hokkien, speaking to friends from English schools of the 1950s and 1960s when they did not learn enough Mandarin in English schools, and were Hokkien and English-speaking. Short-sighted considerations cannot be allowed to decide this vital question of the kind of people we are to be. We must be an educated people. Educated in our own cultures and our own languages. We must also be educated in science, technology, economics, banking, commerce and the contemporary social and political thinking of the English-speaking world, of America, Britain, Australia, New Zealand, Canada, and the rest of the English-speaking Commonwealth, or

American-speaking Philippines. Heaven forbid that we lose our own cultures, and fail to absorb the culture, the spirit, the values, the philosophy of life of the English-speaking civilisations. Then we will only adopt the caricatured, and the superficial manners and mannerisms, the popular trivia we see on television. We must keep the core of our value systems and social mores. To do that, we must have our children literate in Chinese and English. To be literate, they must be Mandarin-speaking, able to read the books, the proverbs, the parables, the stories of heroes and villains, so that they know what a good upright man should do and be. Hence the Mandarin part of our bilingual policy must succeed. To succeed, Mandarin must be used between those who have been educated in our schools, whether English or Chinese stream. It must gradually take over the role of dialects as the *lingua franca* of Chinese Singaporeans.''

In April, the Prime Minister's daughter, Wei Ling, aged 23, topped the University of Singapore's final professional examinations for the degree of Bachelor of Medicine and Bachelor of Surgery. She was the only graduate to pass with honours. She obtained a distinction in surgery.

X

The Prime Minister dipped into history when he addressed the Third Conference of Community Centre Management Committees on 14 April. He said that when Singapore was founded in 1819, Stamford Raffles and his British Officers clearly demarcated various parts of the town for the different racial groups. There was an old map drawn in 1828. It shows the European town in what is today the Bras Basah area, north of the Stamford Canal. Next to the European town to the east was an Arab kampong. It was where Arab Street is today. To the east of the Arab kampong was marked a Bugis kampong. To the west of the European town was the administrative and commercial centre, now the Padang and Empress Place. Across the River, the Chulias (an Indian group) had camps along what is now Chulia Street. Further to the southwest was a Chinese kampong. Further south, a Malay kampong where Tanjong Berlayer now is. Near Selegie Hill was a native cantonment which must have been for Indians. Hence the Indian names of the roads branching from Serangoon Road.

In time, more immigrants came in. The various racial groups spread out. But they lived together in pockets of same dialects and same ethnic groups. Some moved out. The Europeans moved out of the Bras Basah into the Tanglin area. The Indians congregated along the Selegie Road/Serangoon Road area. The Chinese sub-divided themselves, the Cantonese concentrating in Kreta Ayer, the Hokkien around China Street. The Hainanese moved into the Bras Basah area. This went on from 1819 to self-government in 1959. Those who took part in the 1959 elections would remember how compartmentalised voters were by race, language and religion. They lived together in pockets, either in kampongs or in streets, in rows of shophouses. The same race, dialect, language, religious types inevitably drifted together except in the middle-class districts of Holland Park or Katong.

The community centre was first forged in 1960 to provide a meeting-ground for the various ethnic-language-religious groups. "We saw the need for non-partisan or an apolitical social organisation, backed by the elders of the various communities and helped by the resources of the government. It has brought together people with bonds of common economic and social interests. It has engaged people in joint social and recreational activities in each constituency. The PA, through the community centre, has played a catalytic role. It has crystallised the first units of the building bricks for a nation in the making."

Lee observed that if proportional representation, and not repre-sentation by constituencies, single-member constituencies, had been implemented in Singapore elections, the course of history would have been radically different. "It was as well this did not happen, that we followed the British system which was based on geographical delineations, and not on demographic percentages across the whole national constituency. Hence, we avoided the clear-cut divisions of race, language, religion and culture. Voting on proportional representation would have deepened our differences. In some countries, like Guyana, formerly British Guiana, the Indian and African descendants have been unable to reconcile their differ-ences of race, history, language, religion and culture by forging common economic and political, and eventually social, bonds. The British had introduced proportional representation to defeat the Indian majority that tended to support a pro-communist leadership."

Singapore had to work on a single-constituency representation system. So the task had been to get people of different races, languages and religions to overcome prejudices, to get to know each other, to mix freely and to discover how many interests they had in common. This helped to mute and even to reconcile competing, and sometimes contradic-tory, interests between races, dialects and languages. The leadership came from within each constituency, and from each community and each sub-community.

In 1960, there were 28 community centres and 5 youth clubs. In 1963, there were 103 centres. In 1969, there were 186, 90 standard type and 96 rural type. Today, there were 166 community centres, 55 in HDB estates, 37 the old urban constituency types and 74 rural types. Of the 55 in HDB estates, 28 were rented HDB flats in shophouses. 67 others were standard type with brick or concrete buildings. 71 were wooden or zinc structures. To service these centres, there was a staff of 1,483, together with 450 part-time instructors and artistes. To provide community leadership, manage-ment committees were formed in 1964. These committees managed 9 per cent of the 180 community centres. There were 2,189 MC members in the 166 centres in 1978.

The building of new towns and redevelopment of the city centre (urban renewal) had created a totally different demographic picture. That Singapore had changed was stating the obvious. But what was not obvious was that the geographic and the physical changes of new towns, roads, sports-fields, shops and entertainment complexes were superficial. It was not as profound as the change in the nature of the mix or spread of the people. "We no longer live together in groups of Cantonese, Hokkien, Teochew, Hainanese, Malay, Bugis, Arab, Tamil, Punjabi, Bengali or Ceylonese. We have neighbours of all dialects and races in the same block in the new towns. The division is now along educational levels, determining different incomes, which decide who are occupying the 1-, 2-, 3-, 4-, 5-room flats in the towns, and who are living in the HUDC flats adjacent to and later within these new towns. The redistribution is on the basis of educational attainment and incomes. Each new town is more or less a cross-section of Singapore, containing all ethnic, religious, language, cultural and income groups."

The community centre which served each of the constituencies in these new towns would have to reflect the interests of this new Singaporean mix. If the buildings, roads and playing fields were visualised as the bone structure or skeletal framework, and the people who lived in them as the flesh, then what must be achieved was a wide network of nerves all inter-related and inter-linked in one central nervous system. "Such a nerve system will provide us with the sensory perception, the transmission to the central nervous system of signals of pleasure or pain, heat or cold, peace and quiet, or tension and noise, and the signals having been processed in the brain, signals are sent out in response to take the changes and adjustments necessary for effective living." Without the central nervous system, the flesh was just inert, and could not be responsive like muscle. With a wide spread of coordinated nerve network, flesh would become muscle to take care of the body. The CC network was part of this important nerve system of the body of Singapore.

62 per cent of the people were then staying in HDB or JTC flats. By 1988, about 75 per cent would be staying in HDB new towns. There would be no attap or zinc huts in urban Singapore. The only such huts left would be in the rural areas, where some animal husbandry and vegetable farming would continue. "Our people will be concentrated in the rebuilt city centre and the new towns. The PA, through the MCs and the new Residents' Committees, have the task of getting whole segments or resettled people to get to know each other, to adjust to each other's ways and customs, to be considerate and helpful to one another. We can help build self-supporting and closely-knit communities able to look after their own interests. Residents' Committees working with the MCs and the CCCs (Citizens' Consultative Committees) can help to melt away the reserve when strangers are brought suddenly together. They can gradually displace wariness and build up social intimacy and social cohesion." The more energetic and the socially aware and alert, most of whom had been

brought up in squatter huts or dilapidated rent-controlled buildings in which their parents lived, would have to provide this leadership.

The old immigrant pioneers threw up the successful to become clan leaders to look after the interests of their extended family, the clan, people whose ancestors came from the same village or district in China or India or Malaya or Indonesia. Sometimes, they grouped themselves around the same surnames of people from Guangdong or Fujien province, or the same castes from Madras or Kerala. Now the children of the pioneers must throw up new leaders, a new generation of successful Singaporeans, the educated, the socially sensitive, responsible and aware. "We must show the new generation pioneer the way forward into our Singapore of the 1980s. Given some time and sustained effort, we can transform these new towns from just so many flats, into lively, throbbing and closely-interwoven communities. Those who have the ability, the energy and the drive must give the lead in building a sense of community in our new blocks. Marine Parade constituency had pioneered this neighbourhood spirit. Tanjong Pagar Plaza has got its first Residents' Committee. More will follow."

What this conference had to discuss and discover was the way to get the many young and active men and women to come forward and take charge of collective needs and interests. The physical side of community cohesion could be met — better community centres, better facilities, squash courts, libraries, greater range of activities. What could not be easily created was that intricate web of human relationships which would bring strangers together and weld them into a cohesive community. "If we can imagine each of these high-rise blocks as one village or kampong, the question is how to give it a sense of togetherness, how to build a set of defence mechanisms which will enable people in these blocks to look after themselves so that the socially deviant or difficult can be ostracised and, if necessary, removed? If we can do this, we would have succeeded in rebuilding Singapore and remoulding Singapore into new living social units."

It was remarkable, almost a miracle, that within nineteen years, Singapore had achieved this mix without coercion, friction or collision. Instead, there had been tolerance of and accommodation to each other. How to take this one step further, to positive good neighbourliness? How to bring out block leadership, leaders who would look after people not of the same dialect, clan, language or religious group? These old ties would continue to cut across constituencies. The Hainanese were found all over Singapore. Their clan association would probably have headquarters in Bras Basah. But the clan association no longer provided the same leadership. The middleman role it had played, looking after the Hainanese children, setting up Hainanese schools, teaching in Hainanese in the early days, was no longer relevant. The new situation made these old roles redundant. However, they still kept these associations for reasons of sentiment. But their functional role in society as the buffer, the shock absorber, between the poor immigrant, ignorant of local laws and customs, and the colonial government, through their links with the Chinese Chamber and the Chinese Chamber's collaboration with the Secretary for Chinese Affairs, had been overtaken by political and social changes. The immigrant was now a citizen and a voter. He looked to his MP to solve his problems. His MP must help to build a network to cover the interests of all his constituents.

Even if nothing was done, the new mix would settle and find an equilibrium. But by positive encouragement, the new mix could be helped to settle better. "We can build early warnings of new social and economic problems — whether it is families gone too large with time, trapped in one-room flats needing to move out and up into bigger flats, whether it is right to give the younger members of the family priority to move to vacant flats near their parents when these are available as people move out, whether we should not allow greater mobility of people who have bought their flats and find themselves now with greater incomes wanting to sell their old flats and move to one closer to where they work or where their parents live, cannot be done by a government or HDB organisation machine. It is better to have it come up from the ground."

Lee ended on a word of caution. A high percentage on the MCs were over fifty. There was too low a percentage of the 20 – 40 age group. The process of self-renewal was a continuous one. "One of the flaws of our society is the inadequate ability to regenerate itself, the lack of attention it gives to this training and nurturing of the next generation. Maybe it is a traditional weakness. No Chinese *sinseh* will teach anybody, except his son, his secret medicinal herbs. So with each passing generation, there was a loss of knowledge. I detect this same flaw in this problem of transmission of knowledge and experience to those not directly related to the teacher. Too many people are too eager to teach only their own offspring their secrets of success. Let us turn back from this blind alley. We have to get younger men, whether related to us by direct ties of blood or clan or language or religion. Younger men, more alive, more aware of the needs of the younger group, can be enrolled in our ranks. They must express themselves in new ways of community living."

XI

Lee peered into the future in a television appearance on 21 April when he envisaged a Singapore society twenty years hence in which all Chinese would speak Mandarin to each other. He also visualised a Singapore society in which 70 per cent, or perhaps 80 per cent of the people could speak English. Lee was emphatic that Singapore could never become totally English-speaking. Bilingualism was essential in order to maintain links with Chinese, Malay and Indian cultures. He emphasised the importance of speaking a language frequently in order to acquire fluency. Lee said that whenever he went abroad, he always selected a member of his delegation to speak to him every day in Mandarin. In this way he would never forget the language. He also spent twenty minutes a day reading a book, so that he would not become less fluent in Mandarin when he returned.

XII

Lee was in a philosophical mood when he addressed the Tenth Annual Scientific Congress of the Royal Australian College of Ophthalmologists, held in Singapore on 30 April..He said that from time to time, he wondered which of the five senses was the most disabling to lose. A study of the eye alone was a complete specialisation for an ophthalmologist. ENT specialists embraced three sensory organs in one specialisation. He supposed this meant the study of the eye alone was as exacting as a study of the ear, nose and throat. Out of curiosity, he looked up the index of the Matthews Chinese-English dictionary to see how many characters, or ideographs, or words, the Chinese had formed over 4,000 years of writing in the same script, out of the four pictograms of these four organs. Under "eyes", a pictogram of the human eye, there were a hundred and fifty words containing a pictogram called a radical in various ideographic combinations. Under "ear", another pictogram, there were forty ideographic combinations. For "nose" there was no pictogram, but a complex ideograph. There were nine ideographic combinations containing the "nose" ideograph. Under "throat", instead of a pictogram, there were two ideographs. So there were a hundred and fifty characters or words, in which the pictogram "eye" appeared as compared to forty-nine for ENT.

However, in each of the two ideographs for "throat", there was the pictogram of "mouth". It was not unreasonable to assume that the "mouth" was a very early pictogram which included the "throat" in its comprehensive range of meanings. The "mouth" pictogram was found in 225 ideographic combinations, most of them connected with speech, eating or taste. This could reasonably be interpreted to mean that the mouth, and speech, was the most important organ in communication between humans, throughout more than four thousand years, over which these pictograms and then the ideographs evolved and developed.

Lee said that looking up his short book on Chinese proverbs, he discovered under "eye", eleven proverbs; under "ear", six; none for "nose" and "throat". For the "mouth", there were seven. As one who had spent the better part of a life-time having to communicate thoughts, ideas, reasons and arguments to people, he could personally attest to the value of the mouth in forming the oral words as the most important organ for this purpose, and further, that it was the most powerful generator of feelings in and between people, through the use of language, more than sight and the written word could do.

The ideal in human communication, of course, was to use both sight and sound. Hence the immense impact of television, particularly colour television, had displaced the written word for the mass of the people in all countries where the TV was common. Two Chinese proverbs had anticipated this development: "hundred descriptions not equal one sight". Again, "hear reputation not like seeing face". Had the English-speaking peoples found the relative value of the different organs in their civilisation any different? The English language used alphabets which spelt out sounds for different words, not pictograms nor ideographs. Lee believed an analogous, though rough, yardstick would be the frequency these words referring to the five senses were used or referred to in their often-used sayings or saws. A comparable reference could be found in the index to the *Oxford Book of Quotations*. The "eye" had 1½ columns of quotation references, "ear" (under "hark" and "hear") 1½ columns, "nose" (including "smell") ½ column, "throat" ("speak" 1, "speech" ½, "voice" and "voices" 2) equalled 3½ columns. It might not be inaccurate to conclude that the English-speaking peoples also placed more importance to speech than to sight in their language.

"It was my good fortune to have a genetic inheritance which included all five faculties without major defects. However, with the passing of time, malfunctions are occurring with disconcerting frequency, in some more than other of the five senses. I used to have to see my ENT man frequently for complaints of the throat, chest and sinuses. A surgeon introduced me to anti-flu virus vaccine. Contrary to my physician's prediction and advice, the vaccine worked. For I have not had to see the ENT man for more than seven years for these previously recurrent maladies. I have had to see my opthalmologists and my optician once, sometimes twice, a year, particularly in the past five years. I like to believe that it is because I read too much. It is psychologically more comforting to believe this, than to suspect that it comes from 'growing old gracefully', a phrase that could only have been assembled by an idealistic young poet, or more likely, a cynical old satirist. I know humans are mortal, that they must age and die. I comfort myself with the thought that I shall go suddenly, before any of my major organs has begun to malfunction. Recently, after reading a series of articles on gerontology by authors who had spread these interests over the different physiological parts of the human being, I fervently prayed that I shall be fortunate in being cut off whilst most systems are functioning, rather than linger on to disintegrate as all systems finally threaten to go. One article touched upon the subject of loss of hearing. It was most revealing and instructive. The writer recommended that for the sake of the older and deafer people in our midst, we should speak not louder, as this may not really help them. We should rather speak more clearly using our lips to articulate the words, to help the partially deaf to lip-read. I felt consoled that, despite my resolution to go down with all senses functioning, were I to lose my hearing prematurely, I would have the compensatory advantage of my eyes to lip-read the gibberish they are saying on TV. Finally, let me wish you a successful and productive conference. May you help people to keep their eye-sight and make billions of descriptive words unnecessary, and also so that when hearing is impaired, to help those who are disposed to do so, to guess what others are trying to say.''

XIII

"One attribute which has helped us make rapid economic development and social progress,'' declared the Prime Minister in his May Day Message, "is easy social mobility. Another facet of this social mobility, of people of differing family backgrounds moving freely up and down the social and economic ladder, is the absence of strong class divisions. We do not have antagonistic relations between workers and managers. There are no conflicts between those who feel, or are made to feel, that they are exploited; and those who are, or are made out to be, on the side of the exploiters. Had we allowed ourselves to be trapped in these simplistic concepts of the Marxist class struggle, Singapore would have been ruined.''

Lee recalled that they came very close to doing so in the years from 1945 to 1961. In 1961, democratic socialist leaders in the trade unions and in the PAP, who were in a united front with the communists, came into open conflict. The then Singapore Trades Union Congress took a stand against the communists for their anti-national activities. The democratic socialists formed the NTUC (National Trades Union Congress). The communists formed SATU. What followed was a relentless and vicious struggle for the support of the workers. This struggle could so easily have ended with victory for the communists, and a rout of the present leaders in the NTUC. If there had not been enough men with the courage of their convictions, and the strength and stamina to slog it out with the communists, the history of Singapore would have been different.

In the seventeen years since 1961, in 1978, the fruits of this struggle were self-evident. Together, people and government, workers, managers and administrators were rebuilding the old city and creating a new Singapore. Workers and younger union leaders had a completely different outlook, a different view of themselves and society, and their role in the unions. Everyone realised it was vital that the unions be constructive partners in progress. It was possible that Singapore could have achieved progress without the NTUC. "However, without the NTUC, I doubt if we could have given our workers this sense of participation. Only because they were organised in unions, with union leaders being identified in the big decisions which have shaped the new Singapore, do we today have a body of workers who feel themselves a part of Singapore's organic whole. Together, leaders of unions, managements and government, we discuss and settle national wage policies. Together, we keep profiteering down on

519

essential commodities. The government keeps stockpiles of rice and sugar. The NTUC have organised WELCOME to retail essential foodstuff to keep profiteering in check in times of shortage. The lives of our taxi drivers have improved. More drivers have become taxi owners through COMFORT co-op. A whole series of co-operative and union-supported activities help give our workers a sense of co-ownership. People act differently when they know they are joint owners of our national asset, the new towns, with their sports stadiums and playing fields, the schools, community centres, hospitals, and so on. Soon, even the ownership of SBS will be shared by SBS workers and the bus commuters."

Lee said it was worth reminding themselves that these things had come about only because back in 1961, a group of men with the courage of their convictions took their lives into their hands, and stood up against an apparently overwhelmingly powerful communist-controlled pack of unions. They were not intimidated by the fear of vengeance the communists held over the workers, a spell of fear which made workers do the bidding of the communist leaders. That they triumphed over this evil system of compliance through fear of retribution was now part of history. "We cannot afford to forget it. Never must such a perilous situation as that which existed from 1945 – 1961 ever be allowed to recur. The duty of the Government and the NTUC is to create a series of overlapping and re-inforcing organic links through which every worker identifies himself directly with the building of our young nation of which he is a part." Every citizen already felt he had a stake, a sense of proprietorship, in the stability and progress of Singapore. Every citizen could expect to get his commensurate shares of the prosperity to which he had contributed. The task of the unions was to widen this participation in the co-ownership of as many joint enterprises as possible through efficient co-ops. A joint property-owning democracy, giving fair shares to each in accordance with his contribution, was more than a slogan in Singapore.

XIV

INTERVIEW WITH THE PRIME MINISTER, BY MR PADRAIC FALLOW, EDITOR, *EUROMONEY,* ON 2 MAY

Padraic Fallon: You have a reputation as a political visionary, but you also appear to combine that with an impatience of criticism, and a taste for what appears to some to be an excess of regulations. How would you describe your style of government?

Prime Minister: I do not think anybody can be objective in assessing his own style of government. He can be subjective, trying to describe what he is trying to do. What I have been trying to do is to get Singapore — unexpectedly independent on its own in a vastly changed world, politically beyond recognition in the post-empire era. Singapore has been transforming itself very fast to adapt to a changed role in this post-imperial world. Amongst other things, I have had to give diverse ethnic groups who were never intended to be brought together into a nation, a sense of common purpose and destiny. Singapore's unexpected problems have to be solved practically and realistically.

Padraic Fallon: When you say you were left on your own unexpectedly, are you referring to the split with Malaysia?

Prime Minister: Yes. This was the heart of the British Empire in Southeast Asia. From here the British governors ruled Peninsular Malaya, Borneo, the Cocos Islands, the Christmas Islands. Britain cut us off from Peninsular Malaya, after the war, in '45, believing that it was vital for the sea route from Britain through Suez on to Australia. After the Suez crisis in 1956, Britain began to lose interest in Singapore because the sea route to Australia was no longer that vital. Britain was going into Europe.

Padraic Fallon: So, in your view, Singapore's existence is one big, historical, accident?

Prime Minister: Indeed.

Padraic Fallon: But an accident of which you must be very glad?

Prime Minister: I am not sure. We shall leave that to historians. My duty is to make sure it works.

Padraic Fallon: And how do you see yourself going about that?

Prime Minister: You can see for yourself better than I can tell you. You see it from the outside. I am busy working it from the inside.

Padraic Fallon: But would you say that one of your basic philosophies of ruling is one of regulating rather than leaving things to work themselves out?

Prime Minister: Not necessarily. Regulations are necessary if we are to have any order. People who work in a factory must start work at the same time. The workers must be in position before the assembly line begins. We have all to travel either on the left or on the right side of the road. We have got to agree that when the light is red, we stop. When it is amber we take heed. When it is green, we go. I am the product of a transplant — brought up in a Chinese extended family set-up, in a British colony.

Padraic Fallon: But does that give you a taste for regulation?

521

Prime Minister: May be. Certain forms are necessary. For instance, at mealtimes we gather at table. The elder in the family invites you to proceed with the meal. You don't dash to a table and take all the choice bits before your parents have sat down. There are certain forms to be observed.

Padraic Fallon: And you see yourself as the elder of the family in that respect?

Prime Minister: In a vague analogous way.

Padraic Fallon: Is that the Chinese influence?

Prime Minister: Probably, yes.

Padraic Fallon: But not the British one?

Prime Minister: The British influence here was worse. What the Governor's edict stated cannot be challenged. Now that ballot box decides every five years. So that makes the business of government complex.

Padraic Fallon: Let's stay with the ballot box. You run a democratic country, a democratic nation state. But it's been described as the most governed of democratic states.

Prime Minister: That is a subjective appelation. Does it work, does it not work? That is the acid test. If the regulations stifle, we will be strangled, and will perish. If there are no regulations, or not enough regulations, there will be chaos, and we will also perish. We have got to strike a happy medium.

Padraic Fallon: But you appear unduly sensitive to criticism, whether it is in the foreign press or elsewhere. Do you feel that in a sense you have had a bad deal from the foreign press?

Prime Minister: No, not particularly.

Padraic Fallon: Think of the past ten years.

Prime Minister: Not really. It is part of a vogue, a fashion, for Western correspondents to take pot shots at people in authority, especially if they are not respectful of press opinions. I pay due attention to what they write, but do not always change my policies as a result.

Padraic Fallon: You've seen a lot of changes in the years since the withdrawal of the British. Do you think you have lost a lot of your enthusiasm in that time?

Prime Minister: I think I was filled with burning enthusiasm. I was prodded by a deep sense of urgency.

Padraic Fallon: Let's turn to your own vision of Singapore. Are you motivated by a dream of turning it into an Asian centre of influence, a small but rich country which, while it is unable to control the destiny of the area through power, seeks to do so by influence instead?

Prime Minister: I have not thought in those terms at all. My original objective was to have Singapore re-united with Peninsular Malaya, and to build up a multi-racial, tolerant, stable and prosperous society. It would not have been a very strong, not very powerful country, but one which could give an adequate and satisfying life to most of the people. That was not to be. I had to ensure that two million Singaporeans could earn a living on 224 square miles. Fortunately my colleagues and I have not failed them.

Padraic Fallon: Looking at other leaders in the region, recently you have appeared to be on very friendly terms with President Marcos of the Philippines, more so than with any other leader in the region. Would you say that you have a lot in common?

Prime Minister: Why do you say that? I get on well with him, especially in ASEAN, because we share certain ideas of how ASEAN should move forward.

Padraic Fallon: Rather that how your own individual countries should proceed?

Prime Minister: His problems are very different from Singapore's. The Philippines has a different history of American-style "one man one vote", a different culture, and many different problems.

Padraic Fallon: What views do you share on how ASEAN should progress? Let's tackle the political side first. Is ASEAN important politically, rather than economically, or economically rather than politically?

Prime Minister: Both. They are two sides of a coin.

Padraic Fallon: Let's take the political side. How is ASEAN important politically?

Prime Minister: Well, it mutes differences which would otherwise be exploited by those who want to break us up.

Padraic Fallon: Like who?

Prime Minister: Like all those who do not want to see a group of non-communist countries co-operating, helping each other, propelling each other's economy forward.

Padraic Fallon: Who would you single out in particular? The USSR, or China?

Prime Minister: You are not an ignorant man. You read *Tass*, you read *Hsinhua*, you know who supports ASEAN and who does not.

Padraic Fallon: So ASEAN to you is a political grouping as much as an economic grouping?

Prime Minister: Of course.

Padraic Fallon: But can you engineer a mutual defence pact?

Prime Minister: You have moved from the political to the defence arena!

Padraic Fallon: The two are very interconnected, aren't they?

Prime Minister: They are the rim of the coin, to extend the metaphor. When we get the two sides of the coin minted, we can then mill the coin.

Padraic Fallon: So what is on the face of the coin?

Prime Minister: On the one side, closer economic co-operation, complementarity of our economies, our industrialisation, preferences in food supplies, oil supplies in times of scarcity and shortages. On the other side, co-ordination — or rather a greater approximation of our views and policies on the direction in which the region should go, in its relations with the great powers, the kind of arrangements which will enable us, in a tri-polar world, US, USSR, China — quadri-polar if Japan is included — to have the maximum freedom of choice — to choose our partners in economic co-operation, our partners in industrial co-operation, our partners in trade, our partners in progress.

Padraic Fallon: But if we take the other example of a similar form of institution, the EEC, the attempts at political unity have tended to grind to a halt because of one factor and another, and yet those countries are far more similar in terms of political institutions, and in terms of their industrial basis than the countries who are members of ASEAN. Don't you think there are immense obstacles in your way?

Prime Minister: Of course. I think it is nothing short of a miracle that we have been able to get so close to each other so quickly.

Padraic Fallon: Where do you think you will go from here?

Prime Minister: Painfully, laboriously, fitfully, but together, I hope.

Padraic Fallon: What are the main stumbling blocks to becoming more integrated?

Prime Minister: More inter-related is probably more apt. The diversity of our backgrounds, the different stages of economic growth, the different perceptions of ourselves and our separate national aspirations. But we are often brought back to earth by the realities of the common dangers we face, the awesome alternatives if we do not work together.

Padraic Fallon: Economically speaking, how would you like to see Singapore developing? Is your vision, in this respect, one of turning Singapore into the services centre of ASEAN, or of Asia itself?

Prime Minister: The kind of world in which we are living, or in which I find myself living, does not allow me the luxury of painting a pie in the sky and predicting what I would wish to be. In 1973 with the oil crisis, there were times when I doubted whether there would be such a thing called a financial sector, let alone a financial centre. That crisis is not over yet. The meeting that will take place of the seven major industrialised countries in Bonn in July this year could give more confidence to the direction of the world economy than the meeting in last May. Against this world backdrop, to be able to ride out the storms and tornados that blow our way unexpectedly is a fulltime job.

Padraic Fallon: But you have met them very successfully. For instance, Singapore, in particular, came through the recession, and through the worst year of recession, still with some growth left. Aren't you taking too pessimistic a view?

Prime Minister: In the first half of 1975, I thought we were heading for minus growth. We reached zero growth in the first half but fortunately pulled up in the second half because President Ford had stepped on the accelerator for 1976. It was a small plus. This is an inter-related, inter-linked world. We are part of it.

Padraic Fallon: Are you conscious that you are more inter-related and interlinked than most countries?

Prime Minister: Yes. We are plugged into the grid. Our world trade value is twice our GNP. We are a creation of the global economy, or a manifestation of the new global economy, that emerged out of World War Two, out of the IMF, Bretton Woods, GATT — all these institutions are now under great stress and in need of reform.

Padraic Fallon: Is this why you are so worried about protectionism? Because you recently described a "protectionist phobia" that was sweeping the world, didn't you?

Prime Minister: I do not think it is a phobia. I think it is real. Every political leader in office faced with heavy unemployment, faced with declining industries, facing an election, has to cater to his constituents, and that means job protection and import restrictions.

Padraic Fallon: Let's look at your attempt to become a major world banking centre, which has been very successful in many respects, but which is beginning to wane in others. Few, if any, would criticise or question the ability, or even the brilliance of some of the people whom you have appointed to promote that concept. But at the same time, some international banks are beginning to prefer the relatively unregulated atmosphere of Hong Kong from which to do their regional business. Does that development worry you?

Prime Minister: I don't think we can ignore it. But worry is not the right word. I think Hong Kong and Singapore are in many respects complementary. In fact Hong Kong, in a way, makes us think whenever we are not as efficient as we should be.

Padraic Fallon: That point about complementarity is an argument that a lot of people use, and quite frankly I find it a little difficult to accept. Where regional banking headquarters are concerned, some operations can be carried out between one centre and another, and a lot of them are. But for some banking activities people need to congregate in one place where they can see each other as well as talk to each other on the telephone.

Prime Minister: What is the thrust of your argument?

Padraic Fallon: The thrust of my argument is that your banking centre has attracted a lot of foreign banks into Singapore that were very happy to come here and are still very happy. But at the same time, a lot of them are also going to Hong Kong, some of them decidedly in preference to Singapore because Hong Kong is more attractive in some ways, because (a) there is a taxation advantage and (b) there are no regulations in Hong Kong on foreign banks doing foreign business.

Prime Minister: First, we cannot be as unregulated as Hong Kong. That as a fact of life. Hong Kong has not got one man, one vote. It has a different style of government, and a different approach to life and business. There is a distinct disadvantage in being over-regulated. We have looked into this. The MAS, our monetary authority, says that we are not over-regulated compared to Frankfurt or London.

526

Padraic Fallon: Which is true.

Prime Minister: They say that in order to maintain our integrity as a financial centre, we must know what is happening. Hence we must monitor enough banking transactions to ascertain figures to notice when safety margins are being ignored. I do not believe over-regulation is a problem, yet. The problem we face is in tax concessions, the tax-free position in Hong Kong, and also that the Hong Kong Inland Revenue Department has a different philosophy of life. It is a live and let live philosophy, which we cannot afford because we have to pay for so many things in our social system — education, health, social services, the rest. In Hong Kong the user pays for everything. Our users have the vote. This makes us extremely conscious that we must build something which will last. There are two aspects of a financial centre. One is a postbox, a situation, a tax-free haven, a booking centre. The other depends not just on the tax concessions, but more on a geographic imperative, that it serves a certain area, that it is linked to the other world money markets, financial centres, that it has built up banking and financial expertise and it is a plus for the international financial network. Tokyo is three hours ahead of us. We are seven-and-a-half hours ahead of London. Bahrain is three hours ahead of London. New York is nearly twelve hours behind us. Hong Kong is half-an-hour ahead. There is an advantage, in a floating exchange rates regime, of settling accounts on the same day, and not waiting for London to open.

You will notice that the Asian currency unit, or the Asian dollar, is largely based or collected in Singapore. However, the syndication of the loans has tended to be more in Hong Kong recently. There are two reasons for that. First, the tax advantage in Hong Kong for syndication, and secondly, most of recent loans have been to borrowers in South Korea, in Taiwan, or in the Philippines, where Hong Kong enjoys a geographic advantage. The geographic advantage we can do nothing about. In fact Hong Kong and Singapore will complement each other. For instance, before Pertamina's troubles, most syndications were done in Singapore because one could get to Djakarta in 1½ hours, to Kuala Lumpur in 45 minutes. Bangkok is two hours away and so on.

The long-term test will be just how much relevance we have to the economy of the world, and the world network of financial centres, and secondly, how much banking expertise we shall develop and provide. That is the crux of the matter, apart from the infrastructure of good communications, legal facilities, printing facilities, confidence in money moving in and out freely. If we can build up that expertise, attract the money and have the bankers and brokers who know how to put it to good use, then we shall stay as a financial centre.

Padraic Fallon: One of the criticisms is a lack of legal expertise in Singapore, particularly in relation to banking. Do you see this as a disadvantage?

527

Prime Minister: Yes and no. First of all, all former British colonies are beneficiaries of the British legal system, and British lawyers who are qualified to practise in Hong Kong are qualified to practise in Singapore. I do not see any disadvantage or advantage there.

Padraic Fallon: But the fact is that the big London law firms, who specialise in this sort of work, have tended to go to Hong Kong rather than coming here.

Prime Minister: That will depend on the work. If the work is here, then the lawyers will come here. This is the age of the telex. Before you switch off for the night in Singapore, you can leave something on the telex so that your London solicitors or counsel are working on the problem when they go to office and whilst you are asleep. You will have the answer when you wake up first thing tomorrow morning. You can be out in Concorde — I hope in the not-too-distant future — in nine hours, if there is any litigation or argument over what a phrase in a document means. That is not a major problem.

Padraic Fallon: Let me turn to the economy. Your per capita growth has more than doubled in a decade, and is now the highest in Southeast Asia. But when you recently indicated a target of about US$3,000 per head by the early 1980s you added, "and then the real problems will start". What did you mean by that?

Prime Minister: By the early 1980s, assuming that there is no catastrophe and that we grow at say, 4 to 6 per cent, which in turn depends on how the OECD countries are growing, then we would be above US$3,000 per capita. Several problems will then arise. A younger generation entering the labour market, seeking jobs — it has begun to show — that has not known poverty. Attitudes to some types of work may change. I am not sure, but I am fearful. I have already seen signs of these job preferences — preferences decided not by rewards but by working conditions, job status and so on. So we have had our share of guest workers, not because "heavy or dirty" jobs are ill-paid but because the young has been through an educational system influenced by teachers and reinforced by the mass media to consider certain jobs desirable and others undesirable. This means that our work force won't be as flexible. Our manpower planning may have to take this factor into their calculations, that there will not be the same flexibility and adaptability in getting workers to move from one job to another, something which has been a great plus factor so far.

Padraic Fallon: This was something you stressed in your May Day speech.

Prime Minister: Yes. Nobody could have predicted that electronics would give so many lucrative jobs, that ship-repairing was going to thrive, then stall after the oil crisis and now recover, that we would become a major centre for oil refineries, that we would go into petrochemicals from oil refining. These developments were not inevitable. And the flexibility and ease with which our workers moved from job to job enabled this to happen. Now we are getting a touch of calcification, set social attitudes. At about US$3,000 per capita per annum, with one man one vote, our workers may be able to impede our economic development by their job preferences. Every industrialised nation with the exception of Japan has had to face this problem. We have been under-developed. We have got to take this adverse factor in our calculations, when projecting our further development.

Padraic Fallon: Do you think most developed countries did not take this on board?

Prime Minister: No, I don't think they did. That is one of the problems why the developed countries are facing such persistent unemployment. In America, if you play golf you cannot get a caddy. In a hotel you find difficulty in attracting the attention of waiters. In a hospital nurses are not that abundant. Yet, the unemployment shows 6 or 7 per cent, that black unemployment of teenagers is about 40 per cent. So I ask why are these jobs not being done? These are man-made problems, or society-made problems.

Padraic Fallon: You also made a reference in your May Day speech about getting every Singaporean involved in what you termed "nation building", if the situation that existed here in 1945-1961 was never to recur. One of the many outstanding facets of your economy is your complete and utter detestation of communism in any shape or form. Obviously your brushes with the communist movement have left very deep impressions on you. Can you describe those impressions?

Prime Minister: I was in a united front with them for many years, from 1950 onwards. I was dabbling with Marxism as a student before that. But the practice of Leninism and Maoism by the Malayan Communist Party is completely different from the theoretical ideals of Marxism. It is a heartless organisation — a framework designed for the seizure of power by stealth, by force, by every means. The degradation of all human values, the destruction of all humane relationships, are all justified by men who initially must have believed in the sanctity of human life to have had the dedication to want to uplift the human being from the misery of poverty and exploitation of the old colonial society.

Padraic Fallon: Your form of 'dabbling' as you call it, do you see it in retrospect more as a form of anti-imperialism than a pro-Marxist creed?

Prime Minister: It might have been. But I believe I would have gone with them the whole way. Had Britain not handed over power the way she did, had there been a shoot-out, I probably would have been on the other side, too involved, and more deeply involved day by day ever to be able to extricate myself. It did not happen that way.

Padraic Fallon: Did the results of the war in Indo-China ever lead you to believe that the march of Marxism throughout Southeast Asia was inevitable?

Prime Minister: I did not believe it then, and I do not believe it now. These results were determined by men. And they could have been the other way.

Padraic Fallon: Will ASEAN help you to prevent that?

Prime Minister: Undoubtedly. Otherwise why should it be attacked so vehemently?

Padraic Fallon: Do you think that détente is now an empty vessel, in view of what has been happening in Africa?

Prime Minister: Détente, to describe a state of equilibrium in strategic arms of the two super powers, and a common desire to avoid mutual destruction, is the only sane and rational basis on which we can plan the future for the world. But, it is absurd to expect that détente, because it has been called détente by the Americans and not by its Russian name, includes what Giscard d'Estaing has asked of Brezhnev, ideological détente. Brezhnev rejected it. He believes in the class struggle and that history is predetermined with victory to the working classes led by the communist party, fighting by all means, short of nuclear exchange. And the sacred duty of the communist party of the Soviet Union is to help history and bring about the establishment of the dictatorship of the proletariat in all countries in the world. Therefore, although they intend no nuclear war between the super powers, they will contest for the control of hearts, minds, lives, property and territory of other countries, whenever and wherever the opportunity presents itself.

Padraic Fallon: But that is not what President Carter believes.

Prime Minister: I do not know what President Carter believes.

Padraic Fallon: But you know what you read, the same as I do.

Prime Minister: The American view of detente has changed from President Nixon in 1970 – 72 to Ford in election year '76, to Carter in '77 shortly after inauguration, and to Carter-Vance '78 and Carter-Brzezinski '78.

530

Padraic Fallon: Does the Carter-Brzezinski view alarm you?

Prime Minister: I always take a communist leader at face value. If he tells his people, in his official organs, his press, his radio, his books and his publications, that the world will become communist because it is the inevitable march of history, then I must take that seriously at face value. It is his intention to help history. I have never allowed myself to be bemused to the contrary.

Padraic Fallon: Do you think that China under Chairman Hua will now seek to push out beyond its borders?

Prime Minister: It has not done this. I do not think it is in a position to do this even if it wants to.

Padraic Fallon: Does it want to?

Prime Minister: No, I do not think so. At the same time, it does not want to see American influence in the countries along its periphery, particularly in South and Southeast Asia, displaced by Soviet influence. Hence the flurry of activity by China. A new constitution has been promulgated. A new leadership has barely settled its domestic rearrangements before leaders are off on visits to Cambodia and Burma, Nepal and the Philippines.

Padraic Fallon: You mean it is launching a diplomatic offensive?

Prime Minister: They had been too pre-occupied by the Gang of Four, and had neglected their neighbourly relations. It must have been time- and energy-consuming with all this internal feuding.

Padraic Fallon: Do you think there will be an American pull-out of this area?

Prime Minister: The position today is distinctly different from that when President Carter first announced the withdrawal of all ground forces in Korea by 1981. Then, it appeared to be a dramatic off-the-mainland posture. Congressional deliberations have sorted out the fears this policy was thought to mean. I am convinced by what the President and his principal aides have said, and by the interaction between them and Congress, that this is no pull-out from Asia. The United States understand that if there is a fundamental shift in their position which imperils or jeopardizes the Japanese security, then there will be a shift in the Japanese own position. And that could alter the balance of power of the whole world.

Padraic Fallon: Which would be very serious?

531

Prime Minister: Which would be disastrous. I am convinced that America has every intention of maintaining a capacity to project their naval task forces into the region from Pacific to the Indian Oceans, and that they intend to stay in the Philippines for this purpose.

XV

"How has being an intellectual helped you govern and deal with other leaders of the world?" This was one of the questions asked Lee Kuan Yew by *Leaders*, an American quarterly magazine. Lee replied: "I do not think I am an intellectual. What has helped me to get along with other people in government is practical commonsense. Analysis and abstraction of principles. I afford myself in my spare time, reading and ruminating."

"Are you a worrier?"

"Yes, I make a habit of looking out for the troubles and dangers ahead. That has often helped me to avoid or overcome them. However there have been problems which could not be avoided or overcome. I have to live with the consequences. Worrying after the event does not help."

"What are your biggest faults?"

"I do not know or I would have tried to minimise flaws which could be fatal. My friends are too kind or polite to tell me: my enemies mislead me by naming fictitious ones."

XVI

An old friend, Sir Robert Menzies, former Prime Minister of Australia, died on 16 May. Lee sent the following message to the Prime Minister of Australia, Mr. Malcolm Fraser: "I send you my condolences on the death of Sir Robert Menzies. He was one of the great men of his era. He had a commanding presence, a powerful intellect and a rare eloquence. His robust approach to life enabled him to make more than Australia's contribution to the world's quest for peace and stability in an age of rapid and revolutionary changes. He has left his imprint on the history of Australia and of the region."

To Dame Pattie Menzies, GBE, Lee cabled: "I was sad to hear of the death of your husband, Sir Robert Menzies. He was an outstanding leader of men. He presided over two decades of growth and prosperity for Australia. His great stature was justly deserved. His long years as Prime Minister saw Australia grow into an industrial nation. A man fiercely proud of Australia's links with Britain, he was also a realist who set out painstakingly to build up Australia's links with the new countries of Asia, particularly Australia's immediate neighbours in Southeast Asia. I send you and your family my deepest sympathies."

XVII

On 20 May, at the Singapore Registry Office, Mr. and Mrs. Lee Kuan Yew and other relatives, including the Prime Minister's parents, witnessed the wedding of Lee's eldest son, Captain Lee Hsien Loong, to Dr. Wong Ming Yang, a Malaysian. By coincidence, it was the same day fifty-six years ago that Hsien Loong's grandparents married. The newly-married couple met in Cambridge.

XVIII

The Prime Minister, on 31 May, spoke about bilingualism at the Malay Teachers' Union seminar on "Facing Educational Challenges in the 1980s". Lee explained that the implications of bilingualism for the Chinese had cropped up because Nanyang University from 1978 would use English, not Chinese, as the medium of instruction. Thus, it was necessary for Chinese schools to make adjustments from Pre-University 2 down to Secondary 1. They had to prepare their students for English-medium teaching at junior colleges and the universities. This question had been resolved in the Malay community many years ago. By 1970, 92 per cent of Malay parents had opted for the English stream. By 1977, 99 per cent had opted for English.

Malays were fortunate that English was the common working language. The Malay script, in Rumi, was the same as English. Many words, 10½ – 20 per cent, in Malay had come from English or American. Although the spelling might be slightly different, the words were easily recognised as the same. This made bilingualism in Malay-English much easier than bilingualism in Chinese-English or Tamil-English. The Chinese and Tamil scripts were completely different from the English or Rumi alphabets. English-Malay was such a convenient combination that many Chinese and Indian students had opted for Malay instead of Mandarin or Tamil. This had created allegations of unfair treatment, unfair to Chinese students who had to do Mandarin as their second language. Since the bilingual policy was mother tongue and English, this combination had to be discouraged except for those students who spoke Malay at home, for example those whose mother tongue was Malay. However, Singapore needed sufficient numbers of Chinese and Indians competent in Bahasa Melayu.

"To illustrate to Malays how different bilingualism is for the Chinese, let me ask you to imagine what the difficulties would be if, instead of English, we had Japanese as our common language. Then Chinese students learning Chinese-Japanese will have a clear advantage over Malay students learning Malay-Japanese. Malays will have to learn a completely new script of about three thousand Kanji characters. Chinese students would have already learnt them. However, the world that emerged after World War II made English the world's second language for the non-English speaking peoples. This was the curious result of history. The English-speaking colonies in America, founded three hundred years ago, have gradually grown and developed, absorbing large numbers of immigrants from Europe. They all became English-speaking. They have transformed an undeveloped continent into the world's foremost technological and industrial power.''

Most scientists in Japan, Europe and the Soviet Union read and wrote English to keep up with scientific research done by the Americans. The widespread use of the English language, as used by the Americans, was obvious from the number of TV programmes RTS showed from America, as compared to those from Britain, Canada, Australia or New Zealand. That was the reality of the world today. Even big countries, such as China, had to face this reality. So one of the changes after the Gang of Four had been purged was that scientists and students in China were once again busy learning English to catch up in their reading of the latest scientific publications.

"As parents, you should encourage your children to use English with their friends. This will help them develop fluency and a facility for the right words for every occasion. Daily use of a language can guarantee that they will have no difficulty in expressing themselves in English. Malays have no difficulties over learning and speaking Malay. Indeed, Malay has always been widely used in Singapore. Bazaar Malay is better established than English.'' To have English accepted as Singapore's working language was not as easy as it seemed to be today. If they had tried to suppress any language, the consequences would have been disastrous. Suppression of any people's mother tongue led to resistance and antagonism to rational action on language learning and use. "If I were a Malay, and I can speak English, I will make it a point of speaking English to my children, and let my wife speak to them in Malay. In my own home, my wife and I made a habit of getting the children to speak good English, Mandarin and Malay, right from their earliest childhood years. As a result, they have no problems switching over to any of the three languages."

The government's bilingual policy would be fairly and equally implemented for all races. Every Malay would learn English and Malay. No Malay needed to learn Chinese. Malays did not have any difficulty in learning Malay as the second language in the English schools. "What you must make sure is that your children master English for a good education and later a good job.''

Lee said Singapore would never completely and finally settle the problems of a bilingual and bi-cultural society. There was always an undercurrent of competition for dominance between languages and cultures. Singapore's special circumstances lead them rationally to accept the fact that English was the working language of the society. "However, we all want the culture, values and philosophy of life to remain dominant over that of America, Britain or other parts of the English-speaking world.

534

This requires that we know enough of our own mother tongues to appreciate our own traditions and approach to life.'' It was not easy to achieve this balance. And it was aggravated by the vested interests of the monolinguists in each of the language groups, whether it be Chinese, Malay, Tamil or English. Each group believed that emphasis on its language gave the teachers, newspaper editors and reporters, and students and graduates of that language, an advantage over the others. ''From my observation, the monolinguist is more likely to be a language chauvinist and a bigot. He only sees the world through one eye. He does not have binocular vision to see the world in depth, to realise that there are as rich, if not richer, worlds of human experience and knowledge, all expressed in beautiful words, elegantly, vividly and fluently in other languages. He does not understand other great civilisations which have expressed themselves in other languages.''

Bilingualism gave a more balanced and rounded view of the world. The Chinese who only read and spoke Chinese had a sketchy view of the real history of the world outside China. He had little conception of what was happening outside China in the Han and Tang dynasties when equally great civilisations like Greece and Rome had emerged in Europe, from 500 BC to 500 AD. He did not understand how it happened that Europe and then America, through their scientific discoveries and, more important, the practical application of these discoveries to methods of agriculture, transportation, industries and weaponry, enabled the Europeans and Americans to catch up, and overtake the Chinese civilisation. He did not know how the Arabs preserved the science and mathematics of the Greeks and Romans, and developed them further in astronomy and navigation. All the monolingual Chinese knew was that suddenly, in the nineteenth century, the white man came with superior weaponry and manufactured merchandise and carved up China into spheres of economic and political influence, exploiting them from extra-territorial concessions in treaty ports.

The bilinguist saw both sides. A bilingual Chinese Singaporean knew that there was deep wisdom in Chinese culture and philosophy, a result of four thousand years of periods of great achievements and in between long years of chaos and disaster, through wars and foreign conquests, plagues, floods, drought and famine. At the same time, he was also aware that the ritualised, conformist approach to thinking and learning, which was designed to secure the stability of successive dynasties, had prevented innovations in human thought and the discovery of further inventions. The result was that a great civilisation had become stagnant. It failed to rejuvenate itself in time to face the strength of an industrialised Europe.

''We all have seen how, given the will to organise themselves, and to learn science and technology of the West, the Japanese, united in their efforts within the framework of a stable administration, have in just over a hundred years, caught up with the West in many fields. They made original scientific discoveries. They have encouraged this inquisitiveness so

535

crucial to mankind's progress. They have learnt the techniques of mass production, management and marketing. Today, Japanese production and export of steel, ships, cars, TV, VTR, cameras, watches, and so on, are almost unbeatable. If we are to modernise and industrialise, we must be bilingual. If we are to teach the next generation bilingualism effectively, and minimise, even though we may never eliminate, language rivalries and prejudices, we must have more teachers who are bilingual. It is not possible to get teachers who are perfectly bilingual. Moreover, we want teachers, not interpreters or translators." But however imperfect his second language, the bilinguist would be a better teacher because he better understood his students and would be a better model for his students. Those who made the effort to try and learn English would advance the interests of students and themselves. "For you will understand what your students have to learn and, by your example, encourage them to be bilingual and get out of the blinkers of monolingualism."

The more bilingual Singapore teachers were, the more bilingual the next generation would be. Which was the more effective language, the dominant language, might vary from individual to individual. But however inadequate the command of the second language, a teacher or a student was better for knowing some second language. "To achieve this, I am asking the Ministry of Education to provide opportunities for second language learning and to consider giving monthly allowances for adequate mastery of the second language, English for the Malay, Chinese and Tamil stream teachers, and Malay, Mandarin and Tamil for the English stream teachers. I know that lurking at the back of the minds of every monolingual teacher is the hope that his language can become the dominant language, and be the common language. Then he does not have to learn another language. The others will learn his. Let me scotch this silly delusion. No one wants to give up his own. For the average Malay, bilingualism, Malay and English, is practical. For the average Chinese, Mandarin-English. So too for the Indians. A few can be trilingual. Some can and should be encouraged to learn foreign languages like Japanese, French, German or Russian. We need to have some specialists in each of these languages. For all of us, let us press on with English. It is our common working language. It cuts across all racial and linguistic groups. It provides a neutral medium, giving no one any advantage in the competition for knowledge and jobs."

XIX

In early June, the Prime Minister made a four-day official visit to Bahrain. He held talks with the Prime Minister of Bahrain, Sheikh Khalifa bin Sulman Al-Khalifa, and other leaders on measures to promote bilateral co-operation. Lee was accompanied by the Minister for Foreign Affairs. The Prime Minister left Bahrain on 8 June for Iran to attend a seminar held under the auspices of the Aspen Institute for Humanistic Studies from 9 – 11 June.

An "old and treasured" political friend, P. Govindaswamy, died of a heart attack. In a tribute sent from Bahrain, Lee said Govindaswamy did not speak the Queen's English. "But he spoke from the heart, with an openness and sincerity which commanded the respect of the MPs every time he made telling, commonsense points. Most of all, it was his kindly disposition which won him the affection and regard of all Members of the House."

XX

At the end of June, Lee met President Suharto in Bali, and talked with him privately for two days. Lee said it was a meeting of minds. No statement was issued to the press. Lee told reporters that a wide range of subjects, political and economic, had been discussed.

XXI

A meeting of the cadres of the People's Action Party was held on 9 July. *The Straits Times* said that about four hundred representatives from sixty-nine branches attended. Lee told the closed-door meeting that the party must revamp its objectives to meet the changes and political trends of the next twenty-five years. Drafts for the new party policies likely to be adopted at the twenty-fifth anniversary of the PAP in November, 1979, were discussed. Goh Chok Tong, (Senior Minister of State (Finance) was elected the party's deputy organising secretary, Phua Bah Lee, (Senior Parliamentary Secretary (Defence), the organising secretary.

XXII

In July, elections were held in Malaysia. The Prime Minister sent the following congratulatory message to Datuk Hussein bin Onn, Prime Minister of Malaysia: "My warmest congratulations on your decisive victory. It is a vote of confidence on your two and a half years' record as Prime Minister of the National Front Government, and in your integrity and qualities of fairness and firmness. This overwhelming mandate has given you added strength to lead Malaysia to a secure and prosperous future. The leaders of all five ASEAN countries know each other well. All have similar views on the security, stability and economic progress of the region. With your re-election, I am confident we can move steadily forward into more areas of co-operation.''

XXIII

The Government's sudden decision in July that private medical students who took up medical or dental studies after their national service would be bonded to serve the Government for five years after housemanship, was strongly resented by medical students. Students already embarked upon their courses were told that unless they signed the bond they would not be awarded a degree upon the successful completion of their course. A petition on behalf of 395 medical students was sent to the Prime Minister on 12 July by Lim Jin Choon, the honorary secretary of the Medical Club of the University of Singapore.

Lim Siong Guan, the principal private secretary to the Prime Minister, replied a week later. He pointed out that two arguments were advanced as to why there should not be a bond. First, the choice to serve the community. Second, the prediction that compulsory bonding would lead to declining morale and mass exodus from Singapore. The principal private secretary suggested there could be no mass exodus if the main reason students chose medicine was to serve the country. Added Lim Siong Guan: "It is a sad commentary on the moral and ethical qualities of medical students that so many should have signed this petition although it contained such a patent contradiction." In his concluding paragraph, he said: "Our doctors and dentists must be those who have the emotional make-up and aptitudes to care for the sick and the infirm, and not the brightest who calculate what are their best career options." The students duly signed the bond, which became a moral undertaking that they would serve the Government for five years.

XXIV

On 7 August, when Pope Paul died, the Prime Minister sent the following message to Cardinal Jean Villot at the Vatican: "It is with deep regret that I learnt that His Holiness, Pope Paul VI has passed away. During his fifteen-year reign, he worked strenuously and travelled extensively to bring understanding between peoples of different races and religions. He sought to bridge the differences of ideology and religions in his search for peace in our troubled world. Please accept my deepest condolence on behalf of the people and Government of the Republic of Singapore."

Two months later, on 23 October, the Prime Minister on behalf of the Government and people of Singapore sent his congratulations and warmest wishes to Pope John Paul II on the occasion of his inauguration as the Pope of the Roman Catholic Church. "Your election demonstrates the unity and universality of the Roman Catholic Church. As the first non-Italian Pope in more than 450 years, it is also a tribute to your outstanding qualities. For more than three decades, you have cared for the spiritual and religious needs of the Catholics of Poland, a country governed by avowed atheists. In an age when atheism is spreading, your personal experience and example will be a constant source of strength to Catholics, Christians and all other believers of all religions the world over."

XXV

"For the first half of 1978," reported the Prime Minister in his eve of National Day Message "our GDP grew at an annual rate of 8 per cent. Five years after the oil crisis, we have made our adjustments and found a new balance. I believe, barring major setbacks like another international economic crisis, we can make 2 – 3 per cent more growth than the average for the OECD countries. This coming year, OECD countries are expected to make 4½ per cent growth if every country fulfils its promise made in Bonn last month." The international economic situation was very difficult. By way of compensation, the regional situation was favourable. First, economically, the countries of ASEAN had all made good growth rates, averaging between 6 – 9 per cent each year in the five years since the oil crisis. In the developing world, after the oil exporters of the Gulf, East Asia and the ASEAN region had emerged with the best growth record, and the best promise of further growth. Second, politically, three years after the communist victories in Kampuchea, Vietnam and Laos, events had moved in a dramatically unexpected way. After a long and exhausting war, there had been clashes between Vietnam and Kampuchea, and conflict between Vietnam and China.

The peoples and governments of ASEAN had learnt valuable lessons from these events. There was considerable solidarity among ASEAN countries. "We have a common determination to prevent these catastrophes from spreading to us." This contest between the communist countries would consume much of their energies and resources for several years. Until the question of Kampuchea's relationship with Vietnam was resolved, Thailand would have more years of relative respite from external interference in her communist insurgencies.

Lee said that for the next five years, the outlook was more than fair. "Our best use of these years is to get younger men and women of integrity and ability into positions of authority, first into the political leadership, second into the administration. Because of our rapid economic growth, it has not been easy to get good men to take on the burdens and the hazards of political office. It is only in recent years that we have got more young men of quality to take on such responsibilities." Each year, for the past twenty years, the best students had been sent on scholarships to universities in Singapore and abroad. With universal schooling and impartial examinations, it was the best who had won scholarships. About fifty to sixty each year, averaging one in a thousand students. Most of them had chosen to do engineering. In some years, all scholars had studied engineering and applied sciences. Unfortunately, too few took up other disciplines like economics, management, the humanities, law and other professions. This over-concentration on engineering, and now medicine, must be corrected for the future. "Be that as it may, today, we have too many of our best scholars in the engineering profession and not enough in administration and the other professions." Fortunately, engineering was not as narrow and specialised a discipline as medicine. Many engineers had widened their learning to include management and economics. "We are now selecting some of the more promising and versatile of our engineers from the technical services to become administrators. As administrators, their contribution is far more important and valuable than as engineers. For administrators help Ministers formulate policies, policies which shape the kind of Singapore we are going to live in. If they do not include some of our best brains, then Singapore will be the poorer for it."

Lee continued: "You may ask why I am so concerned about our future leaders. Well, because the quality of leadership is decisive. If Singapore is led by men who lack breadth and vision, who do not instinctively place the national interests first and foremost, then the hard-earned gains of the past twenty years will be frittered away. Our achievements as a people are considerable, learning and working the hard way. We have increased our per capita GDP at constant prices from $1,200 in 1960 to $6,500 in 1977, more than five times in seventeen years. True, over 20 per cent of the contribution is due to expatriate managers and professionals. But that still leaves 1977 with four times the 1960 per capita GDP. We have rebuilt Singapore. We are the owners of this new Singapore — something we never were twenty years ago. Then we were squatters — nearly all of us. We have become a more tolerant and a more integrated society. We have got out of our communal, clan, dialect and religious ghettos, to share our lives in our new towns."

The task now was to ensure continuity. If the best, if men with ability, integrity and principles did not take charge and, by default, the mediocre or worse, the opportunists, were left in control, the political and economic system would falter, then fail. Able men and women, however intelligent, well-educated and gifted, had to be tested, trained and tempered in the hard school of experience. Those with the convictions and the strength of character must rapidly take over the responsibilities of high office. "We are in good shape for the next three to five years. To remain in good shape for the next five to ten years, to secure the future, we must ensure that excellence gets to the top as Ministers and administrators."

XXVI

As usual, the Prime Minister addressed a National Day Rally at the National Theatre (on 13 August). He said: "Ten years from now — I will be sixty-four, coming to sixty-five if I am around — I'd like to sit back and hear somebody expound why he is doing what he is doing, why it is good for the country and carry the majority of each language group. That is the business of government — a very complex thing in Singapore. And a very difficult business it is to find people, first, willing; second, able to do this. You think they are able, they are not willing. They are willing, you try them, sometimes something is missing. It can't be helped. You won't know until you have thrown him into the deep end of the pool. Then only you know."

He predicted that Singapore in 1988 would not be facing the problems faced in 1968. He did not really know what kind of world it would be in 1988, but he did know that unless "you've got a population that is well-educated, well-informed, well-knit into a cohesive, integrated community, it cannot maintain this momentum"

Lee dealt at some length with the problem of education, "a most complex series of puzzles". He said if he knew as much today only ten years ago, many errors could have been avoided. Lee emphasized the importance of bilingualism.

"Why do I want this? I say a person who gets deculturalised — and I nearly was, so I know this danger — loses his self-confidence. You get a sense of deprivation. For optimum performance, a man must know himself, know the world. He must know where he stands. I may speak the English language because I learnt English early in life. But I'll never be an Englishman in a thousand generations and I have not got the Western value system inside; it's an Eastern value system. But I use Western concepts, Western words because I understand it. But I also have a different system in my mind."

Lee continued: "I am not saying with the language, you necessarily get the value system; no. But the chances are it will help. And without that value system, I am quite fearful that we will lose this thrust. It is the value system — what is right, what is wrong. You take the Western value system — It is my fundamental right as a citizen. Under the constitution, I am guaranteed all these things; now give me. If you haven't given me, I'll vote you out. Whether the chap who is voted in will give it to him, doesn't matter; wait and see. But the Chinese ethical system is a different one — you owe certain obligations to society. Mind you, when I say this, I am talking about the traditional classical value system; I am not talking of the system today in China. There are completely different systems today in China, in Hong Kong, in Taiwan and what we are trying in Singapore: it is entirely different. We are in Southeast Asian context, we are trying to abstract what is relevant. Confucius says: 'Between government and people, father and son, brothers and sisters, friends.' They are important, fundamental relationships; your obligation to society. And if that is programmed early from the age of six in school, you've got good citizens. If that's not programmed, you have a motley crowd.''

XXVII

"Today, there is little talk of Singapore Malays being left behind in the process of modernisation and industrialisation," said the Prime Minister in his Hari Raya Message on 4 September. Most had made the grade. Yet only ten years ago, many Malays felt most uncertain of their future in a fast changing Singapore. At that time, Lee and his colleagues had urged and encouraged Malay Singaporeans to acquire new skills and disciplines for industry and to break out from the confines of traditional jobs and studies. Gradually, but increasingly, Malays in Singapore responded. "Never have we had so many Malays working in factories in skilled and semi-skilled jobs, as technicians and supervisors, as we have today. Many thousands have succeeded in their courses at the Polytechnic, Ngee Ann Technical College and Industrial Training Board. In the universities, Malay students are no longer confined to Malay studies, but are to be found doing economics, law, accountancy, business management, sociology and political science."

Lee said he could sense the growing self-confidence and pride amongst the Malays. They knew they were making the grade in modern Singapore. They were contributing towards Singapore's economic and social progress. "I also sense that this younger generation is feeling and thinking more and more as Singaporeans, rather than as Malays." There was another healthy development — open discussion on ways and means to cope with problems of high-rise living and seminars on ways and means to generate and to facilitate group cultural and recreational activities in the new towns. It was immensely more satisfying to solve these new problems, which were the result of economic development, than to be stuck with the old problems of stagnation, poverty and unemployment.

Many had become volunteers to assist in social problems of drug addiction. Others had campaigned for the blood bank. Everyone was conscious that these were problems which affected all Singaporeans, and not just Malays. All recognised that they were the result of industrialisation and urbanisation. "We are moving into a different kind of society. There is no going back. For going back means back to unemployment, poverty and the squalor. The significance of the words in our National Anthem is clear for all, that we are making progress together. I wish all Muslims Selamat Hari Raya Aidil Fitri."

542

XXVIII

AN INTERVIEW WITH THE PRIME MINISTER, BY ROY MACKIE, EDITOR, AND QUEK PECK LIM, REPORTER OF *BUSINESS TIMES*, ON 16 SEPTEMBER

Business Times: Can we ask you first to define briefly what you consider to be the prime qualities of leadership in a political sense.

Prime Minister: A political leader must be able to mobilise and move his people in directions which will take them to security and progress. He must create conditions that make achievements possible. He must have the desire to do it, a commitment to his people. He must make decisions in difficult situations and having decided, carry these difficult decisions through.

Business Times: How early in someone's career can this quality of leadership be identified?

Prime Minister: Modern medicine have evidence that most of these characteristics, the emotional make-up of a man — or a woman — his responses, can be observed fairly early in life. I am told by some paediatricians that you can often foretell the kind of person a child is going to grow up to be. I do not know if that is true, but I do know that by the middle twenties a man is complete. His hormonal balance has been reached and the kind of person he is, is set. However, he may not have disclosed what he is because he has not yet been put under severe stress.

Business Times: How adequate is the present population to produce the necessary number of leaders required?

Prime Minister: It depends on the qualities of the population, the genetic pool we have inherited. We get the leaders that we are capable of throwing up.

Business Times: Are you fairly certain, Prime Minister, that there is a second, third or fourth generation of leaders coming along? Is it simply a question of identifying them and persuading them to play an active role?

Prime Minister: I think it is more profitable to discuss only the next generation of leaders rather than the third, fourth or fifth. There is a finite group of people, between the ages of 35 and 45, from which such a leadership must be drawn. Birth rates were about 40,000 per year. On the average, judging from scholastic records, the capacity to digest and expound knowledge, judging from incipient or nascent qualities of leadership, like sport team captains, and presidents of activity groups, there is about one in a thousand — about 40 a year. For the age group 35 to 45 there will be some 400 potentials. What is difficult to pin down is motivation, the emotional make-up of a man, what makes him tick, what makes him do the things he does, how he feels about people and why he feels the way he does. These help to determine how he reacts under pressure and that decides whether he is a leader or a follower.

Business Times: There is also the question of the 400 having to be split over the public and private sectors and between politics and administration. Even 400 looks a little thin?

Prime Minister: Indeed it is.

Business Times: Does it follow then that the rate of growth of the country has got to be structured to suit the availability of top management?

Prime Minister: What does that mean? One has got to make do with lower standards? It has to be so. I hope it is not so.

Business Times: Do you think that those people who will eventually be part of the 400 will be noted in academic terms, that they will show up in schools and universities?

Prime Minister: Each passing year it becomes more so. It is more so in the 35 years group than in the 45 years group because with every passing year the chances of an energetic, intelligent, industrious lad not making it through the school and university system becomes negligible.

Business Times: You have spoken in the past, Prime Minister, about the drift of talent from the public into the private sector. Do you think that this is simply caused by considerations of salaries or is there some deeper reason?

Prime Minister: I think the disparity in rewards has become appreciable in the past six or seven years. It has been an important factor. There are other considerations like more rapid recognition of talent and earlier promotion regardless of seniority in the private sector. We are matching this by changing our own promotion procedures. However, I do not consider any shift of talent from the public to the private sector as a loss. It is still in Singapore. It is part of Singapore's reservoir of experience and talent, therefore part of the total leadership. It is a loss only when they leave the country.

Business Times: So you would consider someone with a lifetime in the private sector still to have, potentially, some political role to play?

Prime Minister: Absolutely. Of my colleagues only Dr. Goh was from the public sector. I wasn't, nor was Dr. Toh, Rajaratnam.

Business Times: To come back to the 400. When you select these men how do you establish priorities. Where do you see leadership to be most critically required? Is it in political leadership, in the Civil Service or in the private sector?

Prime Minister: The political leadership, because they settle the major rules of the game.

Business Times: Therefore if there was a choice the best of the 400 would have to be pulled into the political leadership.

Prime Minister: I have no doubts that if political leadership is not made up of the best we have got, then we will not achieve the best that we are capable of.

Business Times: You said that it is hard to tell motivation and that the only indicator would be academic achievement?

Prime Minister: No, I did not say that. The two are utterly unrelated subjects. Academic achievement just proves ability and application.

Business Times: That would have to be the starting point at which you would start to choose the man for leadership.

Prime Minister: No, I said we came to a rough figure of one in a thousand and that was the way the top scholarships worked out, based on academic performance, on social and group activities, rugger captain, school cadet, secretary of the chess club and so on. They indicate roughly whether he is an activist.

Business Times: And this is the raw material from which you begin your selection process?

Prime Minister: The actual numbers that we give scholarships is about twice that, just to widen the catchment and take in the borderline cases. The subsequent results in University show one good brain in a thousand. These have more than average intelligence, more than average energy, more than average capacity.

Business Times: Some countries have a tradition of leadership, quasi-political leadership, arising through the Trade Union movement. Do you see that being an area where leaders could appear?

Prime Minister: Yes, it used to be. But with universal education and scholarships in secondary schools and universities we have seen a marked change. The NTUC has had to hire their industrial relations officers from the universities. They used to throw them up from the ranks. Now the ranks throw up activists, people with a lot of drive and energy and sometimes dedication. But seldom do they have the intellectual discipline to argue with the employers. So the NTUC have had to employ men from the universities. Twenty years ago the workers would throw up their own negotiators. Take P. Govindaswamy who died recently. I first knew him in 1952 when the postmen were on strike. He was their leader. He did not have much education. He had energy and ability, but no education. However, all his children have been through Secondary schools. Several of them are university graduates. If P. Govindaswamy started life all over again he would probably end up as a university graduate. In a different way that is happening with the British TUC. Len Murray went to Oxford.

Business Times: So basically the same people will come through? They will simply come through in a much more refined way?

Prime Minister: Yes. They will not be denied the educational discipline.

Business Times: Does it matter in any way in which area one learns leadership — whether one comes through the public or the private sector?

Prime Minister: It does not matter. The danger, of course, in the Singapore context, is the longer you are in the private sector and the less self-disciplined you are, the more likely you will disqualify yourself by the social values and habits of the private sector. It requires a strong mind and a strong will to keep high standards of integrity. For example, when we started Intraco we ran into the problems of the private sector i.e. the wheeler dealer problems related to trade. We had absurd situations, where in order to maintain the integrity of the Intraco officers, two officers would have to accompany each other to hand over cash commissions and to countersign that in fact that cash commissions were handed over. In the private sector if you decide to pay, that's that. The converse is also true. If we bring into the political leadership any of these wheeler dealer attributes then Singapore will be ruined. The *raison d'etre*, why there is a Singapore, disappears.

Business Times: Do you feel that in learning leadership you have to go through all these various aspects, — you have to know the trade unions, government, have to know how to deal with the private sector?

Prime Minister: I do not think you learn leadership. You learn about human beings in given cultural, social and economic contexts. You learn to get things done or get people to do things within these contexts. But this attribute called leadership is either in you or it is not.

546

Business Times: If the leadership is there what is the training period supposed to give the man?

Prime Minister: Really to show that he has got it, not that he is hiding the lack thereof behind a show of aplomb and erudition.

Business Times: It is basically a testing period not a training period? Establishing that the qualities that are apparent are also real and that they can be used in decision-making?

Prime Minister: If you want to put it in an unkind way — yes.

Business Times: It is common in Singapore to find multi-function public officers; MPs or administrators running companies. Is this deliberate policy or a consequence of the restricted number of capable people.

Prime Minister: It is the dearth of talent.

Business Times: So ideally administrators would be strictly administrators and not have to be floated off to other semi-commercial activities?

Prime Minister: Yes, if we could find people to do the other jobs.

Business Times: Again on the administration do you feel it is necessary for the top level of the administration to have the same political views as the government?

Prime Minister: Not necessarily. They should not be opposed to it because they then cannot carry out the policies with any conviction. If they are ideologically opposed to a policy they are asked to carry out, they should opt out. But they do not have to be committed to these policies to carry them faithfully out.

XXIX

The London Times on 22 September reported that at least one Asian leader remained "somewhat sceptical" about the overtures then being made by Mr. Pham Van Dong of Vietnam and Mr. Deng Xiao-ping of China to the countries of ASEAN. "He is Singapore's articulate and outspoken Prime Minister, Mr. Lee Kuan Yew, a man who has waged a bitter battle against communist insurgency in the region in the past two decades. Presenting his view to *The Times*, Mr. Lee indicated that he is not convinced that the dispute between China and Vietnam has completely eliminated the spectre of the domino theory ... Mr. Lee believes that the communist nations have not given up their deep-seated plans to under-

547

mine the governments of ASEAN."

The Times continued: "Often criticized because he refuses to tolerate an effective Opposition, Mr. Lee has transformed Singapore into a modern and thriving city. He was asked whether he could have achieved as much under a liberal system of democracy of the British variety. 'If you mean by that whether we could have achieved what we did if we had allowed the communists to run around and organise strikes in the unions to disrupt production — no, then we would not have done it. If we had allowed the communists a free run in our unions as they have in the British unions, then we would have been ruined.' "

Late in September, Lee left Singapore for a two-week visit to Belgium, France and the United States. He was to give a lecture in America. His main purpose in visiting Belgium and France was to remind investors of Singapore opportunities. He told the French Prime Minister, Mr. Raymond Barre, that Singapore was plugged into the global network of giant 'power stations' and could serve a useful role as a service sub-station. The French evening newspaper *Le Monde* described Lee as "the most eager advocate of free enterprise in the ASEAN area".

In Washington, the Prime Minister had an informal meeting with President Carter. He also met the Vice-President and several other members of the Cabinet and congressional leaders. Lee was reported to have discerned a more relaxed American mood in regard to developments in Asia.

XXX

At the Twenty-sixth World Congress of the International Chamber of Commerce held in Orlando, USA on 5 October, the Prime Minister delivered a special lecture, "Extrapolating from the Singapore Experience". He was given a standing ovation. Lee said that three years ago, after the communist victories in Cambodia and Vietnam, the future looked distinctly bleak for non-communist Southeast Asia. The tightly-organised society in North Vietnam had worn down and overcome all that the Americans could do to prevent them from winning. There seemed nothing to prevent Vietnamese drive and zeal from speedily repairing the ravages of war and reconstructing their economy. And in ten to fifteen years, Vietnam could have become an industrialising communist society with capacity to spare to spread revolution and liberation to all the unenlightened, capitalist-ridden countries around them.

But history has its discontinuities. After thirty years of incessant guerilla wars, communist victories in Vietnam and Cambodia did not lead to peace and reconstruction. Instead, there had been violent clashes between Vietnam and Cambodia across their common border, killing and maiming soldiers and civilians and wreaking havoc. On the Cambodian-Thai border, innocent Thai villagers had been butchered and disembowelled. On the Vietnam-China border, border guards and civilians had been killed.

No one could have predicted that after more than twenty years of highly skilled diplomacy in keeping neutral in the Sino-Soviet conflict, and receiving aid from both China and the Soviet Union, Vietnam would become a member of COMECON in June 1978. And in July, Vietnam was in conflict with China, engaged in vociferous acrimony over the fate of ethnic Chinese in Vietnam. "One must assume that the communist leaders of Cambodia, Vietnam and China know that all this feuding and killing is not helping the other communist parties and their liberation forces in non-communist Southeast Asia. Yet, they seem unable to resist their impulses to pre-empt each other's future role and influence in Southeast Asia. The impact on the non-communist peoples of Asia of these unexpected developments has been profound, as they watch in bewilderment, if not disbelief. Communism means something much grimmer, more gruesome than the coloured pictorials depicting gloriously happy workers and peasants working together and enjoying equal happiness and material comforts in a classless society."

When the Chinese Communist Party won in China, communism was equated with agrarian reform, which was humane, gradualist and flexible. Communism was said to have wrought a miracle. Instead of chaos, corruption, hyper-inflation and disintegration, communism was reported to have created a social order in China which enhanced human dignity. China's economic progress and socialist transformation were believed to be making a morally superior society. Some even believed that it made the Chinese super warriors, for how else could the poorly equipped armies of China cross the Yalu River in 1950 to drive the Americans and other UN contingents down the Korean peninsula?

For two decades, China was shrouded in mystery. The world outside believed a great socialist, industrial transformation was taking place. In 1964, the first Chinese atomic bomb was exploded. More news followed of scientific triumphs in advanced nuclear explosives. Who, outside China, really knew that in 1966, China was to be caught in a great internal convulsion? Fewer still expected that the Cultural Revolution was to last more than ten years, causing great social and economic havoc, until Mao died in 1976. People in the world outside had to wait till after President Nixon's visit to China in 1972 before they could gradually piece together the true picture of triumphs and failures of China.

In Indochina, however, communist victories in 1975 had been followed by a dreadful catalogue of displacement of people, inhuman dispersals of city populations, misery, privation, despair and exodus. Communism had had a very different meaning for the world outside. Nowhere else was the impact of these tragedies felt more than in the neighbouring non-communist countries of Southeast Asia. Spasmodic ejections of refugees, already over 350,000, had not stopped. Whole families, whole clans, risked everything to flee from their homeland, although they knew that

549

even if they escaped a watery grave, it would only mean months, if not years, festering away in refugee camps in Thailand, Malaysia or elsewhere.

After the shock of the collapse of the non-communist regimes of South Vietnam, Cambodia and Laos, the other non-communist governments of Southeast Asia, Indonesia, Malaysia, Philippines, Singapore and Thailand, had co-operated more closely together in ASEAN. Differences were reconciled or muted in the quest for peace and harmony, for survival as non-communist societies. All sought greater economic growth, through greater stability, unity and co-operative approach to regional problems. On the other hand, the communist countries of Vietnam and Cambodia, and China and Vietnam, were locked in deep conflict. Had they continued to display the solidarity which Marx attributed to the working classes of the world, as they appeared to do in the long years of the war against America, the future would have been ominous. But long years of war had made them devotees of Mars more than of Marx. Now, both Vietnam and China were seeking the friendship and understanding of each of the ASEAN countries, and of ASEAN as a regional economic organisation. Both Mr. Pham Van Dong, the Vietnamese Prime Minister and Mr. Deng Xiao-ping, China's Vice-Premier, were scheduled to visit the ASEAN countries in October and November respectively. The kaleidoscope had turned once more, and a fascinating, if complicated, pattern was unfolding. It held out the promise of more years of relative peace and stability for the non-communist countries of ASEAN. There was more time for more economic progress to be achieved, and for some of the social and political problems to be lessened, if not resolved.

Lee described these changes as one facet of the overall change in the great power balance in East Asia and the Pacific. After successive shocks from the time of President Nixon to President Carter, Japan had shown a reluctant acceptance of her position in this changed world. Japan was a great economic power in her own right. After six years of dithering since 1972, Japan had signed the treaty of peace and friendship with China. The Chinese made it easier by allowing Japan, first, to subscribe to her clause against hegemonism, and, next, specifically to state that it did not affect Japan's relations with any third party, namely the Soviet Union. Japan seemed poised to be a major exporter of capital equipment and technology to China. At a time when Japanese exports to America and Europe were the cause of friction over huge trade surpluses, this could be one way to redirect her economic activities.

The Japanese had also been forced to rethink their defence posture. President Carter's announcement at the start of his Presidency more than one and a half years ago of total pull-out of American ground troops from South Korea by 1981 was a profound shock. Between Congress and the White House, the pace of the pull-out had been moderated. But the writing was on the wall. Now, China's forthright senior Vice-Premier, Mr.

Deng Xiao-ping, had publicly told Japanese correspondents that Japan was fully justified in preparing to defend herself against "we know who". The most senior Japanese uniformed officer, General Kurisu, allowed himself to be sacked in July 1978 rather than retract his statement that the military forces could not respond adequately to a surprise attack. These developments coincided with a large excess-capacity of steel and other industrial capacity. The proper equipping of a significant Japanese Self-Defence Force made economic, besides strategic, sense. It would help the economy, increase GNP, create jobs, and without exasperating trading partners who continually threatened reprisals for Japan's huge balance of trade surpluses.

If these open discussions had happened five years ago, the people and leaders in ASEAN countries would have expressed alarm at the resurgence of Japanese militarism. All the present generation of ASEAN leaders had personal experience of Japanese militarism and occupation in 1941 – 45. However, thirty-three years after the War, different circumstances and new developments had presented more dangerous threats to relative prosperity and progress. Most leaders realised and accepted the fact that an effective Japanese defence capability was inevitable. Provided the Japan Self-Defence Agency did not have nuclear weapons, and worked under the US nuclear umbrella, it could be a positive contribution to a quadrilateral great power balance in East Asia and the Pacific. "The geopolitical realities of East Asia and the Pacific have changed. They have changed more than that of West Europe and the Atlantic in the past decade."

Lee continued: "I sometimes wonder how much of this change is objective, and how much is subjective, a change in men's minds, their thinking, their perspectives of the future extrapolating from the present. Twenty-four years ago, in 1954, I viewed the Vietnamese communist victory at Dien Bien Phu over the French with very different feelings. I felt exhilaration over the triumph of a subject people over their colonial masters. Better the communists than the colonialists I thought. In Singapore, I was myself in a united front with cadres of the Malayan Communist Party, actively fomenting political unrest to make the British position in Singapore and peninsular Malaysia untenable, and to force them to hand over power."

In the United Front, united against the British, were socialists, communists, and some simply anti-colonialists. Both sides, the non-communist socialists and the communists, knew that the United Front was a convenience. Both knew that after the British had handed over power, they would clash. In 1959, the non-communist socialists won the elections, and Lee took office in an internally self-governing Singapore. And clash with the communists they did. Fortunately, the communists did not come out on top. In 1963, Singapore merged with the Federation of Malaya to form the Federation of Malaysia. Malaysia was "confronted" by Dr. Sukarno's Indonesia. In 1965, Singapore was separated from the Federation of Malaysia. Suddenly, Lee and his colleagues found themselves in a Singapore independent on its own. "On our island of 224 square miles were two million people. We inherited what was the capital of the British Empire in Southeast Asia, but dismembered from the hinterland which was the empire. The question was how to make a living? How to survive? This was not a theoretical problem in the economics of development. It was a matter of life and death for two million people. The realities of the world of 1965 had to be faced. The sole objective was survival. How this was to be achieved, by socialism or free enterprise, was a secondary matter. The answer turned out to be free enterprise, tempered with the socialist philosophy of equal opportunities for education, jobs, health, housing."

Fortunately, an answer was possible, given the favourable economic conditions of the world in the 1960s. A hardworking people, willing and not slow to learn new tasks, given a sense of common purpose, clear direction, and leadership, were the ingredients that turned adversity to advantage. Instead of a capital city suffering from ever increasing pressure from the drift of population from the rural areas in search of jobs in the bright lights of the city, they were able to check the drift of rural people and regulate the flow to such numbers as were manageable and useful to the economy. "We developed an economy in which the enterprise of American, European, and Japanese MNCs transformed British military bases into industrial facilities for manufacturing, and for servicing of ships, oil rigs, aircraft, telecommunications, banking, and insurance." Manufacturing, which formed 11.4 per cent of the GNP in 1960, more than doubled to 25.4 per cent in 1977. When the British decided to withdraw from their bases in January 1968, British military spending constituted 12.7 per cent of Singapore's GNP in 1967. What threatened to be a major economic setback was converted into an economic opportunity, as military facilities and the technicians working them were released for productive civilian industries.

"Did I ever contemplate nationalisation, socialist planning for industrialisation and economic transformation? Frankly, no. For there was precious little to nationalise, apart from office furniture and equipment, bank offices, shops, hotels, and some factories. Further, I had before me, by 1965, the salutory lessons of U Nu's Burma, Bandaranaike's Ceylon, and Sukarno's Indonesia." Some Asian governments took a socialist view of the exploitative nature of private enterprise. That was natural as their economies were dominated by the Europeans and ethnic minorities who came in the wake of the European colonial power. So when they got their independence, they expelled nearly all non-indigenous entrepreneurs, the Europeans, and the other ethnic minorities. They put bureaucrats in charge of enterprises they took over, and established socialism through people's shops and state-corporations. Their economies declined. In some countries, like Indonesia, the army intervened in this madness and set about correcting the errors. The present government of President Suharto reversed these policies of nationalisation. Foreign investments were welcomed. The people benefitted as the economy recovered. Thailand and the Philippines had always allowed free enterprise and their economies had diversified and grown as a result. The Malaysians also upheld the free-enterprise system.

Those countries in Asia that allowed free enterprise had done incomparably better than those that had tried nationalisation and socialist state-corporations. And this was so even where free enterprise had been shackled by legislative and administrative regulations which required the entrepreneur to give a portion of the equity and part of the management to indigenous shareholders and managers. For the period 1960 – 73, Singapore achieved faster economic growth than other countries in Southeast Asia. After the oil crisis in 1973, several countries like Malaysia and Indonesia, both major oil and commodity exporters, recorded higher growth rates than Singapore. Was Singapore's economic growth faster because she had more entrepreneurs per thousand of population than the other countries of Southeast Asia? Lee said he would like to believe that was a reason. But the facts did not bear this out. His Ministers and economic advisers did not take long to convince him that the rate of development necessary if they were to generate the jobs to mop up unemployment, running at 10 per cent of the work force in 1960, could never be achieved at the pace at which Chinese and Indian Singaporean enterprise was slowly moving from traditional retail and entrepot trade to new manufacturing or servicing industries. They saw far greater potential in the expanding subsidiaries of American, European and Japanese corporations.

What made Singapore different in the 1960s from most other countries of Southeast Asia was that she had no xenophobic hangover from colonialism. The statue of the founder of Singapore, Sir Stamford Raffles, still stood in the heart of the city to remind Singaporeans of his vision in 1819 of Singapore becoming, on the basis of free competition, the emporium of the East, on the route between India and China. There were then a hundred and twenty people on the island. They lived by fishing. Within five years of its founding, there were five thousand traders, British, Arabs, Chinese, Indians, and others drawn in by this principle of free and equal competition, regardless of race, language, or religion. Had the Dutch who governed the then Netherlands East Indies accorded those same ground rules for trade and commerce in the Indonesian Archipelago, Singapore might never have got started. Those were Singapore's origins. So Singapore never suffered from any inhibition in borrowing capital, know-how, managers, engineers and marketing capabilities. Far from limiting the entry of foreign managers, engineers and bankers, they were encouraged to come.

Mankind's progress had been what it was because one man's discovery, whether it was the first spark of fire, or the first atomic explosion, did not have to be painfully and painstakingly rediscovered by all those who sought the benefits of the original discovery. "Had we tried to go into industry on our own, working from first principles, we would never had

553

made it. Only continental nations, like China, with massive populations and great national resources, could afford such sturdy self-reliance. And even China, since 1976, seems keen to cut out learning time by importing machines and know-how, if not management.''

Singaporeans were smart enough to recognise those more enterprising than themselves. That was the key to Singapore's rapid development. On paper, the success was enough for the IMF to classify Singapore together with Israel, Greece and Spain, with countries whose per capita GNP exceeded SDR 1,400 (US$1,669) in 1973 and SDR 1,600 (US$1,924) in 1974. As a result, Singapore was to have been promoted, against their own wishes, into the ranks of those countries which could afford not to take their share of the profits arising from the sale of part of the IMF gold holdings. The loss of the gold profits, though not to be sneezed at, did not alarm Singapore half as much as the consequences and implications of this premature promotion into the category of the developed countries, like losing exports under GSP concessions to developing countries. ''These implications made us ferret out the detailed contribution made to our GNP by the enterprise of the industrial countries of America, Europe and Japan. IMF officials, after close examination of the breakdown figures, conceded that value-added accruing to resident foreigners and resident foreign companies amounted to 14.5 per cent in 1973 and 17.7 per cent in 1974 of our GNP. This brought our indigenous per capita GNP for 1973 and 1974 below the cut-off point for promotion into the ranks of the more developed, including now the Mediterranean countries of Israel, Greece and Spain. The IMF Board of Directors, in March 1978, restored our share of the gold profits and restored our name in the list of eligible developing countries.'' Another interesting and significant statistic which turned up in this scrutiny was that 12,000 foreign managers, engineers and technicians, or 20 per cent of the total work force in these categories, had come to Singapore to manage and operate the capital equipment. They and their enterprises in manufacturing, services and commerce, helped to employ some 250,000 workers or 30 per cent of the total work force.

Over the period 1960 – 77, per capita GDP at constant 1968 market prices increased from US$457 (S$1,400) to US$1,422 (S$4,413), more than three times in seventeen years. In current 1977 prices, it was US$2,857 (S$6,971) per capita. This was the result of economic growth plus a family planning programme that reduced birth rates from 38 per 1,000 in 1960 to 17 per 1,000 in 1977, or a reduction in net population increase of 3.5 per cent in 1960 to 1.2 per cent in 1977. The gross fixed assets of foreign investors were US$1 billion (S$2.7 billion) in 1973 and US$1.3 billion (S$3.1 billion) in 1974. The capital could have been raised from domestic savings and foreign loans. However, to acquire the know-how, to develop the management and the markets, would have cost them dearly. ''We would have had to learn the hard way, paying for every mistake. As it was, Singaporeans were being paid whilst learning, and their instructors were making a fair return on investments, whilst instructing them on the job.''

A point worth underlining was that the same 12,000 managers, engineers and technicians, using the same US$1 billion (S$2.7 billion) of capital assets in their various domestic economies in America, Japan, or Europe, could not have generated this value-added of US$0.83 billion (US$1 = S$2.51) (S$2.09 billion) in 1973 and US$1.19 billion (US$1 = S$2.51) (S$2.99 billion) in 1974. They would have been uneconomic because of high labour costs in their home countries. They needed Singaporean workers at lower Singaporean wage costs, stable political and social conditions to be profitable and productive.

In the 1960s, the industries Singapore started with were labour-intensive (wood products, sawmills, plywood and veneer, textiles, garments and plastics). Hong Kong had started these in the 1950s. Singapore learned from the difficulties of other developing countries who had been ahead of them in economic development and industrialisation. As a result, today, textiles and garments constituted about 5 per cent of the domestic exports, compared to 50 per cent of Hong Kong exports. Singapore consciously sought more skill-intensive and less export-sensitive industries like machine tools, electronic meters, miniature ball-bearings. Such industries needed workers who were literate and skilled in working machines. They could employ more managers, engineers and technicians from the two universities and two polytechnics for the same 1,000 workers on the factory floor. Singapore invested heavily in the younger generation since they were the most precious resources. Education was universal and was both academic and technical and from primary to tertiary levels. "Because we had a trained and educated work force ready, industries needing such a work force came and set up operations in Singapore. And because they employed more sophisticated and automated machines, they could pay higher wages. This raised general wage rates and forced the low-wage factories to do likewise, increasing productivity by using better machines, or to move to a low-wage country."

Sample surveys showed that the average monthly wage of production and manual workers was US$62 in 1966 (S$3.06 = US$1) and US$146 in 1977 (S$2.44 = US$1), up two and a half times in US$ and two times in Singapore $ in eleven years. The Singapore dollar had appreciated against the American dollar during this period by 25 per cent. The older factories, whose products had a high labour content, flour mills, sawmills, textiles and simple assembly of integrated circuits, stopped expansion in Singapore. Some moved out, first to Malaysia and later to Indonesia. Some moved to Thailand. Others were planning to move to Sri Lanka and Bangladesh. Small Singapore shipyards were expanding abroad instead of in Singapore. Singaporean ship-builders and ship-repairers were in joint-ventures with Philippines, and were discussing terms with Bangladesh. Singapore entrepreneurs, like the MNCs, were caught in the cycle of change, as rising costs and keener competition forced them to look for new low-wage countries with good workers and stable social and political conditions. Only thus could they stay competitive. The government actively encouraged this, for the transfer of labour-intensive industries freed valuable land and labour in Singapore for higher skill and capital-intensive factories.

An Economic Development Board study of all export-orientated industrial firms set up since 1960 disclosed several significant conclusions on entrepreneurship. First, the bigger and more established an MNC was in his field, the higher his success rate and the bigger his contribution to jobs and GNP. There had been a few casualties, as was inevitable in all risk-taking. But not a single major MNC had failed. The second conclusion was that the less experienced the industrialist and the less advanced his technology, the higher the failure rate. Wholly-owned foreign enterprises from US, Europe and Japan had a failure rate of only 6 per cent. Other wholly-owned foreign enterprises, mainly from Hong Kong and Taiwan, had twice as high a failure rate of 13 per cent. The failure rate for wholly-owned Singaporean enterprise was 38 per cent, six times that of the foreigners from the advanced industrial countries. However, when Singaporeans went into joint ventures with US, European or Japanese foreign entrepreneurs who provided the know-how, the experience and the marketing, their casualty rate went down from 38 per cent to 7 per cent, just 1 per cent higher than the 6 per cent failure rate of the wholly foreign-owned enterprises. When Singaporeans had less advanced partners from Hong Kong and Taiwan, their failure rate was 17 per cent, two and a half times higher than the 7 per cent failure rate with partners from the advanced industrial countries. Lee supposed that one could attribute the lower failure rate where partners were from the advanced industrial countries to the keener enterprise of the Singaporeans in choosing such partners.

Learning from scratch in the Singapore experience proved a costly business. For Singaporean entrepreneurs to go into industry when their past experience had been entrepot trading, the least hazardous way was to choose an experienced guide.

Two examples illustrated how learning was more difficult with a less experienced instructor in a less established business. Singapore wanted to develop its own generation of manager-entrepreneurs. So they started their own shipping line in 1968, under a shrewd and experienced Pakistani. It was called *Neptune Orient Lines*. It owned thirty-one vessels, including five under construction, with a total dead-weight of 927,000 tons. It operated regular scheduled freight runs between Japan-Singapore-Europe, Singapore-West Malaysia-Australia, and Japan-US. The company also operated a tramp fleet comprising both dry cargo freighter and tankers. Singaporeans took six years, 1968 – 1974, to learn to take over the management of a new company. It lost money for eight years until 1976. Only now, after ten years, was it showing profits.

Contrast this with Singapore Airlines. It was started thirty-one years ago by British shipping enterprise. It started under the name "Malayan

Airways''. It made profits right from the start. It become a partly-owned government company in 1969, and a wholly-owned government company since 1972. Today, it operated a fleet of twenty-nine long, medium and short-haul jets (seven Boeing-747s, ten 707s, six 727s, five 737s and one DC10). The management became less British and more Singaporean gradually from 1959 to 1969. From 1972, it became wholly Singaporean. The airline had stayed profitable throughout. Lee described the contrast between the shipping and the airline performance as startling and discomforting. The quality of Singaporean management was the same. What was different was the learning environment between a shipping line started from scratch and an established on-going airline.

What did this add up to? That managers could be trained and educated both at graduate school and on the job. Their function was supposed to be that of risk-analysers and spreaders. Entrepreneurs were defined as risk-takers. Like water-diviners, they were either born with this knack, or, according to professors in Business Schools, teaching would not help. Even if this were more than the natural modesty of teachers in Business Schools, Lee's experience led him to conclude that developing countries could get their industries going with good indigenous managers, provided they had experienced foreign co-managers to show them in the early stages what not to do.

For developing countries without rich natural resources or large domestic markets, the best way forward was to adopt tried and tested methods of production of proven products, adapting work procedures to the local culture and environment, and through lower wage costs and lower overheads, supply a segment of the global market more cheaply and profitably. This was more the business of risk-analysing and spreading.

In today's world of instant communications and jet travel, learning about and from each other was a strong factor for change. It accelerated development and progress. Why try what had repeatedly been shown to be unworkable or impractical, however logical and attractive the theory might be? What policies had succeeded in other countries? Despite differences in geography, history, ethnic characteristics, culture, religion, languages, what were the common features of these more successful developing countries? They had a disciplined, hardworking, increasingly better-educated labour force. The workers were rewarded in accordance with output and performance. They had a stable and orderly society which allowed learning and working to be rewarded. And if the economic benefits of development were spread and enjoyed through all socio-economic groups, then that society was likely to continue to progress with minimal social or political stress.

Several developing countries which had taken the socialist road of nationalisation, like Sri Lanka, Bangladesh, had recently elected governments whose leaders had read the lessons of the past thirty years.

These leaders had experienced what did not work. They had seen what worked and why. The question was how to reproduce some of the essential

557

conditions for successful development in, say, Sri Lanka. How long would it take her to repair the infrastructure of roads, power, water, harbours, telecommunications? If money could be found to finance these, then in only a few years. But other conditions were more difficult to achieve, for they were not like turn-key projects, which consultants and contractors could tender for and carry out. How long would Sri Lanka take to produce a hardworking work force out of voters who had been for over two decades, promised, and given, subsidised rice and sugar? How long would she take to get workers to accept training and discipline seriously after they had played fast and loose with employers for twenty years under communist and Trotskyite union leaders? How long would she take to rebuild an effective administration made flabby and unreliable by nepotism and the intrusion of political partiality and incompetence into the ranks of formerly neutral administrators? How long would she take to persuade her talented and experienced administrators who had emigrated to work for UN and other international agencies to return to help rebuild the administration? They had the human resources. The question was the time required to marshall them, for it had to be done before the next elections due in five years' time.

In the 1950s, there might have been some doubt which of the two economic and political system worked better, free enterprise in a free-market economy, as in America, Europe and Japan, or socialist planning, as in the Soviet Union and China. India, Indonesia and Egypt, the leaders of the non-aligned world, were going for state planning and state-corporations based on Soviet-type five-year plans. By the 1970s, there was no doubt that state planning and state-corporations had not brought about the economic transformation.

The irony was that just as the truth was becoming apparent to the leaders of the developing countries, the new models for growth — South Korea, Taiwan, Hong Kong and Singapore and two others in Latin America — faced the danger of protectionism in the industrial countries. Plagued by high inflation and high unemployment, for which no easy solution had been found since the oil crisis, Lee said he sensed a loss of nerve in some leaders in government and in industry, and amongst some academics in the West. Their confidence in working the free-market system had been shaken. Their despondency had enlarged the threat in their minds of more unemployment over imports like textiles, shoes, electrical and electronic products from NICs (Newly Industrialising Countries). Their reaction had been to heavily protect their no longer competitive industries. Some were using older machinery than those they had exported to the NICs. Some Europeans now proposed organised free trade. The EEC had in disregard of the Multi-Fibre Agreement, forced agreements on a whole group of developing countries to cut back on their exports of textiles and garments. Now, EEC Ministers had proposed in the MTN (Multilateral Trade Negotiations) in Geneva, in July, that there be "safeguard" clauses to enable them to raise tariffs and block imports, not against all countries as required by the present rules of GATT, but only against specific countries, namely the NICs, which were disrupting an industry awaiting restructuring. American unions had urged the cancellation of tax deferrals. They wanted the Administration and Congress to discourage the export of jobs, and to block transfers of capital and technology, which would otherwise take place because they could be more profitable abroad.

The crux of the problem was whether leaders in both industrial and developing countries had adjusted intellectually and emotionally to this being one interdependent world. When the oil crisis came upon them in October 1973, and stock markets in all the capitals of the OECD countries collapsed like nine pins, that was one moment of truth. The world was, all of a sudden, seen and felt as one interdependent world.

Lee said NICs should be encouraged, not obstructed, in their future economic growth. They were demonstration models to other developing countries of how they also could move up the industrial ladder if their leaders and people set out to organise their societies, educate and train their people. Then, they could modernise agriculture and make it productive with less farmers, take their surplus rural population into new towns in which investments in industry could provide jobs. To make it difficult for these countries to export competitively was surely defeatist and self-defeating. For it negated the principles through which all poor and underdeveloped countries had been told they could work their way into the ranks of the developed countries.

In the 1950s, Singapore suffered high unemployment, slow economic growth, social and political unrest. Many bright, "eager-beaver" types joined the communist underground cells for guerilla revolution. Strikes, riots, arson and assassinations were part of the dreadful repetitious calender of weekly events. The same bright, eager-beaver types then went into industry as young engineers and managers. Communist recruitment had dropped in quality and in numbers. This political transformation would not have happened but for Singapore's rapid economic development. This development would not have been possible if Singapore had not been able to plug into the world grid of industrial power-houses in America, Europe and Japan.

Other developing countries should be encouraged and helped to plug into this grid. How soon and how effectively they could plug into this world grid depended upon them, upon how realistic and pragmatic their governments were in their policies, so as to strike a bargain with those who had the capital, technology and management to help produce goods for their own people, and perhaps also for export in the competitive international markets. In other words, the more rationally governments took advantage of their relative backwardness and low wage costs, the more benefits they would derive from the international division of labour. For them not to try was to court more misery, more coups, more totalitarian, and eventually more communist, regimes.

Meanwhile, the problems of slow growth, high inflation and unemployment still troubled the industrialised countries. But this was no reason for the industrialised countries to radically modify the principles of free trade and free capital flows, and technology transfers freely negotiable, except where national security decided otherwise. "Enterprise and the operation of the free market have got us to the highest level of production and consumption ever in man's history. It will be enterprise, operating in a free market, not subsidies and protectionism, which will lead the way out of this present economic trough. This is more than an act of faith. It is the lesson of history, the history of the Great Depression (1929 – 33), followed by protectionism, the rise of intense nationalism, racism and Fascism. There must be a saner and more rational solution to our present problems."

XXXI

Back in Singapore, Lee welcomed the German Chancellor to Singapore. At a dinner in honour of Helmut Schmidt on 13 October, Lee said the Government and people of Singapore were honoured to have him visit them. "You represent a remarkable people. After the devastation of the last war, the Germans have picked themselves up, rebuilt and gone on to greater achievements. It is a proud record of economic and social progress achieved within a democratic framework. You also represent an exceptional social democratic party. The SPD has achieved a more just and equal society in the Federal Republic of Germany without generating and exploiting class hatred and antagonisms. The SPD-FPD Government has recorded the lowest inflation rate of all industrial countries, positive economic growth rates even after the oil crisis, and unemployment lower than most industrial countries. The strength of the Deutsche Mark is an unsolicited, sometimes embarrassing, tribute that the world's bankers pay to the German Government, management and unions, to work together and find some solution to the complex of problems that confront Germany and the world since the oil crisis."

It was not by coincidence that the EEC-ASEAN Ministerial meeting from 20 – 21 November in Brussels was to take place when the EEC Council of Ministers was under the chairmanship of the German Foreign Minister. Lee believed this EEC-ASEAN Ministerial Meeting could chart out the areas in which further and greater co-operation could take place. During his brief stay, Lee hoped that Mr. Schmidt would get a feel of the texture of the society woven in Singapore. Singapore grew out of 140 years of British colonial administration. During that period, Malays, Indians and Chinese migrated to Singapore to seek their fortunes. A few found their fortunes. Most left only their children. In the past twenty years, the descendants of these immigrants had acquired a sense of their own identity. This society had been influenced by men who in turn were

560

influenced by British Labour Party ideals of socialism in the 1940s and '50s. It was a time when most of his colleagues and he were students in Britain. "We were attracted and influenced by the humanitarian instincts and the egalitarian ideas which shaped British Labour Government policies in those years after the last war. None of us foresaw the side-effects of the welfare state on personal motivation and achievement." Fortunately, the Asian philosophy was that life was one hard struggle. This saved them from their early idealistic innocence. "We learned the hard way, that the world does not owe us a living. Our people made the effort to help themselves. So we made some progress."

Now this progress was threatened by slow economic growth in the industrial countries, monetary instability and increasing protectionism. The strong stand against protectionism by the Federal Republic of Germany was reassuring. For industrial countries of the West to con-template retreat behind selective safeguards and other shields or barriers to protect them from competition against old industries in need of restruc-turing was defeatist, and in the end, self-defeating. It was to ignore the lesson of history, history so recent that many present that night could personallly remember the Great Depression, protectionism, nationalism, racism and the terrible consequences of conflict as each major industrial power sought to secure its own base, raw materials and markets. The only sane and rational way forward was an agreement on the Multilateral Trade Negotiations which would increase, not impede, trade.

During a television discussion with Chancellor Schmidt the following day, Lee was asked whether it was realistic to believe that disarmament would set free more money to bridge the gap between the rich and the poor nations. Lee replied that he found this a futile discussion. "It is generally agreed at the UN that the developed countries should try and approximate 0.7 per cent of their GNP for development aid, and very few countries — I think two, three industrial countries — reach that figure. So assuming that you can get the East and the West to reduce their arms and cut down, say, arms expenditure from about 5 per cent of GNP to 2 per cent GNP, then all it will mean will be 0.3 per cent or 0.4 per cent of GNP will be 0.3 per cent of an additional 2 per cent which has been reduced. If you can't get them to reach 0.3 per cent to 0.7 per cent, how do you expect them to cut off their GNP from arms expenditure by 2 per cent or 3 per cent and say, make it 3.7 per cent for development aid, and what will happen? It's a good talking point — it keeps gatherings, when they run out of topics to chase this hare. I find it unproductive and unrealistic. The Soviet Union is unlikely to suddenly say: Let's scrap all these missiles, let's scrap all these tanks. They will always have use for them. They have two long borders — one in Europe, one in the Far East — and that's a fact of life. So I say within those facts the developed countries must strive, if this is one world and we want to keep this system going instead of tearing at each other's throats, then we must show concern for those who have started so late in life and so low down the ladder. Maybe many don't deserve any help; maybe they squander the help, nevertheless, the willingness to help lubricate international relations and lessen international tensions."

XXXII

Within the space of a few weeks, the Prime Minister of the Socialist Republic of Vietnam, Mr. Pham Van Dong, and the Vice-Premier of the People's Republic of China, Mr. Deng Xiao-ping came, to Singapore on official visits. Mr. Dong came first, and on 16 October, was entertained at a dinner in his honour at the Istana.

Lee and his colleagues extended to him a warm welcome. "Until today, our knowledge of each other was limited.to second-hand reports. However accurate and objective, they cannot equal the direct face-to-face encounter. I have learnt more about Vietnam and her distinguished Prime Minister from our two-hour meeting this afternoon than if I had read two books on the subject." The countries of Southeast Asia today were very conscious of each other as neighbours in one region. "We in Singapore are conscious of the need to establish sound and mutually beneficial relationships with all our neighbours, regardless of their economic or political systems. There is no reason why we cannot live in peace with each other, and through trade, economic and cultural co-operation contribute to one another's well-being and progress. To this end we must exorcise preconceived biases, arising from past misconceptions. For these could easily lead us away from a new constructive relationship."

For both, the future was what they chose to make of it. It was for them both to remove difficulties and create opportunities for friendship and co-operation. "If we are to make Southeast Asia a region of peace and prosperity, we must remove distrust and reduce tensions. We must establish confidence in each other by matching words with deeds. As sovereign states we each have the right to solve our problems in our own way, and to establish systems of government which each country believes will satisfy its national aspirations."

Lee said that Singapore was encouraged that, as a result of Mr. Dong's meetings with the leaders of the countries of ASEAN, he had first-hand knowledge of the desire of the leaders of all the countries for peace and stability in order to achieve more economic development. "Your statements in Bangkok, Manila, Jakarta and Kuala Lumpur that Vietnam will not, directly or indirectly, support subversion, were not solicited by the leaders of the countries you visited. This makes the statements all the more significant. If we all uphold and observe this first principle of non-interference, good and constructive relations will develop among us all." Their frank and direct discussions that afternoon were a first and valuable step in establishing a realistic relationship with each other, one which

562

could and would be mutually beneficial.

Mr. Dong, in his reply, said that Singapore, under the leadership of Lee Kuan Yew had recorded important achievements in economic construction. "We want to learn from your experience in construction." He said he desired to promote the ties of friendship and long-term co-operation between Vietnam and Singapore.

XXXIII

A distinctive feature of the Hindu religion and culture, commented the Prime Minister in his Deepavali Message on 29 October, was its tolerance for other religions and cultures. All major religions and cultures met in Singapore. The values and traditions of Christian charity, Islamic brotherhood, Confucian ethics and the Buddhist's search for enlightenment, were all part of Singapore's spiritual milieu. Everyone knew that virtue was not exclusive to any religion. "So long as we preach and practise tolerance and harmony and freedom of religion, we shall continue to be at peace with ourselves and to make progress." He wished all Hindus a Happy Deepavali.

XXXIV

"Just where do the loyalties of overseas-Chinese now lie?" *The Times* of London asked this question on 6 November on the eve of the visit of Mr. Deng Xiao-ping to Singapore. The paper said that the Vice-Premier of China had been well-received in Thailand. In Malaysia, the Chinese community was only barely a minority in the electorate. "Singapore, unlike the rest, may find its own solution through Mr. Lee Kuan Yew's internationalist outlook."

Lee prefaced his speech of welcome to China's Vice-premier, Mr. Deng Xiao-ping, at a dinner at the Istana on 12 November, with the observation that Mr. Deng's visit came at an important time in Asia's history. Many people were re-examining previously unquestioned assumptions, especially in the light of the unexpected developments, in the last three years, between the former countries of Indochina and between them and their neighbours. "We are all trying to fathom the future." What kind of world would it be by the year 2000? What part would East and Southeast Asia play in that world? "However objective we try to be in identifying the key forces which are shaping the future, I suspect we cannot avoid surprises."

For instance, Lee said he could not have anticipated, when he was in

Beijing in May 1976, that he would have had the privilege of welcoming Vice-Premier Deng Xiao-ping to Singapore in November 1978 as the representative of the Government of the People's Republic of China. Surprises added spice to life, provided they were pleasant ones, as in this instance. But it was best not to risk too many surprises. To be accurately appraised of objective facts, and to work out the different possible developments which could flow out of them, was one way of avoiding being taken by surprise. So he welcomed Deng's visit and the opportunity to discuss matters of common concern and interest with him.

The Prime Minister said that the relationship between China and Singapore contained unique elements to which they must address themselves with frankness. "Then there will be no need for ambiguity in our dealings with each other."

Perhaps, he added, he could illustrate this problem by advancing for Mr. Deng's consideration a tantalising thought. "How different would both of us have become had my ancestors stayed on in China and yours emigrated to Singapore?" Lee said he was struck by the first half of this thought when he visited China for the first time in 1976. "I had no doubts that had I been born and bred in China, I would not be the person I had become. I did not know where I would have found myself in a milieu of 900 million Chinese. But whether peasant or worker, political cadre or diligent follower, the spectacles through which I would have viewed the world would have been very different. As it was, having grown up in Singapore, especially my first twenty years, I was conscious that I was looking at China and her people as an outsider. This evening, Your Excellency, permit me some light-hearted speculation as to what would have happened if your ancestors had settled in Singapore and you were born and bred here. Certainly the history of China would not have been the same. Equally, the history of Singapore would have been different. As a Singaporean, you would have found much to admire in the people of China. But you would be much puzzled by some of the events of the past twenty-nine years in China. For, from time to time, China appeared deliberately to choose to travel the longer, rather than the shorter, road to industrialisation."

Lee said Chinese Singaporeans had had their own different experience and history. However short this might be, compared to that of their ancestors in China, it had made them different. More important, they were in the midst of ensuring a separate and durable future for themselves in Southeast Asia. And this future must be shared equally with Malay, Indian and other Singaporeans. "They understand enough of geopolitics to know that their future directly depends on Singapore's future in Southeast Asia, and not on China's future amongst the front rank of industrial nations." Naturally, China's industrialisation would effect the whole of Southeast Asia and so indirectly influence Singapore's future. However, Singaporeans had come to recognise that just as they could not afford to sacrifice their national interests for China, so they could not expect China to sacrifice her national interests for Singapore. "The more both sides are frank with each other over this fact of life, the more constructive and fruitful our bilateral relations will be."

The people of Singapore knew the capabilities of the Chinese nation. "We wish China success in her rapid industrialisation. A prosperous and peaceful country of nearly one billion people is a matter of great consequence for Asia and for the world. Co-operation with such a China becomes desirable, indeed irresistible." Lee said he was confident that Mr. Deng's visit would improve the friendship and understanding between their two peoples and governments.

Mr. Deng, in his reply, paid tribute to "the industrious and valiant people of Singapore" for their marked successes in developing their national economy under the leadership of Prime Minister Lee Kuan Yew. He said that Lee's visit to China in 1976 was a positive contribution to the promotion of China-Singapore friendly relations. He predicted that friendly relations and profound friendship between "our two peoples" would develop further.

XXXV

On 17 November, political detainees Dr. Lim Hock Siew and Said Zahari, detained for fifteen years and nine months, were freed on suspension orders, but confined to Pulau Tekong Besar and Pulau Ubin, two nearby islands.

Lee Kuan Yew told William Buckley, a Washington reporter in an interview, that they had invested many years of their lives to the communist cause and would not write off that investment lightly. Lee added: "But it does look now, after the troubles between Vietnam and Cambodia and Vietnam and China, that the revolution is not going to steamroll out and reach them in time to make it worthwhile to hold out. So it's a question of a test of will."

William Buckley described Lee as "quiet, eloquent, confident, disdainful of demogogic defences. He presides over 520 sq km and two million people, and he will fight for their welfare — on the understanding that he is the ultimate judge of how to define that welfare."

XXXVI

On his way to an official visit to India, the Prime Minister stopped over in Thailand for talks with the Thai Prime Minister, General Kriangsak Chomanan. At a press conference in Bangkok on 11 December, Lee told a Soviet newsman that if ASEAN countries were left to themselves without any outside proposals for collective security, they might find some way of collectively ensuring their future. "The more we have major powers thrusting their energetic, dynamic ideas onto the region, the more strife there seems to be.'' The Soviet newsman had asked Lee for his comments on the Soviet proposal for a zone of peace and security in Asia. Lee said: ''I think we are doing well by ourselves, don't you think? For eleven years, the Soviet Union radio and press had berated ASEAN as a militaristic plot. It took eleven years before the Soviet Union's mass media decided to switch policies and say: 'Yes, it is a promising association'.''

Referring to the invasion of Cambodia by Vietnam, Lee said: ''When one subverts a non-communist neighbour it is called liberation. When one subverts a communist neighbour it is called salvation.'' Lee was meaning the Vietnam-supported Kampuchean United Front for National Salvation.

Asked about the implementation of the five ASEAN joint projects, Lee said: ''We're coming to the agreement that we move much faster if we let the private sector do the job with the government's blessing. Government participation should only be confined to ensuring that no bureaucratic red tape hinders implementation.''

At a dinner hosted by the Indian Prime Minister, Mr. Morarji Desai, on 13 December in New Delhi, Lee said in the seven years since he last visited India, many changes had overtaken the world, especially South and Southeast Asia. Perhaps changes had a deeper imprint on young peoples. He came from a nation which, by Asian standards, had a very short history, just over a hundred and fifty years. ''The distant past of our people lies with their ancestors in China, India, Malaysia and Indonesia. We have no ancient monuments, temples and other glorious antiquities. As a result, we are only too eager to innovate and even to change our way of life.'' This lack of historical ballast could be dangerous at times of crisis. There was not the assurance of a long and splendid history to provide that confidence that destiny was on their side in coping with the next ominous crisis.

''For instance, we in Singapore were startled by the sharp clash between two communist states to our North, for the time being confined to the Indo-Chinese Peninsula. We were startled because we could not believe one communist government had set out deliberately to subvert and overthrow another communist government. When a communist does this to a non-communist government, he calls it 'liberation'. When he does it to another communist government, he calls it 'salvation'. We in Southeast Asia, a member of the countries of ASEAN, want to co-exist peacefully with all the communist states to our North, whatever their ideological idiosyncracies. India's commitment to non-communism and non-alignment makes her a natural friend of the countries of ASEAN. Singapore has always found India a reliable and steadfast friend. It is a friendship that springs from shared values of our common past and shared expectations of one peaceful and stable world in which co-operation in Asia will bring shared benefits. It is therefore a great pleasure for me to be in Delhi again. It is yet another opportunity to meet old friends and renew old friendships."

Lee recalled that when he met Mr. Desai in London eighteen months earlier, after a lapse of nearly eight years, he had left a deep impression on him of a man completely serene and self-contained and none the worse for yet another period of detention. "As you said, it was your conviction that good must triumph over evil which made all difficulties bearable. This is all a part of the Indian tradition, the Hindu ethos. This same ethos is what makes the Indian civilisation so durable. It is this long view of history that has seen India weather many a crisis with equanimity and quiet resolve."

In a joint communique, the two Prime Ministers stated that in their discussions they had reviewed the international situation, with particular reference to the developments in Asia. Bilateral relations between India and Singapore were also considered. "Welcoming the new spirit of co-operation amongst states, both in South Asia and among the ASEAN countries, the two Prime Ministers were of the view that efforts should be made to consolidate regional co-operation as a vital factor for peace, stability and economic development. With reference to the situation in Southeast Asia, the two leaders emphasised the need for peaceful and constructive relations to be developed among all nation states on the basis of the principle of non-interference in internal affairs and respect for sovereignty."

The Prime Minister of Singapore briefed the Prime Minister of India on the progress made by ASEAN. The Prime Minister of India reiterated India's support for ASEAN, and its continued commitment to the establishment of a zone of peace, freedom and neutrality in Southeast Asia. The Prime Minister of India indicated India's desire to establish closer relations with ASEAN. The Prime Ministers felt that increasing co-operation between India and the countries of the ASEAN region was of mutual advantage. Both sides expressed satisfaction that the ASEAN Secretary-General held exploratory talks with the Government of India on possible forms of co-operation between ASEAN and India.

The two Prime Ministers appreciated the successes recorded in developing the respective economies and the priority they attached to raising the living standards of the people. They also noted that the already existing wide range of co-operation between the two countries could be expanded especially in the fields of trade, investment and transfer of technology.

Asked in Singapore by the editor of the *Third World Review* what he thought about the North-South dialogue and the so-called New International Economic Order, Lee said he considered the dialogue futile. Developed countries were not now inclined to be charitable, and the negotiating machinery could offer nothing to the Third World. The dialogue was an exercise in futility.

XXXVII

Opening Parliament on 26 December, President Sheares said three major factors would influence events and help shape the deliberations of the current session. First, most economists forecasted a downturn in the US economy in 1979, but barring a recession, Singapore should still be able to make 6 – 8 per cent economic growth. Second, the conflict between Vietnam and Kampuchea would have important consequences for Thailand and the rest of Southeast Asia. Third, the single most important issue in Singapore was the next political leadership.

On 29 December, the Prime Minister proposed to Parliament that Dr. Benjamin Henry Sheares be elected President of the Republic of Singapore for a further term of four years. "It was eight years ago, in November 1970, that I first moved his election as President. He was then sixty-three. He had a distinguished career as a professor and practitioner of Obstetrics & Gynaecology. He brought to his office a fine intellect and quiet dignity. He keeps himself abreast with all important matters of state. All Cabinet papers and other important subjects go up to him so that he is aware of the background to the decisions he is required by the Constitution to endorse. He also undertakes his social and protocol functions with conscientious interest, never treating them as perfunctory chores. He has done us proud and been an asset to Singapore these past eight years. No distinguished visitor who has called on him has failed to notice the compliment he has paid him by really knowing about him, his country and his major interests. When I asked him in April this year if he would serve as President for a third term, he asked for time to consider it. Characteristically, he wanted to satisfy himself that he could and would discharge his duties to the high standards he sets himself. It was after careful deliberation that he told me in October this year that he was prepared to undertake another term. He said he would do his best. I have no doubts that he will.

"I have less hesitation in commencing his re-election to the office, than he had in accepting the nomination. For me, the question was simple. Is there a better man for the job? There is none. He is the best. However, the question he put to himself was different. Could he discharge his duties in the next four years as well as he had in the past eight? It took time to persuade and convince him that whilst his energy and vigour at seventy-one may not be what it was at sixty-three when he first assumed office, nevertheless, it was more than adequate, given the experience he has acquired, and the routine he has worked out for himself. I am happy that I was able to persuade him to continue. I have no doubts that the habits of a life time will not change. It is part of his nature to apply himself thoroughly to his work. I believe some thoughtfulness on the part of the government can lighten the physical demands of the office. These are the adjustments each of us has to make as the years go by. It is called growing old gracefully, a phrase forged by poetic licence. If we are fortunate to have the right mental approach, we learn to accept these changes without resentment. If we are more fortunate, like the President is, we shall have members of the family and friends who help and encourage us to make these changes as we soldier on."

XXXVIII

Late in December, Lee appeared in the High Court to give evidence in his defamation suit against J.B. Jeyaretnam, Secretary-General of the Workers Party. Lee said Jeyaretnam in an election rally speech on 18 December, 1976 accused him of nepotism and corruption. Mr. Justice F.A. Chua awarded Lee $130,000 damages. In a thirty-two-page judgement, the judge said the slander was grave. Jeyaretnam had used his words "recklessly without an honest belief in their truth". Lee's lawyer said the damages would be given to charity. Jeyaretnam gave notice of appeal: the case was expected to go to the Privy Council.

XXXIX

On the last day of 1978, Lee put out his New Year Message for 1979. He said that 1978 would long be remembered as the year of the refugees. It was the most pitiless in the long chain of calamities that had been suffered by the peoples of Vietnam, Laos and Cambodia. Most of the past sufferings were the results of acts committed in the heat of war. This latest exodus of "boat people" and "ship people" was the result of acts of cold calculation, measured in gold, and long after the heat of battle had cooled. These were victims of peace. What was ominous was that unless world leaders and leader-writers registered their outrage at this cynical disposal of unwanted citizens, many more victims would be sent off on packed boats and ships. They would add to present problems, what with over 120,000, mostly Laotian and Cambodian, refugees in Thailand, 45,000 Vietnamese in Malaysia, several thousands in Indonesia and in the Philippines, and 1,000 in Singapore. If these hapless people knew that this would be their fate, they would have fought with ferocity to prevent their countries and themselves from being overrun. They, 350,000 refugees since 1975, and many millions more stewing away in re-education or work camps in Cambodia, Laos and Vietnam, learned too late that it would have been better to have fought, with many dying, defending their way of life, than to be "liberated" by the communists. Now the choice was to suffer or to die, or both.

"We must always be prepared and ready to stand up and be counted for what we are. Singaporeans have had the opportunity since 1965 to organise themselves into a nation. Time has not been wasted. Today, we have a self-disciplined society, cohesive and united, despite differences in race, language and religion. However, it is not enough to have the capacity to defend what we have worked so hard to build and to create. We must also have the patience and foresight, through diplomacy, to maintain conditions of stability and security over our region, so that more can be achieved in a better life for our like-minded neighbours and ourselves. That the governments of ASEAN, despite their different and sometimes competing interests are like-minded and prepared to set aside differences to unite to defend their larger interests, is not simply a happen-stance. We have all worked together to make it happen."

The outlook for 1979 was fair, with lightning and thunderstorms from time to time. "But we shall make it. Let us work to make it another year of progress and consolidation."

INDEX

575